Contents in *Brief*

The Little, Brown Handbook, *Brief Version*

SIXTH
EDITION

LB
Brief

JANE E. AARON

New!
**2016
MLA
Updates**

PEARSON

Boston   Columbus   Indianapolis   New York   San Francisco
Amsterdam   Cape Town   Dubai   London   Madrid   Milan   Munich
Paris   Montréal   Toronto   Delhi   Mexico City   São Paulo
Sydney   Hong Kong   Seoul   Singapore   Taipei   Tokyo

Vice President and Editor in Chief:
Joseph Opiela
Senior Development Editor: Anne Brunell
Ehrenworth
Program Manager: Eric Jorgensen
Field Marketing Manager: Mark Robinson
Product Marketing Manager: Ali Arnold
Executive Media Producer: Jaclyn Reynen
Content Specialist: Laura Olson
Project Manager: Savoula Amanatidis

Project Coordination, Text Design, and
Electronic Page Makeup: Cenveo
Publisher Services
Program Design Lead and Cover Designer:
Heather Scott
Senior Manufacturing Buyer: Roy L.
Pickering, Jr.
Printer and Binder: LSC Communications
–Crawfordsville
Cover Printer: Lehigh-Phoenix Color
Corporation–Hagerstown

For permission to use copyrighted material, grateful acknowledgment is made to the copyright holders on page 519, which is hereby made part of this copyright page.

PEARSON, ALWAYS LEARNING, and MyWritingLab are exclusive trademarks owned by Pearson Education, Inc. or its affiliates in the United States and/or other countries.

Unless otherwise indicated herein, any third-party trademarks that may appear in this work are the property of their respective owners and any references to third-party trademarks, logos, or other trade dress are for demonstrative or descriptive purposes only. Such references are not intended to imply any sponsorship, endorsement, authorization, or promotion of Pearson's products by the owners of such marks, or any relationship between the owner and Pearson Education, Inc., or its affiliates, authors, licensees, or distributors.

Cataloging in Publication data is on file at the Library of Congress

1   17

Student Edition
ISBN-10: 0-13-467943-1 (tabbed edition)
ISBN-13: 978-0-13-467943-3 (tabbed edition)
ISBN-10: 0-13-467873-7 (untabbed edition)
ISBN-13: 978-0-13-467873-3 (untabbed edition)

A la Carte Edition
ISBN-10: 0-13-470298-0 (untabbed edition)
ISBN-13: 978-0-13-470298-8 (untabbed edition)

www.pearsonhighered.com

Preface for Students

LB Brief contains the basic information you'll need for writing in and out of school. Here you can find out how to get ideas, use commas, search the Web, cite sources, write a résumé, and more—all in a convenient, accessible package.

This book is mainly a reference for you to dip into as needs arise. You probably won't read the book all the way through, nor will you use everything it contains: you already know much of the content anyway, whether consciously or not. The trick is to figure out what you *don't* know—taking cues from your own writing experiences and the comments of others—and then to find the answers to your questions in these pages.

Before you begin using this book, you may need to clear your mind of a very common misconception: that writing is only, or even mainly, a matter of correctness. True, any written message will find a more receptive audience if it is correct in grammar, punctuation, and similar matters. But these concerns should come late in the writing process, after you've allowed yourself to discover what you have to say, freeing yourself to make mistakes along the way. As one writer put it, you need to get the clay on the potter's wheel before you can shape it into a bowl, and you need to shape it into a bowl before you can perfect it. So get your clay on the wheel and work with it until it looks like a bowl. Then worry about correctness.

Finding what you need

You have many ways to find what you need in the handbook:

- **Use a directory.** The brief contents inside the front cover displays all the book's parts and chapters. The more detailed contents inside the back cover provides each chapter's subheadings as well.
- **Use the glossary.** "Commonly Misused Words" (pp. 505–17) clarifies more than 250 words that are often confused.
- **Use the index.** The extensive index lists every topic, term, and problem word or expression mentioned in the book.
- **Use a list.** Two helpful aids fall on the last pages of the book: "CULTURE LANGUAGE Guide" pulls together all the book's material for students using standard American English as a second language or a second dialect. And "Editing Symbols" explains abbreviations often used to mark papers.
- **Use the elements of the page.** As shown on the next page, each page of the handbook tells you what you can find there.

The handbook's page elements

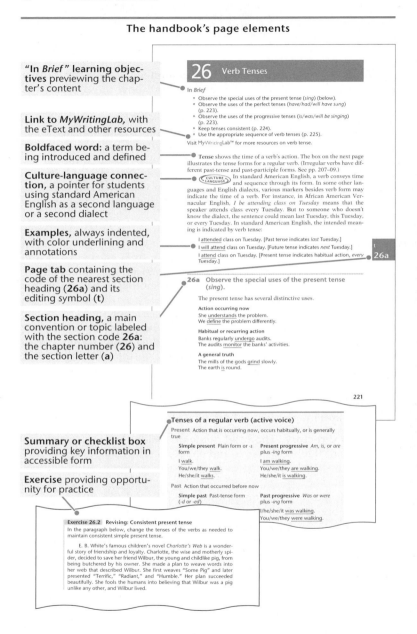

"In *Brief*" learning objectives previewing the chapter's content

Link to *MyWritingLab*, with the eText and other resources

Boldfaced word: a term being introduced and defined

Culture-language connection, a pointer for students using standard American English as a second language or a second dialect

Examples, always indented, with color underlining and annotations

Page tab containing the code of the nearest section heading (**26a**) and its editing symbol (**t**)

Section heading, a main convention or topic labeled with the section code **26a:** the chapter number (**26**) and the section letter (**a**)

Summary or checklist box providing key information in accessible form

Exercise providing opportunity for practice

The annotated page content:

26 Verb Tenses

In *Brief*

- Observe the special uses of the present tense (*sing*) (below).
- Observe the uses of the perfect tenses (*have/had/will have sung*) (p. 223).
- Observe the uses of the progressive tenses (*is/was/will be singing*) (p. 223).
- Keep tenses consistent (p. 224).
- Use the appropriate sequence of verb tenses (p. 225).

Visit MyWritingLab™ for more resources on verb tense.

Tense shows the time of a verb's action. The box on the next page illustrates the tense forms for a regular verb. (Irregular verbs have different past-tense and past-participle forms. See pp. 207–09.)

CULTURE LANGUAGE In standard American English, a verb conveys time and sequence through its form. In some other languages and English dialects, various markers besides verb form may indicate the time of a verb. For instance, in African American Vernacular English, *I be attending class on Tuesday* means that the speaker attends class every Tuesday. But to someone who doesn't know the dialect, the sentence could mean last Tuesday, this Tuesday, or every Tuesday. In standard American English, the intended meaning is indicated by verb tense:

I attended class on Tuesday. [Past tense indicates *last* Tuesday.]
I will attend class on Tuesday. [Future tense indicates *next* Tuesday.]
I attend class on Tuesday. [Present tense indicates habitual action, *every* Tuesday.]

26a Observe the special uses of the present tense (*sing*).

The present tense has several distinctive uses.

Action occurring now
She understands the problem.
We define the problem differently.

Habitual or recurring action
Banks regularly undergo audits.
The audits monitor the banks' activities.

A general truth
The mills of the gods grind slowly.
The earth is round.

221

Tenses of a regular verb (active voice)

Present Action that is occurring now, occurs habitually, or is generally true

Simple present Plain form or -s form	Present progressive *Am, is,* or *are* plus *-ing* form
I walk.	I am walking.
You/we/they walk.	You/we/they are walking.
He/she/it walks.	He/she/it is walking.

Past Action that occurred before now

Simple past Past-tense form (-d or -ed)	Past progressive *Was* or *were* plus *-ing* form
	I/he/she/it was walking.
	You/we/they were walking.

Exercise 26.2 Revising: Consistent present tense
In the paragraph below, change the tenses of the verbs as needed to maintain consistent simple present tense.

E. B. White's famous children's novel *Charlotte's Web* is a wonderful story of friendship and loyalty. Charlotte, the wise and motherly spider, decided to save her friend Wilbur, the young and childlike pig, from being butchered by his owner. She made a plan to weave words into her web that described Wilbur. She first weaves "Some Pig" and later presented "Terrific," "Radiant," and "Humble." Her plan succeeded beautifully. She fools the humans into believing that Wilbur was a pig unlike any other, and Wilbur lived.

Preface for Instructors

LB Brief provides writers with a reliable, accessible, and affordable reference. Merging the authority of its parent, *The Little, Brown Handbook*, and a concise format, this handbook answers questions about the writing process, critical thinking, grammar and style, research writing, documentation, and more. With its cross-curricular outlook, easy-to-use format, and assumption of little or no experience with writing or handbooks, *LB Brief* helps students of varying interests and skills.

This new edition improves on the handbook's strengths while keeping pace with the rapid changes in writing and its teaching. In the context of the handbook's many reference functions, the following pages highlight as New the most significant additions and changes.

An introduction to academic writing

The handbook introduces students to the goals and requirements of college writing.

- New Chapter 9 on academic writing, now at the start of Part 2, greatly expands on common academic genres, such as responses, critical analyses, arguments, informative and personal writing, and research papers and reports. The discussion highlights key features of each genre and points students to examples in the handbook.
- New Chapter 11, "Writing Arguments," emphasizes the features and organization of a successful argument essay. A new checklist on revision helps students read their work critically.
- New Chapter 12, "Reading and Writing about Literature," emphasizes composing a literary analysis, with new discussions of interpretation, evidence, and revision.
- New Throughout the handbook, eight examples of academic writing and seven examples of public writing illustrate varied genres, including a new social-science research report documented in APA style and a sample social-media post for a nonprofit organization.
- New Emphasizing critical analysis and writing, the expanded Chapter 10 on critical reading and writing includes a student's analysis of a Web advertisement and a revised discussion of writing critically about texts and visuals.
- New Pulling together key material on academic integrity, Chapter 9 on academic writing and Chapter 54 on plagiarism and documenting sources discuss developing one's own perspective on a topic, using and managing sources, and avoiding plagiarism.

Other chapters throughout the handbook reinforce these important topics.

- Synthesis receives special emphasis wherever students might need help balancing their own and others' views, such as in responding to texts.
- Part 7 gives students a solid foundation in research writing. Extensive chapters cover documentation and format in MLA and APA styles.

A guide to research writing

With detailed advice and annotated sample MLA and APA papers, the handbook always attends closely to research writing and source citation. The discussion stresses using the library as Web gateway, managing information, evaluating and synthesizing sources, integrating source material, and avoiding plagiarism. The extensive coverage of MLA and APA documentation styles reflects each style's latest version.

- New Coverage of the working bibliography groups sources by books, articles, and other types, reflecting a streamlined approach to source material throughout the handbook.
- New Reflecting the varied ways that students may seek sources, the discussion of libraries' Web portals covers research guides and centralized search engines and also updates the material on databases.
- New A revised discussion of keywords and subject headings helps students develop and refine their search terms.
- New A streamlined discussion of gathering information from sources stresses keeping accurate records of source material, marking borrowed words and ideas clearly, and using synthesis.
- New The discussion of documenting sources explains key features of source documentation, defines the relationship between in-text citations and a bibliography, and presents pros and cons of using bibliography software.
- The discussion of evaluating sources—library, Web, and social media—helps students discern purposes and distinguish between reliable and unreliable sources. Case studies show the application of critical criteria to sample articles, Web documents, and a blog.
- The extensive chapter on avoiding plagiarism discusses deliberate and careless plagiarism, shows examples of plagiarized and revised sentences, and gives updated advice about avoiding plagiarism when using online sources.
- A research paper-in-progress on green consumerism follows a student through the research process and culminates in an annotated paper documented in MLA style.

An updated reference for documenting sources

The extensive coverage of MLA and APA documentation styles reflects each style's latest version.

- New Reorganized chapters for both styles group sources by books, articles, and other types, thus simplifying the search for appropriate models and clarifying differences among print, database, Web, and other media for each type.

- New Updated, annotated samples of key source types illustrate MLA and APA documentation, showing students how to find the bibliographical information needed to cite each type and highlighting the similarities and differences between print and database sources.

- New The chapter on MLA documentation reflects the new eighth edition of the *MLA Handbook*. In addition, the sample papers and other examples that show MLA have been updated to reflect the latest MLA guidelines.

- New A complete APA research report shows the style in the context of student writing.

- Highlighting on all documentation models makes authors, titles, dates, and other citation elements easy to grasp.

A guide to the writing process

The handbook takes a concise, practical approach to assessing the writing situation, generating ideas, developing the thesis statement, revising, and other elements of the writing process.

- New An expanded discussion of the thesis covers using the thesis statement to preview organization.

- New Chapter 7 on paragraphs offers new, relevant examples illustrating paragraph development.

A guide to usage, grammar, and punctuation

The handbook's core reference material reliably and concisely explains basic concepts and common errors, provides hundreds of annotated examples, and offers frequent exercises in connected discourse.

- New Revised explanations of grammar concepts and rules define essential terms in context, simplify the presentation, and emphasize key material.

- New Dozens of new and revised checklist boxes, examples, and exercises clarify and reinforce important concepts.

- New Added examples in Chapter 18 on appropriate language show how to revise common shortcuts of texting and other electronic communication for academic writing.

■ **New** Sentence fragments, a common trouble spot, are discussed in greater detail and illustrated with new and more examples.

■ Hundreds of examples use color underlining to show clearly both the look of errors and the means of correcting them.

A guide for culturally and linguistically diverse writers

At notes and sections labeled ⬮CULTURE LANGUAGE⬮, the handbook provides extensive rhetorical and grammatical help for writers whose first language or dialect is not standard American English.

■ Fully integrated coverage, instead of a separate section, means that students can find what they need without having to know which problems they do and don't share with native SAE speakers.

■ The "⬮CULTURE LANGUAGE⬮ Guide" at the end of the book (pages 562–63) orients students with advice on mastering SAE and pulls all the integrated coverage together in one place.

A guide to using and analyzing media

The handbook helps students think critically about speech, visuals, and other media and use them in their work.

■ **New** A revised and streamlined chapter on presenting writing provides essential information on designing documents, using visuals and other media, and writing for online environments (Chapter 8).

■ **New** A student's analysis of a Web advertisement illustrates critical thinking about a visual (Chapter 10).

■ **New** A new chapter offers a concise guide to planning and delivering an oral presentation with visual aids (Chapter 13).

■ The chapter on finding sources for research gives advice for finding visual, audio, and video sources (Chapter 52).

■ Illustrations in several of the handbook's student papers show various ways to support written ideas with visual information.

A guide for writing beyond the classroom

A chapter on public writing extends the handbook's usefulness beyond academic writing.

■ **New** Discussions of writing for social media encourage students to consider their potential audience now and in the future, whether they are writing to express themselves or to represent an organization.

■ **New** Updated coverage of writing a job application discusses cover letters, résumés, and professional online profiles.

A uniquely accessible reference

LB Brief opens itself to students, featuring not only a convenient spiral binding but also numerous features designed to help students find what they need and then use what they find.

- **New** The approach to terminology facilitates reading and reference, avoiding unnecessary terms, defining needed terms, and boldfacing the key definitions in the index.
- A brief contents inside the front cover shows the book at a glance, while a detailed contents appears inside the back cover.
- "In *Brief*" learning objectives at the start of each chapter provide students with an overview of the handbook's key content.
- A direct organization arranges topics in ways that students can easily grasp.
- More than fifty checklist and summary boxes highlight key reference information, such as questions about audience, uses of the comma, and indexes to documentation formats.
- Annotations on both verbal and visual examples connect concepts and illustrations.
- Highlighting on documentation models distinguishes important elements.
- Dictionary-style headers in the index make it easy to find entries.
- A preface just for students outlines the book's contents, details reference aids, and explains the page layout.

Supplements

- *MyWritingLab* is an online homework, tutorial, and assessment program designed to work with *LB Brief* to engage students and improve results. Within *MyWritingLab*'s structured environment, students practice what they learn, test their comprehension, and pursue personalized study plans that help them absorb course material and understand concepts. Visit *mywritinglab.com* for more information.
- The answer key to *LB Brief* (ISBN 0134123263) includes answers to all of the book's exercises.
- *Developmental Exercises* (ISBN 0134123123) builds on the instruction in *LB Brief* to provide developing writers with extra practice in areas where they need it most. A separate answer key (ISBN 013412328X) is also available.

Acknowledgments

LB Brief remains relevant and useful to students because instructors talk with Pearson's sales representatives and editors, answer questionnaires, write detailed reviews, and send us personal notes. For their helpful feedback, I wish to thank the following instructors who communicated with me directly or through reviews. Their experiences and their insights into the handbook led to the improvements in this new edition: Brooke Anderson, Pima Community College; William R. Black III, Weatherford College; Randy Boone, Northampton Community College; Linda Boynton, Oakland Community College; Misti R. Brock, Vernon College, Century City Center; Nancy C. DeJoy, Michigan State University; Susan Denning, Clark College; Ashley S. Dugas, Copiah-Lincoln Community College; Julie A. Fenton-Glass, Wake Technical Community College; Kristen Garrison, Midwestern State University; Kimberly Hall, Harrisburg Area Community College; Gregg W. Heitschmidt, Surry Community College; David Hennessy, Broward College, Central Campus; Cary Henson, University of Wisconsin, Oshkosh; Calley Hornbuckle, Columbia College; Cynthia Kimball, Portland Community College; Lawrence Morgan, University of Wisconsin, Stevens Point; Andrew Pegman, Cuyahoga Community College; James Price, Navarro College; Julia Ruengert, Pensacola State College; Dia Samuel, Lee College; Jean Sorensen, Grayson College; and Brian Topping, SUNY Jefferson Community College.

In responding to the ideas of these thoughtful critics, I had the help of several creative people. Valerie Vlahakis, John Wood Community College, prompted me to rethink and reorganize the documentation chapters, and she graciously allowed me to adapt her guide to finding appropriate models. Sigrid Anderson Cordell, University of Michigan, guided me through the ever-changing contemporary academic library. Sylvan Barnet, Tufts University, continued to lend his expertise in the chapter "Reading and Writing about Literature," which is adapted from his *Short Guide to Writing about Literature* and *Introduction to Literature* (with William Burto and William E. Cain). Ellen Kuhl provided creative, meticulous, and invaluable help with the material on research writing. And Carol Hollar-Zwick, sine qua non, served brilliantly as originator, sounding board, critic, coordinator, researcher, producer, and friend.

A superb publishing team helped me make this book. At Pearson, editors Joseph Opiela and Anne Brunell Ehrenworth offered perceptive insights into instructors' and students' needs. The project manager at Pearson, Savoula Amanatidis, and the freelance project manager, Susan McIntyre of Essential Edits, shepherded the manuscript skillfully through the many stages of becoming a book. Jerilyn Bockorick once again made the book a pleasure to use. I am grateful to all these collaborators.

1 The Writing Situation

- Analyze the situation (below).
- Choose a subject appropriate to the assignment (p. 4).
- Define your purpose (p. 6).
- Consider your audience (p. 7).
- Understand the genre (p. 9).

Visit MyWritingLab™ for more resources on the writing situation.

Responding to the writing situation is usually the first step in the **writing process**—the term for all the activities, mental and physical, that go into creating what eventually becomes a finished piece of work. There is no universal writing process: no two writers proceed in the same way, and even an individual writer adapts the process to the task at hand. Still, most writers pass through certain stages that overlap and circle back on one another: responding to the writing situation (this chapter) and then inventing and planning (Chapters 2 and 3) and drafting, revising, and editing (Chapters 4–6). As you complete varied assignments and try the many techniques included in this book, you will develop your own writing process.

1a Analyze the writing situation.

Any writing you do for others occurs in a **writing situation** that both limits and clarifies your choices. You are communicating within a particular context, about a particular subject, for a specific reason, to a particular audience of readers. You may be required to write in a particular genre. You may need to conduct research. You probably face a length requirement and a deadline. And you may be expected to present your work in a certain format and medium.

Analyzing the writing situation at the very start of a project can tell you much about how to proceed. (For discussion of the following elements, refer to the page numbers given.)

Assignment (pp. 4–5)

- **What are the basic requirements?** Consider expectations for subject, purpose, audience, genre, and research. What leeway do you have?
- **What other requirements do you have to meet?** How long should your writing be? When is the assignment due? What format does the assignment specify or allow—a printed paper? a Web site? an oral presentation?

Subject (pp. 4–6)

■ **What does your writing assignment instruct you to write about?** If you don't have a specific assignment, what do you want to write about?

■ **What interests you about the subject?** What do you already have ideas about or want to know more about?

Purpose (pp. 6–7)

■ **What aim does your assignment specify?** For instance, does it ask you to explain something or argue a point?

■ **Why are you writing?** What do you want your work to accomplish? What effect do you intend it to have on readers?

■ **How can you best achieve your purpose?**

Audience (pp. 7–9)

■ **Who will read your writing?**

■ **What do your readers already know and think about your subject?** Do they have any characteristics—such as educational background, experience in your field, or political views—that could influence their reception of your writing?

■ **How should you project yourself in your writing?** What role should you play in relation to readers, and what information should you give? How informal or formal should your writing be?

■ **What do you want readers to do or think after they read your writing?**

Genre (pp. 9–10)

■ **What genre, or type of writing, does the assignment call for?** Are you to write an analysis, a report, a proposal, or some other type? Or are you free to choose a genre?

■ **What are the conventions of the genre you are using?** For example, readers might expect a claim supported by evidence, a solution to a defined problem, or easy-to-find information.

Research (pp. 350–415)

■ **What kinds of evidence will best suit your subject, purpose, audience, and genre?** What combination of facts, examples, and expert opinions will support your ideas?

■ **Does your assignment require research?** Will you need to consult sources of information or conduct other research, such as interviews, surveys, or experiments?

■ **Even if research is not required, what additional information do you need to develop your subject?** How will you obtain it?

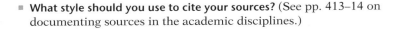

- **What style should you use to cite your sources?** (See pp. 413–14 on documenting sources in the academic disciplines.)

Presentation

- **What format or method of presentation does the assignment require?** (See pp. 61–70 on academic writing, pp. 127–31 on oral presentations, and pp. 132–40 on business and other public writing.)
- **How might you use headings, lists, illustrations, video, and other elements to achieve your purpose?** (See pp. 61–63.)

Exercise 1.1 Analyzing a writing situation

The following assignment was given in a survey course in psychology. What does the assignment specify and imply about the elements of the writing situation? Based on this assignment, how would you answer the questions on the preceding pages and above?

When is psychotherapy most likely to work? That is, what combinations of client, therapist, and theory tend to achieve good results? In your discussion, cite studies supporting your conclusions. Length: 1500 to 1800 words. Post your paper online to me and your discussion group by March 30.

1b   Choose a subject that is appropriate for the assignment.

A subject for writing has several basic requirements:

- **It should be suitable for the purpose, audience, and genre of the assignment.**
- **It should be neither too general nor too limited for the assigned deadline and paper length.**
- **It should be something you are willing to learn more about, even something you care about.**

1 ■ Responding to a specific assignment

When you receive an assignment, study its wording and its implications about your writing situation to guide your choice of subject:

- **What's wanted from you?** Many writing assignments contain words such as *discuss, describe, analyze, report, interpret, explain, define, argue,* or *evaluate.* These words specify the way you are to approach your subject, what kind of thinking is expected of you, and what your general purpose is. (See pp. 6–7.)
- **For whom are you writing?** Many assignments will specify your readers, but sometimes you will have to figure out for yourself who your audience is and what it expects of you. (For more on analyzing your audience, see pp. 7–9.)

■ **What kind of research is required?** An assignment may specify the kinds of sources you are expected to consult, and you can use such information to choose your subject. (If you are unsure whether research is required, check with your instructor.)

■ **Does the subject need to be narrowed?** To do the subject justice in the length and time required, you'll often need to limit it. (See below.)

2 ■ Narrrowing a general subject

Let's say you've decided to write about social-networking Web sites or about a character in a short story. You've got a subject, but it's still broad, worthy of a lengthy article if not a whole book. For a relatively brief paper, you'll need a narrow focus in order to provide the specific details that make writing significant and interesting.

One helpful technique for narrowing a subject is to ask focused questions about it, seeking one that seems appropriate for your assignment and that promises to sustain your interest through the writing process. The following examples illustrate how questioning can scale down broad subjects to specific, manageable subjects:

Broad subjects	Specific subjects
Social-networking sites	What draws people to these sites?
	How do the sites alter the ways people interact?
	What privacy protections should the sites provide for users?
Mrs. Mallard in Kate Chopin's "The Story of an Hour"	What changes does Mrs. Mallard undergo?
	Why does Mrs. Mallard respond as she does to news of her husband's death?
	What does the story's irony contribute to the character of Mrs. Mallard?
Federal aid to college students	Which students should be entitled to federal aid?
	How adequate are the kinds of federal aid available to college students?
	Why should the federal government aid college students?

Use the following guidelines to narrow broad subjects:

■ **Ask as many questions about your broad subject as you can think of.** Make a list.

■ **For each question that interests you and that fits the assignment, roughly sketch out the main ideas.** Consider how many paragraphs or pages of specific facts, examples, and other details you would need to pin those ideas down. This thinking should give you at least a vague idea of how much work you'd have to do and how long the resulting paper might be.

1c

■ **Break a too-broad question down further,** repeating the previous steps.

Exercise 1.2   Narrowing subjects

Choose three of the following broad subjects and, using the guidelines on the previous page and above, narrow each one to at least one specific question that can be answered in a three- to four-page paper.

1. Use of cell phones
2. Training of teachers
3. Dance in America
4. The history of women's suffrage
5. Fad diets
6. Immigrants in the United States
7. Space exploration
8. African Americans and civil rights
9. Child abuse
10. Successes in cancer research
11. Reality TV shows
12. Women writers
13. Political campaigns
14. Genetic engineering
15. Trends in popular music

1c   Define your purpose.

Your **purpose** in writing is your chief reason for communicating something about your subject to a particular audience of readers. Most writing you do will have one of four main purposes:

■ **To entertain readers.**

■ **To express your feelings or ideas.**

■ **To inform or to explain something to readers (exposition).**

■ **To persuade readers to accept or act on your opinion (argument).**

These purposes often overlap in a single essay, but usually one predominates. And the dominant purpose will influence your slant on your subject, the details you choose, and even the words you use.

Many writing assignments narrow the purpose by using a signal word, such as the following:

■ **Report:** Survey, organize, and objectively present the available evidence on the subject.

■ **Summarize:** Concisely state the main points in a text, argument, theory, or other work.

■ **Discuss:** Examine the main points, competing views, or implications of the subject.

■ **Compare and contrast:** Explain the similarities and differences between two subjects. (See also p. 55.)

■ **Define:** Specify the meaning of a term or a concept—distinctive characteristics, boundaries, and so on. (See also p. 53.)

■ **Analyze:** Identify the elements of the subject and discuss how they work together. (See also pp. 54 and 91.)

■ **Interpret:** Infer the subject's meaning or implications.

■ **Evaluate:** Judge the quality or significance of the subject, considering pros and cons. (See also p. 93.)

■ **Argue:** Take a position on the subject and support your position with evidence. (See also pp. 102–17.)

1d

You can conceive of your purpose more specifically, too, in a way that incorporates your particular subject and the outcome you intend:

To explain the steps in a new office procedure so that staffers will be able to follow it without difficulty.

To analyze how Annie Dillard's "Total Eclipse" builds to its climax so that readers appreciate the author's skill.

To persuade readers to support the college administration's plan for more required courses.

To argue against additional regulation of handguns so that readers will perceive the potential disadvantages for themselves and for the nation as a whole.

To argue that gun deaths would be reduced through a new program of background checks.

1d Consider your audience.

The readers likely to see your work—your **audience**—will often be specified or implied in a writing assignment. When you write an editorial for the student newspaper, your audience consists of fellow students. When you analyze a poem in a literature class, your audience consists of your instructor and perhaps your classmates. The box on the next page provides questions that can help you define the audience in most writing situations.

Your sense of your audience will influence three key elements of what you write:

■ **The specific information you use to gain and keep the attention of readers and guide them to accept your conclusions.** This information may consist of details, facts, examples, and other evidence that make your ideas clear, support your assertions, and suit your readers' needs.

■ **The role you choose to play in relation to your readers.** Depending on your purpose, you will want readers to perceive you in a certain way. The possible roles are many and varied—for instance, scholar, storyteller, lecturer, guide, reporter, advocate, inspirer.

■ **The tone you use.** Tone in writing is the attitude conveyed by words and sentence structures. Depending on your aims and what you think your readers will expect and respond to, your

Questions about audience

Identity and expectations

- **Who *are* my readers?**
- **What do my readers expect from the genre of my writing?** Do they expect features such as a particular organization and format, distinctive kinds of evidence, or a certain style of documenting sources?
- **What do I want readers to know or do after reading my work?** How should I make that clear to them?
- **How should I project myself to my readers?** How formal or informal will they expect me to be? What role and tone should I assume?

Characteristics, knowledge, and attitudes

- **What characteristics of readers are relevant for my subject and purpose?** For instance:

  Age and sex
  Occupation: students, professional colleagues, etc.
  Social or economic role: car buyers, potential employers, etc.
  Economic or educational background
  Ethnic background
  Political, religious, or moral beliefs and values
  Hobbies or activities

- **How will the characteristics of readers influence their attitudes toward my subject?**
- **What do readers already know and *not* know about my topic?** How much do I have to tell them? What aspects of my subject will be interesting and relevant to them?
- **How should I handle any specialized terms?** Will readers know them? If not, should I define them?
- **What ideas, arguments, or information might surprise, excite, or offend readers?** How should I handle these points?
- **What misconceptions might readers have about my subject and/or my approach to it?** How can I dispel these misconceptions?

Uses and format

- **What will readers do with my writing?** Should I expect them to read every word from the top, to scan for information, or to look for conclusions? Can I help readers with a summary, headings, illustrations, or other aids? (See pp. 61–70 on presenting writing.)

---

tone may be formal or informal. The attitude you convey may be serious or light, forceful or calm, irritated or cheerful.

Your information, role, and tone contribute to your writer's **voice:** your projection of yourself into your writing. Your voice conveys your sense of the world as it applies to the particular writing situation: this subject, this purpose, this audience. Thus voice can vary quite a bit from one writing situation to another, as the following memos illustrate. Both have the same subject and general purpose, but they address different readers.

To coworkers

Ever notice how much paper collects in your trash basket every day? Well, most of it can be recycled with little effort, I promise. Basically, all you need to do is set a bag or box near your desk and deposit wastepaper in it. I know, space is cramped in these little cubicles. But what's a little more crowding when the earth's at stake? . . .

Voice: a peer who is thoughtful, cheerful, and sympathetic

Information: how employees could handle recycling; no mention of costs

Role: colleague

Tone: informal, personal (*Ever notice; Well; you; I know, space is cramped*)

To management

In my four months here, I have observed that all of us throw out baskets of potentially recyclable paper every day. Considering the drain on our forest resources and the pressure on landfills that paper causes, we could make a valuable contribution to the environmental movement by helping to recycle the paper we use. At the company where I worked before, the employees separate clean wastepaper from other trash at their desks. The maintenance staff collects trash in two receptacles, and the trash hauler (the same one we use here) makes separate pickups. I do not know what the hauler charges for handling recyclable material. . . .

Voice: a subordinate who is thoughtful, responsible, and serious

Information: specific reasons; view of company as a whole; reference to another company; problem of cost

Role: employee

Tone: formal, serious (*Considering the drain; forest resources; valuable contribution; no you*)

1e   Understand the genre.

Writers use familiar **genres,** or types of writing, to express their ideas. You can recognize many genres: the poems and novels of literature, the résumé in business writing, the news article about a sports event. In college you will be asked to write in a wide range of genres, such as analyses, lab reports, reviews, proposals, oral presentations, even blog posts.

Most simply, a genre is the conventional form that writing takes in a certain context. In academic writing, genre conventions help to further the aims of the disciplines; for instance, the features of a chemistry lab report emphasize the procedures, results, and conclusions that are important in scientific investigation. The conventions also help to improve communication because the writer knows what readers expect and readers can predict what they will encounter in the writing.

When you receive a writing assignment, be sure you understand any requirements relating to genre:

- **Is a particular genre being assigned?** An assignment that asks you to write, say, an analysis, an argument, or a report has specified the genre for you to use.
- **What are the conventions of the genre?** Your instructor and/or your textbook will probably outline the requirements for you. You can also learn about a genre by reading samples of it. Consult pages 73–76 for more on genre and descriptions of the sample documents in this handbook.
- **What flexibility do you have?** Within their conventions, most genres still allow plenty of room for your own approach and voice. Again, reading samples will show you much about your options.

2 Invention

In *Brief*

- Keep a journal (facing page).
- Observe your surroundings (p. 12).
- Freewrite or brainstorm (pp. 12 and 13).
- Draw your ideas (p. 14).
- Ask questions (p. 14).

Visit MyWritingLab™ for more resources on invention.

Writers use techniques like those listed above to help invent or discover ideas and information about their subjects. **Whichever of the invention techniques you use, do your work in writing, not just in your head.** Your ideas will then be retrievable, and the very act of writing will lead you to fresh insights.

CULTURE LANGUAGE The discovery process encouraged here rewards rapid writing without a lot of thinking beforehand about what you will write or how. If your first language is not standard American English, you may find it helpful initially to do this exploratory writing in your native language or dialect and then to translate the worthwhile material for use in your drafts. This process can be productive, but it is extra work. You may want to try it at first and gradually move to composing in standard English.

2a   Keep a journal.

A **journal** is a diary of ideas kept on paper or on a computer. It gives you a place to record your responses, thoughts, and observations about what you read, see, hear, or experience. It can also provide ideas for writing. Because you write only for yourself, you can work out your ideas without the pressure of an audience "out there" who will evaluate logic or organization or correctness. If you write every day, even just for a few minutes, the routine will loosen your writing muscles and improve your confidence.

You can use a journal for varied purposes: perhaps to confide your feelings, explore your responses to movies and other media, practice certain kinds of writing (such as poems or news stories), pursue ideas from your courses, or think critically about what you read. One student, Katy Moreno, used her journal for the last purpose. Her composition instructor distributed "It's a Flat World, after All," an essay by Thomas L. Friedman about globalization and the job market, and gave the following assignment, calling for a response to reading.

Instructor's assignment

In "It's a Flat World, after All," Thomas L. Friedman describes today's global job market, focusing not on manufacturing jobs that have been "outsourced" to overseas workers but on jobs that require a college degree and are no longer immune to outsourcing. Friedman argues that keeping jobs in the United States requires that US students, parents, and educators improve math and science education. As a college student, how do you respond to this analysis of the global market for jobs? What do you think today's college students should be learning?

On first reading the essay, Moreno had found it convincing because Friedman's description of the job market matched her family's experience: her mother had lost her job when it was outsourced to India. After rereading the essay, however, Moreno was not persuaded that more math and science would necessarily improve students' opportunities and preserve their future jobs. She compared Friedman's advice with details she recalled from her mother's experience, and in her journal she began to develop her own angle on the topic.

Student's journal entry

Friedman is certainly right that more jobs than we realize are going overseas—that's what happened to Mom's job and we were shocked! But he gives only one way for students like me to compete—take more math and science. At first I thought he's totally right. But then I thought that what he said didn't really explain what happened to Mom—she had lots of math + science + tons of experience, but it was her salary, not better training, that caused her job to be outsourced. An overseas worker would do her job for less money. So she lost her job because of money + because she wasn't a manager. Caught in the middle. I want to major in computer science, but I don't think it's smart to try for the kind of job Mom had—at least not as long as it's so much cheaper for companies to hire workers overseas.

(Further examples of Moreno's writing appear in the next four chapters.)

⟨**CULTURE / LANGUAGE**⟩ A journal can be especially helpful if your first language is not standard American English. You can practice writing to improve your fluency, try out sentence patterns, and experiment with vocabulary words. Equally important, you can experiment with applying what you know from experience to what you read and observe.

2b   Observe your surroundings.

Sometimes you can find a good subject—or gather information about a subject—by looking around you, not in the half-conscious way most of us move from place to place in our daily lives, but deliberately, all senses alert. On a bus, for instance, are there certain types of passengers? What seems to be on the driver's mind? To get the most from observation, you should have a notebook and pen or an electronic device handy for notes and sketches. Back at your desk, study your notes and sketches for oddities or patterns that you'd like to explore further.

2c   Freewrite.

1 ▪ Writing into a subject

Many writers find subjects or discover ideas by **freewriting:** writing without stopping for a certain amount of time (say, ten minutes) or to a certain length (say, one page). The goal of freewriting is to generate ideas and information from *within* yourself by going around the part of your mind that doesn't want to write or can't think of anything to write. You let words themselves suggest other words. *What* you write is not important; that you *keep* writing is. Don't stop, even if that means repeating the same words until new words come. Don't go back to reread, don't censor ideas that seem off-track or repetitious, and above all don't stop to edit: grammar, punctuation, spelling, and the like are irrelevant at this stage.

If you can dim or turn off your computer monitor, you can try **invisible writing** to keep moving forward while freewriting. As you type to a dark screen, the computer will record what you type but keep it from being visible, thus preventing you from tinkering with your prose. Invisible writing may feel uncomfortable at first, but it can free the mind for very creative results.

CULTURE LANGUAGE Invisible writing can be especially helpful if you are uneasy about writing in standard English and you tend to worry about errors while writing: the blank computer screen leaves you no choice but to explore ideas without regard for their expression. If you choose to write with the monitor on, concentrate on *what* you want to say, not *how* you're saying it.

2 ▪ Focused freewriting

Focused freewriting is more concentrated: you start with your question about your subject and answer it without stopping for, say, fifteen minutes or one full page. As in all freewriting, you push to bypass mental blocks and self-consciousness, not debating what to say or editing what you've written. With focused freewriting, though, you let the physical act of writing take you into and around your subject.

An example of focused freewriting can be found in Katy Moreno's journal response to Thomas L. Friedman's "It's a Flat World, after All" on the pages 11–12. Because she already had an idea about Friedman's essay, Moreno was able to start there and expand on the idea.

2d Brainstorm.

A method similar to freewriting is **brainstorming**—focusing intently on a subject for a fixed period (say, fifteen minutes), pushing yourself to list every idea and detail that comes to mind. Like freewriting, brainstorming requires turning off your internal editor so that you keep moving ahead. (The technique of invisible writing, described opposite, can help you move forward.)

Here is an example of brainstorming by a student, Johanna Abrams, on what a summer job can teach:

summer work teaches—
   how to look busy while doing nothing
   how to avoid the sun in summer
   seriously: discipline, budgeting money, value of money
which job? Burger King cashier? baby-sitter? mail-room clerk?
mail room: how to sort mail into boxes: this is learning??
how to survive getting fired—humiliation, outrage
Mrs. King! the mail-room queen as learning experience
the shock of getting fired: what to tell parents, friends?
Mrs. K was so rigid—dumb procedures
initials instead of names on the mail boxes—confusion!

Mrs. K's anger, resentment: the disadvantages of being smarter than your boss
the odd thing about office work: a world with its own rules for how to act
the pecking order—big chick (Mrs. K) pecks on little chick (me)
a job can beat you down—make you be mean to other people

2e   Draw your ideas.

Like freewriting and brainstorming, the technique of **clustering**, or **idea mapping**, uses free association to produce rapid, unedited work. But it emphasizes the relations between ideas by combining writing and nonlinear drawing. Start with your topic at a center point and then radiate outward with ideas. Pursue related ideas in a branching structure until they seem exhausted. Then do the same with other ideas, continuously branching out or drawing arrows to show connections.

The example below shows how a student used clustering for ten minutes to expand on the subject of money in college football.

Clustering or idea mapping

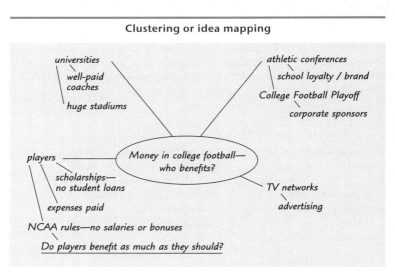

You can use idea-mapping software to draw such diagrams. The software allows you to type your ideas directly into a diagram and then rearrange, delete, and add ideas at any point in the writing process.

2f   Ask questions.

Asking yourself a set of questions about your subject—and writing out the answers—can help you look at the topic objectively and see fresh possibilities in it.

1 ▪ **Journalist's questions**

A journalist with a story to report poses a set of questions:

- **Who was involved?**
- **What happened, and what were the results?**
- **When did it happen?**
- **Where did it happen?**
- **Why did it happen?**
- **How did it happen?**

These questions can also be useful in probing an essay subject, especially when you are examining causes and effects or telling a story.

2 ▪ **Questions about patterns**

We understand a vast range of subjects through patterns such as narration, classification, and comparison and contrast. Asking questions based on patterns can help you view your topic from many angles. Sometimes you may want to develop an entire essay using just one pattern.

- **How did it happen?** (Narration)
- **How does it look, sound, feel, smell, taste?** (Description)
- **What are examples of it or reasons for it?** (Illustration or support)
- **What is it? What does it encompass, and what does it exclude?** (Definition)
- **What are its parts or characteristics?** (Division or analysis)
- **What groups or categories can it be sorted into?** (Classification)
- **How is it like, or different from, other things?** (Comparison and contrast)
- **Why did it happen? What results did or could it have?** (Cause-and-effect analysis)
- **How do you do it, or how does it work?** (Process analysis)

For more on these patterns, including paragraph-length examples, see pages 51–56.

3 Thesis and Organization

- Develop a thesis statement (below).
- Organize your ideas (p. 20).

Visit MyWritingLab™ for more resources on thesis and organization.

You'll form ideas into writing through two main operations. Finding your main idea gives you focus and direction. Organizing your raw material helps you clear away unneeded ideas, spot possible gaps, and energize your subject.

3a Develop a thesis statement.

Your readers will expect your essay to be focused on a main idea, or **thesis**. The thesis is the controlling idea to which all the essay's other ideas and information relate. In your final draft you may express this idea in a **thesis statement**, often at the end of your introduction. You can think of a thesis statement as both a claim about your subject and a promise you make to readers about how you approach the subject. The rest of your essay supports the claim and thus delivers on the promise.

1 ▪ Functions of the thesis statement

The thesis statement serves three crucial functions and one optional one:

The thesis statement

- **The thesis statement narrows your subject to a single, central idea** that you want readers to gain from your essay.
- **It claims something specific and significant about your subject,** a claim that requires support.
- **It conveys your purpose,** your reason for writing.
- **It often concisely previews the arrangement of ideas,** in which case it can also help you organize your essay.

CULTURE LANGUAGE In some cultures it is considered unnecessary or impolite for a writer to have an opinion or to state his or her main idea outright. When writing in standard American English for school or work, you can assume that early in the essay your readers expect a clear idea of what you think. They will not consider you rude if you give your opinion.

2 ▪ Evolution of the thesis statement

Your final thesis statement probably will not leap into your head early in the writing process. You may begin with an idea you want to communicate, but you will need to refine that idea to fit the realities of the paper you write. Often you will have to write and rewrite before you come to a conclusion about your subject.

Even though it will change, a sense of your thesis can give you direction as you proceed through the writing process. Try drafting a tentative thesis statement, or conceive of a **thesis question** that can guide you. This question may arise when you try to narrow your subject (p. 5), and it can sharpen as you develop your ideas. Eventually, you'll be able to answer it in your thesis statement.

Following are examples of questions and answering thesis statements. As assertions, the thesis statements each consist of a topic (usually naming the general subject) and a claim about the topic. Notice how each statement also expresses purpose. Statements 1–3 are **explanatory**: the writers mainly want to explain something to readers, such as the benefits of military service. Statements 4–6 are **argumentative**: the authors mainly want to convince readers of something, such as the need to outlaw drivers' use of cell phones. Most of the thesis statements you write in college papers will be either explanatory or argumentative.

Thesis question	Explanatory thesis statement
1. What are the advantages of serving in the US military?	Military service teaches teamwork, discipline, and job-related skills that transfer well to civilian life. [**Topic:** military service. **Claim:** teaches skills that transfer to civilian life.]
2. What steps can be taken to prevent juvenile crime?	Juveniles can be diverted from crime by active learning programs, full-time sports, frequent contact with positive role models, and intervention by consistent mentors. [**Topic:** juvenile crime. **Claim:** can be prevented in four ways.]
3. Why did Abraham Lincoln delay emancipating the slaves?	Lincoln delayed emancipating any slaves until 1863 because his primary goal was to restore and preserve the Union, with or without slavery. [**Topic:** Lincoln's delay. **Claim:** was caused by his goal of preserving the Union.]

Thesis question	Argumentative thesis statement
4. Why should drivers' use of cell phones be banned?	Drivers' use of cell phones should be outlawed because people who talk or text and drive at the same time cause accidents. [**Topic:** drivers' use of cell phones. **Claim:** should be outlawed because it causes accidents.]

3a

Thesis question	Argumentative thesis statement
5. Which college students should be entitled to federal aid?	As an investment in its own economy, the federal government should provide a tuition grant to any college student who qualifies academically. [**Topic:** federal aid. **Claim:** should be provided to any college student who qualifies academically.]
6. Should the state government play a role in moving consumers to hybrid cars?	Each proposal for the state to encourage purchase of hybrid cars—advertising campaigns, trade-in deals, and tax incentives—needlessly involves government in decisions that consumers are already making on their own. [**Topic:** proposals to encourage hybrid cars. **Claim:** needlessly involve government in consumer decisions.]

Note that statement 2, repeated below, previews the essay's organization. Readers often appreciate a preview, and students often find that it helps them organize their main points during drafting.

Thesis statement
Juveniles can be diverted from crime by <u>active learning programs</u>, <u>full-time sports</u>, <u>frequent contact with positive role models</u>, and <u>intervention by consistent mentors</u>.

Organization of essay
Discussion one by one of four ways to reduce juvenile crime.

3 ▪ Revision of the thesis statement

Before you consider your thesis statement final, ask the following questions about it.

▪ **Does the statement make a concise *claim* about your subject?** That is, does it state an opinion?

Original   Toni Morrison won the Nobel Prize in Literature in 1993.

The original sentence states a fact, not an opinion about Morrison's work. The following revision makes a claim by stating the significance of the prize:

Revised   Toni Morrison's 1993 Nobel Prize in Literature, the first awarded to an African American woman, affirms both the strength of her vivid prose style and the importance of her subject matter.

▪ **Is the claim *limited* to a single specific idea?**

Original   Diets are dangerous.

The original sentence is so broad that it seems insupportable. The revision limits the kinds of diets and their effects:

3a

Revised   Fad diets can be dangerous when they deprive the body of essential nutrients or rely on excessive quantities of potentially harmful foods.

The following original sentence is also too general, whereas the revision specifies differences and their significance:

Original   Televised sports are different from live sports.

Revised   Although television cannot transmit all the excitement of being in a crowd during a game, its close-ups and slow-motion replays reveal much about the players and the strategy of the game.

■ **Is the statement *unified* so that its parts clearly relate to each other?**

Original   Cell phones can be convenient, but they can also be dangerous.

With two facts linked by *but*, the original sentence moves in two directions, not one. The revision clarifies the relation between the parts and their significance:

Revised   The convenience of cell phones does not justify the risks of driving while talking or texting.

■ **Does the statement at least imply your *purpose*?**

Original   Educators' motives for using the Internet vary widely.

The original sentence conveys no hint of the writer's reason for exploring the subject. In contrast, the revision implies a purpose of arguing against a mainly financial motivation for using the Internet in education:

Revised   Too often, educators' uses of the Internet seem motivated less by teaching and learning than by saving money.

Exercise 3.1   Evaluating thesis statements

Evaluate the following thesis statements, considering whether each one makes a claim that is sufficiently limited, specific, and unified. Rewrite the statements as necessary to meet these goals.

1. Aggression usually leads to violence, injury, and even death, and we should use it constructively.
2. The religion of Islam is widely misunderstood in the United States.
3. One evening of a radio talk show amply illustrates both the appeal of such shows and their silliness.
4. Good manners make our society work.
5. The poem is about motherhood.
6. I disliked American history in high school, but I like it in college.

7. Television is useful for children and a mindless escape for adults who do not want to think about their problems.
8. Drunken drivers, whose perception and coordination are impaired, should receive mandatory suspensions of their licenses.
9. Business is a good major for many students.
10. The state's lenient divorce laws undermine the institution of marriage, which is fundamental to our culture, and they should certainly be made stricter for couples who have children.

3b   Organize your ideas.

Most essays share a basic pattern of introduction (states the subject), body (develops the subject), and conclusion (pulls the essay's ideas together). Introductions and conclusions are discussed on pages 57–60. Within the body, every paragraph develops some aspect of the essay's thesis. See pages 40–42 for Katy Moreno's essay, with annotations highlighting the body's support for the thesis statement.

CULTURE • LANGUAGE If you are not used to reading and writing American academic prose, its pattern of introduction-body-conclusion and the organization schemes discussed here may seem unfamiliar. For instance, instead of introductions that focus quickly on the topic and thesis, you may be used to openings that establish personal connections with readers. And instead of body paragraphs that first emphasize general points and then support those points with specific evidence, you may be used to general statements without support (because writers can assume that readers will supply the evidence themselves) or to evidence without explanation (because writers can assume that readers will infer the general points). When writing American academic prose, you need to take into account readers' expectations for directness and for the statement and support of general points.

1 ▪ The general and the specific

Organizing material for an essay requires that you distinguish general and specific ideas and see the relations between ideas. **General** and **specific** refer to the number of instances or objects included in a group signified by a word. The following "ladder" illustrates a general-to-specific hierarchy:

Most general
▲ life form
| plant
| flowering plant
| rose
▼ Uncle Dan's prize-winning American Beauty rose
Most specific

As you arrange your material, pick out the general ideas and then the specific points that support them. Set aside points that seem irrelevant to your key ideas. On a computer, you can easily experiment with various arrangements of general ideas and supporting information: save the master list to a new file and then move material around.

2 ▪ Schemes for organizing essays

An essay's body paragraphs may be arranged in many ways that are familiar to readers. The choice depends on your subject, purpose, and audience.

- **Spatial:** In describing a person, place, or thing, move through space systematically from a starting point to other features—for instance, top to bottom, near to far, left to right.
- **Chronological:** In recounting a sequence of events, arrange the events as they actually occurred in time, first to last.
- **General to specific:** Begin with an overall discussion of the subject; then fill in details, facts, examples, and other support.
- **Specific to general:** First provide the support; then draw a conclusion from it.
- **Climactic:** Arrange ideas in order of increasing importance to your thesis or increasing interest to the reader.
- **Problem-solution:** First outline a problem that needs solving; then propose a solution.

3 ▪ Outlines

It's not essential to craft a detailed outline before you begin drafting an essay; in fact, too detailed a plan could prevent you from discovering ideas while you draft. Still, even a rough scheme can show you patterns of general and specific ideas, suggest proportions, and highlight gaps or overlaps in coverage.

There are several kinds of outlines. Some of them are more flexible than others.

Scratch or informal outline

A scratch or informal outline includes key general points and may suggest specific evidence. Following are Katy Moreno's thesis statement and scratch outline on the global job market:

Thesis statement

My mother's experience of having her job outsourced taught a lesson that Thomas L. Friedman overlooks: technical training by itself can be too narrow to produce the communicators and problem solvers needed by contemporary businesses.

3b

Scratch outline

Mom's outsourcing experience
    Excellent tech skills
    Salary too high compared to overseas tech workers
    Lack of planning + communication skills, unlike managers who kept jobs
Well-rounded education to protect vs. outsourcing
    Tech training, as Friedman says
    Also, communication, problem solving, other management skills

A scratch or informal outline may be all you need to begin drafting. Sometimes, though, it may prove too skimpy a guide, and you may want to develop it into a more detailed outline. Katy Moreno used her scratch outline as a base for a detailed formal outline that gave her an even more definite sense of direction (next page).

Tree diagram

In a tree diagram, ideas and details branch out in increasing specificity. Unlike more linear outlines, this diagram can be supplemented and extended indefinitely, so it is easy to alter. From her brainstorming about a summer job (p. 13), Johanna Abrams developed the following thesis statement and constructed the tree diagram below it.

Thesis statement

Two months working in a large agency taught me that an office's pecking order should be respected.

Tree diagram

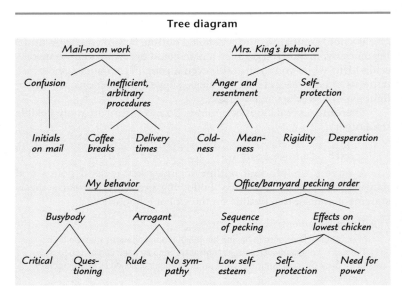

Formal outline

A formal outline not only lays out main ideas and their support but also shows the relative importance of all the essay's elements. On the basis of her scratch outline (previous page), Katy Moreno prepared a detailed formal outline for her essay on the global job market:

Thesis statement

My mother's experience of having her job outsourced taught a lesson that Thomas L. Friedman overlooks: technical training by itself can be too narrow to produce the communicators and problem solvers needed by contemporary businesses.

Formal outline

  I. Summary of Friedman's article
    A. Reasons for outsourcing
      1. Improved technology and access
      2. Well-educated workers
      3. Productive workers
      4. Lower wages
    B. Need for improved technical training in US
  II. Experience of my mother
    A. Outsourcing of job
      1. Mother's education, experience, performance
      2. Employer's cost savings
    B. Retention of managers' jobs
      1. Planning skills
      2. Communication skills
  III. Conclusions about ideal education
    A. Needs of US businesses
      1. Technical skills
      2. Management skills
        a. Communication
        b. Problem solving
        c. Versatility
    B. Consideration of personal goals
      1. Technical training
      2. English and history courses for management skills

This example illustrates several principles of outlining that can ensure completeness, balance, and clear relationships:

- **All parts are systematically indented and labeled:** Roman numerals (I, II) for primary divisions; indented capital letters (A, B) for secondary divisions; further indented Arabic numerals (1, 2) for supporting examples; and small letters (a, b) for details.
- **The outline divides the material into several groups.** A long list of points at the same level should be broken up into groups.
- **Topics of equal generality appear in parallel headings,** with the same indention and numbering or lettering.

3b

- **All subdivided headings break into at least two parts.** A topic cannot logically be divided into only one part.
- **All headings are expressed in parallel grammatical form**—for example, as phrases using nouns plus modifiers.

Note The outline on the previous page is a **topic outline**, with headings expressed as phrases. For an example of a **sentence outline**, with headings expressed as full sentences, see pages 467–68.

Unity and coherence

Two qualities of effective writing relate to organization: unity and coherence. When you perceive that someone's writing "flows well," you are probably appreciating these qualities.

To check an outline or draft for **unity**, ask these questions:

- **Is each section relevant to the main idea (thesis) of the essay?**
- **Within main sections, does each example or detail support the principal idea of that section?**

To check your outline or draft for **coherence**, ask the following questions:

- **Do the ideas follow a clear sequence?**
- **Are the parts of the essay logically connected?**
- **Are the connections clear and smooth?**

Sample essay (informative)

The following essay illustrates some ways of achieving unity and coherence (highlighted in the annotations).

Who Benefits from the Money in College Football?

Introduction establishing subject of essay

Anyone who follows Division 1-A college football cannot fail to notice the money that pours into every aspect of the sport—the lavish stadiums, corporate sponsorships, televised games, and long post-season playoff tournament. The money may seem to flow to everyone, but in reality it doesn't.

Informative thesis statement

Although college football is a multimillion-dollar industry for the schools, conferences, and television networks, the benefits do not extend to the players.

Paragraph idea, linked to thesis statement

Colleges and universities are major players in the for-profit football industry. A vibrant football program attracts not only skilled coaches and talented players but also wealthy, sports-minded donors who give money for state-of-the-

Paragraph developed with evidence supporting its idea

art stadiums and facilities. These great facilities in turn attract fans, some of whom are willing to pay high ticket prices to watch games in luxurious sky boxes and thus generate more profits for the schools' athletic departments.

Paragraph idea, linked to thesis statement

The athletic conferences to which the schools belong—such as the Big Ten, the Atlantic Coast Conference, and the Pac-12—reap financial rewards from college football. Each conference maintains a Web site to post schedules and scores, sell tickets and merchandise, and promote interest in its teams. However, the proceeds from ticket and merchandise sales surely pale in comparison to the money generated by the College Football Playoff—the three-week-long post-season football extravaganza. Each game not only is televised but also carries the name of a corporate sponsor that pays for the privilege of having its name attached to a game.

> Paragraph developed with evidence supporting its idea

Like the schools and athletic conferences, the television networks profit from football. Networks sell advertising slots to the highest bidders for every televised game during the regular season and the College Football Playoff, and they work to sustain fans' interest in football by cultivating viewers on the Web. For instance, one network generates interest in up-and-coming high school players through *Scout.com*, a Web site that posts profiles of boys being recruited by colleges and universities and that is supported, at least in part, through advertising and paid subscriptions.

> Paragraph idea, linked to thesis statement

> Paragraph developed with evidence supporting its idea

Amid these money-making players are the actual football players, the young men who are bound by NCAA rules to play as amateurs and to receive no direct compensation for their hours of practice and field time. They may receive scholarships that cover tuition, room and board, uniforms, medical care, and travel. Yet these payments are a small fraction of the millions of dollars spent on and earned from football.

> Transition and new paragraph idea, linked to thesis statement

> Paragraph developed with evidence supporting its idea

Many critics have pointed out the disparity between players' rewards and the industry's profits. Recent efforts to unionize the players and file lawsuits on their behalf have caused schools, conferences, and the NCAA to make some concessions in scholarship packages and rules. However, these changes do not fundamentally alter a system in which the big benefits go to everyone but the players.

> Conclusion echoing thesis statement and summarizing

—Terrence MacDonald (student)

See also pages 44–50 on unity and coherence in paragraphs.

Exercise 3.2 Organizing ideas

The list of ideas on the next page was extracted by a student from freewriting he did for a brief paper on soccer in the United States. Using his thesis statement as a guide, pick out the general ideas and arrange the relevant specific points under them. In some cases you may have to infer general ideas to cover specific points in the list.

Thesis statement
Although its growth in the United States has been slow and halting, professional soccer may finally be poised to become a major American sport.

4a

List of ideas

In countries of South and Latin America, soccer is the favorite sport.
In the United States the success of a sport depends largely on its ability to attract huge TV audiences.
Soccer was not often presented on US television.
In 2010 and 2014, the World Cup final was broadcast on ABC and on Spanish-language Univision.
In the past, professional soccer could not get a foothold in the United States because of poor TV coverage and lack of financial backing.
The growing Hispanic population in the United States could help soccer grow as well.
Investors have poured hundreds of millions of dollars into the top US professional league.
Potential fans did not have a chance to see soccer games.
Failures of early start-up leagues made potential backers wary of new ventures.
Recently, the outlook for professional soccer has changed dramatically.
The US television audience for the 2014 US-Ghana match was larger than the audience for baseball's World Series.

4   Drafting

In *Brief*

- To begin a draft, just start writing (below).
- To complete a draft, maintain momentum (facing page).

Visit MyWritingLab™ for more resources on drafting.

Drafting is an occasion for exploration. Don't expect to transcribe solid thoughts into polished prose. Instead, let the act of drafting help you find and form your meaning.

4a   Start writing.

Beginning a draft often takes courage, even for seasoned professionals. Procrastination may actually help if you let ideas simmer at the same time. At some point, though, you'll have to face the blank paper or empty screen. The following techniques can help you begin.

- **Read over what you've already written** —notes, outlines, and so on— and immediately start your draft with whatever comes to mind.
- **Freewrite** (see p. 12).
- **Pretend you're writing to a friend about your subject.**

- **Skip the opening and start in the middle.** Or write the conclusion.
- **Write a paragraph.** Explain what you think your essay will be about when you finish it.
- **Start writing the part that you understand best or feel most strongly about.** Using your outline, divide your work into chunks—say, one for the introduction, another for the first point, and so on. One of these chunks may call out to be written.

4b   Maintain momentum.

Drafting requires momentum: the forward movement opens you to fresh ideas and connections. To keep moving while drafting, try one or more of these techniques:

- **Set aside enough time.** For a brief essay, a first draft is likely to take at least an hour or two.
- **Work in a quiet, comfortable place.**
- **If you must stop working, write down what you expect to do next.** Then you can pick up where you stopped with minimal disruption.
- **Be as fluid as possible.** Spontaneity will allow your attitudes toward your subject to surface naturally in your sentences.
- **Keep going.** Skip over sticky spots; leave a blank if you can't find the right word; put alternative ideas or phrasings in brackets so that you can consider them later. If an idea pops out of nowhere but doesn't seem to fit in, quickly jot it down, or write it into the draft and bracket or boldface it for later attention.
- **Resist self-criticism.** Don't worry about your style, grammar, spelling, punctuation, and the like. Don't worry about what your readers will think. These are very important matters, but save them for revision.
- **Use your thesis statement and outline.** They can remind you of your planned purpose, organization, and content. However, if your writing leads you in a direction you find more interesting, then follow.

4c   A sample first draft

Katy Moreno's first-draft response to Thomas L. Friedman's "It's a Flat World, after All" appears on the next two pages. (The first two paragraphs include the page numbers in Friedman's article that Moreno summarized material from.) As part of her assignment, Moreno showed the draft to four classmates, whose suggestions for revision appear in the margin of this draft. They used the Comment function of *Microsoft Word*, which allows users to add comments without inserting words into the document's text. (Notice that the classmates ignore errors in grammar and punctuation, concentrating instead on larger issues such as thesis, clarity of ideas, and unity.)

Title?

In "It's a Flat World, after All," Thomas L. Friedman argues that, most US students are not preparing themselves as well as they should to compete in today's economy. Not like students in India, China, and other countries are (34-37). The outsourcing of my mother's job proves that Thomas L. Friedman's advice to improve students' technical training is too narrow.

> **Comment [Jared]:** Your mother's job being outsourced is interesting, but your introduction seems rushed.

> **Comment [Rabia]:** The end of your thesis statement is a little unclear—too narrow for what?

Friedman describes a "flat" world where technology like the Internet and wireless communication makes it possible for college graduates all over the globe, in particular in India and China, to get jobs that once were gotten by graduates of US colleges and universities (37). He argues that US students need more math and science in order to compete (37).

> **Comment [Erin]:** Can you include the reasons Friedman gives for overseas students' success?

I came to college with first-hand knowledge of globalization and outsourcing. My mother, who worked for sixteen years in the field of information technology (IT), was laid off six months ago when the company she worked for decided to outsource much of its IT work to a company based in India. My mother majored in computer science, had sixteen years of experience, and her bosses always gave her good reviews. She never expected to be laid off and was surprised when she was. She wasn't laid off because of her background and performance. In fact, my mother had a very strong background in math and science and years of training and job experience. The reason was because her salary and benefits cost the company more than outsourcing her job did. Which hurt my family financially, as you can imagine.

> **Comment [Nathaniel]:** Tighten this paragraph to avoid repetition? Also, how does your mother's experience relate to Friedman and your thesis?

A number of well-paid people in the IT department where my mother worked, namely IT managers, were not laid off. As my mother explained at the time, they kept their jobs because they were better at planning and they communicated better, they were better writers and speakers than my mother.

> **Comment [Erin]:** What were the managers better at planning for?

Like my mother, I am more comfortable in front of a computer than I am in front of a group of people. I planned

to major in computer science. Since my mother lost her job,
though, I have decided to take courses in English and history
too, where the classes will require me to do different kinds of
work. When I enter the job market, my well-rounded education will make me a more attractive job candidate, and, will
help me to be a versatile, productive employee.

Comment [Nathaniel]: Can you be more specific about the kinds of work you'll need to do?

Comment [Rabia]: Can you work this point into your thesis?

We know from our history that Americans have been innovative, hard-working people. We students have educational
opportunities to compete in the global economy, but we must
use our time in college wisely. As Thomas L. Friedman says,
my classmates and I need to be ready for a rapidly changing
future. We will have to work hard each day, which means being prepared for class, getting the best grades we can, and
making the most of each class. Our futures depend on the decisions we make today.

Comment [Jared]: Conclusion seems to go off in a
new direction. Friedman
mentions hard work, but it
hasn't been your focus
before.

Comment [Rabia]: Don't
forget your works cited.

5   Revising

In *Brief*

- Read your work critically (next page).
- Use a revision checklist (p. 31).
- Collaborate on revisions (p. 32).

Visit MyWritingLab™ for more resources on revising.

Revising is essential to create an effective piece of writing. During revision—literally, "re-seeing"—you shift your focus outward from yourself and your subject toward your readers, concentrating on what will help them respond as you want. Many writers revise in two stages: first they view the work as a whole, evaluating and improving its over-all meaning and structure (this chapter); then they edit sentences for wording, grammar, punctuation, spelling, and so on (next chapter).

In revising your writing, you may work alone or you may receive input from your instructor and/or other students in a collaborative group. Whether you are responding to your own evaluation or that of readers, you may need to rethink your thesis, move or delete whole paragraphs, clarify how ideas relate to the thesis, or support ideas with details or further research. Knowing that you will edit later gives you the freedom to look beyond the confines of the page or screen to see the paper as a whole.

5a   Read your work critically.

Your first step in revising your writing should be to examine large-scale issues such as whether your purpose and main idea will be clear to readers and whether the draft fully develops the thesis. To evaluate your work in this way, you need to read it critically, and that means you have to create some distance between your draft and yourself. One of the following techniques may help you see your work objectively:

- **Take a break after finishing the draft.** A few hours may be enough; a whole night or day is preferable.
- **Ask someone to respond to your draft.** A roommate, family member, classmate, or tutor in the writing center can call attention to what needs revising.
- **Read your draft in a new medium.** Typing a handwritten draft or printing out a word-processed draft can reveal weaknesses that you didn't see in the original.
- **Outline your draft.** Highlight the main points supporting the thesis, and write these sentences down separately in outline form. Then examine the outline you've made for logical order, gaps, and digressions. A formal outline can be especially illuminating because of its careful structure (see pp. 23–24).
- **Listen to your draft.** Read the draft out loud to yourself or a friend or classmate, record and listen to it, or have someone read the draft to you.
- **Use a revision checklist.** Don't try to re-see everything in your draft at once. Use the checklist on the facing page, making a separate pass through the draft for each item.

Managing drafts

When you revise on a computer, take a few precautions to keep track of your drafts and to avoid losing your work:

- **Work on a copy of your latest draft.** Then the original will remain intact until you're truly finished with it. On the copy you can use your word processor's Track Changes function, which shows changes alongside the original text and allows you to accept or reject revisions later.
- **Save each draft under its own file name.** You may need to consult an earlier draft for ideas or phrasings.
- **Save your work every five to ten minutes.**
- **After doing any major work on a project, create a backup version of the file.**

Checklist for whole-essay revision

Assignment
How have you responded to the assignment for this writing? Verify that your subject, purpose, and genre are appropriate for the requirements of the assignment.

Purpose
What is the purpose of your writing? Does it conform to the assignment? Is it consistent throughout the paper? (See pp. 6–7.)

Audience
How does the writing address the intended audience? How does it meet readers' likely expectations for your subject? Where might readers need more information?

Genre
How does your writing conform to the conventions of the genre you're writing in—features such as organization, kinds of evidence, language, and format?

Thesis
What is the thesis of your writing? Where does it become clear? How well do thesis and paper match: Does any part of the paper stray from the thesis? Does the paper fulfill the commitment of the thesis? (See pp. 16–19.)

Organization
What are the main points of the paper? (List them.) How well does each support the thesis? How effective is their arrangement for the paper's purpose? (See pp. 20–24.)

Development
How well do details, examples, and other evidence support each main point? Where, if at all, might readers find support skimpy or have trouble understanding the content? (See pp. 6–7, 51–56.)

Unity
What does each sentence and paragraph contribute to the thesis? Where, if at all, do digressions occur? Should they be cut, or can they be rewritten to support the thesis? (See pp. 24, 44–45.)

Coherence
How clearly and smoothly does the paper flow? Where does it seem rough or awkward? Can any transitions be improved? (See pp. 24, 45–50.)

Title, introduction, conclusion
How accurately and interestingly does the title reflect the essay's content? (See p. 33.) How well does the introduction engage and focus readers' attention? (See pp. 57–59.) How effective is the conclusion in providing a sense of completion? (See pp. 59–60.)

5b   Collaborate on revisions.

In many writing courses students work together, often commenting on each other's writing to help with revision. This collaborative writing provides experience in reading written work critically and in reaching others through writing. The collaboration may occur face to face in small groups, on paper via drafts and comments, or online, either through a course-management system such as *Blackboard* or *Canvas* or through a class blog, e-mail list, or wiki.

Whatever the medium of collaboration, following a few guidelines will help you gain more from others' comments and become a more constructive reader yourself.

Benefiting from comments on your writing

- **Think of your readers as counselors or coaches.** They can help you see the virtues and flaws in your work and sharpen your awareness of readers' needs.
- **Read or listen to comments closely.**
- **Know what the critic is saying.** If you need more information, ask for it, or consult the appropriate section of this handbook.
- **Don't become defensive.** Letting comments offend you will only erect a barrier to improvement in your writing. As one writing teacher advises, "Leave your ego at the door."
- **Revise your work in response to appropriate comments.** You will learn more from the act of revision than from just thinking about changes.
- **Remember that you are the final authority on your work.** You should be open to suggestions, but you are free to decline advice when you think it is inappropriate.
- **Keep track of both the strengths and the weaknesses others identify.** Then in later assignments you can build on your successes and give special attention to problem areas.

Commenting on others' writing

- **Be sure you know what the writer is saying.** If necessary, summarize the paper to understand its content. (See pp. 89–90.)
- **Address only your most significant concerns with the work.** Focus on the deep issues in other writers' drafts, especially early drafts: thesis, purpose, audience, organization, and support for the thesis. Use the revision checklist on the previous page as a guide to what is significant. Unless you have other instructions, ignore mistakes in grammar, punctuation, spelling, and the like. (The temptation to focus on such errors may be especially strong if the writer is less experienced than you are with standard American English.) Emphasizing mistakes will contribute little to the writer's revision.

- **Remember that you are the reader, not the writer.** Don't edit sentences, add details, or otherwise assume responsibility for the paper.
- **Phrase your comments carefully.** Avoid misunderstandings by making sure comments are both clear and respectful. If you are responding on paper or online, not face to face with the writer, remember that the writer has nothing but your written words to go on. He or she can't ask you for immediate clarification and can't infer your attitudes from gestures, facial expressions, and tone of voice.
- **Be specific.** If something confuses you, say *why*. If you disagree with a conclusion, say *why*.
- **Be supportive as well as honest.** Tell the writer what you like about the paper. Phrase your comments positively: instead of *This paragraph doesn't interest me*, say *You have an interesting detail here that I almost missed.* Question the writer in a way that emphasizes the effect of the work on you, the reader: *This paragraph confuses me because. . . .* And avoid measuring the work against a set of external standards: *This essay is poorly organized. Your thesis statement is inadequate.*
- **While reading, make your comments in writing.** Even if you will be delivering your comments in person later on, the written record will help you recall what you thought.
- **Link comments to specific parts of a paper.** Especially if you are reading the paper on a computer, be clear about what in the paper each comment relates to. You can use a word processor's Comment function, which annotates documents.

CULTURE LANGUAGE   In some cultures writers do not expect criticism from readers, or readers do not expect to think critically about what they read. For example, readers may not question an unclear thesis or evaluate the evidence in an argument. If critical responses are uncommon in your native culture, collaboration may at first be uncomfortable for you. As a writer, consider that readers are responding to your draft or even your final paper more as an exploration of ideas than as the last word on your subject; then you may be more receptive to readers' suggestions. As a reader, ask questions about the focus, content, and organization, such as *How does this general statement support the thesis?* or *How does this example support the general statement?* Know that your tactful questions and suggestions will usually be considered appropriate.

5c   Write a title.

The revision stage is a good time to consider a title because attempting to sum up your essay in a phrase can focus your attention sharply on your subject, purpose, and audience.

Here are suggestions for titling an essay:

- **A *descriptive title* announces the subject clearly and accurately.** Such a title is almost always appropriate and is usually expected for academic writing. Katy Moreno's final title—"Can We Compete? College Education for the Global Economy"—is an example.
- **A *suggestive title* hints at the subject to arouse curiosity.** Such a title is common in popular magazines and may be appropriate for more informal writing. Moreno might have chosen a suggestive title such as "Training for the New World" or "Education for a Flat World" (echoing Thomas L. Friedman's title).

For more information on essay titles, see pages 338 (capitalizing words in a title), 465 (MLA title format), and 498 (APA title format).

5d   A sample revision

Katy Moreno was satisfied with her first draft: she had her ideas down, and the arrangement seemed logical. Still, from the revision checklist she knew the draft needed work, and her classmates' comments (pp. 28–29) highlighted what she needed to focus on. Following is the first half of her revised draft with marginal annotations highlighting the changes. Moreno used the Track Changes function on her word processor, so that deletions are crossed out and additions are in color.

Descriptive title names topic and forecasts approach.

Expanded introduction draws readers into Moreno's topic, clarifies her point of agreement with Friedman, and states her revised thesis.

Can We Compete?

College Education for the Global Economy

~~Title?~~

     Today's students cannot miss news stories about globalization of the economy and outsourcing of jobs, but are students aware of how these trends are affecting the job market? In "It's a Flat World, after All," Thomas L. Friedman argues that most US students are not preparing themselves as well as ~~they should to compete in today's economy. Not like~~ students in India, China, and other countries ~~are~~ to compete in today's economy, which requires hard-working, productive scientists and engineers (34-37). Friedman's article speaks to me because my mother recently lost her job when it was outsourced to India. But her experience taught a lesson Friedman overlooks: technical training by itself can be too narrow to produce the communicators and problem solvers needed by contemporary businesses. ~~My mother lost her job because it was outsourced to India, but not all technical jobs in her company were outsourced. Thomas L. Friedman's advice to improve students' technical training is too narrow.~~

Friedman describes a "flat" world where technology like the Internet and wireless communication makes it possible for college graduates all over the globe, ~~in particular~~ to compete for high paying jobs that once belonged to graduates of US colleges and universities (34). He focuses on workers in India and China, who graduate from college with excellent educations in math and science, who are eager for new opportunities, and who are willing to work exceptionally hard, often harder than their American counterparts and, for less money ~~to get jobs that once were gotten by graduates of US colleges and universities~~ (37). ~~He~~ Friedman argues that US students must be better prepared academically, especially in ~~need more~~ math and science, so that they can get and keep jobs that will otherwise go overseas ~~in order to compete~~ (37).

~~I came to college with first hand knowledge of globalization and outsourcing. My mother, who worked for sixteen years in the field of information technology (IT), was laid off six months ago when the company she worked for decided to outsource much of its IT work to a company based in India. My mother~~ At first glance, my mother's experience of losing her job might seem to support the argument of Friedman that better training in math and science is the key to competing in the global job market. Her experience, however, adds dimensions to the globalization story, which Friedman misses. First my mother had the kind of strong background in math and science that Friedman says, today's workers need. She majored in computer science, rose within the information technology (IT) department of a large company, ~~had sixteen years of experience,~~ and her bosses always gave her good performance reviews. Still, when her employer decided to outsource most of its IT work, my mother lost her job. ~~She never expected to be laid off and was surprised when she was. She wasn't laid off because of her background and performance. In fact, my mother had a very strong background in math and science and years of training and job experience.~~ The reason wasn't because her technical skills were inadequate. Instead, her salary and benefits cost the company more than outsourcing her job did. Until wages rise around the globe, jobs like my mother's will be vulnerable. No matter how well you are trained. ~~Which hurt my family financially, as you can imagine.~~

6 Editing, Formatting, and Proofreading

In *Brief*
- Edit the revised draft (below).
- Use an editing checklist (opposite).
- Format and proofread the final draft (p. 39).

Visit MyWritingLab™ for more resources on editing, formatting, and proofreading.

After you have revised your essay so that all the content is in place, turn to the important work of removing any surface problems that could interfere with the clarity of your ideas.

6a Edit the revised draft.

In your editing, work first for clear and effective sentences that flow smoothly from one to the next. Then check your sentences for correctness. Use the questions in the checklist on the next page to guide your editing.

1 ▪ Discovering what needs editing

Try these approaches to spot possible flaws in your work:

- **Take a break.** Even fifteen or twenty minutes can clear your head.
- **Read the draft slowly, and read what you actually see.** Otherwise, you're likely to read what you intended to write but did not. If you have trouble slowing down, try reading your draft from back to front, sentence by sentence.
- **Listen to the draft.** Read the draft aloud, record the draft and listen to the playback, or use text-to-speech software to create a spoken version. Be alert to awkward rhythms, repetitive sentence patterns, and missing transitions.
- **Ask a classmate, friend, or relative to read your work.** Make sure you understand and consider the reader's suggestions, even if you decide not to take them.
- **Learn from your own experience.** Keep a record of your common problems—certain misspellings, overuse of *there is*, wordy phrases such as *the fact that*, and so on—and check your work against the record. Use a word processor's Find command to locate such problems quickly.

2 ▪ A sample edited paragraph

The third paragraph of Katy Moreno's edited draft appears on page 38. Among other changes, she tightened wording, improved parallelism (with *consistently received*), corrected several comma errors, and repaired the final sentence fragment.

Checklist for editing

Are my sentences clear?

Do my words and sentences mean what I intend them to mean? Is anything confusing? Check especially for these:

Exact language (pp. 166–74)
Parallelism (pp. 151–53)
Clear modifiers (pp. 265–70)
Clear reference of pronouns (pp. 250–53)
Complete sentences (pp. 271–74)
Sentences separated correctly (pp. 276–80)

Are my sentences effective?

How well do words and sentences engage and hold readers' attention? Where does the writing seem wordy, choppy, or dull? Check especially for these:

Expression of voice (pp. 8–9)
Emphasis of main ideas (pp. 142–50)
Smooth and informative transitions (pp. 48–50)
Variety in sentence length and structure (pp. 154–57)
Appropriate language (pp. 158–65)
Concise sentences (pp. 177–81)

Do my sentences contain errors?

Where do surface errors interfere with the clarity and effectiveness of my sentences? Check especially for these:

- **Spelling errors** (pp. 328–32)
- **Sentence fragments** (pp. 271–74)
- **Comma splices** (pp. 276–80)
- **Verb errors**
  Verb forms, especially -s and -ed endings, correct forms of irregular verbs, and appropriate helping verbs (pp. 206–16)
  Verb tenses, especially consistency (pp. 221–27)
  Agreement between subjects and verbs, especially when words come between them or the subject is *each, everyone,* or a similar word (pp. 233–38)
- **Pronoun errors**
  Pronoun forms, especially subjective (*he, she, they, who*) vs. objective (*him, her, them, whom*) (pp. 240–45)
  Agreement between pronouns and antecedents, especially when the antecedent contains *or* or the antecedent is *each, everyone, person,* or a similar word (pp. 246–49)
- **Punctuation errors**
  Commas, especially with comma splices (pp. 276–80) and with *and* or *but,* with introductory elements, with nonessential elements, and with series (pp. 293–303)
  Apostrophes in possessives but not plural nouns (*Dave's/witches*) and in contractions but not possessive personal pronouns (*it's/its*) (pp. 311–15)

At first glance, my mother's experience of losing her job might seem to support ~~the Friedman's~~ argument ~~of Friedman~~ that better training in math and science is the key to competing in the global job market. However, ~~Hh~~er experience~~,~~ ~~however,~~ adds dimensions to the globalization story~~, which~~ that Friedman misses. First, my mother had the kind of strong background in math and science that Friedman says~~,~~ today's workers need. She majored in computer science, rose within the information technology (IT) department of a large company, and consistently received ~~her bosses always gave her~~ good performance reviews. Still, when her employer decided to outsource most of its IT work, my mother lost her job. The reason wasn't ~~because~~that her technical skills were inadequate. Instead, her salary and benefits cost the company more than outsourcing her job did. Until wages rise around the globe, jobs like my mother's will be vulnerable~~,~~ ~~N~~no matter how well ~~you are~~ a person is trained.

3 ▪ Working with spelling and grammar/style checkers

A spelling checker and a grammar/style checker can be helpful *if* you work within their limitations. The programs miss many problems and may even flag items that are actually correct. Further, they cannot make important decisions about your writing because they know nothing of your subject, your purpose, and your audience. Always use these tools critically:

▪ **Read your work yourself to ensure that it's clear and error-free.**
▪ **Consider a checker's suggestions carefully, weighing each one against your intentions.** If you aren't sure whether to accept a checker's suggestion, consult a dictionary, writing handbook, or other source. Your version may be fine.

Using a spelling checker

Your word processor's spelling checker can be a great ally: it will flag words that are spelled incorrectly and will usually suggest alternative spellings that resemble what you've typed. However, this ally also has the potential to undermine you:

▪ **The checker may flag a word that you've spelled correctly** just because the word does not appear in its dictionary.
▪ **The checker may suggest incorrect alternatives.** In providing a list of alternative spellings for your word, the checker may highlight the one it considers most likely to be correct. For example, if you misspell *definitely* by typing *definately*, your checker may highlight *defiantly* as the correct option. You need to verify that the alternative suggested by the checker is actually what you intend before selecting it. Consult an online or printed dictionary when you aren't sure of the checker's recommendations (see pp. 166–67).

▪ **Most important, a spelling checker will not flag words that appear in its dictionary but you have misused.** The paragraph in the following screen shot contains eleven errors that a spelling checker overlooked. Can you spot them?

Spelling checker

The whether effects all of us, though it's affects are different for different people. Some people love a fare day with warm temperatures and sunshine. They revel in spending a hole day outside. Other people enjoy dark, rainy daze. They like to slow down and here they're inner thoughts. Most people agree, however, that to much of one kind of weather makes them board.

A spelling checker failed to catch any of the eleven errors in this jingle.

In the end *the only way to rid your papers of spelling errors is to proofread your papers yourself.* See the next page for proofreading tips. And see Chapter 45 for more advice on spelling.

Using a grammar/style checker

Grammar/style checkers can flag incorrect grammar or punctuation and wordy or awkward sentences. However, these programs can call your attention only to passages that *may* be faulty. They miss many errors because they are not capable of analyzing language in all its complexity. (For instance, they can't accurately distinguish a word's part of speech when there are different possibilities, as *light* can be a noun, a verb, or an adjective.) And they often question passages that don't need editing, such as an appropriate passive verb or a deliberate and emphatic use of repetition.

You can customize a grammar/style checker to suit your needs and habits as a writer. Most checkers allow you to specify whether to check only grammar or both grammar and style. Some style checkers can be set to the level of writing you intend, such as formal, standard, and informal. (For academic writing choose formal.) You can also instruct the checker to flag specific grammar and style problems that tend to bother you, such as apostrophes in plural nouns, overused passive voice, or a confusion between *its* and *it's*.

6b   Format and proofread the final draft.

After editing your essay, format and proofread it before you submit it to your instructor. Follow any required document format, such as MLA (pp. 464–66) or APA (pp. 497–500). See also pages 61–70 for help with document design.

Be sure to proofread the final essay several times to spot and correct errors. To increase the accuracy of your proofreading, you may need to experiment with ways to keep yourself from relaxing into the rhythm and the content of your prose. Here are a few tricks, including some used by professional proofreaders:

- ▪ **Read printed copy,** even if you will eventually submit the paper electronically. Most people proofread more accurately when reading type on paper than when reading it on a computer screen. (At the same time, don't view the printed copy as necessarily error-free just because it's clean. Clean-looking copy may still harbor errors.)
- ▪ **Read the paper aloud,** very slowly, and distinctly pronounce exactly what you see.
- ▪ **Place a ruler under each line as you read it.**
- ▪ **Read "against copy,"** comparing your final draft one sentence at a time against the edited draft.
- ▪ **Ignore content.** To keep the content of your writing from distracting you while you proofread, read the essay backward, end to beginning, examining each sentence as a separate unit. Or, taking advantage of a word processor, isolate each paragraph from its context by printing it on a separate page. (Of course, reassemble the paragraphs before submitting the paper.)

6c   A sample final draft

Katy Moreno's final essay appears on these pages, presented in MLA format except for page numbers. Comments in the margins point out key features of the essay's content.

Katy Moreno

Professor Lacourse

English 110

14 February 2015

Descriptive title

Can We Compete?
College Education for the Global Economy

Introduction

Today's students cannot miss news stories about globalization of the economy and outsourcing of jobs, but are students aware of how these trends are affecting the job market? In "It's a Flat World, after All," Thomas L. Friedman argues that most US students are not preparing themselves as well as students in India, China, and other countries to compete in today's economy, which requires hard-working, productive scientists and engineers (34-37). Friedman's article speaks to me because my mother lost her job when it

Summaries of Friedman cited with parenthetical page numbers using MLA style (p. 419)

was outsourced to India. But her experience taught a lesson that Friedman overlooks: technical training by itself can be too narrow to produce the communicators and problem solvers needed by contemporary businesses.

Friedman describes a "flat" world where technology like the Internet and wireless communication makes it possible for college graduates all over the globe to compete for high-paying jobs that once belonged to graduates of US colleges and universities (34). He focuses on workers in India and China who graduate from college with excellent educations in math and science, who are eager for new opportunities, and who are willing to work exceptionally hard, often harder than their American counterparts, and for less money (37). Friedman argues that US students must be better prepared academically, especially in math and science, so that they can get and keep jobs that will otherwise go overseas (37).

At first glance, my mother's experience of losing her job might seem to support Friedman's argument that better training in math and science is the key to competing in the global job market. However, her experience adds dimensions to the globalization story that Friedman misses. First, my mother had the kind of strong background in math and science that Friedman says today's workers need. She majored in computer science, rose within the information technology (IT) department of a large company, and consistently received good performance reviews. Still, when her employer decided to outsource most of its IT work, my mother lost her job. The reason wasn't that her technical skills were inadequate; instead, her salary and benefits cost the company more than outsourcing her job did. Until wages rise around the globe, jobs like my mother's will be vulnerable, no matter how well a person is trained.

The second dimension that Friedman misses is that a number of well-paid people in my mother's IT department, namely IT managers, were not laid off. As my mother explained at the time, they kept their jobs because they were experienced at figuring out the company's IT needs, planning for changes, researching and proposing solutions, and communicating in writing and speech—skills that her more narrow training and experience had missed. Friedman misses these skills by focusing only on technical training. Without the ability to solve problems creatively and to communicate, people with technical expertise alone may not have enough skills to save their jobs, as my mother learned.

Like my mother, I am more comfortable in front of a computer than I am in front of a group of people, and I had planned to major in computer science. Since my mother lost her job, however, I have decided to take courses

Margin annotations:

- Thesis statement: basic disagreement with Friedman
- Summary of Friedman's article
- Transition to disagreements with Friedman
- First disagreement with Friedman
- Examples to support first disagreement
- Example to qualify first disagreement
- Clarification of first disagreement
- Second disagreement with Friedman
- Explanation of second disagreement
- Conclusion summarizing both disagreements with Friedman

Final point: business needs and author's personal goals	in English and history as well. Classes in these subjects will require me to read broadly, think critically, research, and communicate ideas in writing—in short, to develop skills that make managers. When I enter the job market, my
Explanation of final point	well-rounded education will make me a more attractive job candidate and will help me to become the kind of forward-thinking manager that companies will always need to employ here in the United States.
Conclusion re-capping points of agreement and disagree-ment with Friedman and summarizing essay	Many jobs that require a college degree are indeed going overseas, as Thomas L. Friedman says, and my classmates and I need to be ready for a rapidly changing future. But rather than focus only on math and science, we need to broaden our academic experiences so that the skills we develop make us not only employable but also indispensable.

[New page.]

Work Cited

Work cited in MLA style (p. 429)

Friedman, Thomas L. "It's a Flat World, after All." *The New York Times Magazine,* 3 Apr. 2005, pp. 32-37.

7 Paragraphs

In *Brief*

- Relate each paragraph to the essay as a whole (opposite).
- Unify each paragraph around a central idea (p. 44).
- Make each paragraph coherent (p. 45).
- Develop the central idea of each paragraph (p. 51).
- Create introductory and concluding paragraphs that set up and finish your writing (p. 57).

Visit MyWritingLab™ for more resources on paragraphs.

Paragraphs develop the main ideas that support the thesis of a piece of writing, and they break these supporting ideas into manageable chunks. For readers, paragraphs signal the movement between ideas and provide breathers from long stretches of text.

 Not all cultures share the paragraphing conventions of American academic writing. In some other languages, writing moves differently on the page from English—not left to right, but from right to left or down rows from top to bottom. Even in languages that move as English does, writers may not use paragraphs at all. If your native language is not English and you have difficulty writing paragraphs, don't worry about them during drafting. Instead, during a separate step of revision, divide your text into parts that develop your main points, and mark those parts with indentions.

Checklist for revising paragraphs

- **Does each paragraph contribute to the essay as a whole?** Does each paragraph support the essay's central idea, or thesis? Does it relate to the paragraphs that come before and after it? (See below.)
- **Is each paragraph unified?** Does it focus on one central idea that is either stated in a **topic sentence** or otherwise apparent? (See the next page.)
- **Is each paragraph coherent?** Do the sentences follow a clear sequence? Are the sentences linked as appropriate by parallelism, repetition or restatement, pronouns, consistency, and transitional expressions? (See p. 45.)
- **Is each paragraph developed?** Is the general idea of the paragraph well supported with specific evidence such as details, facts, examples, and reasons? (See p. 51.)

7a   Relate the paragraphs in an essay.

Paragraphs do not stand alone: they are key units of a larger piece of writing. Even if you draft a paragraph separately, it needs to connect to your central idea, or thesis—explaining it and deepening it. Together, paragraphs need to flow from one to the other so that readers easily grasp the points you are making and how each point contributes to the whole essay.

To see how effective body paragraphs work to help both writer and reader, look at the fourth paragraph of Katy Moreno's essay "Can We Compete?" from the previous chapter. Responding to an article by Thomas L. Friedman, Moreno is supporting her thesis that Friedman overlooks the need for technical employees to be good communicators and problem solvers.

The second dimension that Friedman misses is that a number of well-paid people in my mother's IT department, namely IT managers, were not laid off.	New main point linking to previous paragraph and to thesis
As my mother explained at the time, they kept their jobs because they were experienced at figuring out the company's IT needs, planning for changes, researching and proposing solutions, and communicating in writing and speech—skills that her more narrow training and experience had missed. Friedman misses these skills by focusing only on technical training.	Details to support new point
Without the ability to solve problems creatively and to communicate, people with technical expertise alone may not have enough skills to save their jobs, as my mother learned.	Concluding sentence summing up paragraph and linking to previous paragraph and to thesis

7b   Unify the paragraph around a central idea.

Just as readers expect paragraphs to relate clearly to an essay's thesis, they also generally expect each paragraph to be **unified**—that is, to develop a single idea. Often this idea is expressed in a **topic sentence**. For an example, look again at the paragraph by Katy Moreno on the previous page: the opening statement conveys Moreno's promise that she will explain something lacking in Friedman's argument, and the following sentences keep the promise. But what if Moreno had written this paragraph instead?

> The second dimension that Friedman misses is that a number of well-paid people in my mother's IT department, namely IT managers, were not laid off. As my mother explained at the time, they kept their jobs because they were experienced at figuring out the company's IT needs, planning for changes, researching and proposing solutions, and communicating in writing. Like my mother, these managers had families to support, so they were lucky to keep their jobs. Our family still struggles with the financial and emotional effects of my mother's unemployment.

Topic sentence: general statement

Details supporting topic sentence

Digression

By wandering from the topic of why some managers kept their jobs, the paragraph fails to deliver on the commitment of its topic sentence.

A central idea must always govern a paragraph's content as if it were standing guard at the opening, but in fact paragraphs often do not begin with a topic sentence. You may want to start with a transition from the previous paragraph, not stating the central idea until the second or third sentence. You may want to give the evidence for your idea first and let it build to a topic sentence at the end, as in this example about the Civil War general William Tecumseh Sherman:

> Sherman is considered by some to be the inventor of "total war": the first general in human history to carry the logic of war to its ultimate extreme, the first to scorch the earth, the first to consciously demoralize the hostile civilian population in order to subdue its army, the first to wreck an economy in order to starve its soldiers. He has been called our first "merchant of terror" and seen as the spiritual father of our Vietnam War concepts of "search and destroy," "pacification," "strategic hamlets," and "free-fire zones." As such, he remains a cardboard figure of our history: a monstrous arch-villain to unreconstructed Southerners, and an embarrassment to Northerners.
>
> —Adapted from James Reston, Jr., "You Cannot Refine It"

Information supporting and building to topic sentence

Topic sentence

Even when the central idea falls at the end of the paragraph, it must still govern all of the preceding details.

Sometimes you may not state a paragraph's central idea at all, especially in narrative and descriptive writing in which the point becomes clear in the details. But the point must be clear whether it is stated or not.

¶ coh

7c

Exercise 7.1 Writing a unified paragraph

Develop the following topic sentence into a unified paragraph by using the relevant information in the supporting statements. Delete each statement that does not relate directly to the topic, and then rewrite and combine sentences as appropriate. Place the topic sentence in the position that seems most effective to you.

Topic sentence

Mozart's accomplishments in music seem remarkable even today.

Supporting information

Wolfgang Amadeus Mozart was born in 1756 in Salzburg, Austria.
He began composing music at the age of five.
He lived most of his life in Salzburg and Vienna.
His first concert tour of Europe was at the age of six.
On his first tour he played harpsichord, organ, and violin.
He published numerous compositions before reaching adolescence.
He married in 1782.
Mozart and his wife were both poor managers of money.
They were plagued by debts.
Mozart composed over six hundred musical compositions.
His notable works include operas, symphonies, quartets, and concertos.
He died at the age of thirty-five.

7c   Make the paragraph coherent.

When a paragraph is **coherent,** readers can see how it holds together: the sentences seem to flow logically and smoothly into one another. Exactly the opposite happens with this paragraph:

The ancient Egyptians were masters of preserving dead people's bodies by making mummies of them. — Topic sentence

Mummies several thousand years old have been discovered nearly intact. The skin, hair, teeth, finger- and toenails, and facial features of the mummies were evident. It is possible to diagnose the diseases they suffered in life, such as smallpox, arthritis, and nutritional deficiencies. The process was remarkably effective. Sometimes apparent were the fatal afflictions of the dead people: a middle-aged king died from a blow on the head, and polio killed a child king. Mummification consisted of removing the internal organs, applying natural preservatives inside and out, and then wrapping the body in layers of bandages. — Sentences related to topic sentence but disconnected from each other

The paragraph is hard to read. The sentences lurch instead of gliding from point to point.

The paragraph as it was actually written appears below. It is clearer because the writer arranged information differently and also built connections into his sentences to make them flow smoothly:

- After the topic sentence, the writer gives two explanations and four sentences of examples.
- Words in gray repeat or restate key terms or concepts.
- Words in color link sentences and clarify relationships.
- Underlined phrases are in parallel grammatical form to reflect their parallel content.

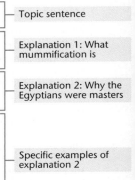

The ancient Egyptians were masters of preserving dead people's bodies by making mummies of them. Basically, mummification consisted of removing the internal organs, applying natural preservatives inside and out, and then wrapping the body in layers of bandages. And the process was remarkably effective. Indeed, mummies several thousand years old have been discovered nearly intact. Their skin, hair, teeth, finger- and toenails, and facial features are still evident. Their diseases in life, such as smallpox, arthritis, and nutritional deficiencies, are still diagnosable. Even their fatal afflictions are still apparent: a middle-aged king died from a blow on the head; a child king died from polio.

Topic sentence

Explanation 1: What mummification is

Explanation 2: Why the Egyptians were masters

Specific examples of explanation 2

—Mitchell Rosenbaum (student),
"Lost Arts of the Egyptians"

1 ■ Paragraph organization

A coherent paragraph organizes information so that readers can easily follow along. These are common paragraph schemes:

- **General to specific:** Sentences downshift from more general statements to more specific ones. (See the example above.)
- **Climactic:** Sentences increase in drama or interest, building to a climax. (See the paragraph by Lawrence Mayer on the facing page.)
- **Spatial:** Sentences scan a person, place, or object from top to bottom, from side to side, or in some other way that approximates the way people actually look at things. (See the paragraph by Virginia Woolf on p. 52.)
- **Chronological:** Sentences present events as they occurred in time, earlier to later. (See the paragraph by Kathleen LaFrank on pp. 48–49.)

2 ▪ Parallelism

One way to achieve paragraph coherence is through **parallelism**, the use of similar grammatical structures for similar elements of meaning within or among sentences. (See Chapter 16.) In the next paragraph the underlined parallel structures link all sentences after the first one, and parallelism also appears within sentences (as in *supporting candidates* and *making speeches* in sentence 5). The paragraph comes from a student's profile of President Ronald Reagan.

Ronald Reagan holds a particularly interesting place in American history, combining successful careers in show business and in politics. After graduating from college in 1932, he worked as a radio sports announcer with an affinity for describing game details. He then launched a successful film career, starring in dozens of movies. After a stint in the US Army, he assumed the role of host for *General Electric Theater*, a weekly TV program that ran from 1953 to 1962. He first entered politics by supporting candidates and making speeches in the 1950s and early 1960s. He became governor of California in 1966 and served for eight years. He ran unsuccessfully for the US presidency in 1976 and then won the job in 1980, when he became the fortieth President. He served two terms, survived an assassination attempt, and earned a popularity that most politicians can only envy.

—William Brooks (student),
"Ronald Reagan, the Actor President"

3 ▪ Repetition and restatement

Repeating or restating key words helps make a paragraph coherent and also reminds readers what the topic is. In the following paragraph note the underlined repetition of *sleep* and restatement of *adults*.

Perhaps the simplest fact about sleep is that individual needs for it vary widely. Most adults sleep between seven and nine hours, but occasionally people turn up who need twelve hours or so, while some rare types can get by on three or four. Rarest of all are those legendary types who require almost no sleep at all; respected researchers have recently studied three such people. One of them—a healthy, happy woman in her seventies—sleeps about an hour every two or three days. The other two are men in early middle age, who get by on a few minutes a night. One of them complains about the daily fifteen minutes or so he's forced to "waste" in sleeping.

—Lawrence A. Mayer,
"The Confounding Enemy of Sleep"

4 ▪ Pronouns

Pronouns such as *she, he, it, they,* and *who* refer to and function as nouns. Thus pronouns naturally help relate sentences to each other. In the paragraph above by William Brooks, *he* works just this way by substituting for *Ronald Reagan.*

5 ▪ Consistency

Consistency (or the lack of it) occurs primarily in the tense of verbs and in the person and number of nouns and pronouns. Any inconsistencies not required by meaning will interfere with a reader's ability to follow the development of ideas.

In the following paragraphs, inconsistencies appear in the underlined words:

Shifts in tense

In the Hopi religion, water is the driving force. Since the Hopi lived in the Arizona desert, they needed water urgently for drinking, cooking, and irrigating crops. They seek the assistance of supernatural forces in obtaining water. Many of the Hopi kachinas, or spirit essences, were directly concerned with clouds, rain, and snow.

Shifts in number

Kachinas represent spiritually the things and events of the real world, such as cumulus clouds, mischief, cornmeal, and even death. A kachina is not worshiped as a god but regarded as an interested friend. They visit the Hopi from December through July in the form of men who dress in kachina costumes and perform dances and other rituals.

Shifts in person

Unlike the man, the Hopi woman does not keep contact with kachinas through costumes and dancing. Instead, one receives a tihu, or small effigy, of a kachina from the man impersonating the kachina. You are more likely to receive a tihu as a girl approaching marriage, though a child or older woman may receive one, too.

6 ▪ Transitional expressions

Transitional expressions such as *therefore, in contrast,* and *meanwhile* can forge specific connections between sentences. Notice the difference in two versions of the same paragraph:

Medical science has succeeded in identifying the hundreds of viruses that can cause the common cold. It has discovered the most effective means of prevention. One person transmits the cold viruses to another most often by hand. An infected person covers his mouth to cough. He picks up the telephone. His daughter picks up the telephone. She rubs her eyes. She has a cold. It spreads. To avoid colds, people should wash their hands often and keep their hands away from their faces.

Paragraph is choppy and hard to follow

Medical science has **thus** succeeded in identifying the hundreds of viruses that can cause the common cold. It has **also** discovered the most effective means of prevention. One person trans-

Transitional expressions (shaded) remove choppiness and spell out relationships

mits the cold viruses to another most often by hand. For instance, an infected person covers his mouth to cough. Then he picks up the telephone. Half an hour later, his daughter picks up the same telephone. Immediately afterward, she rubs her eyes. Within a few days, she, too, has a cold. And thus it spreads. To avoid colds, therefore, people should wash their hands often and keep their hands away from their faces.

—Kathleen LaFrank (student),
"Colds: Myth and Science"

Note that transitional expressions can link paragraphs as well as sentences. In the first sentence of LaFrank's paragraph, the word *thus* signals a connection to an effect discussed in the preceding paragraph. See page 43 for more on such transitions.

The following box lists many transitional expressions by the functions they perform:

Transitional expressions

To add or show sequence
again, also, and, and then, besides, equally important, finally, first, further, furthermore, in addition, in the first place, last, moreover, next, second, still, too

To compare
also, in the same way, likewise, similarly

To contrast
although, and yet, but, but at the same time, despite, even so, even though, for all that, however, in contrast, in spite of, nevertheless, notwithstanding, on the contrary, on the other hand, regardless, still, though, yet

To give examples or intensify
after all, an illustration of, even, for example, for instance, indeed, in fact, it is true, of course, specifically, that is, to illustrate, truly

To indicate place
above, adjacent to, below, elsewhere, farther on, here, near, nearby, on the other side, opposite to, there, to the east, to the left

To indicate time
after a while, afterward, as long as, as soon as, at last, at length, at that time, before, earlier, eventually, formerly, immediately, in the meantime, in the past, lately, later, meanwhile, now, presently, shortly, simultaneously, since, so far, soon, subsequently, suddenly, then, thereafter, until, until now, when

(continued)

Transitional expressions

(continued)

To repeat, summarize, or conclude
all in all, altogether, as has been said, in brief, in conclusion, in other words, in particular, in short, in simpler terms, in summary, on the whole, that is, therefore, to put it differently, to summarize

To show cause or effect
accordingly, as a result, because, consequently, for this purpose, hence, otherwise, since, then, therefore, thereupon, thus, to this end

> **Note** Draw carefully on this list of transitional expressions because the ones within each group are not interchangeable. For instance, *besides, finally,* and *second* may all be used to add information, but each has its own distinct meaning.

CULTURE LANGUAGE If transitional expressions are not common in your native language, you may be tempted to compensate when writing in English by adding them to the beginnings of most sentences. But such explicit transitions aren't needed everywhere, and in fact too many can be intrusive and awkward. When inserting transitional expressions, consider the reader's need for a signal: often the connection from sentence to sentence is already clear from the context or can be made clear by relating the content of sentences more closely (see pp. 144–45). When you do need transitional expressions, try varying their positions in your sentences, as illustrated in LaFrank's paragraph on pages 48–49.

Exercise 7.2 Writing a coherent paragraph

Write a coherent paragraph from the following information, combining and rewriting sentences as necessary. First, begin the paragraph with the topic sentence given and arrange the supporting sentences in a climactic order. Then combine and rewrite the supporting sentences, helping the reader see connections by introducing repetition and restatement, parallelism, pronouns, consistency, and transitional expressions.

Topic sentence
Hypnosis is far superior to drugs for relieving tension.

Supporting information
Hypnosis has none of the dangerous side effects of the drugs that relieve tension.
Tension-relieving drugs can cause weight loss or gain, illness, or even death.
Hypnosis is nonaddictive.
Most of the drugs that relieve tension do foster addiction.
Tension-relieving drugs are expensive.
Hypnosis is inexpensive even for people who have not mastered self-hypnosis.

7d   Develop the central idea.

An effective, well-developed paragraph always provides the specific information that readers need and expect in order to understand and stay interested in what you say. Paragraph length can be a rough gauge of development: anything much shorter than 75 to 125 words may leave readers with a sense of incompleteness. Take this example:

> Untruths can serve as a kind of social oil when they smooth connections between people. In preventing confrontation and injured feelings, they allow everyone to go on as before.

General statements needing examples to be clear and convincing

This paragraph lacks development, or completeness. It does not provide enough information for us to evaluate or even care about the writer's assertions. To improve the paragraph, the writer needs to support the general statements with specific examples, as in this revision:

> Untruths can serve as a kind of social oil when they smooth connections between people. Assuring a worried friend that his haircut is flattering, claiming an appointment to avoid an aunt's dinner invitation, pretending interest in an acquaintance's children—these lies may protect the liar, but they also protect the person lied to. In preventing confrontation and injured feelings, the lies allow everyone to go on as before.
> —Joan Lar (student), "The Truth of Lies"

Examples specifying kinds of lies and consequences

To develop or shape a paragraph's central idea, one or more of the following patterns may help. (These patterns may also be used to develop entire essays. See p. 15.)

1 ▪ Narration

Narration retells a significant sequence of events, usually in the order of their occurrence (that is, chronologically). A narrator is concerned not just with the sequence of events but also with their consequence, their importance to the whole.

> Jill's story is typical for "recruits" to religious cults. She was very lonely in college and appreciated the attention of the nice young men and women who lived in a house near campus. They persuaded her to share their meals and then to move in with them. Between intense bombardments of "love," they deprived her of sleep and sometimes threatened to throw her out. Jill became increasingly confused and dependent, losing touch with any reality besides the one in the group. She dropped out of school and

Important events in chronological order

refused to see or communicate with her family. Before long she, too, was preying on lonely college students.

—Hillary Begas (student), "The Love Bombers"

2 ▪ Description

Description details the sensory qualities of a person, scene, thing, or feeling, using concrete and specific words to convey a dominant mood, to illustrate an idea, or to achieve some other purpose. In the following paragraph, almost every word helps to create a picture in the reader's mind:

> The sun struck straight upon the house, making the white walls glare between the dark windows. Their panes, woven thickly with green branches, held circles of impenetrable darkness. Sharp-edged wedges of light lay upon the window-sill and showed inside the room plates with blue rings, cups with curved handles, the bulge of a great bowl, the criss-cross pattern in the rug, and the formidable corners and lines of cabinets and bookcases. Behind their conglomeration hung a zone of shadow in which might be a further shape to be disencumbered of shadow or still denser depths of darkness.
>
> —Virginia Woolf, *The Waves*

Specific record of sensory details

3 ▪ Illustration or support

An idea may be developed with several specific examples, like those used by William Brooks on page 47 and by Joan Lar on the previous page. Or it may be developed with a single extended example, as in this paragraph:

> Teaching teenagers to drive is a nerve-racking job. During his first lesson, one particularly inept student refused to drive faster than ten miles per hour, forcing impatient drivers behind the car to pass on a residential street with a speed limit of twenty-five and cyclists in the bike lanes. Making a left turn at a four-way stop, the student didn't await his turn and nearly collided with an oncoming car. A few moments later, he jumped the curb when turning right and had to slam on the brakes to avoid hitting a concrete barrier. For a driving instructor, every day is an exercise in keeping one's fear and temper in check.
>
> —Jasmine Greer (student), "Driving School"

Topic sentence

Single detailed example

Sometimes you can develop a paragraph by providing your reasons for stating a general idea. For instance:

> There are three reasons, quite apart from scientific considerations, that mankind needs to travel in space. | Topic sentence
>
> The first reason is the need for garbage disposal: we need to transfer industrial processes into space, so that the earth may remain a green and pleasant place for our grandchildren to live in. The second reason is the need to escape material impoverishment: the resources of this planet are finite, and we shall not forgo forever the abundant solar energy and minerals and living space that are spread out all around us. The third reason is our spiritual need for an open frontier: the ultimate purpose of space travel is to bring to humanity not only scientific discoveries and an occasional spectacular show on television but a real expansion of our spirit. | Three reasons arranged in order of increasing drama and importance
> —Freeman Dyson, "Disturbing the Universe"

4 ▪ Definition

Defining a complicated, abstract, or controversial term often requires extended explanation. The following definition of the professional middle class comes from a book about changes in the American middle class:

> Before this story [of changes in America's middle class] can be told, I must first introduce its central character, the professional middle class. This class can be defined, somewhat abstractly, as all those people whose economic and social status is based on education, rather than on ownership of capital or property. Most professionals are | General definition
>
> included, and so are white-collar managers, whose positions require at least a college degree, and increasingly also a graduate degree. Not all white-collar people are included, though; some of these are entrepreneurs who are better classified as "workers." But the professional middle class is still extremely broad, and includes such diverse types as schoolteachers, anchorpersons, engineers, professors, government bureaucrats, corporate executives (at least up through the middle levels of management), scientists, advertising people, therapists, financial managers, architects, and, I should add, myself. | Specific examples of who is and is not included in the definition
> —Barbara Ehrenreich, *Fear of Falling: The Inner Life of the Middle Class*

5 ▪ Division or analysis

With division or analysis, you separate something into its elements to understand it better—for instance, you might divide a newspaper into its sections, such as national news, regional and local news, sports, lifestyle features, and so on. As in the paragraph below, you may also interpret the meaning and significance of the elements you identify.

> Reality TV shows are anything but "real." Participants are selected from thousands of applicants, and they have auditioned to prove themselves to be competent in front of a camera. The settings for the action are often environments created especially for the shows. Scenes that seem unscripted are often planned to capture entertaining footage. The wardrobes of the participants may be designed to enhance participants' "characters" and to improve their looks on camera. And footage is clearly edited to create scenes that seem authentic and tell compelling stories.
> —Darrell Carter (student), "(Un)Reality TV"

Topic sentence

Elements:
Carefully selected participants
Created environments

Planned scenes

Designed wardrobes

Edited footage

6 ▪ Classification

When you sort many items into groups, you classify the items to see their relations more clearly. The following paragraph identifies three groups, or classes, of parents:

> In my experience, the parents who hire daytime sitters for their school-age children tend to fall into one of three groups. The first group includes parents who work and want someone to be at home when the children return from school. These parents are looking for an extension of themselves, someone who will give the care they would give if they were at home. The second group includes parents who may be home all day themselves but are too disorganized or too frazzled by their children's demands to handle child care alone. They are looking for an organizer and helpmate. The third and final group includes parents who do not want to be bothered by their children, whether they are home all day or not. Unlike the parents in the first two groups, who care for their children whenever and however they can, these parents are looking for a permanent substitute for themselves.
> —Nancy Whittle (student), "Modern Parenting"

Topic sentence

Three groups:
Alike in one way (all hire sitters)
No overlap in groups (each has a different attitude)

Classes arranged in order of increasing drama

7 ▪ Comparison and contrast

Comparison and contrast may be used separately or together to develop an idea. The following paragraph illustrates one of two common ways of organizing a comparison and contrast: **subject by subject,** first one subject and then the other.

¶ dev

7d

Consider the differences also in the behavior of rock and classical music audiences. At a rock concert, the audience members yell, whistle, sing along, and stamp their feet. They may even stand during the entire performance. The better the music, the more active they'll be. At a classical concert, in contrast, the better the performance, the more *still* the audience is. Members of the classical audience are so highly disciplined that they refrain from even clearing their throats or coughing. No matter what effect the powerful music has on their intellects and feelings, they sit on their hands.

— Tony Nahm (student),
"Rock and Roll Is Here to Stay"

Subjects: rock and classical audiences

Rock audience

Classical audience

The next paragraph illustrates the other common organization: **point by point,** with the two subjects discussed side by side and matched feature for feature:

Arguing is often equated with fighting, but there are key differences between the two. Participants in an argument approach the subject to find common ground, or points on which both sides agree, while people engaged in a fight usually approach the subject with an "us-versus-them" attitude. Participants in an argument are careful to use respectful, polite language, in contrast to the insults and worse that people in a fight use to get the better of their opponents. Finally, participants in an argument commonly have the goal of reaching a new understanding or larger truth about the subject they're debating, while those in a fight have winning as their only goal.

— Erica Ito (student),
"Is an Argument Always a Fight?"

Subjects: arguing and fighting

Approach to subject: argument, fight

Language: argument, fight

Goal: argument, fight

8 ▪ Cause-and-effect analysis

When you use analysis to explain why something happened or what did or may happen, then you are determining causes or effects. In the following paragraph the author looks at the cause of an effect—Japanese collectivism.

This *shinkansen* or "bullet train" speeds across the rural areas of Japan giving a quick view of cluster after cluster of farmhouses surrounded by rice paddies.

Effect: pattern of Japanese farming

This particular pattern did not develop purely by chance, but as a consequence of the technology peculiar to the growing of rice, the staple of the Japanese diet. The growing of rice requires the construction and maintenance of an irrigation system, something that takes many hands to build. More importantly, the planting and the harvesting of rice can only be done efficiently with the cooperation of twenty or more people. The "bottom line" is that a single family working alone cannot produce enough rice to survive, but a dozen families working together can produce a surplus.

Causes: Japanese dependence on rice, which requires collective effort

Thus the Japanese have had to develop the capacity to work together in harmony, no matter what the forces of disagreement or social disintegration, in order to survive.

Effect: working in harmony

—William Ouchi, *Theory Z*

9 ▪ Process analysis

When you analyze how to do something or how something works, you explain a process. The following example identifies a process, describes the equipment needed, and details the steps in the process:

As a car owner, you waste money when you pay a mechanic to change the engine oil. The job is not difficult, even if you know little about cars.

Process: changing the oil

All you need is a wrench to remove the drain plug, a large, flat pan to collect the draining oil, plastic bottles to dispose of the used oil, and fresh oil.

Equipment needed

First, warm up the car's engine so that the oil will flow more easily. When the engine is warm, shut it off and remove its oil-filler cap (the owner's manual shows where this cap is). Then locate the drain plug under the engine (again consulting the owner's manual for its location) and place the flat pan under the plug. Remove the plug with the wrench, letting the oil flow into the pan. When the oil stops flowing, replace the plug and, at the engine's filler hole, add the amount and kind of fresh oil specified by the owner's manual. Pour the used oil into the plastic bottles and take it to a waste-oil collector, which any garage mechanic can recommend.

Steps in process

—Anthony Andres (student), "Do-It-Yourself Car Care"

Exercise 7.3   Analyzing and revising skimpy paragraphs

The following paragraphs are not well developed. Rewrite one into a well-developed paragraph, supplying your own concrete details or examples to support general statements.

1.   One big difference between successful and unsuccessful teachers is the quality of communication. A successful teacher is sensitive to students' needs and excited by the course subject. In contrast, an unsuccessful teacher seems uninterested in students and bored by the subject.

2.   Gestures are one of our most important means of communication. We use them instead of speech. We use them to supplement the words we speak. And we use them to communicate some feelings or meanings that words cannot adequately express.

7e   Write introductory and concluding paragraphs.

Introductory paragraphs set up your essay, piquing readers' interest in your topic. Concluding paragraphs finish your essay, giving readers a sense of completion.

1 ▪ Introductions

An introduction draws readers from their world into your world:

- ▪ **It focuses readers' attention on the topic and arouses curiosity about what you have to say.**
- ▪ **It specifies your subject and implies your attitude.**
- ▪ **Often it includes your thesis statement** (see p. 16).
- ▪ **It is concise and sincere.**

To focus readers' attention, you have a number of options:

Some strategies for introductions

- ▪ Ask a question.
- ▪ Relate an incident.
- ▪ Use a vivid quotation.
- ▪ Offer a surprising statistic or other fact.
- ▪ State an opinion related to your thesis.
- ▪ Provide background.

- ▪ Create a visual image that represents your subject.
- ▪ Make a historical comparison or contrast.
- ▪ Outline a problem or dilemma.
- ▪ Define a word central to your subject.
- ▪ In some business or technical writing, summarize your paper.

CULTURE LANGUAGE   These options for an introduction may not be what you are used to if your native language is not English. In other cultures, readers may seek familiarity or reassurance from an author's introduction, or they may prefer an indirect approach to the subject. In academic and business English, however, writers and readers prefer originality and concise, direct expression.

Effective openings

A very common introduction opens with a statement of the essay's general subject, clarifies or limits the subject in one or more sentences, and then asserts the point of the essay in the thesis statement. Here are two examples:

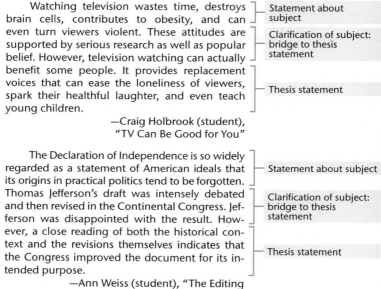

Watching television wastes time, destroys brain cells, contributes to obesity, and can even turn viewers violent. These attitudes are supported by serious research as well as popular belief. However, television watching can actually benefit some people. It provides replacement voices that can ease the loneliness of viewers, spark their healthful laughter, and even teach young children.

Statement about subject

Clarification of subject: bridge to thesis statement

Thesis statement

—Craig Holbrook (student),
"TV Can Be Good for You"

The Declaration of Independence is so widely regarded as a statement of American ideals that its origins in practical politics tend to be forgotten. Thomas Jefferson's draft was intensely debated and then revised in the Continental Congress. Jefferson was disappointed with the result. However, a close reading of both the historical context and the revisions themselves indicates that the Congress improved the document for its intended purpose.

Statement about subject

Clarification of subject: bridge to thesis statement

Thesis statement

—Ann Weiss (student), "The Editing of the Declaration of Independence"

In much public writing, it's more important to tell readers immediately what your point is than to try to engage them. This introduction to a brief memo quickly outlines a problem and (in the thesis statement) suggests a way to solve it:

Starting next month, staff vacations will leave our department short-handed. We need to hire two or perhaps three temporary keyboarders to maintain our schedules for the month.

Thesis statement

Additional examples of effective introductions appear in complete writing samples on pages 24, 40, 100, 118, and 125.

Introduction *don'ts*

When writing and revising your introduction, avoid approaches that are likely to bore readers or make them question your sincerity or control:

- **A vague generality or truth.** Don't extend your reach too wide with a line such as *Throughout human history . . .* or *In today's world. . . .* You may have needed a warm-up paragraph to start drafting, but your readers can do without it.
- **A flat announcement.** Don't start with *The purpose of this essay is . . .*, *In this essay I will . . .*, or any similar presentation of your intention or topic.
- **A reference to the essay's title.** Don't refer to the title of the essay in the first sentence—for example, *This is a big problem* or *This book is about the history of the guitar.*
- *According to Webster.* . . . Don't start by citing a dictionary definition. A definition can be an effective springboard to an essay, but this kind of lead-in has become dull with overuse.
- **An apology.** Don't fault your opinion or your knowledge with *I'm not sure if I'm right, but I think . . .*, *I don't know much about this, but . . .*, or similar lines.

2 ▪ Conclusions

Your conclusion finishes off your essay and tells readers where you think you have brought them. It answers the question "So what?"

Effective conclusions

Usually set off in its own paragraph, the conclusion may consist of a single sentence or a group of sentences. It may take one or more of the following approaches:

Some strategies for conclusions

- Recommend a course of action.
- Summarize the paper.
- Echo the approach of the introduction.
- Restate your thesis and reflect on its implications.
- Strike a note of hope or despair.

- Give a symbolic or powerful fact or other detail.
- Give an especially compelling example.
- Create a visual image that represents your subject.
- Use a quotation.

The following paragraph concludes an essay on the Declaration of Independence (the introduction appears on the facing page):

> The Declaration of Independence has come to be a statement of this nation's political philosophy, but that was not its purpose in 1776. Jefferson had to bow to the goals of the Congress as a whole to forge unity among the colonies and to win the support of foreign nations.
>
> —Ann Weiss (student), "The Editing of the Declaration of Independence"

Echo of introduction: contrast between past and present

Restatement and elaboration of thesis

In the next example the author concludes an essay on environmental protection with a call for action:

> Until we get the answers [about the effects of pollutants], I think we had better keep on building power plants and growing food with the help of fertilizers and such insect-controlling chemicals as we now have. The risks are well known, thanks to the environmentalists. If they had not created a widespread public awareness of the ecological crisis, we wouldn't stand a chance. But such awareness by itself is not enough. Flaming manifestos and prophecies of doom are no longer much help, and a search for scapegoats can only make matters worse. The time for sensations and manifestos is about over. Now we need rigorous analysis, united effort and very hard work.   —Peter F. Drucker, "How Best to Protect the Environment"

— Summary and opinion

— Call for action

Conclusions to avoid

Several kinds of conclusions rarely work well:

- **A repeat of the introduction.** Don't simply replay your introduction. The conclusion should capture what the paragraphs of the body have added to the introduction.
- **A new direction.** Don't introduce a subject that is different from the one your essay has been about.
- **A sweeping generalization.** Don't conclude more than you reasonably can from the evidence you have presented. If your essay is about your frustrating experience trying to clear a parking ticket, you cannot reasonably conclude that *all* local police forces are too tied up in red tape to serve the people.
- **An apology.** Don't cast doubt on your essay. Don't say, *Even though I'm no expert* or *This may not be convincing, but I believe it's true* or anything similar. Rather, to win your readers' confidence, display confidence.

8 Presenting Writing

In *Brief*

- Follow the document format of the discipline you are writing in (below).
- Use visuals and other media appropriately in multimodal writing (p. 63).
- Consider design when writing for the Web (p. 69).

Visit MyWritingLab™ for more resources on presenting writing.

Presenting your writing gives you a chance to display your hard work in the best possible light. This opportunity often comes with challenges as well: to fulfill the requirements of the assignment, the conventions of the genre, and the expectations of your audience.

8a Format academic writing appropriately for each discipline.

Many of the assignments you receive in college will require you to submit a written text either on paper or electronically—for instance, attached to an e-mail or uploaded to a course Web site. For most print papers and files of papers, the example below shows a basic format that will help make your writing attractive and readable.

Many academic style guides recommend specific formats. This book details two such formats:

- **MLA style,** used in English, foreign languages, and some other humanities. MLA style is illustrated on the next page and discussed in detail on pages 464–66.
- **APA style,** used in the social sciences, discussed on pages 497–500. APA style differs from MLA style in specifying a title page, a style for section headings, and other features.

Although they do vary, most academic formats share preferences for the design of standard elements:

- **Margins:** minimum one inch on all sides.
- **Line spacing:** double-spaced throughout.
- **Type fonts and sizes:** standard 10- or 12-point fonts such as Times New Roman and Cambria (serif fonts, with small lines finishing the letters) or Arial and Calibri (sans serif fonts, lacking the small lines). Serif fonts are generally easier to read on paper, while sans serif fonts are easier to read on a screen.
- **Highlighting:** <u>underlining</u>, *italics*, or **boldface** to mark headings and emphasize text elements such as terms being defined.

61

Sample paper in MLA format

Writer's last name and page number.

Identification: writer's name, instructor's name, course title, date.

Title centered.

Double-spaced throughout.

1" margins on top, bottom, and sides.

Indentions marking paragraph breaks.

Source citation in MLA style (see p. 419).

Photograph introduced to indicate its meaning and purpose.

Caption allowing photograph to be read independently from the text.

Torres 1

Mia Torres

Mr. O'Donnell

English 131

14 March 2015

Creating the Next Generation of Smokers

Parents warn their children not to smoke. Schools teach kids and teens about the dangers of smoking. States across the country have enacted smoking bans, making it illegal for adults to smoke in restaurants, bars, workplaces, and public buildings. Yet despite these efforts, smoking among teens and young adults continues, and it does so in part because the film industry creates movies that promote smoking.

According to the organization Smoke Free Movies, a group based in the School of Medicine at the University of California, San Francisco, tobacco companies and filmmakers collaborate to promote smoking: tobacco companies pay filmmakers to feature their products, and filmmakers show celebrity actors smoking in movies and portray smoking as glamorous and socially acceptable (4-5). Stopping young people's exposure to images of smoking in movies requires stopping each of these activities.

Despite proof that showing smoking in movies encourages young people to start smoking, more than half of movies feature well-known stars smoking (Fox). As fig. 1 shows, cigarettes often figure prominently, with the cigarette held close to the celebrity's head so that it is an integral part of the shot.

Fig. 1. The actress Scarlett Johansson in *Black Dahlia*, one of many movies released each year in which characters smoke. From *Daily Mail*. 18 Sept. 2006, www.dailymail.co.uk/article-1602474.html.

- **Headings:** one or two levels as needed to direct readers' attention to significant ideas and transitions. Word headings consistently— for instance, all questions (*What Is Sustainability?*) or all phrases with *-ing* words (*Understanding Sustainability*). Indicate the relative importance of headings with highlighting and position— perhaps bold for first-level headings and lightface italic for second-level headings. (Document format in psychology and some other social sciences requires a particular treatment of headings. See pp. 499–500.)
- **Lists:** numbered or bulleted (as in the list you're reading), to show the relationship of like items, such as the elements of a document or the steps in a process or proposal.

Designing for readers with vision loss

If your audience may include readers who have low vision, problems with color perception, or difficulties processing visual information, adapt your design to meet these readers' needs:

- **Use large type fonts.** Most guidelines call for 14 points or larger.
- **Use standard type fonts.** Many people with low vision find it easier to read sans serif fonts such as Arial than serif fonts. Avoid decorative fonts with unusual flourishes, even in headings.
- **Avoid words in all-capital letters.**
- **Avoid relying on color alone to distinguish elements.** Label elements, and distinguish them by position or size.
- **Use red and green selectively.** To readers who are red-green colorblind, these colors will appear in shades of gray, yellow, or blue.
- **Use contrasting colors.** To make colors distinct, choose them from opposite sides of the color spectrum—violet and yellow, for instance, or orange and blue.
- **Use only light colors for tints behind type.** Make the type itself black or a very dark color.

- **Color:** mainly for illustrations, occasionally for headings, bullets, and other elements. Always use black for the text of a paper, and make sure that any other colors are dark enough to be legible.

8b   Use visuals and other media appropriately in multimodal writing.

Academic writing is often **multimodal**—that is, it includes more than one medium, whether text, charts, photographs, video, or audio. A simple multimodal paper involves just two media—mainly text with some illustrations embedded in the text. A paper submitted online might add links to audio or video files as well. This section provides guidelines for selecting and using such media in your writing.

Caution Any visual or media file you include or link to in your writing requires the same detailed citation as a written source. See pages 410–11 for more on acknowledging sources.

1 ▪ Selection of visuals and other media

Depending on your writing situation, you might use anything from a table to a bar chart to a video to support your writing. The following pages describe and illustrate several options.

Note The Web is an excellent resource for visuals, audio, and video (see pp. 373–75). Your computer may include a program for creating tables, graphs, and other illustrations, or you can work with specialized software such as *Excel* (for graphs and charts) or *Adobe Illustrator* (for diagrams, maps, and the like). Use *PowerPoint* or a similar program for visuals in oral presentations.

Selecting visuals

Visuals can be placed in print or electronic documents. They include tables, pie charts, bar charts, line graphs, infographics, diagrams, flowcharts, and images such as photographs, maps, fine art, advertisements, and cartoons. (See the box on the next two pages.)

Selecting video and audio

You can use video or audio files to emphasize or support points in digital writing, such as Web pages or blogs, and in oral presentations. For example, you might explain a process with a video of how something works, support an interpretation of a play with a video of a scene from a performance, or illustrate a profile of a person by linking to a podcast interview. The screen shot below shows a passage of text from an online paper that links to video of the poet Rita Dove reading her poem "American Smooth."

Link to video file

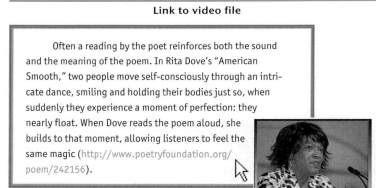

Often a reading by the poet reinforces both the sound and the meaning of the poem. In Rita Dove's "American Smooth," two people move self-consciously through an intricate dance, smiling and holding their bodies just so, when suddenly they experience a moment of perfection: they nearly float. When Dove reads the poem aloud, she builds to that moment, allowing listeners to feel the same magic (http://www.poetryfoundation.org/poem/242156).

2 ▪ Effective use of visuals and other media

An image or a video clip can attract readers' attention, but if it does no more it will amount to mere decoration or, worse, it will distract readers from the substance of your writing. Before using any visual or other media, consider whether it meets the requirements of your assignment, serves a purpose, and is appropriate for your audience.

Selecting visuals

Tables

Tables present raw data to show how variables relate to one another or how two or more groups contrast. Place a descriptive title above the table, and use headings to label rows and columns.

Table 1

Public- and private-school enrollment of US students, 2014

	Number of students (in millions)	Percentage in public school	Percentage in private school
All students	49.7	89	11
Kindergarten through grade 8	35.0	88	12
Grades 9-12	14.7	91	9

Source: Data from *Digest of Education Statistics: 2014*, National Center for Education Statistics, Apr. 2014, nces.ed.gov/tables/dt13_205.10.asp.

Diagrams and flowcharts

Diagrams show concepts visually, such as the structure of an organization or the way something works or looks.

Fig. 4. *MyPlate,* a graphic representation of daily food portions recommended for a healthy diet. From *ChooseMyPlate.gov,* US Dept. of Agriculture, 2011, www.choosemyplate.gov.

Images

Photographs, maps, paintings, advertisements, and cartoons can be the focus of critical analysis or can support points you make.

Fig. 5. View of Saturn from the *Cassini* spacecraft, showing the planet and its rings. From *Cassini-Huygens: Mission to Saturn and Titan*, NASA, Jet Propulsion Laboratory, 24 Feb. 2015, nasa.gov/multimedia/imagegallery/137.html.

(continued)

Selecting visuals
(continued)

Pie charts

Pie charts show how the parts of a whole relate, adding up to 100%. Use a pie chart to show shares of data. Label each pie slice, and make it proportional to its share of the whole.

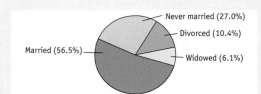

Fig. 1. Marital status in 2014 of adults age eighteen and over. Data from *2014 Statistical Abstract*, US Census Bureau, Jan. 2015, www.census.gov/library/publications/2014/131ed.html.

Bar charts

Bar charts compare groups or time periods. Use a bar chart when relative size is important. On the vertical scale, start with a zero point in the lower left and label the values being measured. On the horizontal scale, label the groups being compared.

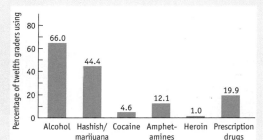

Fig. 2. Lifetime prevalence of use of alcohol, compared with other drugs, among twelfth graders in 2014. Data from *Monitoring the Future: A Continuing Study of American Youth*, U of Michigan, 12 Dec. 2014, www.monitoringthefuture.org/data/data.html.

Line graphs

Line graphs compare many points of data to show change over time. On the vertical scale, start with a zero point in the lower left and label the values being measured. On the horizontal scale, label the range of dates. Label the data lines, and distinguish them with color, dots, or dashes.

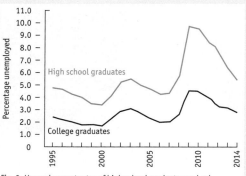

Fig. 3. Unemployment rates of high school graduates and college graduates, 1995-2014. Data from *Economics News Release*, US Dept. of Labor, Bureau of Labor Statistics, 9 Jan. 2015, www.bls.gov/newsrelease/empsit.nr0.htm.

Considering the requirements and limits of your writing situation

What do the type of writing you're doing and its format allow? Look through examples of similar writing to gauge the kinds of media, if any, that readers will expect. It matters, too, how you will present your work: a short animation sequence might be terrific in a *PowerPoint* presentation or on a Web site, but a printed document requires photographs, drawings, and other static means of explanation.

Making visuals and other media support your writing

Ensure that any visual you use relates directly to a point in your writing, adds to that point, and gives your audience something to think about. In an evaluation of an advertisement, the ad itself would support the claim you make about it. In a paper arguing for earthquake preparedness, a photograph could provide a visual record of earthquake damage and a chart could show levels of current preparedness.

The following two images supported a paper with this thesis: *By the mid-1960s, depictions of women in advertising reflected changing attitudes toward the traditional role of homemaker.*

Visuals as support

Visual examples support the thesis about changing attitudes toward women as homemakers.	Caption explains the visuals, tying them to the text of the paper and providing source information.

Fig. 1. An advertisement from 1941 (left) and a brochure illustration from 1965 (right) showing a change in the relationship between homemaking women and their appliances. Left: Bissell advertisement, 1941. Right: *Electric Ranges by Frigidaire*, 1965.

des

8b

Integrating visuals and other media into your writing

Readers should understand why you are including visuals or other media in your writing and how they relate to the overall project:

- **In projects with embedded visuals, connect the visuals to your text.** Refer to visuals at the point(s) where readers will benefit from consulting them—for instance, "See fig. 2" or "See table 1." Number figures and tables separately (Fig. 1, Fig. 2, and so on; Table 1, Table 2, and so on).
- **Always caption visuals.** A caption serves two functions: it says explicitly how the visual relates to your text, so that readers don't have to puzzle out your intentions; and it cites the source of the data or the entire visual. See the examples on pages 65–67.
- **In online projects using audio or video, work the files or links into your text.** Your audience should know what you intend the media to show, whether you link to a photograph from a mainly text document or you integrate text, sound, still images, and video into a complex Web project. For instance, in the sample on page 64, the embedded link invites readers to see and hear Rita Dove reading her poem "American Smooth."

Responsible use of visuals and other media

Visuals and other media require special care to avoid distortion and to ensure honest use of others' material.

- **Create and evaluate tables, charts, and graphs carefully.** Verify that the data you use are accurate and that the highlighted changes, relationships, or trends reflect reality. In a line graph, for instance, starting the vertical axis at zero puts the lines in context (see the sample on p. 66).
- **Be skeptical of digital images.** Altered photographs are posted online and circulated widely. If a photograph seems inauthentic, check into its source or don't use it.
- **Provide a source note.** You must credit the source whenever you use someone else's data to create a visual, embed someone else's visual in your document, or link to someone else's media file. Each discipline has a slightly different style for such source notes: those in the illustrations on pages 65–67 reflect MLA style. See also Chapters 56 and 57.
- **Obtain permission if it is required.** For projects that will reside on the Web, you may need to clear permission from the copyright holder of a visual or a media file. See page 412 for a discussion of copyright and permission.

8c   Consider design when writing for the Web.

When creating blogs, Web sites, wikis, and other types of digital projects, you can use existing templates that simplify the work of design. Even so, you will still have to make choices about how your work will appear on readers' screens. The guidelines below and in the sample blog post can help you make such decisions so that your work achieves its purpose.

- **Consider how design can reflect your purpose for writing and your sense of audience.** Unlike a printed paper, a Web composition allows considerable design freedom. Think about how type fonts and sizes, headings, visuals and other media, color, and other elements can connect with readers and further the purpose of your writing.
- **Anticipate how readers will move within your composition.** A digital document with links to other posts, Web sites, and media can disorient readers. Page length, links, menus, and other cues should work to keep readers oriented.
- **Integrate media into the text.** Any visual or sound element should add essential information that can't be provided in any other way, and it should be well integrated with the rest of your composition. See the guidelines for selecting and using visuals on pages 63–68.

See page 139 for an example of a social-media post. And see pages 129–31 for tips on using slides to support an oral presentation.

Sample blog post

Following is a student's draft of a personal essay, which he posted to his class blog. He composed and edited his text in a word processor and pasted the text into the blog program, adding the title, the comic, and a link to his personal blog.

Literacy narrative posted to a blog

FRIDAY, FEBRUARY 20, 2015
Literacy narrative draft

Comics: Telling Stories in Words and Art

For my seventh birthday, I received a Calvin and Hobbes comic book. I devoured the book, reading it cover to cover countless times, and was instantly attracted to how drawings and words worked together to tell very funny stories about the characters. I didn't always understand the vocabulary, the jokes, and references to the 1980s, but I laughed at what I did get: the funny arguments, crazy games, and hilarious schemes.

Descriptive title.

Anecdote opening the essay.

Standard font for readability.

Paragraph connecting introductory anecdote to writer's life.

Illustration supporting a point in the post.

The summer after my birthday I began drawing my own comics. I created two characters modeled on Calvin and Hobbes—a boy

named Timmy and his dog Snuffy. Over the next five years, I drew hundreds of comics about Timmy, Snuffy, and Timmy's family and friends. I drew the strip shown here, about one of Timmy's many mishaps, when I was ten. I have this strip and some of my other favorites posted on my personal blog: johnsdoodles@blogger.com.

Embedded link to another Web site.

Paragraph expanding previous paragraph with vivid, concrete details.

Timmy experienced much of what I did over the next several years. He went on vacation to places I visited with my family, like New York and San Francisco. He visited aunts, uncles, and grandparents. He exasperated his parents, learned to play an instrument, and dreamed of being a pilot. He also did things I had not experienced: he once trained for the school marathon and came in third, dreamed of going to the prom like his sister, and slid down what seemed like a mile-long hill on a sled. Through Timmy, I used language and drawing to explore ideas, dreams, and experiences, all the time trying to make them funny.

Conclusion pointing out significance of story.

Although I still draw and write, I left Timmy behind the summer I turned twelve. However, occasionally I look back at my Timmy comics and find it interesting to see how I used words and images to develop and display my sense of place in the world.

Posted by John Heywood at 4:23 PM.

PART 2

Writing in and out of College

9   Academic Writing

In *Brief*

- Analyze the purpose and audience in each writing situation (below).
- Use an appropriate academic genre (next page).
- Choose appropriate structure and content (p. 76).
- Use sources with integrity (p. 77).
- Use academic language (p. 79).
- Communicate effectively with instructors and classmates (p. 82).

Visit MyWritingLab™ for more resources on academic writing.

9a

When you take college courses, you enter a community of teachers and students whose basic goal is to share and build knowledge about a subject, whether it is English, history, engineering, or something else. You participate in this community by studying each subject, by asking questions, and by communicating your answers in writing. This chapter gives you ways to approach academic writing situations and make a contribution to knowledge building.

9a   Determine your purpose and audience.

Like any writing, academic writing occurs in a particular situation created by your assignment and by your subject, purpose, audience, and genre. The assignment and subject will be different for each project, but some generalizations can be made about the other elements. (If you haven't already done so, read pp. 2–10 on writing situations and their elements.)

1 ▪ Purpose

For most academic writing, your general purpose will be mainly explanatory or mainly argumentative. That is, you will aim to clarify your subject by analyzing, describing, or reporting on it so that readers understand it as you do; or you will aim to gain readers' agreement with a debatable idea about the subject. (See pp. 6–7 for more on general purposes and pp. 102–17 for more on argument.)

Your specific purpose—including your subject and how you hope readers will respond—depends on the genre, the kind of writing that you're doing. (See the next page.) For instance, in a literature review for a biology class, you want readers to understand the research area you're covering, the recent contributions made by researchers, the issues needing further research, and the sources you consulted. Not coincidentally, these topics correspond to the major sections of a literature review. In following the standard format, you both help to define your purpose and begin to meet the discipline's (and thus your instructor's) expectations.

Your specific purpose will be more complex as well. You take a course to learn about a subject and the ways experts think about it. Your writing, in return, contributes to the discipline through the knowledge you uncover and the lens of your perspective. At the same time, as a student you want to demonstrate your competence with research, evidence, format, and other requirements of the discipline.

2 ▪ Audience

Many academic writing assignments will specify or assume an educated audience or an academic audience. Such readers look for writing that is clear, balanced, well organized, and well reasoned. Other assignments will specify or assume an audience of experts on your subject, readers who look in addition for writing that meets the subject's requirements for claims and evidence, organization, language, format, and other qualities.

9b

Much of your academic writing will have only one reader besides you: the instructor of the course for which you are writing. Instructors fill two main roles as readers:

- **They represent the audience you are addressing.** They may actually be members of the audience, as when you address academic readers or subject experts. Or they may imagine themselves as members of your audience—reading, for instance, as if they sat on the city council. In either case, they're interested in how effectively you write for the audience.

- **They serve as coaches,** guiding you toward achieving the goals of the course and, more broadly, toward the academic aims of building and communicating knowledge.

Like everyone else, instructors have preferences and peeves, but you'll waste time and energy trying to anticipate them. Do attend to written and spoken directions for assignments, of course. But otherwise view your instructors as representatives of the community you are writing for. Their responses will be guided by the community's aims and expectations and by a desire to teach you about them.

9b   Use an appropriate genre.

Many academic writing assignments will suggest the genre in which you are to write—the kind of writing and/or the format. Sometimes the genre is prescribed, such as the literature review mentioned earlier, with its standard content and format. Other assignments imply the genre, such as one that asks you to analyze, compare, and explain. Your response would most likely be a conventional academic essay— introduction, thesis statement, supporting paragraphs, conclusion— that analyzes and compares in order to explain.

Whether genre is specified or implied in your assignment, you are being asked to demonstrate your ability to write competently in that genre. The following sections discuss genres commonly assigned in college courses and point out examples that appear elsewhere in this book. In addition, Chapter 14 contains examples of genres used in public writing: application letter and résumé, memo, report, proposal, social-media post, and newsletter.

1 ▪ Responses to texts or visuals

Responses to texts or visuals involve close reading, summary, and analysis. For more on analyzing and responding to texts and visuals, see Chapter 10.

- **Personal response to a reading:** Use your own experiences, observations, and opinions to explain how and why you agree or disagree (or both) with the author's argument. A personal-response essay usually includes a thesis statement that conveys the essence of your response, a brief summary of the author's main points, and your own main points of agreement or disagreement. (See pp. 40–42 for a response to a reading.)
- **Critical analysis (critique) of a text or a visual:** Closely examine a text or visual, identifying and describing important elements of the work and analyzing how the elements contribute to the whole. Often a critical analysis, or critique, also includes evaluation of the quality and significance of the work. The genre contains an arguable thesis stating your interpretation, a brief summary or description of the work, and examples from the text or visual as support for your thesis and main points. (See pp. 100–02 for a critique of an essay.)
- **Literary analysis:** Argue for an interpretation of a work based on careful reading, giving particular attention to the work's language, structure, meaning, and themes. In a literary analysis, you state your interpretation in a thesis and then support your thesis with examples from the work, usually quotations. Some literary analyses draw on others' views and information, such as a scholar's interpretation of the work or facts about the author's life. (See pp. 125–27 for a literary analysis that draws on such secondary sources.)

2 ▪ Arguments

Argument seeks to persuade readers, moving them to action or convincing them to think as you do. Written arguments contain an arguable thesis statement—a claim reasonable people can disagree over—usually with support for its main points and acknowledgment of opposing views. Arguments often involve research, but not always. For a detailed discussion of writing arguments, see Chapter 11.

- **Proposal argument:** Define a problem, give a solution, explain how the solution can be implemented, and respond to possible objections to the solution. (See pp. 118–21 and 468–76 for two proposal arguments that involve research.)
- **Position argument:** Seek to convince readers to agree with your position on a debatable issue such as lowering the drinking age or requiring military service. A position argument introduces the issue, conveys your position in a thesis statement, makes claims and gives evidence to support your position, and responds to opposing views. Depending on the assignment, evidence may be personal or gathered from research or both. (A type of position argument is literary analysis, described on the previous page, in which you make a case for your interpretation of a work of literature. See pp. 125–27 for an example.)
- **Evaluation argument:** Judge whether something is good or effective. A common type of evaluation argument is a critical analysis of a text or visual, described on the previous page. (See pp. 100–02 for an evaluation of a text.) Reviews of books, movies, exhibits, and so on are also evaluation arguments.

3 ▪ Informative writing

Informative writing seeks to teach readers about a subject. When you write to inform, you explore a subject in depth and provide information that readers may not know. Informative writing often, but not always, involves research. In the social, natural, and applied sciences, informative writing can include summaries and case studies in addition to research-based writing.

- **Informative essay:** Explain a subject such as a situation or a process. Typically, an informative essay begins with an introduction and a thesis statement that previews your major points. Then the body paragraphs support the thesis with evidence. Depending on the assignment, an informative essay may focus on a nonpersonal subject (see the essay on pp. 24–25 about money in college football), or it may arise from personal experience and thus overlap the personal essay (see below).
- **Informative research paper or report:** Draw on research to explain a subject, answer a question, or describe the results of a survey or an experiment. This genre includes research papers and research reports (next page) as well as laboratory reports. (See pp. 501–04 for a sample research report.)

4 ▪ Personal writing

A personal essay often narrates the writer's experience or describes a person or place, usually in vivid detail. What makes a personal essay interesting is the insight the writer provides, showing why the subject is significant to the writer and to readers.

A literacy narrative is a particular kind of personal story: your experience with learning to read and/or write. (See pp. 69–70 for a student's literacy narrative.)

5 ▪ Research papers and reports

Most research projects involve reporting information or results, interpreting a range of views on a topic, or analyzing a problem and arguing for a solution.

- **Research paper:** Develop an informative or argumentative thesis statement, draw on and cite multiple sources to support the thesis, and emphasize synthesis of your sources' views and data from your own perspective. (See pp. 468–76 for a sample research paper.)
- **Research report:** Explain your own original research or your attempt to replicate someone else's research. A research report generally includes an abstract (or summary), an introduction describing your research and reviewing prior research on the subject, a description of methods, the results, discussion of the results, and a list of any sources you have cited. (See pp. 501–04 for a research report.)

9c Choose the structure and content.

Academic writing assignments vary widely, of course, but they tend to share the following key goals.

- **Develop a main point in your writing.** Most academic papers center on a main point, or thesis, and support that thesis with evidence. Depending on the genre you are writing in, the main point may be an opinion, a summary of findings, or a conclusion based on primary research you have conducted, such as an experiment or a survey. (For more on thesis statements, see pp. 16–19.)
- **Support the main point with evidence, usually drawn from your reading, personal experience, or primary research.** The kinds of evidence you use will depend on the discipline you're writing in and the type of paper you're doing. For more on evidence, see pages 105 (argument) and 124 (literature).
- **Synthesize your own and others' ideas.** College writing often involves researching and interacting with the works of other writers—being open to their ideas, responding to them, questioning them, comparing them, and using them to answer questions. Such interaction requires you to read critically (the subject of the next chapter) and to synthesize, or integrate, others' ideas with your own. For more on synthesis in academic writing, see pages 99–100 and 389–91.

▪ **Use academic language.** Unless your instructor specifies otherwise, choose formal, standard English. (For more on academic language, see pages 79–81 and 158–65.)

▪ **Acknowledge sources fully, including online sources.** Academic writers build on the work of others by citing borrowed ideas and information. Always record the publication information for your sources, put other writers' words in quotation marks, and cite the source of every quotation, paraphrase, and summary. *Not* acknowledging sources is plagiarism. See the following section and Chapters 53–54 for more on using and acknowledging sources.

▪ **Organize clearly within the framework of the type of writing you're doing.** Develop your ideas as simply and directly as your purpose and content allow. Relate sentences, paragraphs, and sections clearly so that readers always know where they are in the paper's development.

9d

⟨**CULTURE • LANGUAGE**⟩ These features of academic writing are not universal. In some cultures academic writing may be indirect, may assume that readers will discover the thesis, or may be based only on well-known sources whose ideas are closely adhered to. In US colleges and universities, students are expected to look for relevant and reliable sources, well known or not, and to use sources mainly to support their own ideas.

9d   Use sources with integrity.

Academic integrity is the foundation of academic knowledge building. Trusting in one another's honesty allows students and scholars to examine and extend the work of other scholars, and it allows teachers to guide and assess the progress of their students.

You can build your integrity as a writer by working to develop your own ideas and by handling sources responsibly. The following tips can help. See also Chapters 52–54 for extensive discussions of researching and citing sources.

1 ▪ Avoiding plagiarism

Many writing assignments will require you to consult sources such as journal articles, Web sites, and books. These works belong to their creators; you are free to borrow from them *if* you do so with integrity. That means representing the sources accurately—not misinterpreting or distorting what they say. It also means crediting the sources—not plagiarizing, or presenting sources' ideas and information as if they were your own. On most campuses, plagiarism is a punishable offense.

Plagiarism can be deliberate or careless:

- **Deliberate plagiarism** is outright cheating: copying another writer's sentence or idea and passing it off as your own, buying a paper from the Web, or getting someone else to write a paper for you.
- **Careless plagiarism** is more common among students, often arising from inattentive or inexperienced handling of sources. For instance, you might cut and paste source information into your own ideas without clarifying who said what, or you might present a summary of a source without recognizing that parts of it are actually quoted. In these cases the plagiarism is unintentional, but it is still plagiarism.

9d

See Chapter 54 for more on plagiarism.

2 ▪ Developing perspective on a subject

Consider your own knowledge and perspective on a subject before you start to research. This forethought will make it easier for you to recognize other authors' perspectives and to treat them fairly in your writing—whether or not you agree with them.

- **Before you consult sources, gauge what you already know and think about your subject.** Give yourself time to know your own mind before looking to others for information. Then you'll be able to reflect on how the sources reinforce, contradict, or expand what you already know.
- **Evaluate sources carefully.** Authors generally write from particular perspectives, and some are more overt about their biases than others. You needn't reject a source because it is biased; indeed, often you'll want to consider multiple perspectives. But you do need to recognize and weigh the writer's position. See pages 377–89 for a discussion of evaluating sources.
- **Treat sources fairly.** Represent an author's ideas and perspectives as they were originally presented, without misunderstanding or distortion. Be careful in paraphrasing and summarizing not to misrepresent the author's meaning. Be careful in editing quotations not to omit essential words.

3 ▪ Managing sources

You can avoid plagiarism by keeping track of the sources you consult, the ideas that influence your thinking, and the words and sentences you borrow—and by carefully citing the sources in your writing. If these habits are unfamiliar to you, keep the following list handy.

- **Keep track of source information as you read.** Get in the habit of always recording publication information (the author, title, date, and so on) of any source you read as well as any ideas you glean from it. See the box on page 357 for a list of what to record.

▪ **Be careful with quotations.** If you cut and paste a portion of an article, Web site, or other source into your document, put quotation marks around it so that you don't mix your words and the source's words accidentally. Check any quotation that you use in your own writing against the original source. For a more detailed discussion of how to quote sources, see pages 397–99.

▪ **Use your own words in paraphrases and summaries.** A paraphrase or summary presents the ideas of a source but not in the exact words of the original and not in quotation marks. You will be less likely to use the source author's words (and thus plagiarize) if you look away from the source while you write down what you remember from it. Note, though, that you must still cite the source of a summary or paraphrase, just as you do with a quotation. For a more detailed discussion of how to summarize and paraphrase sources, see pages 393–97.

9e

▪ **Cite your sources.** As you draft, be conscious of when you're using source information and be conscientious about clearly marking where the borrowed material came from. In your final draft you'll use a particular style of citation within your text to refer to a detailed list of sources at the end. This book presents two styles: MLA style for English and some other humanities (pp. 419–64) and APA style for the social sciences (pp. 477–97).

9e   Use academic language.

American academic writing relies on a dialect called standard American English. The dialect is also used in business, the professions, government, the media, and other sites of social and economic power where people of diverse backgrounds must communicate with one another. It is "standard" not because it is better than other forms of English, but because it is accepted as the common language, much as the dollar bill is accepted as the common currency.

In writing, standard American English varies a great deal, from the formality of an academic research report to the more relaxed language of this handbook to informal e-mails between coworkers in a company. Even in academic writing, standard English allows much room for the writer's own tone and voice, as these passages on the same topic show:

More formal

Responsibility for the widespread problem of obesity among Americans depends on the person or group describing the problem and proposing a solution. Some people believe the cause

Drawn-out phrasing, such as *widespread problem of obesity among Americans.*

lies with individuals who make poor eating choices for themselves and parents who feed unhealthy foods to their children. Others take strong issue with the food industry, citing food manufacturers and fast-food chains that create and advertise food that is high in sugar, fat, and sodium. Still others place responsibility on American society as a whole for preferring a sedentary lifestyle centered on screen-based activities such as watching television and using computers for video games and social interaction.

More complicated sentence structures, such as *take strong issue with the food industry, citing food manufacturers and fast-food chains that create and advertise. . . .*

More formal vocabulary: *responsibility, children, television.*

9e

Less formal

Who or what is to blame for the obesity epidemic depends on who is talking and what they want to do about the problem. Some people blame eaters for making bad choices and parents for feeding their kids unhealthy foods. Others demonize food manufacturers and fast-food chains for creating and advertising sugary, fatty, and sodium-loaded food. Still others point to Americans generally for spending too much time in front of screens watching TV, playing video games, or going on *Facebook.*

More informal phrasing, such as *obesity epidemic.*

Less complicated sentence structures, such as *demonize food manufacturers and fast-food chains for creating and advertising. . . .*

More informal vocabulary: *blame, kids, TV.*

As different as they are, both examples illustrate several common features of academic language:

- **It follows the conventions of standard American English for grammar and usage.** These conventions are described in guides to the dialect, such as this handbook.
- **It uses a standard vocabulary,** not one that only some groups understand, such as slang, an ethnic dialect, or another language. (See pp. 158–61 for more on specialized vocabularies.)
- **It does *not* use the informalities of everyday speech, texting, and instant messaging,** including incomplete sentences, slang, no capital letters, and shortened spellings (*u* for *you, b4* for *before, thru* for *through,* and so on). (See pp. 159–60 for more on these forms.)
- **It generally uses the third person (*he, she, it, they*).** The first-person *I* is sometimes appropriate to express personal opinions, but academic writers tend to avoid it and make conclusions speak for themselves. The first-person *we* can connect with readers and invite them to think along, but, again, many academic writers avoid it. The second-person *you* is appropriate only in addressing readers directly (as in this handbook), and even then it may seem condescending or too chummy. Definitely avoid using or implying *you* in conversational expressions such as *You know what I mean* and *Don't take this the wrong way.*

▪ **It is authoritative and neutral.** In the examples opposite, the writers express themselves confidently, not timidly as in *Explaining the causes of obesity requires the reader's patience because. . . .* The writers also refrain from hostility (*The food industry's callous attitude toward health . . .*) and enthusiasm (*The food industry's clever and appealing advertisements . . .*).

At first, the diverse demands of academic writing may leave you groping for an appropriate voice. In an effort to sound fresh and confident, you may write too casually, as if speaking to friends or family:

9e

Too casual

Getting the truth about the obesity epidemic in the US requires some heavy lifting. It turns out that everyone else is to blame for the problem—big eaters, reckless corporations, and all those Americans who think it's OK to be a couch potato.

In an effort to sound "academic," you may produce wordy and awkward sentences:

Wordy and awkward

The responsibility for the problem of widespread obesity among Americans depends on the manner of defining the problem and the proposals for its solution. In some discussions, the cause of obesity is thought to be individuals who are unable or unwilling to make healthy choices in their own diets and parents who similarly make unhealthy choices for their children. [The passive voice in this example—*cause . . . is thought to be* instead of *people blame*—adds to its wordiness and indirection. See pp. 230–32 for more on verb voice.]

A cure for writing too informally or too stiffly is to read academic writing so that the language and style become familiar and to edit your writing (see pp. 36–39).

[CULTURE LANGUAGE] If your first language or dialect is not standard American English, learning to write standard English in no way requires you to abandon your first language. Like most multilingual people, you are probably already adept at switching between languages as the situation demands—speaking one way with your relatives, say, and another way with an employer. As you practice academic writing, you'll develop the same flexibility with it.

Exercise 9.1   Using academic language

Revise the following paragraph to make the language more academic while keeping the factual information the same.

If you buy into the stereotype that teenagers do a lot of texting with their friends, you're right. The Pew Research Center says that teens aged twelve to seventeen text their friends more than sixty times every day on average! Girls aged fourteen to seventeen lead the pack, sending an average of a hundred texts every day. Boys in the same age group aren't as glued to their phones, averaging fifty messages in a day. The research also found that texting is teens' go-to way of sharing with their friends. It outpolls chatting on a cell phone or landline, hanging out on social-networking sites, and getting together.

9f   Communicate effectively in an academic setting.

9f

As a member of an academic community, you will not only write papers and projects but also write directly to instructors, classmates, and other people at your school via e-mail, course-management systems such as *Blackboard* and *Canvas,* and other electronic media. Your written communication with instructors and classmates will rarely be as formal as assigned writing, but it will also rarely be as informal as a text to a friend, a tweet, or a comment on *Facebook.*

Even in a short e-mail, your message will receive a better hearing if you present yourself well and show respect for your reader(s). The following message illustrates an appropriate mix of formality and informality when addressing an instructor.

E-mail message

Uses subject line to describe the content of the message.

Addresses instructor formally with title and last name.

Provides context for request.

Uses complete sentences and words.

Signs with full name and phone number.

> To: cmwhite@cms.edu
>
> Subject: Research paper planning conference
>
> Dear Professor White:
>
> I am in your 8:10 English 111 class, and I'm writing to schedule a planning conference to discuss possible subjects for my research paper. I recently read an article about smoking in movies, and I'm interested in pursuing the topic for my research paper. However, I know I'll have to narrow the topic, and I'm not sure how to do that. Would you be available to meet sometime between 11:00 and 1:00 next Tuesday or Thursday?
>
> Sincerely,
>
> Mia Torres
> 292-8954

Here are guidelines for such communication:

- **Use the medium your instructor prefers.** Don't text, tweet, or use a social-networking site unless you're invited to do so.
- **Use names.** In the body of your message, address your reader(s) by name if possible. Unless your teachers instruct otherwise, always address them formally, using *Professor, Dr., Ms.,* or *Mr.,* as appropriate, followed by the last name. Sign off with your own name and information on how to contact you.

- **Pay attention to tone.** Don't use all capital letters, which SHOUT. And use irony or sarcasm only cautiously: in the absence of facial expressions, either one can lead to misunderstanding.
- **Pay attention to correctness.** Especially when you write to instructors, avoid the shortcuts of texting and tweeting, such as incomplete sentences and abbreviations (*u* for *you*, *r* for *are*, and so on). (See also pp. 159–60.) Proofread for errors in grammar, punctuation, and spelling.
- **Send messages only to the people who need them.** As a general rule, avoid sending messages to many recipients at once—all the students in a course, say—unless what you have to say applies to all of them. Before you hit Reply All in response to a message, ensure that "all" want to see the response.
- **Guard your own and others' privacy.** Online tools allow us to broadcast hurtful information about others—and allow others to do the same to us. Before you post a message about yourself or someone else, consider whether it's worthwhile and who will see it, not only now but in the future. When forwarding messages, make sure not to pass on previous private messages by mistake.
- **Don't write anything that you wouldn't say face to face or wouldn't write in a printed letter.** Electronic messages can be saved and forwarded and can be retrieved in disputes over grades and other matters.

10 Critical Reading and Writing

In *Brief*
- Use techniques of critical reading (next page).
- Summarize (p. 89).
- Form a critical response through analysis, interpretation, synthesis, and sometimes evaluation (p. 91).
- View visuals critically (p. 93).
- Write critical analyses of texts and visuals (p. 98).
- Learn from a sample critical analysis (p. 100).

Visit MyWritingLab™ for more resources on critical reading and writing.

Throughout college and beyond, you will be expected to think, read, and write critically. **Critical** here does not mean "negative" but "skeptical," "exacting," "creative," "curious." You already operate critically every day as you figure out why things happen to you or what your experiences mean. This chapter introduces more formal methods for reading and writing critically.

10a   Use techniques of critical reading.

In college much of your critical thinking will focus on written texts (a short story, a journal article, a blog) or on visual or multimedia texts (a photograph, an advertisement, a film). Like all subjects worthy of critical consideration, such works operate on at least three levels:

1. **What the creator actually says or shows.**
2. **What the creator does not say or show but builds into the work, intentionally or not.**
3. **What you think in response.**

Discovering each level of the work involves a number of reading techniques that are discussed in this chapter.

CULTURE LANGUAGE The idea of reading critically may require you to make some adjustments if readers in your native culture tend to seek understanding or agreement more than engagement from what they read. Readers of English use texts for all kinds of reasons, including pleasure, reinforcement, and information. But they also read questioningly, to uncover the author's motives (*What are this author's biases?*), test their own ideas (*Can I support my point of view as well as this author supports hers?*), and arrive at new knowledge (*Why is the author's evidence so persuasive?*).

1 ▪ Previewing the material

When you're reading a work of literature, such as a short story or a poem, it's often best just to plunge right in. But for critical reading of other works, it's worthwhile to skim before reading word for word, forming expectations and even some preliminary questions. The preview will make your reading more informed and fruitful.

- **Gauge length and level.** Is the material brief and straightforward so that you can read it in one sitting, or will it require more time?
- **Check the facts of publication.** Does the date of publication suggest currency or datedness? Does the publisher or publication specialize in scholarly articles, popular books, or something else? For a Web publication, who or what sponsors the site—an individual? a nonprofit organization? a government body? a college or university?
- **Look for content cues.** What do the title, introduction, headings, illustrations, conclusion, and other features tell you about the topic, the author's approach, and the main ideas?
- **Learn about the author.** Does a biography tell you about the author's publications, interests, biases, and reputation in the field? If there is no biography, what can you gather about the author from his or her words? Use a Web search to trace unfamiliar authors.

- **Consider your preliminary response.** What do you already know about the topic? What questions do you have about either the topic or the author's approach to it? What biases of your own— for instance, curiosity, boredom, or an outlook similar or opposed to the author's—might influence your reading of the work?

Following is an essay by Thomas Sowell, an economist who writes on economics, politics, and education. The essay was first published in the 1990s, but the debate over student loans has hardly subsided. Since Sowell wrote, the number of college graduates with loan debt has increased by a third and the average amount they owe has almost tripled. Preview the essay using the guidelines in the preceding list, and then read it until you think you understand what the author is saying. Note your questions and reactions in writing.

Student Loans

The first lesson of economics is scarcity: There is never enough of 1 anything to fully satisfy all those who want it.

The first lesson of politics is to disregard the first lesson of econom- 2 ics. When politicians discover some group that is being vocal about not having as much as they want, the "solution" is to give them more. Where do politicians get this "more"? They rob Peter to pay Paul.

After a while, of course, they discover that Peter doesn't have 3 enough. Bursting with compassion, politicians rush to the rescue. Needless to say, they do not admit that robbing Peter to pay Paul was a dumb idea in the first place. On the contrary, they now rob Tom, Dick, and Harry to help Peter.

The latest chapter in this long-running saga is that politicians have 4 now suddenly discovered that many college students graduate heavily in debt. To politicians it follows, as the night follows the day, that the government should come to their rescue with the taxpayers' money.

How big is this crushing burden of college students' debt that we 5 hear so much about from politicians and media deep thinkers? For those students who graduate from public colleges owing money, the debt averages a little under $7000. For those who graduate from private colleges owing money, the average debt is a little under $9000.

Buying a very modestly priced automobile involves more debt than 6 that. And a car loan has to be paid off faster than the ten years that college graduates get to repay their student loans. Moreover, you have to keep buying cars every several years, while one college education lasts a lifetime.

College graduates of course earn higher incomes than other peo- 7 ple. Why, then, should we panic at the thought that they have to repay loans for the education which gave them their opportunities? Even graduates with relatively modest incomes pay less than 10 percent of their annual salary on the first loan the first year—with declining percentages in future years, as their pay increases.

Political hysteria and media hype may focus on the low-income stu- 8 dent with a huge debt. That is where you get your heart-rending stories— even if they are not all that typical. In reality, the soaring student loans of the past decade have resulted from allowing high-income people to borrow under government programs.

Before 1978, college loans were available through government pro-   9
grams only to students whose family income was below some cut-off
level. That cut-off level was about double the national average income,
but at least it kept out the Rockefellers and the Vanderbilts. But, in an era
of "compassion," Congress took off even those limits.

That opened the floodgates. No matter how rich you were, it still   10
paid to borrow money through the government at low interest rates. The
money you had set aside for your children's education could be invested
somewhere else, at higher interest rates. Then, when the student loan
became due, parents could pay it off with the money they had set aside—
pocketing the difference in interest rates.

To politicians and the media, however, the rapidly growing loans   11
showed what a great "need" there was. The fact that many students
welshed when time came to repay their loans showed how "crushing"
their burden of debt must be. In reality, those who welsh typically have
smaller loans, but have dropped out of college before finishing. People
who are irresponsible in one way are often irresponsible in other ways.

No small amount of the deterioration of college standards has been 12
due to the increasingly easy availability of college to people who are not
very serious about getting an education. College is not a bad place to
hang out for a few years, if you have nothing better to do, and if someone else is paying for it. Its costs are staggering, but the taxpayers carry
much of that burden, not only for state universities and city colleges, but
also to an increasing extent even for "private" institutions.

Numerous government subsidies and loan programs make it possible 13
for many people to use vast amounts of society's resources at low cost to
themselves. Whether in money terms or in real terms, federal aid to higher education has increased several hundred percent since 1970. That has
enabled colleges to raise their tuition by leaps and bounds and enabled
professors to be paid more and more for doing less and less teaching.

Naturally all these beneficiaries are going to create hype and hyste- 14
ria to keep more of the taxpayers' money coming in. But we would be
fools to keep on writing blank checks for them.

When you weigh the cost of things, in economics that's called   15
"trade-offs." In politics, it's called "mean-spirited." Apparently, if we just
took a different attitude, scarcity would go away.

—Thomas Sowell

2 ▪ Reading

Reading is itself more than a one-step process. You want to understand the first level on which the text operates—what the author
actually says—and begin to form your impressions.

First reading

The first time through new material, read as steadily and smoothly
as possible, trying to get the gist of what the author is saying.

- **Read in a place where you can concentrate.** Choose a quiet environment away from distractions such as music or talking.
- **Give yourself time.** Rushing yourself or worrying about something else you have to do will prevent you from grasping what you read.
- **Try to enjoy the work.** Seek connections between it and what you already know. Appreciate new information, interesting relationships, forceful writing, humor, good examples.
- **Make notes sparingly during this first reading.** Mark major stumbling blocks—such as a paragraph you don't understand—so that you can try to resolve them before rereading.

crit

10a

(**CULTURE**
LANGUAGE) If English is not your first language and you come across unfamiliar words, don't stop and look up every one. You will be distracted from an overall understanding of the text. Instead, try to guess the meanings of the unfamiliar words by using context clues, such as examples and synonyms of the words. Be sure to circle the words and look them up later. You may want to keep a vocabulary log of the words, their definitions, and the sentences in which they appeared.

Rereading and annotating

After the first reading, plan on at least one other. This time read *slowly.* Your main concern should be to grasp the content and how it is constructed. That means rereading a paragraph if you didn't get the point or using a dictionary to look up words you don't know.

Use the tips below to highlight and annotate a text:

- **Distinguish main ideas from supporting ideas.** Mark the central idea (the thesis), the main idea of each paragraph or section, and the evidence supporting ideas.
- **Note key terms.** Understand both their meanings and their applications.
- **Identify the connections among ideas.** Be sure you see why the author moves from point A to point B to point C and how those points relate to support the central idea. It often helps to outline the text or to summarize it (see p. 89).
- **Distinguish between facts and opinions.** Especially when reading an argument, mark the author's opinions as well as the facts on which the opinions are based. (See pp. 104–05 for more on facts and opinions.)
- **Add your own comments.** In the margins or separately, note links to other readings or to class discussions, questions to explore further, possible topics for your writing, points you find especially strong or weak.

An example of critical reading

The following sample shows how a student, Charlene Robinson, approached "Student Loans." After her first reading, Robinson went through Sowell's text more slowly, adding comments and questions in the margin and writing about the essay in her journal. Following are samples of her annotations:

> The first lesson of economics is scarcity: There is never enough of anything to fully satisfy all those who want it.
>   The first lesson of politics is to disregard the first lesson of economics. When politicians discover some group that is being vocal about not having as much as they want, the "solution" is to give them more. Where do politicians get this "more"? They rob Peter to pay Paul.
>   After a while, of course, they discover that Peter doesn't have enough. Bursting with compassion, politicians rush to the rescue. Needless to say, they do not admit that robbing Peter to pay Paul was a dumb idea in the first place. On the contrary, they now rob Tom, Dick, and Harry to help Peter.
>   The latest chapter in this long-running saga is that politicians have now suddenly discovered that many college students graduate heavily in debt. To politicians it follows, as the night follows day, that the government should come to their rescue with the taxpayers' money.

Annotations:
- *fact* ↓
- *related opinion— basic contradiction between economics and politics*
- ← *biblical reference?*
- *ironic and dismissive language*
- *politicians = fools? or irresponsible?*
- *example supporting opinion about economics & politics*

After reading the text, Robinson wrote about it in the journal she kept on her computer. She divided the journal into two columns, one each for the text and her responses. Here is the portion pertaining to the preceding paragraphs:

Text	Responses
Economics teaches lessons (1), and politics (politicians) and economics are at odds.	Is economics truer or more reliable than politics? More scientific?
Politicians don't accept econ. limits—always trying to satisfy "vocal" voters by giving them more of what they want (2).	Politicians do spend tax money, but do they always disregard economics? Evidence?
"Robbing Peter to pay Paul" (2)— the Bible (the Apostles)?	
Politicians support student-loan program with taxpayer refunds bec. of "vocal" voters (2-4): another ex. of not accepting econ. limits.	I support the loan program, too. Are politicians being irresponsible when they do? (Dismissive language underlined on copy.)

You should try to answer the questions about meaning that you raise in your annotations and your journal, and that may take another reading or some digging in other sources, such as dictionaries and encyclopedias. Recording in your journal what you think the author means will help you build an understanding of the text, and a focused attempt to summarize will help even more (see below). Such efforts will resolve any confusion you feel, or they will give you the confidence to say that your confusion is the fault of the author, not the reader.

10b Summarize.

A good way to master the content of a text and to see its strengths and weaknesses is to **summarize** it—that is, distill it to its main points, in your own words. The following box gives a method of summarizing:

crit
10b

Writing a summary

- **Understand the meaning.** Look up words or concepts you don't know so that you understand the author's sentences and how they relate to one another.
- **Understand the organization.** Work through the text to identify its sections—single paragraphs or groups of paragraphs focused on a single topic. To understand how parts of a work relate to one another, try drawing a tree diagram or creating an outline (pp. 20–24).
- **Distill each section.** Write a one- or two-sentence summary of each section you identify. Focus on the main point of the section, omitting examples, facts, and other supporting evidence.
- **State the main idea.** Write a sentence or two capturing the author's central idea.
- **Support the main idea.** Write a full paragraph (or more, if needed) that begins with the central idea and supports it with the sentences that summarize sections of the work. The paragraph should concisely and accurately state the thrust of the entire work.
- *Use your own words.* By writing, you recreate the meaning of the work in a way that makes sense for you. You also avoid plagiarism.
- *Cite the source.* If you use a summary in writing that you do for others, always acknowledge the source.

Summarizing even a passage of text can be tricky. Here we'll look at attempts to summarize the following material from an introductory biology textbook.

Original text

As astronomers study newly discovered planets orbiting distant stars, they hope to find evidence of water on these far-off celestial bodies, for water is the substance that makes possible life as we know it here on Earth. All organisms familiar to us are made mostly of water and live in an environment dominated by water. They require water more than any other substance. Human beings, for example, can survive for quite a few weeks without food, but only a week or so without water. Molecules of water

participate in many chemical reactions necessary to sustain life. Most cells are surrounded by water, and cells themselves are about 70–95% water. Three-quarters of Earth's surface is submerged in water. Although most of this water is in liquid form, water is also present on Earth as ice and vapor. Water is the only common substance to exist in the natural environment in all three physical states of matter: solid, liquid, and gas.
—Neil A. Campbell and Jane B. Reece, *Biology*

The first attempt to summarize the passage accurately restates ideas in the original, but it does not pare the passage to its essence:

Draft summary
Astronomers look for water in outer space because life depends on it. It is the most common substance on Earth and in living cells, and it can be a liquid, a solid (ice), or a gas (vapor).

The work of astronomers and the three physical states of water add color and texture to the original, but they are asides to the key concept that water sustains life because of its role in life. The following revision narrows the summary to this concept:

Revised summary
Water is the most essential support for life, the dominant substance on Earth and in living cells and a component of life-sustaining chemical processes.

When Charlene Robinson summarized Thomas Sowell's "Student Loans," she first drafted this sentence about paragraphs 1–4:

Draft summary
As much as politicians would like to satisfy voters by giving them everything they ask for, the government cannot afford a student loan program.

Reading the sentence and Sowell's paragraphs, Robinson saw that this draft misread the text by asserting that the government cannot afford student loans. She realized that Sowell's point is more complicated than that and rewrote her summary:

Revised summary
As their support of the government's student loan program illustrates, politicians ignore the economic reality that using resources to benefit one group (students in debt) involves taking the resources from another group (taxpayers).

Caution Using your own words when writing a summary not only helps you understand the meaning but also constitutes the first step in avoiding plagiarism. The second step is to cite the source when you use the summary in something written for others. See pages 393–94.

Note Do not count on the AutoSummarize function on your word processor for summarizing texts that you may have copied and pasted into a file. The summaries are rarely accurate, and you will not gain the experience of interacting with the texts on your own.

Exercise 10.1 Summarizing

Start where the preceding summary of Thomas Sowell's essay ends (at paragraph 5) to summarize the entire essay. Your summary, in your own words, should not exceed one paragraph. (For additional exercises in summarizing, see pp. 399–400.)

10c Form a critical response.

Once you've grasped the content of what you're reading—what the author says—then you can turn to understanding what the author does not say outright but suggests or implies or even lets slip. At this stage you are concerned with the purpose or intention of the author and with how he or she carries it out.

Critical thinking and reading consist of four overlapping operations: analyzing, interpreting, synthesizing, and (often) evaluating.

1 ▪ Analyzing

Analysis is the separation of something into its parts or elements, the better to understand it. To see these elements in what you are reading, begin with a question that reflects your purpose in analyzing the text: why you're curious about it or what you're trying to make out of it. This question will serve as a kind of lens that highlights some features and not others.

Analyzing Thomas Sowell's "Student Loans" (pp. 85–86), you might ask one of these questions:

Questions for analysis	Elements
What is Sowell's attitude toward politicians?	References to politicians: content, words, tone
How does Sowell support his assertions about the loan program's costs?	Support: evidence, such as statistics and examples

2 ▪ Interpreting

Identifying the elements of something is only a start: you also need to interpret the meaning or significance of the elements and of the whole. Interpretation usually requires you to infer the author's **assumptions**—opinions or beliefs about what is or what could or should be. (*Infer* means to draw a conclusion based on evidence.)

Assumptions are pervasive: we all adhere to certain values, beliefs, and opinions. But assumptions are not always stated outright. Speakers and writers may judge that their audience already understands and accepts their assumptions; they may not even be aware of their assumptions; or they may deliberately refrain from stating their assumptions for fear that the audience will disagree. That is why your job as a critical thinker is to interpret what the assumptions are.

Thomas Sowell's "Student Loans" is based on certain assumptions, some obvious, some not. Analyzing Sowell's attitude toward politicians requires focusing on the statements about them. They "disregard the first lesson of economics" (paragraph 2), which implies that they ignore important principles (knowing that Sowell is an economist himself makes this a reasonable assumption). Politicians also "rob Peter to pay Paul," are "[b]ursting with compassion," "do not admit . . . a dumb idea," are characters in a "long-running saga," and arrive at the solution of spending taxes "as the night follows the day"—that is, inevitably (paragraphs 2–4). From these statements and others, we can infer the following:

> Sowell assumes that politicians become compassionate when a cause is loud and popular, not necessarily just, and they act irresponsibly by trying to solve the problem with other people's (taxpayers') money.

3 ▪ Synthesizing

If you stopped at analysis and interpretation, critical thinking and reading might leave you with a pile of elements and possible meanings but no vision of the whole. With **synthesis** you make connections among the parts of the text *or* between the text and other texts. You consider the text through the lens of your knowledge and beliefs, drawing conclusions about how the text works as a whole.

A key component of academic reading and writing, synthesis receives attention in this chapter (pp. 99–100) and then in the context of research writing (see pp. 389–91). Sometimes you'll respond directly to a text, as in the following statement about Thomas Sowell's essay "Student Loans," which connects Sowell's assumptions about politicians to a larger idea also implied by the essay:

> Sowell's view that politicians are irresponsible with taxpayers' money reflects his overall opinion that the laws of economics, not politics, should drive government.

Often synthesis will take you outside the text to its surroundings. These questions can help you investigate the context of a work:

- **How does the work compare with similar works?** For instance, how have other writers responded to Sowell's views on student loans?
- **How does the work fit into the context of other works by the same author or group?** How do Sowell's views on student loans typify, or not, the author's other writing on politics and economics?
- **What cultural, economic, or political forces influence the work?** What other examples could illustrate Sowell's view that economics, not politics, should determine government spending?
- **What historical forces influence the work?** How has the indebtedness of college students changed over the past four decades?

4 ▪ Evaluating

Critical reading and writing often end at synthesis: you form and explain your understanding of what the work says and doesn't say. If you are also expected to **evaluate** the work, however, you will go further to judge its quality and significance:

- **Collect and test your judgments.** Determine that they are significant and that they apply to the whole work.
- **Turn the judgments into assertions**—for instance, *The poet creates fresh, intensely vivid images* or *The author does not summon the evidence to support his case.*
- **Support these statements with evidence from the text**—mainly quotations and paraphrases.

Evaluation takes a certain amount of confidence. You may think that you lack the expertise to cast judgment on another's work, especially if the work is difficult or the author well known. True, the more informed you are, the better a critical reader you are. But conscientious reading and analysis will give you the internal authority to judge a work *as it stands* and *as it seems to you*, against your own unique bundle of experiences, observations, and attitudes.

crit

10d

10d   View visuals critically.

Every day we are bombarded with visuals—pictures on billboards, pop-up ads on our devices, graphs in textbooks, and charts on Web sites, to name just a few examples. Most visuals slide by without our noticing them, or so we think. But visuals, sometimes even more than text, can influence us covertly. Their creators have purposes, some worthy, some not, and understanding those purposes requires critical reading. The method parallels that in the previous section for reading text critically: preview, read for comprehension, analyze, interpret, synthesize, and (often) evaluate.

1 ▪ Previewing a visual

Your first step in exploring a visual is to form initial impressions of its origin and purpose and to note its distinctive features. This previewing process is like the one for previewing a text (pp. 84–85):

- **What do you see?** What is most striking about the visual? What is its subject? What is the gist of any text or symbols? What is the overall effect of the visual?
- **What are the facts of publication?** Where did you first see the visual? Was it created especially for that location or for others as well? What can you tell about when the visual was created?

- **What do you know about the person or group that created the visual?** For instance, was the creator an artist, scholar, news organization, or corporation? What seems to have been the creator's purpose?
- **What is your preliminary response?** What about the visual interests, confuses, pleases, or disturbs you? Are the form, style, and subject familiar or unfamiliar? How might your knowledge, experiences, and values influence your reception of the visual?

If possible, print a copy of the visual or scan it into your reading journal, and write comments in the visual's margins or separately.

crit
10d

2 ▪ Reading a visual

Reading a visual requires the same level of concentration as reading a text. Try to answer the following questions about the visual. If some answers aren't clear at this point, skip the question until later.

- **What is the purpose?** Is the visual mainly explanatory, conveying information, or is it argumentative, trying to convince readers of something or to persuade them to act? What information or point of view does it seem intended to get across?
- **Who is the intended audience?** What does the source of the visual, including its publication facts, tell about the expectations of its creator for readers' knowledge, interests, and attitudes? What do the features of the visual itself add to your impression?
- **What do any words or symbols add?** Whether located on the visual or outside it (such as in a caption), do words or symbols add information, focus your attention, or alter your impression?

Annotation of an advertisement

Guy in photo: Eyes focused ahead (on students?). Caught in mid-speech. Clenched hands = intense, engaged, passionate.

Large, white type highlights message. 1st sentence: what kids hear growing up. 2nd sentence: a challenge to be "someone" important, like a celebrity.

"Join us": direct invitation to be like this guy.

What is Teach.org? Recruits new teachers?

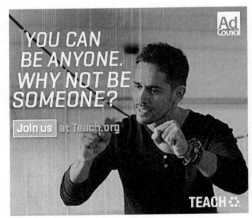

Advertisement for *Teach.org*

- **What action, change, people, places, or things are shown?** Does the visual tell a story? Do its characters or other features tap into your knowledge, or are they unfamiliar?
- **What is the form of the visual?** Is it a photograph, advertisement, painting, graph, diagram, cartoon, or something else? How do its content and apparent purpose and audience relate to its form?

The illustration on the facing page shows the notes that a student, Richard Oliva, made on an advertisement for *Teach.org*.

3 ▪ Analyzing a visual

Elements for analysis

As when analyzing a written work, you analyze a visual by identifying its elements. The visual elements you might consider appear in the box below. Few visuals include all the elements, and you can narrow the list further by posing a question about the visual you are reading, as discussed on the next page.

Elements of visuals

- **Emphasis:** Most visuals pull your eyes to certain features: a graph line moving sharply upward, a provocative figure, bright color, thick lines, and so on.
- **Narration:** Most visuals tell stories, whether in a sequence (a TV commercial or a graph showing changes over time) or at a single moment (a photograph, a painting, or a pie chart). Sometimes dialog or a title or caption contributes to the story.
- **Point of view:** The creator of the visual influences responses by taking account of both the viewer's physical relation to the subject—for instance, whether it is seen head-on or from above—and the viewer's assumed attitude toward the subject.
- **Arrangement:** Pattern, foreground versus background, and separation can contribute to the visual's meaning and effect.
- **Color:** Color can direct the viewer's attention, convey the creator's attitude, and suggest a mood.
- **Characterization:** The qualities of figures and objects—sympathetic or not, desirable or not—reflect their roles in the visual's story.
- **Context:** The source of a visual affects its meaning, whether it is a graph from a scholarly journal or a car ad on the Web.
- **Tension:** Visuals often communicate a problem or seize attention with features that seem wrong, such as misspelled or misaligned words, distorted figures, or controversial relations between characters.
- **Allusions:** An **allusion** is a reference to something the audience is likely to recognize and respond to. Examples include a cultural symbol such as a dollar sign, a mythological figure such as a unicorn, or a familiar movie character such as Darth Vader from *Star Wars*.

Question for analysis

You can focus your analysis of elements by framing your main interest in the visual as a question. Richard Oliva concentrated his analysis of the *Teach.org* ad by asking the question *Does the ad move viewers to imagine themselves as teachers?* The question led Oliva to focus on some elements of the ad and ignore others:

Elements of the ad	Responses
Emphasis	The photo grabs the viewer, placing emphasis on the teacher. Then the lines of white text draw the eye away from the photo to the message.
Narration	In just a few words, the ad tells a story about what viewers could become. It appeals to their wish to be known in some way, like a celebrity, but doing important, interesting work, like the guy in the photo. The invitation "Join us" then urges viewers to take a step toward that dream.
Point of view	The guy is looking down, probably at his students in front of him, not at the viewer. This might be off-putting, but the man is so engaged in speaking that it's not. Instead, the viewer catches his intensity.
Characterization	The guy's intensity about what he's doing is appealing. He seems to have independence and authority—he's not at a desk and is wearing a casual shirt and bracelets, not a suit. He makes teaching look interesting, rewarding, even cool.

Sample visual for analysis

The photograph on the next page gives you a chance to analyze elements of a visual. Try to answer the questions in the annotations.

4 ▪ Interpreting a visual

The strategies for interpreting a visual parallel those for interpreting a written text (pp. 91–92). In this process you look more deeply at the elements, considering them in relation to the likely assumptions and intentions of the visual's creator. You aim to draw reasonable inferences about *why* the visual looks as it does, such as this inference about the *Teach.org* advertisement on page 94:

> The creators of the *Teach.org* ad assume that viewers want careers that make them feel important.

This inference is supported by the second sentence of the ad: "Why not be someone?"

5 ▪ Synthesizing ideas about a visual

As discussed on page 92, with synthesis you take analysis and interpretation a step further to consider how a work's elements and

Elements in a photograph

Emphasis: What is the focus of the photograph? What are your eyes drawn to?

Characterization: What does the man seem to be feeling? Consider especially his mouth and eyes.

Color: The photograph was created in black and white. What does this presentation contribute to the visual? How might it differ in full color?

Narration: What story or stories might the photograph tell?

Arrangement: What is interesting about the arrangement of elements?

Allusion: What symbol do you see? What meaning does it give to the photograph?

Photograph by Steve Simon

underlying assumptions relate and what the overall message is. You may also want to view the visual within the context of similar works of history and culture.

Placing a visual in its context often requires research. For instance, to learn more about the assumptions underlying the *Teach.org* advertisement and the goals of the larger ad campaign, Richard Oliva visited the *Teach.org* Web site. In the following entry from his reading journal, Oliva synthesizes his research and his own ideas about the ad:

The *Teach.org* ad is part of a larger campaign designed to attract young people to careers in teaching. Viewers who go to the *Teach.org* Web site can find information about going to college to become a teacher, getting scholarships for college, and preparing for a job search. They can also watch videos of young teachers talking about what inspired them to choose teaching. The ad with the man talking that popped up on my screen is one of several in the campaign, and the elements of the ad are designed to attract viewers by making teaching look exciting and important.

6 ▪ Evaluating a visual

If your critical reading moves on to evaluation, you'll form judgments about the quality and significance of the visual: Is the message of the visual accurate and fair, or is it distorted and biased? Can you support, refute, or extend the message? Does the visual achieve its apparent purpose, and is the purpose worthwhile? How does the visual affect you?

crit
10e

10e   Write a critical analysis.

Many academic writing assignments ask for **critical analysis**, or **critique**, in which you write critically about texts or visuals. As you form a response to a work, you integrate its ideas and information with yours to come to your own conclusions. As you write your response, you support your ideas about the work by citing evidence from it. (See also pp. 389–91).

Note Critical writing is *not* summarizing. You might summarize to clarify a text or a visual for yourself, and you might briefly summarize a work in your larger piece of writing. But in critical writing you go further to bring your own perspective to the work.

1 ▪ Deciding how to respond

When an assignment asks you to respond directly to a text or a visual, you might take one of the following approaches to decide on your position.

- **Agree with and extend the ideas expressed in the work, exploring related ideas and providing additional examples.**
- **Agree with some of the ideas but disagree with others.**
- **Disagree with one or more ideas.**
- **Explain how the work achieves a particular effect,** such as balancing opposing views or conveying a mood.
- **Analyze the overall effectiveness of the work**—for example, how well a writer supports a thesis with convincing evidence or whether an advertisement succeeds in its unstated purpose.

2 ▪ Shaping a critical analysis

You will likely have an immediate response to at least some of the texts and visuals you analyze: you may agree or disagree strongly with what the author says or shows. But for some other responses, you may need to use the process of critical reading described on pages 84–93 to take notes on the text, summarize it, and develop a view of it. Then, as you write, you can use the tips in the following box to convey your response to readers.

Responding to a text

- **Make sure your writing has a point**—a central idea, or thesis, that focuses your response. (For help with developing a thesis, see pp. 16–19.)
- **Include a very brief summary if readers may be unfamiliar with your subject.** But remember that your job is not just to report what the text says or what a visual shows; it is to *respond* to the work from your own critical perspective. (For more on summary, see pp. 89–90.)
- **Center each paragraph on an idea of your own that supports your thesis.** Generally, state the idea outright, in your own voice.
- **Support the paragraph idea with evidence from the text**—quotations, paraphrases, details, and examples.
- **Conclude each paragraph with your interpretation of the evidence.** As a general rule, avoid ending paragraphs with source evidence; instead, end with at least a sentence that explains what the evidence shows.

crit

10e

3 ▪ Emphasizing synthesis in your response

Following the suggestions in the preceding box will lead you to show readers the synthesis you achieved as you developed a critical response to the text or visual. That is, you integrate your perspective on the work with that of the author or creator in order to support a conclusion of your own.

A key to synthesis is deciding how to present evidence from your critical reading or viewing. Especially when you are writing about a relatively unfamiliar subject, you may be tempted to let a text or other source do the talking for you through extensive summary or quotations. However, readers of your academic writing will expect to see you managing ideas and information to make your points.

A typical paragraph of text-based writing should open with your own idea, give evidence from the text, and conclude with your interpretation of the evidence. You can see this pattern in the following paragraph from an essay that appears later in this chapter.

The most fundamental and most debatable assumption underlying Sowell's essay is that higher education is a kind of commodity that not everyone is entitled to.	Writer's idea
In order to diminish the importance of graduates' average debt from education loans, Sowell claims that a car loan will probably be higher (131).	Evidence
This comparison between education and an automobile implies that the two are somehow equal as products and that an affordable higher education is no more a right than a new car is.	Interpretation
Sowell also condemns the "irresponsible" students who drop out of school and "the increasingly easy availability of college to people who are not very serious about getting an education" (132).	Evidence
But he	Interpretation

overlooks the value of encouraging education, including the education of those who don't finish college or who aren't scholars. For many in the United States, education has a greater value than that of a mere commodity like a car. And even from an economic perspective such as Sowell's, the cost to society of an uneducated public needs to be taken into account. By failing to give education its due, Sowell undermines his argument at its core.

Writer's
conclusion

Note Effective synthesis requires careful handling of evidence from the text (quotations and paraphrases) so that it meshes smoothly into your sentences yet is clearly distinct from your own ideas. See pages 400–03 on integrating borrowed material.

crit
10f

10f   A sample critical analysis

The following essay illustrates a common academic assignment, a critical analysis, or critique, of a text. In the essay, Charlene Robinson responds to Thomas Sowell's essay "Student Loans" (pp. 85–86). Robinson arrived at her response, an argument, through the process of critical reading outlined in this chapter and then by gathering and organizing her ideas, developing a thesis about Sowell's text that synthesized his ideas and hers, and supporting her thesis with evidence from her own experience and from Sowell's text.

Robinson did not assume that her readers would see the same things in Sowell's essay or share her views, so her essay offers evidence of Sowell's ideas in the form of direct quotations, summaries, and paraphrases (restatements in her own words). Robinson documents these borrowings from Sowell using the style of the Modern Language Association (MLA): the numbers in parentheses are page numbers in the book containing Sowell's essay, listed at the end as a work cited. (See pp. 419–64 for more on MLA style.)

Weighing the Costs

Introduction	In the essay "Student Loans," the economist Thomas Sowell challenges the US government's student-loan program for three main reasons: a scarce
Summary of Sowell's essay	resource (taxpayers' money) goes to many undeserving students, a high number of recipients fail to repay their loans, and the easy availability of money has led to both lower academic standards and higher college tuitions. Sowell wants his readers to "weigh the costs of things" (133) in order to see, as he does, that the loan program should not receive so much government funding. Sowell wrote his essay in the 1990s, but the argument he makes
Robinson's critical question	is still heard frequently today and is worth examining. Does Sowell provide the evidence of cost and other problems to lead the reader to agree with his argument? The answer is no, because hard evidence is less common than

debatable and unsupported assumptions about students, scarcity, and the value of education.

Sowell's portrait of student-loan recipients is questionable. It is based on averages, some statistical and some not, but averages are often deceptive. For example, Sowell cites college graduates' low average debt of $7,000 to $9,000 (131) without giving the full range of statistics or acknowledging that when he was writing many students' debt was much higher. (Today the average debt itself is much higher.) Similarly, Sowell dismisses "heart-rending stories" of "the low-income student with a huge debt" as "not at all typical" (132), yet he invents his own exaggerated version of the typical loan recipient: an affluent slacker ("Rockefellers" and "Vanderbilts") for whom college is a "place to hang out for a few years" sponging off the government, while his or her parents clear a profit from making use of the loan program (132). Although such students (and parents) may well exist, are they really typical? Sowell does not offer any data one way or the other—for instance, how many loan recipients come from each income group, what percentage of loan funds go to each group, how many loan recipients receive significant help from their parents, and how many receive none. Together, Sowell's statements and omissions cast doubt on the argument that students don't need or deserve the loans.

Another set of assumptions in the essay has to do with "scarcity": "There is never enough of anything to fully satisfy all those who want it," Sowell says (131). This statement appeals to readers' common sense, but the "lesson" of scarcity does not necessarily apply to the student-loan program. Sowell omits many important figures needed to prove that the nation's resources are too scarce to support the program, such as the total cost of the program, its percentage of the total education budget and the total federal budget, and its cost compared to the cost of defense, Medicare, and other expensive programs. Moreover, Sowell does not mention the interest paid by loan recipients, even though the interest must offset some of the costs of running the program and covering unpaid loans. Thus his argument that there isn't enough money to run the student loan program is unconvincing.

The most fundamental and most debatable assumption underlying Sowell's essay is that higher education is a kind of commodity that not everyone is entitled to. In order to diminish the importance of graduates' average debt from education loans, Sowell claims that a car loan will probably be higher (131). This comparison between education and an automobile implies that the two are somehow equal as products and that an affordable higher education

---

Thesis statement

First main point

Evidence for first point: paraphrases and quotations from Sowell's text

Evidence for first point: Sowell's omissions

Conclusion of first point: Robinson's interpretation

Transition to second main point

Second main point

Evidence for second point: Sowell's omissions

Conclusion of second point: Robinson's interpretation

Third main point

Evidence for third point: paraphrases and quotations from Sowell's text

is no more a right than a new car is. Sowell also condemns the "irresponsible" students who drop out of school and "the increasingly easy availability of college to people who are not very serious about getting an education" (132).

Evidence for third point: Sowell's omissions

But he overlooks the value of encouraging education, including the education of those who don't finish college or who aren't scholars. For many in the United States, education has a greater value than that of a mere commodity like a car.

Conclusion of third point: Robinson's interpretation

And even from an economic perspective such as Sowell's, the cost to society of an uneducated public needs to be taken into account. By failing to give education its due, Sowell undermines his argument at its core.

Conclusion

Sowell writes with conviction, and his concerns are valid: high taxes, waste, unfairness, declining educational standards, obtrusive government. However, the essay's flaws make it unlikely that Sowell could convince readers who do not already agree with him. He does not support his portrait of the typical loan recipient, he fails to demonstrate a lack of resources for the loan program, and he neglects the special nature of education compared to other services and products. Sowell may have the evidence to back up his assumptions, but by omitting it he himself does not truly weigh the costs of the loan program.

Acknowledgment of Sowell's concerns

Summary of three main points

Return to theme of introduction: weighing costs

[New page.]

Work Cited

Work cited in MLA style (p. 429)

Sowell, Thomas. "Student Loans." *Is Reality Optional? and Other Essays*, Hoover Institution Press, 1993, pp. 131-33.

—Charlene Robinson (student)

11 Writing Arguments

In *Brief*

- Choose a subject that can be argued (opposite).
- Make claims about the subject (p. 104).
- Gather and evaluate evidence (p. 105).
- Recognize assumptions (p. 106).
- Write reasonably, with logical thinking, appropriate appeals, acknowledgment of opposing views, and no fallacies (p. 106).
- Organize and revise your argument (p. 115).

Visit MyWritingLab™ for more resources on arguments.

Argument is writing that attempts to solve a problem, open readers' minds to an opinion, change readers' opinions, or move readers to action. Using various techniques, you engage readers to find common ground and narrow the distance between your views and theirs.

⟨**CULTURE LANGUAGE**⟩ The ways of conceiving and writing arguments described here may be initially uncomfortable for you if your native culture approaches such writing differently. In some cultures, for example, a writer is expected to begin indirectly, to avoid asserting his or her opinion outright, to rely on appeals to tradition as evidence, or to establish a compromise rather than argue a position. In American academic and business settings, writers do show respect for readers and their opinions, but the persuasive purpose favors clear statement of an opinion, evidence gathered from many sources, and a direct and concise argument for the opinion.

11a   Choose a subject that can be argued.

An argument starts with a subject and an opinion about the subject—that is, an idea that makes you want to write about the subject. For instance, you might think that your school should do more for energy conservation or more to involve students in clubs and other activities. If you don't have a subject or you aren't sure what you think about it, try some of the invention techniques on pages 11–15.

Your initial opinion should meet several requirements:

- **It can be disputed:** reasonable people can disagree over it.
- **It *will* be disputed:** people on all sides care about the subject.
- **It is narrow enough to argue in the space and time available.**

On the flip side of these requirements, some subjects will not work as the starting place of argument because they concern indisputable facts, such as the functions of the human liver; personal preferences or beliefs, such as a moral commitment to vegetarianism; or ideas that few would disagree with, such as the virtues of a secure home.

> **Exercise 11.1   Testing argument subjects**
> Analyze each subject below to determine whether it is appropriate for argument. Explain your reasoning in each case.
>
> 1. Granting of athletic scholarships
> 2. Care of automobile tires
> 3. Censoring the Web sites of hate groups
> 4. History of the town park
> 5. Housing for the homeless
> 6. Billboards in urban residential areas or in rural areas
> 7. Animal testing for cosmetics research
> 8. Cats versus dogs as pets
> 9. Ten steps in recycling wastepaper
> 10. Benefits of being a parent

11b   Make claims about the subject.

Claims are statements that require support. In an argument the thesis statement makes the central claim that you want readers to accept or act on. This claim is what the argument is about. Then in the body of the argument, supporting claims back up the central claim of the thesis statement.

1 ▪ Thesis statements for argument

A thesis statement is always an **opinion**—that is, a judgment based on facts and arguable on the basis of facts. It may be one of the following:

- ▪ **A claim about past or present reality:** an attempt to convince readers that the writer's perception of something is correct.

  In both the building and the equipment, the exercise facility on this campus is outdated.
  Academic cheating increases with students' economic insecurity.

- ▪ **A claim of value:** an attempt to persuade readers to accept the writer's position.

  Higher user fees are unjustified given the condition of the exercise facility.
  People who pirate music undermine the system that encourages the very creation of music.

- ▪ **A recommendation for a course of action:** often the writer's solution to a perceived problem.

  The administration needs to improve the condition of the exercise facility before it can justify raising user fees.
  Schools and businesses can help to reduce traffic congestion by rewarding people who use public transportation.

2 ▪ Supporting claims

The body of an argument consists of specific claims that support the thesis statement. Supporting claims may be statements of opinion, including claims about past or present reality, claims of value, or recommendations for change (see above). More often, supporting claims are statements of fact. These include facts that are generally known or are verifiable (such as the cost of tuition at your school) and those that can be inferred from verifiable facts (such as the monetary value of a college education).

In an argument that higher fees for the exercise facility are not justified, supporting claims might include the following:

The building is run down.
The equipment is in poor condition.
The facility is overcrowded.

Exercise 11.2   Conceiving a thesis statement

Narrow each arguable subject in Exercise 11.1 to a specific opinion, and draft a tentative thesis statement for each. Make each thesis statement a claim about a past or present reality, a claim of value, or a recommendation for a course of action.

11c   Gather and evaluate evidence.

You show the validity of your claims by supporting them with evidence. To support the claim that higher fees are unjustified given the condition of the exercise facility, you might give the amount students already pay in fees, descriptions of the building and equipment, statistics on overcrowding, testimony of students who exercise on campus, and contrasting examples of exercise facilities and fees on other campuses you have visited.

1 ■ Types of evidence

There are several kinds of evidence:

- **Facts,** statements whose truth can be verified or inferred: *Poland is slightly smaller than New Mexico.*
- **Statistics,** facts expressed as numbers: *Of those polled, 22% prefer a flat tax.*
- **Examples,** specific instances of the point being made: *Some groups, such as graduate and undergraduate students, would benefit from this policy.*
- **Expert opinions,** the judgments formed by authorities on the subject based on their own examination of the facts: *Affirmative action is necessary to right the injustices of the past, a point argued by Howard Glickstein, a past director of the US Commission on Civil Rights.*
- **Appeals to readers' beliefs or needs,** statements that ask readers to accept a claim in part because it states something they already accept as true without evidence: *The crowded, run-down exercise facility makes the school seem a second-rate institution.*

2 ■ Evaluating evidence

Evidence must be reliable to be convincing. Ask these questions about your evidence:

- **Is it accurate**—trustworthy, exact, and undistorted?
- **Is it relevant**—authoritative, pertinent, and current?
- **Is it representative**—true to its context, neither under- nor over-representing any element of the sample it's drawn from?
- **Is it adequate**—plentiful and specific?

11d Recognize assumptions.

Assumptions connect evidence to claims: they are the opinions or beliefs that explain why a particular piece of evidence is relevant to a particular claim. For instance:

> **Claim:** The city should create a plan to preserve historic buildings amid new development.
> **Evidence:** The opinions of local city planners on why both preservation and development are needed.
> **Assumption:** Local experts know this city and also what has worked for other cities.

If readers accept the assumption that local experts are qualified to recommend a certain action, then they are more likely to accept the claim that the city should take that action.

Interpreting a work's assumptions is a significant part of critical reading (see pp. 91–92), and recognizing your own assumptions is important to any argument you write. If readers do not share your assumptions, or if they perceive that you are not forthright about your biases, they will be less receptive to your argument. (See the following discussion of reasonableness.)

11e Write reasonably.

To establish common ground between you and your readers, your argument must be reasonable. Readers expect logical thinking, appropriate appeals, fairness toward the opposition, and, combining all of these, writing that is free of fallacies.

1 ▪ Logical thinking

The thesis of your argument is a conclusion you reach by reasoning about evidence. Two processes of reasoning, induction and deduction, are familiar to you even if you aren't familiar with their names.

Induction

When you're about to buy a used car, you consult friends, relatives, and consumer guides before deciding what kind of car to buy. Using **induction,** or **inductive reasoning,** you make specific observations about cars (your evidence) and you induce, or infer, a **generalization** that Car X is most reliable. The generalization is a claim supported by your observations.

You might also use inductive reasoning in a paper on print advertising:

> **Evidence:** Advertisements in newspapers and magazines
> **Evidence:** Comments by advertisers and publishers

Evidence: Data on the effectiveness of advertising
Generalization or claim: Print remains the most cost-effective medium
for advertising.

Inductive reasoning builds from the evidence to the claim, with the assumptions connecting evidence to claim. In this way, induction creates new knowledge from what is already known.

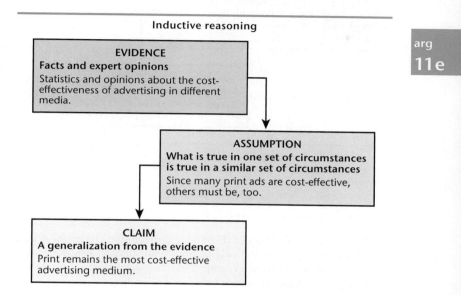

Inductive reasoning

EVIDENCE
Facts and expert opinions
Statistics and opinions about the cost-effectiveness of advertising in different media.

ASSUMPTION
What is true in one set of circumstances is true in a similar set of circumstances
Since many print ads are cost-effective, others must be, too.

CLAIM
A generalization from the evidence
Print remains the most cost-effective advertising medium.

When you reason inductively, you connect your evidence to your generalization by assuming that what is true in one set of circumstances (the ads you look at) is true in a similar set of circumstances (other ads). The more evidence you accumulate, the more probable it is that your generalization is true. Note, however, that absolute certainty is not possible. At some point you must *assume* that your evidence justifies your generalization, for yourself and your readers.

Most errors in inductive reasoning involve oversimplifying either the evidence or the generalization. See pages 111–14 on fallacies.

Deduction

You use **deduction**, or **deductive reasoning**, when you proceed from your generalization that Car X is the most reliable used car to your own specific circumstances (you want to buy a used car) to the conclusion that you should buy a Car X. In deduction your assumption is a generalization, principle, or belief that you think is true. You apply it to the evidence (new information) in order to arrive at your claim (the conclusion you draw). The following diagram corresponds to the one on the previous page for induction, picking up the example of print advertising.

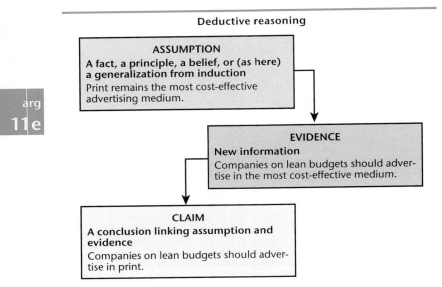

Deductive reasoning

ASSUMPTION
A fact, a principle, a belief, or (as here) a generalization from induction
Print remains the most cost-effective advertising medium.

EVIDENCE
New information
Companies on lean budgets should advertise in the most cost-effective medium.

CLAIM
A conclusion linking assumption and evidence
Companies on lean budgets should advertise in print.

The conventional way of displaying a deductive argument is in a **syllogism.** If you want the school administration to postpone new room fees for one dormitory, your deductive argument might be expressed in the following syllogism:

> **Premise:** The administration should not raise fees on dorm rooms in poor condition. [A generalization or belief that you assume to be true.]
> **Premise:** The rooms in Maroni Hall are in poor condition. [New information: a specific case of the first premise.]
> **Conclusion:** The administration should not raise fees on the rooms in Maroni Hall. [Your claim.]

As long as the premises of a syllogism are true, the conclusion derives logically and certainly from them.

The force of deductive reasoning depends on the reliability of the premises and the care taken to apply them in drawing conclusions. The reasoning process is **valid** if the premises lead logically to the conclusion. It is **true** if the premises are believable. Sometimes the reasoning is true but *not* valid:

> **Premise:** The administration should not raise fees on dorm rooms in bad condition.
> **Premise:** Maroni Hall is a dormitory.
> **Conclusion:** The administration should not raise fees on the rooms in Maroni Hall.

Both premises may be true, but the first does not *necessarily* apply to the second, so the conclusion is invalid. Sometimes, too, the reasoning is valid but *not* true:

> **Premise:** All college administrations are indifferent to students' needs.
> **Premise:** The administration of Valley College is a college administration.
> **Conclusion:** The administration of Valley College is indifferent to students' needs.

This syllogism is valid but useless: the first premise is an untrue assumption, so the entire argument is untrue. Invalid and untrue syllogisms underlie many of the logical fallacies discussed on pages 111–14.

A particular hazard of deductive reasoning is the **unstated premise**: the basic assumption linking evidence and conclusion is not stated but implied. Here the unstated premise is believable and the argument is reasonable:

> Ms. Stein has worked with drug addicts for fifteen years, so she knows a great deal about their problems. [Unstated premise: Anyone who has worked fifteen years with drug addicts knows about their problems.]

But when the unstated premise is wrong or unfounded, the argument is false. For example:

> Since Jane Lightbow is a senator, she must receive money illegally from lobbyists. [Unstated premise: All senators receive money illegally from lobbyists.]

arg
11e

2 ▪ Appeals

Rational and emotional appeals

In most arguments you will combine **rational appeals** to readers' capacities for logical reasoning with **emotional appeals** to readers' beliefs and feelings. In the following example, the second sentence makes a rational appeal (to the logic of financial gain), and the third sentence makes an emotional appeal (to the sense of fairness and open-mindedness):

> Advertising should show more people who are physically challenged. The millions of Americans with disabilities have considerable buying power, yet so far advertisers have made little or no attempt to tap that power. Furthermore, by keeping people with disabilities out of the mainstream depicted in ads, advertisers encourage widespread prejudice against disability, prejudice that frightens and demeans those who hold it.

For an emotional appeal to be successful, it must be appropriate for the audience and the argument:

▪ **It must not misjudge readers' actual feelings.**

- **It must not raise emotional issues that are irrelevant to the claims and the evidence.** See page 113 for a discussion of specific inappropriate appeals, such as bandwagon and ad hominem.

Ethical appeal

A third kind of approach to readers, the **ethical appeal,** is the sense you give of being a competent, fair person who is worth heeding. A rational appeal and an appropriate emotional appeal contribute to your ethical appeal, and so does your acknowledging opposing views (see below). An argument that is concisely written and correct in grammar, spelling, and other matters will underscore your competence. In addition, a sincere and even tone will assure readers that you are balanced and want to reason with them.

A sincere and even tone need not exclude language with emotional appeal—words such as *frightens* and *demeans* at the end of the example about advertising on the previous page. But avoid certain forms of expression that will mark you as unfair:

- **Insulting words** such as *idiotic* or *fascist.*
- **Biased language** such as *fags* or *broads.* (See pp. 162–65.)
- **Sarcasm**—for instance, using the phrase *What a brilliant idea* to indicate contempt for the idea and its originator.
- **Exclamation points!** They'll make you sound shrill!

3 ▪ Acknowledgment of opposing views

A good test of your fairness in argument is how you handle possible objections. Assuming your thesis is indeed arguable, then others can marshal their own evidence to support a different view or views. By dealing squarely with those opposing views, you show yourself to be honest and fair. You strengthen your ethical appeal and thus your entire argument. For more on opposing views, see page 116.

Exercise 11.3   **Logical reasoning**

Convert each of the following statements into a syllogism. (You may have to state unstated assumptions.) Use the syllogism to evaluate both the validity and the truth of the statement.

Example

DiSantis is a banker, so he does not care about the poor.
Premise: Bankers do not care about the poor.
Premise: DiSantis is a banker.
Conclusion: Therefore, DiSantis does not care about the poor.
The statement is untrue because the first premise is untrue.

1. The mayor opposed pollution controls when he was president of a manufacturing company, so he may not support new controls or vigorously enforce existing ones.

2. Information on corporate Web sites is unreliable because the sites are sponsored by for-profit entities.
3. Schroeder is a good artist because she trained at Parsons, like many other good artists.
4. Wealthy athletes who use their resources to help others deserve our particular appreciation.
5. Jimson is clearly a sexist because she has hired only one woman.

Exercise 11.4 Identifying appeals

Identify each passage below as primarily a rational appeal or primarily an emotional appeal. Which passages make a strong ethical appeal as well?

arg
11e

1. The Web may contribute to the global tendency toward breadth rather than depth of knowledge. Using those most essential of skills—pointing and clicking—our brightest minds may now never even hear of, much less read, the works of Aristotle, Shakespeare, and Darwin.
2. Thus the data collected by these researchers indicate that a mandatory sentence for illegal possession of handguns may lead to reduction in handgun purchases.
3. Most broadcasters worry that further government regulation of television programming could breed censorship—certainly, an undesirable outcome. Yet most broadcasters also accept that children's television is a fair target for regulation.
4. Anyone who cherishes life in all its diversity could not help being appalled by the mistreatment of laboratory animals. The so-called scientists who run the labs are misguided.
5. Many experts in constitutional law have warned that the rule violates the right to free speech. Yet other experts have viewed the rule, however regretfully, as necessary for the good of the community as a whole.

4 ■ Fallacies

Fallacies—errors in argument—either evade the issue of the argument or treat the argument as if it were much simpler than it is.

Evasions

An effective argument squarely faces the central issue or question it addresses. An ineffective argument may dodge the issue in one of the following ways:

- **Begging the question:** treating an opinion that is open to question as if it were already proved or disproved. In essence, the writer begs readers to accept his or her claim from the start.

The college library's expenses should be reduced by cutting subscriptions to useless periodicals. [Begged questions: Are some of the library's periodicals useless? Useless to whom?]

The fact is that political financing is too corrupt to be reformed. [Begged questions: How corrupt is political financing? Does corruption, even if extensive, put the system beyond reform?]

- **Non sequitur** (Latin: "It does not follow"): linking two or more ideas that in fact have no logical connection. Usually the problem is an unstated assumption that links the ideas but is false.

  She uses a wheelchair, so she must be unhappy. [Unstated assumption: People who use wheelchairs are unhappy.]

  Kathleen Newsome has my vote for mayor because she has the best-run campaign organization. [Unstated assumption: A good campaign organization means that the candidate is well qualified for the job.]

- **Red herring:** introducing an irrelevant issue intended to distract readers from the relevant issues. (A red herring is a kind of fish that might be used to distract a dog from a scent.)

  A campus speech code is essential to protect students, who already have enough problems coping with rising tuition. [Tuition costs and speech codes are different subjects. What protections do students need that a speech code will provide?]

  Instead of developing a campus speech code that will infringe on students' First Amendment rights, administrators should be figuring out how to prevent another tuition increase. [Again, tuition costs and speech codes are different subjects. How would the code infringe on rights?]

- **False authority:** citing as an expert someone whose expertise is doubtful or nonexistent.

  Jason Bing, a recognized expert in corporate finance, maintains that pharmaceutical companies do not test their products thoroughly enough. [Bing's expertise in corporate finance bears no apparent relation to the testing of pharmaceuticals.]

  According to Helen Liebowitz, the Food and Drug Administration has approved sixty dangerous drugs in the last two years alone. [Who is Helen Liebowitz? On what authority does she make this claim?]

- **Appeal to readers' fear or pity:** substituting emotions for reasoning.

  By electing Susan Clark to the city council, you will prevent the city's economic collapse. [Trades on people's fears. Can Clark single-handedly prevent economic collapse? Is collapse even likely?]

  She should not have to pay taxes because she is an aged widow with no friends or relatives. [Appeals to people's pity. Should age and loneliness, rather than income, determine a person's tax obligation?]

- **Snob appeal:** inviting readers to accept an assertion in order to be identified with others they admire.

  Angelina Jolie has an account at Big City Bank, and so should you. [A celebrity's endorsement does not guarantee the worth of a product, a service, an idea, or anything else.]

- **Bandwagon:** inviting readers to accept a claim because everyone else does.

   As everyone knows, marijuana use leads to heroin addiction. [What is the evidence?]

- **Ad populum** (Latin: "to the people"): asking readers to accept a conclusion based on shared values or even prejudices and nothing else.

   Any truly patriotic American will support the President's action. [But why is the action worth taking?]

- **Ad hominem** (Latin: "to the man"): attacking the qualities of the people holding an opposing view rather than the substance of the view itself.

   One of the scientists has been treated for emotional problems, so his pessimism about nuclear waste merits no attention. [Do the scientist's previous emotional problems invalidate his current views?]

Oversimplifications

In a vain attempt to create something neatly convincing, an ineffective argument may conceal or ignore complexities in one of the following ways:

- **Hasty generalization:** making a claim on the basis of inadequate evidence.

   It is disturbing that several of the youths who shot up schools were users of violent video games. Obviously, these games can breed violence, and they should be banned. [A few cases do not establish the relation between the games and violent behavior. Most youths who play violent video games do not behave violently.]

   From the way it handled this complaint, we can assume that the consumer protection office has little intention of protecting consumers. [One experience with the office does not demonstrate its intention or overall performance.]

- **Sweeping generalization:** making an insupportable statement. Many sweeping generalizations are **absolute statements** involving words such as *all, always, never,* and *no one* that allow no exceptions. Others are **stereotypes,** conventional and oversimplified characterizations of a group of people:

   People who live in cities are unfriendly.
   Californians are fad-crazy.
   Women are emotional.
   Men can't express their feelings.

   (See also pp. 162–65 on sexist and other biased language.)
- **Reductive fallacy:** oversimplifying (reducing) the relation between causes and effects.

Poverty causes crime. [If so, then why do people who are not poor commit crimes? And why aren't all poor people criminals?]

The better a school's athletic facilities are, the worse its academic programs are. [The sentence assumes a direct cause-and-effect link between athletics and scholarship.]

■ **Post hoc fallacy** (from Latin *post hoc, ergo propter hoc,* meaning "after this, therefore because of this"): assuming that because *A* preceded *B*, then *A* must have caused *B*.

In the two months since he took office, Mayor Holcomb has allowed crime in the city to increase 12%. [The increase in crime is probably attributable to conditions existing before Holcomb took office.]

The town council erred in permitting the adult bookstore to open, for shortly afterward two women were assaulted. [It cannot be assumed without evidence that the women's assailants visited or were influenced by the bookstore.]

■ **Either/or fallacy:** assuming that a complicated question has only one good and one bad answer, two good answers, or two bad answers.

City police officers are either brutal or corrupt. [Most city police officers are neither.]

Either we permit mandatory drug testing in the workplace or productivity will continue to decline. [Productivity is not necessarily dependent on drug testing.]

■ **False analogy:** assuming that because two things are alike in one respect, they are *necessarily* alike in other respects as well. Analogy can be useful in argument when the similarities are reasonable. For instance, the "war on drugs" equates a battle against a foe with a program to eradicate (or at least reduce) sales and use of illegal drugs: both involve an enemy, a desired goal, officials in uniform, and other features. But the following passage takes this analogy to a false extreme:

To win the war on drugs, we must wage more of a military-style operation. Prisoners of war are locked up without the benefit of a trial by jury, and drug dealers should be, too. Soldiers shoot their enemy on sight, and officials who encounter big drug operators should be allowed to shoot them, too. Military traitors may be executed, and corrupt law enforcers could be, too.

Exercise 11.5 Identifying and revising fallacies

Identify at least one fallacy illustrated by each of the following sentences. Then revise the sentence to make it more reasonable.

1. A successful marriage demands a maturity that no one under twenty-five possesses.

2. Students' persistent complaints about the grading system prove that it is unfair.

3. The United States got involved in World War II because the Japanese bombed Pearl Harbor.

4. People watch television because they are too lazy to talk or read or because they want mindless escape from their lives.

5. Racial tension is bound to occur when people with different backgrounds are forced to live side by side.

6. Emerging nations should not be allowed to use nuclear technology for creating energy because eventually they will use it to wage war.

7. Mountain climbing has more lasting effects than many people think: my cousin blacked out three times after he climbed Pikes Peak.

8. Failing to promote democracy throughout the Middle East will lose the region forever to American influence.

9. She admits to being an atheist, so how could she be a good philosophy teacher?

10. Teenagers are too young to be encouraged to use contraceptives.

arg
11f

11f Organize and revise your argument.

1 ▪ Organizing your argument

All arguments contain the same parts, but the organization can vary depending on the type of argument.

Introduction

The introduction establishes the significance of the subject and provides background. The introduction generally includes the thesis statement, but the statement may come later if you think readers will have difficulty accepting it before they see at least some support. (See pp. 57–59 for more on introductions.)

Body paragraphs

The body paragraphs state and develop the claims supporting the thesis, using clearly relevant evidence. Each supporting claim will take one or more paragraphs to develop. (See pp. 51–56 on paragraph development.)

You may want to experiment with different ways of organizing the body of your argument. For instance, you can try giving your strongest claims first or last in the body, depending on how you anticipate readers will respond to your argument. You can state claims directly or let the evidence build to them. You may want to address the opposition to your argument claim by claim, or you may prefer to respond to all opposing views near the beginning or end of your paper. See the box on the next page for different ways of organizing claims, evidence, and opposing views in the body of an essay.

arg
11f

Organizing an argument's body and response to opposing views

A common scheme
Claim 1 and evidence
Claim 2 and evidence
Claim X and evidence
Response to opposing views

A variation
Claim 1 and evidence
Response to opposing views
Claim 2 and evidence
Response to opposing views
Claim X and evidence
Response to opposing views

The Rogerian scheme
Common ground and concession
to opposing views
Claim 1 and evidence
Claim 2 and evidence
Claim X and evidence

The problem-solution scheme
The problem: claims and evidence
The solution: claims and evidence
Response to opposing views

Response to opposing views

The body of every argument includes a response to opposing views, which details and addresses counterarguments. Before or while you draft your essay, list for yourself all the opposing views you can think of. You'll find them in your research, by talking to friends and classmates, and by thinking critically about your own ideas.

A common way to handle opposing views is to state them, refute those you can, grant the validity of others, and demonstrate why, despite their validity, the opposing views are less compelling than your own.

A somewhat different approach to addressing opposing views, developed by the psychologist Carl Rogers, emphasizes the search for common ground. A **Rogerian argument** can be especially helpful when you expect readers to resist your claims. You start by showing that you understand readers' views and by establishing points on which you and readers can agree and disagree. Creating a connection in this way can be especially helpful when you expect readers to resist your argument, because it encourages them to hear you out as you make your argument.

See the box above for different ways to place opposing views within an argument.

Conclusion

The conclusion completes the argument. Often it restates the thesis, summarizes the supporting claims, and makes a final appeal to readers. In a Rogerian argument, the conclusion often states the thesis as a solution to the problem discussed, giving ground and inviting readers to do the same. (See pp. 59–60 for more on conclusions.)

2 ▪ Revising your argument

When you revise your argument, do it in at least two stages—first revising underlying meaning and structure and then editing more superficial elements. Use the checklist below to supplement the checklists on pages 31 and 37.

Checklist for revising an argument

Thesis and supporting claims

- What is your thesis? What does it argue? Where is it stated?
- How do supporting claims lay out your argument and connect to the thesis?

Evidence

- What evidence do you give for each supporting claim?
- Where might your evidence *not* be accurate, relevant, representative, or adequate? (Take the position of a neutral or skeptical reader to answer this question.)

Reasoning

- What is the logical structure of your argument?
- Have you avoided fallacies in reasoning?

Appeals

- Where have you considered readers' beliefs and values?
- How will readers respond to your rational and emotional appeals?
- What is your ethical appeal? How can you improve it?

Opposing views

- Which opposing views have you answered? Which have you ignored?
- How have you addressed opposing views in your writing?

Organization

- How clearly does your argument move from one point to the next?
- How appropriate is the organization, given the likely views of your readers?

11g   A sample argument

Aimee Lee, a student, wrote an argument in response to the following assignment:

Select an issue that can be argued, that you care about, and that you know something about through experience, reading, observation, and so on. As you plan and draft your argument, keep the following in mind:

Narrow and shape your subject into a specific thesis statement.
Gather and use evidence to support your claim.
Be aware of assumptions you are making.
Present your claims and evidence reasonably, attempting to establish common ground with your readers.
Acknowledge and try to refute opposing views.
Organize your argument paper straightforwardly and appropriately for your purpose.
The paper should be 900–1200 words in length.

Lee's response to this assignment illustrates the principles discussed in this chapter. Note especially the structure, the relation of claims and supporting evidence, the kinds of appeals Lee makes, and the ways she addresses opposing views.

Awareness, Prevention, Support:

A Proposal to Reduce Cyberbullying

Introduction: identification of the problem

My roommate and I sat in front of her computer staring at the vicious message under her picture. She quickly removed the tag that identified her, but the comments already posted on the photo proved that the damage was done. While she slept, my roommate had become the victim of a cyberbully. She had joined an increasing number of college students who are targeted in texts, e-mails, social-networking sites, and other Web sites that broadcast photographs, videos, and comments. My roommate's experience alerted me that our campus needs

Thesis statement: proposal for a solution to the problem

a program aimed at awareness and prevention of cyberbullying and support for its victims.

Although schoolyard bullying typically ends with high school graduation, cyberbullying continues in college. According to data gathered by re-

Evidence of the problem: information from research

searchers at the Massachusetts Aggression Reduction Center (MARC) of Bridgewater State College, cyberbullying behavior decreases when students enter college, but it does not cease. Examining the experiences of first-year students, the researchers found that 8% of college freshmen had been cyberbullied at college and 3% admitted to having cyberbullied another student (Englander et al. 217-18). In a survey of fifty-two freshmen,

Evidence of the problem: student's own research

I found further evidence of cyberbullying on this campus. I asked two questions: (1) Have you been involved in cyberbullying as a victim, a bully, or both? (2) If you answered "no" to the first question, do you know anyone who has been involved in cyberbullying as a victim, a bully, or both? While a large majority of the students I surveyed (74%) have not been touched by cyberbullying, a significant number (26%) have been involved personally or know someone who has, as shown in fig. 1. Taken together, the evidence demonstrates that cyberbullying is a problem in colleges and specifically on our campus.

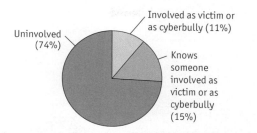

Fig. 1. Involvement in cyberbullying among fifty-two first-year students.

The proposed "Stop Cyberbullying" program aims to reduce the behavior through a month-long campaign of awareness, prevention, and support modeled on the college's "Alcohol Awareness Month" program. The program can raise awareness of cyberbullying by explaining what cyberbullying is and by informing students about the college's code of conduct, which prohibits cyberbullying behavior but which few people read. The program can work to prevent cyberbullying by appealing to students to treat those around them respectfully. And, with the participation of the counseling department, the program can provide support for victims, their friends, and others involved in the behavior.

If adopted, the program can use online and print media to get the message out to the entire college community. For instance, an extensive brochure distributed to first-year students and available through the counseling center can describe cyberbullying and how it violates the college's code of conduct, give strategies for avoiding it, and provide resources for help. During the month-long campaign, flyers posted on campus (see fig. 2) can also raise awareness of the problem, and brief postings to the college's Web site, *Facebook* page, and *Twitter* feed can reach students who take online and hybrid classes as well as those in traditional classes.

Because this college already has a code of conduct in place and because the state has recently enacted anti-bullying legislation that includes cyberbullying, some students and administrators may contend that enough is being done to deal with the problem. To the administration's credit, the code of conduct contains specific language about online behavior, but promises of punishment for proven allegations do not address several aspects of the problem.

First, cyberbullies are sometimes anonymous. To accuse another student of cyberbullying, the victim needs to know the identity of the

Explanation of proposed solution: goals of the program

Explanation of proposed solution: specific actions

Anticipation of objection: code of conduct does enough

Response to objection: anonymity of cyberbullies

Have **YOU** been a victim of cyberbullying?
Have you read something about yourself that made you feel
embarrassed, intimidated, or just bad?

Are **YOU** a cyberbully? Have you sent a message
or posted something that you knew would make someone feel
embarrassed, intimidated, or just bad?

Do **YOU** know someone who is being cyberbullied
or who is bullying someone else?

Together **WE** can **BREAK** the cycle:
- **Wait before you post!** Think about who may read it
  and how they might respond.
- **Be informed about our campus code of conduct** and
  what it says about cyberbullying.
- **Get help if you need it.** The counseling office is available
  to help you cope with or stop cyberbullying.

You can help
stop cyberbullying
STOP
www.mrcc.edu/cyberbullying

Fig. 2. Sample flyer for proposed "Stop Cyberbullying" program.

bully. While postings on *Facebook* are attached to real names, most college gossip sites are anonymous. On such sites, a cyberbully can post photographs, videos, and aggressive messages under the cover of anonymity.

Second, even when the identities of cyberbullies are known, the bullying is often invisible to those in a position to take action against it. According to Ikuko Aoyama and Tony L. Talbert at Baylor University, cyberbullying occurs frequently in groups of people who know each other and who attack and retaliate: students are rarely "pure bullies" or "pure victims" but instead are often part of a "bully-victim group" (qtd. in Laster). Moreover, even if students want to separate from bullying groups, Englander, Mills, and McCoy found that they probably will not report cyberbullying incidents to authorities because students generally believe that administrators are unlikely to do anything about cyberbullying (221). Thus counselors and administrators who may be interested in helping students to cope are often unaware of the problem.

Third, conduct codes rarely affect cyberbullying. While some cyberbullying has resulted in tragedy, many aggressive incidents do not rise to the level of punishable offenses ("Cyberbullying"). More often they consist of a humiliating photograph or a mean message—hurtful, to be sure, but not necessarily in violation of the law or the code of conduct. Indeed, the hurdles to getting recourse through official channels are fairly high.

Visual evidence of program publicity

Response to objection: invisibility of the problem

Response to objection: conduct codes ineffective

Given its hidden nature and the inability of punitive measures to stop it, cyberbullying needs another approach—namely, a program that teaches students to recognize and regulate their own behavior and provides help when they find themselves in a difficult situation. This program will not heal the wound suffered by my roommate, nor will it prevent all cyberbullying. But if adopted, the program will demonstrate to the college community that the administration is aware of the problem, eager to prevent it, and willing to commit resources to support students who are affected by it.

Conclusion

[New page.]

Works Cited

"Cyberbullying Goes to College." *Bostonia*, Boston U, Spring 2009, www.bu.edu/bostonia/spring09/bully/.

Englander, Elizabeth, et al. "Cyberbullying and Information Exposure: User-Generated Content in Post-Secondary Education." *International Journal of Contemporary Society*, vol. 46, no. 2, Oct. 2009, pp. 213–20, www.uef.fi/c/document_library/get_file?uuid=113358&p_l_id=144412.

Laster, Jill. "Two Scholars Examine Cyberbullying among College Students." *The Chronicle of Higher Education*, 6 June 2010, chronicle.com/article/2-Scholars-Examine/65766/.

—Aimee Lee (student)

Works cited in MLA style (p. 429)

12 Reading and Writing about Literature

By Sylvan Barnet

In *Brief*

- Read literary works critically (next page).
- Write a literary analysis (p. 123).
- Examine a sample literary research paper (p. 124).

Visit MyWritingLab™ for more resources on reading and writing about literature.

Writers of literature—stories, novels, poems, and plays—are concerned with presenting human experience concretely, with giving a sense of the feel of life rather than just telling about it. When you read a work of literature, you form an idea of it based on its language and other elements. When you write about literature, you state your idea as your thesis, and you support the thesis with evidence from the work.

12a   Read literary works critically.

Reading literature critically involves interacting with a text in order to understand the work and analyze its significance or quality. It is a process of engagement, of diving into the words themselves.

1 ▪ Writing while reading

You will become more engaged in reading literature if you write while you read. If you own the book you're reading, don't hesitate to underline or highlight passages that especially interest you. Annotate the margins with remarks like *Nice detail* or *This narrator seems unreliable* or *Not believable*. If you don't own the book, make your notes on separate sheets or on your computer.

An effective way to interact with a text is to keep a **reading journal**. A journal is a place to develop and store your reflections on what you read, such as an answer to a question you may have posed in the margin of the text or a response to something said in class. You may, for instance, want to reflect on why your opinion is so different from that of another student. You may even make an entry in the form of a letter to the author or from one character to another. (See pp. 11–12 for more on journal keeping.)

2 ▪ Interpreting meaning

In analyzing any literary work, you face right off the question of *meaning*. Readers disagree all the time over the meanings of works of literature, partly because literature *shows* rather than *tells*: it gives concrete images of imagined human experiences, but it usually does not say how we ought to understand the images. Further, readers bring different experiences to their reading and thus understand images differently. In writing about literature, then, we can offer only our *interpretation* of the meaning rather than *the* meaning. Still, most people agree that there are limits to interpretation: it must be supported by evidence from the work itself that a reasonable person finds at least plausible if not totally convincing.

3 ▪ Analyzing literary elements

One reason interpretations of meaning differ is that readers approach literary works differently. For instance, some approaches focus on the cultural context of a work, others stress readers' responses to the work, and still others view the work as something to be analyzed in itself.

Despite their differences, most critical approaches discuss the following conventional elements of literary works:

- **Plot: patterns of events and relationships.** Plot is essentially what happens in a work. Even a poem has a plot—for instance, a change in mood from grief to resignation.
- **Characters: people the author creates,** including the narrator of a story or the speaker of a poem.
- **Point of view: the perspective or attitude of the speaker in a poem or the voice who tells a story.** The point of view may be **first person** (a participant, using *I*) or **third person** (an outsider, using *he, she, it, they*). A first-person narrator may be a major or a minor character in the narrative and may be **reliable** or **unreliable** (unable to report events wholly or accurately). A third-person narrator may be **omniscient** (knows what goes on in all characters' minds), **limited** (knows what goes on in the mind of only one or two characters), or **objective** (knows only what is external to the characters).
- **Tone: the narrator's or speaker's attitude,** perceived through the words (for instance, joyful, bitter, confident).
- **Imagery: word pictures or details involving the sense of sight, sounds, touch, smell, and taste.**
- **Symbolism: concrete things standing in for larger and more abstract ideas.** For instance, the American flag may symbolize freedom, or a wilted flower may symbolize death.
- **Setting: the place and time where the action happens.**
- **Form: The shape and structure of the work.**
- **Themes: the main ideas about human experience suggested by the work as a whole.** A theme is neither a plot (what happens) nor a subject (such as death or marriage). Rather, it is what the author says with that plot about that subject. For instance, a theme of Agha Shahid Ali's poem "Postcard from Kashmir" (p. 125) is the experience of having more than one home.

12

12b   Write a literary analysis.

The process for writing a literary analysis is similar to that for any other kind of essay: once you've read the work and thought about it, you need to focus your ideas, gather evidence, draft and revise your paper, and cite your sources.

1 ▪ Finding your interpretation

A literary analysis is your interpretation of the work, a claim you make and support about its meaning or effect. As you read, reread, and take notes, seek patterns in the work, such as recurring words, images, symbols, or events. Such patterns can help you see themes both in the work itself and in your ideas about it.

During this process, begin to formulate the main point you want to make about the work. Eventually, this main point will be the thesis statement of your essay—an assertion of the specific idea that you develop and argue with evidence from the literary work. (For more on thesis statements, see pp. 16–19.)

2 ■ Using evidence

The evidence for your literary analysis should be mainly quotations from the work you are discussing, a primary source. Depending on your assignment, you may also draw on secondary sources, such as a biography of the author or other critics' views of the work.

Use the following guidelines when quoting from literary works, and see the sample paper on the following pages for examples.

- **Use quotations to support your assertions.** Quotations provide evidence for your ideas and let readers hear the voice of the work.
- **Specify how each quotation supports your idea.** For instance, *The poet depicts fate as a burden: "..."*
- **Indicate any editing of quotations.** Use ellipsis marks (. . .) to indicate deletions from quotations (pp. 323–25). Use brackets to indicate additions to or changes in quotations (p. 325).
- **Cite sources in MLA style.** Use citations within the text of your paper to refer to a list of works cited at the end (pp. 419–64).

Note A brief plot summary can be helpful to readers who are unfamiliar with the work, but plot summary is not literary analysis. Keep any plot summaries short and to the point.

3 ■ Drafting and revising a literary analysis

Use the first draft of your literary analysis to sharpen your ideas and develop your interpretation of the work. When you revise, attend first to the essay as a whole before turning to smaller surface problems. See pages 31 and 37 and for general revision and editing checklists. The following additional checklist can help you with literary analysis. (To format your paper in MLA style, see pp. 464–66.)

Checklist for revising a literary analysis

- **Introduction:** Does the introductory paragraph name the author and the title so that readers know exactly what work you are discussing? Does it state your thesis?
- **Thesis:** Does the thesis state the interpretation you are arguing for?
- **Organization:** Do the paragraphs lead from one to the next, each one building a case for your interpretation?
- **Quotations:** Do quotations let readers hear the author's voice? Do you introduce each quotation so that it clearly supports one of your ideas?

- **Analysis vs. summary:** Is the essay chiefly devoted to analysis, not summary? Summarize the plot only briefly. A summary is not an essay.
- **Verb tenses:** Have you used the present tense of verbs to describe both the author's work and the action in the work (for example, *The poem's speaker imagines* and *Ali compares*)?
- **Are your sources documented in MLA style?** See pages 419–64.

12c   A sample literary analysis

A poem and a student paper on the work appear on the following pages. The student, Jessie Glenn, makes an argument for a particular interpretation of the poem, developing a thesis and supporting her ideas with quotations from and some paraphrases of the poem, a primary source. Glenn also draws on secondary sources (other critics' views), which test or further support her own views.

Poem

Agha Shahid Ali

Postcard from Kashmir

Kashmir shrinks into my mailbox,
my home a neat four by six inches.
I always loved neatness. Now I hold
the half-inch Himalayas in my hand.

This is home. And this the closest
I'll ever be to home. When I return,   5
the colors won't be so brilliant,
the Jhelum's waters so clean,
so ultramarine. My love
so overexposed.   10

And my memory will be a little
out of focus, in it
a giant negative, black
and white, still undeveloped.

Literary research paper on poetry

Jessie Glenn

Professor Narracci

English 101

14 March 2015

Past and Future in

Agha Shahid Ali's "Postcard from Kashmir"

Most literary critics interpret Agha Shahid Ali's "Postcard from Kashmir" as a longing for a lost home, a poetic expression of the heartbreak of exile. For instance, Maimuna Dali Islam describes the speaker's futile effort "to

Introduction naming author/ title and summarizing other interpretations

capture his homeland" (262). However, such a reading of the poem seems too narrow. "Postcard from Kashmir" does evoke the experience of being displaced from a beloved home, but the speaker does not seem to feel an intense loss. Instead, he seems to reflect on his position of having more than one home.

Thesis statement: student's interpretation

Ali's brief poem consists of three stanzas and divides into two parts. In the first half, the speaker examines a postcard he has received from his former home of Kashmir (lines 1-6). In the second half, the speaker looks forward, imagining how Kashmir will look the next time he sees it and assuming that the place will be different from the idealized view of the postcard and his memory (6-14). The geography is significant. Kashmir has been in the news for many years as the focus of territorial conflict, often violent, among the bordering nations of India, Pakistan, and China. Many residents of the region have been killed, and many have left the region. One of the exiles was Ali: he moved to the United States in 1976 and lived here until his death in 2001, but he also regularly visited his family in Kashmir (Benvenuto 261, 263).

Summary of poem

Background information

In-text citations in MLA style

In the context of Kashmir, the literary theorist Jahan Ramazani concludes that the poem "dramatizes the . . . condition" of losing one's homeland to political turmoil (12). Yet several lines in the poem suggest that the speaker is not mourning a loss but musing about having a sense of home both in Kashmir and in the United States. This sense is evident in the opening stanza: "Kashmir shrinks into my mailbox, / my home a neat four by six inches" (1-2), with "my mailbox" conveying his current residence as home and "my home" referring to Kashmir. The dual sense of home is even more evident in the lines "This is home. And this is the closest / I'll ever be to home" (5-6). Although Maimuna Dali Islam assumes that "This" in these lines refers to the Kashmir pictured on the postcard (262), it could also or instead refer to the home attached to the mailbox.

Critic's interpretation

First point supporting thesis

Quotations from poem

Critic's interpretation

The speaker also seems to perceive that his dual sense of home will continue into the future. The critics do not mention that the second half of the poem is written in the future tense. Beginning with "When I return" (6), the speaker makes it clear that he expects to find himself in Kashmir again, and he imagines how things will be, not how they were. Islam takes the image on the postcard as proof that "there is a place that can be captured in a snapshot" (263), but the poem's speaker compares photography to memory, characterizing both as flawed and deceptive with terms such as "overexposed" (10) and "out of focus" (12). He acknowledges that the place won't be like the photograph: "the colors won't be so brilliant, / the Jhelum's waters so clean, / so ultramarine" (7-9). Kashmir still exists, but not as any

Second point supporting thesis

Quotation from secondary source

photograph or memory has recorded it. And the speaker's relationship to his original home, his "love" (9), is changing with the place itself.

In "Postcard from Kashmir" the speaker reflects on home and displacement as he gazes into a representation of his past and considers the future. If the poem mourns a loss, as the critics suggest, it is a loss that has not happened yet, at least not completely. More convincingly, the poem captures a moment when the two homes and the past, present, and future all meet.

Conclusion restating critics' and student's interpretations

[New page.]

Works Cited

Works cited in MLA style

Ali, Agha Shahid. "Postcard from Kashmir." *The Half-Inch Himalayas*, Wesleyan UP, 1987, p. 1.

Benvenuto, Christine. "Agha Shahid Ali." *Massachusetts Review*, vol. 43, no. 2, Summer 2002, pp. 261–63.

Islam, Maimuna Dali. "A Way in the World of an Asian American Existence: Agha Shahid Ali's Transimmigrant Spacing of North America and India and Kashmir." *Transnational Asian American Literature: Sites and Transits*, edited by Shirley Lim et al., Temple UP, 2006, pp. 257-73.

Ramazani, Jahan. *The Hybrid Muse: Postcolonial Poetry in English*. U of Chicago P, 2001.

13 Oral Presentations

In *Brief*

- Prepare and organize an oral presentation (below).
- Plan the delivery of a presentation, including any visual aids (p. 128).
- Practice in advance (p. 131).

Visit MyWritingLab™ for more resources on oral presentations.

Speaking to a group can produce anxiety, even for those who are experienced at it. This chapter shows how to use organization, voice, and other techniques to present your writing to a listening audience.

13a Plan and organize the presentation.

Give your oral presentation a recognizable shape so that listeners can see how ideas and details relate to each other.

The introduction

The beginning of an oral presentation should try to accomplish three goals:

- **Gain the audience's attention and interest.** Begin with a question, an unusual example or statistic, or a short, relevant story.
- **Put yourself in the speech.** Demonstrate your expertise, experience, or concern to gain the interest and trust of your audience.
- **Introduce and preview your topic and purpose.** By the time your introduction is over, listeners should know what your subject is and the direction you'll take to develop your ideas.

Your introduction should prepare your audience for your main points but not give them away. Think of it as a sneak preview of your speech, not the place for an apology such as *I wish I'd had more time to prepare* . . . or a dull statement such as *My speech is about.* . . .

Supporting material

Just as you do when writing, you should use facts, statistics, examples, and expert opinions to support the main points of your oral presentation. In addition, you can make your points more memorable with vivid description, well-chosen quotations, true or fictional stories, and analogies.

The conclusion

You want your conclusion to be clear, of course, but you also want it to be memorable. Remind listeners of how your topic and main idea connect to their needs and interests. If your speech is motivational, tap an emotion that matches your message. If your speech is informational, give some tips on how to remember important details.

13b Deliver the presentation.

Methods of delivery

You can deliver an oral presentation in several ways:

- **Impromptu, without preparation:** Make a presentation without planning what you will say. Impromptu speaking requires confidence and excellent general preparation.
- **Extemporaneously:** Prepare notes to glance at but not read from. This method allows you to look and sound natural while ensuring that you don't forget anything.
- **Speaking from a text:** Read aloud from a written presentation. You won't lose your way, but you may lose your audience. Avoid reading for an entire presentation.
- **Speaking from memory:** Deliver a prepared presentation without notes. You can look at your audience every minute, but the stress

of retrieving the next words may make you seem tense and un-responsive.

Vocal delivery

The sound of your voice will influence how listeners receive you. Rehearse your presentation several times until you are confident that you are speaking loudly, slowly, and clearly enough for your audience to understand you.

Physical delivery

You are more than your spoken words when you make an oral presentation. If you are able, stand up to deliver your presentation, stepping out from behind any lectern or desk and gesturing as appropriate. Above all, make eye contact with your audience as you speak. Looking directly in your listeners' eyes conveys your honesty, your confidence, and your control of the material.

13b

(CULTURE / LANGUAGE) Eye contact is customary in the United States, both in conversation and in oral presentation. Listeners expect it and may perceive a speaker who doesn't make eye contact as evasive or insincere.

Visual aids

You can supplement an oral presentation with visual aids such as posters, models, slides, or videos.

- **Use visual aids to underscore your points.** Short lists of key ideas, illustrations such as graphs or photographs, and objects such as models can make your presentation more interesting and memorable. But use visual aids judiciously: a constant flow of illustrations or objects will bury your message.
- **Match visual aids and setting.** An audience of five people may be able to see a photograph and share a chart; a classroom or an audience of a hundred will need projected images.
- **Coordinate visual aids with your message.** Time each visual to reinforce a point you're making. Tell listeners what they're looking at. Give them enough viewing time so that they don't mind turning their attention back to you.
- **Show visual aids only while they're needed.** To regain your audience's attention, remove or turn off any aid as soon as you have finished with it.

Many speakers use *PowerPoint*, *Prezi*, or other software to project main points, key images, video, or other elements. To use such software effectively, follow the guidelines with the samples on the next page and also these tips:

- **Don't put your whole presentation on screen.** Select key points and distill them to as few words as possible. Use slides as quick,

Presentation slides

First slide, introducing the project and presentation.

> # Making a Difference?
>
> ## A Service-Learning Project at ReadingWorks
>
> Springfield Veterans Administration Hospital
>
> Jessica Cho
> Nathan Hall
> Alex Ramirez
> Spring 2015

Simple, consistent slide design focusing viewers' attention on information, not software features.

Later slide, including a title and brief, bulleted points to be explained by the speaker.

Link to video about the project's activities.

Photograph reinforcing the project's activities.

> ## Tutor veterans
>
> • Participate in tutor training.
>   http://www.youtube.com/watch?v=526phLMJg
>
> • Get matched with a student.
>
> • Tutor two hours each week at ReadingWorks.

easy-to-remember summaries or ways to present examples. For a twenty-minute presentation, plan to use approximately ten slides.

- **Use a simple design.** Avoid turning your presentation into a show about the software's many capabilities and special effects.
- **Make text readable.** The type should be easy to see for viewers in the back of the room, whether the lights are on or not.
- **Use a consistent design.** For optimal flow through the presentation, each slide should be formatted similarly.
- **Add relevant images and media.** Presentation software allows you to play images, audio, and video as part of your speech. Before you add them, however, be sure each has a point so that you don't overload the presentation. See pages 63–68 on choosing and using visuals and other media.
- **Review all your slides before the presentation.** Make sure they are complete, consistent, and easy to read. Proofread each slide.
- **Don't talk to the computer or the projection during the presentation.** Move away from both and face the audience.

- **Pace your presentation and your slides.** If a section of your presentation doesn't have a slide keyed to it, insert a blank slide to project during that section.

Practice

Take time to rehearse your presentation out loud, with the notes you will be using. Gauge your performance by making an audio- or videotape of yourself or by practicing in front of a mirror. Practicing out loud will also tell you if your presentation is running too long or too short.

If you plan to use visual aids, you'll need to practice with them, too. Your goal is to eliminate hitches (slides in the wrong order, missing charts) and to weave the visuals seamlessly into your presentation.

Stage fright

Many people report that speaking in front of an audience is their number-one fear. Even many experienced and polished speakers have some anxiety about delivering an oral presentation, but they let this nervous energy propel them into working hard on each presentation. Several techniques can help you reduce anxiety:

- **Use simple relaxation exercises.** Deep breathing or tensing and relaxing your stomach muscles can ease some of the physical symptoms of speech anxiety—stomachache, rapid heartbeat, and shaky hands, legs, and voice.
- **Think positively.** Instead of worrying about the mistakes you might make, concentrate on how well you've prepared and practiced your presentation and how significant your ideas are.
- **Don't avoid opportunities to speak in public.** Practice and experience build speaking skills and offer the best insurance for success.

14 Public Writing

In *Brief*

- Consider how to represent yourself on social media (next page).
- Use established formats for business letters (next page).
- When applying for a job, create a cover letter, a résumé, and an online profile that highlight your strengths (p. 134).
- Write focused memos (p. 138).
- Create effective documents and other writing for community work (p. 138).

Visit MyWritingLab™ for more resources on public writing.

At some point in your life, you're likely to write for a public audience—readers beyond your instructor, classmates, family, and friends. The conventions of public writing depend on the purpose of the writing, who will read it, and its genre. This chapter discusses several common public-writing situations.

CULTURE LANGUAGE Public writing in the United States, especially in business, favors efficiency and may seem abrupt or impolite compared with such writing in your native culture. For instance, a business letter elsewhere may be expected to begin with polite questions about the addressee or with compliments for the addressee's company, whereas US business letters are expected to get right to the point.

14a   Consider your audience when writing on social media.

Public writing on social media varies tremendously. It may be thoughtful and carefully crafted, or it may be quick and artless, as in a comment on a Web news story dashed off in frustration or anger. As you make your own writing public—and make yourself public, too—consider these questions:

- **How are you presenting yourself?** How do you want to be viewed by readers—as knowledgable, reasonable, witty, heartfelt, emotional, ranting, or something else? Consider whether your message comes across in the way you intend.
- **Who might read your post?** Once posted, your words may have a very large audience consisting of people whom you do not know and who do not necessarily see things as you do.
- **Are you protecting your own and others' privacy?** Comments, tweets, and photographs that reveal personal information can be hurtful or embarrassing to you and others. Consider who may see your message or photo.
- **How will you feel about the post in the future?** Some online posts, such as comments on news stories, are never fully erased. Think how the message or photo will reflect on you months or years from now.
- **Would you say face to face what you've written?** Imagine saying what you've written to the person your message is about or is addressed to. If you wouldn't say it, don't post it.

14b   Write professional business letters.

When you write for business, you are addressing busy people who want to see quickly why you are writing and how they should respond to you. Follow these general guidelines:

- **State your purpose right at the start.**
- **Be straightforward, clear, concise, objective, and courteous.**
- **Observe conventions of grammar and usage,** which make your writing clear and impress your reader with your care.

1 ▪ Business letter format

Business letters sent on paper or by e-mail have similar formats, with differences for the different media.

Letters on paper

Use either unlined white paper measuring 8½" × 11" or letterhead stationery with your address preprinted at the top of the sheet. Print the letter single-spaced (with double spacing between elements) on one side of a sheet. The sample on the next page shows a common format.

14b

- **The *return-address heading* gives your address and the date.** Do not include your name. If you are using letterhead, add only the date.
- **The *inside address* shows the name, title, and complete address of the person you are writing to.**
- **The *salutation* greets the addressee.** Whenever possible, address your letter to a specific person. (Contact the company or department to ask whom to address.) If you can't find a person's name, then use a job title (*Dear Human Resources Manager, Dear Customer Service Manager*) or use a general salutation (*Dear Smythe Shoes*). Use *Ms.* as the title for a woman.
- **The *body* contains the substance.** Instead of indenting the first line of each paragraph, double-space between paragraphs.
- **The *close* should reflect the level of formality in the salutation:** *Respectfully, Cordially, Yours truly,* and *Sincerely* are more formal closes; *Regards* and *Best wishes* are less formal.
- **The *signature* has two parts:** your name typed four lines below the close, and your handwritten signature in the space between.

Enclose a printed business letter in an envelope that will accommodate the letter once it is folded horizontally in thirds. The envelope should show your name and address in the upper left corner and the addressee's name, title, and address in the center.

Letters by e-mail

An e-mailed business letter lacks some parts of a paper letter: the return-address heading, handwritten signature, and envelope. Your mailing address falls at the end of the letter rather than at the top. Otherwise, it has the same parts listed above: salutation, body, close, and typed signature. And it has two features that paper letters do not:

- **Your e-mail address:** Use a businesslike address that is a variation on your name, such as *john.doe, johndoe,* or *jdoe.* Do not use an address with an anonymous username.

Business letter (cover letter)

Minimum 1"

3712 Swiss Avenue
Dallas, TX 75204 — Return-address heading
March 2, 2015

Double-space

Raymond Chipault
Human Resources Manager
Dallas News — Inside address
Communications Center
Dallas, TX 75222

Double-space

Dear Mr. Chipault: — Salutation

Double-space

In response to your posting in the English Department of Southern Methodist University, I am applying for the summer job of part-time editorial assistant for the Dallas News.

Double-space

1"

I am now enrolled at Southern Methodist University as a sophomore, with a dual major in English literature and journalism. My courses so far have included news reporting, copy editing, and digital publishing. I worked a summer as a copy aide for my hometown newspaper, and for two years I have edited and written sports stories and features for the university newspaper. My feature articles cover subjects as diverse as campus elections, parking regulations, visiting professors, and speech codes.

1"

Body

Double-space

As the enclosed résumé and writing samples indicate, my education and knowledge of newspaper work prepare me for the opening you have.

Double-space

I am available for an interview at your convenience and would be happy to show more samples of my writing. Please e-mail me at ianirvine@mail.smu.edu or call me at 214-744-3816.

Sincerely, — Close

Quadruple space

Ian M. Irvine — Signature

Ian M. Irvine

Enc.

Minimum 1"

■ **The subject line:** Make it short and accurate, reflecting the message of your letter: for instance, *Subscription problem* or *Copy aide position.*

14c Write effective job applications.

In applying for a job or requesting a job interview, you will submit both a résumé and a cover letter, probably in electronic form. You may also create a social-media profile that prospective employers can consult when they are considering your application.

1 ▪ Cover letter

The sample on the facing page illustrates the key features of a cover letter:

- **Interpret your résumé for the particular job.** Don't detail your entire résumé, reciting your job history. Instead, tailor your letter to the job description, highlighting how your qualifications and experience match the job you are applying for.
- **Announce at the outset what job you seek and how you heard about it.**
- **Include any special reason you have for applying,** such as a specific career goal.
- **Summarize your qualifications for this particular job,** including relevant facts about education and employment history and emphasizing notable accomplishments. Mention that additional information appears in an accompanying résumé.
- **Describe your availability.** At the end of the letter, mention that you are free for an interview at the convenience of the addressee, or specify when you will be available (for instance, when your current job or classes leave you free).

14c

2 ▪ Résumé

Your résumé should provide information in table format that allows a potential employer to evaluate your qualifications. The résumé should include your name and address, the position you seek, your education and employment history, any special skills or awards, and how to obtain your references. Fit all the information on one uncrowded page unless your education and experience are extensive.

Most job seekers prepare two versions of their résumé: a formatted version to print and take to in-person interviews (sample on the next page) and a plainer version to submit online (sample on p. 137). Employers may add the electronic version to a computerized database of applicants, so the format and language are important to ensure that your résumé is retrievable:

- **Keep the design simple for accurate scanning or electronic transmittal.** Avoid images, bullets, boldface, italics, underlining, unusual fonts, more than one column, centered headings, and vertical or horizontal lines.
- **Use concise, specific words to describe your skills and experience.** The employer's computer may use keywords (often nouns) to identify the résumés of suitable job candidates, and you want to ensure that your résumé includes keywords that match the field and the job description. Look for likely keywords in the job

---

Résumé (print)

Name and contact information	*Ian M. Irvine*	3712 Swiss Avenue Dallas, TX 75204 214-744-3816 ianirvine@mail.smu.edu
Desired position stated simply and clearly	*Position desired*	Part-time editorial assistant.
Education before work experience for most college students	*Education*	*Southern Methodist University*, 2013 to present. Current standing: sophomore. Major: English literature and journalism. Journalism courses: news reporting, copy editing, digital publishing, communication arts, broadcast journalism. *Abilene (Texas) Senior High School*, 2009-13. Graduated with academic, college-preparatory degree.
Headings marking sections, set off with space and highlighting	*Employment history*	2013 to present. Reporter, *Daily Campus*, student newspaper of Southern Methodist University. Write regular coverage of baseball, track, and soccer teams. Write feature stories on campus policies and events. Edit sports news, campus listings, features.
Conventional use of capital letters: yes for proper nouns and after periods; no for job titles, course names, department names, and so on		Summer 2014. Copy aide, *Abilene Reporter-News*. Assisted reporters with copy routing and research. Summer 2013. Painter, Longhorn Painters, Abilene. Prepared and painted exteriors and interiors of houses.
	Special skills	Fluent in Spanish. Proficient in Internet research and word processing.
Standard, consistent type font	*References*	Available on request: Placement Office Southern Methodist University Dallas, TX 75275

description published by the employer, and use those words in naming your specific skills. Write concretely with words like *manager* (not *person with responsibility for*) and *reporter* (not *staff member who reports*).

3 ▪ Creating an online profile

Many job seekers use social-networking sites such as *LinkedIn* to create online profiles. Like a résumé, an online profile should state the position you seek and use keywords to accurately describe your

Résumé (scannable or electronic)

Ian M. Irvine
3712 Swiss Avenue
Dallas, TX 75204
214-744-3816
ianirvine@mail.smu.edu

KEYWORDS: Editor, editorial assistant, publishing, electronic publishing.

OBJECTIVE
Part-time editorial assistant.

EDUCATION
Southern Methodist University, 2013 to present.
Major: English literature and journalism.
Journalism courses: news reporting, copy editing, digital publishing,
communication arts, broadcast journalism.

Abilene (Texas) Senior High School, 2009-13.
Academic, college preparatory degree.

EMPLOYMENT HISTORY
Reporter, Daily Campus, Southern Methodist University, 2013 to present.
Writer of articles for student newspaper on sports teams, campus policies,
and local events. Editor of sports news, campus listings, and features.

Copy aide, Abilene Reporter-News, Abilene, summer 2014.
Assistant to reporters, routing copy and doing research.

Painter, Longhorn Painters, Abilene, summer 2013.
Preparation and painting of exteriors and interiors of houses.

SPECIAL SKILLS
Fluent in Spanish.
Proficient in Internet research and word processing.

REFERENCES
Available on request:
Placement Office
Southern Methodist University
Dallas, TX 75275

Annotations (right margin):

Accurate keywords, allowing the employer to place the résumé into an appropriate database

Simple design, avoiding unusual fonts, bold, italics, multiple columns, decorative lines, and images

Standard font easily read by scanners

Every line aligning at left margin

---

education, skills, and previous work and volunteer experience. In addition, an online profile often contains the following:

- **A summary of your qualifications, goals, and experience,** similar to the opening paragraphs of a cover letter.
- **A portfolio of your best projects that are relevant to the job you seek**—for instance, writing that you completed for classes, internships, or jobs.
- **A current, high-quality headshot of you,** dressed as you would be for a job.

14d   Writing focused memos.

Business memos address people within the same organization. Most memos deal with a specific topic, such as an answer to a question. The text of a memo comes quickly to the point and discusses it efficiently. State your reason for writing in the first sentence, and in the first paragraph concisely present your answer, conclusion, or evaluation. In the rest of the memo explain your reasoning or evidence. Use headings or lists as appropriate to highlight key information.

Memos are usually sent by e-mail. See the sample below, and consult the guidelines on pages 82–83 for using e-mail and other electronic communication.

Memo

From: pphillips@bigelow.com
To...: Aileen Rosen
Cc...: Larry Mendes; James MacGregor
Subject: 2015 sales of Quick Wax in Territory 12

Names of addressee and people receiving copies.

Subject description providing context for the memo.

Since it was introduced in January 2015, Quick Wax has been unsuccessful in Territory 12 and has not affected the sales of our Easy Shine. Discussions with customers and my own analysis of Quick Wax suggest three reasons for its failure to compete with our product.

Body paragraphs single-spaced with double spacing between them; paragraphs not indented

1. Quick Wax has not received the promotion necessary for a new product. Advertising has been sporadic and has not developed a clear, consistent image for the product. In addition, the Quick Wax representative in Territory 12 is new and inexperienced. He is not known to customers, and his sales pitch (which I once overheard) is weak. As far as I can tell, his efforts are not supported by his home office.

2. When Quick Wax does make it to the store shelves, buyers do not choose it over our product. Though priced competitively with Easy Shine, Quick Wax is poorly packaged. The container seems smaller than ours, though in fact it holds the same eight ounces. The lettering on the package (red on blue) is difficult to read, in contrast to the Easy Shine package.

Numbered list distilling and emphasizing key points

3. Our special purchase offers and my increased efforts to serve existing customers have had the intended effect of keeping customers satisfied with our product and reducing their inclination to stock something new.

Writer's electronic signature giving contact information.

Patricia Phillips
Sales Representative
Bigelow Wax Company
pphillips@bigelow.com
960-556-5565

14e   Write effectively for community work.

At some point in your life, you're likely to volunteer for a community organization such as a soup kitchen, a daycare center, or a literacy program. Many college courses involve service learning, in which you do such volunteer work, write about the experience for your course, and write *for* the organization you're helping.

The writing you do for a community group may range from updating the group's presence on social media to producing a newsletter. The following tips and the samples below and on the next page can help you with such writing:

- **Craft your writing for its purpose and audience.** You are trying to achieve a specific aim with your readers, and the approach and tone you use will influence their responses. For example, a fundraising letter to local businesses would address the readers formally and focus on the group's benefits to them and the community. An appeal for volunteers on the group's *Facebook* page would be more conversational and enthusiastic, emphasizing the rewards of helping out.

- **Remember that your writing represents the organization.** Always be professional. For example, if you respond to a negative comment on your organization's blog, avoid sounding angry.

- **Expect to work with others.** Much public writing is the work of more than one person. Even if you draft the document on your own, others will review the content, tone, and design. Such collaboration is rewarding, but it sometimes requires patience and goodwill. See pages 32–33 for advice on collaborating.

14e

Social-media post

Congratulations to ReadingWorks tutors and students, who last year logged more tutoring hours and passed more levels of proficiency than in any prior year. We are proud of you! We will celebrate your accomplishments at the Annual Awards Dinner on May 23. Please mark your calendars and watch for details—at ReadingWorks.

Online post written in a conversational style

Photograph illustrating information in the post

Like· Comment· Share   📑 12

Newsletter

Multicolumn format allowing room for headings, articles, and other elements on a single page	
Two-column heading emphasizing the main article	
Elements helping readers skim for highlights: spacing, varied font sizes, lines, and a bulleted list	
Color focusing readers' attention on banner, headlines, and table of contents	
Lively but uncluttered overall appearance	
Box in the first column highlighting table of contents	

ReadingWorks

Springfield Veterans Administration Hospital   SUMMER 2015

From the director

Can you help? With more and more learners in the ReadingWorks program, we need more and more tutors. You may know people who would be interested in participating in the program, if only they knew about it.

Those of you who have been tutoring VA patients in reading and writing know both the great need you fulfill and the great benefits you bring to the students. New tutors need no special skills—we'll provide the training—only patience and an interest in helping others.

We've scheduled an orientation meeting for Friday, September 18, at 6:30 PM. Please come and bring a friend who is willing to contribute a couple of hours a week to our work.

Thanks,
Kate Goodman

IN THIS ISSUE

FIRST ANNUAL AWARDS DINNER

A festive night for students and tutors

The first annual Reading-Works Awards Dinner on May 23 was a great success. Springfield's own Golden Fork provided tasty food and Amber Allen supplied lively music. The students decorated Suite 42 on the theme of books and reading. In all, 127 people attended.

The highlight of the night was the awards ceremony. Nine students, recommended by their tutors, received certificates recognizing their efforts and special accomplishments in learning to read and write:

Ramon Berva
Edward Byar
David Dunbar
Tony Garnier
Chris Guigni
Akili Haynes
Josh Livingston
Alex Obeld
B. J. Resnansky

In addition, nine tutors received certificates commemorating five years of service to ReadingWorks:

Anita Crumpton
Felix Cruz-Rivera
Bette Elgen

Kayleah Bortoluzzi
Harriotte Henderson
Ben Obiso
Meggie Puente
Max Smith
Sara Villante

Congratulations to all!

PTSD: New Guidelines

Most of us are working with veterans who have been diagnosed with post-traumatic stress disorder. Because this disorder is often complicated by alcoholism, depression, anxiety, and other problems, the National Center for PTSD has issued some guidelines for helping PTSD patients in ways that reduce their stress.

- The hospital must know your tutoring schedule, and you need to sign in and out before and after each tutoring session.

- To protect patients' privacy, meet them only in designated visiting and tutoring areas, never in their rooms.

- Treat patients with dignity and respect, even when (as sometimes happens) they grow frustrated and angry. Seek help from a nurse or orderly if you need it.

PART **3**

Clarity and Style

15 Emphasis

In *Brief*

- Use subjects and verbs for key actors and actions (below).
- Use sentence beginnings and endings (p. 144).
- Coordinate equally important ideas (p. 146).
- Subordinate less important ideas (p. 148).

Visit MyWritingLab™ for more resources on emphasis.

When you speak, your tone of voice, facial expressions, and even hand gestures work with your words and sentences to convey your meaning. When you write, your words and sentences must do that work alone. To write exactly what you mean, use the advice in this chapter to emphasize the main ideas in your sentences. Also see Chapter 20 on concise writing, which contributes to emphatic writing.

15a Use subjects and verbs for key actors and actions.

emph
15a

The heart of every sentence is its subject, which usually names the actor, and its predicate verb, which asserts something about the subject *Children* [subject] *grow* [predicate verb]. (See p. 191.) When these elements do not identify the key actor and action in the sentence, readers must find that information elsewhere and the sentence may be wordy and unemphatic.

In the next sentences, the subjects and verbs are underlined:

> **Unemphatic** The intention of the company was to expand its workforce. A proposal was also made to diversify the backgrounds and abilities of employees.

These sentences are unemphatic because their key ideas do not appear in their subjects and verbs. Revised, the sentences are not only clearer but more concise:

> **Revised** The company intended to expand its workforce. It also proposed to diversify the backgrounds and abilities of employees.

The constructions discussed below and on the next page usually drain meaning from a sentence's subject and verb.

Nouns made from verbs

Nouns made from verbs can obscure the key actions of sentences and add words. These nouns include *intention* (from *intend*), *proposal* (from *propose*), *decision* (from *decide*), *expectation* (from *expect*), *persistence* (from *persist*), *argument* (from *argue*), and *inclusion* (from *include*).

> **Unemphatic** After the company made a decision to hire more workers with disabilities, its next step was the construction of wheelchair ramps and other facilities.

Revised   After the company <u>decided</u> to hire more workers with disabilities, it next <u>constructed</u> wheelchair ramps and other
facilities.

Weak verbs

Weak verbs, such as *made* and *was* in the previous unemphatic
sentence, tend to stall sentences just where they should be moving
and often bury key actions:

Unemphatic   The company <u>is</u> now the leader among businesses in
complying with the 1990 disabilities act. Its officers <u>make</u>
frequent speeches on the act to business groups.

Revised   The company now <u>leads</u> other businesses in complying
with the 1990 disabilities act. Its officers frequently <u>speak</u>
on the act to business groups.

Forms of *be, have,* and *make* are often weak, but don't try to eliminate every use of them: *be* and *have* are essential as helping verbs (<u>is</u>
<u>going, has written</u>); *be* links subjects and words describing them (*Planes*
<u>are</u> *noisy*); and *have* and *make* have independent meanings (among
them "possess" and "force," respectively). But do consider replacing
forms of *be, have,* and *make* when one of the words after the verb could
be made into a strong verb itself, as in the following examples.

emph

15a

Unemphatic	Emphatic
was influential	influenced
have a preference	prefer
had the appearance	appeared, seemed
made a claim	claimed

Passive voice

Verbs in the passive voice state actions received by, not performed
by, their subjects: *The law was passed.* Thus the passive de-emphasizes
the true actor of the sentence and sometimes omits it entirely, as in the
preceding example. Generally, prefer the **active voice**, in which the
subject performs the action.

Unemphatic   The 1990 <u>law is seen</u> by most businesses as fair, but the
<u>costs</u> of complying <u>have</u> sometimes <u>been objected to</u>.

Revised   Most <u>businesses see</u> the 1990 law as fair, but <u>some have</u>
<u>objected to</u> the costs of complying.

See also pages 230–32 for more on active and passive voice.

Exercise 15.1   Revising: Emphasis of subjects and verbs

Rewrite the following sentences so that their subjects and verbs identify
their key actors and actions.

Example:

The issue of students making a competition over grades is a reason
why their focus on learning may be lost.

Students who compete over grades may lose their focus on learning.

1. The work of many heroes was crucial in helping to emancipate the slaves.
2. The contribution of Harriet Tubman, an escaped slave herself, included the guidance of hundreds of other slaves to freedom on the Underground Railroad.
3. A return to slavery was risked by Tubman or possibly death.
4. During the Civil War she was also a carrier of information from the South to the North.
5. After the war, needy former slaves were helped by Tubman's raising of money.

15b   Use sentence beginnings and endings.

Readers automatically seek a writer's principal meaning in the main clause of a sentence—essentially, in the subject that names the actor and the predicate verb that usually specifies the action (see p. 142). Thus you can help readers understand your intended meaning by controlling the information in your subjects and the relation of the main clause to any modifiers attached to it.

Old and new information

Generally, readers expect the beginning of a sentence to contain information that they already know or that you have already introduced. They then look to the ending for new information. In the unemphatic passage below, the second and third sentences both begin with new topics, while the old topics appear at the ends of the sentences. The pattern of the passage is A→B. C→B. D→A.

Unemphatic $\overset{A}{\underline{\text{Education}}}$ often means $\overset{B}{\underline{\text{controversy}}}$ these days, with rising costs and constant complaints about its inadequacies. But the $\overset{C}{\underset{B}{\underline{\text{value}}}}$ of schooling should not be obscured by the $\underline{\text{controversy}}$. The single best $\overset{D}{\underline{\text{means}}}$ of economic advancement, despite its shortcomings, remains $\overset{A}{\underline{\text{education}}}$.

In the more emphatic revision below, old information begins each sentence and new information ends the sentence. The passage follows the pattern A→B. B→C. A→D.

Revised $\overset{A}{\underline{\text{Education}}}$ often means $\overset{B}{\underline{\text{controversy}}}$ these days, with rising costs and constant complaints about its inadequacies. But the $\overset{B}{\underline{\text{controversy}}}$ should not obscure the $\overset{C}{\underline{\text{value}}}$ of schooling. $\overset{A}{\underline{\text{Education}}}$ remains, despite its shortcomings, the single best $\overset{D}{\underline{\text{means}}}$ of economic advancement.

Cumulative and periodic sentences

You can call attention to information by placing it first or last in a sentence, reserving the middle for incidentals.

Unemphatic	Education remains the single best means of economic advancement, despite its shortcomings. [Emphasizes shortcomings.]
Revised	Despite its shortcomings, education remains the single best means of economic advancement. [Emphasizes advancement more than shortcomings.]
Revised	Education remains, despite its shortcomings, the single best means of economic advancement. [De-emphasizes shortcomings.]

A sentence that begins with the main clause and then adds modifiers is called **cumulative**: it accumulates information as it proceeds.

Cumulative	Education has no equal in opening minds, instilling values, and creating opportunities.
Cumulative	Most of the Great American Desert is made up of bare rock, rugged cliffs, mesas, canyons, mountains, separated from one another by broad flat basins covered with sun-baked mud and alkali, supporting a sparse and measured growth of sagebrush or creosote or saltbush, depending on location and elevation. —Edward Abbey

emph
15b

The opposite kind of sentence, called **periodic**, saves the main clause until just before the end (the period) of the sentence. Everything before the main clause points toward it.

Periodic	In opening minds, instilling values, and creating opportunities, education has no equal.
Periodic	With people from all over the world—Korean doctors, Jamaican cricket players, Vietnamese engineers, Indian restaurant owners—the American mosaic is continually changing.

The periodic sentence creates suspense by reserving important information for the end. But readers should already have an idea of the sentence's subject—because it appeared in the preceding sentence—so that they know what the opening modifiers describe.

Exercise 15.2   Sentence combining: Beginnings and endings

Locate the main idea in each numbered group of sentences. Then combine each group into a single sentence that emphasizes that idea by placing it at the beginning or the end. For sentences 2–5, determine the position of the main idea by considering its relation to the previous sentences: if the main idea picks up a topic that's already been introduced, place it at the beginning; if it adds new information, place it at the end.

Example:

The storm blew roofs off buildings. It caused extensive damage. It knocked down many trees. It severed power lines.

Main idea at beginning: <u>The storm caused extensive damage</u>, blowing roofs off buildings, knocking down many trees, and severing power lines.

Main idea at end: Blowing roofs off buildings, knocking down many trees, and severing power lines, <u>the storm caused extensive damage</u>.

1. Pat Taylor strode into the room. The room was packed. He greeted students called "Taylor's Kids." He nodded to their parents and teachers.
2. This was a wealthy Louisiana oilman. He had promised his "Kids" free college educations. He was determined to make higher education available to all qualified but disadvantaged students.
3. The students welcomed Taylor. Their voices joined in singing. They sang "You Are the Wind beneath My Wings." Their faces beamed with hope. Their eyes flashed with self-confidence.
4. The students had thought a college education was beyond their dreams. It seemed too costly. It seemed too demanding.
5. Taylor had to ease the costs and the demands of getting to college. He created a bold plan. The plan consisted of scholarships, tutoring, and counseling.

coord
15c

15c   Use coordination to relate equal ideas.

Use **coordination** to show that two or more elements in a sentence are equally important in meaning, thus clarifying the relation between them:

- **Link two main clauses with a comma and a coordinating conjunction:** *and, but, or, nor, so, for, yet.*

    equally important

    Independence Hall in Philadelphia is now restored, <u>but</u> fifty years ago it was in bad shape.

- **Link two main clauses with a semicolon alone or with a semicolon and a conjunctive adverb,** such as *therefore* or *however.* (See p. 279 for a list.)

    equally important

    The building was standing; <u>however</u>, it suffered from decay.

- **Within clauses, link words and phrases with a coordinating conjunction.**

    equally important

    The people <u>and</u> officials of the nation were indifferent to Independence Hall <u>or</u> took it for granted.

- **Link main clauses, words, or phrases with a correlative conjunction,** such as *not only . . . but also* and *either . . . or.* (See p. 189 for a list.)

           ⌐⟵ equally important ⟶⌐
People <u>not only</u> took the building for granted <u>but also</u> neglected it.

For the punctuation of coordinate elements, see pages 290–92 (comma and coordinating conjunction), 302 (coordinating conjunction alone), and 305–06 (semicolon alone or with a conjunctive adverb).

1 ▪ Coordinating to smooth sentences

Coordination shows the equality between elements, as illustrated in the preceding examples. At the same time as it clarifies meaning, it can also help smooth choppy sentences like these:

Choppy sentences	We should not rely so heavily on oil. Coal and natural gas are also overused. We have a substantial energy resource in the moving waters of our rivers. Smaller streams add to the total volume of water. The resource renews itself. Coal and oil are irreplaceable. Gas is also irreplaceable. The cost of water does not increase much over time. The costs of coal, oil, and gas fluctuate dramatically.

The following revision groups coal, oil, and natural gas and clearly opposes them to water (the connecting words are underlined):

Ideas coordinated	We should not rely so heavily on coal, oil, <u>and</u> natural gas, <u>for</u> we have a substantial energy resource in the moving waters of our rivers <u>and</u> streams. Coal, oil, <u>and</u> gas are irreplaceable <u>and</u> thus subject to dramatic cost fluctuations; water, <u>however,</u> is self-renewing <u>and</u> more stable in cost.

2 ▪ Coordinating effectively

Use coordination only to express the *equality* of ideas or details. A string of coordinated elements—especially main clauses—implies that all points are equally important:

Excessive coordination	The weeks leading up to the resignation of President Nixon were eventful, and the Supreme Court and the Congress closed in on him, and the Senate Judiciary Committee voted to begin impeachment proceedings, and finally the President resigned on August 9, 1974.

Such a passage needs editing to stress the important points in the main clauses (underlined below) and to de-emphasize the less important information:

Revised	<u>The weeks leading up to the resignation of President Nixon were eventful,</u> as the Supreme Court and the Congress closed in on him and the Senate Judiciary

coor
15

Committee voted to begin impeachment proceedings. Finally, <u>the President resigned on August 9, 1974</u>.

Even within a single sentence, coordination should express a logical equality between ideas:

Faulty	John Stuart Mill was a nineteenth-century utilitarian, and he believed that actions should be judged by their usefulness or by the happiness they cause. [The two clauses are not separate and equal: the second expands on the first by explaining what a utilitarian such as Mill believed.]
Revised	John Stuart Mill, <u>a nineteenth-century utilitarian</u>, believed that actions should be judged by their usefulness or by the happiness they cause.

Exercise 15.3   Revising: Excessive or faulty coordination

Revise the following sentences to eliminate excessive or faulty coordination by adding or subordinating information or by forming more than one sentence. Each item has more than one answer.

Example:

My dog barks, and I have to move out of my apartment.

<u>Because my dog's barking disturbs my neighbors</u>, I have to move out of my apartment.

1. Often soldiers admired their commanding officers, and they gave them nicknames, and these names frequently contained the word *old*, but not all of the commanders were old.
2. General Thomas "Stonewall" Jackson was also called "Old Jack," and he was not yet forty years old.
3. Another Southern general in the Civil War was called "Old Pete," and his full name was James Longstreet.
4. The Union general Henry W. Halleck had a reputation as a good military strategist, and he was an expert on the work of a French military authority, Henri Jomini, and Halleck was called "Old Brains."
5. General William Henry Harrison won the Battle of Tippecanoe, and he received the nickname "Old Tippecanoe," and he used the name in his presidential campaign slogan, "Tippecanoe and Tyler, Too," and he won the election in 1840, but he died of pneumonia a month after taking office.

sub
15d

15d   Use subordination to emphasize ideas.

Use **subordination** to indicate that some elements in a sentence are less important than others for your meaning. Usually, the main idea appears in the main clause, and supporting details appear in subordinate structures.

- Use a subordinate clause beginning with *although, because, if, until, who (whom), that, which,* or another subordinating word. (See pp. 201–03 for more on subordinate clauses.)

more important
⌐less important (subordinate clause)⌐ ⌐(main clause)⌐
Although production costs have declined, they are still high.

less important
⌐(subordinate clause)⌐
Costs, which include labor and facilities, are difficult to control.
◄── more important (main clause)──►

- Use a phrase:

less important   more important
⌐(phrase)⌐   ⌐(main clause)⌐
Despite some decline, production costs are still high.

⌐less important (phrase)⌐
Costs, including labor and facilities, are difficult to control.
◄──more important (main clause)──►

- Use a single word:

Declining costs have not matched prices.

Labor costs are difficult to control.

For punctuating subordinate elements, see pages 293 (comma with introductory elements) and 294–97 (commas with interrupting elements).

1 ▪ Subordinating to distinguish important ideas

A string of main clauses can make everything in a passage seem equally important, as the next example shows.

String of main clauses   Computer prices have dropped, and production costs have dropped more slowly, and computer manufacturers have struggled, for their profits have been declining.

Emphasis comes from keeping the important information in the main clause (underlined) and subordinating less important details:

Revised   Because production costs have dropped more slowly than prices, computer manufacturers have struggled with declining profits.

2 ▪ Subordinating effectively

In subordinating elements within a sentence, be careful to keep relationships clear:

- **Subordinate only the less important information in the sentence.** Faulty subordination reverses the dependent relation that the reader expects.

Faulty	Ms. Angelo was in her first year of teaching, although she was a better instructor than others with many years of experience. [The sentence suggests that Angelo's inexperience is the main idea, whereas the writer meant to stress her skill *despite* her inexperience.]
Revised	Although Ms. Angelo was in her first year of teaching, <u>she was a better instructor than others with many years of experience.</u>

- **Avoid crowding loosely related details into one long sentence.**

Overloaded	The boats that were moored at the dock when the hurricane, which was one of the worst in three decades, struck were ripped from their moorings, because the owners had not been adequately prepared, since the weather service had predicted that the storm would blow out to sea, as storms do at this time of year.
Revised	Struck by one of the worst hurricanes in three decades, <u>the boats at the dock were ripped from their moorings.</u> <u>The owners were unprepared</u> because the weather service had said that hurricanes at this time of year blow out to sea.

- **Avoid a dangling modifier**—that is, a modifier that doesn't relate sensibly to the rest of the sentence. (See pp. 269–70.)

Dangling modifier	Driving through the region, the destruction from the storm was everywhere.
Revised	Driving through the region, <u>we saw</u> destruction from the storm everywhere.

Exercise 15.4   Revising: Faulty or excessive subordination

Revise the following sentences to eliminate faulty or excessive subordination and to achieve appropriate emphasis.

> *Example:*
> Terrified to return home, he had driven his mother's car into a cornfield.
> <u>Having driven his mother's car into a cornfield</u>, he was terrified to return home.

1. Genaro González is a successful writer, which means that his stories and novels have been published to critical acclaim.
2. He loves to write, although he has also earned a doctorate in psychology.
3. His first story, which reflects his growing consciousness of his Aztec heritage and place in the world, is titled "Un Hijo del Sol."
4. González wrote the first version of "Un Hijo del Sol" while he was a

ub
d

sophomore at the University of Texas–Pan American, which is in the Rio Grande Valley of southern Texas, which González calls "el Valle" in the story.

5. González's latest book, which is about a teenager and is titled *A So-Called Vacation*, is a novel about how the teen and his family live for a summer as migrant fruit pickers, which was the experience his father had when he first immigrated from Mexico.

Exercise 15.5   Revising: Coordination and subordination

The following paragraph consists entirely of simple sentences. Use coordination and subordination to combine sentences in the way you think most effective to emphasize main ideas.

Sir Walter Raleigh personified the Elizabethan Age. That was the period of Elizabeth I's rule of England. The period occurred in the last half of the sixteenth century. Raleigh was a courtier and poet. He was also an explorer and entrepreneur. Supposedly, he gained Queen Elizabeth's favor. He did this by throwing his cloak beneath her feet at the right moment. She was just about to step over a puddle. There is no evidence for this story. It does illustrate Raleigh's dramatic and dynamic personality. His energy drew others to him. He was one of Elizabeth's favorites. She supported him. She also dispensed favors to him. However, he lost his queen's goodwill. Without her permission he seduced one of her maids of honor. He eventually married the maid of honor. Elizabeth died. Then her successor imprisoned Raleigh in the Tower of London. Her successor was James I. The king falsely charged Raleigh with treason. Raleigh was released after thirteen years. He was arrested again two years later on the old treason charges. At the age of sixty-six he was beheaded.

//

16

16   Parallelism

In *Brief*

- Use parallelism with *and, but, or, nor,* and *yet* (next page).
- Use parallelism with *both . . . and, not . . . but,* or another correlative conjunction (next page).
- Use parallelism in comparisons, lists, headings, and outlines (p. 153.)

Visit MyWritingLab™ for more resources on parallelism.

When ideas within sentences have the same function and importance, you can show their connection using **parallelism**, or parallel structure, as shown in the following example:

The air is dirtied by <u>factories belching smoke</u> and <u>cars spewing exhaust</u>.

With parallelism, you use the same grammatical forms to express equally important ideas. In the preceding example, the two underlined phrases have the same function and importance (two sources of air pollution), so they also have the same grammatical construction.

16a Use parallelism with *and, but, or, nor, yet.*

The coordinating conjunctions *and, but, or, nor,* and *yet* connect elements of the same kind and importance. These conjunctions always signal a need for parallelism, as shown in the following examples:

> The industrial base was shifting and shrinking. [Parallel words.]
>
> Politicians rarely acknowledged the problem or proposed alternatives. [Parallel phrases.]
>
> Industrial workers were understandably disturbed that they were losing their jobs and that no one seemed to care. [Parallel clauses.]

16b

When sentence elements linked by coordinating conjunctions are not parallel in structure, the sentence is awkward and distracting:

Nonparallel	The reasons steel companies kept losing money were that their plants were inefficient, high labor costs, and foreign competition was increasing.
Revised	The reasons steel companies kept losing money were inefficient plants, high labor costs, and increasing foreign competition.
Nonparallel	Success was difficult even for efficient companies because of the shift away from all manufacturing in the United States and the fact that steel production was shifting toward emerging nations.
Revised	Success was difficult even for efficient companies because of the shift away from all manufacturing in the United States and toward steel production in emerging nations.

All the words required by idiom or grammar must be stated in compound constructions (see also pp. 175–76):

Faulty	Given training, workers can acquire the skills and interest in other jobs. [Idiom dictates different prepositions with *skills* and *interest*.]
Revised	Given training, workers can acquire the skills for and interest in other jobs.

16b Use parallelism with *both . . . and* or another correlative conjunction.

Correlative conjunctions include *both . . . and, either . . . or,* and *not only . . . but also.* They stress equality and balance between elements, and parallelism confirms the equality.

It is not a tax bill but a tax relief bill, providing relief not for the needy but for the greedy.
—Franklin Delano Roosevelt

With correlative conjunctions, the element after the second connector must match the element after the first connector:

Nonparallel	Huck Finn learns not only that human beings have an enormous capacity for folly but also enormous dignity. [The first element includes *that human beings have*; the second element does not.]
Revised	Huck Finn learns that human beings have not only an enormous capacity for folly but also enormous dignity. [Repositioning *that human beings have* makes the two elements parallel.]

16c Use parallelism in comparisons.

Parallelism confirms the likeness or difference between two elements being compared using *than* or *as*.

Nonparallel	Huck Finn proves less a bad boy than to be an independent spirit. In the end he is every bit as determined in rejecting help as he is to leave for "the territory."
Revised	Huck Finn proves less a bad boy than an independent spirit. In the end he is every bit as determined to reject help as he is to leave for "the territory."

(See also pp. 257–58 on making comparisons logical.)

16d Use parallelism in lists, headings, and outlines.

The items in a list or outline are coordinate and should be parallel. Parallelism is essential in the headings that divide a paper into sections (see p. 62) and in a formal topic outline (see pp. 23–24).

Nonparallel	Revised
Changes in Renaissance England	Changes in Renaissance England
1. Extension of trade routes	1. Extension of trade routes
2. Merchant class became more powerful	2. Increased power of the merchant class
3. The death of feudalism	3. Death of feudalism
4. Upsurging of the arts	4. Upsurge of the arts
5. Religious quarrels began	5. Rise of religious quarrels

Exercise 16.1 Revising: Parallelism

Revise the following sentences to create parallelism wherever it is required for grammar and coherence. Add or delete words or rephrase as necessary.

// 16d

Example:

After emptying her bag, searching the apartment, and she called the library, Jennifer realized she had lost the book.

After emptying her bag, searching the apartment, and <u>calling</u> the library, Jennifer realized she had lost the book.

1. The ancient Greeks celebrated four athletic contests: the Olympic Games at Olympia, the Isthmian Games were held near Corinth, at Delphi the Pythian Games, and the Nemean Games were sponsored by the people of Cleonae.
2. Each day the games consisted of either athletic events or holding ceremonies and sacrifices to the gods.
3. In the years between the games, competitors were taught wrestling, javelin throwing, and how to box.
4. Competitors participated in running sprints, spectacular chariot and horse races, and running long distances while wearing full armor.
5. The purpose of such events was to develop physical strength, demonstrating skill and endurance, and to sharpen the skills needed for war.
6. Events were held for both men and for boys.
7. At the Olympic Games the spectators cheered their favorites to victory, attended sacrifices to the gods, and they feasted on the meat not burned in offerings.
8. The athletes competed less to achieve great wealth than for gaining honor both for themselves and their cities.
9. Of course, exceptional athletes received financial support from patrons, poems and statues by admiring artists, and they even got lavish living quarters from their sponsoring cities.
10. With the medal counts and flag ceremonies, today's Olympians sometimes seem to be proving their countries' superiority more than to demonstrate individual talent.

17   Variety and Details

In *Brief*

- Vary sentence length (facing page).
- Vary sentence structure with subordination, sentence combining, and sentence beginnings (facing page).
- Add relevant and informative details (p. 157).

Visit MyWritingLab™ for more resources on variety and details.

Writing that is interesting as well as clear has at least two features: the length and structure of sentences suit their meaning and importance, and details provide information and texture.

17a   Vary sentence length.

Sentences generally vary from about ten to about forty words, with an average between fifteen and twenty-five words. If your sentences are all at one extreme or the other, your readers may have difficulty focusing on main ideas and seeing the relations among them.

- **Long sentences.** If most of your sentences contain thirty-five words or more, your main ideas may not stand out from the details that support them. To give the main ideas more emphasis, separate them from the details by breaking them out into their own shorter, simpler sentences.

- **Short sentences.** If most of your sentences contain fewer than ten or fifteen words, all your ideas may seem equally important and the links between them may not be clear. Try combining sentences with coordination (p. 146) and subordination (p. 148) to show relationships and stress main ideas over supporting information.

17b   Vary sentence structure.

var

17b

A passage will be monotonous if all its sentences follow the same pattern, like soldiers marching in a parade. To vary structure, try subordination, sentence combining, varying sentence beginnings, and varying word order.

1 ▪ Subordination

A string of main clauses—subject-verb, subject-verb—can make all ideas seem equally important and can be especially plodding:

Monotonous	The moon is now drifting away from the earth. It moves away at the rate of about one inch a year. This movement is lengthening our days. They increase a thousandth of a second every century. Forty-seven of our present days will someday make up a month. We might eventually lose the moon altogether. Such great planetary movement rightly concerns astronomers, but it need not worry us. It will take 50 million years.

Enliven such writing—and make the main ideas stand out—by subordinating the less important information with phrases and subordinate clauses. (See pp. 197–203 for more on these structures.) In the following revision, underlining indicates subordinate structures that used to be main clauses:

Revised	The moon is now drifting away from the earth <u>about one inch a year</u>. <u>At a thousandth of a second every century</u>, this movement is lengthening our days. Forty-seven of our present days will someday make up a month, <u>if we</u>

don't eventually lose the moon altogether. Such great planetary movement rightly concerns astronomers, but it need not worry us. It will take 50 million years.

2 ▪ Sentence combining

As the preceding example shows, subordinating to achieve variety often involves combining short, choppy sentences into longer units that link related information and stress main ideas. Here is another example of such sentence combining:

Monotonous   Astronomy may seem a remote science. It may seem to have little to do with people's daily lives. Many astronomers find otherwise. They see their science as soothing. It gives perspective to everyday routines and problems.

Combining five sentences into one, the revision below is both clearer and easier to read. Underlining highlights the changes.

Revised   Astronomy may seem a remote science <u>having</u> little to do with people's daily lives, <u>but</u> many astronomers <u>find their</u> science soothing <u>because</u> it gives perspective to everyday routines and problems.

3 ▪ Varying sentence beginnings

An English sentence often begins with its subject, which generally captures old information from a preceding sentence (see pp. 144–45):

The defendant's <u>lawyer</u> was determined to break the prosecution's witness. <u>He</u> relentlessly cross-examined the stubborn witness for a week.

However, an unbroken sequence of sentences beginning with the subject quickly becomes monotonous:

Monotonous   The defendant's lawyer was determined to break the prosecution's witness. He relentlessly cross-examined the witness for a week. The witness had expected to be dismissed within an hour and was visibly irritated. She did not cooperate. She was reprimanded by the judge.

Beginning some of these sentences with other expressions improves readability and clarity:

Revised   The defendant's lawyer was determined to break the prosecution's witness. <u>For a week</u> he relentlessly cross-examined the witness. <u>Expecting to be dismissed within an hour</u>, the witness was visibly irritated. She did not cooperate. <u>Indeed</u>, she was reprimanded by the judge.

 In standard American English, placing some negative adverb modifiers at the beginning of a sentence requires you to use the word order of a question, in which the verb or a part of it precedes the subject. These negative modifiers include *never, rarely, seldom,* and phrases beginning with *no, not since,* and *not until.*

                              verb
          adverb   subject phrase

Faulty   Seldom a witness has held the stand so long.

                   helping   main
         adverb verb subject verb

Revised   Seldom has a witness held the stand so long.

4 ▪ Varying word order

Occasionally, you can vary a sentence and emphasize it at the same time by inverting the usual order of parts:

A dozen witnesses testified for the prosecution, and the defense attorney barely questioned eleven of them. The twelfth, however, he grilled. [Normal word order: *He grilled the twelfth, however.*]

Inverted sentences used without need are artificial. Use them only when emphasis demands.

17c

17c   Add details.

Relevant details such as facts and examples create the texture and life that keep readers awake and help them grasp your meaning. Notice the difference in the following two examples:

Flat   Constructed after World War II, Levittown, New York, consisted of thousands of houses in two basic styles. Over the decades, residents have altered the houses so dramatically that the original styles are often unrecognizable.

Detailed Constructed on potato fields after World War II, Levittown, New York, consisted of more than seventeen thousand houses in Cape Cod and ranch styles. Over the decades, residents have added expansive front porches, punched dormer windows through roofs, converted garages to sun porches, and otherwise altered the houses so dramatically that the original styles are often unrecognizable.

Note The details in the revised passage are effective because they relate to the writer's point and make that point clearer. Details that don't support and clarify your points will likely distract or annoy readers.

Exercise 17.1   Revising: Variety

The following paragraph consists entirely of simple sentences that begin with their subjects. Use the techniques discussed in this chapter to vary the sentences. Delete, add, change, and rearrange words to make the paragraph more readable and to make important ideas stand out clearly.

> The Italian volcano Vesuvius had been dormant for many years. It then exploded on August 24 in the year AD 79. The ash, pumice, and mud from the volcano buried two busy towns. Herculaneum is one. The more famous is Pompeii. Both towns lay undiscovered for many centuries. Herculaneum and Pompeii were discovered in 1709 and 1748, respectively. The excavation of Pompeii was the more systematic. It was the occasion for initiating modern methods of conservation and restoration. Herculaneum was simply looted of its more valuable finds. It was then left to disintegrate. Pompeii appears much as it did before the eruption. A luxurious house opens onto a lush central garden. An election poster decorates a wall. A dining table is set for breakfast.

18 Appropriate and Exact Words

In *Brief*
- Choose words that are appropriate for your writing situation (below).
- Avoid sexist and biased language (p. 162).
- Choose words that express your meaning exactly (p. 166).

Visit MyWritingLab™ for more resources on appropriate and exact words.

To write clearly and effectively, choose words that fit both the context in which you are writing and the meaning that you are trying to convey.

18a Choose appropriate words.

Appropriate words suit your writing situation—your subject, purpose, and audience. In most college and career writing you should rely on what's called **standard American English,** the dialect of English normally expected and used in schools, businesses, government, and the communications media. (For more on its role in academic writing, see pp. 79–81.)

The vocabulary of written standard English is huge, allowing you to express an infinite range of ideas and feelings. However, it does exclude words that are too imprecise for writing and that only some groups of people use, understand, or find inoffensive. The types of excluded words are discussed in this section. Whenever you doubt a word's status, consult a dictionary (see pp. 166–67). A label such as *nonstandard, slang,* or *colloquial* tells you that the word is not generally appropriate in academic or business writing.

1 ■ Dialects other than standard English ⟨CULTURE LANGUAGE⟩

Like many countries, the United States includes scores of regional, social, or ethnic groups with their own distinct **dialects,** or versions of English. Standard American English is one of those dialects, and so are African American Vernacular English, Appalachian English, Creole, and the English of coastal Maine. All the dialects of English share many features, but each also has its own vocabulary, pronunciation, and grammar.

If you speak a dialect other than standard English, you are probably already adept at moving between your dialect and standard English in speech and writing. Dialects are not wrong in themselves, but forms imported from one dialect into another may still be perceived as unclear or incorrect. When standard English is expected, such as in academic and public writing, edit your work to revise expressions in your dialect that you know (or have been told) differ from standard English. These expressions may include *theirselves, hisn, them books,* and others labeled *nonstandard* by a dictionary. They may also include certain verb forms, as discussed on pages 211–20. For help identifying and editing nonstandard language, see the "⟨CULTURE LANGUAGE⟩ Guide" just before the back endpapers of this book.

appr
18a

Your participation in the community of standard American English does not require you to abandon your own dialect. You may want to use it in writing you do for yourself, such as journals, notes, and drafts, which should be composed as freely as possible. You may want to quote it in an academic paper, as when analyzing or reporting conversation in dialect. And, of course, you will want to use it with others who speak it.

2 ■ Shortcuts of texting and other electronic communication

Rapid communication by e-mail and text or instant messaging encourages some informalities that are inappropriate for academic writing. If you use these media frequently, you may need to proofread your academic papers especially to identify and revise errors such as the following:

- **Sentence fragments.** Make sure every sentence has a subject and a predicate. (See pp. 271–73.)

  Not   Observed the results.
  But   <u>Researchers</u> observed the results.

- **Missing punctuation.** Between and within sentences, use standard punctuation marks. Check especially for missing commas within sentences and missing apostrophes in possessives and contractions. (See pp. 290–301 and 311–15.)

  Not   The dogs bony ribs visible through its fur were evidence of neglect.

But   The dog⊙'s bony ribs⊙ visible through its fur⊙ were evidence of neglect.

■ **Missing capital letters.** Use capital letters at the beginnings of sentences, for proper nouns and adjectives, and in titles. (See pp. 335–39.)

Not   scholars have written about abraham lincoln more than any other american.

But   Scholars have written about Abraham Lincoln more than any other American.

■ **Nonstandard abbreviations and spellings.** Write out most words, avoiding forms such as *2* for *to* or *too, b4* for *before, bc* for *because, ur* for *you are* or *you're,* and *+* or *&* for *and.* (See pp. 342–45 and 328–32.)

Not   Students + tutors need to meet b4 the third week of the semester.
But   Students and tutors need to meet before the third week of the semester.

appr
18a

3 ■ Slang

Slang is the language used by a group, such as musicians or computer programmers, to reflect common experiences and to make technical references efficient. The following example is from an essay on the slang of "skaters" (skateboarders):

> Curtis slashed ultra-punk crunchers on his longboard, while the Rubeman flailed his usual Gumbyness on tweaked frontsides and lofty fakie ollies.   —Miles Orkin, "Mucho Slingage by the Pool"

Among those who understand it, slang may be vivid and forceful. It often occurs in dialog, and an occasional slang expression can enliven an informal essay. But most slang is too flippant and imprecise for effective communication, and it is generally inappropriate for college or business writing. Notice the gain in seriousness and precision achieved in the following revision:

Slang   Many students start out pretty together but then get weird.
Revised   Many students start out with clear goals but then lose their direction.

4 ■ Colloquial language

Colloquial language is the everyday spoken language, including expressions such as *get together, go nuts,* and *chill out.*

When you write informally to friends and family, colloquial language can help you achieve the casual, relaxed effect of conversation. In academic, public, and professional writing, however, colloquial language is not precise enough to convey meaning exactly. Generally avoid any words and expressions labeled *informal* or *colloquial* in your dictionary.

| Colloquial | According to a Native American myth, the Great Creator had a dog hanging around with him when he created the earth. |
| Revised | According to a Native American myth, the Great Creator was accompanied by a dog when he created the earth. |

Note See also pages 79–81 for a discussion of formal and informal language in academic writing.

5 ▪ Technical words

All disciplines and professions rely on specialized language that allows the members to communicate precisely and efficiently with each other. Chemists, for instance, have their *phosphatides,* and literary critics have their *motifs* and *subtexts.* Without explanation, technical words are meaningless to nonspecialists. When you are writing for nonspecialists, avoid unnecessary technical terms and carefully define terms you must use.

For revising the overly complicated language that is also sometimes called jargon, see page 181.

appr

18a

6 ▪ Indirect and pretentious writing

In most writing, small, plain, and direct words are preferable to evasive or showy words.

▪ **Euphemisms** are presumably inoffensive words that substitute for words deemed potentially offensive or too direct, such as *passed away* for "died." Euphemisms can soften the truth, but they are appropriate only when blunt, truthful words would needlessly hurt or offend your audience.

▪ **Double talk** (also called *doublespeak* or *weasel words*) is language intended to confuse or be misunderstood. It is unfortunately common in politics and advertising—the *revenue enhancement* that is really a tax, for example. Double talk has no place in honest writing.

▪ **Pretentious writing** is excessively showy. Such writing is more fancy than its subject requires. Choose your words for their exactness and economy. The big, ornate word may be tempting, but pass it up. Your readers will be grateful.

| Pretentious | Hardly a day goes by without a new revelation about the devastation of the natural world, and to a significant extent our dependence on the internal combustion engine is the culprit. Respected scientific minds coalesce around the argument that carbon dioxide emissions, such as those |

from automobiles imbibing gasoline, are responsible for a gradual escalation in temperatures on the earth.

Revised   Much of the frequent bad news about the environment can be blamed on the internal combustion engine. Respected scientists maintain that carbon dioxide emissions, such as those from gasoline-powered cars, are warming the earth.

7 ▪ Sexist and other biased language

Even when we do not mean it to, our language can reflect and perpetuate hurtful prejudices toward groups of people. Such biased language can be obvious—words such as *nigger, honky, mick, kike, fag, dyke,* and *broad*. But it can also be subtle, generalizing about groups in ways that may be familiar but that are also inaccurate or unfair.

Biased language reflects poorly on the user, not on the person or persons whom it mischaracterizes or insults. Unbiased language does not submit to false generalizations. It treats people respectfully as individuals and labels groups as they wish to be labeled.

appr
18a

Stereotypes of race, ethnicity, religion, age, and other characteristics

A **stereotype** is a generalization based on poor evidence, a kind of formula for understanding and judging people simply because of their membership in a group:

Men are uncommunicative.
Women are emotional.
Liberals want to raise taxes.
Conservatives are affluent.

At best, stereotypes betray a noncritical writer, one who is not thinking beyond notions received from others. In your writing, be alert for statements that characterize whole groups of people.

Stereotype   Elderly drivers should have their licenses limited to daytime driving only. [Asserts that all elderly people are poor night drivers.]

Revised   Drivers with impaired night vision should have their licenses limited to daytime driving only.

Some stereotypes have become part of the language, but they are still potentially offensive:

Stereotype   The administrators are too blind to see the need for a new gymnasium. [Equates vision loss and lack of understanding.]

Revised   The administrators do not understand the need for a new gymnasium.

Sexist language

Among the most subtle and persistent biased language is that expressing narrow ideas about men's and women's roles, position, and value in society. Like other stereotypes, this **sexist language** can wound or irritate readers, and it indicates the writer's thoughtlessness or unfairness. The following box suggests some ways of eliminating sexist language.

Eliminating sexist language

■ **Avoid demeaning and patronizing language:**

Sexist   Dr. Keith Kim and Lydia Hawkins coauthored the article.
Revised   Dr. Keith Kim and Dr. Lydia Hawkins coauthored the article.
Revised   Keith Kim and Lydia Hawkins coauthored the article.

Sexist   Ladies are entering almost every occupation formerly filled by men.

Revised   Women are entering almost every occupation formerly filled by men.

■ **Avoid occupational or social stereotypes:**

Sexist   The considerate doctor commends a nurse when she provides his patients with good care.

Revised   The considerate doctor commends a nurse who provides good care for patients.

Sexist   The grocery shopper should save her coupons.
Revised   Grocery shoppers should save their coupons.

■ **Avoid referring needlessly to a person's sex:**

Sexist   Marie Curie, a woman chemist, discovered radium.
Revised   Marie Curie, a chemist, discovered radium.

Sexist   The patients were tended by a male nurse.
Revised   The patients were tended by a nurse.

However, don't overcorrect by avoiding appropriate references to a person's sex: *Pregnant women* [not *people*] *should avoid drinking alcohol and smoking cigarettes.*

■ **Avoid using *man* or words containing *man* to refer to all human beings.** Here are a few alternatives:

businessman   businessperson
chairman   chair, chairperson
congressman   representative, congressperson, legislator
craftsman   craftsperson, artisan
layman   layperson

(continued)

Eliminating sexist language

(continued)

mankind	humankind, humanity, human beings, humans
manmade	handmade, manufactured, synthetic, artificial
manpower	personnel, human resources
policeman	police officer
salesman	salesperson

Sexist   Man has not reached the limits of social justice.

Revised   Humankind [or Humanity] has not reached the limits of social justice.

Sexist   The furniture consists of manmade materials.

Revised   The furniture consists of synthetic materials.

■ **Avoid the *generic he*, the male pronoun used to refer to both sexes.**
(See also pp. 248–49.)

Sexist   The newborn child explores his world.

Revised   Newborn children explore their world. [Use the plural for the pronoun and the word it refers to.]

Revised   The newborn child explores the world. [Avoid the pronoun altogether.]

Revised   The newborn child explores his or her world. [Substitute male and female pronouns.]

Use the last option sparingly—only once in a group of sentences and only to stress the singular individual.

CULTURE LANGUAGE   Forms of address vary widely from culture to culture. In some cultures, for instance, one shows respect by referring to all older women as if they were married, using the equivalent of *Mrs.* Usage in the United States is changing toward making no assumptions about marital status, rank, or other characteristics—for instance, addressing a woman as *Ms.* unless she is known to prefer *Mrs.* or *Miss.*

Appropriate labels

We often need to label groups: *swimmers, politicians, mothers, Christians, Westerners, students.* But labels can be shorthand stereotypes, slighting the person labeled and ignoring the preferences of the group members themselves. Although sometimes dismissed as "political correctness," showing sensitivity about labels hurts no one and helps gain your readers' trust and respect.

■ **Avoid labels that (intentionally or not) insult the person or group you refer to.** A person with emotional problems is not a *mental patient.* A person with cancer is not a *cancer victim.* A person using a wheelchair is not *wheelchair-bound.*

- Use names for racial, ethnic, and other groups that reflect the preferences of each group's members, or at least many of them. Examples of current preferences include *African American* or *black* and *people with disabilities* (rather than *the disabled* or *the handicapped*). But labels change often. To learn how a group's members wish to be labeled, ask them directly, attend to usage in reputable periodicals, or check a recent dictionary.
- Identify a person's group only when it is relevant to the point you're making. Consider the context of the label: Is it a necessary piece of information? If not, don't use it.

Exercise 18.1 Revising: Appropriate words

Rewrite the following sentences as needed for standard American English, focusing on inappropriate slang, technical or pretentious language, and biased language. Consult a dictionary to determine whether particular words are appropriate and to find suitable substitutes.

Example:

If negotiators get hyper during contract discussions, they may mess up chances for a settlement.

If negotiators <u>become excited or upset</u> during contract discussions, they may <u>harm</u> chances for a settlement.

appr
18a

1. Vaccinations to prevent serious diseases have been a huge deal for public health since they became widely available in the 1920s.
2. Diseases such as polio, measles, and whooping cough that used to sicken and kill many children have been pronounced mostly dead.
3. Measles is making a comeback because some moms do not vaccinate their kids.
4. Despite evidence to the contrary, some of these overprotective mothers claim that the measles vaccine, which is combined with vaccines for mumps and rubella, causes autism.
5. Some anti-vaccine types buy into the idea that vaccines are not necessary because other children's vaccines will protect their children from coming into contact with disease.
6. Measles is a serious and highly contagious disease. Victims often exhibit multiple symptoms including high fever, conjunctivitis, nasal secretions, white spots in the mouth, cough, depressed appetite, vomiting, diarrhea, and full-body rash.
7. Respected scientific and medical professionals coalesce around evidence showing that vaccines are not effective at eradicating disease unless 95% of the population receives these life-saving injections.
8. To immunize a child, a doctor must discuss the necessary vaccines with the child's mother. If she agrees to the vaccines, he orders the shots while the child is in the office for a check up.
9. A nurse typically administers vaccines. She gives the shots quickly to minimize the pain.
10. Kids often scream bloody murder when they feel the shot, but they usually calm down right away when their moms comfort them.

Exercise 18.2   Revising: Sexist language

Revise the following sentences to eliminate sexist language. If you change a singular noun or pronoun to plural, be sure to make any needed changes in verbs or other pronouns.

Example:

The career placement officer at most colleges and universities spends part of his time advising students how to write successful résumés.

Career placement officers at most colleges and universities spend part of their time advising students how to write successful résumés.

1. When a person applies for a job, he should represent himself with the best possible résumé.
2. A person applying for a job as a mailman should appear to be honest and responsible.
3. A girl applying for a position as an in-home nurse should also represent herself as honest and responsible.
4. Of course, she should also have a background of capable nursing.
5. The businessman who is scanning a stack of résumés will, of necessity, read them all quickly.
6. The person who wants his résumé to stand out will make sure it highlights his best points.
7. The Web designer will highlight his experience with computers.
8. Volunteer work may be appropriate, too, such as being chairman of a student organization.
9. If the student has been secretary for a campus organization, she could include that volunteer experience in her résumé.
10. If the applicant writing a résumé would keep in mind the man who will be reading it, he might know better what he should include.

exact
18b

18b   Choose exact words.

To write clearly and effectively, you will want to find the words that fit your meaning exactly and convey your attitude precisely.

1 ▪ Word meanings and synonyms

For writing exactly, a dictionary is essential and a thesaurus can be helpful.

Dictionaries

A dictionary defines words and provides pronunciation, grammatical functions, synonyms, etymology (word history), and other information. The sample opposite is part of the entry for *reckon* from *Merriam-Webster Online*. Other useful online sites are *Dictionary.com* and *The Free Dictionary*.

If you prefer a print dictionary, good ones include *Merriam Webster's Collegiate Dictionary, American Heritage College Dictionary, Random House Webster's College Dictionary,* and *Webster's New World College Dictionary.*

Partial online dictionary entry

reck·on ◄))   *verb* \re-kən\

reck·oned │ reck·on·ing ◄))

Definition of RECKON ·······························

transitive verb

1 a : COUNT *<reckon* the days till Christmas>

  b : ESTIMATE, COMPUTE *<reckon* the height of a building>

  c : to determine by reference to a fixed basis <the existence of the United States is *reckoned* from the Declaration of Independence>

2 : to regard or think of as : CONSIDER

3 *chiefly dialect* : THINK, SUPPOSE <I *reckon* I've outlived my time — Ellen Glasgow>

(**CULTURE LANGUAGE**) If English is not your native language, you probably should have a dictionary prepared especially for students using English as a second language (ESL). Such a dictionary contains special information on prepositions, count versus noncount nouns, and many other matters. The following are reliable ESL dictionaries, each available both online and in print: *Longman Dictionary of Contemporary English, Oxford Advanced Learner's Dictionary,* and *Merriam-Webster Advanced Learner's English Dictionary.*

exact
18b

Thesauruses

To find a word with the exact shade of meaning you intend, you may want to consult a thesaurus, or collection of **synonyms**—words with approximately the same meaning. A print or online thesaurus lists most imaginable synonyms for thousands of words. For instance, on the site *Thesaurus.com*, the word *reckon* has nearly fifty synonyms, including *account, evaluate,* and *judge.*

Because a thesaurus aims to open up possibilities, its lists of synonyms include approximate as well as precise matches. The thesaurus does not define synonyms or distinguish among them, however, so you need a dictionary to discover exact meanings. In general, don't use a word from a thesaurus—even one you like the sound of—until you are sure of its appropriateness for your meaning.

2 ▪ The right word for your meaning

All words have one or more basic meanings, called **denotations**—the meanings listed in the dictionary, without reference to emotional associations. If readers are to understand you, you must use words according to their established meanings.

▪ **Consult a dictionary whenever you are unsure of a word's meaning.**

■ **Distinguish between similar-sounding words that have widely different denotations:**

Inexact   Older people often suffer infirmaries [places for the sick].
Exact   Older people often suffer infirmities [disabilities].

Some words, called **homonyms**, sound exactly alike but differ in meaning: for example, *principal/principle* or *rain/reign/rein*. (See pp. 328–29 for a list of commonly confused homonyms.)

■ **Distinguish between words with related but distinct meanings:**

Inexact   Television commercials continuously [unceasingly] interrupt programming.
Exact   Television commercials continually [regularly] interrupt programming.

In addition to their emotion-free meanings, many words carry related meanings that evoke specific feelings. These **connotations** can shape readers' responses and are thus a powerful tool for writers. The following word pairs have related denotations but very different connotations:

> *pride:* sense of self-worth
> *vanity:* excessive regard for oneself

> *firm:* steady, unchanging, unyielding
> *stubborn:* unreasonable, bullheaded

> *lasting:* long-lived, enduring
> *endless:* without limit, eternal

> *enthusiasm:* excitement
> *mania:* excessive interest or desire

A dictionary can help you track down words with the exact connotations you want. Besides providing meanings, your dictionary may also list and distinguish synonyms to guide your choices. A thesaurus can also help if you use it carefully, as discussed on the previous page.

exact
18b

Exercise 18.3   Revising: Denotation

In the following sentences, revise any underlined word that is used incorrectly. Consult a dictionary if you are uncertain of a word's meaning.

Example:

Sam and Dave are going to Bermuda and Hauppage, respectfully, for spring vacation.

Sam and Dave are going to Bermuda and Hauppage, respectively, for spring vacation.

1. Maxine Hong Kingston was rewarded many prizes for her first two books, *The Woman Warrior* and *China Men*.

2. Kingston <u>sites</u> her mother's tales about ancestors and ancient Chinese customs as the sources of these memoirs.

3. Two of Kingston's <u>progeny</u>, her great-grandfathers, are focal points of *China Men.*

4. Both men led rebellions against <u>suppressive</u> employers: a sugar-cane farmer and a railroad-construction engineer.

5. In her childhood Kingston was greatly <u>effected</u> by her mother's tale about a pregnant aunt who was <u>ostracized</u> by villagers.

6. The aunt gained <u>avengeance</u> by drowning herself in the village's water supply.

7. Kingston decided to make her nameless relative <u>infamous</u> by giving her <u>immortality</u> in *The Woman Warrior.*

8. Kingston's novel *Tripmaster Monkey* has been called the <u>premier</u> novel about the 1960s.

9. Her characters <u>embody</u> the <u>principles</u> that led to her own protest against the Vietnam War.

10. Kingston's innovative books <u>infer</u> her opposition to racism and sexism both in the China of the past and in the United States of the present.

Exercise 18.4   Considering the connotations of words

Fill in the blank in each sentence below with the most appropriate word from the list in parentheses. Consult a dictionary to be sure of your choices.

Example:

Channel 5 _____ Oshu the winner before the polls closed. (*advertised, declared, broadcast, promulgated*)

Channel 5 <u>declared</u> Oshu the winner before the polls closed.

1. AIDS is a serious health _____. (*problem, worry, difficulty, plight*)

2. Once the virus has entered the blood system, it _____ T-cells. (*murders, destroys, slaughters, executes*)

3. The _____ of T-cells is to combat infections. (*ambition, function, aim, goal*)

4. Without enough T-cells, the body is nearly _____ against infections. (*defenseless, hopeless, desperate*)

5. To prevent exposure to the disease, one should be especially _____ in sexual relationships. (*chary, circumspect, cautious, calculating*)

3 ▪ Concrete and specific words

Clear, exact writing balances abstract and general words, which outline ideas and objects, with concrete and specific words, which sharpen and solidify.

▪ **Abstract words** name ideas: *beauty, inflation, management, culture, liberal.* **Concrete words** name qualities and things we can know by our five senses of sight, hearing, touch, taste, and smell: *sleek, humming, rough, salty, musty.*

- **General words** name classes or groups of things, such as *buildings, weather,* or *birds,* and include all the varieties of the class. **Specific words** limit a general class, such as *buildings,* by naming one of its varieties, such as *skyscraper* or *my house on Emerald Street.*

Abstract and general words are useful in the broad statements that set the course for your writing:

> The wild horse in America has a <u>romantic</u> history.
>
> <u>Relations</u> between the sexes today are more <u>relaxed</u> than they were in the past.

But such statements need development with concrete and specific detail. Detail can turn a vague sentence into an exact one:

> **Vague**   The size of his hands made his smallness real. [How big were his hands? How small was he?]
>
> **Exact**   Not until I saw his delicate, doll-like hands did I realize that he stood a full head shorter than most other men.

Note If you write on a computer, you can use its Find function to help you find and revise abstract and general words that you tend to overuse. Examples of such words include *nice, interesting, things, very, good, a lot, a little,* and *some.*

Exercise 18.5   Revising: Concrete and specific words

Make the following paragraph vivid by expanding the sentences with appropriate details of your own choosing. Substitute concrete and specific words for the abstract and general ones that are underlined.

I remember <u>clearly</u> how <u>awful</u> I felt the first time I <u>attended</u> Mrs. Murphy's second-grade class. I had <u>recently</u> moved from a <u>small</u> town in Missouri to a <u>crowded</u> suburb of Chicago. My new school <u>looked</u> <u>big</u> from the outside and seemed <u>dark</u> inside as I <u>walked</u> down the <u>long</u> corridor toward the classroom. The class was <u>noisy</u> as I neared the door; but when I <u>entered</u>, <u>everyone</u> became <u>quiet</u> and <u>looked</u> at me. I felt <u>uncomfortable</u> and <u>wanted</u> a place to hide. However, in a <u>loud</u> voice Mrs. Murphy <u>directed</u> me to the front of the room to introduce myself.

---

4 ▪ Idioms

Idioms are expressions in any language that do not fit the rules for meaning or grammar—for instance, *put up with, plug away at, make off with.*

Idioms that involve prepositions can be especially confusing for both native and nonnative speakers of English. Some idioms with prepositions are listed in the following box. (More appear on pp. 219–20.)

Idioms with prepositions

abide by a rule
    in a place or state
according to
accords with
accuse of a crime
accustomed to
adapt from a source
    to a situation
afraid of
agree on a plan
    to a proposal
    with a person
angry with
aware of
based on
capable of
certain of
charge for a purchase
    with a crime
concur in an opinion
    with a person
contend for a principle
    with a person
dependent on
differ about or over a question
    from in some quality
    with a person
disappointed by or in a person
    in or with a thing
familiar with
famous for

identical with or to
impatient for a raise
    with a person
independent of
infer from
inferior to
involved in a task
    with a person
oblivious of or to one's surroundings
    of something forgotten
occupied by a person
    in study
    with a thing
opposed to
part from a person
    with a possession
prior to
proud of
related to
rewarded by the judge
    for something done
    with a gift
similar to
sorry about an error
    for a person
superior to
tired of
wait at, beside, by, under a place or
    thing
    for a train, a person
    in a room
    on a customer

exact
18b

CULTURE LANGUAGE   If you are learning standard American English, you may find its prepositions difficult: their meanings can shift depending on context, and they have many idiomatic uses. In mastering English prepositions, you probably can't avoid memorization. But you can help yourself by memorizing related groups, such as *at/in/on* and *for/since*:

At, in, or *on* in expressions of time

- Use *at* before actual clock time: <u>at</u> *8:30.*
- Use *in* before a month, year, century, or period: <u>in</u> *April,* <u>in</u> *2018,* <u>in</u> *the twenty-first century,* <u>in</u> *the next month.*
- Use *on* before a day or date: <u>on</u> *Tuesday,* <u>on</u> *August 3,* <u>on</u> *Labor Day.*

At, in, or *on* in expressions of place

- Use *at* before a specific place or address: <u>at</u> *the school,* <u>at</u> *511 Iris Street.*
- Use *in* before a place with limits or before a city, state, country, or continent: <u>in</u> *the house,* <u>in</u> *a box,* <u>in</u> *Oklahoma City,* <u>in</u> *China,* <u>in</u> *Asia.*
- Use *on* to mean "supported by" or "touching the surface of": <u>on</u> *the table,* <u>on</u> *Iris Street,* <u>on</u> *page 150.*

For or *since* in expressions of time

- Use *for* before a period of time: <u>for</u> *an hour,* <u>for</u> *two years.*
- Use *since* before a specific point in time: <u>since</u> *1999,* <u>since</u> *Friday.*

exact

18b

A dictionary of English as a second language is the best source for the meanings of prepositions; see the suggestions on page 167.

Exercise 18.6   Using prepositions in idioms

In the sentences below, insert the preposition that correctly completes each idiom. Consult the box on the previous page or a dictionary as needed.

Example:

I disagree _____ many feminists who say women should not be homemakers.

I disagree <u>with</u> many feminists who say women should not be homemakers.

1. Children are waiting longer to become independent _____ their parents.
2. According _____ US Census data for young adults ages eighteen to twenty-four, 57% of men and 47% of women live full-time with their parents.
3. Some of these adult children are dependent _____ their parents financially.
4. In other cases, the parents charge their children _____ housing, food, and other living expenses.
5. Many adult children are financially capable _____ living independently but prefer to save money rather than contend _____ high housing costs.

Exercise 18.7   Using prepositions in idioms   ⬭ CULTURE LANGUAGE

Complete the following sentences by filling in the blanks with the appropriate prepositions from this list: *at, by, for, from, in, of, on, to, with.*

Example:

The most recent amendment to the US Constitution, ratified
_____ May 18, 1992, was first proposed _____ 1789.

The most recent amendment to the US Constitution, ratified <u>on</u>
May 18, 1992, was first proposed <u>in</u> 1789.

1. The Eighteenth Amendment _____ the Constitution _____ the
   United States was ratified _____ 1919.
2. It prohibited the "manufacture, sale, or transportation _____ in-
   toxicating liquors."
3. It was adopted _____ response _____ a nationwide crusade
   _____ temperance groups.
4. The amendment did not prevent Americans _____ drinking, and
   the sale _____ alcoholic beverages was taken over _____ organized crime.
5. Wide-scale smuggling and bootlegging came _____ the demand
   _____ liquor.

5 ▪ Figurative language

Figurative language (or a **figure of speech**) departs from the literal meanings of words, usually by comparing very different ideas or
objects:

Literal   As I try to write, I can think of nothing to say.
Figurative   As I try to write, <u>my mind is a slab of black slate.</u>

Imaginatively and carefully used, figurative language can capture
meaning more precisely and emotionally than literal language. Here
is a figure of speech at work in technical writing (paraphrasing the
physicist Edward Andrade):

The molecules in a liquid move continuously like couples on an overcrowded dance floor, jostling each other.

The two most common figures of speech are the simile and the
metaphor. Both compare two things of different classes, often one
abstract and the other concrete.

▪ **A *simile* stresses the comparison.** It usually begins with *like* or *as*:

Whenever we grow, we tend to feel it, <u>as</u> a young seed must feel the
weight and inertia of the earth when it <u>seeks</u> to break out of its shell on
its way to becoming a plant.   —Alice Walker

▪ **A *metaphor* claims that the two things are identical.** It omits such
words as *like* and *as*:

A school is a hopper into which children are heaved while they are
young and tender; therein they are pressed into certain standard shapes
and covered from head to heels with official rubber stamps.
                                                    —H. L. Mencken

Successful figurative language is fresh and unstrained, calling attention not to itself but to the writer's meaning. Be wary of mixed metaphors, which combine two or more incompatible figures:

Mixed   Various thorny problems that we try to sweep under the rug continue to bob up all the same.

Improved   Various thorny problems that we try to weed out continue to thrive all the same.

Exercise 18.8   Using figurative language

Invent appropriate similes or metaphors of your own to describe each scene or quality below, and use the figure in a sentence.

Example:

The attraction of a lake on a hot day
The small waves like fingers beckoned us irresistibly.

1. The sound of a kindergarten classroom
2. People waiting in line to buy tickets to a rock concert
3. The politeness of strangers meeting for the first time
4. A streetlight seen through dense fog
5. The effect of watching television for ten hours straight

exact
18b

6 ▪ Trite expressions

Trite expressions, or **clichés,** are phrases so old and so often repeated that they have become stale. They include the following:

add insult to injury	needle in a haystack
better late than never	point with pride
crushing blow	pride and joy
easier said than done	ripe old age
face the music	rude awakening
few and far between	sadder but wiser
green with envy	shoulder the burden
hard as a rock	shoulder to cry on
heavy as lead	sneaking suspicion
hit the nail on the head	stand in awe
hour of need	thin as a rail
ladder of success	tried and true
moving experience	wise as an owl

To edit clichés, listen to your writing for any expressions that you have heard or used before. You can also try using a style checker, which may flag clichés. When you find a cliché, substitute fresh words of your own or restate the idea in plain language.

Exercise 18.9   Revising: Trite expressions

Revise the following sentences to eliminate trite expressions.

Example:

The basketball team had almost seized victory, but it faced the test of truth in the last quarter of the game.

The basketball team <u>seemed about to win</u>, but the <u>real test</u> came in the last quarter of the game.

1. The disastrous consequences of the war have shaken the small nation to its roots.
2. Prices for food have shot sky high, and citizens have sneaking suspicions that others are making a killing on the black market.
3. Medical supplies are so few and far between that even civilians who are as sick as dogs cannot get treatment.
4. With most men fighting or injured or killed, women have had to knuckle down and bear the men's burden in farming and manufacturing.
5. Last but not least, the war's heavy drain on the nation's pocketbook has left the economy in shambles.
6. Our reliance on foreign oil to support our driving habit has hit record highs in recent years.
7. Gas-guzzling vehicles are responsible for part of the increase.
8. In the future, we may have to bite the bullet and use public transportation or drive only fuel-efficient cars.
9. Both solutions are easier said than done.
10. But it stands to reason that we cannot go on using the world's oil reserves at such a rapid rate.

inc
19a

19 Completeness

In *Brief*

- Write complete compounds (below).
- Add needed words (next page).

Visit MyWritingLab™ for more resources on completeness.

Sometimes, omitting even a little word like *of* or *in* can make a sentence unclear. In editing, check your sentences to be sure you've included all the words they need. For additional help with complete sentences, see Chapter 35 on sentence fragments.

19a   Write complete compounds.

A **compound construction** combines words that are closely related and equally important. You may omit words from a compound construction when the omission will not confuse readers:

Environmentalists have hopes for alternative fuels and [for] public transportation.

Some automobiles will run on electricity and some [will run] on hydrogen.

Such omissions are possible only when the words omitted are common to all the parts of a compound construction. When the parts differ in any way, all words must be included in all parts.

> One new hybrid car g̲e̲ts eighty miles per gallon; some old cars g̲e̲t as little as five miles per g̲allon. [One verb is singular, the other plural.]

> Environmentalists believe i̲n̲ and work f̲o̲r fuel conservation. [Idiom requires different prepositions with *believe* and *work*.]

19b Add needed words.

In haste or carelessness, do not omit small words that are needed for clarity:

Incomplete	Regular payroll deductions are a type painless savings. You hardly notice missing amounts, and after period of years the contributions can add a large total.
Revised	Regular payroll deductions are a type o̲f̲ painless savings. You hardly notice t̲h̲e̲ missing amounts, and after a̲ period of years the contributions can add u̲p̲ t̲o̲ a large total.

inc
19b

Attentive proofreading is the only insurance against this kind of omission. *Proofread all your papers carefully*. See page 40 for proofreading suggestions.

CULTURE LANGUAGE If your native language is not English, you may have difficulty knowing when to use the English articles *a, an,* and *the.* For guidelines on using articles, see pages 260–62.

Exercise 19.1 Revising: Completeness

Add words to the following sentences so that the sentences are complete and clear.

Example:
The fruit this plant is edible.
The fruit o̲f̲ this plant is edible.

1. The first ice cream, eaten China in about 2000 BC, was lumpier than modern ice cream.
2. The Chinese made their ice cream of milk, spices, and overcooked rice and packed in snow to solidify.
3. In the fourteenth century ice milk and fruit ices appeared in Italy and the tables of the wealthy.
4. At her wedding in 1533 to the king of France, Catherine de Médicis offered several flavors fruit ices.
5. Modern sherbets resemble her ices; modern ice cream her soft dessert of thick, sweetened cream.

20 Conciseness

In *Brief*

- Focus on the subject and verb (below).
- Cut empty words and unneeded repetition (next two pages).
- Tighten modifiers (p. 180).
- Revise *there is* or *it is* constructions (p. 180).
- Combine sentences (p. 180).
- Avoid jargon (p. 181).

Visit MyWritingLab™ for more resources on conciseness.

Concise writing makes every word count. Conciseness is not the same as mere brevity: detail and originality should not be cut with needless words. Rather, the length of an expression should be appropriate to the thought.

You may find yourself writing wordily when you are unsure of your subject or when your thoughts are tangled. It's fine, even necessary, to stumble and grope while drafting. But you should straighten out your ideas and eliminate wordiness during revision and editing. CULTURE LANGUAGE Wordiness is not a problem of incorrect grammar. A sentence may be perfectly grammatical but still contain unneeded words that make it unclear or awkward.

con
20a

20a Focus on the subject and verb.

Using the subjects and verbs of your sentences for the key actors and actions will reduce words and emphasize important ideas. (See pp. 142–43 for more on this topic.)

Wordy	The reason why most of the country shifts to daylight time is that summer days are much longer than winter days.
Concise	Most of the country shifts to daylight time because summer days are much longer than winter days.

Focusing on subjects and verbs will also help you avoid several other causes of wordiness discussed further on pages 142–43:

Nouns made from verbs

Wordy	The occurrence of the winter solstice, the shortest day of the year, is an event taking place about December 22.
Concise	The winter solstice, the shortest day of the year, occurs about December 22.

Weak verbs

Wordy	The earth's axis has a tilt as the planet is in orbit around the sun so that the northern and southern hemispheres are alternately in alignment toward the sun.

Ways to achieve conciseness

Wordy (87 words)

The highly pressured <u>nature</u> of critical-care nursing is <u>due to the fact that</u> the patients have life-threatening illnesses. Critical-care	Focus on subject and verb, and cut or shorten empty words and phrases.
nurses must have possession of steady nerves	Avoid nouns made from verbs.
to care for patients who are critically ill and	Cut unneeded repetition.
very sick. The nurses must also have posses-	Combine sentences.
sion of interpersonal skills. They must also have medical skills. It is considered by most	Change passive voice to active voice.
health-care professionals that these nurses are essential if there is to be improvement of	Eliminate *there is* constructions.
patients who are now in critical care from that status to the status of intermediate care.	Cut unneeded repetition, and reduce clauses and phrases.

con
20b

Concise (37 words)
Critical-care nursing is highly pressured because the patients have life-threatening illnesses. Critical-care nurses must possess steady nerves and interpersonal and medical skills. Most health-care professionals consider these nurses essential if patients are to improve to intermediate care.

Concise   The earth's axis <u>tilts</u> as the planet <u>orbits</u> around the sun so that the northern and southern hemispheres alternately <u>align</u> toward the sun.

Passive voice

Wordy   During its winter the northern hemisphere <u>is tilted</u> farthest away from the sun, so the nights <u>are made</u> longer and the days <u>are made</u> shorter.

Concise   During its winter the northern hemisphere <u>tilts</u> away from the sun, which <u>makes</u> the nights longer and the days shorter.

See also pages 230–32 on active and passive voice.

20b   Cut empty words.

Empty words walk in place, gaining little or nothing in meaning. Many of them can be cut entirely. The following are just a few examples:

all things considered	for all intents and purposes
as far as I'm concerned	for the most part

in a manner of speaking   last but not least
in my opinion   more or less

Other empty words can also be cut, usually along with some of the words around them:

angle	character	kind	situation
area	element	manner	thing
aspect	factor	nature	type
case	field		

Still others can be reduced from several words to a single word:

For	Substitute
at all times	always
at the present time	now, yet
because of the fact that	because
by virtue of the fact that	because
due to the fact that	because
for the purpose of	for
in order to	to
in the event that	if
in the final analysis	finally
in today's society	now

con
20c

Cutting or reducing such words and phrases will make your writing move faster and work harder:

Wordy   In my opinion, the council's proposal to improve the nature of the city center is inadequate, for the reason that it ignores pedestrians.

Concise   The council's proposal to improve the city center is inadequate, because it ignores pedestrians.

20c   Cut unneeded repetition.

Deliberate repetition and restatement can make writing more coherent by linking sentences (see p. 47). But unnecessary repetition weakens sentences:

Wordy   Many unskilled workers without training in a particular job are unemployed and do not have any work.

Concise   Many unskilled workers are unemployed.

Be especially alert to phrases that say the same thing twice. In the examples below, the unneeded words are underlined:

circle around	important [basic] essentials
consensus of opinion	puzzling in nature
cooperate together	repeat again
final completion	return again
frank and honest exchange	square [round] in shape
the future to come	surrounding circumstances

CULTURE LANGUAGE The preceding phrases are redundant because the main word already implies the underlined word or words. A dictionary will tell you what meanings a word implies. *Assassinate*, for instance, means "murder someone well known," so the following sentence is redundant: *Julius Caesar was <u>assassinated and killed</u> in 44 BCE.*

20d Tighten modifiers.

Modifiers can be expanded or contracted depending on the emphasis you want to achieve. When editing your sentences, consider whether any modifiers can be tightened without loss of emphasis or clarity.

Wordy   The weight-loss industry faces new competition from lipolysis, <u>which is</u> a cosmetic procedure <u>that is</u> relatively noninvasive.

Concise   The weight-loss industry faces new competition from lipolysis, <u>a relatively noninvasive cosmetic procedure.</u>

20e Revise *there is* and *it is* constructions.

You can postpone the sentence subject with the words *there* and *it*: *There are three points made in the text. It was not fair that only seniors could vote.* These **expletive constructions** can be useful to emphasize the subject (as when introducing it for the first time) or to indicate a change in direction. But often they just add words and weaken sentences:

Wordy   <u>There is</u> a completely noninvasive laser treatment <u>that</u> makes people thinner by rupturing fat cells and releasing the fat into the spaces between cells. <u>It is the expectation of some doctors</u> that the procedure will replace liposuction.

Concise   <u>A completely noninvasive laser treatment</u> makes people thinner by rupturing fat cells and releasing the fat into the spaces between cells. <u>Some doctors expect</u> that the procedure will replace liposuction.

CULTURE LANGUAGE When you must use an expletive construction, be careful to include *there* or *it*. Only commands and some questions can begin with verbs.

20f Combine sentences.

Often the information in two or more sentences can be combined into one tight sentence:

Wordy   People who receive fat-releasing laser treatments can lose inches from their waists. They can also lose inches from their

hips and thighs. They do not lose weight. The released fat
remains in their bodies.

Concise   People who receive fat-releasing laser treatments can lose
inches from their <u>waists, hips, and thighs;</u> <u>but</u> they do not
lose weight <u>because</u> the released fat remains in their bodies.

(See also p. 156 on combining sentences to achieve variety.)

20g Avoid jargon.

Jargon can refer to the special vocabulary of any discipline or profession (see p. 161). But it has also come to describe vague, inflated
language that is overcomplicated, even incomprehensible. When it
comes from government or business, we call it **bureaucratese**.

Jargon   The necessity for individuals to become separate entities in
their own right may impel children to engage in open re-
belliousness against parental authority or against sibling
influence, with resultant bewilderment of those being re-
belled against.

Translation Children's natural desire to become themselves may make
them rebel against bewildered parents or siblings.

Exercise 20.1   **Revising: Writing concisely**

Make the following sentences more concise.

Example:

It is thought by some people that there is gain from exercise only
when it involves pain.

<u>Some people think</u> that <u>gain comes</u> from exercise only <u>with</u> pain.

1. If sore muscles after exercising are a problem for you, there are
   some measures that can be taken by you to ease the discomfort.
2. First, the immediate application of cold will help to reduce
   inflammation.
3. Blood vessels are constricted by cold. Blood is kept away from the
   injured muscles.
4. It is advisable to avoid heat for the first day.
5. The application of heat within the first twenty-four hours can cause
   an increase in muscle soreness and stiffness.
6. There are two ways the application of cold can be made: you can
   take a cold shower or use an ice pack.
7. Inflammation of muscles can also be reduced with aspirin, ibupro-
   fen, or another anti-inflammatory medication.
8. There is the idea that muscle soreness can be worsened by power
   lifting.
9. While healing is occurring, you need to take it easy.
10. A day or two after overdoing exercise, it is advisable for you to get
    some light exercise and gentle massage.

co

20g

Exercise 20.2   Revising: Conciseness
Make the following paragraph as concise as possible. Be merciless.

At the end of a lengthy line of reasoning, he came to the conclusion that the situation with carcinogens [cancer-causing substances] should be regarded as similar to the situation with the automobile. Instead of giving in to an irrational fear of cancer, we should consider all aspects of the problem in a balanced and dispassionate frame of mind, making a total of the benefits received from potential carcinogens (plastics, pesticides, and other similar products) and measuring said total against the damage done by such products. This is the nature of most discussions about the automobile. Instead of responding irrationally to the visual, aural, and air pollution caused by automobiles, we have decided to live with them (while simultaneously working to improve on them) for the benefits brought to society as a whole.

PART 4

Sentence Parts and Patterns

21 Parts of Speech

In *Brief*

- Learn to recognize nouns and pronouns (below and opposite).
- Learn to recognize verbs (opposite).
- Learn to recognize adjectives and adverbs (p. 187).
- Learn to recognize prepositions, conjunctions, and interjections (pp. 188, 190).

Visit MyWritingLab™ for more resources on parts of speech.

All English words fall into eight groups, or **parts of speech,** such as nouns, verbs, adjectives, and adverbs. A word's part of speech determines its form and its position in a sentence. The same word may even serve as different parts of speech in different sentences, as these examples show:

> The government sent aid to the city. [*Aid* is a noun.]
> Governments aid citizens. [*Aid* is a verb.]

The *function* of a word in a sentence always determines its part of speech in that sentence.

21a Learn to recognize nouns.

Nouns name. They may name a person (*Helen Mirren, Jay-Z, astronaut*), a thing (*chair, book, Mt. Rainier*), a quality (*pain, mystery, simplicity*), a place (*city, Washington, ocean, Red Sea*), or an idea (*reality, peace, success*).

The forms of nouns depend partly on where they fit in certain groups, such as those following. As the examples indicate, the same noun may appear in more than one group.

- **Common nouns** name general classes of things and do not begin with capital letters: *dog, citizen, earth, fortitude, army.*
- **Proper nouns** name specific people, places, and things and begin with capital letters: *Angelina Jolie, Washington Monument, El Paso, US Congress.*
- **Count nouns** name things considered countable in English. Most add *-s* or *-es* to distinguish between singular (one) and plural (more than one): *citizen, citizens; city, cities.* Some count nouns form irregular plurals: *woman, women; child, children.*
- **Noncount nouns** name things that aren't considered countable in English (*earth, sugar*), or they name qualities (*chaos, fortitude*). Noncount nouns do not form plurals.

■ **Collective nouns** are singular in form but name groups: *army, family, herd, US Congress.*

In addition, most nouns form the **possessive** by adding -*'s* to show ownership (*Nadia's books, citizen's rights*), source (*Auden's poems*), and some other relationships.

21b Learn to recognize pronouns.

Most **pronouns** substitute for nouns and function in sentences as nouns do: *Susanne Ling enlisted in the Navy when she graduated.*

Pronouns fall into several subclasses depending on their form or function:

■ **Personal pronouns** refer to a specific individual or to individuals: *I, you, he, she, it, we,* and *they.* (See p. 240 for the forms of personal pronouns.)

■ **Indefinite pronouns,** such as *everybody* and *some,* do not substitute for any specific nouns, though they function as nouns (*Everybody speaks*).

■ **Relative pronouns**—*who, whoever, which, that*—relate groups of words to nouns or other pronouns (*The book that won is a novel*). (See p. 240 for the forms of relative pronouns.)

■ **Interrogative pronouns,** such as *who, which,* and *what,* introduce questions (*Who will contribute?*).

■ **Demonstrative pronouns,** including *this, that,* and *such,* identify or point to nouns (*This is the problem*).

■ **Intensive pronouns**—a personal pronoun plus -*self* or -*selves* (*himself, ourselves*)—emphasize a noun or other pronoun (*He himself asked that question*).

■ **Reflexive pronouns** have the same form as intensive pronouns but indicate that the sentence subject also receives the action of the verb (*They injured themselves*).

The personal pronouns *I, he, she, we,* and *they* and the relative pronouns *who* and *whoever* change form depending on their function in the sentence. (See Chapter 30.)

gram
21c

21c Learn to recognize verbs.

Verbs express an action (*bring, change, grow, consider*), an occurrence (*become, happen, occur*), or a state of being (*be, seem, remain*).

1 ■ Forms of verbs

Verbs have five distinctive forms. If the form can change as described in the following list, the word is a verb:

- **Plain form:** *love, forget.*
- **-s form:** *loves, forgets.*
- **Past-tense form:** *loved* (regular verb), *forgot* (irregular verb).
- **Past participle:** *loved* (regular verb), *forgotten* (irregular verb).
- **Present participle:** *loving, forgetting.*

The verb *be* has eight forms rather than five: *be, am, is, are, was, were, been, being.*

See pages 206–12 for more on verb forms and regular vs. irregular verbs.

2 ▪ Helping verbs

Some verb forms combine with **helping verbs** to indicate time, possibility, obligation, necessity, and other kinds of meaning: *can run, was sleeping, had been working.* In these **verb phrases** *run, sleeping,* and *working* are **main verbs**—they carry the principal meaning.

<table>
<tr><td colspan="2" align="center">**Verb phrase**</td></tr>
<tr><td>*Helping*</td><td>*Main*</td></tr>
<tr><td>Artists can</td><td><u>train</u> others to draw.</td></tr>
<tr><td>The techniques <u>have</u></td><td><u>changed</u> little.</td></tr>
</table>

The most common helping verbs are listed in the box below. See pages 212–16 for more on helping verbs.

Common helping verbs

Forms of *be*: be, am, is, are, was, were, been, being
Forms of *have*: have, has, had, having
Forms of *do*: do, does, did

be able to	could	may	ought to	used to
be supposed to	had better	might	shall	will
can	have to	must	should	would

Exercise 21.1   **Identifying nouns, pronouns, and verbs**
Identify the words that function as nouns (N), pronouns (P), and verbs (V) in the following sentences.

Example:

$$\underset{\text{Ancestors}}{\text{N}} \text{ of the gingko } \underset{\text{tree}}{\text{N}} \underset{\text{lived}}{\text{V}} \text{ 175 to 200 million } \underset{\text{years}}{\text{N}} \text{ ago.}$$

1. The gingko tree, which is one of the world's oldest trees, is large and picturesque.
2. Gingko trees may grow to over a hundred feet in height.
3. Their leaves look like fans and are about three inches wide.
4. The leaves turn yellow in the fall.
5. Because it tolerates smoke, low temperatures, and low rainfall, the gingko appears in many cities.

6. A shortcoming, however, is the foul odor of its fruit.
7. Inside the fruit is a large white seed, which some people value as food.
8. The fruit often does not appear until the tree is mature.
9. The tree's name means "apricot" in the Japanese language.
10. Originally, the gingko grew only in China, but it has now spread throughout the world.

21d Learn to recognize adjectives and adverbs.

Adjectives describe or modify nouns and pronouns. They specify which one, what quality, or how many.

old	city	generous	one	two	pears
adjective	noun	adjective	pronoun	adjective	noun

Adverbs describe or modify verbs, adjectives, other adverbs, and whole groups of words. They specify when, where, how, and to what extent.

nearly	destroyed		too	quickly
adverb	verb		adverb	adverb

very	generous	Unfortunately,	taxes will rise.
adverb	adjective	adverb	word group

An *-ly* ending often signals an adverb, but not always: *friendly* is an adjective; *never* is an adverb. The only way to tell whether a word is an adjective or an adverb is to determine what it modifies.

Adjectives and adverbs appear in three forms: **positive** (*green, angrily*), **comparative** (*greener, more angrily*), and **superlative** (*greenest, most angrily*).

See Chapter 33 for more on adjectives and adverbs.

gr
21d

Exercise 21.2 Identifying adjectives and adverbs

Identify the adjectives (ADJ) and adverbs (ADV) in the following sentences. Mark *a, an,* and *the* as adjectives.

Example:

ADV
Stress can hit people when they least expect it.

1. You can reduce stress by making a few simple changes.
2. Get up fifteen minutes earlier than you ordinarily do.
3. Eat a healthy breakfast, and eat it slowly so that you enjoy it.
4. Do your more unpleasant tasks early in the day.
5. Every day, do at least one thing you really enjoy.
6. If waiting in lines is stressful for you, carry something to read when you know you'll have to wait.
7. Make promises sparingly and keep them faithfully.
8. Plan ahead to prevent the most stressful situations.
9. For example, carry spare keys so you won't be locked out of your car or house.
10. See a doctor and a dentist regularly.

21e   Learn to recognize connecting words: Prepositions and conjunctions.

Connecting words are mostly small words that link parts of sentences. They never change form.

1 ■ Prepositions

Prepositions form nouns or pronouns (plus any modifiers) into word groups called **prepositional phrases**: *about* love, *down the stairs*. These phrases usually serve as modifiers in sentences, as in *The plants trailed down the stairs*. (See also p. 198.)

Common prepositions

about	before	except for	of	throughout
above	behind	excepting	off	till
according to	below	for	on	to
across	beneath	from	onto	toward
after	beside	in	on top of	under
against	between	in addition to	out	underneath
along	beyond	inside	out of	unlike
along with	by	inside of	outside	until
among	concerning	in spite of	over	up
around	despite	instead of	past	upon
as	down	into	regarding	up to
aside from	due to	like	round	with
at	during	near	since	within
because of	except	next to	through	without

CULTURE LANGUAGE The meanings and uses of English prepositions can be difficult to master. See pages 170–72 for a discussion of prepositions in idioms, such as *proud of* and *angry with*. See pages 219–20 for two-word verbs that include prepositions, such as *look after* and *look up*.

2 ■ Subordinating conjunctions

Subordinating conjunctions form sentences into word groups called **subordinate clauses**, such as *when the meeting ended*. These clauses serve as parts of sentences: *Everyone was relieved when the meeting ended*. (See pp. 201–03 for more on subordinate clauses.)

Common subordinating conjunctions

after	as	as long as	because
although	as if	as though	before

even if	once	that	whenever
even though	provided	though	where
if	rather than	till	whereas
if only	since	unless	wherever
in order that	so that	until	whether
now that	than	when	while

CULTURE LANGUAGE Learning the meanings of subordinating conjunctions can help you to express your ideas clearly. Note that each one conveys its meaning on its own. It does not need help from another function word, such as the coordinating conjunctions *and, but, for,* or *so*:

Faulty	Even though the parents cannot read, but their children may read well. [*Even though* and *but* have the same meaning, so both are not needed.]
Revised	Even though the parents cannot read, their children may read well.

3 ▪ Coordinating and correlative conjunctions

Coordinating and correlative conjunctions connect words or word groups of the same kind, such as nouns, adjectives, or sentences.

Coordinating conjunctions consist of a single word:

Coordinating conjunctions

and	nor	for	yet
but	or	so	

Dieting or exercise alone is not enough for most people to maintain a healthy weight.

Dieting takes discipline, but exercise takes discipline and time.

Correlative conjunctions are combinations of coordinating conjunctions and other words:

Common correlative conjunctions

both . . . and	neither . . . nor
not only . . . but also	whether . . . or
not . . . but	as . . . as
either . . . or	

Both a balanced diet and regular exercise are necessary to maintain a healthy weight.

Neither diet nor exercise alone will substantially improve a person's health.

Exercise 21.3   Adding connecting words

Fill each blank in the following sentences with the appropriate connecting word: a preposition, a subordinating conjunction, or a coordinating conjunction. Consult the lists on the previous two pages if you need help.

Example:

A Trojan priest warned, "Beware _____ Greeks bearing gifts." (*preposition*)

A Trojan priest warned, "Beware of Greeks bearing gifts."

1. Just about everyone has heard the story _____ the Trojan Horse. (*preposition*)
2. This incident happened at the city of Troy _____ was planned by the Greeks. (*coordinating conjunction*)
3. The Greeks built a huge wooden horse _____ a hollow space big enough to hold many men. (*preposition*)
4. At night, they rolled the horse to the gate of Troy _____ left it there filled with soldiers. (*coordinating conjunction*)
5. _____ the morning, the Trojans were surprised to see the enormous horse. (*preposition*)
6. They were amazed _____ they saw that the Greeks were gone. (*subordinating conjunction*)
7. _____ they were curious to examine this gift from the Greeks, they dragged the horse into the city and left it outside the temple. (*subordinating conjunction*)
8. In the middle of the night, the hidden Greeks emerged _____ the horse and began setting fires all over town. (*preposition*)
9. _____ the Trojan soldiers awoke and came out of their houses, the Greeks killed them one by one. (*subordinating conjunction*)
10. By the next morning, the Trojan men were dead _____ the women were slaves to the Greeks. (*coordinating conjunction*)

21f   Learn to recognize interjections.

Interjections express feeling or command attention. They are rarely used in academic or business writing.

Oh, the meeting went fine.
They won seven thousand dollars! Wow!

22 The Sentence

In *Brief*

- Learn to recognize subjects and predicates (below).
- Learn the basic predicate patterns (p. 193).
- Learn alternative sentence patterns (p. 195).

Visit MyWritingLab™ for more resources on the sentence.

The **sentence** is the basic unit of expression, forming a complete thought. Its subject and predicate usually name an actor and an action.

22a Learn to recognize subjects and predicates.

Most sentences make statements. First the **subject** names something; then the **predicate** makes an assertion about the subject or describes an action by the subject.

Subject	Predicate
Art	thrives.

The **simple subject** consists of one or more nouns or pronouns, whereas the **complete subject** also includes any modifiers. The **simple predicate** consists of one or more verbs, whereas the **complete predicate** adds any words needed to complete the meaning of the verb plus any modifiers.

Sometimes, as in the short example *Art thrives,* the simple and complete subject and predicate are the same. More often, they are different:

Subject	Predicate
┌──────complete──────┐	┌──complete──┐
simple	simple
Some contemporary <u>art</u>	<u>stirs</u> controversy.
┌──────complete──────┐	┌──────complete──────┐
◄─simple─►	◄─simple─►
<u>Critics</u> and the <u>media</u>	<u>discuss</u> and <u>dispute</u> its value.

In the second example, the simple subject and simple predicate are both **compound:** in each, two words joined by a coordinating conjunction (*and*) serve the same function.

> **CULTURE LANGUAGE** The subject of an English sentence may be a noun (*art*) or a pronoun that refers to the noun (*it*), but not both. (See p. 285.)

Faulty	<u>Art</u> it can stir controversy.
Revised	<u>Art</u> can stir controversy.
Revised	<u>It</u> can stir controversy.

Tests to find subjects and predicates

The tests below use the following example:

> Art that makes it into museums has often survived controversy.

Identify the subject.

■ Ask *who* or *what* is acting or being described in the sentence.

Complete subject   art that makes it into museums

■ **Isolate the simple subject by deleting modifiers**—words or word groups that don't name the actor of the sentence but give information about it. In the example, the word group *that makes it into museums* does not name the actor but modifies it.

Simple subject   art

Identify the predicate.

■ **Ask what the sentence asserts about the subject:** what is its action, or what state is it in? In the example, the assertion about *art* is that it *has often survived controversy.*

Complete predicate   has often survived controversy

■ **Isolate the verb, the simple predicate, by changing the time of the subject's action.** The simple predicate is the word or words that change as a result.

Example	Art . . . has often survived controversy.
Present	Art . . . often survives controversy.
Future	Art . . . will often survive controversy.
Simple predicate	has survived

When identifying the subject and the predicate of a sentence, be aware that some English words can serve as both nouns and verbs. For example, *visits* in the following sentences functions as a verb and as a noun:

> She visits the museum every Saturday. [Verb.]
> Her visits are enjoyable. [Noun.]

Note If a sentence contains a word group such as *that makes it into museums* or *because viewers agree about its quality,* you may be tempted to mark the subject and verb in the word group as the subject and verb of the sentence. But these word groups are subordinate clauses, made into modifiers by the words they begin with: *that* and *because.* Subordinate clauses are not sentences. See pages 201–03 for more on these clauses.

Identifying subjects and predicates

In the following sentences, insert a line between the complete subject and the complete predicate. Underline each simple subject once and each simple predicate twice.

Example:

The pony, the light <u>horse</u>, and the draft <u>horse</u> | <u><u>are</u></u> the three main types of domestic horses.

1. The horse has a long history of service to humanity but today is mainly a show and sport animal.
2. A member of the genus *Equus*, the domestic horse shares its lineage with the ass and the zebra.
3. The domestic horse and its relatives are all plains-dwelling herd animals.
4. The modern horse evolved in North America.
5. It migrated to other parts of the world and then became extinct in the Americas.
6. The Spaniards reintroduced the domestic horse to the Americas.
7. North American wild horses are actually descended from escaped domestic horses.
8. An average-sized adult horse may require twenty-six pounds or more of pasture feed or hay per day.
9. According to records, North Americans hunted and domesticated horses as early as four to five thousand years ago.
10. The earliest ancestor of the modern horse may have been eohippus, approximately 55 million years ago.

22b Learn the basic predicate patterns.

English sentences usually follow one of five patterns, each differing in the complete predicate (the verb and any words following it).

(CULTURE LANGUAGE) Word order in English sentences may not correspond to word order in the sentences of your native language or dialect. For instance, some other languages prefer the verb first in the sentence, whereas English strongly prefers the subject first.

Pattern 1: The earth trembled.

In the simplest pattern the predicate consists only of an **intransitive verb,** a verb that does not require a following word to complete its meaning.

Subject	Predicate
	Intransitive verb
The earth	trembled.
The hospital	may close.

Pattern 2: The earthquake destroyed the city.

In pattern 2 the verb is followed by a **direct object,** a noun or pronoun that identifies who or what receives the action of the verb. A verb that requires a direct object to complete its meaning is called **transitive**.

Subject	Predicate	
	Transitive verb	*Direct object*
The earthquake	destroyed	the city.
Education	opens	doors.

CULTURE LANGUAGE Only transitive verbs can be used in the passive voice, when the subject names the receiver of the verb's action: *The city was destroyed by the earthquake.* Your dictionary says whether a verb is transitive or intransitive, often with an abbreviation such as *tr.* or *intr.* Some verbs (*begin, learn, read, write,* and others) can be either transitive or intransitive.

Pattern 3: The result was chaos.

In pattern 3 the verb is followed by a **subject complement**, a word that renames or describes the subject. A verb in this pattern is called a **linking verb** because it links its subject to the description following. The linking verbs include *be, seem, appear, become, grow, remain, stay, prove, feel, look, smell, sound,* and *taste.* Subject complements are usually nouns or adjectives.

Subject	Predicate	
	Linking verb	*Subject complement*
The result	was	chaos. [Noun.]
The man	became	an accountant. [Noun.]
The car	seems	expensive. [Adjective.]

gram
22b

Pattern 4: The government sent the city aid.

In pattern 4 the verb is followed by a direct object and an **indirect object**, a word identifying to or for whom the action of the verb is performed. The direct object and indirect object refer to different things, people, or places.

Subject	Predicate		
	Transitive verb	*Indirect object*	*Direct object*
The government	sent	the city	aid.
One company	offered	its employees	bonuses.

A number of verbs can take indirect objects, including *allow, bring, buy, deny, find, get, give, leave, make, offer, pay, read, sell, send, show, teach,* and *write.*

CULTURE LANGUAGE With some verbs that express action done to or for someone, the indirect object must be turned into a phrase beginning with *to* or *for*. In addition, the phrase must come after the direct object. The verbs that require these changes include *admit, announce, demonstrate, explain, introduce, mention, prove, recommend, say,* and *suggest*.

indirect object   direct object

Faulty   The manual explains workers the new procedure.

direct object   *to* phrase

Revised   The manual explains the new procedure to workers.

Pattern 5: The citizens considered the earthquake a disaster.

In pattern 5 the verb is followed by a direct object and an **object complement**, a word that renames or describes the direct object. Object complements may be nouns or adjectives.

Subject	Predicate		
	Transitive verb	*Direct object*	*Object complement*
The citizens	considered	the earthquake	a disaster.
Success	makes	some people	nervous.

Exercise 22.2   Identifying sentence parts

In the following sentences identify the subject (S) and verb (V) as well as any direct objects (DO), indirect objects (IO), subject complements (SC), or object complements (OC).

Example:

S   V   V   DO

Crime statistics can cause surprise.

1. The number of serious crimes in the United States decreased.
2. A decline in serious crimes occurred each year.
3. The Crime Index measures serious crime.
4. The FBI invented the index.
5. The four serious violent crimes are murder, robbery, forcible rape, and aggravated assault.
6. The Crime Index calls auto theft, burglary, arson, and larceny-theft the four serious crimes against property.
7. The Crime Index gives the FBI a measure of crime.
8. The index shows trends in crimes and criminals.
9. The nation's largest cities showed the largest decline in crime.
10. However, crime actually increased in smaller cities, proving that the decline in crime is unrepresentative of the nation.

22c   Learn alternative sentence patterns.

Most English sentences first name the actor in the subject and then assert something about the actor in the predicate. But four kinds of sentences alter this basic pattern.

1 ▪ Questions

In most questions the predicate verb or a part of it precedes the subject:

<pre>
                                          sub-
  verb   subject ___verb___   verb ject verb
  Have interest rates been rising?   Why did rates rise today?
</pre>

<pre>
  subject verb
  What is the answer? [Normal subject-verb order.]
</pre>

2 ▪ Commands

Construct a command simply by deleting the subject of the sentence, *you*:

Think of options.   Eat your spinach.
Watch the news.   Leave me alone.

3 ▪ Passive sentences

In the basic subject-predicate pattern, the subject performs the action of the verb. The verb is in the **active voice**:

<pre>
             active
  subject   verb   object
  Kyong wrote the paper.
</pre>

In the **passive voice,** the subject *receives* the action of the verb:

<pre>
              passive
  subject   verb
  The paper was written by Kyong.
</pre>

In the passive voice, the object of the active verb (*paper*) becomes the subject of the passive verb.

Passive verbs always consist of a form of *be* plus the past participle of the main verb (*paper was written, absences were excused*). The actual actor (the person or thing performing the action of the verb) may be expressed in a phrase (as in the example above: *by Kyong*) or may be omitted entirely if it is unknown or unimportant: *The house was flooded.*

For more on the formation and uses of the passive voice, see pages 230–32.

4 ▪ Sentences with postponed subjects

Two kinds of sentences state the subject after the predicate. In one, the normal word order reverses for emphasis:

The cause of the problem lies here. [Normal order.]
Here lies the cause of the problem. [Reversed order.]

The second kind of sentence starts with *there* or *it* and postpones the subject:

> verb   subject
> There <u>will be</u> eighteen <u>people</u> at the meeting. [Normal order: *Eighteen people will be at the meeting.*]

> verb   subject
> It <u>was</u> surprising <u>that Marinetti was nominated</u>. [Normal order: *That Marinetti was nominated was surprising.*]

The words *there* and *it* in such sentences are **expletives**. Their only function is to postpone the sentence subject. Expletive sentences do have their uses (see p. 180), but they are often just wordy.

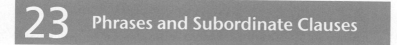 When you use an expletive construction, be careful to include *there* or *it*. Only commands and some questions can begin with verbs (see the previous page).

Faulty   No one predicted the nomination. Were no polls showing Marinetti ahead.

Revised No one predicted the nomination. <u>There</u> were no polls showing Marinetti ahead.

Exercise 22.3   Rewriting passives and expletives

Rewrite each passive sentence as active, and rewrite each expletive construction to restore normal subject-predicate order. For additional exercises with the passive voice and with expletives, see pages 143–44, 181, and 232.

> *Example:*
> All the trees in the park were planted by the city.
> <u>The city planted</u> all the trees in the park.

1. The screenplay for *Monster's Ball* was cowritten by Milo Addica and Will Rokos.
2. The film was directed by Marc Foster.
3. There was only one performance in the movie that received an Academy Award.
4. It was Halle Berry who won the award for best actress.
5. Berry was congratulated by the press for being the first African American to win the award.

---

23   Phrases and Subordinate Clauses

In *Brief*

- Learn to recognize phrases: prepositional, verbal, absolute, appositive (next page).
- Learn to recognize subordinate clauses (p. 201).

Visit MyWritingLab™ for more resources on phrases and subordinate clauses.

Most sentences contain word groups that serve as adjectives, adverbs, or nouns. These phrases and subordinate clauses add color and meaning to writing, but they cannot stand alone as complete sentences (see Chapter 35 on sentence fragments).

23a Learn to recognize phrases.

A **phrase** lacks either a subject or a predicate or both: *in a panic* (prepositional), *fearing an accident* (verbal), *alarms having sounded* (absolute), *night, that dark blanket* (appositive).

1 ▪ Prepositional phrases

A **prepositional phrase** consists of a preposition plus a noun, pronoun, or word group serving as a noun, called the **object of the preposition**. Prepositions include *about, at, by, for, to, under,* and *with*. A fuller list appears on page 188.

Preposition	Object
of	spaghetti
on	the surface
with	great satisfaction
upon	entering the room
from	where you are standing

Prepositional phrases usually function as adjectives or adverbs, adding details and making sentences more interesting for readers. An adjective phrase usually falls immediately after the word it modifies, but an adverb phrase need not.

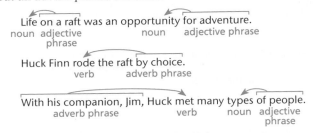

Life on a raft was an opportunity for adventure.
noun adjective   noun   adjective phrase
      phrase

Huck Finn rode the raft by choice.
              verb   adverb phrase

With his companion, Jim, Huck met many types of people.
     adverb phrase   verb   noun adjective
                                                 phrase

2 ▪ Verbal phrases

Certain forms of verbs, called **verbals,** can serve as modifiers or nouns. Often these verbals appear with their own modifiers and objects in **verbal phrases.**

Note A verbal is not a verb: it cannot serve as the complete verb of a sentence. *The sun rises over the dump* is a sentence; *The sun rising over the dump* is a sentence fragment. (See pp. 271–72.)

Participial phrases

Present participles end in *-ing*: *living, walking.* **Past participles** usually end in *-d* or *-ed*: *lived, walked.* **Participial phrases** are made from participles plus modifiers and objects. Participles and participial phrases usually serve as adjectives.

Strolling shoppers fill the malls.
participle   noun

They make selections determined by personal taste.
            noun   participial phrase

Note With irregular verbs, the past participle may have a different ending—for instance, *hidden funds.* (See pp. 207–09.)

CULTURE LANGUAGE The present and past participles of verbs that express feelings have different meanings. The present participle modifies the thing that causes the feeling: *It was a boring lecture.* The past participle modifies the thing that experiences the feeling: *The bored students slept.* (See p. 259.)

Gerund phrases

A **gerund** is the *-ing* form of a verb when it serves as a noun. Gerunds and gerund phrases replace nouns and can do whatever nouns can do.

sentence
subject
Shopping satisfies personal needs.
noun

                              object of
                              preposition
Malls are good at creating such needs.
                        noun phrase

Infinitive phrases

An **infinitive** is the plain form of a verb plus *to: to hide.* Infinitives and infinitive phrases serve as adjectives, adverbs, or nouns. A noun or noun phrase replaces a noun:

sentence
subject   subject complement
To design a mall is to create an artificial environment.
noun phrase   noun phrase

An adverb or adverb phrase modifies a verb, adjective, other adverb, or entire word group and may fall near or away from the word it modifies:

To achieve this goal, designers emphasize the familiar.
adverb phrase   verb

Malls are designed to make shoppers feel safe.
verb   adverb phrase

gram
23a

An adjective or adjective phrase modifies a noun or pronoun and usually falls immediately after the word it modifies:

The environment supports the impulse to shop.
                             noun   adjective

> **CULTURE LANGUAGE** Infinitives and gerunds may follow some verbs and not others and may differ in meaning after a verb:

The cowboy stopped to sing. [He stopped to do the activity.]
The cowboy stopped singing. [He finished the activity.]

(See pp. 217–18.)

3 ■ Absolute phrases

An **absolute phrase** consists of a noun or pronoun and a participle, plus any modifiers. It modifies the rest of its sentence and may fall in more than one place in the sentence.

Their own place established, many ethnic groups are making way for
         absolute phrase

new arrivals.

Unlike a participial phrase, an absolute phrase always contains a noun that serves as its subject:

Learning English, many immigrants discover American culture.
participial phrase

Immigrants having learned English, their opportunities widen.
                absolute phrase

gram
23a

4 ■ Appositive phrases

An **appositive** is usually a noun that renames another noun. An appositive phrase includes modifiers as well. Both appositives and appositive phrases usually fall immediately after the nouns they rename.

Bizen ware, a dark stoneware, is produced in Japan.
   noun   appositive phrase

Appositives and appositive phrases sometimes begin with *that is, such as, for example,* or *in other words.*

Bizen ware is used in the Japanese tea ceremony, that is, the Zen Bud-
                         noun   appositive phrase

dhist observance that links meditation and art.

Exercise 23.1 Identifying phrases

In each of the following sentences, identify every verbal and appositive and every verbal, appositive, prepositional, and absolute phrase. All the sentences include at least two such words or phrases.

Example:

```
                        ┌────participial phrase────┐
Modern English contains words borrowed from many sources.
                        └prepositional phrase┘
```

1. With its many synonyms, or words with similar meanings, English can make choosing the right word a difficult task.
2. Borrowing words from other languages such as French and Latin, English acquired an unusual number of synonyms.
3. Having so many choices, how does a writer decide between *motherly* and *maternal* or among *womanly, feminine,* and *female*?
4. Some people prefer longer and more ornate words to avoid the flatness of short words.
5. During the Renaissance a heated debate occurred between the Latinists, favoring Latin words, and the Saxonists, preferring Anglo-Saxon words derived from Germanic roots.
6. Students in writing classes are often told to choose the shorter word, generally an Anglo-Saxon derivative.
7. Better advice, wrote William Hazlitt, is the principle of choosing "the best word in common use."
8. Keeping this principle in mind, a writer would choose either *womanly,* the Anglo-Saxon word, or *feminine,* a French derivative, according to meaning and situation.
9. Synonyms rarely have exactly the same meaning, usage having created subtle but real differences over time.
10. To take another example, the meaning of *handbook,* an old English word, is slightly different from that of *manual,* a French derivative.

23b   Learn to recognize subordinate clauses.

A **clause** is any group of words that contains both a subject (naming an actor) and a predicate verb (asserting something about the subject). (See p. 191.) There are two kinds of clauses, and the distinction between them is important:

- A *main clause* makes a complete statement and can stand alone as a sentence: *The sky darkened.*
- A *subordinate clause* is just like a main clause except that it begins with a subordinating word: *when the sky darkened*; *whoever calls.* The subordinating word reduces the clause from a complete statement to a single part of speech: an adjective, adverb, or noun.

Note   A subordinate clause punctuated as a sentence is a sentence fragment. (See pp. 272–73.)

Adjective clauses

An **adjective clause** modifies a noun or pronoun. It usually begins with the relative pronoun *who, whom, whose, which,* or *that* but may also begin with *where, when,* or *why.* The clause ordinarily falls immediately after the word it modifies.

Parents who cannot read may have bad memories of school.
noun   adjective clause

Children whom the schools fail sometimes have illiterate parents.
noun   adjective clause

One school, which is open year-round, helps parents learn to read.
noun   adjective clause

The school is in a city where the illiteracy rate is high.
noun   adjective clause

In the first three examples, the relative pronouns *who, whom,* and *which* refer to the nouns modified by the clause (*Parents, Children, school*). The relative pronoun serves as the subject of its clause (*who cannot read, which is open year-round*) or as an object (*whom the schools fail*). In the last example, *where* substitutes for *in which* (*a city in which the illiteracy rate is high*).

See pages 295–96 for advice on punctuating adjective clauses.

Adverb clauses

An **adverb clause** modifies a verb, an adjective, another adverb, or a whole word group. It always begins with a subordinating conjunction, such as *after, although, as, because, even though, how, if, until, when,* or *while.* (See pp. 188–89 for a fuller list.) The clause may fall in more than one place in its sentence (but see pp. 266–68 for limitations).

gram
23b

The school began teaching parents when adult illiteracy gained na-
verb   adverb clause
tional attention.

At first the program was not as successful as its founders had hoped.
adjective   adverb clause

Because it was directed at people who could not read, advertising had
adverb clause   main clause
to be inventive.

Noun clauses

A **noun clause** replaces a noun in a sentence and does anything a noun can do. It begins with *that, what, whatever, who, whom, whoever, whomever, when, where, whether, why,* or *how.*

____sentence subject____
Whether the program would succeed depended on door-to-door adver-
noun clause
tising.

┌─────object of verb─────┐
Teachers explained in person how the program would work.
                              noun clause

┌────sentence subject────┐
Whoever seemed slightly interested was invited to an open meeting.
    noun clause

                         ┌────object of preposition────┐
A few parents were anxious about what their children would think.
                              noun clause

                    ┌────subject complement────┐
The children's needs were what the parents asked most about.
                         noun clause

Exercise 23.2   Identifying clauses

Underline the subordinate clauses in the following sentences. Then identify each one as adjective (ADJ), adverb (ADV), or noun (N) by determining how it functions in its sentence.

Example:

>   N
> Whoever follows the Koran refers to God as *Allah,* the Arabic word for his name.

1. The Prophet Muhammad, who was the founder of Islam, was born about 570 CE in the city of Mecca.
2. He grew up in the care of his grandfather and an uncle because both of his parents had died.
3. His family was part of a powerful Arab tribe that lived in western Arabia.
4. When Muhammad was about forty years old, he had a vision while he was in a cave outside Mecca.
5. He believed that God had selected him to be the prophet of a true religion for the Arab people.
6. Throughout his life he continued to have revelations, which have been written in the Koran.
7. The Koran is the sacred book of Muslims, who as adherents of Islam view Muhammad as God's messenger.
8. When he no longer had the support of the clans of Mecca, Muhammad and his followers moved to Medina.
9. There they established an organized Muslim community that sometimes clashed with the Meccans and with Jewish clans.
10. Throughout his life Muhammad continued as the religious, political, and military leader of Islam as it spread in Asia and Africa.

gram
23b

24 Sentence Types

In *Brief*
- Learn to recognize simple sentences (below).
- Learn to recognize compound sentences (below).
- Learn to recognize complex sentences (below).
- Learn to recognize compound-complex sentences (opposite).

Visit MyWritingLab™ for more resources on sentence types.

The four basic sentence structures vary in the number of main and subordinate clauses they contain. Each structure gives different emphasis to the main and supporting information in a sentence.

24a Learn to recognize simple sentences.

A **simple sentence** consists of a single main clause and no subordinate clause:

┌─────main clause─────┐
Last summer was unusually hot.

┌────────────────main clause────────────────┐
The summer made many farmers leave the area for good or reduced them to bare existence.

24b Learn to recognize compound sentences.

A **compound sentence** consists of two or more main clauses and no subordinate clause.

┌─main clause─┐ ┌────main clause────┐
Last July was hot, but August was even hotter.

┌──────── main clause ────────┐ ┌────main clause────┐
The hot sun scorched the earth, and the lack of rain killed many crops.

24c Learn to recognize complex sentences.

A **complex sentence** consists of one main clause and one or more subordinate clauses:

┌─main clause─┐ ┌──────subordinate clause──────┐
Rain finally came, although many had left the area by then.

┌─────────── main clause ───────────┐ ┌subordinate clause─
Those who remained were able to start anew because the govern-
        subordinate clause

ment came to their aid.

204

24d Learn to recognize compound-complex sentences.

A **compound-complex sentence** has the characteristics of both the compound sentence (two or more main clauses) and the complex sentence (at least one subordinate clause):

```
┌──────────subordinate clause────────┐  ┌────────main clause──────────
When government aid finally came, many people had already been
────────────────────────┐  ┌──────────main clause──────────┐
reduced to poverty and others had been forced to move.
```

Exercise 24.1 Identifying sentence structures

Mark the main clauses and subordinate clauses in the following sentences. Then identify each sentence as simple, compound, complex, or compound-complex.

Example:

```
┌─────────── main clause ──────────────┐  ┌─subordinate clause─
The human voice is produced in the larynx, which has two bands
───────────────────┐
called vocal chords. [Complex.]
```

1. Our world has many sounds, but they all have one thing in common.
2. The one thing that all sounds share is that they are produced by vibrations.
3. The vibrations make the air move in waves, and these sound waves travel to the ear.
4. When sound waves enter the ear, the auditory nerves convey them to the brain, and the brain interprets them.
5. Sound waves can also travel through other material, such as water and even the solid earth.
6. Some sounds are pleasant, and others, which we call noise, are not.
7. Most noises are produced by irregular vibrations at irregular intervals; an example is the barking of a dog.
8. Sounds have frequency and pitch.
9. When an object vibrates rapidly, it produces high-frequency, high-pitched sounds.
10. People can hear sounds over a wide range of frequencies, but dogs, cats, and many other animals can hear high frequencies that humans cannot.

gram

24d

25   Verb Forms

In *Brief*

- Use the correct forms of *sing/sang/sung* and other irregular verbs (opposite).
- Distinguish between *sit* and *set*, *lie* and *lay*, and *rise* and *raise* (p. 210).
- Use the *-s* and *-ed* forms of the verb when they are required (p. 211).
- Use helping verbs with main verbs appropriately (p. 212).
- Use a gerund or an infinitive after a verb as appropriate (p. 217).
- Use the appropriate particles with two-word verbs (p. 219).

Visit MyWritingLab™ for more resources on verb forms.

Verbs have five distinctive forms:

- **The *plain form* is the dictionary form of the verb: *watch, break.*** When the subject is a plural noun or the pronoun *I, we, you,* or *they,* the plain form indicates action that occurs in the present, occurs habitually, or is generally true.
- **The *-s form* ends in *-s* or *-es*: *watches, breaks.*** When the subject is a singular noun, a pronoun such as *everyone,* or the personal pronoun *he, she,* or *it,* the *-s* form indicates action that occurs in the present, occurs habitually, or is generally true.
- **The *past tense form* indicates that the action of the verb occurred before now: *watched, broke.*** It usually adds *-d* or *-ed* to the plain form, although most irregular verbs create it in different ways.
- **The *past participle* is usually the same as the past-tense form, except in most irregular verbs: *watched, broken.*** It combines with forms of *have* or *be* (*has watched*, *was broken*), or by itself it modifies nouns and pronouns (*my broken heart*).
- **The *present participle* adds *-ing* to the verb's plain form: *watching, breaking.*** It combines with forms of *be* (*is watching*), modifies nouns and pronouns (*the boiling water*), or functions as a noun (*Running exhausts me*).

The verb *be* has eight forms rather than the five forms of most other verbs:

Plain form	be		
Present participle	being		
Past participle	been		
	I	*he, she, it*	*we, you, they*
Present tense	am	is	are
Past tense	was	was	were

**vb
25**

This chapter focuses on the verb forms that most often cause difficulty.

25a   Use the correct forms of *sing/sang/sung* and other irregular verbs.

Most verbs are **regular**: they form their past tense and past participle by adding *-d* or *-ed* to the plain form.

Plain form	Past tense	Past participle
live	lived	lived
act	acted	acted

About two hundred English verbs are **irregular**: they form their past tense and past participle in some irregular way. Check a dictionary under the verb's plain form if you have any doubt about its other forms. If the verb is irregular, the dictionary will list the plain form, the past tense, and the past participle in that order (*go, went, gone*). If the dictionary gives only two forms (as in *think, thought*), then the past tense and the past participle are the same.

Common irregular verbs

Plain form	Past tense	Past participle
arise	arose	arisen
be	was, were	been
become	became	become
begin	began	begun
bend	bent	bent
bid	bid	bid
bite	bit	bitten, bit
blow	blew	blown
break	broke	broken
bring	brought	brought
build	built	built
burst	burst	burst
buy	bought	bought
catch	caught	caught
choose	chose	chosen
come	came	come
cut	cut	cut
dig	dug	dug
dive	dived, dove	dived
do	did	done
draw	drew	drawn
dream	dreamed, dreamt	dreamed, dreamt
drink	drank	drunk

(continued)

vb
25a

Common irregular verbs
(continued)

Plain form	Past tense	Past participle
drive	drove	driven
eat	ate	eaten
fall	fell	fallen
find	found	found
fly	flew	flown
forget	forgot	forgotten, forgot
freeze	froze	frozen
get	got	got, gotten
give	gave	given
go	went	gone
grow	grew	grown
hang (suspend)	hung	hung
hang (execute)	hanged	hanged
have	had	had
hear	heard	heard
hide	hid	hidden
hold	held	held
hurt	hurt	hurt
keep	kept	kept
know	knew	known
lay	laid	laid
lead	led	led
leave	left	left
let	let	let
lie	lay	lain
lose	lost	lost
pay	paid	paid
read	read	read
ride	rode	ridden
ring	rang	rung
rise	rose	risen
run	ran	run
say	said	said
see	saw	seen
set	set	set
shake	shook	shaken
shrink	shrank, shrunk	shrunk, shrunken
sing	sang, sung	sung
sink	sank, sunk	sunk
sit	sat	sat
sleep	slept	slept
speak	spoke	spoken
stand	stood	stood
steal	stole	stolen
swim	swam	swum
swing	swung	swung

vb
25a

Plain form	Past tense	Past participle
take	took	taken
teach	taught	taught
tear	tore	torn
throw	threw	thrown
wear	wore	worn
write	wrote	written

CULTURE LANGUAGE Some English dialects use verb forms that differ from those of standard American English: for instance, *drug* for *dragged*, *growed* for *grew*, *come* for *came*, or *went* for *gone*. In situations requiring standard American English, use the forms in the preceding list or in a dictionary.

Faulty   They have <u>went</u> to the movies.
Revised   They have <u>gone</u> to the movies.

Exercise 25.1   Using irregular verbs

For each irregular verb in brackets, supply either the past tense or the past participle, as appropriate, and identify the form you used.

Example:

Though we had [hide] the cash box, it was [steal].

Though we had <u>hidden</u> the cash box, it was <u>stolen</u>. [Two past participles.]

1. The world population has [grow] by two-thirds of a billion people in less than a decade.
2. Recently it [break] the 7 billion mark.
3. Experts have [draw] pictures of a crowded future.
4. They predict that the world population may have [slide] up to as much as 9.5 billion by the year 2050.
5. Though the food supply [rise] in the last decade, the share to each person [fall].
6. At the same time the water supply, which had actually [become] healthier in the twentieth century, [sink] in size and quality.
7. The number of species on earth [shrink] by 20%.
8. Changes in land use [run] nomads and subsistence farmers off the land.
9. Yet all has not been [lose].
10. Recently human beings have [begin] to heed these and other problems and to explore how technology can be [drive] to help the earth and all its populations.
11. Some new techniques for waste processing have [prove] effective.
12. Crop management has [take] some pressure off lands with poor soil, allowing their owners to produce food.
13. Genetic engineering could replenish food supplies that have [shrink].
14. Population control has [find] adherents all over the world.
15. Many endangered species have been [give] room to thrive.

vb

25a

25b   Distinguish between *sit* and *set, lie* and *lay*, and *rise* and *raise*.

The forms of *sit* and *set, lie* and *lay,* and *rise* and *raise* are easy to confuse.

Plain form	Past tense	Past participle
sit	sat	sat
set	set	set
lie	lay	lain
lay	laid	laid
rise	rose	risen
raise	raised	raised

In each of these confusing pairs, one verb is intransitive (it does not take an object) and one is transitive (it does take an object). (See pp. 193–94 for more on this distinction.)

Intransitive

The patients lie in their hospital beds. [*Lie* means "recline" and takes no object.]

Visitors sit with them. [*Sit* means "be seated" or "be located" and takes no object.]

Patients' temperatures rise. [*Rise* means "increase" or "get up" and takes no object.]

Transitive

Nursing aides lay the dinner trays on tables. [*Lay* means "place" and takes an object, here *trays*.]

The aides set the trays down. [*Set* means "place" and takes an object, here *trays*.]

The aides raise the patients' beds. [*Raise* means "lift" or "bring up" and takes an object, here *beds*.]

Note   The verb *lie* meaning "to tell an untruth" is a regular verb. Its past tense and past participle forms are *lied*: *Nikki lied to us. She has lied to us for many years.*

Exercise 25.2   **Distinguishing between *sit/set, lie/lay, rise/raise***

Choose the correct verb from the pair given in brackets. Then supply the past tense or past participle, as appropriate.

Example:

After I washed all the windows, I [lie, lay] down the squeegee and then I [sit, set] the table.

After I washed all the windows, I laid down the squeegee and then I set the table.

1. Yesterday afternoon the child [lie, lay] down for a nap.
2. The child has been [rise, raise] by her grandparents.
3. Most days her grandfather has [sit, set] with her, reading her adventure stories.
4. She has [rise, raise] at dawn most mornings.
5. Her toys were [lie, lay] on the floor.

25c **Use the -s and -ed forms of the verb when they are required.**

Speakers of some English dialects and nonnative speakers of English sometimes omit the -s and -ed verb endings when they are required in standard American English.

Note If you tend to omit these endings in writing, practice pronouncing them when speaking or when reading correct verbs aloud, such as those in the examples here. The spoken practice can help you remember the endings in writing.

1 ▪ Required -s ending

Use the -s form of a verb when *both* of these situations hold:

▪ **The subject is a singular noun (*boy*), an indefinite pronoun (*everyone*), or *he*, *she*, or *it*.** These subjects are **third person,** used when someone or something is being spoken about.
▪ **The verb's action occurs in the present.**

The letter asks [not ask] for a quick response.
Delay costs [not cost] money.

Be especially careful with the -s forms of *be* (*is*), *have* (*has*), and *do* (*does, doesn't*). These forms should always be used to indicate present time with third-person singular subjects.

The company is [not be] late in responding.
It has [not have] problems.
It doesn't [not don't] have the needed data.
The contract does [not do] depend on the response.

In addition, *be* has the -s form *was* in the past tense with *I* and third-person singular subjects:

The company was [not were] in trouble before.

Except for the past-tense *I was*, the pronouns *I* and *you* and all plural subjects do *not* take the -s form of verbs:

I am [not is] a student.
You are [not is] also a student.
They are [not is] students, too.

vb
25c

2 ▪ Required -ed or -d ending

The -ed or -d verb form is required in *any* of these situations:

▪ **The verb's action occurred in the past:**

The company <u>asked</u> [not <u>ask</u>] for more time.

▪ **The verb form functions as a modifier:**

The data <u>concerned</u> [not <u>concern</u>] should be retrievable.

▪ **The verb form combines with a form of *be* or *have*:**

The company is <u>supposed</u> [not <u>suppose</u>] to be the best.
It has <u>developed</u> [not <u>develop</u>] an excellent reputation.

Watch especially for a needed -ed or -d ending when it isn't pronounced clearly in speech, as in *asked, discussed, mixed, supposed, walked,* and *used.*

Exercise 25.3 Using -s and -ed verb endings (CULTURE LANGUAGE)

Supply the correct form of each verb in brackets. Be careful to include -s and -ed (or -d) endings where they are needed for standard English.

Example:

Unfortunately, the roof on our new house already [<u>leak</u>].
Unfortunately, the roof on our new house already <u>leaks</u>.

1. A teacher sometimes [<u>ask</u>] too much of a student.
2. In high school I was once [<u>punish</u>] for being sick.
3. I had [<u>miss</u>] a week of school because of a serious case of the flu.
4. I [<u>realize</u>] that I would fail a test unless I had a chance to make up the class work.
5. I [<u>discuss</u>] the problem with the teacher.
6. He said I was [<u>suppose</u>] to make up the work while I was sick.
7. At that I [<u>walk</u>] out of the class.
8. I [<u>receive</u>] a failing grade then, but it did not change my attitude.
9. I [<u>work</u>] harder in the courses that have more understanding teachers.
10. Today I still balk when a teacher [<u>make</u>] unreasonable demands or [<u>expect</u>] miracles.

---

vb

25d

25d Use helping verbs with main verbs appropriately. (CULTURE LANGUAGE)

Helping verbs combine with main verbs in verb phrases: *The line <u>should have been cut</u>. Who <u>was calling</u>?*

1 ▪ Required helping verbs

Standard American English requires helping verbs in certain situations:

- **The main verb ends in -*ing*:**

  Researchers are conducting fieldwork all over the world. [Not Researchers conducting. . . .]

- **The main verb is *been* or *be*:**

  Many have been fortunate in their discoveries. [Not Many been. . . .]
  Some could be real-life Indiana Joneses. [Not Some be. . . .]

- **The main verb is a past participle,** such as *talked, begun,* or *thrown*:

  Their discoveries were covered in newspapers and magazines. [Not Their discoveries covered. . . .]
  The researchers have given interviews. [Not The researchers given. . . .]

The omission of a helping verb may create an incomplete sentence, or **sentence fragment,** because a present participle (*conducting*), an irregular past participle (*been*), or the plain form *be* cannot stand alone as the only verb in a sentence (see pp. 271–72). To work as sentence verbs, these verb forms need helping verbs.

2 ▪ Combination of helping verb + main verb

Helping verbs and main verbs combine into verb phrases in specific ways.

Note   The main verb in a verb phrase (the one carrying the main meaning) does not change to show a change in subject or time: *she has sung, you had sung.* Only the helping verb may change.

Form of *be* + present participle

The progressive tenses indicate action in progress. Create them with *be, am, is, are, was, were,* or *been* followed by the main verb's present participle (*-ing* form):

She is working on a new book.

Be and *been* require additional helping verbs to form the progressive tenses:

can	might	should		have		
could	must	will	be working	has		been working
may	shall	would		had		

When forming the progressive tenses, be sure to use the *-ing* form of the main verb:

Faulty	Her ideas are grow more complex. She is developed a new approach to ethics.
Revised	Her ideas are growing more complex. She is developing a new approach to ethics.

vb
25d

Form of *be* + past participle

The passive voice of the verb indicates that the subject *receives* the action of the verb. Create the passive voice with *be, am, is, are, was, were, being,* or *been* followed by a past participle:

Her latest book was completed in four months.

Be, being, and *been* require additional helping verbs to form the passive voice:

have ⎫
has ⎬ been completed
had ⎭

am   was ⎫
is   were ⎬ being completed
are   ⎭

will be completed

Be sure to use the main verb's past participle for the passive voice:

Faulty   Her next book will be publish soon.
Revised Her next book will be published soon.

Note Only verbs that take objects (transitive verbs) may form the passive voice. See pages 193–94 for more on these verbs.

Faulty   A philosophy conference will be occurred in the same week that the book comes out. [*Occur* is not a transitive verb.]
Revised A philosophy conference will occur in the same week that the book comes out.

See pages 230–32 for advice on when to use and when to avoid the passive voice.

Forms of *have*

Four forms of *have* serve as helping verbs: *have, has, had, having.* One of these forms plus the main verb's past participle creates one of the perfect tenses, those expressing action completed before another specific time or action:

Some students have complained about the laboratory.
Others had complained before.

Will and other helping verbs sometimes accompany forms of *have* in the perfect tenses:

Several more students will have complained by the end of the week.

Forms of *do*

Do, does, and *did* have three uses as helping verbs, always with the plain form of the main verb:

- **To pose a question:** *How did the trial end?*
- **To emphasize the main verb:** *It did end eventually.*

- **To negate the main verb, along with *not* or *never*:** *The judge did not withdraw.*

Be sure to use the main verb's plain form with any form of *do*:

Faulty   The judge did remained in court.
Revised The judge did remain in court.

Modals

The modal helping verbs include *can, may, should, would,* and several two- and three-word combinations, such as *have to* and *be supposed to.* (See p. 186 for a list of helping verbs.)

Modals convey various meanings, with these being most common:

- **Ability:** *can, could, be able to*

  The equipment can detect small vibrations. [Present.]
  The equipment could detect small vibrations. [Past.]
  The equipment is able to detect small vibrations. [Present. Past: *was able to.* Future: *will be able to.*]

- **Possibility:** *could, may, might; could/may/might have* + past participle

  The equipment could fail. [Present.]
  The equipment may fail. [Present or future.]
  The equipment might fail. [Present or future.]
  The equipment may have failed. [Past.]

- **Necessity or obligation:** *must, have to, be supposed to*

  The lab must purchase a backup. [Present or future.]
  The lab has to purchase a backup. [Present or future. Past: *had to.*]
  The lab will have to purchase a backup. [Future.]
  The lab is supposed to purchase a backup. [Present. Past: *was supposed to.*]

- **Permission:** *may, can, could*

  The lab may spend the money. [Present or future.]
  The lab can spend the money. [Present or future.]
  The lab could spend the money. [Present or future, more tentative.]
  The lab could have spent the money. [Past.]

- **Intention:** *will, shall, would*

  The lab will spend the money. [Future.]
  Shall we offer advice? [Future. Use *shall* for questions requesting opinion or consent.]
  We would have offered advice. [Past.]

vb
25d

- **Request:** *could, can, would*

  Could [or Can or Would] you please <u>obtain</u> a bid? [Present or future.]

- **Advisability:** *should, had better, ought to; should have* + past participle

  You <u>should obtain</u> three bids. [Present or future.]
  You <u>had better obtain</u> three bids. [Present or future.]
  You <u>ought to obtain</u> three bids. [Present or future.]
  You <u>should have obtained</u> three bids. [Past.]

- **Past habit:** *would, used to*

  In years past we <u>would obtain</u> five bids.
  We <u>used to obtain</u> five bids.

Exercise 25.4 Using helping verbs (CULTURE LANGUAGE)

Add helping verbs to the following sentences where they are needed for standard American English.

> *Example:*
> The school be opened to shelter storm victims.
> The school <u>will</u> be opened to shelter storm victims.

1. For as long as I can remember, I been writing stories.
2. While I living with my grandparents one summer, I wrote mystery stories.
3. Nearly every afternoon I sat at the computer and wrote about two brothers who solved mysteries while their mother be working.
4. By the end of the summer, I written four stories.
5. I was very happy when one of my stories published in the school newspaper.

Exercise 25.5 Revising: Helping verbs plus main verbs (CULTURE LANGUAGE)

Revise the following sentences so that helping verbs and main verbs are used correctly. If a sentence is correct as given, mark the number preceding it.

> *Example:*
> The college testing service has test as many as five hundred students at one time.
>
> The college testing service has <u>tested</u> as many as five hundred students at one time.

1. A report from the Bureau of the Census has confirm a widening gap between rich and poor.
2. As suspected, the percentage of people below the poverty level did increased over the last decade.
3. The richest 1% of the population is make 24% of all the income.
4. These households will keeping an average of $1.3 million each after taxes.
5. The other 99% all together will average about $300,000.

25e Use a gerund or an infinitive after a verb as appropriate.

CULTURE / LANGUAGE

A **gerund** is the -*ing* form of a verb used as a noun: *Smoking* is *unhealthful*. An **infinitive** is the plain form of a verb preceded by *to*: *Try not to smoke*. Gerunds and infinitives may follow certain verbs but not others. Sometimes the use of a gerund or an infinitive with the same verb changes the meaning of the verb.

1 ▪ Either gerund or infinitive

A gerund or an infinitive may come after the following verbs with no significant difference in meaning:

begin	continue	intend	prefer
can't bear	hate	like	start
can't stand	hesitate	love	

The pump began working. The pump began to work.

2 ▪ Meaning change with gerund or infinitive

With four verbs, a gerund has quite a different meaning from an infinitive:

forget	stop
remember	try

The man stopped eating. [He no longer ate.]
The man stopped to eat. [He stopped in order to eat.]

vb
25e

3 ▪ Gerund, not infinitive

Do not use an infinitive after these verbs:

admit	discuss	mind	recollect
adore	dislike	miss	resent
appreciate	enjoy	postpone	resist
avoid	escape	practice	risk
consider	finish	put off	suggest
deny	imagine	quit	tolerate
detest	keep	recall	understand

Faulty   He finished to eat lunch.
Revised   He finished eating lunch.

4 ▪ Infinitive, not gerund

Do not use a gerund after the verbs below and on the next page:

agree	ask	claim	expect
appear	assent	consent	have
arrange	beg	decide	hope

manage	plan	promise	wait
mean	prepare	refuse	want
offer	pretend	say	wish

Faulty   He decided <u>checking</u> the meter.
Revised   He decided <u>to check</u> the meter.

5 ▪ Noun or pronoun + infinitive

Some verbs may be followed by an infinitive alone or by a noun or pronoun and an infinitive. The presence of a noun or pronoun changes the meaning.

ask	dare	need	wish
beg	expect	promise	would like
choose	help	want	

He expected <u>to wait</u>.
He expected <u>his friends</u> <u>to wait</u>.

Some verbs *must* be followed by a noun or pronoun before an infinitive:

admonish	encourage	oblige	require
advise	forbid	order	teach
allow	force	permit	tell
cause	hire	persuade	train
challenge	instruct	remind	urge
command	invite	request	warn
convince			

He told <u>his friends</u> <u>to wait</u>.

Do not use *to* before the infinitive when it follows one of the next verbs and a noun or pronoun:

feel	make ("force")
have	see
hear	watch
let	

He watched his friends <u>leave</u> without him.

Exercise 25.6   **Revising: Verbs plus gerunds or infinitives**

Revise the following sentences so that gerunds or infinitives are used correctly with verbs. Mark the number preceding any sentence that is already correct.

Example:

A politician cannot avoid to alienate some voters.
A politician cannot avoid <u>alienating</u> some voters.

1. A program called *Boostup.org* aims to improve students' school attendance.
2. The goal is to encourage students stopping skipping school.
3. Parents who want to help can choose tracking their child's attendance.
4. The program persuades parents signing up via its Web site, *Facebook* page, and *Twitter* feed.
5. Because of *Boostup.org*, many students who might have dropped out now plan going to college.

25f Use the appropriate particles with two-word verbs. CULTURE LANGUAGE

Standard American English includes some verbs that consist of two words: the verb itself and a **particle**, another word that changes the meaning of the verb. For example:

<u>Look up</u> the answer. [Research the answer.]
<u>Look over</u> the answer. [Examine the answer.]

The meanings of these two-word verbs are often quite different from the meanings of the individual words that make them up. (There are some three-word verbs, too, such as *look out for* and *run out of*.)

A dictionary of English as a second language will define two-word verbs for you and say whether the verbs may be separated in a sentence, as explained below and on the next page. (See p. 167 for a list of ESL dictionaries.)

Note Many two-word verbs are more common in speech than in more formal academic or public writing. For formal writing, consider using *research* instead of *look up, examine* or *inspect* instead of *look over*.

1 ▪ Inseparable two-word verbs

Verbs and particles that may not be separated by any other words include the following:

catch on	go over	play around	stay away
come across	grow up	run into	stay up
get along	keep on	run out of	take care of
give in	look into	speak up	turn up at

Faulty Children <u>grow</u> quickly <u>up</u>.
Revised Children <u>grow up</u> quickly.

2 ▪ Separable two-word verbs

Most two-word verbs that take direct objects may be separated by the object.

Parents help out their children.
Parents help their children out.

If the direct object is a pronoun, the pronoun *must* separate the verb from the particle.

Faulty Parents help out them.
Revised Parents help them out.

The separable two-word verbs include the following:

bring up	give back	make up	throw out
call off	hand in	point out	try on
call up	hand out	put away	try out
drop off	help out	put back	turn down
fill out	leave out	put off	turn on
fill up	look over	take out	turn up
give away	look up	take over	wrap up

Exercise 25.7 Revising: Verbs plus particles (CULTURE · LANGUAGE)

The two- and three-word verbs in the sentences below are underlined. Some are correct as given, and some are not because they should or should not be separated by other words. Revise the verbs and other words that are incorrect. Consult the preceding lists or an ESL dictionary if necessary to determine which verbs are separable.

Example:

Hollywood producers never seem to come up with entirely new plots, but they also never run new ways out of to present old ones.

Hollywood producers never seem to come up with [correct] entirely new plots, but they also never run out of new ways to present old ones.

1. American movies treat everything from going out with someone to making up an ethnic identity, but few people look their significance into.
2. While some viewers stay away from topical films, others turn at the theater up simply because a movie has sparked debate.
3. Some movies attracted rowdy spectators, and the theaters had to throw out them.
4. Filmmakers have always been eager to point their influence out to the public.
5. Everyone agrees that filmmakers will keep creating controversy on, if only because it can fill up theaters.

vb
25f

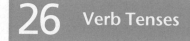

26 Verb Tenses

In *Brief*

- Observe the special uses of the present tense (*sing*) (below).
- Observe the uses of the perfect tenses (*have/had/will have sung*) (p. 223).
- Observe the uses of the progressive tenses (*is/was/will be singing*) (p. 223).
- Keep tenses consistent (p. 224).
- Use the appropriate sequence of verb tenses (p. 225).

Visit MyWritingLab™ for more resources on verb tense.

Tense shows the time of a verb's action. The box on the next page illustrates the tense forms for a regular verb. (Irregular verbs have different past-tense and past-participle forms. See pp. 207–09.)

CULTURE LANGUAGE In standard American English, a verb conveys time and sequence through its form. In some other languages and English dialects, various markers besides verb form may indicate the time of a verb. For instance, in African American Vernacular English, *I be attending class on Tuesday* means that the speaker attends class every Tuesday. But to someone who doesn't know the dialect, the sentence could mean last Tuesday, this Tuesday, or every Tuesday. In standard American English, the intended meaning is indicated by verb tense:

I attended class on Tuesday. [Past tense indicates *last* Tuesday.]

I will attend class on Tuesday. [Future tense indicates *next* Tuesday.]

I attend class on Tuesday. [Present tense indicates habitual action, *every* Tuesday.]

t
26a

26a Observe the special uses of the present tense (*sing*).

The present tense has several distinctive uses.

Action occurring now
She understands the problem.
We define the problem differently.

Habitual or recurring action
Banks regularly undergo audits.
The audits monitor the banks' activities.

A general truth
The mills of the gods grind slowly.
The earth is round.

Tenses of a regular verb (active voice)

Present Action that is occurring now, occurs habitually, or is generally true

Simple present Plain form or -s form

I walk.
You/we/they walk.
He/she/it walks.

Present progressive *Am, is,* or *are* plus -*ing* form

I am walking.
You/we/they are walking.
He/she/it is walking.

Past Action that occurred before now

Simple past Past-tense form (-*d* or -*ed*)

I/he/she/it walked.
You/we/they walked.

Past progressive *Was* or *were* plus -*ing* form

I/he/she/it was walking.
You/we/they were walking.

Future Action that will occur in the future

Simple future *Will* plus plain form

I/you/he/she/it/we/they will walk.

Future progressive *Will be* plus -*ing form*

I/you/he/she/it/we/they will be walking.

Present perfect Action that began in the past and is linked to the present

Present perfect *Have* or *has* plus past participle (-*d* or -*ed*)

I/you/we/they have walked.
He/she/it has walked.

Present perfect progressive *Have been* or *has been* plus -*ing* form

I/you/we/they have been walking.
He/she/it has been walking.

Past perfect Action that was completed before another past action

Past perfect *Had* plus past participle (-*d* or -*ed*)

I/you/he/she/it/we/they had walked.

Past perfect progressive *Had been* plus -*ing* form

I/you/he/she/it/we/they had been walking.

Future perfect Action that will be completed before another future action

Future perfect *Will have* plus past participle (-*d* or -*ed*)

I/you/he/she/it/we/they will have walked.

Future perfect progressive *Will have been* plus -*ing* form

I/you/he/she/it/we/they will have been walking.

Discussion of literature, film, and so on

Huckleberry Finn <u>has</u> adventures we all envy.

In that article the author <u>examines</u> several causes of crime in very rural areas.

Future time

Next week we <u>draft</u> a new budget.
Funding <u>ends</u> in less than a year.

The present tense shows future time with expressions like those in the examples above: *next week, in less than a year.*

26b   Observe the uses of the perfect tenses (*have/had/will have sung*).

The **perfect tenses** consist of a form of *have* plus the verb's past participle (*closed, hidden*). They indicate an action that is completed before another specific time or action. The present perfect tense also indicates action that is begun in the past and continued into the present.

present perfect
The dancer <u>has performed</u> here only once. [The action is completed at the time of the statement.]

present perfect
Critics <u>have written</u> about the performance ever since. [The action began in the past and continues now.]

past perfect
The dancer <u>had trained</u> in Asia before his performance. [The action was completed before another past action.]

future perfect
He <u>will have danced</u> here again by the end of the year. [The action begins now or in the future and will be completed by a specific time in the future.]

CULTURE
LANGUAGE   With the present perfect tense, the words *since* and *for* are followed by different information. After *since*, give a specific point in time: *The play has run <u>since 1989</u>.* After *for*, give a span of time: *It has run <u>for decades</u>.*

26c   Observe the uses of the progressive tenses (*is/was/will be singing*).   CULTURE LANGUAGE

The **progressive tenses** indicate continuing (therefore progressive) action. They consist of a form of *be* plus the verb's *-ing* form. (The words *be* and *been* must be combined with other helping verbs. See p. 213.)

t
26c

present progressive
The team is improving.

past progressive
Last year the team was losing.

future progressive
The owners will be watching for signs of improvement.

present perfect progressive
Sports writers have been expecting an upturn.

past perfect progressive
New players had been performing well.

future perfect progressive
If the season goes badly, fans will have been watching their team lose for ten years straight.

Note Verbs that express unchanging conditions (especially mental states) rather than physical actions do not usually appear in the progressive tenses. These verbs include *adore, appear, believe, belong, care, hate, have, hear, know, like, love, mean, need, own, prefer, remember, see, sound, taste, think, understand,* and *want.*

Faulty	She is wanting to study ethics.
Revised	She wants to study ethics.

26d Keep tenses consistent.

Within a sentence, the tenses of verbs and verb forms need not be identical as long as they reflect actual changes in time: *Ramon will graduate from college thirty years after his father arrived in America.* In speech we often shift tenses even when they don't reflect changes in time. But in writing, such needless shifts in tense will confuse or distract readers:

Inconsistent tense	Immediately after Booth shot Lincoln, Major Rathbone threw himself upon the assassin. But Booth pulls a knife and plunges it into the major's arm.
Revised	Immediately after Booth shot Lincoln, Major Rathbone threw himself upon the assassin. But Booth pulled a knife and plunged it into the major's arm.
Inconsistent tense	The main character in the novel suffers psychologically because he has a clubfoot, but he eventually triumphed over his disability.
Revised	The main character in the novel suffers psychologically because he has a clubfoot, but he eventually triumphs over his disability. [Use the present tense when discussing the content of literature, film, and so on.]

Exercise 26.1 Revising: Consistent past tense
In the following paragraph, change the tenses of the verbs as needed to maintain consistent simple past tense.

The 1960 presidential race between Richard Nixon and John F. Kennedy was the first to feature a televised debate. Despite his extensive political experience, Nixon perspires heavily and looks haggard and uneasy in front of the camera. By contrast, Kennedy was projecting cool poise and providing crisp answers that made him seem fit for the office of President. The public responded positively to Kennedy's image. His poll ratings shoot up immediately, while Nixon's take a corresponding drop. The popular vote was close, but Kennedy won the election.

Exercise 26.2   Revising: Consistent present tense

In the paragraph below, change the tenses of the verbs as needed to maintain consistent simple present tense.

E. B. White's famous children's novel *Charlotte's Web* is a wonderful story of friendship and loyalty. Charlotte, the wise and motherly spider, decided to save her friend Wilbur, the young and childlike pig, from being butchered by his owner. She made a plan to weave words into her web that described Wilbur. She first weaves "Some Pig" and later presented "Terrific," "Radiant," and "Humble." Her plan succeeded beautifully. She fools the humans into believing that Wilbur was a pig unlike any other, and Wilbur lived.

26e   Use the appropriate sequence of verb tenses.

The **sequence of tenses** is the relation between the verb tense in a main clause and the verb tense in a subordinate clause. The tenses often differ to reflect differences in relative time:

Ramon's father <u>arrived</u> in the United States thirty years ago, after he <u>had married</u>, and now Ramon <u>has decided</u> that he <u>will return</u> to his father's homeland.

English tense sequence can be tricky for native speakers and especially challenging for nonnative speakers. The main difficulties are discussed on the following pages.

1 ▪ Past or past perfect tense in main clause

When the verb in the main clause is in the past or past perfect tense, the verb in the subordinate clause must also be past or past perfect.

> main clause: subordinate clause:
>   past   past
> The researchers <u>discovered</u> that people <u>varied</u> widely in their knowledge of public events.

> main clause: subordinate clause:
>   past   past perfect
> The variation <u>occurred</u> because respondents <u>had been born</u> in different decades.

> main clause: subordinate clause:
> past perfect   past
> None of them <u>had been born</u> when Eisenhower <u>was</u> President.

t seq

26e

Exception Always use the present tense for a general truth, such as *The earth is round*:

> main clause: subordinate clause:
>   past   present
> Most <u>understood</u> that popular Presidents <u>are</u> not necessarily good Presidents.

2 ■ Conditional sentences

A **conditional sentence** states a factual relation between cause and effect, makes a prediction, or speculates about what might happen. Such a sentence usually consists of a subordinate clause beginning with *if, when,* or *unless* and a main clause stating the result. The three kinds of conditional sentences use distinctive verbs.

Factual relation

For statements asserting that something always or usually happens whenever something else happens, use the present tense in both clauses:

> subordinate clause: main clause:
>   present   present
> When a voter <u>casts</u> a ballot, he or she <u>has</u> complete privacy.

If the linked events occurred in the past, use the past tense in both clauses:

> subordinate clause: main clause:
>   past   past
> When voters <u>registered</u> in some states, they <u>had</u> to pay a poll tax.

Prediction

For a prediction, generally use the present tense in the subordinate clause and the future tense in the main clause:

> subordinate clause: main clause:
>   present   future
> Unless citizens <u>regain</u> faith in politics, they <u>will</u> not <u>vote</u>.

Sometimes the verb in the main clause consists of *may, can, should,* or *might* plus the verb's plain form: *If citizens <u>regain</u> faith, they <u>may vote</u>.*

Speculation

Speculations are mainly of two kinds, each with its own verb pattern. For events that are possible in the present but unlikely, use the past tense in the subordinate clause and *would, could,* or *might* plus the verb's plain form in the main clause:

> subordinate clause: main clause:
>   past   *would* + verb
> If voters <u>had</u> more confidence, they <u>would vote</u> more often.

Use *were* instead of *was* when the subject is *I, he, she, it,* or a singular noun. (See pp. 228–29 for more on this distinctive verb form.)

subordinate clause: main clause:
    past   *would* + verb
If the voter <u>were</u> more confident, he or she <u>would vote</u> more often.

Use the same forms for events that are impossible now, that are contrary to fact (including the distinctive *were* when applicable):

subordinate clause: main clause:
   past   *might* + verb
If Lincoln <u>were</u> alive, he <u>might inspire</u> confidence.

For events that were impossible in the past, use the past perfect tense in the subordinate clause and *would, could,* or *might* plus the present perfect tense in the main clause:

subordinate clause: main clause:
   past   *might* + present perfect
If Lincoln <u>had lived</u> past the Civil War, he <u>might have helped</u> stabilize the country.

Exercise 26.3   Adjusting tense sequence: Past or past perfect tense

The tenses in the following sentences are in correct sequence. Change the tense of one verb as instructed. Then change the other verb tenses as needed to restore correct sequence. Some items have more than one possible answer.

Example:

Delgado will call when he reaches his destination. (*Change <u>will call</u> to <u>called</u>.*)

Delgado <u>called</u> when he <u>reached</u> [or <u>had reached</u>] his destination.

1. Diaries that Adolf Hitler is supposed to have written have surfaced in Germany. (*Change <u>have surfaced</u> to <u>had surfaced</u>.*)
2. Many people believe that the diaries are authentic because a well-known historian has declared them so. (*Change <u>believe</u> to <u>believed</u>.*)
3. However, the historian's evaluation has been questioned by other authorities, who call the diaries forgeries. (*Change <u>has been questioned</u> to <u>was questioned</u>.*)
4. They claim, among other things, that the paper is not old enough to have been used by Hitler. (*Change <u>claim</u> to <u>claimed</u>.*)
5. Eventually, the doubters will win the debate because they have the best evidence. (*Change <u>will win</u> to <u>won</u>.*)

Exercise 26.4   Revising: Tense sequence with conditional sentences

Supply the appropriate tense for each verb in brackets.

Example:

If Babe Ruth or Jim Thorpe [be] athletes today, they [remind] us that even sports heroes must contend with a harsh reality.

If Babe Ruth or Jim Thorpe <u>were</u> athletes today, they <u>might</u> [or could or would] remind us that even sports heroes must contend with a harsh reality.

t seq

26e

1. When an athlete [turn] professional, he or she commits to a gruel-ing regimen of mental and physical training.
2. If athletes [be] less committed, they [disappoint] teammates, fans, and themselves.
3. If professional athletes [be] very lucky, they may play until age forty.
4. Unless an athlete achieves celebrity status, he or she [have] few em-ployment choices after retirement.
5. If professional sports [be] less risky, athletes [have] longer careers and more choices after retirement.
6. If you think you [be] exposed to the flu in the winter, you [get] a flu shot.
7. If you are allergic to eggs, you [have] an allergic reaction to the flu shot.
8. If you get the flu after having a flu shot, your illness [be] milder.
9. If you had had a flu shot last year, you [avoid] the illness.
10. If you [be] not so afraid of shots, you [will] get a flu shot every year.

27   Verb Mood

In *Brief*

- Use the subjunctive verb forms appropriately, as in *I wish I were* (be-low).
- Keep mood consistent (opposite).

Visit MyWritingLab™ for more resources on verb mood.

Mood in grammar is a verb form that indicates the writer's atti-tude:

- **The** *indicative mood* **states a fact or opinion or asks a question:** *The theater needs support.*
- **The** *imperative mood* **expresses a command or gives direction:** *Sup-port the theater.*
- **The** *subjunctive mood* **expresses wishes, suggestions, requirements, and other attitudes,** using *he were* and other distinctive verb forms described here.

27a   Use the subjunctive verb forms appropriately, as in *I wish I were.*

The subjunctive mood expresses a suggestion, requirement, or desire, or it states a condition that is contrary to fact (that is, imagi-nary or hypothetical).

▪ **A request or requirement often includes a verb such as** *ask, insist,*
urge, require, recommend, **or** *suggest.* After the verb, a subordinate
clause beginning with *that* contains the substance of the request
or requirement. For all subjects, the verb in the *that* clause is the
plain form:

plain form
Rules require that every donation <u>be</u> mailed.

▪ **A contrary-to-fact clause states an imaginary or hypothetical condi-**
tion and usually follows *wish* **or starts with** *if* **or** *unless.* For a present
contrary-to-fact clause, use the verb's past-tense form (for *be,* use
the past-tense form *were* for all subjects):

past
I wish I <u>were</u> able to donate money to the theater.

past   past
If the theater <u>were</u> in better shape and <u>had</u> more money, its future
would be assured.

For a past contrary-to-fact clause, use *had* plus the verb's past participle:

had + past participle
The theater would be better funded if it <u>had been</u> better managed last
year.

Note Do not use the helping verb *would* or *could* in a contrary-to-
fact clause beginning with *if*:

| Not | Many people would have helped if they <u>would have</u> known. |
| But | Many people would have helped if they <u>had</u> known. |

See also page 227 for more on verb tenses in contrary-to-fact sentences like these.

vb
27b

27b Keep mood consistent.

Shifts in mood within a sentence or among related sentences can
be confusing. Such shifts occur most frequently in directions.

| Inconsistent mood | <u>Cook</u> the mixture slowly, and <u>you should stir</u> it until the sugar is dissolved. [Mood shifts from imperative to indicative.] |
| Revised | <u>Cook</u> the mixture slowly, and <u>stir</u> it until the sugar is dis-solved. [Consistently imperative.] |

Exercise 27.1 Revising: Subjunctive mood
Revise the following sentences with appropriate subjunctive verb forms.

Example:

I would help the old man if I was able to reach him.

I would help the old man if I <u>were</u> able to reach him.

1. If John Hawkins would have known of all the dangerous side effects of smoking tobacco, would he have introduced the dried plant to England in 1565?
2. Hawkins noted that if a Florida Indian man was to travel for several days, he would have smoked tobacco to satisfy his hunger and thirst.
3. Early tobacco growers feared that their product would not gain acceptance unless it was perceived as healthful.
4. To prevent fires, in 1646 the General Court of Massachusetts passed a law requiring that colonists smoked tobacco only if they were five miles from any town.
5. To prevent decadence, in 1647 Connecticut passed a law mandating that one's smoking of tobacco was limited to once a day in one's own home.

---

28   Verb Voice

In *Brief*
- Prefer the active voice (opposite).
- Use the passive voice when the actor is unknown or unimportant (opposite).
- Keep voice consistent (p. 232).

Visit MyWritingLab™ for more resources on verb voice.

The **voice** of a verb tells whether the subject of the sentence performs the action (**active**) or is acted upon (**passive**).

Active voice   She wrote the book. [The subject performs the action.]
subject verb

Passive voice   The book was written by her. [The subject receives the action.]
subject   verb

 A passive verb always consists of a form of *be* plus the past participle of the main verb: *Rents are controlled.* Other helping verbs must also be used with *be, being,* and *been*: *Rents will be controlled. Rents are being controlled. Rents have been controlled.* Only a transitive verb (one that takes an object) may be used in the passive voice. (See pp. 193–94.)

Active and passive voice

Active voice The subject acts.

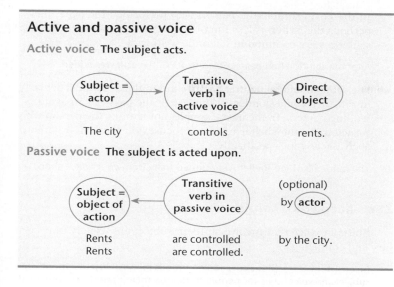

The city   controls   rents.

Passive voice The subject is acted upon.

Rents   are controlled   by the city.
Rents   are controlled.

28a Prefer the active voice.

The active voice is usually clearer, more concise, and more forthright than the passive voice.

Weak passive The library is used by both students and teachers for studying and research, and the plan to expand it has been praised by many.

Strong active Both students and teachers use the library for studying and research, and many have praised the plan to expand it.

28b Use the passive voice when the actor is unknown or unimportant or when naming the actor might be offensive.

The passive voice can be useful when naming the actor is not possible or desirable.

■ **The actor is unknown, unimportant, or less important than the object of the action.** In the following sentences, the writer wishes to stress the Internet rather than the actors.

The Internet was established in 1969 by the US Department of Defense. The network has been extended internationally to governments, universities, corporations, and private individuals.

In the next example the person who performed the experiment, perhaps the writer, is less important than the procedure. Passive sentences are common in scientific writing.

After the solution <u>had been cooled</u> to 10°C, the acid <u>was added</u>.

■ **The actor should be neutral background to the action.** Particularly in sensitive correspondence, this use of the passive can avoid offending readers. In the next example, not naming the person who turned away the shelter residents focuses on the action without accusing anyone specifically.

The residents of the shelter <u>were turned away</u> from your coffee shop.

28c Keep voice consistent.

Shifts in voice that involve shifts in subject are usually unnecessary and confusing.

Inconsistent subject and voice	Blogs <u>cover</u> an enormous range of topics. <u>Opportunities</u> for people to discuss their interests <u>are provided</u> on these sites.
Revised	Blogs <u>cover</u> an enormous range of topics <u>and provide</u> opportunities for people to discuss their interests.

A shift in voice is appropriate when it helps focus the reader's attention on a single subject, as in *The* <u>*candidate*</u> *campaigned vigorously and* <u>*was nominated*</u> *on the first ballot.*

Exercise 28.1 Revising: Using the active voice

Rewrite each of the following passive sentences into the active voice, adding a subject as necessary.

Example:

Contaminants are removed from water by treatment plants.
Treatment <u>plants</u> <u>remove</u> contaminants from water.

1. Water quality is determined by many factors.
2. Suspended and dissolved substances are contained in all natural waters.
3. The amounts of the substances are controlled by the environment.
4. Some dissolved substances are produced by pesticides.
5. Sediment is deposited in water by fields, livestock feedlots, and other sources.
6. The bottom life of streams and lakes is affected by sediment.
7. Light penetration is reduced by sediment, and bottom-dwelling organisms may be smothered.
8. The quality of water in city systems is measured frequently.
9. If legal levels are exceeded by pollutants, the citizens must be notified by city officials.
10. The chlorine taste of water is disliked by many people.

29 Agreement of Subject and Verb

In *Brief*

- Make the subject and verb agree even when other words come between them (next page).
- Make the verb agree with a subject joined by *and, or,* or *nor* (p. 235).
- Make the verb agree when the subject is *everyone* or another indefinite pronoun (p. 235).
- Make the verb agree when the subject is *team* or another collective noun (p. 236).
- Make the verb agree with the antecedent of *who, which,* or *that* (p. 237).
- Use a singular verb for *news* and other singular nouns ending in *-s* (p. 237).
- Make the verb and subject agree even when the verb comes first (p. 238).
- Make *is, are,* and other linking verbs agree with their subjects (p. 238).
- Use a singular verb with titles and words being defined (p. 238).

Visit MyWritingLab™ for more resources on subject-verb agreement.

A subject and its verb should agree in number and person:

Daniel Inouye was the first Japanese American in Congress.
subject   verb

More Japanese Americans live in Hawaii and California than elsewhere.
    subject   verb

	Number	
Person	*Singular*	*Plural*
First	I eat.	We eat.
Second	You eat.	You eat.
Third	He/she/it eats.	They eat.
	The bird eats.	Birds eat.

Most problems of subject-verb agreement arise when endings are omitted from subjects or verbs or when the relation between sentence parts is uncertain.

vb agr
29a

29a   The *-s* and *-es* endings work differently for nouns and verbs.

An *-s* or *-es* ending does opposite things to nouns and verbs: it usually makes a noun *plural,* but it always makes a present-tense verb *singular.* Thus a singular-noun subject will not end in *-s,* but its verb will. A plural-noun subject will end in *-s,* but its verb will not. Between them, subject and verb use only one *-s* ending.

Singular subject	Plural subject
The boy plays.	The boys play.
The bird soars.	The birds soar.

The only exceptions to these rules involve the nouns that form irregular plurals, such as *child/children, woman/women*. The irregular plural still requires a plural verb: *The children play. The women sing.*

CULTURE LANGUAGE If your first language or dialect is not standard American English, subject-verb agreement may be difficult, especially for the following reasons.

- **Some English dialects omit the -s ending for singular verbs or use the -s ending for plural verbs:**

Nonstandard	The voter resist change.
Standard	The voter resists change.
Standard	The voters resist change.

  The verb *be* changes spelling for singular and plural in both present and past tense. (See also p. 206.)

Nonstandard	Taxes is high. They was raised just last year.
Standard	Taxes are high. They were raised just last year.

  Have also has a distinctive -s form, *has*:

Nonstandard	The new tax have little chance of passing.
Standard	The new tax has little chance of passing.

- **Some other languages change all parts of verb phrases to match their subjects.** In English verb phrases, however, only the helping verbs *be, have,* and *do* change for different subjects. The modal helping verbs—*can, may, should, will, would,* and others—do not change:

Nonstandard	The tax mays pass next year.
Standard	The tax may pass next year.

  The main verb in a verb phrase also does not change for different subjects:

Nonstandard	The tax may passes next year.
Standard	The tax may pass next year.

29b Subject and verb should agree even when other words come between them.

The survival of hibernating frogs in freezing temperatures is [not are] fascinating.

A chemical reaction inside the cells of the frogs stops [not stop] the formation of ice crystals.

Note Phrases beginning with *as well as, together with, along with,* and *in addition to* do not change the number of the subject:

The president, together with the deans, has [not have] agreed to revise the catalog.

29c   Subjects joined by *and* usually take plural verbs.

Frost and Roethke were contemporaries.

Exceptions When the parts of the subject form a single idea or refer to a single person or thing, they take a singular verb:

Avocado and bean sprouts is a California sandwich.

When a compound subject is preceded by the adjective *each* or *every*, the verb is usually singular:

Each man, woman, and child has a right to be heard.

29d   When parts of a subject are joined by *or* or *nor*, the verb agrees with the nearer part.

Either the painter or the carpenter knows the cost.

The cabinets or the bookcases are too costly.

When one part of the subject is singular and the other plural, avoid awkwardness by placing the plural part closer to the verb so that the verb is plural:

Awkward   Neither the owners nor the contractor agrees.

Revised   Neither the contractor nor the owners agree.

29e   With *everyone* and other indefinite pronouns, use a singular or plural verb as appropriate.

An **indefinite pronoun** does not refer to a specific person or thing. Most indefinite pronouns are singular in meaning (they refer to a single unspecified person or thing), and they take a singular verb. These include *anybody, anyone, anything, each, either, everybody, everyone, everything, much, neither, nobody, no one, nothing, one, somebody, someone,* and *something.*

Something smells.   Neither is right.

Four indefinite pronouns are always plural in meaning: *both, few, many, several.*

Both are correct.   Several were invited.

Six indefinite pronouns may be either singular or plural in meaning: *all, any, more, most, none, some.* The verb with one of these pronouns depends on what the pronoun refers to:

All of the money is reserved for emergencies. [*All* refers to *money.*]

All of the funds are reserved for emergencies. [*All* refers to *funds.*]

None may be singular even when referring to a plural word, especially to emphasize the meaning "not one": *None* [*Not one*] *of the animals has a home.*

> **CULTURE LANGUAGE** See page 263 for the distinction between *few* ("not many") and *a few* ("some").

29f Collective nouns such as *team* take singular or plural verbs depending on meaning.

A **collective noun** has singular form and names a group of persons or things: for instance, *army, audience, committee, crowd, family, group, team.* Use a singular verb with a collective noun when the group acts as a unit:

The team has won five of the last six meets.

But when the group's members act separately, not together, use a plural verb:

The old team have gone to various colleges.

If a combination such as *team have* seems awkward, reword the sentence: *The members of the old team have gone to various colleges.*

The collective noun *number* may be singular or plural. Preceded by *a,* it is plural; preceded by *the,* it is singular:

A number of people are in debt.

The number of people in debt is very large.

> **CULTURE LANGUAGE** Some noncount nouns (nouns that don't form plurals) are collective nouns because they name groups: for instance, *furniture, clothing, mail.* These noncount nouns usually take singular verbs: *Mail arrives daily.* But some of these nouns take plural verbs, including *clergy, military, people, police,* and any collective noun that comes from an adjective, such as *the poor, the rich, the young, the elderly.* If you mean one representative of the group, use a singular noun such as *police officer* or *poor person.*

29g   *Who, which,* and *that* take verbs that agree with their antecedents.

When used as subjects, *who, which,* and *that* refer to another word in the sentence, called the **antecedent**. The verb agrees with the antecedent.

Mayor Garber ought to listen to the people who work for her.

Bardini is the only aide who has her ear.

Agreement problems often occur with *who* and *that* when the sentence includes *one of the* or *the only one of the*:

Bardini is one of the aides who work unpaid. [Of the aides who work unpaid, Bardini is one.]

Bardini is the only one of the aides who knows the community. [Of the aides, only one, Bardini, knows the community.]

> ⟨**CULTURE LANGUAGE**⟩ In phrases beginning with *one of the*, be sure the noun is plural: *Bardini is one of the aides* [not *aide*] *who work unpaid.*

29h   *News* and other singular nouns ending in *-s* take singular verbs.

vb agr
29h

Singular nouns ending in *-s* include *athletics, economics, linguistics, mathematics, measles, mumps, news, physics, politics,* and *statistics,* as well as place names such as *Athens, Wales,* and *United States.*

Measles is a serious illness.

After so long a wait, the news has to be good.

Statistics is required of psychology majors.

Politics requires compromise.

A few of these words also take plural verbs, but only when they describe individual items rather than whole bodies of activity or knowledge: *The statistics prove him wrong. The mayor's politics make compromise difficult.*

Measurements and figures ending in *-s* may also be singular when the quantity they refer to is a unit:

Three years is a long time to wait.

Three-fourths of the library consists of reference books.

29i   The verb agrees with the subject even when it precedes the subject.

The verb precedes the subject mainly in questions and in constructions beginning with *there* or *here* and a form of *be*:

Is voting a right or a privilege?

Are a right and a privilege the same thing?

There are differences between them.

29j   *Is, are,* and other linking verbs agree with their subjects.

A linking verb such as *is* or *are* connects and equates the sentence subject and a word or words describing the subject (see p. 194). Make a linking verb agree with its subject, usually the first element in the sentence, not with the word or words that describe the subject.

The child's sole support is her court-appointed guardians.

Her court-appointed guardians are the child's sole support.

29k   Use singular verbs with titles and with words being defined.

Hakada Associates is a new firm.

Dream Days remains a favorite book.

Folks is a down-home word for *people*.

Exercise 29.1   Revising: Subject-verb agreement

Revise the verbs in the following sentences as needed to make subjects and verbs agree in number. If the sentence is already correct as given, mark the number preceding it.

Example:

Each of the job applicants type sixty words per minute.
Each of the job applicants types sixty words per minute.

1. Weinstein & Associates are a consulting firm that try to make businesspeople laugh.
2. Results from recent research shows that humor relieves stress.
3. Reduced stress in businesses in turn reduce illness and absenteeism.
4. In special conferences held by one consultant, each of the participants practice making others laugh.

5. "Isn't there enough laughs within you to spread the wealth?" the consultant asks his students.

6. The consultant quotes Casey Stengel's rule that the best way to keep your management job is to separate the underlings who hate you from the ones who have not decided how they feel.

7. Such self-deprecating comments in public is uncommon among business managers, the consultant says.

8. When a manager laughs at himself or herself, a grumpy employee becomes one of those who hides bad temper.

9. Reduced stress can reduce friction within an employee group, which then work together more productively.

10. Every one of the consultants caution, however, that humor has no place in life-affecting corporate situations such as employee layoffs.

Exercise 29.2   Adjusting for subject-verb agreement

Rewrite the following paragraphs to change the underlined words from plural to singular. (You will sometimes need to add *a* or *the* for the singular, as in the example.) Then change verbs as necessary so that they agree with their new subjects.

Example:

Siberian tigers are an endangered subspecies.
The Siberian tiger is an endangered subspecies.

Siberian tigers are the largest living cats in the world, much bigger than their relative the Bengal tiger. They grow to a length of nine to twelve feet, including their tails, and to a height of about three and a half feet. They can weigh over six hundred pounds. These carnivorous hunters live in northern China and Korea as well as in Siberia. During the long winter of this Arctic climate, the yellowish striped coats get a little lighter in order to blend with the snow-covered landscape. The coats also grow quite thick because the tigers have to withstand temperatures as low as −50°F.

Siberian tigers sometimes have to travel great distances to find food. They need about twenty pounds of food a day because of their size and the cold climate, but when they have fresh food they may eat as much as a hundred pounds at one time. They hunt mainly deer, boars, and even bears, plus smaller prey such as fish and rabbits. They pounce on their prey and grab them by the back of the neck. Animals that are not killed immediately are thrown to the ground and suffocated with a bite to the throat. Then the tigers feast.

vb agr

29

30 Pronoun Case

In *Brief*

- Distinguish between compound subjects and compound objects: *she and I* vs. *her and me* (opposite).
- Use the subjective case for subject complements: *It was she* (opposite).
- Use *who* or *whom* depending on the pronoun's function in its clause (p. 242).
- Use the appropriate case in other constructions, such as after *than* or *as* or with an infinitive (p. 244).

Visit MyWritingLab™ for more resources on pronoun case.

Choosing the right **case** of a pronoun—the right form, such as *she* or *her*—requires understanding how the pronoun functions in its sentence.

- **The subjective case** indicates that the pronoun is a subject (*She spoke*) or a subject complement (*It was she*). (See pp. 191 and 194.)
- **The objective case** indicates that the pronoun is an object of a verb (*They hired him*) or preposition (*She spoke to us*). (See pp. 193–95 and 198.)
- **The possessive case** indicates that the pronoun owns or is the source of a noun in the sentence (*Its fur is smooth*).

case
30

Subjective	Objective	Possessive
I	me	my, mine
you	you	your, yours
he	him	his
she	her	her, hers
it	it	its
we	us	our, ours
you	you	your, yours
they	them	their, theirs
who	whom	whose
whoever	whomever	—

CULTURE LANGUAGE In standard American English, *-self* pronouns do not change form to show function. Their only forms are *myself, yourself, himself, herself, itself, ourselves, yourselves, themselves*. Avoid nonstandard forms such as *hisself, ourself,* and *theirselves*.

Faulty   Novick presented the proposal hisself.
Revised   Novick presented the proposal himself.

30a Distinguish between compound subjects and compound objects: *she and I* vs. *her and me.*

Compound subjects and compound objects—those consisting of two or more nouns or pronouns—have the same case forms as they would if one noun or pronoun stood alone.

<u>compound
subject
She and Novick</u> discussed the proposal.

<u>compound
object</u>
The proposal disappointed <u>her and him.</u>

If you are in doubt about the correct form of a pronoun, try the following test.

A test for case forms in compound subjects or objects

1. **Identify a compound subject or object** (one connected by *and, but, or, nor*):

   [He, Him] and [I, me] won the prize.
   The prize went to [he, him] and [I, me].

2. **Write a separate sentence for each part of the compound:**

   [He, Him] won the prize. [I, Me] won the prize.
   The prize went to [he, him]. The prize went to [I, me].

3. **Choose the pronouns that sound correct:**

   <u>He</u> won the prize. <u>I</u> won the prize. [Subjective.]
   The prize went to <u>him.</u> The prize went to <u>me.</u> [Objective.]

4. **Put the separate sentences back together:**

   <u>He and I</u> won the prize.
   The prize went to <u>him and me.</u>

case
30b

Note Avoid using the pronoun *myself* in place of the personal pronoun *I* or *me*: *Stephen and I* [not *myself*] *trained. Everyone went except me* [not *myself*]. For more on the *-self* pronouns, see pages 512–13.

30b Use the subjective case for subject complements: *It was she.*

After a linking verb such as *is* or *are*, a pronoun renaming the subject (a subject complement) should be in the subjective case:

subject
complement
The ones who care most are <u>she and Novick</u>.

subject
complement
It was <u>they</u> whom the mayor appointed.

If this construction sounds stilted to you, use the more natural order: *She and Novick* *are the ones who care most. The mayor appointed* <u>*them*</u>.

Exercise 30.1   Choosing between subjective and objective pronouns

From the pairs in brackets, select the appropriate subjective or objective pronoun(s) for each of the following sentences.

Example:

"Between you and [I, me]," the seller said, "this deal is a steal."
"Between you and <u>me</u>," the seller said, "this deal is a steal."

1. Kayla and [<u>I</u>, me] were competing for places on the relay team.
2. The fastest runners at our school were [<u>she</u>, her] and [<u>I</u>, me], so [<u>we</u>, us] expected to make the team.
3. [<u>She</u>, Her] and [<u>I</u>, me] were friends but also intense rivals.
4. The time trials went badly, excluding both [she, <u>her</u>] and [I, <u>me</u>] from the team.
5. Next season [<u>she</u>, her] and [<u>I</u>, me] are determined to earn places on the team.

30c   The use of *who* vs. *whom* depends on the pronoun's function in its clause.

1 ▪ Questions

At the beginning of a question, use *who* for a subject and *whom* for an object:

subject
Who wrote the policy?

object
Whom does it affect?

To find the correct case of *who* in a question, follow the steps below:

1. **Pose the question:**

   [Who, Whom] makes that decision?
   [Who, Whom] does one ask?

2. **Answer the question, using a personal pronoun.** Choose the pronoun that sounds correct, and note its case:

   [She, Her] makes that decision. <u>She</u> makes that decision. [Subjective.]
   One asks [she, her]. One asks <u>her</u>. [Objective.]

3. **Use the same case (*who* or *whom*) in the question:**

Who makes that decision? [Subjective.]
Whom does one ask? [Objective.]

2 ▪ Subordinate clauses

A subordinate clause contains a subject and a predicate but begins with a subordinating word (see pp. 188–89). When that word is a form of *who* or *whoever,* you need to determine whether it serves as the subject of the clause or as an object.

subject ⟍
Give old clothes to whoever needs them.

object ⟵
I don't know whom the mayor appointed.

To determine which form to use, try the following test:

1. **Locate the subordinate clause:**

Few people know [who, whom] they should ask.
They are unsure [who, whom] makes the decision.

2. **Rewrite the subordinate clause as a separate sentence, substituting a personal pronoun for *who, whom.*** Choose the pronoun that sounds correct, and note its case:

They should ask [she, her]. They should ask her. [Objective.]

[She, her] usually makes the decision. She usually makes the decision. [Subjective.]

case
30c

3. **Use the same case (*who* or *whom*) in the subordinate clause:**

Few people know whom they should ask. [Objective.]
They are unsure who makes the decision. [Subjective.]

Note Don't let expressions such as *I think* and *she says* mislead you into using *whom* rather than *who* for the subject of a clause.

subject ⟍
He is the one who I think is best qualified.

To choose between *who* and *whom* in such constructions, delete the interrupting phrase so that you can see the true relation between parts: *He is the one who is best qualified.*

Exercise 30.2 Choosing between *who* and *whom*

From the pairs in brackets, select the appropriate form of the pronoun in each of the following sentences.

Example:

My mother asked me [who, whom] I was meeting.
My mother asked me whom I was meeting.

1. The school administrators suspended Jurgen, [who, whom] they suspected of setting the fire.
2. Jurgen had been complaining to other custodians, [who, whom] reported him.
3. He constantly complained of unfair treatment from [whoever, whomever] happened to be passing in the halls, including pupils.
4. "[Who, Whom] here has heard Mr. Jurgen's complaints?" the police asked.
5. "[Who, Whom] did he complain most about?"
6. His coworkers agreed that Jurgen seemed less upset with the staff or students, most of [who, whom] he did not even know, than with the building itself.
7. "He took out his aggression on the building," claimed one coworker [who, whom] often witnessed Jurgen's behavior.
8. "He cursed and kicked the walls and [whoever, whomever] he saw nearby."
9. The coworker thought that Jurgen might have imagined people [who, whom] instructed him to behave the way he did.
10. "He's someone [who, whom] other people can't get next to," said the coworker.

30d   Use the appropriate case in other constructions.

1 ▪ *We* or *us* with a noun

The choice of *we* or *us* before a noun depends on the use of the noun:

> object of
> preposition

Freezing weather is welcomed by us skaters.

> subject

We skaters welcome freezing weather.

2 ▪ Pronoun in an appositive

An appositive renames the noun immediately before it (see p. 200). The case of a pronoun in an appositive depends on the function of the word the appositive describes or identifies:

> appositive
> identifies object

The class elected two representatives, DeShawn and me.

> appositive
> identifies subject

Two representatives, DeShawn and I, were elected.

3 ▪ Pronoun after *than* or *as*

When a pronoun follows *than* or *as* in a comparison, the case of the pronoun indicates what words may have been omitted. A subjective pronoun must be the subject of the omitted verb:

subject
Some critics like Glass more than <u>he</u> [does].

An objective pronoun must be the object of the omitted verb:

object
Some critics like Glass more than [they like] <u>him</u>.

4 ■ Subject and object of infinitive

An infinitive is the plain form of the verb plus *to*: *to run* (see p. 199). Both the object *and* the subject of an infinitive are in the objective case.

subject
of infinitive
The school asked <u>him</u> to speak.

object
of infinitive
Students chose to invite <u>him</u>.

5 ■ Case before a gerund

A gerund is the *-ing* form of a verb used as a noun: *I enjoy* <u>cooking</u> (see p. 199). Ordinarily, use the possessive form of a pronoun or noun immediately before a gerund:

The coach disapproved of <u>their</u> lifting weights.

The <u>coach's</u> disapproving was a surprise.

Exercise 30.3   **Revising: Pronoun case**

Revise all inappropriate case forms in the sentences below. If a sentence is already correct as given, mark the number preceding it.

case

30d

Example:

Convincing we veterans to vote yes will be difficult.
Convincing <u>us</u> veterans to vote yes will be difficult.

1. Written four thousand years ago, *The Epic of Gilgamesh* tells of a bored king who his people thought was too harsh.
2. Gilgamesh found a source of entertainment when he met Enkidu, a wild man who had lived with the animals in the mountains.
3. Him and Gilgamesh wrestled to see whom was more powerful.
4. After hours of struggle, Enkidu admitted that Gilgamesh was stronger than he.
5. The friendship of the two strong men was sealed by them fighting.
6. Gilgamesh said, "Between you and I, mighty deeds will be accomplished, and our fame will be everlasting."
7. Among their glorious acts, Enkidu and him defeated a giant bull, Humbaba, and cut down the bull's cedar forests.
8. Their bringing back cedar logs to Gilgamesh's treeless land won great praise from the people.

9. When Enkidu died, Gilgamesh mourned his death, realizing that no one had been a better friend than him.
10. When Gilgamesh himself died many years later, his people raised a monument praising Enkidu and he for their friendship and their mighty deeds of courage.

31 Agreement of Pronoun and Antecedent

In *Brief*

- Make a pronoun agree with an antecedent joined by *and, or,* or *nor* (opposite).
- Make a pronoun agree when the antecedent is *everyone* or another indefinite pronoun (opposite).
- Make a pronoun agree when the antecedent is *team* or another collective noun (p. 249).

Visit MyWritingLab™ for more resources on pronoun-antecedent agreement.

pn agr
31

The **antecedent** of a pronoun is the noun or other pronoun to which the pronoun refers:

Students fret over their tuition bills.
antecedent   pronoun

Its yearly increases make the tuition bill a dreaded document.
pronoun   antecedent

For clarity, a pronoun should agree with its antecedent in person and number as well as in gender (masculine, feminine, neuter).

	Number	
Person	*Singular*	*Plural*
First	*I*	*we*
Second	*you*	*you*
Third	*he, she, it,* indefinite pronouns, singular nouns	*they,* plural nouns

CULTURE LANGUAGE   The gender of a pronoun should match its antecedent, not a noun that the pronoun may modify: *Sara asked her* [not *his*] *son.* Also, nouns in English have only neuter gender unless they specifically refer to males or females. Thus nouns such as *book, sun,* and *earth* take the pronoun *it*: *Read this book. It is inspiring.*

31a   Antecedents joined by *and* usually take plural pronouns.

Mr. Bartos and I cannot settle our dispute.

The dean and my adviser have offered their help.

Exceptions When the compound antecedent refers to a single idea, person, or thing, then the pronoun is singular:

My friend and adviser offered her help.

When the compound antecedent follows *each* or *every*, the pronoun is singular:

Every girl and woman took her seat.

31b   When parts of an antecedent are joined by *or* or *nor*, the pronoun agrees with the nearer part.

Tenants or owners must present their grievances.

Either the tenant or the owner will have her way.

When one subject is plural and the other singular, the sentence will be awkward unless you put the plural subject second:

Awkward	Neither the tenants nor the owner has yet made her case.
Revised	Neither the owner nor the tenants have yet made their case.

31c   With *everyone, person,* and other indefinite words, use a singular or plural pronoun as appropriate.

Indefinite words do not refer to a specific person or thing. **Indefinite pronouns** include *anybody, anyone, anything, each, either, everybody, everyone, everything, much, neither, nobody, no one, nothing, one, somebody, someone,* and *something.* **Generic nouns** are words such as *person, individual,* and *student* when they refer to a typical member of a group, not to a particular individual.

Most indefinite pronouns and all generic nouns are singular in meaning. When they serve as antecedents, they take singular nouns:

Each of the animal shelters has its population of homeless pets.
indefinite pronoun

Every worker in our shelter cares for his or her favorite animal.
generic noun

Four indefinite pronouns are plural in meaning: *both, few, many, several*. As antecedents, they take plural pronouns:

Many of the animals show affection for their caretakers.

Six indefinite pronouns may be singular or plural in meaning: *all, any, more, most, none, some*. As antecedents, they take singular pronouns if they refer to singular words, plural pronouns if they refer to plural words:

Most of the shelter's equipment was donated by its original owner. [*Most* refers to *equipment*.]

Most of the veterinarians donate their time. [*Most* refers to *veterinarians*.]

None may be singular even when referring to a plural word, especially to emphasize the meaning "not one": *None* [*Not one*] *of the shelters has increased its capacity.*

Most agreement problems arise with the singular indefinite words. We often use these words to mean something like "many" or "all" rather than "one" and then refer to them with plural pronouns, as in *Everyone has their own locker* or *A person can padlock their locker*. Often, too, we mean indefinite words to include both masculine and feminine genders and thus resort to *they* instead of the generic *he*—the masculine pronoun referring to both genders, as in *Everyone deserves his privacy*. (For more on the generic *he*, which many readers view as sexist, see p. 164.)

(For more on the generic *he*, which many readers view as sexist, see p. 164.)

Although some experts accept *they, them,* and *their* with singular indefinite words, most do not, and many teachers and employers regard the plural as incorrect. To be safe, work for agreement between singular indefinite words and the pronouns that refer to them. You have several options:

Ways to correct agreement with indefinite words

- **Change the indefinite word to a plural, and use a plural pronoun to match:**

  Faulty   Every athlete deserves their privacy.
  Revised   Athletes deserve their privacy.

- **Rewrite the sentence to omit the pronoun:**

  Faulty   Everyone is entitled to their own locker.
  Revised   Everyone is entitled to a locker.

- **Use *he or she* (*him or her, his or her*) to refer to the indefinite word:**

  Faulty   Now everyone has their private space.
  Revised   Now everyone has his or her private space.

However, used more than once in several sentences, *he or she* quickly becomes awkward. (Many readers do not accept the alternative *he/she*.) In most cases, using the plural or omitting the pronoun will not only correct agreement problems but also create more readable sentences.

31d Collective nouns such as *team* take singular or plural pronouns depending on meaning.

A **collective noun** has singular form and names a group of persons or things: *army, audience, family, group, team.* Use a singular pronoun with a collective noun when referring to the group as a unit:

The committee voted to disband itself.

When referring to the individual members of the group, use a plural pronoun:

The old team have gone their separate ways.

If a combination such as *team have . . . their* seems awkward, reword the sentence: *The members of the old team have gone their separate ways.*

CULTURE LANGUAGE In standard American English, collective nouns that are noncount nouns (they don't form plurals) usually take singular pronouns: *The mail sits in its own basket.* A few noncount nouns take plural pronouns, including *clergy, military, police, the rich,* and *the poor: The police support their unions.*

pn agr
31d

Exercise 31.1 Revising: Pronoun-antecedent agreement
Revise the following sentences so that pronouns and their antecedents agree in person and number. Some items have more than one possible answer. Try to avoid the generic *he* (see opposite). If you change the subject of a sentence, be sure to change the verb as necessary for agreement. If a sentence is already correct as given, mark the number preceding it.

Example:

Each of the Boudreaus' children brought their laundry home at Thanksgiving.

All of the Boudreaus' children brought their laundry home at Thanksgiving. *Or:* Each of the Boudreaus' children brought laundry home at Thanksgiving. *Or:* Each of the Boudreaus' children brought his or her laundry home at Thanksgiving.

1. Each girl raised in a Mexican American family in the Rio Grande Valley of Texas hopes that one day they will be given a *quinceañera* party for their fifteenth birthday.
2. Such celebrations are very expensive because it entails a religious service followed by a huge party.

3. A girl's immediate family, unless they are wealthy, cannot afford the party by themselves.
4. The parents will ask each close friend or relative if they can help with the preparations.
5. Surrounded by her family and attended by her friends and their escorts, the *quinceañera* is introduced as a young woman eligible for Mexican American society.
6. Almost any child will quickly astound observers with their capabilities.
7. Despite their extensive research and experience, neither child psychologists nor parents have yet figured out how children become who they are.
8. Of course, the family has a tremendous influence on the development of a child in their midst.
9. Each member of the immediate family exerts their own unique pull on the child.
10. Other relatives, teachers, and friends also can affect the child's view of the world and of themselves.
11. The workings of genetics also strongly influence the child, but it may never be fully understood.
12. The psychology community cannot agree in its views of whether nurture or nature is more important in a child's development.
13. Another debated issue is whether the child's emotional development or their intellectual development is more central.
14. Just about everyone has their strong opinion on these issues, often backed up by evidence.
15. Neither the popular press nor scholarly journals devote much of their space to the wholeness of the child.

ref
32

32 Reference of Pronoun to Antecedent

In *Brief*

- Make a pronoun refer clearly to one antecedent (opposite).
- Place a pronoun close enough to its antecedent to ensure clarity (opposite).
- Make a pronoun refer to a specific antecedent (opposite).
- Use *you* only to mean "you, the reader" (p. 253).
- Keep pronouns consistent (p. 253).

Visit MyWritingLab™ for more resources on pronoun reference.

A pronoun should refer clearly to its **antecedent,** the noun or nouns it refers to. Otherwise, readers will have difficulty grasping the pronoun's meaning. In editing your writing, make sure that each pronoun refers to an obvious, close, and specific antecedent.

⟨CULTURE LANGUAGE⟩ In standard American English, a pronoun needs a clear antecedent nearby, but don't use both a pronoun and its antecedent as the subject of the same clause: *James* [not *James he*] *told Victor to go alone.* (See also p. 285.)

32a Make a pronoun refer clearly to one antecedent.

When either of two nouns can be a pronoun's antecedent, the reference will not be clear.

> **Confusing** Emily Dickinson is sometimes compared with Jane Austen,
> but <u>she</u> led a more reclusive life.

Revise such a sentence in one of two ways:

- Replace the pronoun with the appropriate noun.

  > **Clear** Emily Dickinson is sometimes compared with Jane Austen,
  > but <u>Dickinson</u> led a more reclusive life.

- **Avoid repetition by rewriting the sentence.** If you use the pronoun, make sure it has only one possible antecedent.

  > **Clear** Despite occasional comparison of their lives, Emily Dickinson was more reclusive than Jane Austen.

  > **Clear** Though sometimes compared with <u>her</u>, Emily Dickinson led a more reclusive life than Jane Austen.

32b Place a pronoun close enough to its antecedent to ensure clarity.

A clause beginning with *who, which,* or *that* should generally fall immediately after the word to which it refers:

> **Confusing** Jody found a lamp in the attic <u>that</u> her aunt had used.
> **Clear** In the attic Jody found a lamp <u>that</u> her aunt had used.

32c Make a pronoun refer to a specific antecedent, not an implied one.

A pronoun should refer to a specific noun or other pronoun. A reader can only guess at the meaning of a pronoun when its antecedent is implied by the context, not stated outright.

1 ▪ Vague *this, that, which,* or *it*

This, that, which, or *it* should refer to a specific noun, not to a whole word group expressing an idea or situation.

Confusing	The faculty agreed on changing the requirements, but it took time.
Clear	The faculty agreed on changing the requirements, but the agreement took time.
Clear	The faculty agreed on changing the requirements, but the change took time.
Confusing	The British knew little of the American countryside, and they had no experience with the colonists' guerrilla tactics. This gave the colonists an advantage.
Clear	The British knew little of the American countryside, and they had no experience with the colonists' guerrilla tactics. This ignorance and inexperience gave the colonists an advantage.

2 ▪ Indefinite antecedents with *it* and *they*

It and *they* should have definite noun antecedents. Rewrite the sentence if the antecedent is missing.

Confusing	In Chapter 4 of this book it describes the early flights of the Wright brothers.
Clear	Chapter 4 of this book describes the early flights of the Wright brothers.

Confusing	Even in TV reality shows, they present a false picture of life.
Clear	Even TV reality shows present a false picture of life.
Clear	Even in TV reality shows, the producers present a false picture of life.

3 ▪ Implied nouns

A noun may be implied in some other word or phrase, such as an adjective (*happiness* implied in *happy*), a verb (*driver* implied in *drive*), or a possessive (*mother* implied in *mother's*). But a pronoun cannot refer clearly to an implied noun, only to a specific, stated one.

Confusing	In Cohen's report she made claims that led to a lawsuit.
Clear	In her report Cohen made claims that led to a lawsuit.
Confusing	Her reports on psychological development generally go unnoticed outside it.
Clear	Her reports on psychological development generally go unnoticed outside the field.

32d   Use *you* only to mean "you, the reader."

In all but formal academic writing, *you* is acceptable when the meaning is clearly "you, the reader." But the context must be appropriate for such a meaning:

Inappropriate	In the fourteenth century <u>you</u> had to struggle simply to survive.
Revised	In the fourteenth century <u>one</u> [or <u>a person</u>] had to struggle simply to survive.

Writers sometimes drift into *you* because *one, a person,* or a similar indefinite word can be difficult to sustain. Sentence after sentence, the indefinite word may sound stuffy, and it requires *he* or *he or she* for pronoun-antecedent agreement (see pp. 247–49). To avoid these problems, try using plural nouns and pronouns:

Original	In the fourteenth century <u>one</u> had to struggle simply to survive.
Revised	In the fourteenth century <u>people</u> had to struggle simply to survive.

32e   Keep pronouns consistent.

Within a sentence or a group of related sentences, pronouns should be consistent. Partly, consistency comes from making pronouns and their antecedents agree (see Chapter 31). In addition, the pronouns within a passage should match each other.

Inconsistent pronouns	<u>One</u> finds when reading that <u>your</u> concentration improves with practice, so that <u>I</u> now comprehend more in less time.
Revised	<u>I</u> find when reading that <u>my</u> concentration improves with practice, so that <u>I</u> now comprehend more in less time.

Exercise 32.1   Revising: Pronoun reference

Many of the pronouns in the following sentences do not refer to clear, specific, and appropriate antecedents. Revise the sentences as necessary to correct the errors.

Example:

In Grand Teton National Park they have moose, elk, and trumpeter swans.

<u>Moose, elk, and trumpeter swans live</u> in Grand Teton National Park.

1. "Life begins at forty" is a cliché many people live by, and this may or may not be true.
2. Living successfully or not depends on one's definition of it.
3. When she was forty, Pearl Buck's novel *The Good Earth* won the Pulitzer Prize.

4. Buck was raised in a missionary family in China, and she wrote about it in her novels.
5. In *The Good Earth* you have to struggle, but fortitude is rewarded.
6. Buck received much critical praise and earned over $7 million, but she was very modest about it.
7. Pearl Buck donated most of her earnings to a foundation for Asian American children that proves her generosity.
8. In the *Book of Romance* it reserves a chapter for the story of Elizabeth Barrett, who at forty married Robert Browning against her father's wishes.
9. In the 1840s they did not normally defy their fathers, but Elizabeth was too much in love to obey.
10. She left a poetic record of her love for Robert, and readers still enjoy reading them.

Exercise 32.2 Revising: Pronoun reference

Revise the following paragraph so that each pronoun refers clearly to a single, specific, and appropriate antecedent.

In Charlotte Brontë's *Jane Eyre*, she is a shy young woman that takes a job as governess. Her employer is a rude, brooding man named Rochester. He lives in a mysterious mansion on the English moors, which contributes an eerie quality to Jane's experience. Eerier still are the fires, strange noises, and other unexplained happenings in the house; but Rochester refuses to discuss this. Eventually, they fall in love. On the day they are to be married, however, she learns that he has a wife hidden in the house. She is hopelessly insane and violent and must be guarded at all times, which explains his strange behavior. Heartbroken, Jane leaves the moors, and many years pass before they are reunited.

ad
33

——— MODIFIERS ———

33 Adjectives and Adverbs

In *Brief*

- Use adjectives only to modify nouns and pronouns (opposite).
- Use an adjective after a linking verb to modify the subject; use an adverb to modify a verb (opposite).
- Use comparative and superlative forms appropriately (p. 256).
- Avoid most double negatives (p. 258).
- Distinguish between present and past participles as adjectives (p. 259).
- Use *a, an, the,* and other determiners appropriately (p. 260).

Visit MyWritingLab™ for more resources on adjectives and adverbs.

Adjectives modify nouns (*happy child*) and pronouns (*special someone*). **Adverbs** modify verbs (*almost see*), adjectives (*very happy*), other adverbs (*not very*), and whole word groups (*Otherwise, I'll go*). The only way to tell whether a modifier should be an adjective or an adverb is to determine its function in the sentence.

CULTURE LANGUAGE In standard American English, an adjective does not change along with the noun it modifies to show plural number: *white* [not *whites*] *shoes, square* [not *squares*] *spaces, better* [not *betters*] *chances*. Only nouns form plurals.

33a Use adjectives only to modify nouns and pronouns.

Using adjectives instead of adverbs to modify verbs, adverbs, or other adjectives is nonstandard.

Faulty   Educating children good should be everyone's focus.

Revised   Educating children well should be everyone's focus.

Faulty   Some children suffer bad.

Revised   Some children suffer badly.

CULTURE LANGUAGE Choosing between *not* and *no* can be a challenge. *Not* is an adverb, so it makes a verb or an adjective negative:

They do not learn. They are not happy. They have not been in class.

(See pp. 267–68 for where to place *not* in relation to verbs and adjectives.) *No* is an adjective, so it makes a noun negative:

No child likes to fail. No good school fails children.

Place *no* before the noun or any other modifier.

ad
33b

33b Use an adjective after a linking verb to modify the subject. Use an adverb to modify a verb.

A linking verb connects the subject and a word that describes the subject—for instance, *seem, become, look,* and forms of *be*. Some verbs may or may not be linking verbs, depending on their meaning in the sentence. When the word after the verb modifies the subject, the verb is linking and the word should be an adjective: *He looked happy. The milk turned sour*. When the word modifies the verb, however, it should be an adverb: *He looked carefully. The car turned suddenly*.

Two word pairs are especially tricky. One is *bad* and *badly*:

The weather grew bad.
linking adjective
verb

She felt bad.
linking adjective
verb

Flowers grow badly in such soil.
verb adverb

The other tricky pair is *good* and *well*. *Good* serves only as an adjective. *Well* may serve as an adverb with a host of meanings or as an adjective meaning only "fit" or "healthy."

Decker felt well.
linking adjective
verb

Her health was good.
linking adjective
verb

She trained well.
verb adverb

Exercise 33.1   Revising: Adjectives and adverbs

Revise the following sentences to use adjectives and adverbs appropriately. If any sentence is already correct as given, mark the number preceding it.

Example:

The announcer warned loud and clear that traffic was stopped on the bridge.

The announcer warned loudly and clearly that traffic was stopped on the bridge.

1. People who take their health serious often believe that movie-theater popcorn is a healthy snack.
2. Nutrition information about movie popcorn may make these people feel different.
3. One large tub of movie popcorn has twelve hundred calories and sixty grams of saturated fat—both surprisingly high numbers.
4. Once people are aware of the calories and fat, they may feel badly about indulging in this classic snack.
5. People who want to eat good should think twice before ordering popcorn at the movies.

ad
33c

33c   Use the comparative and superlative forms of adjectives and adverbs appropriately.

Adjectives and adverbs can show degrees of quality or amount with the endings *-er* and *-est* or with the words *more* and *most* or *less* and *least*. Most modifiers have three forms.

Positive The basic form listed in the dictionary	**Comparative** A greater or lesser degree of the quality	**Superlative** The greatest or least degree of the quality
Adjectives		
red	redder	reddest
awful	more/less awful	most/least awful
Adverbs		
soon	sooner	soonest
quickly	more/less quickly	most/least quickly

If sound alone does not tell you whether to use *-er/-est* or *more/ most,* consult a dictionary. If the endings can be used, the dictionary will list them. Otherwise, use *more* or *most.*

1 ▪ Irregular adjectives and adverbs

Irregular modifiers change the spelling of their positive form to show comparative and superlative degrees.

Positive	Comparative	Superlative
Adjectives		
good	better	best
bad	worse	worst
little	littler, less	littlest, least
many ⎫		
some ⎬	more	most
much ⎭		
Adverbs		
well	better	best
badly	worse	worst

2 ▪ Double comparisons

A double comparative or double superlative combines the *-er* or *-est* ending with the word *more* or *most.* It is redundant.

Chang was the <u>wisest</u> [not <u>most wisest</u>] person in town.
He was <u>smarter</u> [not <u>more smarter</u>] than anyone else.

3 ▪ Logical comparisons

Absolute modifiers

Some adjectives and adverbs cannot logically be compared—for instance, *perfect, unique, dead, impossible, infinite.* These absolute words can be preceded by adverbs like *nearly* or *almost* that mean "approaching," but they cannot logically be modified by *more* or *most* (as in *most perfect*).

Not	He was the <u>most unique</u> teacher we had.
But	He was a <u>unique</u> teacher.

Completeness

To be logical, a comparison must also be complete in the following ways:

▪ **The comparison must state a relation fully enough for clarity.**

Unclear	Carmakers worry about their industry more than environmentalists.
Clear	Carmakers worry about their industry more than environmentalists <u>do</u>.

Clear   Carmakers worry about their industry more than <u>they worry about</u> environmentalists.

■ **The items being compared should in fact be comparable.**

Illogical   The cost of a hybrid car can be greater than a gasoline-powered car. [Illogically compares a cost and a car.]

Revised   The cost of a hybrid car can be greater than <u>the cost of</u> [or <u>that of</u>] a gasoline-powered car.

See also page 153 on parallelism with comparisons.

Any vs. *any other*

Use *any other* when comparing something with others in the same group. Use *any* when comparing something with others in a different group.

Illogical   Los Angeles is larger than <u>any</u> city in California. [Since Los Angeles is itself a city in California, the sentence seems to say that Los Angeles is larger than itself.]

Revised   Los Angeles is larger than <u>any other</u> city in California.

Illogical   Los Angeles is larger than <u>any other</u> city in Canada. [The cities in Canada constitute a group to which Los Angeles does not belong.]

Revised   Los Angeles is larger than <u>any</u> city in Canada.

33d Watch for double negatives.

In a **double negative** two negative words such as *no, not, none, barely, hardly,* or *scarcely* cancel each other out. Some double negatives are intentional: for instance, *She was <u>not unhappy</u>* indicates with understatement that she was indeed happy. But most double negatives say the opposite of what is intended: *Nadine did <u>not</u> feel <u>nothing</u>* asserts that Nadine felt other than nothing, or something. For the opposite meaning, one of the negatives must be eliminated (*She felt nothing*) or one of them must be changed to a positive (*She did not feel anything*).

Faulty   The IRS <u>cannot hardly</u> audit all tax returns. <u>None</u> of its audits <u>never</u> touch many cheaters.

Revised   The IRS <u>cannot</u> audit all tax returns. Its audits <u>never</u> touch many cheaters.

Exercise 33.2 **Revising: Double negatives**

Identify and revise the double negatives in the following sentences. Each error may have more than one correct revision. If a sentence is already correct as given, mark the number preceding it.

1. Interest in books about the founding of the United States is not hardly consistent among Americans: it seems to vary with the national mood.
2. Americans show barely any interest in books about the founders when things are going well in the United States.
3. However, when Americans can't hardly agree on major issues, sales of books about the Revolutionary War era increase.
4. During such periods, one cannot go to no bookstore without seeing several new volumes about John Adams, Thomas Jefferson, and other founders.
5. When Americans feel they don't have nothing in common, their increased interest in the early leaders may reflect a desire for unity.

33e Distinguish between present and past participles as adjectives. (CULTURE LANGUAGE)

Both present participles and past participles may serve as adjectives: *a burning building* (present), *a burned building* (past). As in the examples, the two participles usually differ in the time they indicate.

But some present and past participles—those derived from verbs expressing feeling—can have altogether different meanings. The present participle modifies something that causes the feeling: *That was a frightening storm* (the storm frightens). The past participle modifies something that experiences the feeling: *They quieted the frightened horses* (the horses feel fright).

The following participles are among those likely to be confused:

amazing/amazed	fascinating/fascinated
amusing/amused	frightening/frightened
annoying/annoyed	frustrating/frustrated
astonishing/astonished	interesting/interested
boring/bored	pleasing/pleased
confusing/confused	satisfying/satisfied
depressing/depressed	shocking/shocked
embarrassing/embarrassed	surprising/surprised
exciting/excited	tiring/tired
exhausting/exhausted	worrying/worried

ad
33e

Exercise 33.3 Revising: Present and past participles (CULTURE LANGUAGE)
Revise the adjectives in the following sentences as needed to distinguish between present and past participles. If a sentence is already correct as given, mark the number preceding it.

Example:

The subject was embarrassed to many people.
The subject was <u>embarrassing</u> to many people.

1. Several critics found Alice Walker's *The Color Purple* to be a fascinated book.

2. One confused critic wished that Walker had deleted the scenes set in Africa.
3. Another critic argued that although the book contained many depressed episodes, the overall effect was excited.
4. Since other readers found the book annoyed, this critic pointed out its many surprising qualities.
5. In the end most critics agreed that the book was a satisfied novel about the struggles of an African American woman.

33f Use *a, an, the,* and other determiners appropriately.   CULTURE LANGUAGE

Determiners are special kinds of adjectives that mark nouns because they always precede nouns. Some common determiners are *a, an,* and *the* (called **articles**) and *my, their, whose, this, these, those, one, some,* and *any.*

Native speakers of standard American English can rely on their intuition when using determiners, but speakers of other languages and dialects often have difficulty with them. In standard American English, the use of determiners depends on the context they appear in and the kind of noun they precede:

- A *proper noun* **names a particular person, place, or thing and begins with a capital letter:** *February, Joe Allen, Red River.* Most proper nouns are not preceded by determiners.

- A *count noun* **names something that is countable in English and can form a plural:** *girl/girls, apple/apples, child/children.* A singular count noun is always preceded by a determiner; a plural count noun sometimes is.

- A *noncount noun* **names something not usually considered countable in English, and so it does not form a plural.** A noncount noun is sometimes preceded by a determiner. Here is a sample of noncount nouns, sorted into groups by meaning:

Abstractions: advice, confidence, democracy, education, equality, evidence, health, information, intelligence, knowledge, luxury, peace, pollution, research, success, supervision, truth, wealth, work
Food and drink: bread, candy, cereal, flour, meat, milk, salt, water, wine
Emotions: anger, courage, happiness, hate, joy, love, respect, sadness, satisfaction
Natural events and substances: air, blood, dirt, gasoline, gold, hair, heat, ice, oil, oxygen, rain, silver, smoke, weather, wood
Groups: clergy, clothing, equipment, furniture, garbage, jewelry, junk, legislation, machinery, mail, military, money, police, vocabulary
Fields of study: accounting, architecture, biology, business, chemistry, engineering, literature, psychology, science

A dictionary of English as a second language will tell you whether a noun is a count noun, a noncount noun, or both. (See p. 167 for recommended dictionaries.)

Note Many nouns are sometimes count nouns and sometimes noncount nouns:

> The library has a room for readers. [*Room* is a count noun meaning "walled area."]
>
> The library has room for reading. [*Room* is a noncount noun meaning "space."]

1 ▪ *A, an,* and *the*

With singular count nouns

A or *an* precedes a singular count noun when the reader does not already know its identity, usually because you have not mentioned it before:

> A scientist in our chemistry lab developed a process to strengthen metals. [*Scientist* and *process* are being mentioned for the first time.]

The precedes a singular count noun that has a specific identity for the reader, for one of the following reasons:

▪ **You have mentioned the noun before:**

> A scientist in our chemistry lab developed a process to strengthen metals. The scientist patented the process. [*Scientist* and *process* were identified in the preceding sentence.]

▪ **You identify the noun immediately before or after you state it:**

> The most productive lab is the research center in the chemistry department. [*Most productive* identifies *lab. In the chemistry department* identifies *research center.* And *chemistry department* is a shared facility—see below.]

▪ **The noun names something unique—the only one in existence:**

> The sun rises in the east. [*Sun* and *east* are unique.]

▪ **The noun names an institution or facility that is shared by the community of readers:**

> Many men and women aspire to the presidency. [*Presidency* is a shared institution.]
>
> The cell phone has changed communication. [*Cell phone* is a shared facility.]

The is not used before a singular noun that names a general category:

> Wordsworth's poetry shows his love of nature [not the nature].

det

33f

General Sherman said that war is hell. [*War* names a general category.]
The war in Iraq has left many wounded. [*War* names a specific war.]

With plural count nouns

A or *an* never precedes a plural noun. *The* does not precede a plural noun that names a general category. *The* does precede a plural noun that names specific representatives of a category.

Men and women are different. [*Men* and *women* name general categories.]

The women formed a team. [*Women* refers to specific people.]

With noncount nouns

A or *an* never precedes a noncount noun. *The* does precede a noncount noun that names specific representatives of a general category.

Vegetation suffers from drought. [*Vegetation* names a general category.]

The vegetation in the park withered or died. [*Vegetation* refers to specific plants.]

With proper nouns

A or *an* never precedes a proper noun. *The* generally does not precede proper nouns.

Garcia lives in Boulder.

There are exceptions, however. For instance, we generally use *the* before plural proper nouns (*the Murphys, the Boston Celtics*) and before the names of groups and organizations (*the Department of Justice, the Sierra Club*), ships (*the Lusitania*), oceans (*the Pacific*), mountain ranges (*the Alps*), regions (*the Middle East*), rivers (*the Mississippi*), and some countries (*the United States, the Netherlands*).

2 ▪ Other determiners

The uses of English determiners besides articles also depend on context and kind of noun. The following determiners may be used as indicated with singular count nouns, plural count nouns, or noncount nouns.

With any kind of noun (singular count, plural count, noncount)

my, our, your, his, her, its, their, possessive nouns (*boy's, boys'*)
whose, which(ever), what(ever)
some, any, the other
no

Their account is overdrawn. [Singular count.]
Their funds are low. [Plural count.]
Their money is running out. [Noncount.]

Only with singular nouns (count and noncount)
this, that

This account has some money. [Count.]
That information may help. [Noncount.]

Only with noncount nouns and plural count nouns
most, enough, other, such, all, all of the, a lot of

Most funds are committed. [Plural count.]
Most money is needed elsewhere. [Noncount.]

Only with singular count nouns
one, every, each, either, neither, another

One car must be sold. [Singular count.]

Only with plural count nouns
these, those
both, many, few, a few, fewer, fewest, several
two, three, and so forth

Two cars are unnecessary. [Plural count.]

Note *Few* means "not many" or "not enough." *A few* means "some" or "a small but sufficient quantity."

Few committee members came to the meeting.
A few members can keep the committee going.

Do not use *much* with a plural count noun.

Many [not much] members want to help.

det
33f

Only with noncount nouns
much, more, little, a little, less, least, a large amount of

Less luxury is in order. [Noncount.]

Note *Little* means "not many" or "not enough." *A little* means "some" or "a small but sufficient quantity."

Little time remains before the conference.
The members need a little help from their colleagues.

Do not use *many* with a noncount noun.

Much [not many] work remains.

Exercise 33.4 Revising: Articles (CULTURE LANGUAGE)
For each blank, indicate whether *a, an, the,* or no article should be inserted.

Example:

On our bicycle trip across _____ country, we carried _____ map and plenty of _____ food and _____ water.

On our bicycle trip across the country, we carried a map and plenty of food and water.

From _____ native American Indians who migrated from _____ Asia 20,000 years ago to _____ new arrivals who now come by _____ planes, _____ United States is _____ nation of foreigners. It is _____ country of immigrants who are all living under _____ single flag.

Back in _____ seventeenth and eighteenth centuries, at least 75% of the population came from _____ England. However, between 1820 and 1975 more than 38 million immigrants came to this country from elsewhere in Europe. Many children of _____ immigrants were self-conscious and denied their heritage; many even refused to learn _____ native language of their parents and grandparents. They tried to "Americanize" themselves. The so-called Melting Pot theory of _____ social change stressed _____ importance of blending everyone together into _____ kind of stew. Each nationality would contribute its own flavor, but _____ final stew would be something called "American."

This Melting Pot theory was never completely successful. In the last half of the twentieth century, _____ ethnic revival changed _____ metaphor. Many people now see _____ American society as _____ mosaic. Americans are once again proud of their heritage, and _____ ethnic differences make _____ mosaic colorful and interesting.

det
33f

Exercise 33.5   Revising: Adjectives and adverbs

Revise the sentences below to correct errors in the use of adjectives and adverbs. If a sentence is already correct as given, mark the number preceding it.

Example:

Sports fans always feel happily when their team wins.
Sports fans always feel happy when their team wins.

1. Americans often argue about which professional sport is better: basketball, football, or baseball.
2. Basketball fans contend that their sport offers more action because the players are constant running and shooting.
3. Because it is played indoors in relative small arenas, basketball allows fans to be more closer to the action than the other sports do.
4. Football fanatics say they don't hardly stop yelling once the game begins.
5. They cheer when their team executes a real complicated play good.
6. They roar more louder when the defense stops the opponents in a goal-line stand.
7. They yell loudest when a fullback crashes in for a score.
8. In contrast, the supporters of baseball believe that it might be the most perfect sport.

9. It combines the one-on-one duel of pitcher and batter struggling valiant with the tight teamwork of double and triple plays.
10. Because the game is played slow and careful, fans can analyze and discuss the manager's strategy.

34   Misplaced and Dangling Modifiers

In *Brief*

- Reposition misplaced modifiers so that they clearly relate to the words you intend (below).
- Relate dangling modifiers to their sentences by rewriting (p. 269).

Visit MyWritingLab™ for more resources on misplaced and dangling modifiers.

The arrangement of words in a sentence is an important clue to their relationships. Modifiers will be unclear if readers can't connect them to the words they describe.

34a   Reposition misplaced modifiers.

A misplaced modifier falls in the wrong place in a sentence. It is usually awkward or confusing. It may even be unintentionally funny.

mm
34a

1 ▪ Clear placement

Readers tend to link a modifier to the nearest word it could modify. Any other placement can link the modifier to the wrong word.

Confusing   He served steak to the men on paper plates.

Clear   He served the men steak on paper plates.

Confusing   According to the police, many dogs are killed by automobiles and trucks roaming unleashed.

Clear   According to the police, many dogs roaming unleashed are killed by automobiles and trucks.

2 ▪ *Only* and other limiting modifiers

Limiting modifiers include *almost, even, exactly, hardly, just, merely, nearly, only, scarcely,* and *simply.* For clarity, place such a modifier immediately before the word or word group you intend it to limit.

Unclear	The archaeologist only found the skull on her last dig.
Clear	The archaeologist found only the skull on her last dig.
Clear	The archaeologist found the skull only on her last dig.

3 ■ Adverbs with sentence elements

Adverbs modify verbs, adjectives, other adverbs, and whole word groups. They can often move around in sentences, but some will be awkward if they interrupt certain sentence elements.

■ **A long adverb stops the flow from subject to verb:**

subject ┌——adverb——┐ verb
Awkward   The city, after the hurricane, began massive rebuilding.

┌——adverb——┐ subject verb
Revised   After the hurricane, the city began massive rebuilding.

■ **Any adverb is awkward between a verb and its direct object:**

┌——verb——┐ adverb   object
Awkward   The hurricane had damaged badly many homes in the city.

┌—verb—→   object
Revised   The hurricane had badly damaged many homes in the city.
adverb

■ **A *split infinitive*—an adverb placed between *to* and the verb—annoys many readers:**

◄infinitive►
Awkward   The weather service expected temperatures to not rise.

infinitive
Revised   The weather service expected temperatures not to rise.

A split infinitive may sometimes be natural and preferable, though it may still bother some readers:

◄—infinitive—→
Several US industries expect to more than triple their use of robots.

Here the split infinitive is more economical than the alternatives, such as *Several US industries expect to increase their use of robots by more than three times.*

■ **A long adverb is usually awkward inside a verb phrase:**

helping
verb ┌——adverb——┐
Awkward   People who have osteoporosis can, by increasing their daily
————————————, main verb
intake of calcium and vitamin D, improve their bone density.

┌——adverb——————┐
Revised   By increasing their daily intake of calcium and vitamin D,
verb phrase
people who have osteoporosis can improve their bone density.

> **CULTURE LANGUAGE** In a question, place a one-word adverb immediately after the subject.

helping
verb subject adverb verb phrase
rest of
Will spacecraft <u>ever</u> be able to leave the solar system?

4 ▪ Other adverb positions **CULTURE LANGUAGE**

A few adverbs are subject to special conventions for placement:

▪ **Adverbs of frequency** include *always, never, often, rarely, seldom, sometimes,* and *usually.* They generally appear at the beginning of a sentence, before a one-word verb, or after the helping verb in a verb phrase:

helping
verb adverb verb
main
Robots have <u>sometimes</u> put humans out of work.

adverb verb phrase
<u>Sometimes</u> robots have put humans out of work.

Adverbs of frequency always follow the verb *be*:

verb adverb
Robots are <u>often</u> helpful to workers.

When *rarely, seldom,* and other negative adverbs of frequency begin a sentence, the normal subject-verb order changes. (See also pp. 156–57.)

adverb verb subject
<u>Rarely</u> are robots simple machines.

▪ **Adverbs of degree** include *absolutely, almost, certainly, completely, definitely, especially, extremely, hardly,* and *only.* They fall just before the word modified (an adjective, another adverb, sometimes a verb):

adverb adjective
Robots have been <u>especially</u> useful in making cars.

▪ **Adverbs of manner** include *badly, beautifully, openly, tightly, well,* and others that describe how something is done. They usually fall after the verb:

verb adverb
Robots work <u>smoothly</u> on assembly lines.

▪ **The adverb *not*** changes position depending on what it modifies. When it modifies a verb, place it after the helping verb (or the first helping verb if more than one):

helping
verb
main
verb
Robots do <u>not</u> think.

When *not* modifies another adverb or an adjective, place it before the other modifier:

adjective
Robots are <u>not</u> sleek machines.

5 ▪ Order of adjectives ⟨CULTURE LANGUAGE⟩

Adjectives modify nouns and pronouns. English follows distinctive rules for arranging two or three adjectives before a noun. (A string of more than three adjectives before a noun is rare.) The adjectives follow this order:

Determiner	Opinion	Size or shape	Color	Origin	Material	Noun used as adjective	Noun
many						state	**laws**
	lovely		green	Thai			**birds**
a		square			wooden		**table**
all						business	**reports**
the			blue		litmus		**paper**

See pages 298–99 on punctuating adjectives before a noun.

mm
34a

Exercise 34.1 Revising: Misplaced modifiers
Revise the following sentences so that modifiers clearly and appropriately describe the intended words.

Example:

Although at first I feared the sensation of flight, I came to enjoy flying over time.

Although at first I feared the sensation of flight, <u>over time</u> I came to enjoy flying.

1. Women have contributed much to American culture of great value.
2. For example, Elizabeth Pinckney during the colonial era introduced indigo, the source of a valuable blue dye.
3. Emma Willard founded the Troy Female Seminary, the first institution to provide a college-level education for women in 1821.
4. Mary Lyon founded Mount Holyoke Female Seminary as the first true women's college with directors and a campus who would sustain the college even after Lyon's death.
5. *Una* was the first US newspaper, which was founded by Paulina Wright Davis in 1853, that was dedicated to gaining women's rights.
6. Mitchell's Comet was discovered in 1847, which was named for Maria Mitchell.

7. Mitchell was the first American woman astronomer who lived from 1818 to 1889.
8. She was a member at Vassar College of the first faculty.
9. She was when elected to the American Academy of Arts and Sciences in 1848 the first woman to join the prestigious organization.
10. Mitchell said that she was persistent rather than especially capable when asked about her many accomplishments.

Exercise 34.2   Revising: Placement of adverbs and adjectives   (CULTURE LANGUAGE)

Revise the following sentences to correct the positions of adverbs or adjectives. Mark the number preceding any sentence that is correct as given.

Example:

Gasoline high prices affect usually car sales.
High gasoline prices usually affect car sales.

1. Some years ago Detroit cars often were praised.
2. Luxury large cars especially were prized.
3. Then a serious oil shortage led drivers to value small foreign cars that got good mileage.
4. When gasoline ample supplies returned, consumers bought again American large cars and trucks.
5. Consumers not were loyal to the big vehicles when gasoline prices dramatically rose.

34b   Relate dangling modifiers to their sentences.

dm
34b

A **dangling modifier** does not sensibly modify anything in its sentence.

Dangling   Passing the building, the vandalism became visible.

Dangling modifiers usually introduce sentences, contain a verb form, and imply but do not name a subject. In the example above, the implied subject is the someone or something passing the building. Readers assume that this implied subject is the same as the subject of the sentence (*vandalism* in the example), but vandalism does not pass buildings. The modifier "dangles" because it does not connect sensibly to the rest of the sentence. Here is another example:

Dangling   Although intact, graffiti covered every inch of the walls and windows. [The walls and windows, not the graffiti, were intact.]

To revise a dangling modifier, you have to rewrite the sentence. (Revising just by moving the modifier will still leave it dangling: *The vandalism became visible passing the building.*) You can rewrite in one

Identifying and revising dangling modifiers

- **Find a subject.** If the modifier lacks a subject of its own (e.g., *when in diapers*), identify what it describes.
- **Connect the subject and modifier.** Verify that what the modifier describes is in fact the subject of the main clause. If it is not, the modifier is probably dangling:

  ┌──modifier──┐ subject
  Dangling When in diapers, my mother remarried.

- **Revise as needed.** Revise a dangling modifier (*a*) by recasting it with a subject of its own or (*b*) by changing the subject of the main clause:

  Revision *a* When I <u>was</u> in diapers, my mother remarried.
  Revision *b* When in diapers, <u>I attended my mother's second wedding.</u>

of two ways, depending on what you want to emphasize in the sentence:

- **Rewrite the dangling modifier as a complete clause with its own stated subject and verb.** Readers can accept that the new subject and the sentence subject are different.

  Dangling Passing the building, the vandalism became visible.

  Revised As <u>we passed</u> the building, the vandalism became visible.

- **Change the subject of the sentence to a word the modifier properly describes.**

  Dangling Trying to understand the causes, vandalism has been extensively studied.

  Revised Trying to understand the causes, <u>researchers have</u> extensively <u>studied</u> vandalism.

Exercise 34.3 Revising: Dangling modifiers

Revise the following sentences to eliminate any dangling modifiers. Each item has more than one possible answer.

> *Example:*
> Driving north, the vegetation became more sparse.
> Driving north, <u>we noticed that</u> the vegetation became more sparse. *Or:* <u>As we drove north</u>, the vegetation became more sparse.

1. Drawing conclusions from several formal studies, pets can improve people's emotional well-being.
2. Suffering from Alzheimer's and unable to recognize her husband, one woman's ability to identify her beloved dog was unaffected.

3. Once subject to violent outbursts, a companion dog calmed an autistic boy.
4. Facing long hospital stays, pet-therapy dogs can cheer up patients.
5. To understand why people with serious illnesses often respond well to animals, pet therapy is being studied.
6. After accomplishing many deeds of valor, Andrew Jackson's fame led to his election to the presidency in 1828 and 1832.
7. To aid the American Revolution, service as a mounted courier was Jackson's choice.
8. Earning the nicknames "Old Hickory" and "Sharp Knife," the War of 1812 established Jackson's military prowess.
9. Losing only six dead and ten wounded, the triumph of the Battle of New Orleans burnished Jackson's reputation.
10. Winning many military battles, the American public believed in Jackson's leadership.

——— SENTENCE FAULTS ———

35 Sentence Fragments

In *Brief*

- Test your sentences for completeness (below).
- Revise sentence fragments (p. 273).
- Be aware of the acceptable uses of incomplete sentences (p. 274).

Visit MyWritingLab™ for more resources on sentence fragments.

frag

35a

A **sentence fragment** is part of a sentence that is set off as if it were a whole sentence by an initial capital letter and a final period or other end punctuation. Readers perceive most fragments as serious errors.

35a Test your sentences for completeness.

A word group punctuated as a sentence requires two elements: a subject (naming who or what performs the action) and a predicate verb (asserting something about the subject). In addition, the word group cannot be a subordinate clause (beginning with a subordinating word such as *because* or *who*). A complete sentence should pass *all three* of the following tests.

Test 1: Find the predicate verb.

Look for a verb that can serve as the predicate of a sentence. Some fragments lack any verb at all.

Fragment   Millions of sites on the Web.

Revised   Millions of sites make up the Web.

Other sentence fragments contain a verb form, but it is not a predicate verb. Instead, it is often the *-ing* or *to* form (for instance, *walking, to walk*):

Fragment   The Web growing with new sites and users every day.

Revised   The Web grows with new sites and users every day.

CULTURE LANGUAGE   Some languages allow forms of *be* to be omitted, but English requires stating forms of *be*, as shown in the following revised example.

Fragments   The network growing. It much larger than anticipated.

Revised   The network is growing. It is much larger than anticipated.

Test 2: Find the subject.

The subject of the sentence will usually come before the verb. If there is no subject, the word group is probably a fragment:

Fragment   The Web continues to grow. And shows no sign of slowing down.

Revised   The Web continues to grow. And it shows no sign of slowing down.

In one kind of complete sentence, a command, the subject *you* is understood: [*You*] *Try this recipe.*

CULTURE LANGUAGE   Some languages allow the omission of the sentence subject, especially when it is a pronoun. But in English, except in commands, the subject is always stated:

Fragment   Web shopping has exploded. Has hurt traditional stores.

Revised   Web shopping has exploded. It has hurt traditional stores.

Test 3: Make sure the clause is not subordinate.

A subordinate clause usually begins with a subordinating word, such as one of the following:

Subordinating conjunctions			Relative pronouns	
after	once	until	that	who/whom
although	since	when	which	whoever/whomever
as	than	where		whose
because	that	whereas		
if	unless	while		

Subordinate clauses serve as parts of sentences (as nouns or modifiers), not as whole sentences:

Fragment   When the government devised the Internet.

Revised   The government devised the Internet.

frag
35a

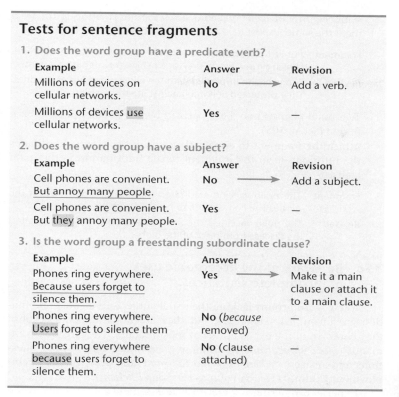

Tests for sentence fragments

1. Does the word group have a predicate verb?

Example	Answer	Revision
Millions of devices on cellular networks.	No ⟶	Add a verb.
Millions of devices use cellular networks.	Yes	—

2. Does the word group have a subject?

Example	Answer	Revision
Cell phones are convenient. But annoy many people.	No ⟶	Add a subject.
Cell phones are convenient. But they annoy many people.	Yes	—

3. Is the word group a freestanding subordinate clause?

Example	Answer	Revision
Phones ring everywhere. Because users forget to silence them.	Yes ⟶	Make it a main clause or attach it to a main clause.
Phones ring everywhere. Users forget to silence them	No (*because* removed)	—
Phones ring everywhere because users forget to silence them.	No (clause attached)	—

Revised   When the government devised the Internet, <u>no expansive computer network existed</u>.

Fragment   The reason that the government devised the Internet.

Revised   The reason that the government devised the Internet <u>was to link departments and defense contractors</u>.

Note Questions beginning with *how, what, when, where, which, who, whom, whose,* and *why* are not sentence fragments: *Who was responsible? When did it happen?*

35b   Revise sentence fragments.

Most sentence fragments can be corrected in one of two ways. The choice depends on the importance of the information in the fragment and thus how much you want to stress it.

- **Rewrite the fragment as a complete sentence.** Add a predicate verb or a subject as needed, or change a subordinate clause into a complete sentence. Any of these revisions gives the information in the fragment the same importance as that in other complete sentences.

Fragment   Public health improved with the widespread use of vaccines. <u>Which protected children against life-threatening diseases</u>.

Revised   Public health improved with the widespread use of vaccines. <u>They</u> protected children against life-threatening diseases.

Two main clauses may be separated by a semicolon instead of a period (see p. 305).

■ **Attach the fragment to a main clause.** This revision subordinates the information in the fragment to the information in the main clause.

Fragment   The polio vaccine eradicated the disease from most of the globe. <u>The first vaccine to be used widely</u>.

Revised   The polio vaccine_⊙ <u>the first to be used widely</u>_⊙ eradicated the disease from most of the globe.

35c   Be aware of the acceptable uses of incomplete sentences.

A few word groups lacking the usual subject-predicate combination are incomplete sentences, but they are not fragments because they conform to the expectations of most readers. They include commands (*Move along. Shut the window.*); exclamations (*Oh no!*); questions and answers (*Where next? To Kansas.*); and descriptions in employment résumés (*Weekly volunteer in soup kitchen.*).

Experienced writers sometimes use sentence fragments when they want to achieve a special effect. Such fragments appear more in informal than in formal writing. Unless you are experienced and thoroughly secure in your own writing, however, you should avoid all fragments and concentrate on writing clear, well-formed sentences.

Exercise 35.1   Revising: Sentence fragments

Correct any sentence fragment in the following items either by combining it with a complete sentence or by making it a complete sentence. If an item contains no sentence fragment, mark the number preceding it.

> *Example:*
> Jujitsu is good for self-protection. Because it enables one to overcome an opponent without the use of weapons.
>
> Jujitsu is good for self-protection◯because it enables one to overcome an opponent without the use of weapons. *Or:* Jujitsu is good for self-protection. <u>It</u> enables one to overcome an opponent without the use of weapons.

1. Human beings who perfume themselves. They are not much different from other animals.

2. Animals as varied as insects and dogs release pheromones. Chemicals that signal other animals.
3. Human beings have a diminished sense of smell. And do not consciously detect most of their own species' pheromones.
4. The human substitute for pheromones may be perfumes. Most common in ancient times were musk and other fragrances derived from animal oils.
5. Some sources say that people began using perfume to cover up the smell of burning flesh. During sacrifices to the gods.
6. Perfumes became religious offerings in their own right. Being expensive to make, they were highly prized.
7. The earliest historical documents from the Middle East record the use of fragrances. Not only in religious ceremonies but on the body.
8. In the nineteenth century, chemists began synthesizing perfume oils. Which previously could be made only from natural sources.
9. The most popular animal oil for perfume today is musk. Although some people dislike its heavy, sweet odor.
10. Synthetic musk oil would help conserve a certain species of deer. Whose gland is the source of musk.

Exercise 35.2   Revising: Sentence fragments

Revise the following paragraphs to eliminate sentence fragments by combining them with main clauses or rewriting them as main clauses.

Example:

Gymnosperms, the most advanced of nonflowering plants. They thrive in diverse environments.

Gymnosperms, the most advanced of nonflowering plants⊙ thrive in diverse environments. *Or:* Gymnosperms are the most advanced of nonflowering plants. They thrive in diverse environments.

frag

35

People generally avoid eating mushrooms except those they buy in stores. But in fact many varieties of mushrooms are edible. Mushrooms are members of a large group of vegetation called nonflowering plants. Including algae, mosses, ferns, and coniferous trees. Even the giant redwoods of California. Most of the nonflowering plants prefer moist environments. Such as forest floors, fallen timber, and still water. Mushrooms, for example. They prefer moist, shady soil. Algae grow in water.

Most mushrooms, both edible and inedible, are members of a class called basidium fungi. A term referring to their method of reproduction. The basidia produce spores. Which can develop into mushrooms. This classification including the prized meadow mushroom, cultivated commercially, and the amanitas. The amanita group contains both edible and poisonous species. Another familiar group of mushrooms, the puffballs. They are easily identified by their round shape. Their spores are contained under a thick skin. Which eventually ruptures to release the spores. The famous morels are in still another group. These pitted, spongy mushrooms called sac fungi because the spores develop in sacs.

Anyone interested in mushrooms as food should heed the US Public Health Service warning. Not to eat any wild mushrooms unless their identity and edibility are established without a doubt.

36 Comma Splices and Fused Sentences

In *Brief*

- Separate main clauses that are not joined by *and*, *but*, or another coordinating conjunction (p. 278).
- Separate main clauses that are related by *however*, *for example*, or a similar expression (p. 279).

Visit MyWritingLab™ for more resources on comma splices and fused sentences.

The kernel of a sentence is the main clause consisting of a subject and its predicate, which together express a complete thought that can stand alone. To know that one main clause is ending and another is beginning, readers expect one of these signals:

- **A period,** creating two separate sentences:

  The ship was huge⊙ Its mast stood eighty feet high.

- **A comma and a coordinating conjunction such as *and* or *but*,** linking two clauses in one sentence:

  The ship was huge⊘ <u>and</u> its mast stood eighty feet high.

- **A semicolon,** separating two clauses within one sentence:

  The ship was huge⊙ its mast stood eighty feet high.

cs/fs
36

Readers may be confused if two main clauses run together in a sentence *without* the second or third signal. The result may be a **comma splice,** in which the clauses are joined (or spliced) *only* with a comma:

Comma splice
The ship was huge, its mast stood eighty feet high.

Or the result may be a **fused sentence** (or **run-on sentence**), in which no punctuation or conjunction appears between the clauses:

Fused sentence
The ship was huge its mast stood eighty feet high.

The usual repairs for comma splices and fused sentences are shown in the box opposite and discussed on pages 278–79.

CULTURE LANGUAGE In standard American English, a sentence may not include more than one main clause unless the clauses are separated by a comma and a coordinating conjunction or by a semicolon. If your native language does not have such a rule or has accustomed you to writing long sentences, you may need to edit your English writing especially to correct comma splices and fused sentences.

Finding and revising comma splices and fused sentences

The following steps can help you identify and revise comma splices and fused sentences.

1. **Underline the main clauses in your draft.**

   <u>Sailors trained on the ship</u>. <u>They learned about wind and sails</u>. <u>Trainees who took the course ranged from high school students to Navy officers</u>. <u>The ship was built in 1910</u>, <u>it had sailed ever since</u>. In almost a century, <u>it had circled the globe forty times</u>. <u>It burned in 2001</u> its cabins and decks were destroyed.

2. **Are consecutive main clauses separated by periods?**

   If **yes,** OK.
   If **no,** go to question 3.

   Comma splice The ship was built in 1910, it had sailed ever since.
   Fused sentence It burned in 2001 its cabins and decks were destroyed.

3. **Are consecutive main clauses linked by a comma?**

   If **yes,** go to question 4.

   Comma splice The ship was built in 1910, it had sailed ever since.

   If **no,** go to question 5.

   Fused sentence It burned in 2001 its cabins and decks were destroyed.

4. **Does a coordinating conjunction follow the comma between main clauses?**

   If **yes,** OK.
   If **no,** add a coordinating conjunction: *and, but, or, nor, for, so, yet.*

   Revised The ship was built in 1910, and it had sailed ever since.

5. **Are consecutive main clauses separated by a semicolon?**

   If **yes,** OK.
   If **no,** add a semicolon.

   Revised It burned in 2001; its cabins and decks were destroyed.

As an alternative to these revision methods, you can also subordinate one clause to another:

   Revised When it burned in 2001, its cabins and decks were destroyed.

36a   Separate main clauses not joined by *and, but,* or another coordinating conjunction.

If your readers point out comma splices or fused sentences in your writing, you're not creating enough separation between main clauses in your sentences. Separate main clauses in the following ways.

Separate sentences

Make the clauses into separate sentences when the ideas expressed are only loosely related:

Comma splice	Chemistry has contributed much to our understanding of foods, many foods such as wheat and beans can be produced in the laboratory.
Revised	Chemistry has contributed much to our understanding of foods⊙ Many foods such as wheat and beans can be produced in the laboratory.

⟨CULTURE LANGUAGE⟩ Making separate sentences may be the best option if you are used to writing very long sentences in your native language but often write comma splices in English.

Coordinating conjunction

The coordinating conjunctions are *and, but, or, nor, for, so,* and *yet.* Insert a coordinating conjunction in a comma splice when the ideas in the main clauses are closely related and are equally important:

cs/fs
36a

Comma splice	Some laboratory-grown foods taste good, they are nutritious.
Revised	Some laboratory-grown foods taste good, <u>and</u> they are nutritious.

In a fused sentence insert a comma and a coordinating conjunction:

Fused sentence	Chemists have made much progress they still have a way to go.
Revised	Chemists have made much progress⊙ <u>but</u> they still have a way to go.

Semicolon

Insert a semicolon between clauses if the relation between the ideas is very close and obvious without a conjunction:

Comma splice	Good taste is rare in laboratory-grown vegetables, they are usually bland.
Revised	Good taste is rare in laboratory-grown vegetables⨀ they are usually bland.

Subordination

Subordination is often more effective than forming separate sentences because it defines the relations between ideas more precisely. When one idea is less important than the other, express the less important idea in a subordinate clause:

Comma splice	The vitamins are adequate, the flavor is deficient.
Revised	<u>Even though</u> the vitamins are adequate, the flavor is deficient.

See pages 201–03 for more on subordinate clauses.

36b   Separate main clauses related by *however, for example,* or a similar expression.

Two groups of words that are not conjunctions describe how one main clause relates to another: **conjunctive adverbs** and other **transitional expressions**. (See pp. 49–50 for a longer list.)

Common conjunctive adverbs and transitional expressions

accordingly	for instance	in the meantime	otherwise
anyway	further	in the past	similarly
as a result	furthermore	likewise	so far
at last	hence	meanwhile	still
at length	however	moreover	that is
besides	incidentally	namely	then
certainly	in contrast	nevertheless	thereafter
consequently	indeed	nonetheless	therefore
even so	in fact	now	thus
finally	in other words	of course	to this end
for all that	in short	on the contrary	undoubtedly
for example	instead	on the whole	until now

---

cs/fs

36b

When two main clauses are related by a conjunctive adverb or another transitional expression, they must be separated by a period or by a semicolon. The adverb or expression is also generally set off by a comma or commas.

Comma splice	Healthcare costs are higher in the United States than in many other countries, <u>consequently</u> health insurance is also more costly.
Revised	Healthcare costs are higher in the United States than in many other countries⊙ <u>Consequently</u>⊙ health insurance is also more costly.

Revised	Healthcare costs are higher in the United States than in many other countries⨀ consequently⨀ health insurance is also more costly.

A conjunctive adverb or transitional expression can often move around within a clause:

Healthcare costs are higher in the United States than in many other countries⨀ health insurance⨀ consequently⨀ is also more costly.

No matter where in the clause the adverb or expression falls, the clause must be separated from another main clause by a period or a semicolon.

Note The ability to move distinguishes conjunctive adverbs and other transitional expressions from coordinating conjunctions (*and, but,* and so on) and subordinating conjunctions (*although, because,* and so on). The conjunctions cannot move.

Exercise 36.1   Sentence combining to avoid comma splices and fused sentences

Using the method suggested in parentheses, combine each of the following pairs of sentences into one sentence without creating a comma splice or a fused sentence.

Example:

The sun sank lower in the sky. The colors gradually faded. (*Subordinate one clause to the other.*)

As the sun sank lower in the sky⨀ the colors gradually faded.

1. The exact origin of paper money is unknown. It has not survived as coins, shells, and other durable objects have. (*Subordinate one clause to the other.*)
2. Scholars disagree over where paper money originated. Many believe it was first used in Europe. (*Subordinate one clause to the other.*)
3. Perhaps goldsmiths were also bankers. Thus they held the gold of their wealthy customers. (*Supply a semicolon.*)
4. The goldsmiths probably gave customers receipts for their gold. These receipts were then used in trade. (*Supply a comma and coordinating conjunction.*)
5. The goldsmiths were something like modern-day bankers. Their receipts were something like modern-day money. (*Supply a semicolon.*)
6. The goldsmiths became even more like modern-day bankers. They began issuing receipts for more gold than they actually held in their vaults. (*Subordinate one clause to the other.*)
7. Today's bankers owe more to their customers than they actually have in reserve. They keep enough assets on hand to meet reasonable withdrawals. (*Supply a semicolon and a conjunctive adverb or transitional expression.*)
8. In economic crises, bank customers sometimes fear the loss of their money. Consequently, they demand their deposits. (*Supply a semicolon.*)

9. Depositors' demands may exceed a bank's reserves. The bank may collapse. (*Supply a comma and coordinating conjunction.*)
10. The government now regulates banks to protect depositors. Bank failures are less frequent than they once were. (*Supply a semicolon and a conjunctive adverb or transitional expression.*)

Exercise 36.2 Revising: Comma splices and fused sentences

Correct each of the following comma splices or fused sentences in two of the following ways: (1) make separate sentences of the main clauses; (2) insert an appropriate coordinating conjunction or both a comma and a coordinating conjunction between the main clauses; (3) insert a semicolon and a conjunctive adverb or transitional expression between the main clauses; (4) subordinate one clause to another. If an item contains no comma splice or fused sentence, mark the number preceding it.

Example:

Carolyn still had a headache, she could not get the child-proof cap off the aspirin bottle.

Carolyn still had a headache because she could not get the child-proof cap off the aspirin bottle. (*Subordination.*)

Carolyn still had a headache, for she could not get the child-proof cap off the aspirin bottle. (*Coordinating conjunction.*)

1. Money has a long history, it goes back at least as far as the earliest records.
2. Many of the earliest records concern financial transactions, indeed, early history must often be inferred from traces of commercial activity.
3. Every known society has had a system of money, though the objects serving as money have varied widely.
4. Sometimes the objects have had real value, in modern times their value has been more abstract.
5. Cattle, fermented beverages, and rare shells have served as money each one had actual value for the society.
6. As money, these objects acquired additional value they represented other goods.
7. Today money may be made of worthless paper, it may even consist of a bit of data in a computer's memory.
8. We think of money as valuable only our common faith in it makes it valuable.
9. That faith is sometimes fragile, consequently, currencies themselves are fragile.
10. Economic crises often shake the belief in money, indeed, such weakened faith helped cause the Great Depression of the 1930s.

Exercise 36.3 Revising: Comma splices and fused sentences

Revise each comma splice and fused sentence in the following paragraphs using the technique that seems most appropriate for the meaning.

cs/fs

36

What many call the first genocide of modern times occurred during World War I, the Armenians were deported from their homes in Anatolia, Turkey. The Turkish government assumed that the Armenians were sympathetic to Russia, with whom the Turks were at war. Many Armenians died because of the hardships of the journey many were massacred. The death toll was estimated at between 600,000 and 1 million.

Many of the deported Armenians migrated to Russia, in 1918 they established the Republic of Armenia, they continued to be attacked by Turkey, in 1920 they became the Soviet Republic of Armenia rather than surrender to the Turks. Like other Soviet republics, Armenia became independent in 1991, about 3.4 million Armenians live there now.

The Armenians have a long history of conquest by others. As a people, they formed a centralized state in the seventh century BC then they were ruled by the Persian empire until it was conquered by Alexander the Great. Greek and Roman rule followed, internal clan leadership marked by disunity and strife was next. In AD 640 the country was invaded by the Arabs in the eleventh century it was conquered by the Byzantines and then by the Turks, who controlled it until 1920.

37 Mixed Sentences

In *Brief*

- Match subjects and predicates in meaning (below).
- Untangle sentences that are mixed in grammar (facing page).
- State parts of clauses, such as subjects, only once (p. 285).

Visit MyWritingLab™ for more resources on mixed sentences.

A **mixed sentence** contains parts that do not fit together. The misfit may be in meaning or in grammar.

37a Match subjects and predicates in meaning.

In a sentence with mixed meaning, the subject is said to do or be something illogical. Such a mixture is sometimes called **faulty predication** because the predicate conflicts with the subject.

1 ▪ Illogical equation with *be*

When a form of *be* connects a subject and a word that describes the subject (a complement), the subject and complement must be logically related:

Mixed	A <u>compromise</u> between the city and the country would be the ideal <u>place</u> to live.

Revised   A community that offered the best qualities of both city and
country would be the ideal place to live.

2 ▪ *Is when, is where*

Definitions require nouns on both sides of *be*. Clauses that define
and begin with *when* or *where* are common in speech but should be
avoided in writing.

Mixed   An examination is when you are tested on what you know.

Revised   An examination is a test of what you know.

3 ▪ *Reason is because*

The commonly heard construction *reason is because* is redundant
since *because* means "for the reason that":

Mixed   The reason the temple requests donations is because the
school needs expansion.

Revised   The reason the temple requests donations is that the school
needs expansion.

Revised   The temple requests donations because the school needs expansion.

4 ▪ Other mixed meanings

Faulty predications are not confined to sentences with *be*:

Mixed   The use of emission controls was created to reduce air pollution.

Revised   Emission controls were created to reduce air pollution.

37b   Untangle sentences that are mixed in grammar.

Many mixed sentences start with one grammatical plan or construction but end with a different one:

            ┌──────── modifier (prepositional phrase) ────────┐ predicate
Mixed   By paying more attention to impressions than facts causes us
to misjudge others.

This mixed sentence makes a prepositional phrase work as the subject
of *causes*, but prepositional phrases function as modifiers, not as
nouns, and thus not as sentence subjects.

                ┌──────── modifier (prepositional phrase)────────┐ subject
Revised   By paying more attention to impressions than facts, we
predicate
misjudge others.

Constructions that use *Just because* clauses as subjects are common in speech but should be avoided in writing:

          ⎡—modifier (subordinate clause)—⎤ ⎡—predicate—⎤

Mixed   Just because no one is watching does not mean we have license to break the law.

          ⎡—modifier (subordinate clause)—⎤ subject + predicate

Revised   Even when no one is watching, we do not have license to break the law.

A mixed sentence is especially likely when you are working on a computer and connect parts of two sentences or rewrite half a sentence but not the other half. A mixed sentence may also occur when you don't make the subject and predicate verb carry the principal meaning. (See p. 142.)

Exercise 37.1   **Revising: Mixed sentences**

Revise the following sentences so that their parts fit together both in grammar and in meaning. Each item has more than one possible answer. If a sentence is already correct as given, mark the number preceding it.

Example:

When they found out how expensive pianos are discouraged them from buying one.

When they found out how expensive pianos are, they were discouraged from buying one. *Or:* Finding out how expensive pianos are discouraged them from buying one.

1. A hurricane is when the winds in a tropical depression rotate counterclockwise at more than seventy-four miles per hour.
2. Because hurricanes can destroy so many lives and so much property is why people fear them.
3. Through high winds, storm surge, floods, and tornadoes is how hurricanes have killed thousands of people.
4. Storm surge is where the hurricane's winds whip up a tide that spills over seawalls and deluges coastal islands.
5. The winds themselves are also destructive, uprooting trees and smashing buildings.
6. Many scientists observe that hurricanes in recent years they have become more ferocious and destructive.
7. However, in the last half-century, with improved communication systems and weather satellites have made hurricanes more predictable and less deadly.
8. The reason is because people have more time to escape.
9. The emphasis on evacuation is in fact the best way for people to avoid a hurricane's force.
10. Simply boarding up a house's windows will not protect a family from wind, water surges, and flying debris.

mixed
37b

37c State parts of clauses, such as subjects, only once.

<CULTURE-LANGUAGE>

In some languages other than English, certain parts of sentences may be repeated. These include the subject in any kind of clause or an object or adverb in an adjective clause. In English, however, these parts are stated only once in a clause.

1 ▪ Repetition of subject

You may be tempted to restate a subject as a pronoun before the verb. But the subject needs stating only once in its clause:

Faulty	The liquid it boiled.
Revised	The liquid boiled.

Faulty	Gases in the liquid they escaped.
Revised	Gases in the liquid escaped.

2 ▪ Repetition in an adjective clause

Adjective clauses begin with *who, whom, whose, which, that, where,* and *when* (see also pp. 201–02). The beginning word replaces another word: the subject (*He is the person who called*), an object (*He is the person whom I mentioned*), or a phrase such as *in which, at which,* or *on which* (*He knows the office where [in which] the meeting is*).

Do not state the word being replaced in an adjective clause:

Faulty	The technician whom the test depended on her was burned. [*Whom* should replace *her.*]
Revised	The technician whom the test depended on was burned.

Adjective clauses beginning with *where* or *when* do not need an adverb such as *there* or *then*:

Faulty	Gases escaped at a moment when the technician was unprepared then.
Revised	Gases escaped at a moment when the technician was unprepared.

Note *Whom, which,* and similar words are sometimes omitted but are still understood by the reader. Thus the word being replaced should not be stated:

Faulty	Accidents rarely happen to technicians the lab has trained them. [*Whom* is understood: . . . *technicians whom the lab has trained.*]
Revised	Accidents rarely happen to technicians the lab has trained.

mixed

37c

Exercise 37.2 Revising: Repeated subjects and other parts

Revise the following sentences to eliminate any unneeded words.

Example:

Scientists they use special instruments for measuring the age of artifacts.

Scientists use special instruments for measuring the age of artifacts.

1. Archaeologists and other scientists they can often determine the age of their discoveries by means of radiocarbon dating.
2. This technique it can be used on any material that once was living.
3. This technique is based on the fact that all living organisms they contain carbon.
4. The most common isotope is carbon 12, which it contains six protons and six neutrons.
5. A few carbon atoms are classified as the isotope carbon 14, where the nucleus consists of six protons and eight neutrons there.

38 **End Punctuation**

In *Brief*

- Use periods after most sentences and with some abbreviations (below).
- Use a question mark after a direct question and sometimes to indicate doubt (facing page).
- Use an exclamation point occasionally for emphasis (facing page).

Visit MyWritingLab™ for more resources on end punctuation.

End a sentence with one of three punctuation marks: a period (.), a question mark (?), or an exclamation point (!).

38a Use periods after most sentences and in many abbreviations.

1 ▪ Statements, mild commands, and indirect questions

Statement

The airline went bankrupt⊙   It no longer flies⊙

Mild command

Think of the possibilities⊙   Please consider others⊙

Indirect question

An **indirect question** reports what someone asked but not in the exact form or words of the original question:

The judge asked why I had been driving with my lights off⊙
No one asked how we got home⊙

⟨**CULTURE LANGUAGE**⟩ In standard American English, the reporting verb in an indirect question (for example, *asked* or *said*) usually precedes a clause that contains a subject and verb in normal order, not question order: *The reporter asked why the bank failed*, not *why did the bank fail*.

2 ▪ Abbreviations

Use periods with abbreviations that consist of or end in small letters. Otherwise, omit periods from abbreviations.

Dr.	Mr., Mrs.	e.g.	Feb.	ft.
St.	Ms.	i.e.	p.	a.m., p.m.
PhD	BC, AD	USA	IBM	JFK
BA	AM, PM	US	USMC	AIDS

Note When an abbreviation falls at the end of a sentence, use only one period: *My first class is at 8 a.m⊙*

. ? !
38a

288

38b Use a question mark after a direct question and sometimes to indicate doubt.

1 ▪ Direct questions

Who will follow her(?)
What is the difference between these two people(?)

After indirect questions, use a period: *We wondered who would follow her*⊙ (See the facing page.)

Questions in a series are each followed by a question mark:

The officer asked how many times the suspect had been arrested. Three times(?) Four times(?) More than that(?)

Note A question mark falls inside or outside a closing quotation mark depending on whether it is part of a quoted question or part of the larger sentence. (See also pp. 319–20.)

He asked, "Who will go(?)" [Question mark part of the quoted question.]
Did he say, "I will go"(?) [Question mark part of the larger sentence, a question.]

2 ▪ Doubt

A question mark within parentheses can indicate doubt about a number or date.

The Greek philosopher Socrates was born in 470 (?) BC and died in 399 BC. [Socrates's birthdate is not known for sure.]

However, don't use a question mark to express sarcasm or irony.

Not   Stern's friendliness (?) bothered Crane.
But   Stern's insincerity bothered Crane.

38c Use an exclamation point after an emphatic statement, interjection, or command.

No(!) We must not lose this election(!)
Come here immediately(!)

Follow mild interjections and commands with commas or periods, as appropriate: *Oh*, *call whenever you can*⊙

Use exclamation points sparingly, even in informal writing. Frequent use will make you sound overemphatic.

Note An exclamation point falls inside or outside a closing quotation mark depending on whether it is part of the quotation or part of the larger sentence. (See also pp. 319–20.)

. ? !
38c

Exercise 38.1   Revising: End punctuation

Insert appropriate end punctuation (periods, question marks, or exclamation points) where needed in the following paragraph.

When visitors first arrive in Hawaii, they often encounter an unexpected language barrier Standard English is the language of business and government, but many of the people speak Pidgin English Instead of an excited "Aloha" the visitors may be greeted with an excited Pidgin "Howzit" or asked if they know "how fo' find one good hotel" Many Hawaiians question whether Pidgin will hold children back because it prevents communication with *haoles,* or Caucasians, who run many businesses Yet many others feel that Pidgin is a last defense of ethnic diversity on the islands To those who want to make Standard English the official language of the state, these Hawaiians may respond, "Just 'cause I speak Pidgin no mean I dumb" They may ask, "Why you no listen" or, in standard English, "Why don't you listen"

---

39   The Comma

In *Brief*

To use the comma correctly,

- Separate main clauses linked by *and, but,* and other coordinating conjunctions (below).
- Set off most introductory elements (p. 293).
- Set off nonessential elements (p. 294).
- Separate items in a series and coordinate adjectives (p. 298).
- Separate parts of dates, addresses, place names, and long numbers (p. 300).
- Separate signal phrases and quotations (p. 300).
- Avoid common misuses, such as between subjects and verbs, after conjunctions, and around essential elements (p. 301).

Visit MyWritingLab™ for more resources on the comma.

The comma (,) is the most common punctuation mark within sentences. Its main uses are shown in the box opposite.

39a   Use a comma before *and, but,* or another coordinating conjunction linking main clauses.

The coordinating conjunctions are *and, but, or, not, for, so,* and *yet.* When one of these links words or phrases, do not use a comma: *The band plays and records Irish and Scottish folk songs.* However, *do* use a comma when a coordinating conjunction joins main clauses—that is, word groups that can stand alone as sentences because they contain a subject and a predicate and do not begin with a subordinating word.

Main uses of the comma

■ **Separate main clauses linked by a coordinating conjunction** (opposite and next page).

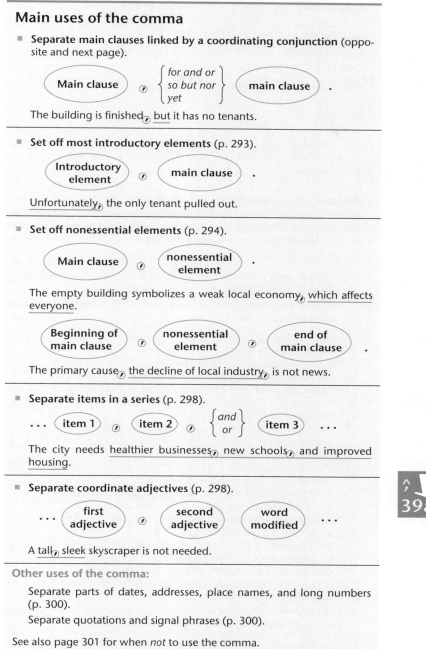

The building is finished, but it has no tenants.

■ **Set off most introductory elements** (p. 293).

Unfortunately, the only tenant pulled out.

■ **Set off nonessential elements** (p. 294).

The empty building symbolizes a weak local economy, which affects everyone.

The primary cause, the decline of local industry, is not news.

■ **Separate items in a series** (p. 298).

The city needs healthier businesses, new schools, and improved housing.

■ **Separate coordinate adjectives** (p. 298).

A tall, sleek skyscraper is not needed.

Other uses of the comma:

Separate parts of dates, addresses, place names, and long numbers (p. 300).

Separate quotations and signal phrases (p. 300).

See also page 301 for when *not* to use the comma.

^ ,
39a

Caffeine can keep coffee drinkers alert‸ and it may elevate their mood.

Caffeine was once thought to be safe‸ but now researchers warn of harmful effects.

Coffee drinkers may suffer sleeplessness‸ for the drug acts as a stimulant to the nervous system.

Note The comma goes *before*, not after, the coordinating conjunction: *Caffeine increases heart rate‸ and⌒it* [not *and, it*] *constricts blood vessels*.

Exception Some writers omit the comma between main clauses that are very short and closely related in meaning: *Caffeine helps but it also hurts*. If you are in doubt about whether to use the comma in such a sentence, use it. It will always be correct.

Exercise 39.1   Punctuating linked main clauses

Insert a comma before each coordinating conjunction that links main clauses in the following sentences. If a sentence is already correct as given, mark the number preceding it.

> *Example:*
>
> I would have attended the concert and the reception but I had to baby-sit for my niece.
>
> I would have attended the concert and the reception‸ but I had to baby-sit for my niece.

1. Parents once automatically gave their children the father's last name but some no longer do.
2. Parents were once legally required to give their children the father's last name but these laws have been contested in court.
3. Parents may now give their children any last name they choose and the arguments for choosing the mother's last name are often strong and convincing.
4. Parents who choose the mother's last name may do so because they believe that the mother's importance should be recognized or because the mother's name is easier to pronounce.
5. The child's last name may be just the mother's or it may link the mother's and the father's with a hyphen.
6. Sometimes the first and third children will have the mother's last name and the second child will have the father's.
7. Occasionally, the mother and father combine parts of their names and a new last name is formed.
8. Critics sometimes point out that unusual names confuse others and can create difficulties for children.
9. Children with last names different from their fathers' may find the difference awkward since most children in the United States still bear their fathers' names.
10. Hyphenated names are awkward and difficult to pass on so some observers think they will die out in a generation or two.

39a

39b Use a comma to set off most introductory elements.

An **introductory element** begins a sentence and modifies a word or words in the main clause that follows. It is usually followed by a comma.

Subordinate clause (pp. 201–03)

<u>Even when identical twins are raised apart</u>, they grow up very like each other.

Verbal or verbal phrase (pp. 198–200)

<u>Explaining the similarity</u>, some researchers claim that one's genes are one's destiny.

<u>Concerned</u>, other researchers deny the claim.

Prepositional phrase (p. 198)

<u>In a debate that has lasted centuries</u>, scientists use identical twins to argue for or against genetic destiny.

Transitional expression (pp. 48–50)

<u>Of course</u>, scientists can now look directly at the genes themselves to answer questions.

You may omit the comma after a short subordinate clause or prepositional phrase if its omission does not create confusion: *When snow falls the city collapses. By the year 2000 the world population had topped 6 billion.* You may also omit the comma after some transitional expressions when they start sentences: *Thus the debate about education continues* (see pp. 296–97). However, in both situations the comma is never wrong.

Note Take care to distinguish *-ing* words used as modifiers from *-ing* words used as subjects. The former almost always take a comma; the latter never do.

    ┌────── modifier ──────┐   subject   verb
Studying identical twins, geneticists learn about inheritance.

    ┌────── subject ──────┐   verb
Studying identical twins helps geneticists learn about inheritance.

^
,
39b

Exercise 39.2 Punctuating introductory elements

In the following sentences, insert commas where needed after introductory elements. If a sentence is already correct as given, mark the number preceding it.

Example:

After the new library opened the old one became a student union.
After the new library opened, the old one became a student union.

1. Veering sharply to the right a large flock of birds neatly avoids a high wall.
2. Moving in a fluid mass is typical of flocks of birds and schools of fish.
3. With the help of complex computer simulations zoologists are learning more about this movement.
4. Because it is sudden and apparently well coordinated the movement of flocks and schools has seemed to be directed by a leader.
5. Almost incredibly the group could behave with more intelligence than any individual seemed to possess.
6. However new studies have discovered that flocks and schools are leaderless.
7. As it turns out evading danger is really an individual response.
8. When each bird or fish senses a predator it follows individual rules for fleeing.
9. To keep from colliding with its neighbors each bird or fish uses other rules for dodging.
10. Multiplied over hundreds of individuals these responses look as if they have been choreographed.

39c   Use a comma or commas to set off nonessential elements.

Commas around part of a sentence often signal that the element is not necessary to the meaning. This **nonessential element** may modify or rename the word it refers to, but it does not limit the word to a particular individual or group. The meaning of the word would still be clear if the element were deleted:

Nonessential element

The company, which is located in Oklahoma, has an excellent reputation.

(Because it does not restrict meaning, a nonessential element is also called a **nonrestrictive element**.)

In contrast, an **essential** (or **restrictive**) **element** *does* limit the word it refers to: the element cannot be omitted without leaving the meaning too general. Because it is essential, such an element is *not* set off with commas.

Essential element

The company rewards employees who work hard.

Omitting the underlined words would distort the meaning: the company doesn't necessarily reward *all* employees, only the hardworking ones.

The same element in the same sentence may be essential or nonessential depending on your meaning and the context:

Essential

Not all the bands were equally well received, however. The band playing old music held the audience's attention. The other groups created

---

A test for nonessential and essential elements

1. **Identify the element:**

   Hai Nguyen <u>who emigrated from Vietnam</u> lives in Denver.
   Those <u>who emigrated with him</u> live elsewhere.

2. **Remove the element.** Does the fundamental meaning of the sentence change?

   Hai Nguyen lives in Denver. **No.**
   Those live elsewhere. **Yes.** [Who are *Those*?]

3. **If *no*, the element is *nonessential* and *should* be set off with punctuation:**

   Hai Nguyen⌒ who emigrated from Vietnam⌒ lives in Denver.

   If *yes*, the element is *essential* and should *not* be set off with punctuation:

   Those⌒who emigrated with him⌒live elsewhere.

---

much less excitement. [*Playing old music* distinguishes a particular band from all possible bands, so the information is essential.]

Nonessential

A new band called Fats made its debut on Saturday night. The band⌒ <u>playing old music</u>⌒ held the audience's attention. [*Playing old music* adds information about a band already named and thus already familiar to readers, so the phrase is nonessential.]

Note When a nonessential element falls in the middle of a sentence, be sure to set it off with a pair of commas, one *before* and one *after* the element.

1 ▪ Nonessential phrases and clauses

Most nonessential phrases and subordinate clauses function as adjectives or, less commonly, as adverbs. In each of the following examples, the underlined words could be omitted with no loss of clarity.

Elizabeth Blackwell was the first woman to graduate from an American medical school⌒ <u>in 1849</u>. [Adverb phrase.]

She was a medical pioneer⌒ <u>helping to found the first medical college for women</u>. [Adjective phrase.]

She taught at the school⌒ <u>which was affiliated with the New York Infirmary</u>. [Adjective clause.]

Blackwell⌒ <u>who published books and papers on medicine</u>⌒ practiced pediatrics and gynecology. [Adjective clause.]

She moved to England in 1869⌒ <u>when she was forty-eight</u>. [Adverb clause.]

^
,
39c

Note Use *that* only in an essential clause, never in a nonessential clause.

Faulty The tree, <u>that</u> is 120 years old, shades the house.

Revised The tree, <u>which</u> is 120 years old, shades the house.

Many writers reserve *which* for nonessential clauses.

2 ▪ Nonessential appositives

An appositive is a noun or a noun substitute that renames another noun just before it. (See p. 200.) A nonessential appositive merely adds information about the word it refers to:

Toni Morrison's fifth novel, *Beloved,* won the Pulitzer Prize in 1988. [The word *fifth* identifies the novel, so the book's title simply adds a detail.]

In contrast, an essential appositive limits or defines the word it refers to:

Morrison's novel *The Bluest Eye* is about an African American girl who longs for blue eyes. [Morrison has written more than one novel, so the title is essential to identify the intended one.]

3 ▪ Other nonessential elements

Like nonessential modifiers or appositives, many other elements contribute to texture, tone, or overall clarity but are not essential to the meaning. Unlike nonessential modifiers or appositives, these other nonessential elements generally do not refer to any specific word in the sentence.

Note Use a pair of commas—one before, one after—when any of these elements falls in the middle of a sentence.

Absolute phrases (p. 200)

Household recycling having succeeded, the city now wants to extend the program to businesses.

Many businesses, their profits already squeezed, resist recycling.

Transitional and parenthetical expressions (pp. 48–50, 322)

Generally, set off transitional and parenthetical expressions with commas:

US workers, for example, receive fewer holidays than European workers do. [Transitional expression.]

Indeed, Americans have relatively few holidays. [Transitional expression.]

The world's most celebrated holiday is, perhaps surprisingly, New Year's Day. [Parenthetical expression.]

(Dashes and parentheses may also set off parenthetical expressions. See pp. 321–22.)

When a transitional expression links main clauses, precede it with a semicolon and follow it with a comma (see p. 305):

European workers often have long paid vacations⨀ indeed⨀ they may receive a full month after just a few years with a company.

Exception The conjunctions *and* and *but*, sometimes used as transitional expressions, are never followed by commas (see p. 302). Usage varies with some other transitional expressions, depending on the expression and the writer's judgment. Many writers omit commas with expressions that we read without pauses, such as *also, hence, next, now, then,* and *thus.* The same applies to *therefore* and *instead* when they fall inside or at the ends of clauses.

US workers⨀thus⨀put in more work days. But⨀the days themselves may be shorter.

Then⨀the total hours worked would come out roughly the same for US and European workers.

Phrases of contrast

The substance⨀ not the style⨀ is important.
Substance⨀ unlike style⨀ cannot be faked.

Tag questions

They don't stop to consider others⨀ do they?
Jones should be allowed to vote⨀ shouldn't he?

Yes and *no*

Yes⨀ the writer did have a point.
No⨀ that can never be.

Words of direct address

Cody⨀ please bring me the newspaper.
With all due respect⨀ sir⨀ I will not.

Mild interjections

Well⨀ you will never know who did it.
Oh⨀ they forgot all about the baby.

∧
,
39c

Exercise 39.3   Punctuating essential and nonessential elements

Insert commas in the following sentences to set off nonessential elements, and delete any commas that incorrectly set off essential elements. If a sentence is already correct as given, mark the number preceding it.

Example:

Elizabeth Blackwell who attended medical school in the 1840s was the first American woman to earn a medical degree.

Elizabeth Blackwell⨀ who attended medical school in the 1840s⨀ was the first American woman to earn a medical degree.

1. Many colleges have started campus garden programs, that aim to teach students about the benefits of sustainable farming methods and locally grown food.
2. These gardens which use organic farming techniques also provide fresh produce for the college cafeteria.
3. A garden, that is big enough to grow produce for a college cafeteria, requires a large piece of land.
4. Such a garden also needs a leader, who can choose crops that will thrive in local growing conditions.
5. Volunteers, willing to work in the garden every week, are essential as well.
6. Some campus gardeners distribute produce to people in the community who live far from a grocery store.
7. Some urban neighborhoods are called "food deserts," because they lack grocery stores that residents can reach easily on foot.
8. The colleges may distribute produce with special trucks or "veggie wagons" that drive through the urban neighborhoods.
9. The wagons deliver produce once a week although they may make two deliveries during peak harvest time.
10. A community garden planted during the academic year will fare better in the southern states where the growing season is longer than in northern states.

39d   Use commas between items in a series.

A **series** consists of three or more items of equal importance. The items may be words, phrases, or clauses.

> Anna Spingle married at the age of seventeen, had three children by twenty-one, and divorced at twenty-two.

> She worked as a cook, a baby-sitter, and a crossing guard.

Some writers omit the comma before the last item in a series (*Breakfast consisted of coffee, eggs and kippers*). But the final comma is never wrong, and it always helps the reader see the last two items as separate.

39e   Use commas between two or more adjectives that equally modify the same word.

Adjectives that equally modify the same word—**coordinate adjectives**—may be separated either by *and* or by a comma.

> Spingle's scratched and dented car is old, but it gets her to work.
> She dreams of buying a sleek, shiny car.

Adjectives are not coordinate—and should not be separated by commas—when the adjective nearer the modified word is more closely related to the word in meaning.

Spingle's children work at various⌒part-time jobs.
They all expect to go to a nearby⌒community college.

Tests for commas with adjectives

1. **Identify the adjectives:**

   She was a faithful sincere friend.
   They are dedicated medical students.

2. **Can the adjectives be reversed without changing meaning?**

   She was a sincere faithful friend. *Yes.*
   They are medical dedicated students. *No.*

3. **Can the word *and* be sensibly inserted between the adjectives?**

   She was a faithful and sincere friend. *Yes.*
   They are dedicated and medical students. *No.*

4. **If *yes* to both questions, the adjectives *should* be separated by a comma:**

   She was a faithful⌒sincere friend.

5. **If *no* to both questions, the adjectives should *not* be separated by a comma:**

   They are dedicated⌒medical students.

Exercise 39.4 **Punctuating series and coordinate adjectives**

Insert commas in the following sentences to separate coordinate adjectives or elements in a series. If a sentence is already correct as given, mark the number preceding it.

> *Example:*
>
> Quiet by day, the club became a noisy smoky dive at night.
> Quiet by day, the club became a noisy⌒smoky dive at night.

1. Shoes with high heels were originally designed to protect feet from mud garbage and animal waste in the streets.
2. The first known high heels worn strictly for fashion appeared in the sixteenth century.
3. The heels were worn by men and made of colorful silk fabrics soft suedes or smooth leathers.
4. High-heeled shoes became popular when the short powerful King Louis XIV of France began wearing them.
5. Louis's influence was so strong that men and women of the court priests and cardinals and even household servants wore high heels.
6. Eventually only wealthy fashionable French women wore high heels.
7. In the seventeenth and eighteenth centuries, French culture represented the one true standard of elegance and refinement.

39e

8. High-heeled shoes for women spread to other courts of Europe among the Europeans of North America and to almost all social classes.
9. Now high heels are common, though depending on the fashion they range from short squat thick heels to tall skinny spikes.
10. A New York boutique recently showed a pair of purple satin pumps with tiny jeweled bows and four-inch stiletto heels.

39f Use commas in dates, addresses, place names, and long numbers.

When they appear within sentences, elements punctuated with a comma also end with a comma, as in the following examples.

Dates

July 4, 1776, is the date the Declaration was signed.
The bombing of Pearl Harbor on Sunday, December 7, 1941, prompted American entry into World War II.

Do not use commas between the parts of a date in inverted order (*15 December 1992*) or in dates consisting of a month or season and a year (*December 1941*).

Addresses and place names

Use the address 220 Cornell Road, Woodside, California 94062, for all correspondence.
Columbus, Ohio, is the location of Ohio State University.

Do not use a comma between a state name and a zip code.

Long numbers

Use the comma to separate the figures in long numbers into groups of three, counting from the right. With numbers of four digits, the comma is optional.

The new assembly plant cost $7,525,000.
A kilometer is 3,281 feet [*or* 3281 feet].

 Usage in standard American English differs from that in some other languages, which use a period, not a comma, to separate the figures in long numbers.

39g Use commas with quotations according to standard practice.

The words *she said, he writes,* and so on, identify the source of a quotation. These **signal phrases** should be separated from the quotation by punctuation, usually a comma or commas.

Eleanor Roosevelt said⊙ "You must do the thing you think you cannot do."

"Knowledge is power⊙" wrote Francis Bacon.

"The shore has a dual nature⊙" observes Rachel Carson⊙ "changing with the swing of the tides." [The signal phrase interrupts the quotation at a comma and thus ends with a comma.]

Exceptions Do not use commas with signal phrases in some situations:

- **Use a semicolon or a period after a signal phrase that interrupts a quotation between main clauses.** (Main clauses can stand alone as complete sentences.) The use of a semicolon or a period depends on the punctuation of the original:

Not	"That part of my life was over," she wrote, "his words had sealed it shut."
But	"That part of my life was over," she wrote⊙ "His words had sealed it shut." [*She wrote* interrupts the quotation at a period.]
Or	"That part of my life was over," she wrote⊙ "his words had sealed it shut." [*She wrote* interrupts the quotation at a semicolon.]

- **Omit a comma when a signal phrase follows a quotation ending in an exclamation point or a question mark:**

  "Claude⊙" Mrs. Harrison called.
  "Why must I come home⊙" he asked.

- **Use a colon when a complete sentence introduces a quotation:**

  Her statement was clear⊙ "I will not resign."

- **Omit commas when a quotation is integrated into your sentence structure,** including a quotation introduced by *that*:

  James Baldwin insists that⊙"one must never, in one's life, accept . . . injustices as commonplace."

  Baldwin thought that the violence of a riot⊙"had been devised as a corrective⊙ to his own violence."

- **Omit commas with a quoted title unless it is a nonessential appositive (p. 296):**

  The Beatles recorded⊙"She Loves You⊙" in the early 1960s.
  The Beatles' first huge US hit⊙ "She Loves You⊙" appeared in 1963.

no ⌃
39h

See Exercise 43.1, page 320, for practice with punctuating quotations.

39h Delete commas where they are not required.

Commas can make sentences choppy and even confusing if they are used more often than needed. Following are the most common spots for misused commas.

1 ▪ No comma between subject and verb, verb and object, or preposition and object

                          subject   verb
Not   The returning <u>soldiers, received</u> a warm welcome. [Separated subject and verb.]

But   The returning <u>soldiers⌒received</u> a warm welcome.

                    verb   object   preposition object
Not   They had <u>chosen, to fight</u> for their country <u>despite, the risks</u>. [Separated verb *chosen* and its object; separated preposition *despite* and its object.]

But   They had <u>chosen⌒to fight</u> for their country <u>despite⌒the risks</u>.

2 ▪ No comma in most compound constructions

A compound construction consists of two or more words, phrases, or clauses connected usually by *and, but, or,* or *nor.* A compound consisting of two elements almost never requires a comma. The only exception is the sentence consisting of two main clauses linked by a coordinating conjunction: *The network failed⌒, but employees kept working* (see p. 290).

                 ┌────── compound subject ──────┐
Not   <u>Banks, and other financial institutions</u> have helped older people
                 ┌── compound object of preposition ──┐
with <u>money management, and investment.</u>

But   <u>Banks⌒and other financial institutions</u> have helped older people
with <u>money management⌒and investment.</u>

                         ┌────── compound predicate ──────→
Not   One bank <u>created</u> special accounts for older people, <u>and held</u>
compound object of verb
<u>classes, and workshops.</u>

But   One bank <u>created</u> special accounts for older people⌒<u>and held</u>
<u>classes⌒and workshops.</u>

3 ▪ No comma after a conjunction

A comma does not follow a coordinating conjunction (*and, but,* and so on) or a subordinating conjunction (*although, because,* and so on):

Not   Parents of adolescents notice increased conflict at puberty, <u>and, they</u> complain of bickering.

But   Parents of adolescents notice increased conflict at puberty, <u>and⌒they</u> complain of bickering.

Not   <u>Although,</u> other primates leave the family at adolescence, humans do not.

But   <u>Although⌒</u>other primates leave the family at adolescence, humans do not.

4 ▪ No comma around essential elements

Commas do not set off an essential element, which limits the meaning of the word to which it refers (see p. 294):

Not   Hawthorne's work, *The Scarlet Letter,* was the first major American novel. [The title is essential to distinguish the novel from the rest of Hawthorne's work.]

But   Hawthorne's work⌒*The Scarlet Letter*⌒was the first major American novel.

Not   The symbols, that Hawthorne uses, have influenced other novelists. [The clause identifies which symbols were influential.]

But   The symbols⌒that Hawthorne uses⌒have influenced other novelists.

Not   Published in 1850, *The Scarlet Letter* is still popular, because its theme of secret sin resonates with contemporary readers. [The clause is essential to explain why the novel is popular.]

But   Published in 1850, *The Scarlet Letter* is still popular⌒because its theme of secret sin resonates with contemporary readers.

Note Like the *because* clause in the preceding example, most clauses functioning as adverbs are essential because they describe conditions necessary to the main clause.

5 ▪ No comma around a series

Commas separate the items *within* a series (p. 298), but do not separate the series from the rest of the sentence.

Not   The skills of, hunting, herding, and agriculture, sustained the Native Americans.

But   The skills of⌒hunting, herding, and agriculture⌒sustained the Native Americans.

6 ▪ No comma before an indirect quotation

Not   The report concluded, that dieting could be more dangerous than overeating.

But   The report concluded⌒that dieting could be more dangerous than overeating.

no ⌃
39h

Exercise 39.5   Revising: Needless and misused commas

Revise the following sentences to eliminate needless or misused commas. If a sentence is already correct as given, mark the number preceding it.

Example:

Aquifers can be recharged by rainfall, but, the process is slow.
Aquifers can be recharged by rainfall, but⌒the process is slow.

1. Underground aquifers are deep, and sometimes broad layers of water, that are trapped between layers of rock.
2. Porous rock, or sediment holds the water.
3. Deep wells drilled through the top layers of solid rock, produce a flow of water.
4. Such wells are sometimes called, artesian wells.
5. One of the largest aquifers in North America, the Ogallala aquifer, is named after the Ogallala Indian tribe, which once lived in the region and hunted buffalo there.
6. The Ogallala aquifer underlies a region from western Texas through northern Nebraska, and has a huge capacity of fresh water, that is contained in a layer of sand and gravel.
7. But, the water in the Ogallala is being removed at a rate faster than it is being replaced.
8. Water is pumped from the aquifer for many purposes, such as drinking and other household use, industrial use, and, agricultural use.
9. Scientists estimate that, at the present consumption rate the Ogallala will be depleted in forty years.
10. Water table levels are receding from six inches to three feet a year, the amount depending on location.

Exercise 39.6   Revising: Commas

Insert commas in the following paragraphs wherever they are needed, and eliminate any misused or needless commas.

Ellis Island New York reopened for business in 1990 but now the customers are tourists not immigrants. This spot which lies in New York Harbor was the first American soil seen, or touched by many of the nation's immigrants. Though other places also served as ports of entry for foreigners none has the symbolic power of, Ellis Island. Between its opening in 1892 and its closing in 1954, over 20 million people about two-thirds of all immigrants were detained there before taking up their new lives in the United States. Ellis Island processed over 2000 newcomers a day when immigration was at its peak between 1900 and 1920.

As the end of a long voyage and the introduction to the New World Ellis Island must have left something to be desired. The "huddled masses" as the Statue of Liberty calls them indeed were huddled. New arrivals were herded about kept standing in lines for hours or days yelled at and abused. Assigned numbers they submitted their bodies to the pokings and proddings of the silent nurses and doctors, who were charged with ferreting out the slightest sign, of sickness disability or insanity. But, millions survived the examination humiliation and confusion, to take the last short boat ride to New York City, and begin new lives.

40 The Semicolon

In *Brief*

To use the semicolon correctly,

- Separate main clauses that are not joined by *and, but,* or another coordinating conjunction (below).
- Separate main clauses that are related by *however, for example,* or a similar expression (below).
- Separate main clauses or series items that contain commas (p. 307).
- Avoid the common misuses: with phrases and subordinate clauses and before series and explanations (p. 307).

Visit MyWritingLab™ for more resources on the semicolon.

The semicolon (;) separates equal and balanced elements—usually main clauses and occasionally items in a series.

40a Use a semicolon between main clauses not joined by *and, but,* or another coordinating conjunction.

Main clauses contain a subject and a predicate and do not begin with a subordinating word (see p. 201). When no coordinating conjunction links two main clauses, the clauses should be separated by a semicolon.

> A new ulcer drug arrived on the market with a mixed reputation; doctors find that the drug works but worry about its side effects.

> The side effects are not minor; some leave the patient quite uncomfortable or even ill.

Note This rule prevents the errors known as comma splices and fused sentences. (See pp. 278–79.)

40b Use a semicolon between main clauses related by *however, for example,* and so on.

Two kinds of words can relate main clauses: conjunctive adverbs, such as *consequently, hence, however, indeed,* and *thus* (see p. 279); and other transitional expressions, such as *even so, for example,* and *of course* (see pp. 48–50). When either type of word connects two main clauses, the clauses should be separated by a semicolon:

> An American immigrant, Levi Strauss, invented blue jeans in the 1860s; eventually, his product clothed working men throughout the West.

The position of the semicolon between main clauses never changes, but the conjunctive adverb or transitional expression may

;
40b

move around within the second clause. Wherever the adverb or expression falls, it is usually set off with a comma or commas.

> Blue jeans have become fashionable all over the world⊙ however⊙ the American originators still wear more jeans than anyone else.

> Blue jeans have become fashionable all over the world⊙ the American originators⊙ however⊙ still wear more jeans than anyone else.

> Blue jeans have become fashionable all over the world⊙ the American originators still wear more jeans than anyone else⊙ however.

Note This rule prevents the errors known as comma splices and fused sentences. (See pp. 279–80.)

Exercise 40.1   Sentence combining: Related main clauses

Combine each of the following sets of sentences into one sentence containing only two main clauses. As indicated in parentheses, connect the clauses with a semicolon alone or with a semicolon plus a conjunctive adverb or transitional expression followed by a comma. You will have to add, delete, change, and rearrange words. Each item has more than one possible answer.

Example:

The Albanians censored their news. We got little news from them. And what we got was unreliable. (*Therefore and semicolon.*)

The Albanians censored their news⊙ therefore⊙ the little news we got from them was unreliable.

1. Electronic instruments are prevalent in jazz. They are also prevalent in rock music. They are less common in classical music. (*However and semicolon.*)

2. Jazz and rock change rapidly. They nourish experimentation. They nourish improvisation. (*Semicolon alone.*)

3. The notes and instrumentation of traditional classical music were established by a composer. The composer was writing decades or centuries ago. Such music does not change. (*Therefore and semicolon.*)

4. Contemporary classical music not only can draw on tradition. It can also respond to innovations. These are innovations such as jazz rhythms and electronic sounds. (*Semicolon alone.*)

5. Much contemporary electronic music is more than just one type of music. It is more than just jazz, rock, or classical. It is a fusion of all three. (*Semicolon alone.*)

6. Most music computers are too expensive for the average consumer. Digital keyboard instruments can be inexpensive. They are widely available. (*However and semicolon.*)

7. Inside the keyboard is a small computer. The computer controls a sound synthesizer. The instrument can both process and produce music. (*Consequently and semicolon.*)

8. The person playing the keyboard presses keys or manipulates other controls. The computer and synthesizer convert these signals. The signals are converted into vibrations and sounds. (*Semicolon alone.*)

;
40b

9. The inexpensive keyboards can perform only a few functions. To the novice computer musician, the range is exciting. The range includes drum rhythms and simulated instruments. (*Still and semicolon.*)
10. Would-be musicians can orchestrate whole songs. They start from just the melody lines. They need never again play "Chopsticks." (*Semicolon alone.*)

40c   Use semicolons between main clauses or series items containing commas.

Normally, commas separate main clauses linked by coordinating conjunctions (*and, but, or, nor*) and separate items in a series. But when the clauses or series items contain commas, a semicolon between them makes the sentence easier to read.

Lewis and Clark led the men of their party with consummate skill, inspiring and encouraging them, doctoring and caring for them⟨;⟩ and they kept voluminous journals.   —Page Smith

The custody case involved Amy Dalton, the child⟨;⟩ Ellen and Mark Dalton, the parents⟨;⟩ and Ruth and Hal Blum, the grandparents.

40d   Delete or replace unneeded semicolons.

Semicolons are often misused in certain constructions that call for other punctuation or no punctuation.

1 ▪ No semicolon between a main clause and subordinate clause or phrase

The semicolon does not separate unequal parts, such as main clauses and subordinate clauses or phrases.

Not   Pygmies are in danger of extinction; because of encroaching development.

But   Pygmies are in danger of extinction⟨ ⟩because of encroaching development.

Not   According to African authorities; only about 35,000 Pygmies exist today.

But   According to African authorities⟨,⟩ only about 35,000 Pygmies exist today.

2 ▪ No semicolon before a series or explanation

Colons and dashes, not semicolons, introduce series, explanations, and so forth. (See pp. 309 and 321.)

Not   Teachers have heard many reasons why students do poorly; psychological problems, family illness, too much work, too little time.

;
40d

But   Teachers have heard many reasons why students do poorly⊙ psychological problems, family illness, too much work, too little time.

Exercise 40.2   Revising: Semicolons

Insert semicolons in the following paragraph wherever they are needed.
Also eliminate any misused or needless semicolons, substituting other
punctuation as appropriate.

The set, sounds, and actors in the movie captured the essence of
horror films. The set was ideal; dark, deserted streets, trees dipping their
branches over the sidewalks, mist hugging the ground and creeping up
to meet the trees, looming shadows of unlighted, turreted houses. The
sounds, too, were appropriate, especially terrifying was the hard, hollow sound of footsteps echoing throughout the film. But the best feature of the movie was its actors; all of them tall, pale, and thin to the
point of emaciation. With one exception, they were dressed uniformly in
gray and had gray hair. The exception was an actress who dressed only
in black; as if to set off her pale yellow, nearly white, long hair; the only
color in the film. The glinting black eyes of another actor stole almost
every scene, indeed, they were the source of the film's mischief.

---

41   The Colon

In *Brief*

To use the colon correctly,

- Introduce a concluding explanation, series, or appositive and some
  concluding quotations (below).
- Conclude a business-letter salutation, separate a title and subtitle, and
  separate divisions of time (facing page).
- Avoid common misuses: after a verb, preposition, *such as,* or *including*
  (p. 310).

Visit MyWritingLab™ for more resources on the colon.

The colon (:) is mainly a mark of introduction: it signals that the
words following it will explain or amplify. It also has several conventional uses, such as in expressions of time.

41a   Use a colon before a concluding explanation, series, or appositive and before some quotations.

As an introducer, a colon is always preceded by a complete main
clause—a word group that can stand alone as a sentence because it

contains a subject and a predicate verb and does not start with a subordinating word (see pp. 188–89). A colon may or may not be followed by a main clause. This is one way the colon differs from the semicolon, which generally separates main clauses only. (See p. 305.)

Explanation

Soul food has a deceptively simple definition⟨:⟩ the ethnic cooking of African Americans.

Sometimes a concluding explanation is preceded by *the following* or *as follows* and a colon:

A more precise definition might be the following⟨:⟩ soul food draws on ingredients, cooking methods, and dishes that originated in Africa, were brought to the New World by slaves, and were modified in the Caribbean and the American South.

Note A complete sentence *after* a colon may begin with a capital letter or a small letter. Just be consistent throughout an essay.

Series (p. 298)

At least three soul food dishes are familiar to most Americans⟨:⟩ fried chicken, barbecued spareribs, and sweet potatoes.

Appositive (p. 200)

Soul food has one disadvantage⟨:⟩ fat.

Namely, that is, and other expressions that introduce appositives *follow* the colon: *Soul food has one disadvantage⟨:⟩ namely, fat.*

Quotation

Use a colon before a quotation when the introduction is a complete sentence.

One soul food chef has a solution⟨:⟩ "Soul food doesn't have to be greasy to taste good. Instead of using ham hocks to flavor beans, I use smoked turkey wings. The soulful, smoky taste remains, but without all the fat."

41b Use a colon after the salutation of a business letter, between a title and subtitle, and between divisions of time.

41b

Salutation of business letter
Dear Ms. Burak⟨:⟩

Title and subtitle
Charles Dickens⟨:⟩ An Introduction to His Novels

Time
12⟨:⟩26 AM   6⟨:⟩00 PM

41c Delete or replace unneeded colons.

Use the colon only at the end of a main clause, not in the following situations:

▪ **Delete a colon after a verb.**

Not The best-known soul food dishes <u>are:</u> fried chicken and barbecued spareribs.

But The best-known soul food dishes <u>are</u>◯fried chicken and barbecued spareribs.

▪ **Delete a colon after a preposition, such as** *at, for,* **and** *in* (see p. 188).

Not Soul food recipes can be found <u>in:</u> mainstream cookbooks as well as specialized references.

But Soul food recipes can be found <u>in</u>◯mainstream cookbooks as well as specialized references.

▪ **Delete a colon after** *such as* **or** *including.*

Not Many Americans have not tasted delicacies <u>such as:</u> chitlins and black-eyed peas.

But Many Americans have not tasted delicacies <u>such as</u>◯chitlins and black-eyed peas.

Exercise 41.1 **Revising: Colons and semicolons**

In the following sentences, use colons or semicolons where they are needed, and delete or replace them where they are incorrect. If a sentence is already correct as given, mark the number preceding it.

> *Example:*
> Mix the ingredients as follows sift the flour and salt together, add the milk, and slowly beat in the egg yolk.
> Mix the ingredients as follows⊙ sift the flour and salt together, add the milk, and slowly beat in the egg yolk.

1. Sunlight is made up of three kinds of radiation; visible rays; infrared rays, which we cannot see; and ultraviolet rays, which are also invisible.
2. Especially in the ultraviolet range; sunlight is harmful to the eyes.
3. Ultraviolet rays can damage the retina: furthermore, they can cause cataracts on the lens.
4. Infrared rays are the longest; measuring 700 nanometers and longer, while ultraviolet rays are the shortest; measuring 400 nanometers and shorter.
5. The lens protects the eye by: absorbing much of the ultraviolet radiation and thus protecting the retina.
6. By protecting the retina, however, the lens becomes a victim; growing cloudy and blocking vision.
7. The best way to protect your eyes is: to wear hats that shade the face and sunglasses that screen out the ultraviolet rays.

8. Many sunglass lenses have been designed as ultraviolet screens; many others are extremely ineffective.

9. Sunglass lenses should screen out ultraviolet rays and be dark enough so that people can't see your eyes through them, otherwise, the lenses will not protect your eyes, and you will be at risk for cataracts later in life.

10. People who spend much time outside in the sun; really owe it to themselves to buy a pair of sunglasses that will shield their eyes.

42 The Apostrophe

In *Brief*

- Use the apostrophe to show possession in singular and plural words (below).
- Do not use the apostrophe in plural nouns or in singular verbs ending in -*s* (p. 314).
- Do not use the apostrophe in possessive personal or relative pronouns (p. 314).
- Use the apostrophe to show omissions in contractions (p. 314).

Visit MyWritingLab™ for more resources on the apostrophe.

The apostrophe (') appears as part of a word to indicate possession, the omission of one or more letters, or sometimes plural number.

42a Use the apostrophe to show possession.

A noun or an indefinite pronoun (such as *everyone*) shows possession with an apostrophe and, usually, an -*s*: *the dog's hair, everyone's hope*. Only certain pronouns do not use apostrophes for possession: *mine, yours, his, hers, its, ours, theirs,* and *whose*.

Note Remember that the apostrophe or apostrophe-plus-*s* is an *addition*. Before this addition, always spell the name of the owner or owners without dropping or adding letters.

42a

1 ▪ Singular words: Add -'*s*.

Bill Boughton's skillful card tricks amaze children.
Some of the earth's forests are regenerating.
Everyone's fitness can be improved through exercise.

The -'*s* ending for singular words pertains also to singular words ending in -*s*, as the next examples show.

Uses and misuses of the apostrophe

Uses of the apostrophe

- Use an apostrophe to form the possessives of nouns and indefinite pronouns (pp. 311–13).

Singular	Plural
Ms. Park's	the Parks'
lawyer's	lawyers'
everyone's	two weeks'

- Use an apostrophe to form contractions (p. 314).

it's a girl	shouldn't
you're	won't

- The apostrophe is optional for plurals of abbreviations, dates, and words or characters named as words (p. 315).

MAs or MA's	Cs or C's
1960s or 1960's	ifs or if's

Misuses of the apostrophe

- Do not use an apostrophe plus -s to form the possessives of plural nouns (p. 315). Instead, first form the plural with -s and *then* add an apostrophe.

Not	But
the Kim's car	the Kims' car
boy's fathers	boys' fathers
babie's care	babies' care

- Do not use an apostrophe to form plurals of nouns (p. 314).

Not	But
book's are	books are
the Freed's	the Freeds

- Do not use an apostrophe with verbs ending in -s (p. 314).

Not	But
swim's	swims

- Do not use an apostrophe to form the possessives of personal and relative pronouns (p. 314).

Not	But
it's toes	its toes
your's	yours
who's car	whose car

Henry James's novels reward the patient reader.
The business's customers filed suit.

Exception An apostrophe alone may be added to a singular word ending in *-s* if another *s* would make the word difficult to say:

Moses' mother concealed him in the bulrushes.
Joan Rivers' career spanned nearly six decades.

However, the added -s is never wrong (*Moses's, Rivers's*).

2 ▪ **Plural words ending in -s: Add -' only.**

Workers' incomes have fallen slightly over the past year.
Many students benefit from several years' work after high school.
The Jameses' talents are extraordinary.

Note the difference in the possessives of singular and plural words ending in -s. The singular form usually takes -s: *James's*. The plural takes only the apostrophe: *Jameses'*.

3 ▪ **Plural words not ending in -s: Add -'s.**

Children's educations are at stake.
We need to attract the media's attention.

4 ▪ **Compound words: Add -'s only to the last word.**

The brother-in-law's business failed.
Taxes are always somebody else's fault.

5 ▪ **Two or more owners: Add -'s depending on possession.**

Individual possession
Zimbale's and Mason's comedy techniques are similar. [Each comedian has his own technique.]

Joint possession
The children recovered despite their mother and father's neglect. [The mother and father were jointly neglectful.]

Exercise 42.1   **Forming possessives**
Form the possessive of each word or word group in brackets.

Example:
The [men] blood pressures were higher than the [women].
The men's blood pressures were higher than the women's.

1. In works for adults and teens, fiction writers often explore [people] relationship to nature and the environment.
2. For example, [Carl Hiaasen] inventive and humorous plots often revolve around endangered [species] habitats.
3. In *Hoot*, [Hiaasen] first novel for younger readers, endangered [owls] habitat will be destroyed if a [business] plans to build a new restaurant proceed.
4. In *Scat* two [students] investigation into a [teacher] disappearance leads to an environmental mystery.
5. Three of [Margaret Atwood] recent novels are about several [individuals] survival following a devastating environmental crisis and a plague that has killed nearly all of the residents of a city.

✓
42a

6. The first of the three books, *Oryx and Crake*, involves characters with those names but is told from one [man] perspective, that of a character named Jimmy.

7. Gradually readers learn about [Oryx and Crake] lives and why they are not struggling for survival along with Jimmy.

8. In the second Atwood book, *The Year of the Flood*, readers encounter a similar story, but through two [women] experiences.

9. In the third book, *Maddaddam*, the [characters] stories come together. [Everyone] life must start anew.

10. Some readers may be unsettled by these [books] visions of the future.

42b   Delete apostrophes where they are not required.

1 ▪ No apostrophe with a plural noun

The plurals of nouns are generally formed by adding *-s* or *-es*: *boys, families, Joneses*. Don't add an apostrophe to form the plural:

Not   The Jones' controlled the firm's until 2011.
But   The Joneses controlled the firms until 2011.

2 ▪ No apostrophe with a singular verb

Verbs ending in *-s* *never* take an apostrophe:

Not   The subway break's down less often now.
But   The subway breaks down less often now.

3 ▪ No apostrophe with a possessive personal or relative pronoun

His, hers, its, ours, yours, and *theirs*—all without apostrophes—are possessive forms of the personal pronouns *he, she, it, we, you,* and *they*. Likewise, *whose*—without an apostrophe—is the possessive of the relative pronoun *who*.

Not   Who's house is it? The house is her's. It's roof leaks.
But   Whose house is it? The house is hers. Its roof leaks.

Don't confuse possessive pronouns with contractions. See the examples on the facing page.

42c

42c   Use the apostrophe to form contractions.

Standard contractions

A **contraction** replaces one or more letters, numbers, or words with an apostrophe, as in the following examples:

it is	its	cannot	cant
they are	theyre	does not	doesnt
you are	youre	were not	werent
who is	whos	class of 2019	class of 19

Contractions vs. possessive pronouns

Don't confuse contractions with possessive pronouns:

Contractions	**Possessive pronouns**
Its a book.	Its cover is green.
Theyre coming.	Their car broke down.
Youre right.	Your idea is good.
Whos coming?	Whose party is it?

Exercise 42.2   Revising: Contractions and possessive pronouns

Revise the following sentences for correct use of contractions and possessive pronouns. Mark the number preceding any sentence that is already correct.

Example:

The agencies give they're employees they're birthdays off.
The agencies give their employees their birthdays off.

1. Many students seek help from the college writing center when their writing papers for their classes.
2. The writing center has expanded it's hours: it's now open until 10 PM every night.
3. The writing center also offers online tutoring to students whose schedules make face-to-face meetings difficult.
4. For online tutoring, students can submit they're papers by computer when they're ready to receive help.
5. In a survey, students who use the writing center responded that it's a good source of feedback for they're writing.

42d The apostrophe is optional in plural abbreviations, dates, and words or characters named as words.

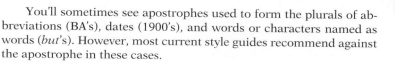

You'll sometimes see apostrophes used to form the plurals of abbreviations (BA's), dates (1900's), and words or characters named as words (*but's*). However, most current style guides recommend against the apostrophe in these cases.

BAs	PhDs
1990s	2000s

The sentence has too many *buts*.
Two *3s* end the zip code.

Note Italicize or underline a word or character named as a word (see p. 341), but not the added -*s*.

Exercise 42.3 **Revising: Apostrophes**

In the following paragraph, correct any mistakes in the use of apostrophes or any confusion between contractions and possessive personal pronouns.

People who's online experiences include blogging, Web cams, and social-networking sites are often used to seeing the details of other peoples private lives. Many are also comfortable sharing they're own opinions, photographs, and videos with family, friend's, and even stranger's. However, they need to realize that employers and even the government can see they're information, too. Employers commonly search for applicants names on social-networking Web sites such as *Facebook* and *Twitter*. Many companies monitor their employees outbound e-mail. People can take steps to protect their personal information by adjusting the privacy settings on their social-networking pages. They can avoid posting photos of themselves that they wouldnt want an employer to see. They can avoid sending personal e-mail while their at work. Its the individuals responsibility to keep certain information private.

---

43 Quotation Marks

In *Brief*

- Use quotation marks around direct quotations (facing page).
- Use quotation marks around titles of works that are parts of other works (facing page).
- Use quotation marks around words used in a special sense (p. 318).
- Do not use quotation marks with the title of your own paper, common nicknames, or slang (p. 318).
- Place quotation marks inside or outside other marks according to standard practice (p. 319).

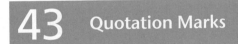

Visit MyWritingLab™ for more resources on quotation marks.

Quotation marks—either double (" ") or single (' ')—mainly enclose direct quotations and certain titles. Additional issues with quotations are discussed elsewhere in this book:

- **Punctuating** *she said* **and other signal phrases with quotations** (pp. 300–01).
- **Altering quotations using the ellipsis mark or brackets** (pp. 323–25).
- **Quoting sources versus paraphrasing or summarizing them** (pp. 393–99).
- **Integrating quotations into your text** (pp. 400–03).

- Avoiding plagiarism when quoting (pp. 405–11).
- Formatting long prose quotations and poetry quotations in MLA style or in APA style (pp. 466 and 500).

43a   Use double quotation marks to enclose direct quotations.

A **direct quotation** reports what someone said or wrote, in the exact words of the original:

> "Life," said the psychoanalyst Karen Horney, "remains a very efficient therapist."

When quoting dialog, begin a new paragraph for each speaker.

> "What shall I call you? Your name?" Andrews whispered rapidly, as with a high squeak the latch of the door rose.
> "Elizabeth," she said. "Elizabeth."
>
> —Graham Greene, *The Man Within*

Note   Do not use quotation marks with a direct quotation that is set off from your text. See pages 466 and 500 for handling such quotations in MLA and APA styles, respectively. Also do not use quotation marks with an **indirect quotation,** which reports what someone said or wrote but not in the exact words:

> The psychoanalyst Karen Horney claimed that life is a good therapist.

43b   Use single quotation marks to enclose a quotation within a quotation.

> "In formulating any philosophy," Woody Allen writes, "the first consideration must always be: What can we know? Descartes hinted at the problem when he wrote, 'My mind can never know my body, although it has become quite friendly with my leg.'"

Notice that two different quotation marks appear at the end of the sentence—one single (to finish the interior quotation) and one double (to finish the main quotation).

43c   Use quotation marks around the titles of works that are parts of other works.

Use quotation marks to enclose the titles of works that are published or released within larger works. (See the box on the next page.) Use single quotation marks for a quotation within a quoted title, as in the article title and essay title in the box. And enclose all punctuation in the title within the quotation marks, as in the article title.

Titles to be enclosed in quotation marks

Other titles should be italicized or underlined. (See p. 340.)

Song
"The Star-Spangled Banner"

Short story
"The Gift of the Magi"

Short poem
"Stopping by Woods on a Snowy Evening"

Article in a periodical
"Does 'Scaring' Work?"

Essay
"Joey: A 'Mechanical Boy'"

Unpublished speech
"Horses and Healing"

Page or work on a Web site
"Readers' Page" (on the site *Friends of Prufrock*)

Episode of a television or radio program
"The Mexican Connection" (on *Sixty Minutes*)

Subdivision of a book
"The Mast Head" (Chapter 35 of *Moby-Dick*)

Note Some academic disciplines do not require quotation marks for titles within source citations. See page 482 on the style of the American Psychological Association (APA).

43d Quotation marks may enclose words being used in a special sense.

On movie sets movable "wild walls" make a one-walled room seem four-walled on film.

Note Use italics or underlining for words you are defining or emphasizing. (See p. 341.)

43e Delete quotation marks where they are not required.

Title of your paper

Not "The Death Wish in One Poem by Robert Frost"
But The Death Wish in One Poem by Robert Frost
Or The Death Wish in "Stopping by Woods on a Snowy Evening"

Common nickname

Not When he was President, "Jimmy" Carter preferred to use his nickname.
But When he was President, Jimmy Carter preferred to use his nickname.

Slang or trite expression

Quotation marks will not excuse slang or a trite expression that is inappropriate to your writing. If slang is appropriate, use it without quotation marks.

Not We should support the President in his "hour of need" rather than "wimp out on him."

But We should give the President the support he needs rather than turn away like cowards.

43f Place other punctuation marks inside or outside quotation marks according to standard practice.

1 ▪ Commas and periods: Inside quotation marks

Swift uses irony in his essay "A Modest Proposal."

Many first-time readers are shocked to see infants described as "delicious."

"'A Modest Proposal,'" wrote one critic, "is so outrageous that it cannot be believed."

Exception When a source citation in your text immediately follows a quotation, place any period or comma *after* the citation:

One critic calls the essay "outrageous" (Olms 26).

Partly because of "the cool calculation of its delivery" (Olms 27), the satire still chills a modern reader.

2 ▪ Colons and semicolons: Outside quotation marks

A few years ago the slogan in elementary education was "learning by playing"; now educators are concerned with teaching basic skills.

We all know the meaning of "basic skills": reading, writing, and arithmetic.

3 ▪ Dashes, question marks, and exclamation points: Inside quotation marks only if part of the quotation

When a dash, question mark, or exclamation point is part of the quotation, place it *inside* quotation marks. Don't use any other punctuation, such as a period or comma:

"But must you—" Marcia hesitated, afraid of the answer.

"Go away!" I yelled.

Did you say, "Who is she?" [When both your sentence and the quotation would end in a question mark or exclamation point, use only the mark in the quotation.]

When a dash, question mark, or exclamation point applies only to the larger sentence, not to the quotation, place it *outside* quotation marks—again, with no other punctuation:

> Another evocative line in English poetry—"Now slides the silent meteor on"—comes from Alfred, Lord Tennyson.
>
> Who said, "Now cracks a noble heart"?
>
> The woman called me "stupid"!

Exercise 43.1 Revising: Quotation marks

Insert quotation marks as needed in the following paragraph.

> In a history class we talked about a passage from Abraham Lincoln's *Gettysburg Address*, delivered on November 19, 1863:
>
> > Four score and seven years ago our fathers brought forth on this continent, a new nation, conceived in Liberty, and dedicated to the proposition that all men are created equal. Now we are engaged in a great civil war, testing whether that nation, or any nation so conceived and so dedicated, can long endure.
>
> What was Lincoln referring to in the first sentence? the teacher asked. Perhaps we should define *score* first. Explaining that a score is twenty years, she said that Lincoln was referring to the document in which the colonies had declared independence from England eighty-seven years earlier, in 1776.
>
> One student commented, Lincoln's decision to end slavery is implied in that first sentence. The President was calling on the authority of the Founding Fathers.
>
> Lincoln gave the speech at the dedication of the National Cemetery in Gettysburg, Pennsylvania, which was the site of a very bloody Civil War battle, another student added.
>
> A third student noted that in the second sentence Lincoln was posing the central question of the war: whether a nation founded on equality can long endure.

44 Other Marks

In *Brief*

- Use the dash (—) to set off interruptions (opposite).
- Use parentheses (()) to enclose parenthetical expressions and labels for lists within sentences (p. 322).
- Use the ellipsis mark (. . .) to indicate omissions from quotations (p. 323).
- Use brackets ([ ]) mainly to indicate changes in quotations (p. 325).
- Use the slash (/) to separate options and lines of poetry (p. 326).

Visit MyWritingLab™ for more resources on other punctuation marks.

44a   Use the dash or dashes to indicate shifts and to set off some sentence elements.

The **dash** is mainly a mark of interruption: it signals a shift, insertion, or break. Form a dash with two hyphens (--), or use the character called an em dash on your word processor. Do not add extra space around or between the hyphens or around the em dash.

Note When an interrupting element starting with a dash falls in the middle of a sentence, be sure to add the closing dash to signal the end of the interruption. See the first example below.

1 ▪ Shifts and hesitations

The novel—if one can call it that—appeared in 2012.

If the book had a plot—but a plot would be conventional.

"I was worried you might think I had stayed away because I was influenced by—" He stopped and lowered his eyes.
Astonished, Howe said, "Influenced by what?"
"Well, by—" Blackburn hesitated and for an answer pointed to the table.   —Lionel Trilling

2 ▪ Nonessential elements (p. 294)

Dashes may be used instead of commas to set off modifiers, parenthetical expressions, and other nonessential elements. The dashes emphasize the elements more than commas do.

Though they are close together—separated by only a few blocks—the two neighborhoods could be in different countries.

Dashes are especially useful when a nonessential element contains punctuation of its own:

The qualities Monet painted—sunlight, rich shadows, deep colors— abounded near the rivers and gardens he used as subjects.

3 ▪ Introductory series and concluding series and explanations

Shortness of breath, skin discoloration or the sudden appearance of moles, persistent indigestion, the presence of small lumps—all these may signify cancer. [Introductory series.]

The patient undergoes a battery of tests—imaging, blood tests, perhaps even biopsy. [Concluding series.]

Many patients are disturbed by MRI imaging—by the need to keep still for long periods in an exceedingly small space. [Concluding explanation.]

A colon could be used instead of a dash in the last two examples. The dash is more informal.

44a

4 ■ Overuse

Too many dashes can make writing jumpy or breathy:

Not In all his life—eighty-seven years—my great-grandfather never allowed his picture to be taken—not even once. He claimed the "black box"—the camera—would steal his soul.

But In all his eighty-seven years, my great-grandfather did not allow his picture to be taken even once. He claimed the "black box"—the camera—would steal his soul.

44b Use parentheses to enclose parenthetical expressions and labels for lists within sentences.

Note Parentheses *always* come in pairs, one before and one after the punctuated material.

1 ■ Parenthetical expressions

Parenthetical expressions include explanations, facts, digressions, and examples that may be helpful or interesting but are not essential to meaning. Parentheses de-emphasize parenthetical expressions. (Commas emphasize them more and dashes still more.)

The population of Philadelphia (now about 1.5 million) has declined since 1950.

Note Don't put a comma before a parenthetical expression enclosed in parentheses. Punctuation after the parenthetical expression should be placed outside the closing parenthesis.

Not The population of Philadelphia compares with that of Phoenix, (about 1.5 million.)

But The population of Philadelphia compares with that of Phoenix (about 1.5 million).

If you enclose a complete sentence in parentheses, capitalize the sentence and place the closing period *inside* the closing parenthesis:

In general, coaches will tell you that scouts are just guys who can't coach. (But then, so are brain surgeons.)   —Roy Blount

2 ■ Labels for lists within sentences

Outside the Middle East, the following countries have the largest oil reserves: (1) Venezuela (297 billion barrels), (2) Canada (197 billion barrels), and (3) Russia (116 billion barrels).

When you set a list off from your text, do not enclose such labels in parentheses.

44c Use the ellipsis mark to indicate omissions from quotations.

The **ellipsis mark,** consisting of three periods separated by space (...), generally indicates an omission from a quotation. The following examples quote from or refer to this passage:

Original quotation

"At the heart of the environmentalist world view is the conviction that human physical and spiritual health depends on sustaining the planet in a relatively unaltered state. Earth is our home in the full, genetic sense, where humanity and its ancestors existed for all the millions of years of their evolution. Natural ecosystems—forests, coral reefs, marine blue waters—maintain the world exactly as we would wish it to be maintained. When we debase the global environment and extinguish the variety of life, we are dismantling a support system that is too complex to understand, let alone replace, in the foreseeable future."

—Edward O. Wilson, "Is Humanity Suicidal?"

1. Omission of the middle of a sentence
Wilson writes, "Natural ecosystems . . . maintain the world exactly as we would wish it to be maintained."

2. Omission of the end of a sentence, without source citation
Wilson writes, "Earth is our home . . . ." [The sentence period, closed up to the last word, precedes the ellipsis mark.]

3. Omission of the end of a sentence, with source citation
Wilson writes, "Earth is our home . . ." (27). [The sentence period follows the source citation.]

4. Omission of parts of two or more sentences
Wilson writes, "At the heart of the environmentalist world view is the conviction that human physical and spiritual health depends on sustaining the planet . . . where humanity and its ancestors existed for all the millions of years of their evolution."

5. Omission of one or more sentences
As Wilson puts it, "At the heart of the environmentalist world view is the conviction that human physical and spiritual health depends on sustaining the planet in a relatively unaltered state. . . . When we debase the global environment and extinguish the variety of life, we are dismantling a support system that is too complex to understand, let alone replace, in the foreseeable future."

6. Omission from the middle of a sentence through the end of another sentence
"Earth is our home. . . . When we debase the global environment and extinguish the variety of life, we are dismantling a support system that

is too complex to understand, let alone replace, in the foreseeable future."

7. Omission of the beginning of a sentence, leaving a complete sentence

a. Bracketed capital letter

"[H]uman physical and spiritual health," Wilson writes, "depends on sustaining the planet in a relatively unaltered state." [No ellipsis mark is needed because the brackets around the *H* indicate that the letter was not capitalized originally and thus that the beginning of the sentence has been omitted.]

b. Small letter

According to Wilson, "human physical and spiritual health depends on sustaining the planet in a relatively unaltered state." [No ellipsis mark is needed because the small *h* indicates that the beginning of the sentence has been omitted.]

c. Capital letter from the original

One reviewer comments, "...Wilson argues eloquently for the environmentalist world view" (Hami 28). [An ellipsis mark *is* needed because the quoted part of the sentence begins with a capital letter and it's otherwise not clear that the beginning of the original sentence has been omitted.]

8. Use of a word or phrase

Wilson describes the earth as "our home in the full, genetic sense." [No ellipsis mark is needed.]

Note these features of the examples:

- **Use an ellipsis mark when it is not otherwise clear that you have left out material from the source,** as when you omit one or more sentences (examples 5 and 6) or when the words you quote form a complete sentence that is different in the original (examples 1–4 and 7c).
- **You don't need an ellipsis mark when it is obvious that you have omitted something,** such as when a bracketed capital or small letter indicates omission (examples 7a and 7b) or when a phrase clearly comes from a larger sentence (example 8).
- **Place an ellipsis mark after any sentence period** *except* **when a parenthetical source citation follows the quotation,** as in examples 3 and 7c. Then the sentence period falls after the citation.

If you omit one or more lines of poetry or paragraphs of prose from a quotation, use a separate line of ellipsis marks across the full width of the quotation to show the omission. (See pp. 466 and 500, respectively, for the format of such set-off quotations in MLA and APA styles.)

In "Song: Love Armed" from 1676, Aphra Behn contrasts two lovers'
experiences of a romance:

> Love in fantastic triumph sate,
>> Whilst bleeding hearts around him flowed,
>
> . . . .
>
> But my poor heart alone is harmed,
>> Whilst thine the victor is, and free. (lines 1-2, 15-16)

Exercise 44.1   Using ellipsis marks

Use ellipsis marks and any other needed punctuation to follow the numbered instructions for quoting from the following paragraph.

> Women in the sixteenth and seventeenth centuries were educated
> in the home and, in some cases, in boarding schools. Men were edu-
> cated at home, in grammar schools, and at the universities. The universi-
> ties were closed to female students. For women, "learning the Bible," as
> Elizabeth Joceline puts it, was an impetus to learning to read. To be able
> to read the Bible in the vernacular was a liberating experience that freed
> the reader from hearing only the set passages read in the church and
> interpreted by the church. A Protestant woman was expected to read
> the scriptures daily, to meditate on them, and to memorize portions of
> them. In addition, a woman was expected to instruct her entire house-
> hold in "learning the Bible" by holding instructional and devotional
> times each day for all household members, including the servants.
>> —Charlotte F. Otten, *English Women's Voices, 1540–1700*

1. Quote the fifth sentence, but omit everything from *that freed the
   reader* to the end.
2. Quote the fifth sentence, but omit the words *was a liberating experience that.*
3. Quote the first and sixth sentences together.

44d   Use brackets to indicate changes in quotations.

Brackets have specialized uses in mathematical equations, but
their main use for all kinds of writing is to indicate that you have altered a quotation to explain, clarify, or correct it.

[ ]
44d

> "That Chevron station [just outside Dallas] is one of the busiest in the
> nation," said a company spokesperson.

The word *sic* (Latin for "in this manner") in brackets indicates
that an error in the quotation appeared in the original and was not
made by you. Do not underline or italicize *sic* in brackets.

> According to the newspaper report, "The car slammed thru [sic] the
> railing and into oncoming traffic."

Do not use *sic* to make fun of a writer or to note errors in a passage that is clearly nonstandard.

44e Use the slash between options and between lines of poetry run into the text.

Option

Some teachers oppose pass⊘fail courses.

Poetry

Many readers have sensed a reluctant turn away from death in Frost's lines "The woods are lovely, dark and deep, ⊘ But I have promises to keep" (13–14).

When separating lines of poetry in this way, leave a space before and after the slash. (See p. 466 for more on quoting poetry.)

> **Exercise 44.2 Revising: Dashes, parentheses, ellipsis marks, brackets, slashes**
>
> Insert dashes, parentheses, ellipsis marks, brackets, or slashes as needed in the following paragraph. In some cases, two or more different marks could be correct.
>
> "Let all the learned say what they can, 'Tis ready money makes the man." These two lines of poetry by the Englishman William Somerville 1645–1742 may apply to a current American economic problem. Non-American investors with "ready money" pour some of it as much as $1.3 trillion in recent years into the United States. Stocks and bonds, savings deposits, service companies, factories, artworks, political campaigns the investments of foreigners are varied and grow more numerous every day. Proponents of foreign investment argue that it revives industry, strengthens the economy, creates jobs more than 3 million, they say, and encourages free trade among nations. Opponents caution that the risks associated with heavy foreign investment namely decreased profits at home and increased political influence from outside may ultimately weaken the economy. On both sides, it seems, "the learned say, 'Tis ready money makes the man or country." The question is, whose money theirs or ours?

45 Spelling

In *Brief*
- Anticipate typical spelling problems, such as misleading pronunciation (below).
- Follow spelling rules for *ie* vs. *ei*, attaching endings or prefixes to words, and forming plurals (p. 330).

Visit MyWritingLab™ for more resources on spelling.

You can train yourself to spell better by following this chapter's tips for pinpointing and fixing your spelling problems. But you can improve your spelling instantly by adopting three habits:

- **Carefully proofread all of your writing.**
- **Cultivate a healthy suspicion of your spellings.**
- **Check a dictionary *every time* you doubt a spelling.**

45a Anticipate typical spelling problems.

Misspellings often result from misleading pronunciation, different forms of the same word, and the confusion of British and American spellings.

1 ▪ Pronunciation

In English, pronunciation of words is an unreliable guide to their spelling. Pronunciation is especially misleading with **homonyms,** words that are pronounced the same but spelled differently. Some homonyms and near-homonyms appear in the following box. (For more confusing pairs, see "Commonly Misused Words," pp. 505–17.)

Words commonly confused

accept (to receive)
except (other than)

affect (to have an influence on)
effect (result)

all ready (prepared)
already (by this time)

allusion (an indirect reference)
illusion (an erroneous belief or perception)

ascent (a movement up)
assent (to agree, or an agreement)

bare (unclothed)
bear (to carry, or an animal)

board (a plane of wood)
bored (uninterested)

brake (to stop)
break (to smash)

buy (to purchase)
by (next to)

capital (the seat of government)
capitol (the building where a legislature meets)

cite (to quote an authority)
sight (the ability to see)
site (a place)

---

desert (to abandon)
dessert (after-dinner course)

discreet (reserved, respectful)
discrete (individual, distinct)

elicit (to draw out)
illicit (illegal or immoral)

eminent (prominent, respected)
imminent (about to occur)

fair (average, or lovely)
fare (a fee for transportation)

forth (forward)
fourth (after *third*)

hear (to perceive by ear)
here (in this place)

heard (past tense of *hear*)
herd (a group of animals)

hole (an opening)
whole (complete)

its (possessive of *it*)
it's (contraction of *it is* or *it has*)

know (to be certain)
no (the opposite of *yes*)

lead (heavy metal)
led (past tense of *lead*)

lessen (to reduce)
lesson (something learned)

meat (flesh)
meet (to encounter, or a competition)

passed (past tense of *pass*)
past (after, or a time gone by)

patience (forbearance)
patients (persons under medical care)

peace (the absence of war)
piece (a portion of something)

plain (clear)
plane (a carpenter's tool, or an airborne vehicle)

presence (the state of being at hand)
presents (gifts)

principal (most important, or the head of a school)
principle (a basic truth or law)

rain (precipitation)
reign (to rule)
rein (a strap for an animal)

raise (to lift up)
raze (to tear down)

right (correct)
rite (a religious ceremony)
write (to make letters)

road (a surface for driving)
rode (past tense of *ride*)

scene (where an action occurs)
seen (past participle of *see*)

stationary (unmoving)
stationery (writing paper)

their (possessive of *they*)
there (opposite of *here*)
they're (contraction of *they are*)

to (toward)
too (also)
two (following *one*)

waist (the middle of the body)
waste (discarded material)

weak (not strong)
week (Sunday through Saturday)

weather (climate)
whether (*if,* or introducing a choice)

which (one of a group)
witch (a sorcerer)

who's (contraction of *who is* or *who has*)
whose (possessive of *who*)

your (possessive of *you*)
you're (contraction of *you are*)

---

2 ▪ Different forms of the same word

sp
45a

Spellings often differ for the same word's noun and verb forms or noun and adjective forms: for example, *advi̲ce* (noun) and *advi̲se* (verb); *description* (noun) and *describe* (verb); *height* (noun) and *high* (adjective); *generosity* (noun) and *generous* (adjective). Similar differences occur in the parts of some irregular verbs (*know, knew, known*) and the plurals of irregular nouns (*man, men*).

3 ■ American vs. British spellings (CULTURE LANGUAGE)

When writing for an American audience, use American spellings instead of their British equivalents.

American	British
color, humor	colour, humour
theater, center	theatre, centre
canceled, traveled	cancelled, travelled
judgment	judgement
realize, civilize	realise, civilise
connection	connexion

Your dictionary may list both spellings, but it will specially mark the British one with *chiefly Brit* or a similar label.

45b Follow spelling rules.

1 ■ *ie* vs. *ei*

To distinguish between *ie* and *ei*, use the familiar jingle:

I before *e*, except after *c*, or when pronounced "ay" as in *neighbor* and *weigh*.

i before *e*	believe	thief	hygiene
ei after *c*	ceiling	conceive	perceive
ei sounded as "ay"	sleigh	eight	beige

Exceptions For some exceptions, remember this sentence:

The weird foreigner neither seizes leisure nor forfeits height.

2 ■ Final *e*

When adding an ending to a word with a final *e*, drop the *e* if the ending begins with a vowel:

advise + able = advisable   surprise + ing = surprising

Keep the *e* if the ending begins with a consonant:

care + ful = careful   like + ly = likely

Exceptions Retain the *e* after a soft *c* or *g*, to keep the sound of the consonant soft rather than hard: *courageous, changeable.* And drop the *e* before a consonant when the *e* is preceded by another vowel: *argue + ment = argument, true + ly = truly.*

3 ▪ Final *y*

When adding an ending to a word with a final *y*, change the *y* to *i* if it follows a consonant:

beauty, beauties   worry, worried   supply, supplies

But keep the *y* if it follows a vowel, if it ends a proper name, or if the added ending is *ing*:

day, days   Minsky, Minskys   cry, crying

4 ▪ Final consonants

When adding an ending to a one-syllable word ending in a consonant, double the final consonant when it follows a single vowel. Otherwise, don't double the consonant.

slap, slapping   park, parking   pair, paired

In words of more than one syllable, double the final consonant when it follows a single vowel *and* ends a stressed syllable once the new ending is added. Otherwise, don't double the consonant.

refer, referring   refer, reference   relent, relented

5 ▪ Prefixes

When adding a prefix, do not drop a letter from or add a letter to the original word:

unnecessary   disappoint   misspell

6 ▪ Plurals

Most nouns form plurals by adding *s* to the singular form. Add *es* for the plural of nouns ending in *s, sh, ch,* or *x*.

boy, boys   kiss, kisses   church, churches

Nouns ending in *o* preceded by a vowel usually form the plural with *s*. Those ending in *o* preceded by a consonant usually form the plural with *es*.

ratio, ratios   hero, heroes

Some very common nouns form irregular plurals.

child, children   woman, women   mouse, mice

Some English nouns that were originally Italian, Greek, Latin, or French form the plural according to their original language:

analysis, analyses   criterion, criteria   piano, pianos
basis, bases   datum, data   thesis, theses
crisis, crises   medium, media

sp
45b

A few such nouns may form irregular *or* regular plurals: for instance, *index, indices, indexes; curriculum, curricula, curriculums.* The regular plural is more contemporary.

With compound nouns, add *s* to the main word of the compound. Sometimes this main word is not the last word.

city-states   fathers-in-law   passersby

CULTURE LANGUAGE Noncount nouns do not form plurals, either regularly (with an added *s*) or irregularly. Examples of noncount nouns are *air, intelligence,* and *wealth.* See pages 260–61.

Exercise 45.1   Using correct spellings

Select the correct spelling from the choices in brackets, referring as needed to the list of words on pages 328–30, the preceding rules, or a dictionary.

Example:

The boat [passed, past] us so fast that we rocked violently in [its, it's] wake.

The boat passed us so fast that we rocked violently in its wake.

1. Science [affects, effects] many [important, importent] aspects of our lives.
2. Many people have a [pore, poor] understanding of the [role, roll] of scientific breakthroughs in [their, they're] health.
3. Many people [beleive, believe] that [docters, doctors] are more [responsable, responsible] for [improvements, improvments] in health care than scientists are.
4. But scientists in the [labratory, laboratory] have made crucial steps in the search for [knowlege, knowledge] about human health and [medecine, medicine].
5. For example, one scientist [who's, whose] discoveries have [affected, effected] many people is Ulf Von Euler.
6. In the 1950s Von Euler's discovery of certain hormones [lead, led] to the invention of the birth control pill.
7. Von Euler's work was used by John Rock, who [developed, developped] the first birth control pill and influenced family [planing, planning].
8. Von Euler also discovered the [principal, principle] neurotransmitter that controls the heartbeat.
9. Another scientist, Hans Selye, showed what [affect, effect] stress can have on the body.
10. His findings have [lead, led] to methods of [baring, bearing] stress.

Exercise 45.2   Working with a spelling checker

Try your computer's spelling checker on the following paragraph. Type the paragraph exactly as it appears here, and run it through your spelling checker. Then proofread it to correct the errors missed by the checker. (Hint: There are fourteen errors in all.)

sp
45b

The whether effects all of us, though it's affects are different for different people. Some people love a fare day with warm temperatures
and sunshine. They revel in spending a hole day outside without the
threat of rein. Other people prefer dark, rainy daze. They relish the opportunity to slow down and here they're inner thoughts. Most people
agree, however, that to much of one kind of whether—reign, sun, snow,
or clouds—makes them board.

46   The Hyphen

In *Brief*

- Use the hyphen in some compound words (below).
- Use the hyphen to divide words (next page).

Visit MyWritingLab™ for more resources on the hyphen.

46a   Use the hyphen in some compound words.

1 ■ Compound adjectives

When two or more words serve together as a single modifier before a noun, a hyphen forms the modifying words clearly into a unit.

She is a well⊖known actor.

Some Spanish⊖speaking students work as translators in the admission
and finance offices.

When such a compound adjective follows the noun, the hyphen is
unnecessary.

The actor is well◯known.

Many students are Spanish◯speaking.

The hyphen is also unnecessary in a compound adjective containing
an -*ly* adverb, even before the noun: *clearly◯defined terms.*
When part of a compound adjective appears only once in two or
more parallel compounds, hyphens indicate which words the reader
should mentally join with the missing part.

School-age children should have eight⊖ or nine⊖o'clock bedtimes.

2 ■ Fractions and compound numbers

Hyphens always join the numerator and denominator of fractions: *two⊖thirds, three⊖fourths.* Hyphens also join the parts of the
whole numbers *twenty⊖one* to *ninety⊖nine.*

3 ▪ Prefixes and suffixes

Do not use hyphens with prefixes except as follows:

- **With the prefixes *self-*, *all-*, and *ex-*:** *self-control, all-inclusive, ex-student.*
- **With a prefix before a capitalized word:** *un-American.*
- **With a capital letter before a word:** *T-shirt.*
- **To prevent misreading:** *de-emphasize, re-create a story.*

The only suffix that regularly requires a hyphen is *-elect,* as in *president-elect.*

46b Use the hyphen to divide words at the ends of lines.

You can avoid very short lines in your documents by dividing some words between the end of one line and the beginning of the next. You can set a word processor to divide words automatically at appropriate breaks. To divide words manually, follow these guidelines:

- **Divide words only between syllables**—for instance, *win-dows,* not *wi-ndows.* Check a dictionary for correct syllable breaks.
- **Never divide a one-syllable word.**
- **Leave at least two letters on the first line and three on the second line.** If a word cannot be divided to follow this rule (for instance, *a-bus-er*), don't divide it.
- **Do not use a hyphen in breaking a URL** because readers may perceive any added hyphens as part of the address. The documentation styles differ in where they allow breaks in URLs. For example, MLA style allows a break only after a slash, while APA style allows a break before most punctuation marks.

Exercise 46.1   Using hyphens

Insert hyphens wherever they are needed, and delete them where they are not needed. If a sentence is already correct as given, mark the number preceding it.

> *Example:*
> Elephants have twelve inch long teeth, but they have only four of them.
> Elephants have twelve-inch-long teeth, but they have only four of them.

1. The African elephant is well known for its size.
2. Both male and female African elephants can grow to a ten-foot height.

3. The non African elephants of south central Asia are somewhat smaller.
4. A fourteen or fifteen year old elephant has reached sexual maturity.
5. The elephant life span is about sixty five or seventy years.
6. A newborn elephant calf weighs two to three hundred pounds.
7. It stands about thirty three inches high.
8. A two hundred pound, thirty three inch baby is quite a big baby.
9. Unfortunately, elephants are often killed for their ivory tusks, and partly as a result they are an increasingly-endangered species.
10. African governments have made tusk and ivory selling illegal.

47 Capital Letters

In *Brief*

- Capitalize the first word of every sentence (below).
- Capitalize proper nouns, proper adjectives, and words used as essential parts of proper nouns (next page).
- Capitalize most words in titles and subtitles of works (p. 338).
- Capitalize words according to convention in online communication (p. 338).

Visit MyWritingLab™ for more resources on capital letters.

The conventions described in this chapter and a desk dictionary can help you decide whether to capitalize a particular word in most writing. Consult the style guides listed on page 414 for the requirements of particular disciplines.

⟨CULTURE ᐱLANGUAGE⟩ Conventions of capitalization vary from language to language. English, for instance, is the only language to capitalize the first-person singular pronoun (*I*), and its practice of capitalizing proper nouns but not most common nouns also distinguishes it from some other languages.

common noun	proper noun	pronoun	common noun
My <u>friend</u> <u>Nathaniel</u> and <u>I</u> both play the <u>drums</u>.

47a Capitalize the first word of every sentence.

No one expected the outcome.
Will inflation result?
Watch out!

When quoting other writers, you should reproduce the capital letters beginning their sentences or indicate that you have altered the source's capitalization. Whenever possible, integrate the quotation into your own sentence so that its capitalization coincides with yours:

> "Psychotherapists often overlook the benefits of self-deception," the author argues (122).

> The author argues that "the benefits of self-deception" are not always recognized by psychotherapists (122). [Do not capitalize a phrase quoted from inside a sentence.]

If you need to alter the capitalization in the source, indicate the change with brackets.

> "[T]he benefits of self-deception" are not always recognized by psychotherapists, the author argues. (122).

> The author argues that "[p]sychotherapists often overlook the benefits of self-deception" (122).

Note Capitalization of questions in a series is optional. Both of the following examples are correct:

> Is the population a hundred? Two hundred? More?
> Is the population a hundred? two hundred? more?

Also optional is capitalization of the first word in a complete sentence after a colon.

47b Capitalize proper nouns, proper adjectives, and words used as essential parts of proper nouns.

1 ▪ Proper nouns and proper adjectives

Proper nouns name specific persons, places, and things: *Shakespeare, China, World War I.* **Proper adjectives** are formed from some proper nouns: *Shakespearean, Chinese.* Capitalize all proper nouns and proper adjectives but not the articles (*a, an, the*) that precede them.

Proper nouns and adjectives to be capitalized

Specific persons and things

Oprah Winfrey	Boulder Dam
Napoleon Bonaparte	the Empire State Building

Specific places and geographical regions

New York City	the Mediterranean Sea
China	the Northeast, the South

But: northeast of the city, going south, northern

Days of the week, months, holidays

Monday	Yom Kippur
May	Christmas

Historical events, documents, periods, movements

Vietnam War	Renaissance
Constitution	Romantic Movement

Government offices, departments, and institutions

House of Representatives	Polk Municipal Court
Department of Defense	Sequoia Hospital

Academic institutions and departments

University of Kansas	Department of Nursing
Santa Monica College	Haven High School

But: the university, college course, high school diploma

Political, social, athletic, and other organizations and associations and their members

Democratic Party, Democrats	League of Women Voters
Sierra Club	Boston Celtics
B'nai B'rith	Chicago Symphony Orchestra

Races, nationalities, and their languages

Native American	Germans
African American	Swahili
Caucasian	Italian

But: blacks, whites

Religions, their followers, and terms for the sacred

Christianity, Christians	God
Catholicism, Catholics	Allah
Judaism, Orthodox Jews	the Bible [but biblical]
Islam, Muslims	the Koran, the Qur'an

---

2 ▪ Common nouns used as essential parts of proper nouns

Capitalize the common nouns *street, avenue, park, river, ocean, lake, company, college, county,* and *memorial* when they are part of proper nouns naming specific places or institutions:

Main Street	Ford Motor Company
Central Park	Madison College
Mississippi River	George Washington Memorial

3 ▪ Relationships

Capitalize the names of relationships only when they precede or replace proper names:

Our aunt scolded us for disrespecting Father and Uncle Jake.

cap

47b

4 ▪ Titles with persons' names

Before a person's name, capitalize his or her title. After or apart from the name, do not capitalize the title.

Professor Otto Osborne	Otto Osborne, a professor
Doctor Jane Covington	Jane Covington, a doctor
Governor Ella Moore	Ella Moore, the governor

Note Many writers capitalize a title denoting very high rank even when it follows a name or is used alone: *Ronald Reagan, past President of the United States*.

47c Capitalize most words in titles and subtitles of works.

Within your text, capitalize all the words in a title *except* the following: articles (*a, an, the*), *to* in infinitives, coordinating conjunctions (*and, but*, etc.), and prepositions (*with, between*, etc.). Capitalize even these words when they are the first or last word in a title or when they fall after a colon or semicolon.

"Courtship through the Ages"	*Management: A New Theory*
A Diamond Is Forever	"Once More to the Lake"
"Knowing Whom to Ask"	*An End to Live For*
Learning from Las Vegas	*File under Architecture*

Note The style guides of the academic disciplines have their own rules for capitals in titles. For instance, the preceding guidelines reflect MLA style for English and some other humanities. In contrast, APA style for the social sciences capitalizes only the first word and proper names in book and article titles within source citations (see p. 482).

47d Use capitals according to convention in electronic communication.

Electronic messages written in all-capital letters or with no capital letters are difficult to read. Further, messages in all-capital letters may be taken as rude (see also pp. 82–83).

> **Exercise 47.1   Revising: Capitals**
>
> Edit the following sentences to correct errors in capitalization. Consult a dictionary if you are in doubt. If a sentence is already correct as given, mark the number preceding it.
>
> *Example:*
>
> The first book on the reading list is mark twain's *a connecticut yankee in king arthur's court*.

The first book on the reading list is Mark Twain's *A Connecticut Yankee in King Arthur's Court*.

1. San Antonio, texas, is a thriving city in the southwest.
2. The city has always offered much to tourists interested in the roots of spanish settlement in the new world.
3. The alamo is one of five Catholic Missions built by Priests to convert native americans and to maintain spain's claims in the area.
4. But the alamo is more famous for being the site of an 1836 battle that helped to create the republic of Texas.
5. Many of the nearby Streets, such as Crockett street, are named for men who died in that Battle.
6. The Hemisfair plaza and the San Antonio river link tourist and convention facilities.
7. Restaurants, Hotels, and shops line the River. the haunting melodies of "Una paloma blanca" and "malagueña" lure passing tourists into Casa rio and other mexican restaurants.
8. The university of Texas at San Antonio has expanded, and a Medical Center lies in the Northwest part of the city.
9. A marine attraction on the west side of San Antonio entertains grandparents, fathers and mothers, and children with the antics of dolphins and seals.
10. The City has attracted high-tech industry, creating a corridor between san antonio and austin.

48 Italics or Underlining

In *Brief*

Italicize or underline the following:

- Titles of works that appear independently (next page).
- Names of ships, aircraft, spacecraft, and trains (next page).
- Foreign words that are not part of the English language (p. 341).
- Words or characters named as words (p. 341).
- Occasionally, words that you are emphasizing (p. 341).

Visit MyWritingLab™ for more resources on italics or underlining.

Italic type and underlining indicate the same thing: the word or words are being distinguished or emphasized. Always use one or the other consistently throughout a document in both text and source citations:

Text

Growing older is one of several themes that Joan Didion explores in *Blue Nights*.

Source citation (MLA style)
Didion, Joan. *Blue Nights.* Vintage, 2011.

48a   Italicize or underline the titles of works that appear independently.

Within your text italicize or underline the titles of works, such as books and periodicals, that are published, released, or produced separately from other works. (See the following box.) Use quotation marks for all other titles.

Titles to be italicized or underlined

Other titles should be placed in quotation marks (see p. 318).

Books	**Long musical works**
War and Peace	Tchaikovsky's *Swan Lake*
And the Band Played On	**But:** Symphony in C
Plays	**Television and radio programs**
Hamlet	*NBC Sports Hour*
The Phantom of the Opera	*Radio Lab*
Pamphlets	**Long poems**
The Truth about Alcoholism	*Beowulf*
	Paradise Lost
Web sites	
Friends of Prufrock	**Published speeches**
YouTube	Lincoln's *Gettysburg Address*
Computer software	**Movies and videos**
Microsoft Word	*Schindler's List*
Google Chrome	*How to Relax*
Periodicals	**Works of visual art**
Time	Michelangelo's *David*
Philadelphia Inquirer	the *Mona Lisa*

Exceptions Legal documents, the Bible, the Koran, and their parts are generally not italicized or underlined:

Not   We studied the *Book of Revelation* in the *Bible.*
But   We studied the Book of Revelation in the Bible.

48b   Italicize or underline the names of ships, aircraft, spacecraft, and trains.

Challenger	*Orient Express*	*Queen Mary 2*
Apollo XI	*Montrealer*	*Spirit of St. Louis*

48c   Italicize or underline foreign words that are not part of the English language.

Italicize or underline a foreign expression that has not been absorbed into English. A dictionary will say whether a word is still considered foreign to English.

The scientific name for the brown trout is *Salmo trutta*. [The Latin scientific names for plants and animals are always italicized or underlined.]

The Latin *De gustibus non est disputandum* translates roughly as "There's no accounting for taste."

48d   Italicize or underline words or characters named as words.

Use italics or underlining to indicate that you are citing a character or word as a word rather than using it for its meaning. Words you are defining fall under this convention.

The word *syzygy* refers to a straight line formed by three celestial bodies, as in the alignment of the earth, sun, and moon.

Some people say *th*, as in *thought*, with a faint *s* or *f* sound.

48e   Occasionally, italics or underlining may be used for emphasis.

Italics or underlining can stress an important word or phrase, especially in reporting how someone said something. But use such emphasis very rarely, or your writing may seem overemotional.

48f   In electronic communication, use alternatives for italics or underlining.

Some forms of electronic communication do not allow conventional highlighting such as italics or underlining for the purposes described in this chapter. If you can't use italics or underlining to distinguish book titles and other elements that usually require highlighting, type an underscore before and after the element: *Measurements coincide with those in _Joule's Handbook_.* You can also emphasize words with asterisks before and after: *I *will not* be able to attend.*

Don't use all-capital letters for emphasis; they yell too loudly. (See also pp. 82–83.)

ital

48f

Exercise 48.1   Revising: Italics or underlining

In the following paragraph, underline the words and phrases that need highlighting with italics or underlining and place a check mark before words and phrases that are highlighted unnecessarily. If a sentence is correct as given, mark the number preceding it.

Example:

Of Hitchcock's movies, Psycho is the scariest.
Of Hitchcock's movies, *Psycho* is the scariest.

1. Of the many Vietnam veterans who are writers, Oliver Stone is perhaps the most famous for writing and directing the films Platoon and Born on the Fourth of July.
2. Tim O'Brien has written short stories for Esquire, GQ, and Massachusetts Review.
3. Going after Cacciato is O'Brien's dreamlike novel about the horrors of combat.
4. The word Vietnam is technically two words (*Viet* and *Nam*), but most American writers spell it as *one* word.
5. American writers use words or phrases borrowed from Vietnamese, such as di di mau ("go quickly") or dinky dau ("crazy").
6. Philip Caputo's *gripping* account of his service in Vietnam appears in the book *A Rumor of War*.
7. Caputo's book was made into a television movie, also titled *A Rumor of War*.
8. David Rabe's plays—including The Basic Training of Pavlo Hummel, Streamers, and Sticks and Bones—depict the effects of the war *not only* on the soldiers *but also* on their families.
9. Called "the poet laureate of the Vietnam war," Steve Mason has published two collections of poems: Johnny's Song and Warrior for Peace.
10. The Washington Post published *rave* reviews of Veteran's Day, an autobiography by Rod Kane.

49   Abbreviations

In *Brief*

- Use abbreviations only if they are familiar to your readers (opposite).
- Generally spell out units of measurement and names of places, calendar designations, people, and courses (opposite).
- Use abbreviations for titles only just before and after proper names (p. 344).
- Use BC, BCE, AD, CE, AM, PM, no., and $ only with specific dates and numbers (p. 344).
- Use *Inc., Bros., Co.,* or & (for *and*) only in official names of business firms (p. 344).

Visit MyWritingLab™ for more resources on abbreviations.

In academic writing, appropriate abbreviations depend partly on the discipline, with nontechnical fields using fewer than technical fields.

The guidelines in this chapter pertain to the text of a nontechnical document. Consult one of the style guides listed on page 414 for the requirements of the discipline you are writing in.

Usage varies, but writers increasingly omit periods from abbreviations of two or more words written in all-capital letters: *US*, *BA*, *USMC*. See page 288 on punctuating abbreviations.

49a Familiar abbreviations and acronyms are acceptable in most writing.

An **acronym** is an abbreviation that spells a pronounceable word, such as WHO, NATO, SWAT, and AIDS. These and other abbreviations using initials are acceptable in most writing as long as they are familiar to readers.

Institutions	LSU, UCLA, TCU
Organizations	CIA, FBI, YMCA, AFL-CIO
Corporations	IBM, CBS, ITT
People	JFK, LBJ, FDR
Countries	US, USA

Note If a name or term (such as *operating room*) appears often in a piece of writing, then its abbreviation (*OR*) can cut down on extra words. Spell out the full term at its first appearance, indicate its abbreviation in parentheses, and then use the abbreviation.

49b Spell out most units of measurement and names of places, calendar designations, people, and courses.

In most academic, general, and business writing, the following types of words should always be spelled out. (In source citations and technical writing, however, the first three categories are more often abbreviated.)

Units of measurement
The dog is thirty inches [not in.] high.

Geographical names
The publisher is in Massachusetts [not Mass. or MA].

Names of days, months, and holidays
The truce was signed on Tuesday [not Tues.], April [not Apr.] 16.

ab
49b

Names of people
Robert [not <u>Robt.</u>] Frost wrote accessible poems.

Courses of instruction
I'm majoring in <u>political science</u> [not <u>poli. sci.</u>].

49c **Generally reserve Latin abbreviations for source citations and comments in parentheses.**

i.e.	*id est:* that is
cf.	*confer:* compare
e.g.	*exempli gratia:* for example
et al.	*et alii:* and others
etc.	*et cetera:* and so forth
NB	*nota bene:* note well

He said he would be gone a fortnight (i.e., two weeks).
Bloom et al., editors, *Anthology of Light Verse*
Trees, too, are susceptible to disease (e.g., Dutch elm disease).

Some writers avoid these abbreviations in formal writing, even within parentheses.

49d **Use standard abbreviations for titles immediately before and after proper names.**

Before the name	After the name
Dr. Michael Hsu	Michael Hsu, MD
Mr., Mrs., Ms., Hon.,	DDS, DVM, PhD,
St., Rev., Msgr., Gen.	EdD, OSB, SJ, Sr., Jr.

Do not use abbreviations such as *Rev., Hon., Prof., Rep., Sen., Dr.,* and *St.* (for *Saint*) unless they appear before a proper name.

49e **Use *BC, BCE, AD, CE, AM, PM, no.,* and *$* only with specific dates and numbers.**

44 BC	AD 1492	11:26 AM (*or* a.m.)	no. 36 (*or* No. 36)
44 BCE	1492 CE	8:05 PM (*or* p.m.)	$7.41

BC ("before Christ"), BCE ("before the common era"), and CE ("common era") always follow a date. In contrast, AD (*anno Domini,* Latin for "in the year of the Lord") precedes a date.

49f **Use *Inc., Bros., Co.,* or *&* (for *and*) only in official names of business firms.**

Not The Santini <u>bros.</u> run a moving firm in New York City <u>&</u> environs.

But   The Santini <u>brothers</u> run a moving firm in New York City <u>and</u> environs.

Or   Santini <u>Bros.</u> is a moving firm in New York City <u>and</u> environs.

Exercise 49.1   Revising: Abbreviations

Revise the following sentences as needed to correct inappropriate use of abbreviations for nontechnical writing. If a sentence is already correct as given, mark the number preceding it.

Example:

One prof. lectured for five hrs.
One <u>professor</u> lectured for five <u>hours.</u>

1. In an issue of *Science* magazine, Dr. Virgil L. Sharpton discusses a theory that could help explain the extinction of dinosaurs.
2. About 65 mill. yrs. ago, a comet or asteroid crashed into the earth.
3. The result was a huge crater about 10 km. (6.2 mi.) deep in the Gulf of Mex.
4. Sharpton's new measurements suggest that the crater is 50 pct. larger than scientists had previously believed.
5. Indeed, 20-yr.-old drilling cores reveal that the crater is about 186 mi. wide, roughly the size of Conn.
6. The space object was traveling more than 100,000 miles per hour and hit the earth with the impact of 100 to 300 megatons of TNT.
7. On impact, 200,000 cubic km. of rock and soil were vaporized or thrown into the air.
8. That's the equivalent of 2.34 bill. cubic ft. of matter.
9. The impact would have created 400-ft. tidal waves across the Atl. Ocean, temps. higher than 20,000 degs., and powerful earthquakes.
10. Sharpton theorizes that the dust, vapor, and smoke from this impact blocked the sun's rays for mos., cooled the earth, and thus resulted in the death of the dinosaurs.

---

50   Numbers

In *Brief*

- Use numerals according to standard practice in your field (next page).
- Use numerals according to convention for dates, addresses, and other information (next page).
- Spell out numbers that begin sentences (p. 347).

Visit MyWritingLab™ for more resources on numbers.

Expressing numbers in numerals (*28*) or in words (*twenty-eight*) is often a matter of style in a discipline: the technical disciplines more often prefer numerals, and the nontechnical disciplines more often prefer words. All disciplines use many more numerals in source citations than in the document text.

50a Use numerals according to standard practice in the field you are writing in.

Always use numerals for numbers that require more than two words to spell out.

The leap year has <u>366</u> days.
The population of Minot, North Dakota, is about <u>32,800</u>.

In nontechnical academic writing, spell out numbers of one or two words. A hyphenated number may be considered one word.

The waiting period is <u>eighteen</u> to <u>twenty-four</u> days.
The ball game drew <u>forty-two thousand</u> people.
Jenson lived to be <u>ninety-nine</u> or <u>one hundred</u>.

In much business writing, use numerals for all numbers over ten: *five reasons, 11 participants*. In technical academic and business writing, such as in science and engineering, use numerals for all numbers over ten, and use numerals for zero through nine when they refer to exact measurements: *2 liters, 1 hour*. (Consult one of the style guides listed on p. 414 for more details.)

Notes Use a combination of numerals and words for round numbers over a million: *26 million, 2.45 billion*. And use either all numerals or all words when several numbers appear together in a passage, even if convention would require a mixture. Be careful to avoid using two numbers in a row, which can be confusing. Rewrite to separate the numbers:

Confusing Out of 530, 101 children caught the virus.

Clear Out of 530 <u>children</u>, 101 caught the virus.

(CULTURE LANGUAGE) In standard American English, a comma separates the numerals in long numbers (26ͺ000), and a period functions as a decimal point (2.06).

50b Use numerals according to convention for dates, addresses, and other information.

Days and years		Addresses
June 18, 1985	AD 12	355 Clinton Avenue
456 BC	2010	Washington, DC 20036

Exact amounts of money		The time of day	
$3.5 million	$4.50	9:00 AM	3:45 PM

Decimals, percentages, and fractions	Pages, chapters, volumes, acts, scenes, lines
22.5 $3\frac{1}{2}$	Chapter 9, page 123
48% (*or* 48 percent)	*Antony and Cleopatra*, act 5, scene 2, lines 124–32
Scores and statistics	*The Collected Works of Abraham Lincoln*,
21 to 7 a ratio of 8 to 1	volume 4
a mean of 26	

Exceptions Round dollar or cent amounts of only a few words may be expressed in words: *seventeen dollars*; *sixty cents*. When the word *o'clock* is used for the time of day, also express the number in words: *two o'clock* (not *2 o'clock*).

50c   Spell out numbers that begin sentences.

For clarity, spell out any number that begins a sentence. If the number requires more than two words, reword the sentence so that the number falls later and can be expressed as a numeral.

Not   3.9 billion people live in Asia.

But   The population of Asia is 3.9 billion.

Exercise 50.1   Revising: Numbers

Revise the following sentences so that numbers are used appropriately for nontechnical writing. If a sentence is already correct as given, mark the number preceding it.

Example:

Addie paid two hundred and five dollars for used scuba gear.
Addie paid $205 for used scuba gear.

1. The planet Saturn is nine hundred million miles, or nearly one billion five hundred million kilometers, from the sun.
2. A year on Saturn equals almost thirty of our years.
3. Thus, Saturn orbits the sun only two and four-tenths times during the average human life span.
4. It travels in its orbit at about twenty-one thousand six hundred miles per hour.
5. 15 to 20 times denser than Earth's core, Saturn's core measures 17,000 miles across.
6. The temperature at Saturn's cloud tops is minus one hundred seventy degrees Fahrenheit.
7. In nineteen hundred thirty-three, astronomers found on Saturn's surface a huge white spot 2 times the size of Earth and 7 times the size of Mercury.
8. Saturn's famous rings reflect almost seventy percent of the sunlight that approaches the planet.
9. The ring system is almost forty thousand miles wide, beginning

num
50c

8,800 miles from the planet's visible surface and ending forty-seven thousand miles from that surface.

10. The spacecraft *Cassini* traveled more than eight hundred and twenty million miles to explore and photograph Saturn.

Research and Documentation

In *Brief*

- Plan your project (below).
- Keep a research journal (facing page).
- Find a researchable subject and question (facing page).
- Set goals for sources (p. 353).
- Keep a working, annotated bibliography (p. 356).

Visit MyWritingLab™ for more resources on research strategy.

Like many writers, you may find it helpful to approach research writing as a detective approaches a new case. The mystery is the answer to a question you care about. The search for an answer leads you to consider what others think about your subject, but you do more than simply report their views. You build on them to develop and support your own opinion.

Your investigation will be more productive and enjoyable if you take the steps described in this chapter.

51a Plan the research process.

Research writing is a *writing* process:

- **You work within a particular situation of subject, purpose, audience, genre, and other factors** (see Chapter 1).
- **You gather ideas and information about your subject** (Chapter 2).
- **You focus and arrange your ideas** (Chapter 3).
- **You draft to explore your meaning** (Chapter 4).
- **You revise to develop and shape your writing** (Chapter 5).
- **You edit to refine and polish your writing** (Chapter 6).

Although the process seems neatly sequential in this list, you know from experience that the stages overlap—that, for instance, you may begin drafting before you've gathered all the information you expect to find, and then while drafting you may discover a source that causes you to rethink your approach. Anticipating the process of research writing can free you to be flexible in your search and open to discoveries.

A thoughtful plan and systematic procedures can help you follow through on the diverse activities of research writing. One step is to make a schedule like the one opposite that apportions the available time to the necessary work. You can estimate that each segment marked off by a horizontal line will occupy *roughly* one-quarter of the total time—for example, a week in a four-week assignment. The most unpredictable segments are the first two, so it's wise to get started early enough to accommodate the unexpected.

Scheduling steps in research writing

Complete
by:

_____   1. Setting a schedule and beginning a research journal (here
            and below)
_____   2. Finding a researchable subject and question (below)
_____   3. Setting goals for sources (p. 353)
_____   4. Finding print and electronic sources (p. 358), and making a
            working, annotated bibliography (p. 356)

_____   5. Evaluating and synthesizing sources (pp. 377, 389)
_____   6. Gathering information from sources (p. 392), often using
            summary, paraphrase, and direct quotation (p. 393)
_____   7. Taking steps to avoid plagiarism (p. 405)

_____   8. Developing a thesis statement and creating a structure (p. 415)
_____   9. Drafting the paper (p. 416), integrating summaries, para-
            phrases, and direct quotations into your ideas (p. 400)
_____   10. Citing sources in your text (p. 413)

_____   11. Revising and editing the paper (p. 417)
_____   12. Finalizing text citations and preparing the list of works cited
            or references (p. 413)
_____   13. Preparing the final manuscript (p. 418)
_____ Final paper due

51c

51b   Keep a research journal.

While working on a research project, carry a notebook or a computer with you at all times to use as a **research journal,** a place to record your activities and ideas. (See pp. 11–12 on journal keeping.) In
the journal's dated entries, you can write about the sources you consult, the leads you want to pursue, and any difficulties you encounter.
Most important, you can record your thoughts about sources, leads,
difficulties, new directions, relationships, and anything else that
strikes you. The very act of writing in the journal can expand and
clarify your thinking.

Note The research journal is the place to track and develop your
own ideas. To avoid mixing up your thoughts and those of others, keep
separate notes on what your sources actually say, following the guidelines on pages 392–93.

51c   Find a researchable subject and question.

Before reading this section, review the suggestions in Chapter 1
for finding and narrowing a writing subject (pp. 4–6). Generally, the

same procedure applies to writing any kind of research paper. However, selecting and limiting a subject for a research paper can present special opportunities and problems. And before you proceed with your subject, you'll want to transform it into a question that can guide your search for sources.

1 ▪ Appropriate subject

Seek a research subject that you want to learn more about. (It may be a subject you've already written about without benefit of research.) Starting with your own views will motivate you, and you will be a participant in a dialog when you begin examining sources.

When you settle on a subject, ask the following questions about it. For each requirement, there are corresponding pitfalls.

▪ **Are ample sources of information available on the subject?**

Avoid a very recent subject, such as a newly announced medical discovery or a breaking story in today's news, unless you are placing it in a larger context.

▪ **Does the subject encourage research in the kinds and number of sources required by the assignment?**

Avoid (*a*) a subject that depends entirely on personal opinion and experience, such as the virtues of your hobby, and (*b*) a subject that requires research in only one source, such as a straight factual biography.

▪ **Will the subject lead you to an objective assessment of sources and to defensible conclusions?**

Avoid a subject that rests entirely on belief or prejudice, such as when human life begins or why women (or men) are superior. Your readers are unlikely to be swayed from their own beliefs.

▪ **Does the subject suit the length of paper assigned and the time given for research and writing?**

Avoid a broad subject that has too many sources to survey adequately, such as a major event in history.

2 ▪ Research question

Asking a question or questions about your subject opens avenues of inquiry. In asking questions, you can consider what you already know about the subject, explore what you don't know, and begin to develop your own perspective. (See the next page for suggestions on using your own knowledge.)

Try to narrow your research question so that you can answer it in the time and space you have available. The question *How does human activity affect the environment?* is very broad, encompassing issues as diverse as pollution, distribution of resources, climate change, population growth, land use, biodiversity, and the ozone layer. In contrast, the question *How can buying environmentally friendly products help the environment?* or *How, if at all, should carbon emissions be taxed?* is much narrower. Each question also requires more than just a *yes* or *no* answer, so that answering, even tentatively, demands thought about pros and cons, causes and effects.

As you read and write, your question will undoubtedly evolve to reflect your increasing knowledge of the subject, and eventually its answer will become your main idea, or thesis statement (see pp. 415–16).

51d Set goals for your sources.

Before you start looking for sources, consider what you already know about your subject and where you are likely to find information on it.

1 ▪ Your own knowledge

Discovering what you already know about your subject will guide you in discovering what you don't know. Take some time at the start to write down everything you know about the subject: facts you have learned, opinions you have heard or read elsewhere, and of course your own opinions. Use one or more of the discovery techniques discussed in Chapter 2 to explore and develop your ideas: keeping a journal, observing your surroundings, freewriting, brainstorming, drawing, asking questions, and thinking critically.

When you've explored your thoughts, make a list of questions for which you don't have answers, whether factual (*How much do Americans spend on green products?*) or more open-ended (*Are green products worth the higher prices?*). These questions will give you clues about the sources you need to look for first.

2 ▪ Kinds of sources

For many research projects, you'll want to consult a mix of sources, as described on the next two pages. You may start by seeking the outlines of your subject—the range and depth of opinions about it—in reference works and articles in popular periodicals or through a Web search. Then, as you refine your views and your research question, you'll move on to more specialized sources, such as scholarly books and periodicals and your own interviews or surveys. (See pp. 363–77 for more on each kind of source.)

The mix of sources you choose depends heavily on your subject. For example, a paper on green consumerism would require the use of very recent sources because environmentally friendly products are fairly new to the US marketplace. Your mix of sources may also be specified or limited by your assignment.

Sources through the library or the open Web

The print and electronic sources available at your library or through its Web site—mainly reference works, books, and articles in periodicals—have two big advantages over most of what you'll find on the open Web: library sources are cataloged and indexed for easy retrieval; and they are generally reliable, having been screened first by their publishers and then by the library's staff. In contrast, the retrieval systems of the open Web are more difficult to use effectively, and the sources themselves tend to be less reliable because most do not pass through any screening before being posted. (There are many exceptions, such as online scholarly journals and reference works. But these sources are generally available through your library's Web site as well.)

Most instructors expect research writers to consult library sources. But they'll accept sources from the open Web, too, if you have used them judiciously. Even with its disadvantages, the Internet can be a valuable resource for primary sources, current information, and a diversity of views. For guidelines on evaluating both library and open-Web sources, see pages 377–89.

Primary and secondary sources

Use **primary sources** when they are required by the assignment or are appropriate for your subject. Primary sources are documents and objects that were created during the period you are studying. They consist of firsthand or original accounts, such as works of literature, historical documents (letters, speeches, and so on), eyewitness reports (including articles by journalists who are on location), reports on experiments or surveys conducted by the writer, and sources you originate (interviews, experiments, observations, or correspondence).

Many assignments will allow you to use **secondary sources,** which report and analyze information drawn from other sources, often primary ones. Examples include a reporter's summary of a controversial issue, a historian's account of a battle, a critic's reading of a poem, and a psychologist's evaluation of several studies. (Sometimes a secondary source may actually be your primary source, as when you analyze a historian's account or respond to a critic's interpretation.) In themselves, secondary sources may contain helpful summaries and interpretations that direct, support, and extend your own thinking. However, most research-writing assignments require your own ideas to go beyond those in such sources.

Scholarly and popular sources

The scholarship of acknowledged experts is essential for depth, authority, and specificity. Most instructors expect students to emphasize scholarly sources in their research. But the general-interest views and information of popular sources can provide everyday examples, anecdotes, and stories that can help you apply scholarly approaches to your subject, and they can provide context for very recent topics.

Use the following guidelines to determine whether a source is scholarly or popular.

- **Check the title.** Is it technical, or does it use a general vocabulary?
- **Check the publisher.** Is it a scholarly journal (such as *Cultural Geographies*) or a publisher of scholarly books (such as Harvard University Press), or is it a popular magazine (such as *Consumer Reports* or *Time*) or a publisher of popular books (such as Little, Brown)? For more on the distinction between scholarly and popular sources, see pages 364–65 and 378.
- **Check the length of periodical articles.** Scholarly articles are generally much longer than magazine and newspaper articles.
- **Check the author.** Search the Web for the author. Is he or she an expert on the topic?
- **Check the URL.** A Web site's URL, or electronic address, includes an abbreviation that can tell you something about the origin of the source: scholarly sources usually end in *edu, org,* or *gov,* while popular sources usually end in *com.* (See pp. 383 and 386–89 for more on types of online sources.)
- **Check for sources.** Scholarly authors cite their sources formally in notes or a bibliography.

51d

Older and newer sources

Check the publication date. For most subjects a combination of older, established sources (such as books) and current sources (such as newspaper articles, interviews, or Web sites) will provide both background and up-to-date information. Only historical subjects or very current subjects require an emphasis on one extreme or another.

Impartial and biased sources

Seek a range of viewpoints. Sources that attempt to be impartial can offer an overview of your subject and trustworthy facts. Sources with clear biases can give you a range of views about a subject and enrich your understanding of it. Of course, to discover bias, you may have to read the source carefully (see pp. 377–89); but you can infer quite a bit just from a bibliographical listing.

- **Check the author.** Do a Web search to find out more about the author. Is he or she a respected researcher (thus more likely to be objective) or a leading proponent of a certain view (less likely to be objective)?
- **Check the title.** It may reveal something about point of view. (Consider these contrasting titles: "Go for the Green" versus "Green Consumerism and the Struggle for Northern Maine.")

Sources with helpful features

Depending on your topic and how far along your research is, you may want to look for sources with features such as illustrations (which can clarify important concepts), bibliographies (which can direct you to other sources), and indexes (which can help you develop keywords for electronic searches; see pp. 361–63).

51e Keep a working, annotated bibliography.

To track where sources are, compile a **working bibliography** as you uncover possibilities. When you have a substantial file—say, ten to thirty sources—you can decide which ones seem most promising and look them up first.

1 ▪ Source information

When you turn in your paper, you will be expected to attach a list of the sources you have used. Your list must include all the information needed to find the sources, in a format readers can understand. (See pp. 413–14.) The box on the next page shows the information you should record for each type of source so that you will not have to retrace your steps later.

Note Recording source information meticulously will help you avoid careless plagiarism because you will be less likely to omit the information in your paper. Careful records will also help you avoid omitting or mixing up numbers, dates, and other data when it's time to write your citations. This book describes two documentation styles: MLA (p. 419) and APA (p. 477). For other styles, consult one of the guides listed on page 414.

2 ▪ Annotations

Your instructor may ask you to prepare an **annotated bibliography** as part of the research process or as a separate assignment. Creating annotations converts your bibliography into a tool for assessing sources, helping you discover gaps that may remain in your sources and helping you decide which sources to pursue in depth.

As you find and evaluate each source, record not only its publication information but also the following:

- **What you know about the content of the source.** Periodical databases and book catalogs generally include abstracts, or summaries, of sources that can help with this part of the annotation.
- **How you think the source may be helpful in your research.** Does it offer expert opinion, statistics, an important example, or a range of views? Does it place your subject in a historical, social, or economic context?
- **Your assessment of the source.** Consider how reliable the source is and how it might fit into your research. (See pp. 377–91 for more on evaluating and synthesizing sources.)

Information for a working bibliography

For a print or electronic book

Library call number

Name(s) of author(s), editor(s), translator(s), and other contributors

Title and subtitle

Publication data: (1) place of publication; (2) publisher's name; (3) date of publication; (4) title of any database or Web site used to reach the book; (5) publisher and date of any Web site used to find the book

Other important data, such as edition or volume number

Format (print, Web, Kindle file, etc.)

DOI or complete URL (see the note below)

For periodical articles in print, in online databases, or in Web journals

Name(s) of author(s)

Title and subtitle of article

Title of periodical

Publication data: (1) volume number and issue number (if any) in which the article appears; (2) date of issue; (3) page numbers on which article appears

Title of any database used to reach the source

DOI or complete URL (see the note below)

For Web material and other electronic sources

Name(s) of author(s) and other contributors

Title and subtitle of source

Title of Web site

Publication data: publisher and date of publication

Any publication data for the source in another medium (print, film, etc.)

Format of online source (Web site or page, podcast, e-mail, etc.)

Date you consulted the source

Title of any database used to reach the source

Complete URL or DOI (see the note below)

For other sources

Name(s) of author(s) or creator(s) and other contributors

Title of the source

Title of any larger work of which the source is a part (television series, album, etc.)

Publication or production data: (1) publisher's or producer's name; (2) date of publication, release, or production; (3) identifying numbers (if any)

Format or medium (live performance, lecture, DVD, map, TV episode, etc.)

51e

Note Documentation styles generally require DOIs (Digital Object Identifiers) or URLs for citations of electronic sources. Always record the DOI (if one is available) and the complete URL so that you'll have whatever is needed for your final citation of a source. For more on DOIs and URLs, see pages 433 (MLA style) and 482 (APA style).

Taking the time with your annotations can help you discover gaps that may remain in your sources and will help you decide which sources to pursue in depth. The following entry from an annotated bibliography shows one student's annotation of a source, including a summary, a note on the source features the student thought would be helpful, and an assessment of the source's strength and weakness for his purposes.

Annotated bibliography entry with assessment

Publication information for source

> Gore, Al. *Our Choice: A Plan to Solve the Climate Crisis*. Emmaus, PA: Rodale Books, 2009.

Summary of source

> A sequel to Gore's *An Inconvenient Truth* that emphasizes solutions to global warming. Expands on the argument that global warming is a serious threat, with recent examples of natural disasters. Proposes ways that governments, businesses, and individuals can reduce or reverse the risks of global warming.

Helpful features

> Includes helpful summaries of scientific studies, short essays on various subjects, and dozens of images, tables, charts, and graphs.

Assessment of source

> Compelling overview of possible solutions, with lots of data that seem thorough and convincing. But the book is aimed at a general audience and doesn't have formal source citations. Can use it for broad concepts, but for data I'll have to track down Gore's scholarly sources.

---

52   Finding Sources

In *Brief*

- Start with your library's Web site (opposite).
- Plan electronic searches (p.360).
- Consult reference works (p. 363).
- Consult books (p. 363).
- Find articles in periodicals (p. 364).
- Explore the Web and social media (pp. 368, 371).
- Consult government publications (p. 372).
- Locate visuals, audio, and video (p. 373).
- Generate your own sources through interviews, surveys, and observation (p. 375).

Visit MyWritingLab™ for more resources on finding sources.

Your library and a computer connected to the Internet give you access to an almost infinite range of sources. The challenge, of course, is to find the most worthy and appropriate sources for your needs and then to use them effectively. This chapter shows you how.

Note As you look for sources, avoid the temptation to seek a "silver bullet"—that is, to locate two or three perfect sources that already say everything you want to say about your subject. Instead of merely repeating others' ideas, read and synthesize many sources so that you enter into a dialog with them and develop your own ideas. For more on synthesis, see pages 389–91.

52a   Start with your library's Web site.

As you conduct academic research, your library's Web site will be your gateway to ideas and information. Always start with your library's Web site, not with a public search engine such as *Google*.

Advantages of a library search

The library site will lead you to vast resources, including books, periodical articles, and reference works that aren't available on the open Web. More important, every source you find on the library site will have passed through filters to ensure its value. A scholarly journal article, for instance, undergoes at least three successive reviews: subject-matter experts first deem it worth publishing in the journal; then a database vendor deems the journal worth including in the database; and finally your school's librarians deem the database worth subscribing to.

Note Start with the library's Web site, but don't stop there. Many books, periodicals, and other excellent sources are available only on library shelves, not online, and most instructors expect research papers to be built to some extent on these resources. When you spot promising print sources while browsing the library's online databases, make records of them and then look them up at the library.

Disadvantages of an open-Web search

Google and other public search engines do have benefits: they may seem more user-friendly than the library's Web site, they can

---

A tip for researchers

Take advantage of two valuable resources offered by your library:

- **An orientation,** which will introduce you to the resources available through your library and help you navigate the library's Web site.
- **Reference librarians,** whose job it is to help you and others navigate the library's resources. All libraries offer face-to-face consultations, and many offer e-mail and chat services. Even very experienced researchers often consult reference librarians.

help you get a quick sense of how your subject is talked about, and they may locate some reliable and relevant sources for your research.

However, for academic research these search engines have more drawbacks than benefits. They are not geared toward academic research, so most of the sources they find will be unsuitable for your project. And the sources will not be filtered as library materials are: no one ensures their basic reliability. In the end, a library Web search will be more efficient and more effective than an open-Web search. (For help with evaluating sources from any resource, see pp. 377–89.)

52b   Plan electronic searches.

An electronic search requires planning. A search that is too broad can miss helpful sources while returning hundreds, even thousands, of irrelevant sources. A search that is too narrow can exclude important sources.

1 ▪ Print and electronic resources available through your library

Your library's Web site will lead you to many kinds of print and electronic resources suitable for academic research.

- **The library catalog.** Searchable from the library's Web site, the catalog is a database that lists all the resources the library owns or subscribes to. At many libraries, the catalog finds books, e-books, and the titles of periodicals but not individual articles within online databases. At other libraries, the catalog functions as a centralized search engine that covers all the library's holdings and subscriptions and locates articles in online databases. Either type of catalog may also include the holdings at other libraries in your college's system or in your state.

- **Online databases.** Also searchable from the library's Web site, databases include a wide range of source types, from journal collections and full-text resources to reference works and primary sources. Your library's Web site will likely list databases alphabetically and by discipline. (You may discover some of the same databases on the open Web, but unless you retrieve articles through your library's Web site, you will probably have to pay for what you find.) As you use a database, be aware of what it does and does not offer, and keep track of whether you are looking at an article, a book, an archival document, or something else. Ask a librarian if you're not sure. For help with selecting databases, see pages 365–66.

- **Research guides.** Some libraries provide guides that direct users to resources on particular subjects, such as twentieth-century English literature or social psychology.
- **Google Scholar.** Available on the open Web, *Google Scholar* is a search engine that seeks out scholarly books and articles. It is particularly useful for subjects that range across disciplines, for which discipline-specific databases can be too limited. *Google Scholar* can connect to your library's holdings if you set it to do so under Scholar Preferences. Keep in mind, however, that *Google Scholar*'s searches may list books that are unavailable to you and articles that you cannot obtain in full text. Your library is still the best resource for material that is easily available to you, so begin there.

52b

2 ▪ Development of search terms

Take time early in your research to develop search terms that describe your subject effectively. For this step, it helps to understand the difference between keywords and subject headings:

- **Keywords** are the terms you type when you begin a search. In a library catalog or an online database, a keyword search looks for that word (or words) in titles, authors, and subject headings and sometimes within lists of keywords supplied by the author or in user tags added by readers. On the open Web, a keyword search looks for your terms anywhere in the record. In any case, the process is entirely automatic, so as a researcher your challenge is to find keywords that others have used to describe the same subject.
- **Subject headings** (also called *subject terms*) tell you what a source is about. They are assigned to books and articles by people who have read the sources and categorized them, so they can be more efficient than keywords at finding relevant sources. To find subject headings, use and refine your keywords until you find a promising source. On the source's full record, check the list of subject headings to see how the source is categorized. (See p. 364 for an illustration.) Building the subject headings that most closely match your subject into your search terms can improve your searches.

3 ▪ Refinement of search terms

Databases, catalogs, and search engines provide systems that you can use to refine your search terms for your purposes. The basic operations appear in the following box, but resources do differ. For instance, some assume that *AND* should link keywords, while others provide options specifying "Must contain all the words" and other equivalents for the operations in the box. You can learn a search engine's system by consulting its Advanced Search page.

Ways to refine keywords

Most databases and many search engines work with **Boolean operators,** terms or symbols that allow you to expand or limit your keywords and thus your search.

- Use *AND* or + to narrow the search by including only sources that use all the given words. The keywords *green AND products* request only the sources in the shaded area.

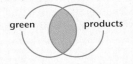

- Use *NOT* or – ("minus") to narrow the search by excluding irrelevant words. The keywords *green AND products NOT guide* exclude sources that use the word *guide*:

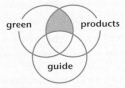

- Use *OR* to broaden the search by giving alternative keywords. The keywords *green AND products OR goods* allow for sources that use a synonym for *products*:

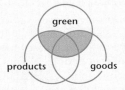

- Use quotation marks or parentheses to form search phrases. For instance, *"green products"* requests the exact phrase, not the separate words. Only sources using *green products* would turn up.
- Use wild cards to permit different versions of the same word. In *consum**, for instance, the wild card * indicates that sources may include *consume, consumer, consumerism,* and *consumption* as well as *consumptive, consumedly,* and *consummate.* The example suggests that you have to consider all the variations allowed by a wild card and whether it opens up your search too much. If you seek only two or three from many variations, you may be better off using *OR: consumption OR consumerism.* (Note that some systems use ?, :, or + for a wild card instead of *.)

- **Be sure to spell your keywords correctly.** Some search tools will look for close matches or approximations, but correct spelling gives you the best chance of finding relevant sources.

Note You will probably have to use trial and error in developing your terms because library catalogs, databases, and search engines may all use slightly different words to describe your subject. If you are having trouble finding appropriate sources, try using subject headings, and be flexible in your search terms. The process is not busywork—far from it. Besides leading you eventually to worthwhile sources, it can also teach you a great deal about your subject: how you can or should narrow it, how it is and is not described by others, what others consider interesting or debatable about it, and what the major arguments are. See pages 370–71 for an example of a student's keyword search of the Web.

52d

52c Consult reference works.

Reference works, available through your library and on the open Web, include encyclopedias, dictionaries, digests, bibliographies, indexes, atlases, almanacs, and handbooks. Your research *must* go beyond these sources, but they can help you decide whether your topic really interests you and whether it meets the requirements for a research paper (p. 352). Preliminary research in reference works can also help you develop keywords for electronic searches and can direct you to more detailed sources on your topic.

Note The Web-based encyclopedia *Wikipedia* (at *wikipedia.org*) is one of the largest reference sites on the Internet. Like any encyclopedia, *Wikipedia* can provide background information for research on a topic. But unlike other encyclopedias, *Wikipedia* is a **wiki,** a kind of Web site that can be contributed to or edited by anyone. Ask your instructor whether *Wikipedia* is an acceptable source before you use it. If you do use it, you must carefully evaluate any information you find, following the guidelines on pages 377–87.

52d Consult books.

Your library's catalog is searchable via the library's Web site. Unless you seek a specific author or title, you'll want to search for books by using keywords or subject headings. In a keyword search, you start with your own search terms. In a subject-heading search, you use the headings on the records of promising sources to locate similar sources. The screen shot below shows the complete record for a book, including the subject headings and the call number for finding the book on the library's shelves.

Full catalog record

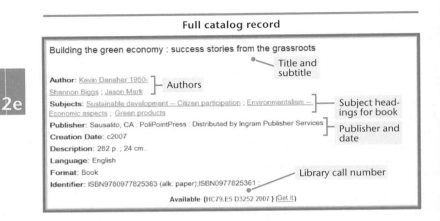

52e   Consult periodicals.

Periodicals include newspapers, academic journals, and magazines, either print or online. Newspapers are useful for detailed accounts of past and current events. Journals and magazines can be harder to distinguish, but their differences are important. Most college instructors expect students' research to rely more on journals than on magazines.

Journals	Magazines
Examples	
American Anthropologist, Journal of Black Studies, Journal of Chemical Education	*The New Yorker, Time, Rolling Stone, People*
Availability	
Mainly college and university libraries, either on library shelves or in online databases	Public libraries, newsstands, bookstores, the open Web, and online databases
Purpose	
Advance knowledge in a particular field	Express opinion, inform, or entertain
Authors	
Specialists in the field	May or may not be specialists in their subjects

Journals	Magazines
Readers	
Often specialists in the field	Members of the general public or a subgroup with a particular interest
Source citations	
Source citations always included	Source citations rarely included
Length of articles	
Usually long, ten pages or more	Usually short, fewer than ten pages
Frequency of publication	
Quarterly or less often	Weekly, biweekly, or monthly
Pagination of issues	
May be paged separately (like a magazine) or may be paged sequentially throughout an annual volume, so that issue number 3 (the third issue of the year) could open on page 373	Paged separately, each beginning on page 1

52e

1 ▪ Periodical databases

Periodical databases index articles in journals, magazines, and newspapers. Often these databases include abstracts, or summaries, of the articles, and they may offer the full text of the articles as well. Your library subscribes to many periodical databases and to services that offer multiple databases. (See p. 368 for a list.) Most databases will be searchable through the library's Web site.

Selection of databases

To decide which databases to consult, you'll need to consider what you're looking for:

▪ **Does your research subject span more than one discipline?** If so, start with a broad database such as *Academic Search Complete, ProQuest Research Library,* or *JSTOR.* A broad database covers many subjects and disciplines but does not index the full range of periodicals in each subject. If your library offers a centralized search engine that searches across multiple databases, you can start there.

▪ **Does your research subject focus on a single discipline?** If so, start with a discipline-specific database such as *Historical Abstracts, MLA International Bibliography, Biological Abstracts,* or *Education Search Complete.* A specific database covers few subjects but includes most of the available periodicals in each subject. If you don't know the name of an appropriate database, the library's Web site probably lists possibilities by discipline.

- **Do you need primary sources?** Some specialized databases collect primary sources—for instance, historical newspapers, literary works not available in print, diaries, letters, music recordings, album liner notes. To determine whether you have access to such materials through your library, consult the list of databases on your library's Web site and read the descriptions to find out what each offers.

- **Which databases most likely include the kinds of resources you need?** The Web sites of most libraries provide lists of databases organized alphabetically and by discipline. Some libraries also provide research guides, which list potentially helpful databases for your search terms. To determine each database's focus, check the description of the database or the list of indexed resources. The description will also tell you the time period the database covers, so you'll know whether you also need to consult older print indexes at the library.

Database searches

When you first search a database, use your own keywords to locate sources. The procedure is illustrated in the three screen shots shown on these two pages. Your goal is to find at least one source that seems just right for your subject, so that you can see what subject headings the database itself uses for such sources (screen 3). Picking up one or more of those headings for your search terms will focus and speed your search.

---

1. Initial keyword search of a periodical database

2. Partial keyword search results

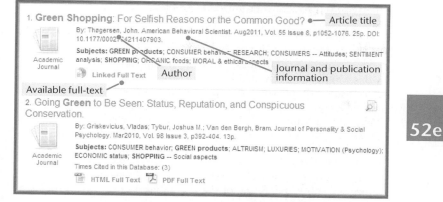

1. **Green Shopping**: For Selfish Reasons or the Common Good? •— Article title

By: Thøgersen, John. American Behavioral Scientist. Aug2011, Vol. 55 Issue 8, p1052-1076. 25p. DOI: 10.1177/0002764211407903.

Subjects: GREEN products; CONSUMER behavior; RESEARCH; CONSUMERS -- Attitudes; SENTIMENT analysis; SHOPPING; ORGANIC foods; MORAL & ethical aspects

Academic Journal

Linked Full Text — Author — Journal and publication information

Available full-text

2. Going **Green** to Be Seen: Status, Reputation, and Conspicuous Conservation.

By: Griskevicius, Vladas; Tybur, Joshua M.; Van den Bergh, Bram. Journal of Personality & Social Psychology. Mar2010, Vol. 98 Issue 3, p392-404. 13p.

Subjects: CONSUMER behavior; GREEN products; ALTRUISM; LUXURIES; MOTIVATION (Psychology); ECONOMIC status; SHOPPING -- Social aspects

Academic Journal

Times Cited in this Database: (3)

HTML Full Text PDF Full Text

52e

3. Full article record with abstract

Green Shopping: For Selfish Reasons or the Common Good? •- Article title

Authors: Thøgersen, John[1] •— Author

Source: American Behavioral Scientist. Aug2011, Vol. 55 Issue 8, p1052-1076. 25p.

Journal and publication information

Document Type: Article

Subject Terms: *GREEN products
*CONSUMER behavior
*RESEARCH
*CONSUMERS -- Attitudes
*SENTIMENT analysis
*SHOPPING
*ORGANIC foods
MORAL & ethical aspects

— Database subject headings

— Abstract

Abstract: Findings suggesting that consumers buy "green" products, such as organic foods, for selfish reasons are usually accepted at face value. In this article, the author argues that the evidence backing this claim is questionable and that it reflects post hoc rationalizations and self-presentation biases on behalf of respondents. Knowing that one has incurred substantial personal costs by contributing to a worthy cause can create an uneasiness that one is motivated to relieve, especially when one is uncertain about the ultimate impact of this contribution. A possible coping strategy is to adjust one's beliefs about intangible private benefits in a way that justifies (bolsters) one's purchasing decision. A survey study among a representative sample of approximately 4,000 respondents from four European countries (Denmark, Germany, United Kingdom, and Italy) confirmed that this is exactly what "green" consumers do.

Author Affiliations: [1]Aarhus University, Aarhus, Denmark jbt@asb.dk

Full Text Word Count: 9918

ISSN: 0002-7642

DOI: 10.1177/0002764211407903 •— Digital Object Identifier (DOI)

Note Many databases allow you to limit your search to so-called peer-reviewed or refereed journals—that is, scholarly journals whose articles have been reviewed before publication by experts in the field and then revised by the author. Limiting your search to peer-reviewed journals (screen 1) can help you navigate huge databases that might otherwise return scores of unusable articles.

The use of abstracts

In screen 3 the full article record shows a key feature of many databases' periodical listings: an **abstract** that summarizes the article. By describing research methods, conclusions, and other information, an abstract can tell you whether you want to pursue an article and thus save you time. However, the abstract cannot replace the actual article. If you want to use the work as a source, you must consult the full text.

Helpful databases

The following list includes databases to which academic libraries commonly subscribe. Some of these databases cover much the same material, so your library may not subscribe to all of them.

> *EBSCOhost Academic Search.* A periodical index covering magazines and journals in the social sciences, sciences, arts, and humanities. Many articles are available full-text.
>
> *Expanded Academic ASAP.* The Gale Group's general periodical index covering the social sciences, sciences, arts, and humanities as well as national news periodicals. It includes full-text articles.
>
> *LexisNexis Academic.* An index of news and business, legal, and reference information, with full-text articles. *LexisNexis* includes international, national, and regional newspapers, news magazines, legal and business publications, and court cases.
>
> *ProQuest Research Library.* A periodical index covering the sciences, social sciences, arts, and humanities, including many full-text articles.

2 ▪ Locations of periodicals

Many article listings you find will include or link directly to the full text of the article, which you'll be able to read online and print or e-mail to yourself. If the full text is not available online, usually you can click on a link within the article record to see whether your library has the article in print or another format. Recent issues of periodicals are probably held in the library's periodical room. Back issues are usually stored elsewhere, either in bound volumes or on film that requires a special machine to read. A librarian will show you how to operate the machine.

52f Search the Web.

As an academic researcher, you enter the Web in two ways: through your library's Web site and through public search engines such as *Firefox* and *Google*. The library entrance, covered in the preceding sections, is your main path to the books and periodicals that, for most subjects, should make up most of your sources. The open Web, discussed here, can lead to a wealth of information and ideas, but it also has disadvantages that limit its usefulness for academic research:

- **The Web is a wide-open network.** Anyone with the right tools can place information on the Internet, and even a carefully conceived search can turn up sources with widely varying reliability: journal articles, government documents, scholarly data, term papers written by high school students, sales pitches masked as objective reports, wild theories. You must be especially diligent about evaluating open-Web sources (see pp. 382–89).

- **The Web changes constantly.** No search engine can keep up with the Web's daily additions and deletions, and a source you find today may be updated or gone tomorrow. You should not put off consulting an online source that you think you may want to use.

- **The Web is not all-inclusive.** Most books and many periodicals are available only via the library, not directly via the Web.

52f

Clearly, the Web warrants cautious use. It should not be the only resource you work with.

1 ▪ Public search engines

To find sources on the Web, you use a **search engine** that catalogs Web sites in a series of directories and conducts keyword searches. For a good range of sources, try out more than a single search engine, perhaps as many as four or five, because no search engine can catalog the entire Web. In addition, most search engines accept paid placements, giving higher billing to sites that pay a fee. These so-called sponsored links are usually marked as such, but they can compromise a search engine's method for arranging sites in response to your keywords.

Customized searches

The home page of a search engine includes a field for you to type your keywords into. Generally, it will also include an Advanced Search link that you can use to customize your search. For instance, you may be able to select a range of dates, a language, or a number of results to see. Advanced Search will also explain how to use operators such as *AND*, *OR*, and *NOT* to limit or expand your search.

Search records

No matter which search engine you use, your Web browser includes functions that allow you to keep track of Web sources and your search:

- **Use *Favorites* or *Bookmarks* to save site addresses as links.** Click one of these terms near the top of the browser screen to add a site you want to return to. A favorite or bookmark remains on file until you delete it.
- **Use *History* to locate sites you have visited before.** The browser records visited sites for a certain period, such as a single online session or a week's sessions. (After that period, the history is deleted.) If you forgot to bookmark a site, you can click History or Go to locate your search history and recover the site.

52f

2 ▪ A sample search

The following sample Web search illustrates how the refinement of keywords can narrow a search to maximize the relevant hits and minimize the irrelevant ones. Justin Malik, a student researching the environmental effects of green consumer products, first used the keywords *green products* on *Google*. But, as shown on screen 1 below, the search produced more than *1.5 billion* items, with the first page consisting entirely of sites selling products.

1. First *Google* search results

Malik realized he had to alter his strategy to get more useful results. He experimented with combinations of synonyms and narrower terms and arrived at *"green consumerism"* and *products*, which refined the search but still produced 130,000 results. Adding *site:.gov* limited the results to government sites, whose URLs end in *.gov*. With *"green consumerism" products site:.gov*, Malik received 8,780 results (see screen 2 opposite). He continued to limit the search by replacing *site:.gov* with *site:.org* (nonprofit organizations), *site:.edu* (educational institutions), and *site:.com* (commercial organizations).

2. *Google* results with refined keywords

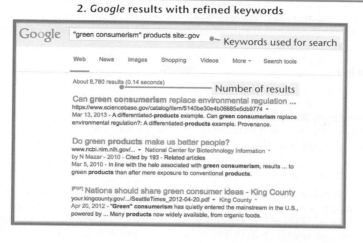

Google   "green consumerism" products site:.gov ●— Keywords used for search

Web   News   Images   Shopping   Videos   More ▾   Search tools

About 8,780 results (0.14 seconds) ————— Number of results

Can green consumerism replace environmental regulation ...
https://www.sciencebase.gov/catalog/item/5140be30e4b06685e5db9774 ▾
Mar 13, 2013 - A differentiated-**products** example. Can **green consumerism** replace
environmental regulation?: A differentiated-**products** example. Provenance.

Do green products make us better people?
www.ncbi.nlm.nih.gov/... ▾ National Center for Biotechnology Information ▾
by N Mazar - 2010 - Cited by 193 - Related articles
Mar 5, 2010 - In line with the halo associated with **green consumerism**, results ... to
green **products** than after mere exposure to conventional **products**.

[PDF] Nations should share green consumer ideas - King County
your.kingcounty.gov/.../SeattleTimes_2012-04-20.pdf ▾ King County ▾
Apr 20, 2012 - "**Green**" consumerism has quietly entered the mainstream in the U.S.,
powered by ... Many **products** now widely available, from organic foods.

52g

52g   Explore social media.

Online sources that you reach through social media can put you directly in touch with experts and others whose ideas and information may inform your research. These media include e-mail, blogs, social-networking sites, and discussion groups. Like Web sites, they are unfiltered, so you must always evaluate them carefully. (See pp. 387–89.)

Note If your paper includes social-media correspondence that is not already public—for instance, an e-mail or a discussion-group posting—ask the author for permission to use it. Doing so advises the author that his or her ideas are about to be distributed more widely and lets the author verify that you have not misrepresented the ideas. (See also pp. 375–76 on interviews.)

1 ▪ E-mail

As a research tool, e-mail allows you to communicate with others who are interested in your topic. You might, for instance, carry on an e-mail conversation with a teacher at your school or interview an expert in another state to follow up on a scholarly article he or she published.

2 ▪ Blogs and social-networking sites

Blogs are Web sites on which an author or authors post time-stamped comments, generally centering on a common theme, in a format that allows readers to respond to the writer or to one another. You can find directories of blogs at *blogcatalog.com*.

Somewhat similar to blogs, social-networking sites such as *Twitter*, *Instagram*, and *Facebook* are increasingly being used by organizations, businesses, individuals, and even scholars to communicate with others. Like all other social media discussed in this section, blogs and posts on social-networking sites must be evaluated carefully as potential sources. Some are reliable sources of opinion and evolving scholarship, and many refer to worthy books, articles, Web sites, and other resources. But just as many are little more than outlets for their authors' gripes or self-marketing. See pages 387–89 for tips on telling the good from the bad.

52h

3 ▪ Discussion lists

A **discussion list** (sometimes called a **listserv** or just a **list**) uses e-mail to connect individuals who are interested in a common subject, often with a scholarly or technical focus. By sending a question to an appropriate list, you may be able to reach scores of people who know something about your topic. For an index of discussion lists, see *tile.net/lists*.

Begin research on a discussion list by consulting the list's archive to ensure that the discussion is relevant to your topic and to see whether your question has already been answered. When you write to the list, follow the guidelines for writing e-mail on pages 82–83. And always evaluate messages you receive, following the guidelines on pages 387–89. Although many contributors are reliable experts, almost anyone with an Internet connection can post a message.

4 ▪ Web forums and newsgroups

Web forums and newsgroups are more open and less scholarly than discussion lists, so their messages require even more diligent evaluation. **Web forums** allow participants to join a conversation simply by selecting a link on a Web page. For a directory of forums, see *delphiforums.com*. **Newsgroups** are organized under subject headings such as *soc* for social issues and *biz* for business. For a directory of newsgroups, see *giganews.com*.

52h   Consult government publications.

Government publications provide a vast array of data, reports, policy statements, public records, and other historical and contemporary information. For US government publications, consult the Government Printing Office's *GPO Access* at *www.gpoaccess.gov*. Also helpful is *www.usa.gov*, a portal to a range of documents and information.

Many federal, state, and local government agencies post important publications—legislation, reports, press releases—on their own Web sites. You can find lists of sites for various federal agencies by using the keywords *United States federal government* with a search engine. Use the name of a state, city, or town with *government* for state and local information.

52i   Locate visuals, audio, and video.

52i

Visuals, audio, and video can be used as both primary and secondary sources in a research project. A painting, an advertisement, or a video of a speech might be the subject of your writing and thus a primary source. A podcast of a radio interview with an expert on your subject or a college lecture might serve as a secondary source. Because many of these sources are unfiltered—they can be posted by anyone—you must always evaluate them as carefully as you would any source you find on the open Web. (See pp. 382–89.)

Caution You must cite every visual, audio, and video source fully in your paper, just as you cite text sources, with author, title, and publication information. In addition, some sources will require that you seek permission from the copyright holder, such as a publisher or a photographer. To avoid having to seek permission, you can search Web sites such as *Google, Flickr Creative Commons,* and *Wikimedia Commons* for media that are not protected by copyright. On *Google,* for instance, go to "Search tools" and select "Labeled for reuse." Consult a librarian at your school if you have questions.

1 ▪ Visuals

The use of visuals to support your writing is discussed on pages 63–68. To find visuals, you have a number of options:

- ▪ **Scout for visuals while reading print or online sources.** While you are examining your sources, you may see charts, graphs, photographs, and other visuals that can support your ideas. When you find a visual you may want to use, photocopy or download it so you'll have it available later.

- ▪ **Create your own visuals,** such as photographs or charts. See pages 65–66 for suggestions on creating visuals.

- ▪ **Use an image search engine.** Web search engines can be set to find visuals, and they allow you to restrict your search to visuals that don't require reuse permission. Although search engines can find scores of visuals, the results will be only as accurate or complete as the information is in the sources surveyed. (The engines search file names and any text accompanying the visuals.)

- **Use a public image database.** The following sites generally conduct accurate searches because their images are filed with information such as a description of the visual, the artist's name, and the visual's date:

  Digital Public Library of America. Maps, documents, photographs, advertisements, and more from libraries throughout the United States.
  Duke University, *Ad*Access.* Print advertisements spanning 1911–55.
  Library of Congress, *American Memory.* Maps, photographs, prints, cartoons, and advertisements documenting the American experience.
  Library of Congress, *Prints and Photographs Online Catalog.* Visuals from the library's collection, including those available through *American Memory.*
  New York Public Library Digital Gallery. Maps, drawings, photographs, and paintings from the library's collection.

- **Use a public image directory.** The following sites collect links to image sources:

  Art Project—Google Cultural Institute. Selections of fine art from major museums in the United States and Europe.
  MuseumLink's Museum of Museums. Links to museums all over the world.
  Cultural Politics: Resources for Critical Analysis. Sources on advertising, fashion, magazines, toys, and other artifacts of popular culture.
  Yale University Robert B. Haas Family Arts Library, *Image Resources.* Sources on the visual and performing arts.

- **Use a library database.** Your library may subscribe to the following resources:

  ARTstor. Museum collections and a database of images typically used in art history courses.
  Associated Press, *AccuNet/AP Multimedia Archives.* Historical and contemporary news images.
  Grove Art Online. Art images and links to museum sites.

Many visuals you find will be available at no charge for copying or downloading, but some sources do charge a fee for use. Before paying for a visual, check with a librarian to see if it is available elsewhere for free.

2 ▪ Audio and video

Audio and video, widely available on the Web and on disc, can provide your readers with the experience of "being there." For example, if you write about the media response to the *I Have a Dream* speech of Martin Luther King, Jr., and you will submit your paper electronically, you might insert links to the speech and to TV and radio coverage of it.

- **Audio files** such as podcasts, Webcasts, and CDs record radio programs, interviews, speeches, lectures, and music. They are available on the Web and through your library. Online sources of audio include the Library of Congress's *American Memory*, the *Internet Archive*, and *Podcastdirectory.com*.

■ **Video files** capture performances, speeches and public presentations, news events, and other activities. They are available on the Web and on DVD or Blu-ray disc from your library. Online sources of video include the Library of Congress's *American Memory*; *YouTube* and the *Internet Archive*, which include commercials, historical footage, current events, and much more; and search engines such as *Google*.

52j   Generate your own sources.

For some papers you will need to conduct primary research to support, extend, or refute the ideas of others. For example, if you were writing about cyberbullying among college students, you might want to survey students on your campus as well as consult published research on the subject. Three common forms of primary research are personal interviews, surveys, and observation.

1 ■ Personal interviews

An interview can be especially helpful for a research project because it allows you to ask questions precisely geared to your topic. You can conduct an interview in person, over the telephone, or online. A personal interview is preferable if you can arrange it, because you can see the person's expressions and gestures as well as hear his or her tone.

Here are a few guidelines for interviews:

■ **Call or write for an appointment.** Tell the person exactly why you are calling, what you want to discuss, and how long you expect the interview to take. Be true to your word on all points.

■ **Prepare a list of open-ended questions to ask**—perhaps ten or twelve for a one-hour interview. Do some research on these questions before the interview to discover background on the issues and your subject's published views on the issues.

■ **Pay attention to your subject's answers** so that you can ask appropriate follow-up questions. Take care in interpreting answers, especially if you are online and can't infer the subject's attitudes from facial expressions, gestures, and tone of voice.

■ **Keep thorough notes.** Take notes during an in-person or telephone interview, or record the interview if you have the equipment and your subject agrees. For online interviews, save the discussion in a file of its own.

■ **Verify quotations.** Before you quote your subject in your paper, check with him or her to ensure that the quotations are accurate.

- **Send a thank-you note immediately after the interview.** Promise your subject a copy of your finished paper, and send the paper promptly.

See page 473 for an example of an interview used as a research source.

2 ▪ Surveys

Asking questions of a defined group of people can provide information about respondents' attitudes, behavior, backgrounds, and expectations. Use the following tips to plan and conduct a survey:

- **Decide what you want to find out.** The questions you ask should be dictated by your purpose. Formulating a **hypothesis** about your subject—a generalization that can be tested—will help you refine your purpose.
- **Define your population.** Think about the kinds of people your hypothesis is about—for instance, college men or preschool children. Plan to sample this population so that your findings will be representative.
- **Write your questions.** Surveys may contain closed questions that direct the respondent's answers (checklists and multiple-choice, true/false, or yes/no questions) or open-ended questions that allow brief, descriptive answers. Avoid loaded questions that reveal your own biases or make assumptions about subjects' answers.
- **Test your questions.** Use a few respondents with whom you can discuss the answers. Eliminate or recast questions that respondents find unclear, discomforting, or unanswerable.
- **Tally the results.** Count the actual numbers of answers, including any nonanswers.
- **Seek patterns in the raw data.** Such patterns may confirm or contradict your hypothesis. Revise the hypothesis or conduct additional research if necessary.

See pages 118–19 for an example of a survey used as a research source.

3 ▪ Observation

Observation can be an effective way to gather fresh information on your subject. You may observe in a controlled setting—for instance, watching children at play in a child-development lab. Or you may observe in a more open setting—for instance, watching the interactions among students at a cafeteria on your campus. Use these guidelines for planning and gathering information through observation:

- **Be sure that what you want to learn *can* be observed.** You can observe people's choices and interactions, but you would need an interview or a survey to discover people's attitudes or opinions.

52j

▪ **Allow ample time.** Observation requires several sessions of several hours in order to be reliable.

▪ **Record your impressions.** Throughout the observation sessions, take careful notes on paper, a computer, or a mobile device. Always record the date, time, and location for each session.

▪ **Be aware of your own bias.** Such awareness will help you avoid the common pitfall of seeing only what you expect or want to see.

53 Working with Sources

In *Brief*

▪ Use the criteria for reading sources critically (below).
▪ Evaluate library sources (p. 379).
▪ Evaluate Web sources and social media (pp. 382, 387).
▪ Synthesize information from sources (p. 389).
▪ Gather information, carefully summarizing, paraphrasing, and quoting (pp. 392, 393).
▪ Integrate source information into your writing (p. 400).

Visit MyWritingLab™ for more resources on working with sources.

Research writing is much more than finding sources and reporting their contents. The challenge and interest come from interacting with and synthesizing sources. Reading sources critically will help you discover their meanings, judge their relevance and reliability, and create relationships among them. Using sources to extend and support your own ideas will lead you to make your subject your own.

(CULTURE LANGUAGE) Making a subject your own requires thinking critically about sources and developing independent ideas. These goals may at first be uncomfortable for you if your native culture emphasizes understanding and respecting established authority more than questioning and enlarging it. The information here will help you work with sources so that you can become an expert in your own right and convincingly convey your expertise to others.

53a Evaluate sources.

Before you gather ideas and information from your sources, scan them to evaluate what they offer and how you might use them. As you evaluate each source, add an assessment of it to your annotated bibliography, as shown on page 358.

Note In evaluating sources, you need to consider how they come to you. The sources you find through the library, both print and online, have been previewed for you by their publishers and by the library's staff. They still require your critical reading, but you can have some confidence in the information they contain. With online sources you reach directly, however, you can't assume similar previewing, so your critical reading must be especially rigorous. Special tips for evaluating Web sites and other online sources begin on page 382.

1 ▪ Relevance and reliability

Not all the sources you find will prove worthwhile: some may be irrelevant to your project, and others may be unreliable. Gauging the relevance and reliability of sources is the essential task of evaluating them. If you haven't already done so, read this book's Chapter 10 on critical thinking and reading. It provides a foundation for answering the questions in the following box.

Questions for evaluating sources

For online sources, supplement these questions with those on pages 382 and 387.

Relevance

▪ **Does the source devote some attention to your subject?** Does it focus on your subject or cover it marginally? How does it compare to other sources you've found?

▪ **Is the source appropriately specialized for your needs?** Check the source's treatment of a topic you know something about, to ensure that it is neither too superficial nor too technical.

▪ **Is the source up to date enough for your subject?** When was it published? If your subject is current, your sources should be, too.

Reliability

▪ **Where does the source come from?** Did you find it through your library or directly through the Internet? (If the latter, see pp. 382–89.) Is the source popular or scholarly?

▪ **Is the author an expert in the field?** Check the author's credentials in a biography (if the source includes one), in a biographical reference, or by a keyword search of the Web.

▪ **What is the bias of the source?** How do the author's ideas relate to those in other sources? What areas does the author emphasize, ignore, or dismiss?

▪ **Is the source fair, reasonable, and well written?** Does it provide sound reasoning and a fair picture of opposing views? Is the tone calm and objective? Is the source logically organized and error-free?

▪ **Are the claims well supported, even if you don't agree with the author?** Does the author provide accurate, relevant, representative, and adequate evidence to back up his or her claims? Does the author cite sources, and if so are they reliable?

---

2 ▪ Evaluating library sources

To evaluate sources you find through your library—either in print or on the library's Web site—look at dates, titles, summaries, introductions, headings, author biographies, and any source citations. The following criteria expand on the most important tips in the preceding box. The next two pages show how the student Justin Malik applied these criteria to two print sources, a magazine article and a journal article, that he consulted while researching green consumerism.

Identify the origin of the source.

Check whether a library source is popular or scholarly. Scholarly sources, such as refereed journals and university press books, are generally deeper and more reliable. But some popular sources, such as firsthand newspaper accounts and books for a general audience, are often appropriate for research projects.

Check the author's expertise.

The authors of scholarly publications tend to be experts whose authority can be verified. Check the source to see whether it contains a biographical note about the author, check a biographical reference, or check the author's name in a keyword search of the Web. Look for other publications by the author and for his or her job and any affiliation, such as teacher at a university, researcher with a nonprofit organization, author of general-interest books, or writer for popular magazines.

Identify the bias.

Every author has a point of view that influences the selection and interpretation of evidence. You may be able to learn about an author's bias from biographies or from citation indexes and review indexes, which list references to and reviews of articles and books. But also look at the source itself. How do the author's ideas relate to those in other sources? What areas does the author emphasize, ignore, or dismiss? When you're aware of sources' biases, you can acknowledge them in your writing and try to balance them.

Determine whether the source is fair, reasonable, and well written.

Even a strongly biased work should present solid reasoning and give balanced coverage to opposing views—all in an objective tone. Any source should be organized logically and should be written in clear, error-free sentences. The absence of any of these qualities should raise a warning flag.

Analyze support for the author's claims.

Whether or not you agree with the author, evidence should be accurate, relevant to the argument, representative of its context, and

(continued on p. 382)

Evaluating library sources

Opposite are sample pages from two library sources that Justin Malik considered for his paper on green consumerism. Malik evaluated the sources using the questions and guidelines starting on page 378.

(questions and guidelines starting on page 378)

Makower	Jackson
Origin	
Interview with Joel Makower published in *Vegetarian Times*, a popular magazine.	Article by Tim Jackson published in *Journal of Industrial Ecology*, a scholarly journal sponsored by two reputable universities: MIT and Yale.
Author	
Gives Makower's credentials at the beginning of the interview: the author of a book on green products and of a monthly newsletter on green businesses. Quotes another source that calls Makower the "guru of green business practice."	Includes a biography at the end of the article that describes Jackson as a professor at the University of Surrey (UK) and lists his professional activities related to the environment.
Bias	
Describes and promotes green products. Concludes with an endorsement of a for-profit Web site that tracks and sells green products.	Presents multiple views of green consumerism. Argues that a solution to environmental problems will involve green products and less consumption but in different ways than currently proposed.
Reasonableness and writing	
Presents Makower's data and perspective on distinguishing good from bad green products, using conversational writing in an informal presentation.	Presents and cites opposing views objectively, using formal academic writing.
Source citations	
Lacks source citations for claims and data.	Includes more than three pages of source citations, many of scholarly and government sources and all cited within the article.
Assessment	
Unreliable for academic research: Despite Makower's reputation, the article comes from a nonscholarly source, takes a one-sided approach to consumption, and depends on statistics credited only to Makower.	**Reliable for academic research:** The article comes from a scholarly journal, the author is an expert in the field, he discusses many views and concedes some, and his source citations confirm evidence from reliable sources.

53a

Unreliable source for academic research:
An interview with Joel Makower, published in *Vegetarian Times*

Reliable source for academic research:
An article by Tim Jackson, published in the *Journal of Industrial Ecology*

(continued from p. 379)
adequate for the point being made. (See p. 105.) The author's sources should themselves be reliable.

3 ▪ Evaluating Web sites

The same critical reading that helps you evaluate library sources will help you evaluate Web sites that you reach directly. You would not use a popular magazine such as *People* in academic research—unless, say, you were considering it as a primary source in a paper analyzing popular culture. Similarly, you would not use a celebrity's Web site, a fan site, or a gossip site as a source unless you were placing it in a larger academic context.

Even Web sites that seem worthy pose challenges for evaluation because they have not undergone prior screening by editors and librarians. On your own, you must distinguish scholarship from corporate promotion, valid data from invented statistics, well-founded opinion from clever propaganda.

The strategy summarized in the following box can help you make such distinctions. On pages 384–85 you can see how Justin Malik applied this strategy to two Web sites that he consulted while researching green consumerism.

Questions for evaluating Web sites

Supplement these questions with those on pages 378 and 387.

- **What type of site are you viewing**—for example, is it scholarly, informational, or commercial?
- **Who is the author or publisher?** How credible is the person or group responsible for the site?
- **What is the purpose of the site?** What does the site's author or publisher intend to achieve? Are there ads on the site, signaling that the site is trying to make money from its content?
- **What is the bias of the site?** Does the site advocate for one side or another of a particular issue?
- **What does context tell you?** What do you already know about the site's subject that can inform your evaluation? What kinds of support or other information do the site's links provide?
- **What does presentation tell you?** Is the site's design well thought out and effective? Is the writing clear and error-free?
- **How worthwhile is the content?** Are the site's claims well supported by evidence from reliable sources? When was the site posted or last updated?

Note To evaluate a Web document, you'll often need to travel to the site's home page to discover the author or publisher, date of publication, and other relevant information. The page you're reading may include a link to the home page. If it doesn't, you can find it by editing the URL in the Address or Location field of your browser. Working backward, delete the end of the URL up to the last slash and hit Enter. Repeat this step until you reach the home page. There you may also find a menu option, often labeled "About," that will lead you to a description of the site's author or publisher.

Determine the type of site.

When you search the Web, you're likely to encounter various types of sites. Although they sometimes overlap, the types can usually be identified by their content and purposes. Here are the main types of Web sites you will find using a search engine:

- **Scholarly sites:** These sites have a knowledge-building interest, and they are likely to be reliable. They include research reports with supporting data and extensive documentation of scholarly sources. For such sites originating in the United States, the URLs generally end in *edu* (originating from a college or university), *org* (a nonprofit organization), or *gov* (a government department or agency). Sites originating in other countries will end differently, usually with a country code such as *uk* (United Kingdom), *de* (Germany), or *kr* (South Korea).

- **Informational sites:** Individuals, nonprofit organizations, corporations, schools, and government bodies all produce sites intended to centralize information on subjects as diverse as astronomy, hip-hop music, and zoo design. The sites' URLs may end in *edu*, *org*, *gov*, or *com* (originating from a commercial organization). Such sites generally do not have the knowledge-building focus of scholarly sites and may omit supporting data and documentation, but they can provide useful information and sometimes include links to scholarly and other sources.

- **Advocacy sites:** Many sites present the views of individuals or organizations that promote certain policies or actions, such as the National Rifle Association or People for the Ethical Treatment of Animals. Their URLs usually end in *org*, but they may end in *edu* or *com*. Most advocacy sites have a strong bias. Some sites include serious, well-documented research to support their positions, but others select or distort evidence.

- **Commercial sites:** Corporations and other businesses such as automakers, electronics manufacturers, and booksellers maintain Web sites to explain themselves, promote themselves, or sell goods and services. URLs of commercial sites usually end in *com*; however, some end in *biz*, and those of businesses based outside the United States often end in the country code. Although business sites intend to further the publishers' profit-making purposes, they can include reliable data.

(continued on p. 386)

Evaluating Web sites

Opposite are screen shots from two Web sites that Justin Malik consulted for his paper on green consumerism. Malik evaluated the sources using the questions in the boxes on pages 378 and 382.

Wikipedia	*Center for Climate and Energy Solutions*
Author and publisher	
Author of the page is not given. Web site is *Wikipedia*, the online encyclopedia to which anyone can contribute anonymously.	Author is an expert on energy and public policy. (His biography can be found online.) Publisher is the Center for Climate and Energy Solutions, a nonprofit group specializing in energy and climate change.
Purpose and bias	
Informational page with no stated or obvious bias.	Informational site with the stated purpose of "working to promote sound policy on the challenges of energy and climate change." Report expresses bias toward sustainable electricity production.
Context	
An encyclopedia site publishing information on a wide variety of topics.	Nonprofit organization's site dedicated to publishing current research on energy and climate issues.
Presentation	
Clean, professional-looking page with mostly error-free writing.	Clean, professionally designed site with error-free writing.
Content	
Article gives basic information about energy use and provides links to other pages that expand on its claims. Probably because of the intended general audience, the page does not link to extensive citations of scholarly research.	Report is current (date below the author's name), it describes scenarios for meeting future electricity needs, and it cites scholarly sources.
Assessment	
Unreliable for academic research: The page has no listed author and few scholarly citations. A *Wikipedia* page is suitable for background information but not as evidence in an academic paper.	**Reliable for academic research:** The report has a bias toward sustainable electricity production, but the publisher is reputable and the author is an expert and cites scholarly sources.

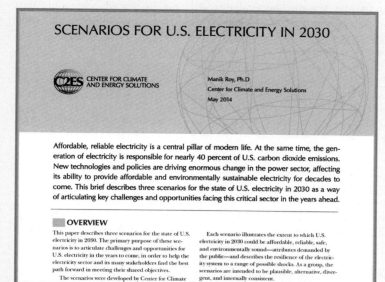

Create account   Log in

Article Talk   Read Edit View history Search

Electric energy consumption

From Wikipedia, the free encyclopedia

Main page
Contents
Featured content
Current events
Random article
Donate to Wikipedia
Wikimedia Shop

Interaction
Help
About Wikipedia
Community portal
Recent changes
Contact page

Tools
What links here
Related changes
Upload file
Special pages
Permanent link
Page information
Wikidata item
Cite this page

Print/export

Electric energy consumption is the form of energy consumption that uses electric energy. Electric energy consumption is the actual energy demand made on existing electricity supply.

Overview [edit]

Consumption of electric energy is measured in watt-hours (written W-h, equal to Watt x Hour)

  1 W-h = 3600 joule = 859.8 calorie.

Electric and electronic devices consume electric energy to generate desired output (i.e. light, heat, motion, etc.). During operation, some part of the energy is consumed in unintended output, such as waste heat. See Electrical Efficiency .

In 2008, the world total of electricity production and consumption was 20.279 TWh (terawatt-hours). This number corresponds to an average consumption rate of around 2.3 terawatts continuously during the year. The total energy needed to produce this power is roughly a factor 2 to 3 higher because the efficiency of power plants is roughly 30-50%, see Electricity generation. The generated power is thus in the order of 5 TW. This is approximately a third of the total energy consumption of 15 TW, see World energy consumption.

In 2005, the primary energy used to generate electricity was 41.60 Quadrillion BTU (Coal 21.01 quads, Natural Gas 6.69 quads, Petroleum 1.32 quads, Nuclear electric power 8.13 quads, Renewable energy 4.23 quads respectively). The gross consumption of electricity in that year was 14.50 Quads; the difference, 27.10 Quads, was conversion losses. Among all electricity, 4.84 Quads was used in residential area, 4.32 Quads used in commercial, 3.47 Quads used in industrial and 0.03 Quads used in transportation.

16816TWh(83%) of electric energy was consumed by final users. The difference of 3464TWh(17%)was consumed in the process of generating power and consumed as transmission loss and all most consumed at misuse.

Unreliable source for academic research: A page on the Web site *Wikipedia.* Source: Courtesy of Wikipedia.org. http://en.wikipedia.org/wiki/ Electric_energy_consumption.

SCENARIOS FOR U.S. ELECTRICITY IN 2030

C2ES CENTER FOR CLIMATE
AND ENERGY SOLUTIONS

Manik Roy, Ph.D
Center for Climate and Energy Solutions
May 2014

Affordable, reliable electricity is a central pillar of modern life. At the same time, the generation of electricity is responsible for nearly 40 percent of U.S. carbon dioxide emissions. New technologies and policies are driving enormous change in the power sector, affecting its ability to provide affordable and environmentally sustainable electricity for decades to come. This brief describes three scenarios for the state of U.S. electricity in 2030 as a way of articulating key challenges and opportunities facing this critical sector in the years ahead.

▮ OVERVIEW

This paper describes three scenarios for the state of U.S. electricity in 2030. The primary purpose of these scenarios is to articulate challenges and opportunities for U.S. electricity in the years to come, in order to help the electricity sector and its many stakeholders find the best path forward in meeting their shared objectives.

  The scenarios were developed by Center for Climate

Each scenario illustrates the extent to which U.S. electricity in 2030 could be affordable, reliable, safe, and environmentally sound—attributes demanded by the public—and describes the resilience of the electricity system to a range of possible shocks. As a group, the scenarios are intended to be plausible, alternative, divergent, and internally consistent.

Reliable source for academic research: A report published on the Web site *Center for Climate and Energy Solutions*

(continued from p. 383)

- **Personal sites:** The sites maintained by individuals range from diaries of a family's travels to opinions on political issues to reports on evolving scholarship. The sites' URLs usually end in *com* or *edu*. Personal sites are only as reliable as their authors, but some do provide valuable eyewitness accounts, links to worthy sources, and other usable information. Personal sites are often blogs or social-networking pages, discussed on pages 371–72.

53a

Identify the author and publisher.

A reputable site lists its authors, names the group responsible for the site, and provides information for contacting the author and the publisher. If none of this information is provided, you should not use the source. If you have only the author's or the publisher's name, you may be able to discover more in a biographical dictionary, through a keyword search, or in another source. Make sure the author and the publisher have expertise on the subject they're presenting: if an author is a doctor, for instance, what is he or she a doctor of?

Gauge purpose and bias.

A Web site's purpose determines what ideas and information it offers. Inferring that purpose tells you how to interpret what you see on the site. If a site is intended to sell a product or advocate a particular position, it may emphasize favorable ideas and information while ignoring or even distorting unfavorable information or opposing views. In contrast, if a site is intended to build knowledge—for instance, a scholarly project or journal—it will likely acknowledge diverse views and evidence.

Determining the purpose and bias of a site often requires looking beyond the first page and beneath the surface of words and images. To start, read critically what the site says about itself, usually on a page labeled "About." Be suspicious of any site that doesn't provide information about itself and its goals.

Consider context.

Your evaluation of a Web site should be informed by considerations outside the site itself. Chief among these considerations is your own knowledge. What do you already know about the site's subject and the prevailing views of it? Where does this site seem to fit into that picture? What can you learn from this site that you don't already know?

In addition, you can follow some of the site's links to see how they support, or don't support, the site's credibility. For instance, links to scholarly sources lend authority to a site—but *only* if the scholarly sources actually relate to and back up the site's claims.

Look at presentation.

Considering both the look of a site and the way it's written can illuminate its intentions and reliability. Do the site's elements all support its purpose, or is the site cluttered with irrelevant material and graphics? Is the text clearly written and focused on the purpose? Is it relatively error-free, or does it contain typos and grammatical errors? Does the site seem carefully constructed and well maintained, or is it sloppy? How intrusive are any pop-up advertisements?

Analyze content.
With information about a site's author, purpose, and context, you're in a position to evaluate its content. Are the ideas and information current, or are they dated? (Check the publication date.) Are they slanted and, if so, in what direction? Are the views and data authoritative, or do you need to balance them—or even reject them? Are claims made on the site supported by evidence drawn from reliable sources? These questions require close reading of both the text and its sources.

53a

4 ▪ Evaluating other online sources

Social media and multimedia require the same critical scrutiny as Web sites do. Social media—including e-mail, blogs, *Twitter*, discussion groups, *Facebook* pages, and wikis—can be sources of reliable data and opinions, but they can also contain wrong or misleading data and skewed opinions. Multimedia—visuals, audio, and video—can provide valuable support for your ideas, but they can also mislead or distort. For example, a *YouTube* search using "I have a dream" brings up videos of Martin Luther King, Jr., delivering his famous speech as well as videos of people speaking hatefully about King and the speech.

Answer the following questions when evaluating social media and multimedia.

Questions for evaluating social media and multimedia

Supplement these questions with those on pages 378 and 382.

- ▪ **Who is the author or creator?** How credible is he or she?
- ▪ **What is the author's or creator's purpose?** What can you tell about why the author or creator is publishing the work?
- ▪ **What does the context reveal?** What do reasonable responses to the work, such as comments on a blog or a news site, indicate about the source's balance and reliability?
- ▪ **How worthwhile is the content?** Are the claims made by the author or creator supported by evidence? Is the evidence from reliable sources?
- ▪ **How does the source compare with other sources?** Do the claims made by the author or creator seem accurate and fair given what you've seen in sources you know to be reliable?

Identify the author or creator.

Checking out the author or creator of a potential source can help you judge its reliability. The author may be identified on the source—for instance, the blog posting shown below includes a biographical note at the end saying that the author is a professor writing on behalf of the American Anthropological Association's Task Force on Global Climate Change. You may also be able to learn about the author with a keyword search of the Web. If you can't identify the author or creator at all, you can't use the source.

You can also get a sense of the interests and biases of an author or creator by tracking down his or her other work. For instance, you might check whether a blog author cites or links to other publications, look for other postings by the same author in a discussion-group archive, or try to gain an overview of a photographer's work.

Analyze the author's or creator's purpose.

What can you tell about *why* the author or creator is publishing the work? The blog posting below provides a quick answer in the title, which indicates the author's negative view of green products. You can

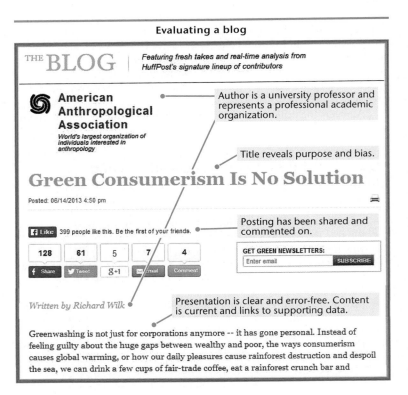

Evaluating a blog

THE **BLOG** | Featuring fresh takes and real-time analysis from HuffPost's signature lineup of contributors

American Anthropological Association
World's largest organization of individuals interested in anthropology

Author is a university professor and represents a professional academic organization.

Title reveals purpose and bias.

Green Consumerism Is No Solution

Posted: 06/14/2013 4:50 pm

Like 399 people like this. Be the first of your friends.

| 128 | 61 | 5 | 7 | 4 |

Share Tweet 8+1 Email Comment

Posting has been shared and commented on.

GET GREEN NEWSLETTERS:
Enter email   SUBSCRIBE

Written by Richard Wilk

Presentation is clear and error-free. Content is current and links to supporting data.

Greenwashing is not just for corporations anymore -- it has gone personal. Instead of feeling guilty about the huge gaps between wealthy and poor, the ways consumerism causes global warming, or how our daily pleasures cause rainforest destruction and despoil the sea, we can drink a few cups of fair-trade coffee, eat a rainforest crunch bar and

also dig to discover purpose, looking for claims, the use (or lack) of evidence, and the treatment of opposing views. All these factors convey the person's stand on the subject and general fairness, and they will help you position the source among your other sources.

Consider the context.

Social media and multimedia are often difficult to evaluate in isolation. Looking beyond a contribution to the responses of others can give you a sense of context by indicating how the author or creator is regarded. On a *Facebook* page or a blog, look at the comments others have posted. If you discover negative or angry responses, try to understand why: sometimes online anonymity encourages hateful responses to even quite reasonable postings.

53b

Analyze content.

A reliable source will offer evidence for claims and will list the sources of its evidence. The blog posting on the facing page, for example, links to information about carbon dioxide emissions. If you don't see such support, then you probably shouldn't use the source. However, when the source is important to you and biographical information or context indicates that the author or creator is serious and reliable, you might ask him or her to direct you to supporting information.

The tone of writing can also be a clue to its purpose and reliability. In most social media, the writing tends to be more informal and may be more heated than in other kinds of sources; but look askance at writing that's contemptuous, dismissive, or shrill.

Compare with other sources.

Always consider social-media and multimedia sources in comparison to other sources so that you can distinguish singular, untested views from more mainstream views that have been subject to verification. Don't assume that a blog author's information and opinions are mainstream just because you see them on other blogs. The technology allows content to be picked up instantly by other blogs, so widespread distribution indicates only popular interest, not reliability.

Be wary of blogs that reproduce periodical articles, reports, or other publications. Try to locate the original version of the publication to be sure it has been reproduced fully and accurately, not quoted selectively or distorted. If you can't locate the original version, don't use the publication as a source.

53b Synthesize sources.

When you begin to see the differences and similarities among sources, you move into the most significant part of research writing:

forging relationships for your own purpose. This **synthesis** is an essential step in reading sources critically, and it continues through the drafting and revision of a research paper. As you infer connections—say, between one writer's opinions and another's or between two works by the same author—you shape your own perspective on your subject and create new knowledge.

Your synthesis of sources will grow more detailed and sophisticated as you proceed through the process of working with sources described in the balance of this chapter: gathering information from sources (pp. 392–93); deciding whether to summarize, paraphrase, or quote directly from sources (pp. 393–99); and integrating sources into your sentences (pp. 400–03). Unless you are analyzing primary sources such as the works of a poet, at first read your sources quickly and selectively to obtain an overview of your topic and a sense of how the sources approach it. Don't get bogged down in taking detailed notes, but *do* record your ideas about sources in your research journal (p. 351) or your annotated bibliography (pp. 356–58).

Respond to sources.

One way to find your own perspective on a topic is to write down what your sources make you think. Do you agree or disagree with the author? Why do you agree or disagree? What new approaches to your subject does each source open for you? Is there anything in the source that you need to research further before you can understand it? Does the source prompt questions that you should keep in mind while reading other sources?

Connect sources.

When you notice a link between sources, write about it. Do two sources differ in their theories or their interpretations of facts? Does one source illuminate another—perhaps commenting or clarifying or supplying additional data? Do two or more sources report studies that support a theory you've read about or an idea of your own?

Heed your own insights.

Apart from ideas prompted by your sources, you are sure to come up with independent thoughts: a conviction, a point of confusion that suddenly becomes clear, a question you haven't seen anyone else ask. These insights may occur at unexpected times, so it's good practice to keep a notebook or computer handy to record them.

Draw your own conclusions.

As your research proceeds, the responses, connections, and insights you form through synthesis will lead you to answer your starting research question with a statement of your thesis (see pp. 415–16). They will also lead you to the main ideas supporting your thesis—conclusions you have drawn from your synthesis of sources, forming the main divisions of your paper. Be sure to write them down as they occur to you.

Use sources to support your conclusions.

Effective synthesis requires careful handling of evidence from sources so that it meshes smoothly into your sentences and yet is clearly distinct from your own ideas. When drafting your paper, make sure that each paragraph focuses on an idea of your own, with the support for the idea coming from your sources. Generally, open each paragraph with your idea, provide evidence from a source or sources with appropriate citations, and close with an interpretation of the evidence. (Avoid ending a paragraph with a source citation; instead, end with your own idea.) In this way, your paper will synthesize others' work into something wholly your own. (For more on structuring paragraphs in academic writing, see pp. 99–100.)

53b

Exercise 53.1   Synthesizing sources

The following three passages address the same issue, the legalization of drugs. What similarities do you see in the authors' ideas? What differences? Write a paragraph of your own in which you use these authors' views as a point of departure for your own view about drug legalization.

Perhaps the most unfortunate victims of drug prohibition laws have been the residents of America's ghettos. These laws have proved largely futile in deterring ghetto-dwellers from becoming drug abusers, but they do account for much of what ghetto residents identify as the drug problem. Aggressive, gun-toting drug dealers often upset law-abiding residents far more than do addicts nodding out in doorways. Meanwhile other residents perceive the drug dealers as heroes and successful role models. They're symbols of success to children who see no other options. At the same time the increasingly harsh criminal penalties imposed on adult drug dealers have led drug traffickers to recruit juveniles. Where once children started dealing drugs only after they had been using them for a few years, today the sequence is often reversed. Many children start using drugs only after working for older drug dealers for a while. Legalization of drugs, like legalization of alcohol in the 1930s, would drive the drug-dealing business off the streets and out of apartment buildings and into government-regulated, tax-paying stores. It also would force many of the gun-toting dealers out of the business and convert others into legitimate businessmen.

—Ethan A. Nadelmann, "Shooting Up"

Statistics argue against legalization. The University of Michigan conducts an annual survey of twelfth graders, asking the students about their drug consumption. In 1980, 56.4% of those polled said they had used marijuana in the past twelve months, whereas in 2013 only 45.5% had done so. Cocaine use was also reduced in the same period (22.6% to 5.2%). At the same time, twelve-month use of legally available drugs—alcohol and nicotine-containing cigarettes—remained constant at about 70% and 50%, respectively. The numbers of illegal drug users haven't declined nearly enough: those teenaged marijuana and cocaine users are still vulnerable to addiction and even death, and they threaten to infect their impressionable peers. But clearly the prohibition of illegal drugs has helped, while the legal status of alcohol and cigarettes has not made them less popular.

—Sylvia Smith, "The Case against Legalization"

I have to laugh at the debate over what to do about the drug problem. Everyone is running around offering solutions—from making drug use a more serious criminal offense to legalizing it. But there isn't a real solution. I know that. I used and abused drugs, and people, and society, for two decades. Nothing worked to get me to stop all that behavior except just plain being sick and tired. Nothing. Not threats, not ten-plus years in prison, not anything that was said to me. I used until I got through. Period. And that's when you'll win the war. When all the dope fiends are done. Not a minute before.

—Michael W. Posey, "I Did Drugs Until They Wore Me Out. Then I Stopped."

53c

53c Gather information from sources.

You can collect and store source information in a number of ways: handwrite notes, type notes into a file, copy and paste chunks of text from online articles into a file, annotate print or electronic documents such as PDF files, or scan or photocopy pages from books and other print sources.

Whatever method you use to gather information, you have four main goals:

- **Keep accurate records of what sources say.** Accuracy helps prevent misrepresentation and plagiarism. If you write notes by hand or type them into a file, do so carefully to avoid introducing errors.

- **Keep track of others' words and ideas.** Put quotation marks around any words you take from a source, and always include a source citation that ties the quotation to the publication information you have recorded. Also include a source citation for any idea you summarize or paraphrase so that you know the idea is not your own but came from a specific source. For more on summarizing, paraphrasing, and quoting sources, see the next section.

- **Keep accurate records of how to find sources.** Whether you handwrite notes or work with an electronic file, always link the source material to its complete publication information. These records are essential for retracing steps and for citing sources in your drafts and in the final paper. If you have the complete information in your working bibliography (see pp. 356–57), you can use a shorthand reference to it on the source material, such as the author's name and any page or other reference number. (See the examples on pp. 394–96.)

■ **Synthesize sources.** Information gathering is a critical process in which you learn from sources, understand the relationships among them, and develop your own ideas about your subject and your sources. Analyze and interact with your sources by highlighting their key information and commenting on what they say.

53d Use summary, paraphrase, and quotation.

Deciding whether to summarize, paraphrase, or quote directly from sources is an important step in synthesizing the sources' ideas and your own. You engage in synthesis when you use your own words to summarize an author's argument or paraphrase a significant example or when you select a significant passage to quote. Choosing summary, paraphrase, or quotation should depend on why you are using a source.

Caution Summaries, paraphrases, and quotations all require source citations in your paper. A summary or paraphrase without a source citation or a quotation without quotation marks is plagiarism. (See pp. 405–11 for more on plagiarism.)

1 ■ Summary

When you **summarize**, you condense an extended idea or argument into a sentence or more in your own words. (See pp. 89–90 for tips.) Summary is most useful when you want to record the gist of an author's idea without the background or supporting evidence. The following passage comes from a source that Justin Malik used for his paper on green consumerism: a scholarly essay about consumption and its impact on the environment.

Original quotation

Such intuition is even making its way, albeit slowly, into scholarly circles, where recognition is mounting that ever-increasing pressures on ecosystems, life-supporting environmental services, and critical natural cycles are driven not only by the sheer number of resource users and the inefficiencies of their resource use, but also by the patterns of resource use themselves. In global environmental policymaking arenas, it is becoming more and more difficult to ignore the fact that overdeveloped countries must restrain their consumption if they expect underdeveloped countries to embrace a more sustainable trajectory. And while global population growth still remains a huge issue in many regions around the world—both rich and poor—per-capita growth in consumption is, for many resources, expanding eight to twelve times faster than population growth.

—Thomas Princen, Michael Maniates, and Ken Conca,
Confronting Consumption, p. 4

In the following one-sentence summary, Malik picks out the kernel of the authors' passage and expresses it in his own words:

Summary of source

> Environmental consequences of consumption
>
> Princen et al. 4
>
> Overconsumption may be a more significant cause of environmental problems than increasing population is.

53d

Notice how Malik records the authors of the source and the page number in his note to avoid accidentally plagiarizing the authors' idea in his paper.

The examples below show the preceding summary in the context of a draft. The first lacks proper citation and thus is plagiarism. The second has proper citation (in MLA style).

Summary with no citation (plagiarized)

Always seeking newer and better things, we consume without regard for the resources we use or the waste we leave behind. In fact, overconsumption may be a more significant cause of environmental problems than increasing population is.

Summary with proper citation (not plagiarized)

Always seeking newer and better things, we consume without regard for the resources we use or the waste we leave behind. In fact, according to Thomas Princen, Michael Maniates, and Ken Conca, overconsumption may be a more significant cause of environmental problems than increasing population is (4).

See pages 405–11 for more on plagiarism.

2 ▪ Paraphrase

When you **paraphrase**, you follow much more closely the author's original presentation, but you restate it using your own words and sentence structures. Paraphrase is most useful when you want to present or examine an author's line of reasoning but you don't feel the original words merit direct quotation.

The note on the facing page shows how Malik might have paraphrased the passage by Princen, Maniates, and Conca given on the previous page. Notice the record of the authors' names and the page number, which would help Malik avoid confusing the paraphrase with his own ideas and then inadvertently plagiarizing the source in his paper.

Complete paraphrase of source

Environmental consequences of consumption

Princen et al. 4

Scholars are coming to believe that consumption is partly to blame for changes in ecosystems, reduction of essential natural resources, and changes in natural cycles. Policy makers increasingly see that developing nations will not adopt practices that reduce pollution and waste unless wealthy nations consume less. Rising population around the world does cause significant stress on the environment, but consumption is increasing even more rapidly than population.

53d

This paraphrase uses simpler sentences and more common terms than the original passage, in effect translating it as shown in the following comparison. Only words that lack satisfactory synonyms— such as *ecosystems, natural, cycles, population,* and *consumption*— remain the same.

Source authors' words	Malik's paraphrase
Such intuition is even making its way, albeit slowly, into scholarly circles, where recognition is mounting that	Scholars are coming to believe that
ever-increasing pressures on ecosystems, life-supporting environmental services, and critical natural cycles are driven not only by the sheer number of resource users and the inefficiencies of their resource use, but also by the patterns of resource use themselves.	consumption is partly to blame for changes in ecosystems, reduction of essential natural resources, and changes in natural cycles.
In global environmental policy-making arenas, it is becoming more and more difficult to ignore the fact that	Policy makers increasingly see that
overdeveloped countries must restrain their consumption if they expect underdeveloped countries to embrace a more sustainable trajectory.	developing nations will not adopt practices that reduce pollution and waste unless wealthy nations consume less.
And while global population growth still remains a huge issue in many regions around the world—both rich and poor—	Rising population around the world does cause significant stress on the environment,

Source authors' words	Malik's paraphrase
per-capita growth in consumption is, for many resources, expanding eight to twelve times faster than population growth.	but consumption is increasing even more rapidly than population.

Follow these guidelines when paraphrasing:

53d

- **Read the material several times to be sure you understand it.** Then you will find it easier to use your own words.
- **Restate the main ideas in your own words and sentence structures.** You do not have to follow the organization of the original or restate all of it. Select and restate only what you need. If complete sentences seem too detailed or cumbersome, use phrases. Justin Malik might have written the following briefer paraphrase of the quotation by Princen, Maniates, and Conca.

Abbreviated paraphrase of source

Environmental consequences of consumption

Princen et al. 4

Consumption is increasing more rapidly than population and contributing to major ecological crises. Wealthy nations have to start consuming less.

- **Be careful not to distort meaning.** Don't change the source's emphasis or omit connecting words, qualifiers, and other material whose absence will confuse you later or cause you to misrepresent the source.
- **Be careful not to plagiarize the source.** Use your own words and your own sentence structures, and always record a source citation in your notes. Especially if your source is difficult or complex, you may be tempted to change just a few words or to modify the sentence structure just a bit. But that is plagiarism, not paraphrase.

The following examples show the preceding paraphrase in the context of a draft. The first lacks proper citation and is plagiarism. The second has proper citation (in MLA style).

Paraphrase with no citation (plagiarized)

Always seeking newer and better things, we consume without regard for the resources we use or the waste we leave behind. In fact, overconsumption is increasing more rapidly than population and contributing to major ecological crises. Wealthy nations have to start consuming less.

Paraphrase with proper citation (not plagiarized)
Always seeking newer and better things, we consume without regard for the resources we use or the waste we leave behind. In fact, according to Thomas Princen, Michael Maniates, and Ken Conca, overconsumption is increasing more rapidly than population and contributing to major ecological crises. Wealthy nations have to start consuming less (4).

See pages 405–11 for more on plagiarism.

CULTURE · LANGUAGE If English is not your native language and you have difficulty paraphrasing the ideas in sources, try this: Before attempting a paraphrase, read the original passage several times. Then, instead of "translating" line by line, try to state the gist of the passage without looking at it. Check your effort against the original to be sure you have captured the source author's meaning and emphasis without using his or her words and sentence structures. If you need a synonym for a word, look it up in a dictionary.

53d

3 ▪ Direct quotation

Your notes from sources may include many quotations, especially if you rely on photocopies, printouts, or downloads. Whether to use a quotation in your draft, instead of a summary or paraphrase, depends on whether the source is primary or secondary and on how important the exact words are:

▪ **Quote extensively when you are analyzing primary sources**—firsthand accounts such as literary works, eyewitness reports, and historical documents. The quotations will often be both the target of your analysis and the chief support for your ideas.

▪ **Quote selectively when you are drawing on secondary sources**—reports or analyses of other sources, such as a critic's view of a poem or a historian's synthesis of several eyewitness reports. Favor summaries and paraphrases over quotations, and put every quotation to each test in the box on the next page. Most papers of ten or so pages should not need more than two or three quotations that are longer than a few lines each.

When you quote a source, either in your notes or in your draft, take precautions to avoid plagiarism or misrepresentation of the source:

▪ **Copy the material carefully.** Take down the author's exact wording, spelling, capitalization, and punctuation.

▪ **Proofread every direct quotation at least twice.**

▪ **Use quotation marks around the quotation** so that later you won't confuse it with a paraphrase or summary. Be sure to transfer the quotation marks into your draft as well, unless the quotation is long and is set off from your text. For advice on when to set off

---

Tests for direct quotations from secondary sources

The author's original satisfies one of these requirements:

- The language is unusually vivid, bold, or inventive.
- The quotation cannot be paraphrased without distortion or loss of meaning.
- The words themselves are at issue in your interpretation.
- The quotation represents and emphasizes a body of opinion or the view of an important expert.
- The quotation emphatically reinforces your own idea.
- The quotation is an illustration, such as a graph, diagram, or table.

The quotation is as short as possible:

- It includes only material relevant to your point.
- It is edited to eliminate examples and other unneeded material, using brackets and ellipsis marks (pp. 323–25).

---

quotations and how to format them, see pages 466 (MLA style) and 500 (APA style).

- **Use brackets** to add words for clarity or to change the capitalization of letters (see pp. 325, 336).
- **Use ellipsis marks** to omit material that is irrelevant to your point (see pp. 323–25).
- **Cite the source of the quotation in your draft.** See pages 413–14 on documentation.

The note below shows how Justin Malik might have quoted part of the passage on page 393 by Princen, Maniates, and Conca, using brackets and an ellipsis mark to make the quotation more concise. Notice the record of the authors' names and the page number as well as the quotation marks around the authors' exact words. All of these notations would help Malik avoid plagiarizing the source in his paper.

Quotation of source

Environmental consequences of consumption

Princen et al. 4

"[E]ver-increasing pressures on ecosystems, life-supporting environmental services, and critical natural cycles are driven not only by the sheer number of resource users . . . but also by the patterns of resource use themselves."

The following examples show the quotation as part of a draft. The first is plagiarism, lacking appropriate punctuation and proper citation. The second is corrected (in MLA style).

Quotation lacking quotation marks, an ellipsis mark, and a citation (plagiarized)

Increasing consumption may be as much of a threat to the environment as increasing population. In fact, ever-increasing pressures on ecosystems, life-supporting environmental services, and critical natural cycles are driven not only by the sheer number of resource users but also by the patterns of resource use themselves.

Quotation with quotation marks, an ellipsis mark, and proper citation (not plagiarized)

Increasing consumption may be as much of a threat to the environment as increasing population. According to Thomas Princen, Michael Maniates, and Ken Conca, "ever-increasing pressures on ecosystems, life-supporting environmental services, and critical natural cycles are driven not only by the sheer number of resource users . . . but also by the patterns of resource use themselves" (4).

See pages 405–11 for more on plagiarism.

53d

Exercise 53.2   Summarizing and paraphrasing

Prepare two source notes, one summarizing the entire following paragraph and the other paraphrasing the first four sentences (ending with the word *autonomy*). Be sure to record the source author's name and the page number.

Federal organization [of the United States] has made it possible for the different states to deal with the same problems in many different ways. One consequence of federalism, then, has been that people are treated differently, by law, from state to state. The great strength of this system is that differences from state to state in cultural preferences, moral standards, and levels of wealth can be accommodated. In contrast to a unitary system in which the central government makes all important decisions (as in France), federalism is a powerful arrangement for maximizing regional freedom and autonomy. The great weakness of our federal system, however, is that people in some states receive less than the best or the most advanced or the least expensive services and policies that government can offer. The federal dilemma does not invite easy solution, for the costs and benefits of the arrangement have tended to balance out.   —Peter K. Eisinger et al., *American Politics*, p. 44

Exercise 53.3   Combining summary, paraphrase, and direct quotation

Prepare a source note containing a combination of paraphrase or summary along with direct quotation that states the main idea of the following passage. Be sure to record the source author's name and the page number.

> Most speakers unconsciously duel even during seemingly casual conversations, as can often be observed at social gatherings where they show less concern for exchanging information with other guests than for asserting their own dominance. Their verbal dueling often employs very subtle weapons like mumbling, a hostile act which defeats the listener's desire to understand what the speaker claims he is trying to say (but is really not saying because he is mumbling!). Or the verbal dueler may keep talking after someone has passed out of hearing range—which is often an aggressive challenge to the listener to return and acknowledge the dominance of the speaker.   —Peter K. Farb, *Word Play*, p. 107

53e   Integrate sources into your text.

Integrating source material into your sentences is key to synthesizing others' ideas and information with your own. Evidence drawn from sources should *back up* your conclusions, not *be* your conclusions: you don't want to let your evidence overwhelm your own point of view. To keep your ideas in the forefront, you do more than merely present borrowed material; you introduce and interpret it as well.

Note   The examples in this section use the MLA style for citing sources in the text of a paper and also present-tense verbs (such as *disagrees*). See pages 403–04 for specific variations in documentation style and verb tense within the academic disciplines. Several other conventions governing quotations are discussed elsewhere in this book:

- **Using commas to punctuate signal phrases** (pp. 300–01).
- **Placing other punctuation marks with quotation marks** (pp. 319–20).
- **Using brackets and the ellipsis mark to indicate changes in quotations** (pp. 323–25).
- **Punctuating and placing parenthetical citations** (pp. 426–28).
- **Formatting long prose quotations and poetry quotations** (MLA style, p. 466; APA style, p. 500).

1 ▪ Introduction of borrowed material

Always introduce a summary, a paraphrase, or a quotation by identifying it and by providing a smooth transition between your words and ideas and those of your source. In the following passage, the writer has not meshed the structures of her own and her source's sentences:

> Awkward   One editor disagrees with this view and "a good reporter does not fail to separate opinions from facts" (Lyman 52).

In the revision below, the writer adds words to integrate the quotation into her sentence:

> Revised   One editor disagrees with this view, maintaining that "a good reporter does not fail to separate opinions from facts" (Lyman 52).

To mesh your own and your source's words, you may sometimes need to make a substitution or addition to the quotation, signaling your change with brackets:

Words added	"The tabloids [of England] are a journalistic case study in bad reporting," claims Lyman (52).
Verb form changed	A bad reporter, Lyman implies, is one who "[fails] to separate opinions from facts" (52). [The bracketed verb replaces *fail* in the original.]
Capitalization changed	"[T]o separate opinions from facts" is the work of a good reporter (Lyman 52). [In the original, *to* is not capitalized.]
Noun supplied for pronoun	The reliability of a news organization "depends on [reporters'] trustworthiness," says Lyman (52). [The bracketed noun replaces *their* in the original.]

53e

2 ▪ Interpretation of borrowed material

You need to work borrowed material into your sentences so that readers see without effort how it contributes to the points you are making. If you merely dump source material into your paper without explaining how you intend it to be interpreted, readers will have to struggle to understand your sentences and the relationships you are trying to establish. For example, the following passage forces us to figure out for ourselves that the writer's sentence and the quotation state opposite points of view:

Dumped	Many news editors and reporters maintain that it is impossible to keep personal opinions from influencing the selection and presentation of facts. "True, news reporters, like everyone else, form impressions of what they see and hear. However, a good reporter does not fail to separate opinions from facts" (Lyman 52).

In the revision, the underlined additions tell us how to interpret the quotation:

Revised	Many news editors and reporters maintain that it is impossible to keep personal opinions from influencing the selection and presentation of facts. Yet not all authorities agree with this view. One editor grants that "news reporters, like everyone else, form impressions of what they see and hear." But, he insists, "a good reporter does not fail to separate opinions from facts" (Lyman 52).

Signal phrases

The words *One editor grants* and *he insists* in the preceding revised passage are **signal phrases**: they tell readers who the source is and what to expect in the quotations that follow. Signal phrases usually contain (1) the source author's name (or a substitute for it, such as *One editor* and *he*) and (2) a verb that indicates the source author's attitude or approach to what he or she says.

Some verbs for signal phrases appear below. These verbs are in the present tense, typical of writing in the humanities. In the social and natural sciences, the past tense (*asked*) or present perfect tense (*has asked*) is more common. See page 404.

Author is neutral	Author infers or suggests	Author argues	Author is uneasy or disparaging
comments	analyzes	claims	belittles
describes	asks	contends	bemoans
explains	assesses	defends	complains
illustrates	concludes	holds	condemns
notes	considers	insists	deplores
observes	demonstrates	maintains	deprecates
points out	finds		derides
records	predicts	**Author agrees**	disagrees
relates	proposes		laments
reports	reveals	admits	warns
says	shows	agrees	
sees	speculates	concedes	
thinks	suggests	concurs	
writes	supposes	grants	

53e

Vary your signal phrases to suit your interpretation of borrowed material and also to keep readers' interest. A signal phrase may precede, interrupt, or follow the borrowed material:

Precedes   Lyman insists that "a good reporter does not fail to separate opinions from facts" (52).

Interrupts   "However," Lyman insists, "a good reporter does not fail to separate opinions from facts" (52).

Follows   "[A] good reporter does not fail to separate opinions from facts," Lyman insists (52).

Background information

You can add information to a signal phrase to inform readers why you are using a source. In most cases, provide the author's name in the text, especially if the author is an expert or readers will recognize the name:

Author named   Harold Lyman grants that "news reporters, like everyone else, form impressions of what they see and hear." But, Lyman insists, "a good reporter does not fail to separate opinions from facts" (52).

If the source title contributes information about the author or the context of the quotation, you can provide it in the text:

Title	Harold Lyman, <u>in his book *The Conscience of the Journalist*</u>,
given	grants that "news reporters, like everyone else, form im-
	pressions of what they see and hear." But, Lyman insists,
	"a good reporter does not fail to separate opinions from
	facts" (52).

If the quoted author's background and experience reinforce or clarify the quotation, you can provide those credentials in the text:

Credentials	Harold Lyman, <u>a newspaper editor for more than forty</u>
given	<u>years</u>, grants that "news reporters, like everyone else, form
	impressions of what they see and hear." But, Lyman in-
	sists, "a good reporter does not fail to separate opinions
	from facts" (52).

You need not name the author, source, or credentials in your text when you are simply establishing facts or weaving together facts and opinions from varied sources. In the following passage, the information is more important than the source, so the name of the source is confined to a parenthetical acknowledgment:

> To end the abuses of the British, many colonists were urging three ac-
> tions: forming a united front, seceding from Britain, and taking control
> of their own international relations (Wills 325–36).

3 ▪ Discipline styles for integrating sources

The preceding guidelines for introducing and interpreting borrowed material apply generally across academic disciplines, but the
disciplines do differ in verb tenses and documentation style.

English and some other humanities

Writers in English, foreign languages, and related disciplines use
MLA style for documenting sources (see Chapter 56) and generally
use the present tense of verbs in signal phrases. In discussing sources
other than works of literature, the present perfect tense is also sometimes appropriate:

> Lyman <u>insists</u> . . . [present].
> Lyman <u>has insisted</u> . . . [present perfect].

In discussing works of literature, use only the present tense to describe both the work of the author and the action in the work:

> Kate Chopin <u>builds</u> irony into every turn of "The Story of an Hour." For
> example, Mrs. Mallard, the central character, <u>finds</u> joy in the death of
> her husband, whom she <u>loves</u>, because she <u>anticipates</u> "the long pro-
> cession of years that <u>would belong</u> to her absolutely" (23).

Avoid shifting tenses in writing about literature. You can, for instance, shorten quotations to avoid their past-tense verbs:

Shift	Her freedom <u>elevates</u> her, so that "she <u>carried</u> herself unwittingly like a goddess of victory" (24).
No shift	Her freedom <u>elevates</u> her, so that she <u>walks</u> "unwittingly like a goddess of victory" (24).

History and other humanities

Writers in history, art history, philosophy, and related disciplines generally use the present tense or present perfect tense of verbs in signal phrases:

> Lincoln persisted, as Haworth <u>has noted</u>, in "feeling that events controlled him."[3]
>
> What Miller <u>calls</u> Lincoln's "severe self-doubt"[6] undermined his effectiveness on at least two occasions.

The raised numbers after the quotations are part of the Chicago documentation style, used in history and other disciplines. You can find information on Chicago style and sample student papers documented in Chicago style at *mywritinglab.com*.

Social and natural sciences

Writers in the sciences generally use a verb's present tense just for reporting the results of a study (*The data suggest* . . .). Otherwise, they use a verb's past or present perfect tense in a signal phrase, as when introducing an explanation, interpretation, or other commentary. (Thus when you are writing in the sciences, generally convert the list of signal-phrase verbs on p. 402 from the present to the past or present perfect tense.)

> Lin (2001) <u>has suggested</u> that preschooling may significantly affect children's academic performance not only in elementary school but through high school (pp. 22–23).
>
> In an exhaustive survey of the literature published between 1990 and 2005, Walker (2006) <u>found</u> "no proof, merely a weak correlation, linking place of residence and rate of illness" (p. 121).

These examples conform to APA documentation style, discussed in Chapter 57. APA style, or one quite similar to it, is also used in sociology, education, nursing, biology, and many other social and natural sciences.

Exercise 53.4   Introducing and interpreting borrowed material

Drawing on the ideas in the following paragraph and using examples from your own observations and experiences, write a paragraph about anxiety. Integrate at least one direct quotation and one paraphrase from the following paragraph into your own sentences. In your paragraph identify the author by name and give his credentials: he is a professor of psychiatry and a practicing psychoanalyst.

> There are so many ways in which human beings are different from all the lower forms of animals, and almost all of them make us uniquely susceptible to feelings of anxiousness. Our imagination and reasoning powers facilitate anxiety; the anxious feeling is precipitated not by an absolute impending threat—such as the worry about an examination, a speech, travel—but rather by the symbolic and often unconscious representations. We do not have to be experiencing a potential danger. We can experience something related to it. We can recall, through our incredible memories, the original symbolic sense of vulnerability in childhood and suffer the feeling attached to that. We can even forget the original memory and be stuck with the emotion—which is then compounded by its seemingly irrational quality at this time. It is not just the fear of death which pains us, but the anticipation of it; or the anniversary of a specific death; or a street, a hospital, a time of day, a color, a flower, a symbol associated with death.
>
> —Willard Gaylin, "Feeling Anxious," p. 23

plag
54

54 Avoiding Plagiarism and Documenting Sources

In *Brief*

- Know what plagiarism is, and do not plagiarize sources deliberately or carelessly (next two pages).
- Know which sources you do not need to cite (p. 408).
- Know which sources you *must* cite (p. 409).
- Obtain necessary permission if you intend to publish your work (p. 412).
- Document your sources (p. 413).

Visit MyWritingLab™ for more resources on avoiding plagiarism and documenting sources.

The knowledge building that is the focus of academic writing depends on the integrity of everyone who participates, including students, in using and crediting sources. The work of a writer or creator is his or her intellectual property. You and others may borrow the work's ideas and even its words or an image, but you *must* acknowledge that what you are presenting came from and belongs to someone else.

When you acknowledge sources in your writing, you are doing more than giving credit to the writer or creator of the work you consulted. You are also showing what your own writing is based on, which in turn adds to your integrity as a researcher and writer. Acknowledging sources creates the trust among scholars, students, writers, and readers that knowledge building requires.

Plagiarism (from a Latin word for "kidnapper") is the presentation of someone else's work as your own. Whether deliberate or careless, plagiarism is a serious offense. It breaks trust, and it undermines or even destroys your credibility as a researcher and writer. In most colleges, a code of academic honesty calls for severe consequences for plagiarism: a reduced or failing grade, suspension from school, or expulsion. The way to avoid plagiarism is to acknowledge your sources: keep track of the ones you consult for each paper you write, and document them within the paper and in a list of works cited.

⟨CULTURE / LANGUAGE⟩ The concepts of originality, intellectual property, and plagiarism are not universal. In some other cultures, for instance, students may be encouraged to copy the words of scholars without acknowledging the sources, in order to demonstrate their mastery of or respect for the scholars' work. In the United States, however, using an author's work without a source citation is a

---

Checklist for avoiding plagiarism

Know your source.
Are you using

- your own experience,
- common knowledge, or
- someone else's material?

You must acknowledge someone else's material.

Quote carefully.

- Check that every quotation exactly matches its source.
- Insert quotation marks around every quotation that you run into your text. (A quotation set off from the text does not need quotation marks. See pp. 466 and 500.)
- Indicate any omission from a quotation with an ellipsis mark and any addition with brackets.
- Acknowledge the source of every quotation.

Paraphrase and summarize carefully.

- Use your own words and sentence structures for every paraphrase and summary. If you have used the author's words, add quotation marks around them.
- Acknowledge the source of the idea(s) in every paraphrase or summary.

Cite sources responsibly.

- Acknowledge every use of someone else's material in each place you use it.
- Include all your sources in your list of works cited. See Chapters 56 and 57 for citing sources in MLA and APA documentation styles.

serious offense, whether it is careless or intentional. If you have questions about the guidelines in this chapter, ask your instructor for advice.

54a   Avoid both deliberate and careless plagiarism.

Instructors usually distinguish between deliberate plagiarism, which is cheating, and careless plagiarism, which often stems from a writer's inexperience with managing sources.

1 ▪ Deliberate plagiarism

Deliberate plagiarism is intentional: the writer chooses to cheat by turning in someone else's work as his or her own. Students who deliberately plagiarize deprive themselves of an education in honest research. When their cheating is detected, the students often face stiff penalties, including expulsion.

Following are examples of deliberate plagiarism:

Copying a phrase, a sentence, or a longer passage from a source and passing it off as your own by not adding quotation marks and a source citation.

Summarizing or paraphrasing someone else's ideas without acknowledging the source in a citation.

Handing in as your own work a paper you have copied off the Web, had a friend write, or accepted from another student.

Handing in as your own work a paper you have purchased from a paper-writing service. **Paying for research or a paper does not make it your work.**

2 ▪ Careless plagiarism

Careless plagiarism is unintentional: grappling with complicated information and ideas in sources, the writer neglects to put quotation marks around a source's exact words or neglects to include a source citation for a quotation, paraphrase, or summary. Most instructors and schools do not permit careless plagiarism, but they treat it less harshly than deliberate plagiarism—at least the first time it occurs.

Here are examples of careless plagiarism:

Reading sources without taking notes on them and then not distinguishing what you recently learned from what you already knew.

Copying and pasting material from a source into your document without placing quotation marks around the other writer's work.

Forgetting to add a source citation for a paraphrase. Even though a paraphrase casts another person's idea in your own words, you still need to cite the source of the idea.

Omitting a source citation for another's idea because you are unaware of the need to acknowledge the idea.

Plagiarism and the Internet

The Internet has made it easier to plagiarize than ever before: with just a few clicks, you can copy and paste passages or whole documents into your own files. If you do so without quoting and acknowledging your source, you plagiarize.

The Internet has also made plagiarism easier to detect. Instructors can use search engines to find specific phrases or sentences anywhere on the Web, including among scholarly publications, all kinds of Web sites, and term-paper collections. They can search term-paper sites as easily as students can, looking for similarities with papers they've received. They can also use detection software—such as *Turnitin*, *PlagiServe*, and *Glatt Plagiarism Services*—which compares students' work with other work anywhere on the Internet, seeking matches as short as a few words.

Some instructors suggest that their students use plagiarism-detection programs to verify that their own work does not include careless plagiarism, at least not from the Internet.

54b Know what you need not acknowledge.

1 ▪ Your independent material

Your own observations, thoughts, compilations of facts, or experimental results—expressed in your words and format—do not require acknowledgment. You should describe the basis for your conclusions so that readers can evaluate your thinking, but you need not cite sources for them.

2 ▪ Common knowledge

Common knowledge consists of the standard information on a subject as well as folk literature and commonsense observations.

- **Standard information** includes the major facts of history, such as the dates during which Charlemagne ruled as emperor of Rome (800–14). It does *not* include interpretations of facts, such as a historian's opinion that Charlemagne was sometimes needlessly cruel in extending his power.
- **Folk literature,** such as the fairy tale "Snow White," is popularly known and cannot be traced to a particular writer. Literature traceable to a writer is *not* folk literature, even if it is very familiar.
- **Commonsense observations** are things most people know, such as that inflation is most troublesome for people with low and fixed incomes. However, a particular economist's argument about the effects of inflation on Chinese immigrants is *not* a commonsense observation.

If you do not know a subject well enough to determine whether a piece of information is common knowledge, make a record of the source as you would for any other quotation, paraphrase, or summary. As you read more about the subject, the information may come up repeatedly without acknowledgment, in which case it is probably common knowledge. But if you are still in doubt when you finish your research, always acknowledge the source.

54c Know what you *must* acknowledge.

You must always acknowledge other people's independent material—that is, any facts, ideas, or opinions that are not common knowledge or your own. The source may be a formal publication or release, such as a book, an article, a movie, an interview, an artwork, a comic strip, a map, a Web page, or a blog. The source may also be informal, such as a tweet, a post on *Facebook*, an opinion you heard on the radio, or a comment by your instructor or a classmate that substantially shaped your argument. You must acknowledge summaries or paraphrases of ideas or facts as well as quotations of the language and format in which ideas or facts appear: wording, sentence structures, arrangement, and special graphics (such as a diagram). You must acknowledge another's material no matter how you use it, how much of it you use, or how often you use it.

1 ▪ Using copied language: Quotation marks and a source citation

The following example baldly plagiarizes the original quotation from Jessica Mitford's *Kind and Usual Punishment*, page 9. Without quotation marks or a source citation, the example matches Mitford's wording (underlined) and closely parallels her sentence structure:

Original quotation	"The character and mentality of the keepers may be of more importance in understanding prisons than the character and mentality of the kept."
Plagiarism	But the character of prison officials (the keepers) is of more importance in understanding prisons than the character of prisoners (the kept).

To avoid plagiarism, the writer can paraphrase and cite the source (see the examples on the next page) or use Mitford's actual words *in quotation marks* and *with a source citation* (here, in MLA style):

Revision (quotation)	According to Mitford, a critic of the penal system, "The character and mentality of the keepers may be of more importance in understanding prisons than the character and mentality of the kept" (9).

Even with a source citation and with a different sentence structure, the next example is still plagiarism because it uses some of Mitford's words (underlined) without quotation marks:

Plagiarism	According to Mitford, a critic of the penal system, the psychology of <u>the kept</u> may say less about prisons than the psychology of <u>the keepers</u> (9).
Revision (quotation)	According to Mitford, a critic of the penal system, the psychology of *"*the kept*"* may say less about prisons than the psychology of *"*the keepers*"* (9).

plag
54c

2 ▪ Using paraphrase or summary: Your own words and sentence structure and a source citation

The following example changes the sentence structure of the original Mitford quotation above, but it still uses Mitford's words (underlined) without quotation marks and without a source citation:

Plagiarism	<u>In understanding prisons</u>, we should know more about <u>the character and mentality of the keepers</u> than <u>of the kept</u>.

To avoid plagiarism, the writer can use quotation marks and cite the source (see the previous page) or *use his or her own words* and still *cite the source* (because the idea is Mitford's, not the writer's):

Revision (paraphrase)	Mitford holds that we may be able to learn more about prisons from the psychology of the prison officials than from that of the prisoners (9).
Revision (paraphrase)	We may understand prisons better if we focus on the personalities and attitudes of the prison workers rather than those of the inmates (Mitford 9).

In the next example, the writer cites Mitford and does not use her words but still plagiarizes her sentence structure. The revised paraphrase changes the sentence structure as well as the words.

Plagiarism	Mitford, a critic of the penal system maintains that <u>the psychology of prison officials may be more informative about prisons than the psychology of prisoners</u> (9).
Revision (paraphrase)	Mitford, a critic of the penal system maintains that we may be able to learn less from the psychology of prisoners than from the psychology of prison officials (9).

3 ▪ Using online sources

Online sources are so accessible and so easy to copy into your own documents that it may seem they are freely available, exempting you from the obligation to acknowledge them. They are not. Acknowledging online sources is somewhat trickier than acknowledging print sources, but it is no less essential: when you use someone else's independent material from an online source, you must acknowledge the source.

Citing online sources is easier when you keep track of them as you work:

- **Record complete publication information each time you consult an online source.** Online sources may change from one day to the next or even disappear entirely. See page 357 for the information to record, such as the publication date. Without the proper information, you *may not* use the source.
- **Immediately put quotation marks around any text that you copy and paste into your document.** If you don't add quotation marks right away, you risk forgetting which words belong to the source and which are yours. If you don't know whose words you are using, recheck the source or *do not* use them.
- **Acknowledge linked sites.** If you use not only a Web site but also one or more of its linked sites, you must acknowledge the linked sites as well. The fact that one person has used a second person's work does not release you from the responsibility to cite the second work.

plag
54c

Exercise 54.1   Recognizing plagiarism

The following numbered items show various attempts to quote or paraphrase the passage below. Carefully compare each attempt with the original passage. Which attempts are plagiarized, inaccurate, or both, and which are acceptable? Why?

I would agree with the sociologists that psychiatric labeling is dangerous. Society can inflict terrible wounds by discrimination, and by confusing health with disease and disease with badness.
—George E. Vaillant, Adaptation to Life, p. 361

1. According to George Vaillant, society often inflicts wounds by using psychiatric labeling, confusing health, disease, and badness (361).
2. According to George Vaillant, "psychiatric labeling [such as 'homosexual' or 'schizophrenic'] is dangerous. Society can inflict terrible wounds by . . . confusing health with disease and disease with badness" (361).
3. According to George Vaillant, when psychiatric labeling discriminates between health and disease or between disease and badness, it can inflict wounds on those labeled (361).
4. Psychiatric labels can badly hurt those labeled, says George Vaillant, because they fail to distinguish among health, illness, and immorality (361).
5. Labels such as "homosexual" and "schizophrenic" can be hurtful when they fail to distinguish among health, illness, and immorality.
6. "I would agree with the sociologists that society can inflict terrible wounds by discrimination, and by confusing health with disease and disease with badness" (Vaillant 361).

54d   Obtain permission when publishing your work.

When you use material from print or online sources in a project that will be published, you must not only acknowledge your sources but also take care to observe copyright restrictions.

Publication means that your work will circulate outside the limited circle of a class or other group. It may appear in print media, such as magazines and newspapers, or it may appear on the Web, which is a publication medium as well. (The exception is a password-protected Web site, such as a course site, which many copyright holders regard as private.)

When you publish your work, borrowing certain kinds or amounts of material requires you to obtain the permission of the copyright holders. You can find information about copyright holders and permissions on the copyright page of a print publication (following the title page) and on a page labeled something like "Terms of Use" on a Web site. If you don't see an explicit release for student use or publication on private Web sites, assume that you must seek permission.

The legal convention of **fair use** allows an author to use a small portion of copyrighted material without obtaining the copyright holder's permission, as long as the author acknowledges the source. The standards of fair use are not fixed, so the following guidelines are conservative:

- **Text from print sources:** Quote without permission fewer than fifty words from an article or fewer than three hundred words from a book. You'll need permission to use any longer quotation from an article or a book or any quotation at all from a play, poem, or song.

- **Text from online sources:** Quote without permission text that represents just a small portion of the whole—say, up to forty words out of three hundred. As with print texts, seek permission for any use of a play, poem, or song that you find online.

- **Visuals, audio, and video:** Seek permission to use any copyrighted media from either print or online sources: photographs, charts, maps, cartoons, paintings, audio files, video files, and so on.

Note   Much valuable material is not copyrighted and can be used without permission, although *you must still cite the source*. Uncopyrighted sources fall into two groups:

- **The creator does not claim copyright.** This category includes most government documents and material labeled for reuse, such as some of the media on *Google, Flikr Creative Commons,* and *Wikimedia Commons.*

- **The copyright has lapsed.** Material in the public domain includes most works by authors who have been dead at least fifty years.

54e   Document sources carefully.

Every time you borrow the words, facts, or ideas of others, you must **document** the source—that is, supply a reference (or document) telling readers that you borrowed the material and where you borrowed it from.

Editors and teachers in most academic disciplines require special documentation formats (or styles) in their scholarly journals and in students' papers. All the styles share two common features:

plag
54e

- **Citations in the text signal that material is borrowed and refer readers to detailed information about the sources.** The following text citation, in MLA style, gives the source author's last name and the page number in the source. Other styles add a publication date. Some styles use raised numerals to refer to numbered source information.

  Veterans are more likely to complete college degrees if they have not only professional support but also a community of peers (Dao A16).

- **Detailed source information, either in footnotes or at the end of the paper, tells how to locate sources.** The following source listing, also in MLA style, provides detailed publication information for the source summarized above. Most styles provide the same information, but they may organize and punctuate it differently.

  Dao, James. "Getting Them Through: Helping Veterans Graduate." *The New York Times*, 5 Feb. 2013, pp. A16+.

1 ▪ Discipline styles for documentation

Aside from the similarities of citations in the text and detailed source information, the disciplines' documentation styles vary markedly in citation form, arrangement of source information, and other particulars. Each discipline's style reflects the needs of its practitioners for certain kinds of information presented in specific ways. For instance, the currency of a source is important in the social sciences, where studies build on and correct each other; thus in-text citations in the social sciences include a source's date of publication. In the humanities, however, currency is less important, so in-text citations do not include date of publication.

The disciplines' documentation formats are described in style guides, including those in the box on the next page. This book presents the styles of the *MLA Handbook* and the *Publication Manual of the American Psychological Association*. In addition, you can find information about *The Chicago Manual of Style* (for the humanities) and *Scientific Style and Format: The CSE Manual for Authors, Editors, and Publishers* (for the natural sciences) at *mywritinglab.com*.

Style guides for documenting sources

Humanities
The Chicago Manual of Style. 16th ed. 2010.
A Manual for Writers of Research Papers, Theses, and Dissertations, by Kate L. Turabian, 8th ed., rev. Wayne C. Booth, Gregory G. Colomb, Joseph M. Williams, and the University of Chicago Press Editorial Staff. 2013.
MLA Handbook. 8th ed. 2016. (See pp. 419–66.)

Social sciences
American Anthropological Association. *AAA Style Guide.* 2009. *www.aaanet.org/publications/style_guide.pdf*
American Political Science Association. *Style Manual for Political Science.* 2006. *www.apsanet.org/media/PDFs/Publications/APSAStyleManual2006.pdf*
Publication Manual of the American Psychological Association. 6th ed. 2010. (See pp. 477–500.)
American Sociological Association. *ASA Style Guide.* 5th ed. 2014.
Linguistic Society of America. "LSA Style Sheet." Published every December in *LSA Bulletin*.
A Uniform System of Citation (law). 20th ed. 2015.

Sciences and mathematics
American Chemical Society. *ACS Style Guide: A Manual for Authors and Editors.* 3rd ed. 2006.
American Medical Association Manual of Style. 10th ed. 2007.
Council of Science Editors. *Scientific Style and Format: The CSE Manual for Authors, Editors, and Publishers.* 8th ed. 2014.

Always ask your instructor which documentation style you should use. If your instructor does not require a particular style, use the one in this book that's appropriate for the discipline you're writing in. Be sure to follow a single system for citing sources so that you provide all the necessary information in a consistent format.

2 ▪ Bibliography software

Bibliography software can help you format your source citations in the style of your choice, and some programs can help you keep track of sources as you research. Your library may offer one or more bibliography programs, such as *RefWorks* or *Endnote,* or you can find free options on the Web, such as *Zotero, Bibme,* and *EasyBib.*

The programs vary in what they can do. Some simply prompt you for needed information (author's name, book title, and so on) and then format the information into a bibliography following the format of your documentation style. Others go beyond formatting to help you organize your sources, export citations from databases, and insert in-text citations as you write.

As helpful as bibliography programs can be, they don't always work the way they're advertised, and they can't substitute for your own care and attention in giving your sources accurate and complete acknowledgment. Always ask your instructors if you may use such software for your papers, and always review the citations compiled by any software to ensure that they meet your instructors' requirements.

55 Writing the Paper

In *Brief*

- Focus your material with a thesis statement (below).
- Organize your material (next page).
- Write a first draft, including source citations (next page).
- Revise and edit the draft (pp. 417, 418).
- Use an appropriate document format (p. 418).

Visit MyWritingLab™ for more resources on writing the paper.

Like other kinds of writing, research writing involves focusing on a main idea, organizing ideas, expressing ideas in a draft, revising and editing drafts, and formatting the final paper. Because research writing draws on others' work, however, its stages also require attention to interpreting, integrating, and citing sources.

This chapter complements and extends the detailed discussion of the writing situation and the writing process in Chapters 1–6. If you haven't already done so, read those chapters before this one.

55a Focus and organize the paper.

Before you begin using your source notes in a draft, give some thought to your main idea and your organization.

1 ▪ Thesis statement

You began research with a question about your subject (see pp. 352–53). Though your question may have evolved during research, you should be able to answer it once you've consulted most of your sources. Try to state that answer in a **thesis statement,** a claim that narrows your subject to a single assertion. For example, following are the research question and thesis statement of Justin Malik, whose final paper appears on pages 468–76:

Research question
How can green consumerism help the environment?

Thesis statement
Although green consumerism can help the environment, consumerism itself is the root of some of the most pressing ecological problems. To make a real difference, humans must consume less.

(Malik's thesis statement consists of two sentences, the first setting up the second. Many instructors allow statements of two or more sentences as long as they build a single idea and the final sentence presents the key assertion of the paper. However, other instructors require thesis statements of a single sentence. Ask your instructor for his or her preference.)

A precise and focused thesis statement will guide you as you organize and draft your paper. For more on thesis statements, see pages 16–19.

2 ▪ Organization

To structure your paper, you'll need to synthesize, or forge relationships among ideas (see pp. 389–91). Here is one approach:

- **Arrange source information in categories.** Each category should correspond to a main section of your paper: a key idea of your own that supports the thesis. Within each category, you may have source views that differ from your own and that you intend to discuss or refute.

- **Review your research journal** for connections between sources and other thoughts that can help you organize your paper.

- **Look objectively at your categories.** If some are skimpy, with little information, consider whether you should drop the categories or conduct more research to fill them out. If most of your information falls into one or two categories, consider whether they are too broad and should be divided. (If any of this rethinking affects your thesis statement, revise it accordingly.)

- **Within each group, distinguish between the main idea and the supporting ideas and evidence.** Only the support should come from your sources. The main idea should be your own.

See pages 20–24 for more on organizing a paper, including samples of both informal and formal outlines.

55b   Draft, revise, edit, and format the paper.

1 ▪ First draft

In drafting your paper, you do not have to proceed methodically from introduction to conclusion. Instead, draft in sections, beginning with the one you feel most confident about. Each section should center on a principal idea contributing to your thesis, a conclusion you have drawn from reading and responding to sources. Start the section by stating the idea; then support it with information, summaries, paraphrases, and quotations from your notes. Remember to insert source information from your notes as well.

- **Weave the sections together with transitions and other signposts.** As the sections of your paper develop, you will see relationships emerging among them. Spell these relationships out, and highlight them with transitions (see pp. 43 and 48–50). Headings may be appropriate to highlight your organization and signal direction. These signposts will help your readers perceive a coherent whole.

55b

- **Track source citations.** As you draft your paper, insert the source of each summary, paraphrase, and quotation in parentheses in the text—for instance, "(Frankel 42)," referring to page 42 in a work by Frankel. If you are conscientious about inserting these notes and carrying them through successive drafts, you will be less likely to plagiarize carelessly and you will have little difficulty documenting your sources in the final paper.

2 ▪ Revision

Always revise your draft first, satisfying yourself with the content and shape of the whole before trying to edit sentences or refine word choices. Begin with the advice on pages 29–34, and supplement it with the following checklist.

Checklist for revising a research paper

Assignment

How does the draft satisfy all of the criteria stated in your instructor's assignment?

Thesis statement

How well does your thesis statement describe your subject and your perspective as they emerged during drafting?

Structure

(Outlining your draft can help you see structure at a glance. See p. 30.)

How consistently does borrowed material illuminate and support—not lead and dominate—your own ideas? How well is the importance of ideas reflected in the emphasis they receive? Will the arrangement of ideas be clear to readers?

(continued)

Checklist for revising a research paper
(continued)

Evidence
Where might supporting evidence seem weak or irrelevant to readers?

Reasonableness and clarity
How reasonable will readers find your argument? (See pp. 106–14.)

Where do you need to define terms or concepts that readers may not know or may dispute?

55b

Source citations
Have you provided an in-text citation for every use of someone else's material and provided a complete list of all your sources?

---

3 ▪ Editing

For editing, consult the advice and checklist on pages 36–39. Try to read your work from the point of view of someone who has not spent hours planning and researching but instead has come fresh to the paper. Look for lapses in sense, awkward passages, wordiness, poor transitions between ideas and evidence, unnecessary repetition, wrong or misspelled words, and errors in grammar, punctuation, or mechanics—in short, anything that is likely to interfere with a reader's understanding of your meaning.

4 ▪ Format

The final draft of your paper should conform to the document format recommended by your instructor or by the style guide of the discipline in which you are writing (see p. 414). This book details two common formats: Modern Language Association (pp. 464–66) and American Psychological Association (pp. 497–500).

In any discipline you can present your ideas effectively and attractively with readable type fonts, headings, illustrations, and other elements. See pages 61–70 for ideas.

56 MLA Documentation and Format

In *Brief*

- In your text, document your sources with citations (below).
- Place text citations so that they are clear and unobtrusive (p. 426).
- Use supplemental notes as needed (p. 428).
- Prepare an MLA list of works cited (p. 429). (See the index to models on pp. 434–35.)
- Format your paper, attending to margins, spacing, long quotations, and other elements (p. 464).

Visit MyWritingLab™ for more resources on MLA documentation and format.

English, foreign languages, and some other humanities use the documentation style of the Modern Language Association, described in the *MLA Handbook* (8th ed., 2016).

In MLA style, you twice acknowledge the sources of borrowed material:

- **In your text, a brief citation adjacent to the borrowed material directs readers to a complete list of all the works you cite.** The citation consists of the author's last name and usually the page number in the source where the borrowed material appears. If the author's name is not mentioned in your sentence, it appears in parentheses with the page number:

In-text citation

Among African cities, says one observer, in Johannesburg "a spirit of optimism glows" (Gaddis 155).

- **At the end of your paper, the list of works cited includes complete bibliographical information for every source.**

Works-cited entry

Gaddis, Anicee. "Johannesburg." *Transculturalism: How the World Is Coming Together*, edited by Claude Grunitzky, True Agency, 2008, pp. 154-57.

56a Use MLA style for in-text citations.

1 ▪ Formats for in-text citations

In-text citations of sources must include just enough information for the reader to locate both of the following:

- The *source* in your list of works cited.
- The *place* in the source where the borrowed material appears.

For any kind of source, you can usually meet both these requirements by providing the author's last name and (if the source uses
them) the page numbers where the material appears. The reader can
find the source in your list of works cited and find the borrowed material in the source itself.

The following box is a guide to all the models of in-text citations.

MLA in-text citations

1. Author not named in your text 420
2. Author named in your text 421
3. Work with two authors 421
4. Work with more than two authors 421
5. Work by an author of two or more cited works 421
6. Anonymous work 422
7. Work with a corporate author 422
8. Electronic or other nonprint source 422
   a. Work with a named author and stable page numbers 422
   b. Work with a named author and no page numbers 422
   c. Work with a named author on an e-reader or other device 423
   d. Work with a named author and numbered paragraphs or sections 423
   e. Work with no named author 423
   f. Audio or video 423
9. One-page work or entire work 424
10. Work with no page or other reference numbers 424
11. Multivolume work 424
12. Source referred to by another source (indirect source) 424
13. Literary work 425
14. The Bible 425
15. Two or more works in the same citation 425

Note Models 1 and 2 show the direct relationship between what
you include in your text and what you include in a parenthetical
citation. If you do *not* name the author in your text, you include the
name in parentheses before the page reference (model 1). If you *do*
name the author in your text, you do not include the name in parentheses (model 2).

1. Author not named in your text

When you have not already named the author in your sentence,
provide the author's last name and the page number(s), with no punctuation between them, in parentheses.

> One researcher concludes that "women impose a distinctive construction on
> moral problems, seeing moral dilemmas in terms of conflicting responsibilities"
> (Gilligan 105-06).

See models 6 and 8–10 for the forms to use when the source does not list an author or provide page numbers.

2. Author named in your text

When you have already given the author's name with the material you're citing, do not repeat it in the parenthetical citation. Give just the page number(s).

Carol Gilligan concludes that "women impose a distinctive construction on moral problems, seeing moral dilemmas in terms of conflicting responsibilities" (105-06).

See models 6 and 8–10 for the forms to use when the source does not list an author or provide page numbers.

3. Work with two authors

If the source has two authors, give both of their last names in the text or in the citation. Separate the names with and:

As Frieden and Sagalyn observe, "The poor and the minorities were the leading victims of highway and renewal programs" (29).

According to one study, "The poor and the minorities were the leading victims of highway and renewal programs" (Frieden and Sagalyn 29).

4. Work with more than two authors

If the source has more than two authors, give only the first author's name followed by et al. (the abbreviation for the Latin *et alii*, "and others").

Increased competition means that employees of public relations firms may find their loyalty stretched in more than one direction (Wilcox et al. 417).

5. Work by an author of two or more cited works

If your list of works cited includes two or more works by the same author, then your citation must tell the reader which of the author's works you are referring to. Give the title either in the text or in a parenthetical citation. In a parenthetical citation, omit any *A*, *An*, or *The* and shorten the title if it is longer than a noun preceded by its modifiers, if any. For instance, *Time's Arrow, Time's Cycle* shortens to *Time's Arrow*. In the following example, *Arts* is short for Gardner's full title, *The Arts and Human Development*.

At about age seven, children begin to use appropriate gestures with their stories (Gardner, *Arts* 144-45).

If the title does not start with a noun or a noun preceded by modifiers, shorten the title to the first word (again excluding *A*, *An*, or *The*): for instance, shorten *As the Eye Moves* to *As*.

6. Anonymous work

For a work with no named author or editor (whether an individual or an organization), use a full or shortened version of the title, as explained with the previous model. In your list of works cited, you alphabetize an anonymous work by the first word of the title excluding *A*, *An*, or *The* (see p. 437), and the first word of a shortened title will be the same. The following citations refer to an unsigned source titled "The Right to Die." The title appears in quotation marks because the source is a periodical article.

> One article notes that a death-row inmate may demand his own execution to achieve a fleeting notoriety ("Right" 16).

> "The Right to Die" notes that a death-row inmate may demand execution to achieve a fleeting notoriety (16).

If two or more anonymous works have the same title, distinguish them with additional information in the text citation, such as the publication date.

7. Work with a corporate author

Some works list as author a government body, association, committee, company, or other group. Cite such a work by the organization's name except when it and the publisher are the same. When the organization and publisher have the same name, omit the author and cite the work by the title (see model 6 above).

If the organization's name is long, work it into the text to avoid an intrusive parenthetical citation:

> A 2014 report by the Nevada Department of Education provides evidence of an increase in graduation rates (12).

8. Electronic or other nonprint source

Electronic or other nonprint sources vary widely, including articles in databases, e-books, Web pages, *Facebook* posts, films or videos, and tweets. If possible, cite such a source as you would any other source, giving author and page number; but often these elements and others are lacking. The following models give a range of possibilities.

a. Work with a named author and stable page numbers

> Brannon observes that students respond readily to some poets (53).

If the work you cite has stable page numbers, like those in a PDF file, give them in your citation.

b. Work with a named author and no page numbers

> Smith reports that almost 20% of commercial banks are audited each year.

When you cite a passage from a work with no page or other reference numbers, such as a Web source or an article in HTML format, try to give the author's name in your text. You will not need a parenthetical citation then, but you must list the source in your works cited.

If the author's name does not appear in your text, give it in a parenthetical citation:

> Clean cars are defined as vehicles with low pollution emissions and high fuel economy (Hagedorn).

c. Work with a named author on an e-reader or other device

> Writing about post-Saddam Iraq, the journalist George Packer describes the tense relationship that existed between Kurdistan and the rest of the country (ch. 1).

Page numbers are not always the same on Kindles, iPads, and other e-readers and tablets. For a book you read on such a device, give the chapter number, not the device's page numbers.

d. Work with a named author and numbered paragraphs or sections

> Twins reared apart report similar feelings (Palfrey, pars. 6-7).

If the work gives numbered paragraphs or sections, use the abbreviation par., pars., sec., or secs. to tell readers that you are citing one or more paragraphs or sections rather than page numbers.

e. Work with no named author

> Many decades after its release, *Citizen Kane* is still remarkable for its rich black-and-white photography.

When your works-cited entry lists the work under its title, cite the work by title in your text, as explained in model 6. This example, a film, gives the title in the text, so it omits a parenthetical citation (see model 9).

f. Audio or video

> In an episode of *Master of None*, the characters recognize how little they know about the lives of their fathers in their native countries of India and China ("Parents" 14:02-27).

You may view or listen to a video or audio source on a device that displays the time span of the recording you are citing. Give the start and stop times of your source in hours (if any), minutes, and seconds, separated by colons. The numbers above cite 14 minutes, 2 to 27 seconds.

9. One-page work or entire work

When you cite a work that's a single page long or cite an entire work—for instance, a one-page article, a tweet, a Web site, a book, or a film—you may omit any page or other reference number. If the work you cite has an author, try to give the name in the text. If the work does not have an author, give the title.

> Boyd deals with the need to acknowledge and come to terms with our fear of nuclear technology.

10. Work with no page or other reference numbers

When the work you cite, print or nonprint, has no page or other reference numbers, give the author's name, if available, in your text or in a parenthetical citation. (If no author is listed, give the title.)

> In the children's classic picture book *The Very Busy Spider,* hard work and patience are rewarded when the spider catches a fly in her web (Carle).

11. Multivolume work

If you consulted only one volume of a multivolume work, your list of works cited will say so (see model 20 on p. 448), and you can treat the volume as you would any book.

If you consulted more than one volume of a multivolume work, give the appropriate volume before the page number (here volume 5):

> After issuing the Emancipation Proclamation, Lincoln said, "What I did, I did after very full deliberations, and under a very heavy and solemn sense of responsibility" (5: 438).

The number 5 indicates the volume from which the quotation was taken; the number 438 indicates the page number in that volume. When the author's name appears in such a citation, place it before the volume number with no punctuation: (Lincoln 5: 438).

If you are referring generally to an entire volume of a multivolume work and are not citing specific page numbers, add the abbreviation vol. before the volume number, as in (vol. 5) or (Lincoln, vol. 5) (note the comma after the author's name). Then readers will not misinterpret the volume number as a page number.

12. Source referred to by another source (indirect source)

When you want to use a quotation that is already in quotation marks—indicating that the author you are reading is quoting someone else—try to find the original source and quote directly from it. If you can't find the original source, then your citation must indicate that your quotation of it is indirect. In the following citation, qtd. in ("quoted in") says that Davino was quoted by Boyd.

MLA
56a

George Davino maintains that "even small children have vivid ideas about nuclear energy" (qtd. in Boyd 22).

The list of works cited then includes only Boyd (the work consulted), not Davino.

13. Literary work

Novels, plays, and poems are often available in many editions, so your instructor may ask you to provide information that will help readers find the passage you cite no matter what edition they consult.

a. Novel

Toward the end of James's novel, Maggie suddenly feels "the thick breath of the definite—which was the intimate, the immediate, the familiar, as she hadn't had them for so long" (535; pt. 6, ch. 41).

Give the page number first, followed by a semicolon and then information on the appropriate part or chapter of the work.

b. Poem not divided into parts

In Shakespeare's Sonnet 73 the speaker identifies with the trees of late autumn, "Bare ruined choirs, where late the sweet birds sang" (line 4). "In me," Shakespeare writes, "thou seest the glowing of such fire / That on the ashes of his youth doth lie . . ." (9-10).

You may omit the page number and supply the line number(s) for the quotation. To prevent confusion with page numbers, precede the numbers with line or lines in the first citation; then use just the numbers. (See pp. 125–27 for a sample paper on a poem.)

c. Verse play or poem divided into parts

Later in Shakespeare's *King Lear* the disguised Edgar says, "The prince of darkness is a gentleman" (3.4.147).

Omit a page number and cite the appropriate part—act (and scene, if any), canto, book, and so on—plus the line number(s). Use Arabic numerals for parts, including acts and scenes (3.4), unless your instructor specifies Roman numerals (III.iv).

d. Prose play

In Miller's *Death of a Salesman,* Willie Loman's wife, Linda, acknowledges her husband's failings but also the need for him to be treated with dignity: "He's not the finest character that ever lived. But he's a human being, and a terrible thing is happening to him" (56; act 1).

Provide the page number followed by the act and scene, if any.

14. The Bible

When you cite passages of the Bible in parentheses, abbreviate the title of any book longer than four letters—for instance, Gen. (Genesis), 1 Sam. (1 Samuel), Ps. (Psalms), Prov. (Proverbs), Matt. (Matthew), Rom. (Romans), 2 Cor. (2 Corinthians). Then give the chapter and verse(s) in Arabic numerals.

> According to the Bible, at Babel God "did . . . confound the language of all the earth" (Gen. 11.9).

15. Two or more works in the same citation

When you refer to more than one work in a single parenthetical citation, separate the references with a semicolon.

> Two recent articles point out that a computer badly used can be less efficient than no computer at all (Gough and Hall 201; Richards 162).

Since long citations in the text can distract the reader, you may choose to cite several or more works in an endnote or footnote rather than in the text. See page 428.

2 ▪ Placement and punctuation of in-text citations

The following guidelines will help you place and punctuate text citations to distinguish between your own and your sources' ideas and to make your own text readable. See also pages 400–03 on editing quotations and using signal phrases to integrate source material into your sentences.

Where to place citations

Position text citations to accomplish two goals:

- **Make it clear exactly where your borrowing begins and ends.**
- **Keep the citation as unobtrusive as possible.**

You can accomplish both goals by placing the parenthetical citation at the end of the sentence element containing the borrowed material. This sentence element may be a phrase or a clause, and it may begin, interrupt, or conclude the sentence. Usually, as in the following examples, the element ends with a punctuation mark.

> The inflation rate might climb as high as 30 percent (Kim 164), an increase that could threaten the small nation's stability.

> The inflation rate, which might climb as high as 30 percent (Kim 164), could threaten the small nation's stability.

> The small nation's stability could be threatened by its inflation rate, which, one source predicts, might climb as high as 30 percent (Kim 164).

In the last example the addition of one source predicts clarifies that Kim is responsible only for the inflation-rate prediction, not for the statement about stability.

When your paraphrase or summary of a source runs longer than a sentence, clarify the boundaries by using the author's name in the first sentence and placing the parenthetical citation at the end of the last sentence.

> Juliette Kim studied the effects of acutely high inflation in several South American and African countries since World War II. She discovered that a major change in government accompanied or followed the inflationary period in 56% of cases (22-23).

When you cite two or more sources in the same paragraph, position authors' names and parenthetical citations so that readers can see who said what. In the following example, the beginnings and ends of sentences clearly mark the different sources.

> Schools use computers extensively for drill-and-practice exercises, in which students repeat specific skills such as spelling words, using the multiplication facts, or, at a higher level, doing chemistry problems. But many education experts criticize such exercises for boring students and failing to engage their critical thinking and creativity. Jane M. Healy, a noted educational psychologist and teacher, takes issue with "interactive" software for children as well as drill-and-practice software, arguing that "some of the most popular 'educational' software . . . may be damaging to independent thinking, attention, and motivation" (20). Another education expert, Harold Wenglinsky of the Educational Testing Service, found in a well-regarded study that fourth and eighth graders who used computers frequently, including for drill and practice, actually did worse on tests than their peers who used computers less often (*Does* 21). In a later article, Wenglinsky concludes that "the quantity of use matters far less than the quality of use." In schools, he says, high-quality computer work, involving critical thinking, is still rare ("In" 17).

How to punctuate citations

Generally place a parenthetical citation *before* any punctuation required by your sentence. If the borrowed material is a quotation, place the citation *between* the closing quotation mark and the punctuation:

> Spelling argues that during the 1970s American automobile manufacturers met consumer needs "as well as could be expected" (26), but not everyone agrees with him.

The exception is a quotation ending in a question mark or exclamation point. Then use the appropriate punctuation inside the closing quotation mark, and follow the quotation with the text citation and a period.

> "Of what use is genius," Emerson asks, "if the organ . . . cannot find a focal distance within the actual horizon of human life?" ("Experience" 60). Mad genius is no genius.

When a citation appears at the end of a quotation set off from the text, place it one space *after* the punctuation ending the quotation. Do not use additional punctuation with the citation or quotation marks around the quotation.

> In Charles Dickens's *A Christmas Carol,* Scrooge and the Ghost of Christmas Past visit Scrooge's childhood boarding school. They watch as the schoolmaster offers young Ebenezer and his sister some unappealing food and drink:
>
>> Here he produced a decanter of curiously light wine, and a block of curiously heavy cake, and administered installments of those dainties to the young people: at the same time, sending out a meager servant to offer a glass of the "something" to the postboy, who answered that he thanked the gentleman, but if it was the same tap as he had tasted before, he had rather not. (34)

See the sample research paper starting on page 468 for further examples of placing parenthetical references in relation to summaries, paraphrases, and quotations.

3 ■ Footnotes or endnotes in special circumstances

Occasionally you may want to use footnotes or endnotes in place of parenthetical citations. If you need to refer to several sources at once, listing them in a long parenthetical citation could be intrusive. In that case, signal the citation with a numeral raised above the appropriate line of text and write a note beginning with the same numeral to cite the sources:

> **Text**   At least five studies have confirmed these results.[1]
>
> **Note**   1. Abbott and Winger 266-68; Casner 27; Hoyenga 78-79; Marino 36; Tripp et al. 179-83.

You may also use a footnote or endnote to comment on a source or to provide information that does not fit easily in the text:

> **Text**   So far, no one has confirmed these results.[2]
>
> **Note**   2. Manter tried repeatedly to replicate the experiment, but he was never able to produce the high temperatures (616).

If the note appears as a footnote, use the footnote feature of your word processor to set it at the bottom of the page on which the citation appears. If the note appears as an endnote, place it in numerical order with the other endnotes on a page between the text and the list of works cited. Double-space all footnotes and endnotes.

56b   Prepare an MLA list of works cited.

At the end of your paper, a list titled Works Cited includes all the sources you quoted, paraphrased, or summarized in your paper. (If your instructor asks you to include sources you examined but did not cite, title the list Works Consulted.)

Format of the list of works cited

To format the list of works cited, use the following illustration and guidelines. For an example of a complete list of works cited, see pages 475–76.

Arrangement Arrange sources alphabetically by the author's last name. If there is no author, alphabetize by the first main word of the title (excluding *A*, *An*, or *The*).

Spacing Double-space everything in the list.

Indention Begin each entry at the left margin, and indent the second and subsequent lines one-half inch. Your word processor can create this so-called hanging indent automatically.

MLA
56b

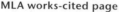

MLA works-cited page

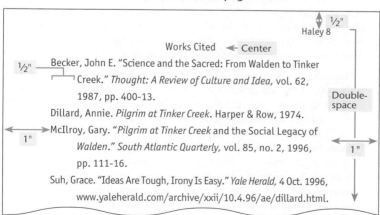

Elements of works-cited entries

The eighth edition of the *MLA Handbook* simplifies writing works-cited entries by building them on the core, visible elements in sources. In the following description and the box on the next page, these core elements are listed in order of their appearance in a works-cited entry. Few sources include all of the listed elements: as you build works-cited entries, give the elements that you find in your sources. For more information from MLA, go to *style.mla.org*.

Author Begin each entry with the author's last name, a comma, and the author's first name and middle name or initial, if any—for instance, Hohulin, John D. End the author's name with a period. See models 1–6 for how to cite various numbers and kinds of authors.

Title of source After the author, give the full title and any subtitle of the source, separating them with a colon. End the title with a period.

- **Quotation marks for shorter works:** Use quotation marks around titles of works that are part of larger works, such as articles, pages on Web sites, and selections from anthologies: "A Rose for Emily." (See pp. 317–18 for titles to enclose in quotation marks.)

- **Italics for longer works:** Use italics for the titles of longer, independent works such as books and films: Do the Right Thing. Containers (next item) also have italic titles. (See p. 340 for titles to italicize.)

- **Descriptions for untitled works:** For works that do not have titles, such as interviews, give a description of the work after the name of the author. (See models 32, 34, 47, and 50 for examples of descriptions of untitled works.)

Title of container Many sources used in research are shorter works, such as articles and Web pages, that are published in larger works, such as journals and Web sites. In MLA style, the larger publication is called the **container**. In your works-cited entry, give the title of the container in italics, followed by a comma.

- **Container 1:** Some works fall in one container. For example, if you are citing an article on a Web site, the container is the Web site (see model 34). If you are citing a short story or a chapter from a print anthology, the container is the anthology (see models 27 and 28).

- **Container 2:** Many sources have more than one container—in essence, the source is inside container 1, which is inside container 2. For example, if you are citing an article from a scholarly journal that you found in a database, container 1 is the journal and container 2 is the database (see pp. 438–39). If your source is an episode of a television series that you watched on *Netflix*,

Building MLA works-cited entries

Following are the core elements and their order in works-cited entries. Most sources will not contain every element. The colors correspond to the highlight colors in the models on pages 433–63.

Author's last name, First name.
"Title of Shorter Work." or *Title of Longer Work.*

Container 1
Give these elements in this order if they are available. Skip "Title of Container" for self-contained works.

Title of Container 1,
Other contributors,
Version,
Number,
Publisher,
Publication date,
Location.

Container 2
Give these elements in this order if they are available.

Title of Container 2,
Other contributors,
Version,
Number,
Publisher,
Publication date,
Location.

container 1 is the television series and container 2 is *Netflix* (see model 48b).

- **Self-contained works:** Note that some sources are self-contained. These include books such as novels, manuals, works of nonfiction, and the like.

The models on the following pages give examples of many short works in containers such as books, journals, databases, and Web sites, as well as longer, self-contained works such as books, films, Web sites, music albums, and so on.

Other contributors Some sources and some containers, such as anthologies and edited collections, may include the work of people besides the author. If a person's contribution to a work is important to your research, add the contributor's name to your works-cited entry preceded by a description such as adapted by, directed by, edited by, illustrated by, interviewed by, introduction by, narrated by, performance by, or translated by. Follow the name of a contributor with a comma. For examples of works-cited entries showing contributors, see models 16, 17, 19 (books), 48 (television episodes and series), 49 (radio programs), 51 (films and videos), 52 (sound recordings), and 54 (live performances).

Version Books, films, and computer software such as games and apps often appear in updated or revised editions and versions. If your source or its container gives a version or edition, add it to your works-cited entry, followed by a comma—for instance, version 8.1, or 3rd ed., (ed. stands for "edition"). For examples of works-cited entries showing editions and versions, see models 14 (book) and 56 (app).

Number in a sequence Some sources and containers are published in a numbered sequence. Examples include academic journals, which often have volume and issue numbers (models 7 and 8). Some books are published in sets consisting of multiple volumes (model 20). Television series and episodes are typically numbered by season and by episode (model 48). In your works-cited entry, follow a sequence number with a comma—for example, season 1, episode 6, or vol. 32, no. 6, (vol. and no. stand for "volume" and "number," respectively).

Publisher Give the publisher followed by a comma. For instance, the publisher of a book is the company that issued the book (see pp. 444–45), the publisher of a Web site is the organization that sponsors the site (see p. 454), and the publisher of a TV series is generally the main studio that produced the series (see model 48). If the source has more than one publisher, separate the names with a forward slash: Vertigo / DC Comics.

You do not need to list a publisher for some kinds of sources or containers, including periodicals (journals, newspapers, and magazines), databases, self-published works, and Web sites whose titles and publishers are the same.

Publication date Give the date of publication followed by a comma. Publication dates vary considerably depending on the type of source you are citing. To identify and cite the publication date, see the box on pages 434–35 to locate a model that most closely matches your source. Abbreviate all months except May, June, and July. See also model 37 to cite an undated source you find on the Web.

Location Give a location telling where you found the source or its container so that other researchers can find the source, too. Follow the location with a period.

- **Page numbers:** For a source within a container with page numbers, such as a chapter of a book or an article in a periodical, provide the page numbers. Use the abbreviation p. or pp. before the page numbers: p. 72 or pp. 210-13. See pages 438–39 and 442 for examples of page numbers.

- **Digital Object Identifer (DOI):** Many journal articles, books, and other documents have a DOI attached to them, a permanent URL that links to the text and functions as a unique identifier. When a DOI is available, include it at the end of your works-cited entry and follow it with a period: doi:10.1682/JRRD.2010.03.0024. Usually a DOI will follow the title of a container such as a database or a Web site. See pages 438–39 for an example of a DOI.

- **URL:** If a DOI is not available for a source you found in a database or on the Web, copy and paste the URL from your browser into your works-cited entry, deleting "http://"—for instance, harpers. org/archive/2012/10/contest-of-words/. If your source gives a stable URL, such as a *permalink*, give it instead.

- **Name and city:** If you viewed an object in a museum or an archive or attended a performance or lecture, give the name of the institution or venue and the city in which it is located—for instance, DeYoung Museum, San Francisco. For examples, see models 44, 54, and 58.

Models of MLA works-cited entries

Unlike earlier editions of the *MLA Handbook*, which gave numerous examples of works-cited entries organized by the type of source, the eighth edition emphasizes building entries based on the elements described in the preceding section. This chapter blends the two approaches, applying the new guidelines to a wide variety of sources you may encounter during your research. The models here are extensive but not exhaustive, and you will surely come across sources that do not match exactly. For such sources, refer to the list of core elements on page 431 and give whatever information you can find in the source.

The box on the next two pages will help you find appropriate MLA works-cited models for your sources.

1 ▪ Authors

The following models show how to handle authors' names in citing any kind of source.

1. One author

Ehrenreich, Barbara. *Dancing in the Streets: A History of Collective Joy.* Henry
    Holt, 2006.

Give the author's full name—last name first, a comma, first name, and any middle name or initial. Omit any title, such as *Dr.* or *PhD.* End the name with a period. If your source lists an editor as author, see model 15.

Index to models of MLA works-cited entries

MLA

56b

2. Two authors

Lifton, Robert Jay, and Greg Mitchell. *Who Owns Death: Capital Punishment, the American Conscience, and the End of Executions*. William Morrow, 2000.

Give the authors' names in the order provided on the title page. Reverse the first and last names of the first author *only*, not of the other author. Separate the authors' names with a comma and and. If your source lists two editors as authors, see model 15.

3. More than two authors

Wilcox, Dennis L., et al. *Think Public Relations*. 2nd ed., Allyn & Bacon, 2013.

Give the name of the first author only, and follow the name with a comma and the abbreviation et al. (for the Latin *et alii*, meaning "and others"). If your source lists more than two editors as authors, see model 15.

4. The same author(s) for two or more works

Gardner, Howard. *The Arts and Human Development*. John Wiley & Sons, 1973.

---. *Five Minds for the Future*. Harvard Business School P, 2007.

Give the author's name only in the first entry. For the second and any subsequent works by the same author, substitute three hyphens for the author's name, followed by a period. Note that the three hyphens may substitute only for *exactly* the same name or names. If the second Gardner source were by Gardner and somebody else, both names would have to be given in full.

Place an entry or entries using three hyphens immediately after the entry that names the author. Within the set of entries by the same author, arrange the sources alphabetically by the first main word of the title, as in the Gardner examples (*Arts*, then *Five*).

If you cite two or more sources that list as author(s) exactly the same editor(s), follow the hyphens with a comma and editor or editors as appropriate. (See model 15.)

5. A corporate author

Corporate authors include associations, committees, institutions, government bodies, companies, and other groups. When a source gives only the name of the organization as author and not an individual's name, the source has a corporate author.

a. Source cited by author

Vault Technologies. *Turnkey Parking Solutions*. Mills, 2014.

When the corporate author and the publisher are different, start with the name of the author.

b. Source cited by title

"Thailand's Campaign for Tobacco Control." *Center for Global Development*, 2015, millionssaved.cgdev.org/case-studies/thailands-campaign-for-tobacco-control.

When the corporate author and the publisher are the same, omit the author and start with the title. Omit the publisher as well when its name is the Web site title, as in the preceding example. (For examples of government documents cited in this way, see model 33b.)

6. Author not named (anonymous)

The Dorling Kindersley World Atlas. DK Publishing, 2014.

List a work that names no author—neither an individual nor a group—by its full title. If the work is a book, italicize the title. If the work is a periodical article or other short work, enclose the title in quotation marks:

"Case Dismissed." The Economist, 24 Apr. 2015, p. 12.

Alphabetize the work by the title's first main word, excluding *A, An,* or *The* (*Dorling* in the first example and Case in the second).

2 ▪ Articles in journals, newspapers, and magazines

Articles in scholarly journals, in newspapers, and in magazines appear in print periodicals, in online databases available through your library, and on the Web.

Articles in scholarly journals

To cite an article in a scholarly journal, give the author and the title of the article. Enclose the title in quotation marks. Then give information about the container(s), depending on what is available. In container 1, give the title of the journal, any volume and issue numbers, the publication date, and the location of the source, such as page numbers of the article or possibly a URL. Add a container 2 if you reached the source electronically—for instance, through a library database—and give the source's location, such as a Digital Object Identifier (DOI) or a URL.

You do not need to give a publisher for articles in academic journals in print, in online databases such as *EBSCOhost* or *ProQuest,* or on Web sites.

MLA
56b

7. Article in a scholarly journal with volume and issue numbers

a. Print journal article

Mattingly, Carol. "Telling Evidence: Rethinking What Counts in Rhetoric."
Rhetoric Society Quarterly, vol. 32, no. 1, Winter 2002, pp. 99-108.

See the next two pages for an explanation of this format and where to find the required information in a print journal.

b. Database journal article

Neves, Joshua. "Cinematic Encounters in Beijing." Film Quarterly, vol. 67, no. 1,
Fall 2013, pp. 27-40. EBSCOhost, doi:10.1525/FQ.2.13.67.1.27.

(text continues on p. 440)

Citing journal articles: Print and database

Print journal article

First page of article

THE IMPORTANCE OF PRESERVING PAPER-BASED ARTIFACTS IN A
DIGITAL AGE

② **Title of article**

Robert Bee[1] ●—— ① **Author**

The preservation of paper-based ④ **Volume and** ial issue for collection management in academic libraries. I **issue numbers** brary science profession has

③ **Title of con-** ●— *[Library Quarterly,* vol. 78, no. 2, pp. 179–194] ●—— ⑥ **Location**
tainer 1 (journal) © 2008 by The University of Chicago. All rights reserved. **(page numbers)**
                    0024-2519/2008/7802-0002$10.00
⑤ **Publication date**
                              179

MLA
56b

Database journal article

⑦ **Title of container 2 (database)**

Searching: Academic Search Complete │ Choose Databases

Detailed record

② **Title of article**

THE IMPORTANCE OF PRESERVING PAPER-BASED
ARTIFACTS IN A **DIGITAL** AGE.

⑥ **Location
(page numbers)**

① **Author**

Authors: Bee, Robert *Robb37@hotmail.com*

③ **Title of con-**
tainer 1 (journal)   Source: Library Quarterly. Apr2008, Vol. 78 Issue 2, p179-194. 16p.

Docum ⑤ **Publication date**

④ **Volume and
issue numbers**

Subject Terms: *DIGITAL preservation
               *ACADEMIC librarians
               *LIBRARY science
               *MICROFILMS
               *CHANGE

*TEXTBOOKS
*ABSTRACTING
DOI: 10.1086/528888 ●—— ⑧ **Location (DOI)**

Works-cited entry: Print journal article

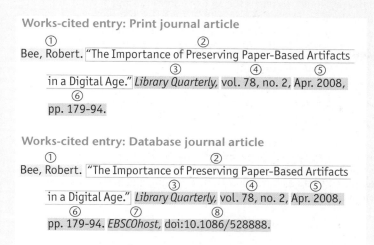

Bee, Robert. "The Importance of Preserving Paper-Based Artifacts in a Digital Age." *Library Quarterly,* vol. 78, no. 2, Apr. 2008, pp. 179-94.

Works-cited entry: Database journal article

Bee, Robert. "The Importance of Preserving Paper-Based Artifacts in a Digital Age." *Library Quarterly,* vol. 78, no. 2, Apr. 2008, pp. 179-94. *EBSCOhost,* doi:10.1086/528888.

① **Author.** Give the full name—last name first, a comma, first name, and any middle name or initial. Omit *Dr., PhD,* or any other title. End the name with a period.

② **Title of article,** in quotation marks. Give the full title and any subtitle, separating them with a colon. End the title with a period inside the final quotation mark.

③ **Title of container 1 (journal),** in italics. End with a comma.

④ **Volume and issue numbers,** in Arabic numerals, preceded by vol. and no. and followed by commas.

⑤ **Publication date,** preceded by the month or season, if available. Abbreviate all months except May, June, and July. End with a comma.

⑥ **Location (page numbers of the article),** preceded by pp. and ending with a period. Provide only as many digits in the last number as needed for clarity, usually two.

⑦ **Title of container 2 (database),** in italics. End with a comma.

⑧ **Location.** If available, give a Digital Object Identifier (DOI), preceded by doi:. End with a period. If no DOI is available, give the URL without "http://." (For more on DOIs and URLs, see p. 433.)

See p. 440 for how to cite a journal article you find on the open Web.

MLA

56b

(continued from p. 437)
See the previous two pages for an explanation of this format and where to find the required information in a database. Basically, start with the information for a print article (previous model), and add the information for container 2—the title of the database and the DOI or URL.

c. Web journal article

Aulisio, George J. "Green Libraries Are More Than Just Buildings." *Electronic Green Journal,* vol. 35, no. 1, 2013, escholarship.org/uc/ item/3x11862z#page-1.

For a scholarly article you find in a Web journal, begin with the author and title. Then give available information about the container: the title of the journal, the volume and issue numbers, the publication date, and a URL, as here, or a DOI. If the journal article does not have page numbers, omit them from the works-cited entry.

8. Article in a journal with only issue numbers

Dobozy, Tomas. "The Writing of Trespass." *Canadian Literature,* no. 218, Autumn 2013, pp. 11-28. *EBSCOhost,* web.a.ebscohost.com/ehost/detail/ AN=94425037&db=aph.

MLA
56b

If a scholarly journal numbers only issues, not volumes, give the issue alone after the journal title.

Articles in newspapers

To cite an article in a newspaper, give the author and the title of the article. Enclose the title in quotation marks. Then give information about the container(s), depending on what is available. In container 1, give the title of the newspaper, the publication date, and the location of the article (generally page numbers or a URL). Add information for a container 2 if you used another source, such as a library database, to reach the article.

You do not need to give a publisher for newspaper articles that appear in print, in online databases such *LexisNexis,* or on Web sites.

9. Article in a national newspaper

a. Print newspaper article

Lowery, Annie. "Cities Advancing Inequality Fight." *The New York Times,* 7 Apr. 2014, pp. A1+.

If the newspaper is divided into lettered sections, provide the section designation before the page number when the newspaper does the same: A1+ above. The plus sign indicates that the article continues on a later page.

b. Database newspaper article

Stein, Rob. "Obesity May Stall Trend of Increasing Longevity." *The Washington Post,* 15 Mar. 2015, p. A2. *LexisNexis Academic,* www.lexisnexis.com/ lnacademic/HEADLINE(Obesity+may+stall%2C+trend+of+increasing%2C+ longevity)%2BDATE%2B2015.

See the next page for an explanation of this format and where to find the required information in a database. Basically, start with the information for a print article (previous model), and add the information for container 2—the title of the database and the URL or DOI.

c. Web news article

Jarvie, Jenny. "What Life Is Like on $7.25 Per Hour." *Los Angeles Times,* 6 Apr. 2016, www.latimes.com/nation/la-na-minimum-wage-life-20160405-story.html.

To cite a newspaper article that you find on the open Web, follow the author and title with the information for the container: the title of the newspaper, the publication date (day, month, year), and the URL. To cite a reader's comment on an article, see model 40.

10. Article in a local newspaper

Beckett, Lois. "The Ignored PTSD Crisis: Americans Wounded in Their Own Neighborhoods." *The Louisiana Weekly* [New Orleans], 17 Feb. 2014, pp. 12-13.

If the city of publication does not appear in the title of a local newspaper, follow the title with the city name in brackets, not italicized.

Articles in magazines

To cite an article in a magazine, give the author and the title of the article. Enclose the title in quotation marks. Then give information about the container(s), depending on what is available. For container 1, give the title of the magazine, the publication date, and the location of the article (page numbers, a URL, or a DOI). Add information for a container 2 if you used another source, such as a library database, to reach the article.

You do not need to give a publisher for magazine articles that appear in print, in online databases such *EBSCOhost,* or on Web sites.

11. Article in a weekly or biweekly magazine

a. Print magazine article

Toobin, Jeffrey. "Justice Delayed." *The New Yorker,* 22 Aug. 2016, pp. 38-47.

Following the author and title, give information for the container: the title of the magazine, the publication date (day, month, year), and the page numbers.

Citing a newspaper article: Database

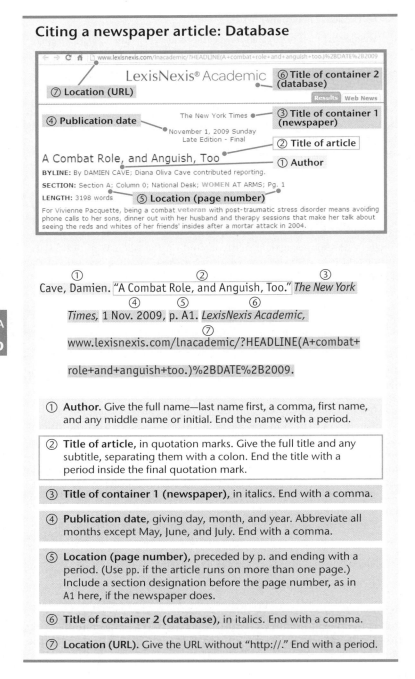

① **Author.** Give the full name—last name first, a comma, first name, and any middle name or initial. End the name with a period.

② **Title of article,** in quotation marks. Give the full title and any subtitle, separating them with a colon. End the title with a period inside the final quotation mark.

③ **Title of container 1 (newspaper),** in italics. End with a comma.

④ **Publication date,** giving day, month, and year. Abbreviate all months except May, June, and July. End with a comma.

⑤ **Location (page number),** preceded by p. and ending with a period. (Use pp. if the article runs on more than one page.) Include a section designation before the page number, as in A1 here, if the newspaper does.

⑥ **Title of container 2 (database),** in italics. End with a comma.

⑦ **Location (URL).** Give the URL without "http://." End with a period.

b. Database magazine article

Barras, Colin. "Right on Target." *New Scientist*, 25 Jan. 2014, pp. 40-43.
EBSCOhost, web.a.ebscohost.com/ehost/detail/AN=93983067&db=aph.

To cite a magazine article you found in an online database, start with the information for a print article (model a on p. 441). Then add the information for the second container—the title of the database and the DOI or URL.

c. Web magazine article

Stampler, Laura. "These Cities Have the Most Open-Minded Daters." *Time*, 14 Apr.
2014, time.com/61947/these-cities-have-the-most-open-minded-daters/.

To cite a magazine article you find on the open Web, follow the author and title with information for the container: the title of the magazine, the publication date (day, month, year), and the URL. To cite a reader's comment on an article, see model 40.

12. Article in a monthly or bimonthly magazine

Wong, Kate. "Secrets of Neanderthal Cognition Revealed." *Scientific American*,
Apr. 2015, pp. 46-51.

Follow the magazine title with the month and the year of publication. If the date on the magazine spans two months, give both months: Jan.-Feb. 2016.

3 ■ Books and government publications

Complete books

A complete, stand-alone book is self-contained, so the title of a book is followed by the names of other contributors (if any) and publication information. A book in a library database or on the Web requires information for the container: the name of the database or Web site and a DOI or URL after the publication information.

13. Basic format for a complete book

To cite a book, give the author, the title, the publisher, and the date. When other information is present, give it between the author's name and the title, between the title and the publication information, or at the end of the entry, as in models 14–23.

a. Print book or book on an e-reader

Shteir, Rachel. *The Steal: A Cultural History of Shoplifting*. The Penguin Press, 2011.

See the next two pages for an explanation of this format and where to find the required information in a print book or an e-book with print publication information.

(text continues on p. 446)

MLA
56b

Citing books: Print and database

Print book

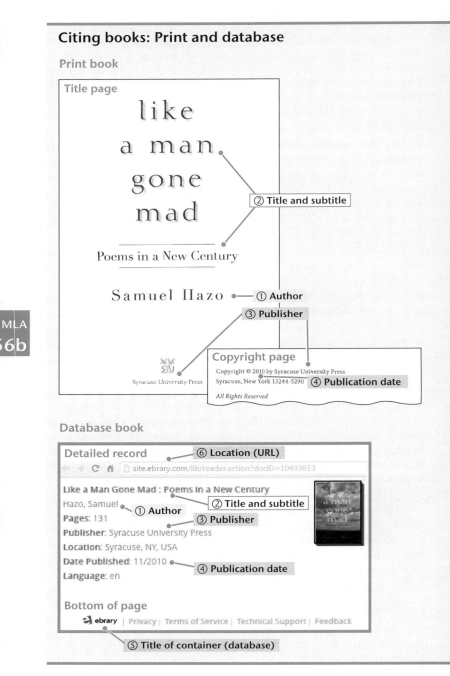

Title page

like
a man.
gone
mad

② Title and subtitle

Poems in a New Century

Samuel Hazo ● ① Author

③ Publisher

SU
Syracuse University Press

Copyright page

Copyright © 2010 by Syracuse University Press
Syracuse, New York 13244-5290   ④ Publication date
All Rights Reserved

Database book

Detailed record ● ⑥ Location (URL)

← → C ⌂ ⌗ site.ebrary.com/lib/reader.action?docID=10493613

Like a Man Gone Mad : Poems in a New Century
Hazo, Samuel ● ① Author   ② Title and subtitle
Pages: 131   ③ Publisher
Publisher: Syracuse University Press
Location: Syracuse, NY, USA
Date Published: 11/2010 ● ④ Publication date
Language: en

Bottom of page

ebrary | Privacy | Terms of Service | Technical Support | Feedback

⑤ Title of container (database)

Works-cited entry: Print book

① ②
Hazo, Samuel. *Like a Man Gone Mad: Poems in a New Century.*
③ ④
Syracuse UP, 2010.

Works-cited entry: Database book

① ②
Hazo, Samuel. *Like a Man Gone Mad: Poems in a New Century.*
③ ④ ⑤ ⑥
Syracuse UP, 2010. *Ebrary,* site.ebrary.com/lib/reader.

action?docID=10493613.

① **Author.** Give the full name—last name first, a comma, first name, and any middle name or initial. Omit *Dr., PhD,* or any other title. End the name with a period.

② **Title,** in italics. Give the full title and any subtitle, separating them with a colon. Capitalize all significant words of the title even if the book does not. End the title with a period.

③ **Publisher.** Give the name as it appears on the title page or copyright page, followed by a comma. Shorten "University Press" to UP and omit "Company," "Co.," and "Inc." from other publishers' names. If two publisher names are listed on the title or copyright page, determine their relationship: If they are both independent entities, list them both with a forward slash between the names (see model 19). If one is a division of the other (for instance, Scribner is a division of Simon & Schuster), cite only the division.

④ **Publication date.** If the date doesn't appear on the title page, look for it on the next page. End with a period.

⑤ **Title of container (database),** in italics. End with a comma.

⑥ **Location (URL).** Give the URL without "http://," ending with a period. If the database record gives a DOI, provide it instead. (For more on DOIs, see p. 443.)

See pp. 446–51 for how to cite other types of books.

MLA
56b

(continued from p. 443)

b. Database book

Levine, Daniel. *Bayard Rustin and the Civil Rights Movement.* Rutgers UP, 2000.
eBook Collection, web.a.ebscohost.com/ehost/ebookviewer/ebook/
e6967d23-394e-41d9-ab54-d292ebd6287b =2.

See the previous pages for an explanation of this format and where to
find the required information in a database. Basically, give any print
publication information before the information about the container—
the name of the database and a DOI or URL.

c. E-book

Booth, Marilyn. *May Her Likes Be Multiplied: Biography and Gender Politics in
Egypt.* Kindle ed., U of California P, 2001.

Give the type of e-book after the title, followed by the publication information. If you do not know the type you consulted, give E-book instead.

d. Web book

Cather, Willa. *One of Ours.* Alfred A. Knopf, 1922. *Bartleby.com,* 2000, www.
bartleby.com/1006/1.html.

MLA
56b

Providing print publication information for a book on the Web is not
required, but it can be helpful to readers. This example gives the original publisher and publication date followed by information for the
container: the title of the Web site and the URL. (The title of the Web
site and the name of the publisher are the same, so only the Web site
is given.)

14. Second or subsequent edition

Bolinger, Dwight L. *Aspects of Language.* 3rd ed., Harcourt Brace Jovanovich,
1981.

Books are often revised and published in new editions. For any edition after the first, place the edition number after the title. Use the
designation given in the source, such as Expanded ed., Updated ed., or 3rd
ed., as in the example.

15. Book with an editor

Holland, Merlin, and Rupert Hart-Davis, editors. *The Complete Letters of Oscar
Wilde.* Henry Holt, 2000.

Handle editors' names like authors' names (models 1–4), but add a
comma and editor or editors after the last editor's name.

16. Book with an author and an editor

Mumford, Lewis. *The City in History.* Edited by Donald L. Miller, Pantheon, 1986.

When citing the work of the author, give the author's name first. After the title, give the editor's name (another contributor) preceded by Edited by.

When citing the work of the editor, use model 15 for a book with an editor, adding By and the author's name after the title:

> Miller, Donald L., editor. *The City in History.* By Lewis Mumford, Mariner Books, 1968.

17. Book with a translator

> Alighieri, Dante. *The Inferno.* Translated by John Ciardi, New American Library, 1971.

When citing the work of an author, shown above, give his or her name first, and give the translator's name (another contributor) after the title, preceded by Translated by.

When citing the work of the translator, give his or her name first, followed by a comma and translator. Follow the title with By and the author's name.

> Ciardi, John, translator. *The Inferno.* By Dante Alighieri, New American Library, 1971.

When a book you cite by the author's name has a translator *and* an editor, give the translator's and the editor's names in the order used on the book's title page.

18. Anthology

> Kennedy, X. J., and Dana Gioia, editors. *Literature: An Introduction to Fiction, Poetry, Drama, and Writing.* 13th ed., Pearson, 2016.

Cite an entire anthology only when citing the work of the editor or editors or when your instructor permits cross-referencing like that shown in model 28. Give the name of the editor or editors (followed by editor or editors) and then the title of the anthology.

19. Illustrated book or graphic narrative

> Wilson, G. Willow. *Cairo.* Illustrated by M. K. Perker, Vertigo / DC Comics, 2005.

When citing the work of the writer of a graphic narrative or illustrated book, follow the example above: the author's name, the title, Illustrated by, and the illustrator's name (another contributor). This book's two publishers, Vertigo and DC Comics, are separated by a forward slash.

When citing the work of an illustrator, list his or her name first, followed by a comma and illustrator. After the title and By, list the author's name.

> Williams, Garth, illustrator. *Charlotte's Web.* By E. B. White, Harper & Brothers, 1952.

20. Multivolume work

> Lincoln, Abraham. *The Collected Works of Abraham Lincoln.* Edited by Roy P.
>
> Basler, vol. 5, Rutgers UP, 1953. 8 vols.

When the work you cite is one volume in a set of numbered volumes, give the volume number before the publication information (vol. 5 in the example). The total number of volumes at the end of the entry is optional (8 vols. in the example).

If you use two or more volumes of a multivolume work, give the work's total number of volumes before the publication information (8 vols. in the following example). Your in-text citation will indicate which volume you are citing (see p. 424).

> Lincoln, Abraham. *The Collected Works of Abraham Lincoln.* Edited by Roy P.
>
> Basler, 8 vols., Rutgers UP, 1953.

21. Book in a series

> Bergman, Ingmar. *The Seventh Seal.* Simon and Schuster, 1960. Modern Film
>
> Scripts Series 12.

When you cite a work in a series, you may give the name of the series, not italicized or in quotation marks, at the end of the entry.

22. Book published before 1900

> James, Henry. *The Bostonians.* London, 1886.

Although the city of publication is not required in most works-cited entries, MLA recommends giving the city rather than the publisher for books published before 1900 because such books are usually associated with the cities in which they were published.

23. Republished book

> Achebe, Chinua. *Things Fall Apart.* 1958. Anchor Books, 1994.

Many books, especially classic literary works, are republished and reissued by publishers. If the original publication date of a book is important to your use of it, give the date after the title. Then provide the publication information for the source you are using.

24. Sacred works

> *The Bible: Authorized King James Version with Apocrypha.* Edited by Robert
>
> Carroll and Stephen Prickett, Oxford UP, 2008.
>
> *The Koran.* Translated by N. J. Dawood, rev. ed., Penguin, 2015.

When citing a sacred work, give the edition you consulted, beginning with the title unless you are citing the work of an editor or translator.

25. Book with a title in its title

Eco, Umberto. *Postscript to* The Name of the Rose. Translated by William Weaver, Harcourt Brace Jovanovich, 1983.

When a book's title contains another book title (here *The Name of the Rose*), do not italicize the second title. When a book's title contains a quotation or the title of a work normally placed in quotation marks, keep the quotation marks and italicize both titles: *Critical Response to Henry James's "The Beast in the Jungle."*

26. Book lacking publication information or pagination

Carle, Eric. *The Very Busy Spider*. Philomel Books, 1984, n. pag.

Some books are not paginated or do not list a publisher or date of publication. Although MLA style no longer requires you to indicate missing information, your instructor may ask you to do so for clarity. These abbreviations are conventional: n.p. if no publisher, n.d. if no publication date, and n. pag. if no page numbers.

Parts of books

Parts of books include selections from anthologies, articles and chapters in scholarly collections and reference works, and the like. Works-cited entries for these short works include the author and title as well as information about the container in which they appear: the title, any other contributors, publication information, and page numbers, if available.

27. Selection from an anthology

Munro, Alice. "How I Met My Husband." *Literature: An Introduction to Fiction, Poetry, Drama, and Writing*, edited by X. J. Kennedy and Dana Gioia, 13th ed., Pearson, 2016, pp. 189-201.

This listing adds to the anthology entry in model 18: author of the selection, title of the selection (in quotation marks), and inclusive page numbers for the selection. If you wish, you may also supply the original date of publication for the work you are citing, after its title (see model 23).

If the work you cite comes from a collection of works by one author that has no editor, use the following form:

Hempel, Amy. "San Francisco." *The Collected Stories of Amy Hempel*, Scribner, 2006, pp. 27-28.

28. Two or more selections from the same anthology

Bradstreet, Anne. "The Author to Her Book." Kennedy and Gioia, pp. 657-58.

Kennedy, X. J., and Dana Gioia, editors. *Literature: An Introduction to Fiction, Poetry, Drama, and Writing*. 13th ed., Pearson, 2016.

Merwin, W. S. "For the Anniversary of My Death." Kennedy and Gioia, p. 828.

Stevens, Wallace. "Thirteen Ways of Looking at a Blackbird." Kennedy and Gioia,
pp. 831-33.

When you are citing more than one selection from the same anthology, your instructor may allow you to avoid repetition by giving the anthology information in full (the Kennedy and Gioia entry) and then simply cross-referencing it in entries for the works you used. Thus the Bradstreet, Merwin, and Stevens examples replace full publication information with Kennedy and Gioia and the appropriate pages in that book. Note that each entry appears in its proper alphabetical place among other works cited.

29. Work from a collection of scholarly articles

Molloy, Francis C. "The Suburban Vision in John O'Hara's Short Stories."
*Short Story Criticism: Excerpts from Criticism of the Works of Short Fiction
Writers,* edited by David Segal, Gale, 1989, pp. 287-92. Originally published in *Critique: Studies in Modern Fiction,* vol. 25, no. 2, 1984,
pp. 101-13.

Scholarly articles may be in collections like the one in the preceding example, *Short Story Criticism.* If the articles were written for the collection, you can follow model 27 for a selection from an anthology. However, if the articles were previously printed elsewhere—for instance, in scholarly journals—your instructor may ask you to provide the information for the earlier publication of articles you cite. Add Originally published in to the end of the entry and then give information for the earlier publication.

30. Article in a reference work

List an article in a reference work by the title if no author is given (models a and b) or by the author (model c). Then give the information for the container.

a. Print reference work

"Fortune." *Encyclopedia of Indo-European Culture,* edited by J. P. Malloy and D. Q.
Adams, Fitzroy, 1997, pp. 211-12.

b. Web reference work

"Ming Dynasty." *Encyclopaedia Britannica,* 14 Dec. 2015, www.britannica.com/
topic/Ming-dynasty-Chinese-history.

c. CD-ROM or DVD-ROM reference work

Nunberg, Geoffrey. "Usage in the Dictionary." *The American Heritage Dictionary of
the English Language,* 4th ed., Houghton Mifflin, 2000.

Single-issue CD-ROMs may be encyclopedias, dictionaries, books, and other resources that are published just once. Cite such sources like print books.

31. Introduction, preface, foreword, or afterword

Quindlen, Anna. Foreword. *A Tree Grows In Brooklyn,* by Betty Smith, HarperCollins, 2011, pp. vii-xv.

An introduction, foreword, or afterword is often written by someone other than the book's author. When citing such a piece, give its name without quotation marks or italics, as with Foreword in the example. (If the piece has a title of its own, provide it, in quotation marks, between the name of the author and the title of the book.) Give the inclusive page numbers of the part you cite.

When the author of a preface or introduction is the same as the author of the book, give only the last name after the title:

Gould, Stephen Jay. Prologue. *The Flamingo's Smile: Reflections in Natural History,* by Gould, W. W. Norton, 1985, pp. 13-20.

32. Published letter

Buttolph, Mrs. Laura E. Letter to Reverend and Mrs. C. C. Jones. 20 June 1857. *The Children of Pride: A True Story of Georgia and the Civil War,* edited by Robert Manson Myers, Yale UP, 1972, pp. 334-35.

List a published letter under the writer's name. Give it a descriptive label, specifying that the source is a letter and to whom it was addressed, and give the date of the letter. Do not put this description in quotation marks or italics. Treat the rest of the information like a selection from an anthology (model 27), giving the title of collection, the editor, publication information, and any page numbers.

Government publications

33. Government publication

a. Publication cited by author

Gray, Colin S. *Defense Planning for National Security: Navigation Aids for the Mystery Tour.* United States Army War College P, 2014.

United States, Dept. of Defense, Office of Civil Defense. *Fallout Protection: What to Know and Do about Nuclear Attack.* US Government Printing Office, 1961.

If a government publication lists a person as author or editor, treat the source as an authored or edited book (first example). If a publication does not list an author or editor, give the government and the agency as author (second example).

For a congressional publication, give the house and committee involved before the title. Then give the title (in italics) and information for the container: the title of the Web site, the date, and the URL.

United States, Congress, Senate, Committee on Veterans' Affairs. *Post-9/11*

Veterans Educational Assistance Improvements Act of 2010. US Government

Printing Office, 2010, www.gpo.gov/fdsys/pkg/BILLS-111s3447.

If you like, after the URL you may include the number and session of Congress, the chamber (House of Representatives or Senate), and the type and number of the publication—for instance, 111th Congress, 2nd session, Senate Bill 3447.

b. Publication cited by title

"Autism Spectrum Disorder." *National Institute of Mental Health,* Sept. 2015,

www.nimh.nih.gov/health/publications/autism-spectrum-disorder-qf-

15-5511/index.shtml.

"A Comprehensive Approach to Bullying Prevention." *Wisconsin Dept. of*

Public Instruction, 24 Feb. 2016, dpi.wi.gov/sspw/safe-schools/

bullying-prevention.

MLA
56b

MLA style recommends omitting a corporate author when it is the same as the publisher and omitting the publisher when it has the same name as its Web site. The preceding examples begin with the title and then give information for the container: the title of the Web site, the date, and the URL. (For more on corporate authors, see model 5.)

4 ▪ Web sources and social media

Web sites and parts of Web sites

The following models encompass pages, essays, articles, stories, poems, plays, and other works that you find on larger Web sites. To cite journal, newspaper, and magazine articles that you find on the open Web, see, respectively, models 7c, 9c, and 11c. To cite books that you find on the open Web, see model 13c. To cite a government document on a Web site, see model 33. To cite a complete Web site, see model 35.

34. Page or work on a Web site

When you cite a page or work on a Web site, treat the Web site as the container of the source. After the author and title, give the title of the Web site, in italics, any other contributors (such as an editor of the site), the publisher (if different from the site title), the publication date, and the location of the source (the URL).

a. Work with an author and a title

Murray, Amanda. "Invention Hot Spot: Birth of Hip-Hop in the Bronx, New York, in the 1970s." *Lemelson Center for the Study of Invention and Innovation,* Smithsonian Institution, 15 Oct. 2010, invention.si.edu/invention-hot -spot-birth-hip-hop-bronx-new-york-1970s.

See the next page for an explanation of this format and where to find the required information on a Web site.

Most works on Web sites are brief, and their titles should be placed in quotation marks. However, some works, such as books and plays, are longer, and their titles should be italicized. (See pp. 317–18 and 340 for titles to be quoted or italicized.) The work cited below is a collection of poems:

Wheatley, Phillis. *Poems on Various Subjects, Religious and Moral.* London, 1773. *Bartleby.com,* www.bartleby.com/150/.

b. Work without an author

"Eliminating Polio in Haiti." *Center for Global Development,* 2015, millionssaved. cgdev.org/case-studies/eliminating-polio-in-haiti.

If the work lacks an author, start with the title.

c. Work without a title

Cyberbullying Research Center. Home page. 2016, cyberbullying.org/.

If you are citing an untitled work from a Web site, such as the home page or an untitled blog posting, give the name of the site followed by Home page, Online posting, or another descriptive label. Do not use quotation marks or italics for this label.

d. Work with print publication information

Herodotus. *The Histories.* Translated by A. D. Godley, Harvard UP, 1920. *Perseus Digital Library,* Tufts U, Dept. of Classics, www.perseus.tufts.edu/hopper/ text?doc=Perseus:text:1999.01.0126.

If the print information for a source is relevant to your research, give it after the title of the work. In this example, the name of the translator and the publication information identify a specific version of the work. The title of the Web site, the publisher, and the URL follow. For more examples of digital books, see model 13.

35. Entire Web site

a. Web site with an author or an editor

Crane, Gregory, editor. *The Perseus Digital Library.* Tufts U, Dept. of Classics, 1985-2016, www.perseus.tufts.edu/hopper/.

MLA
56b

Citing a page or work on a Web site

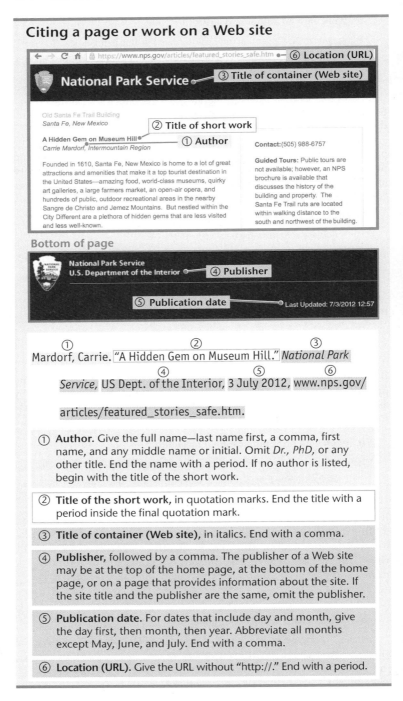

Mardorf, Carrie. "A Hidden Gem on Museum Hill." *National Park Service*, US Dept. of the Interior, 3 July 2012, www.nps.gov/articles/featured_stories_safe.htm.

① **Author.** Give the full name—last name first, a comma, first name, and any middle name or initial. Omit *Dr., PhD,* or any other title. End the name with a period. If no author is listed, begin with the title of the short work.

② **Title of the short work,** in quotation marks. End the title with a period inside the final quotation mark.

③ **Title of container (Web site),** in italics. End with a comma.

④ **Publisher,** followed by a comma. The publisher of a Web site may be at the top of the home page, at the bottom of the home page, or on a page that provides information about the site. If the site title and the publisher are the same, omit the publisher.

⑤ **Publication date.** For dates that include day and month, give the day first, then month, then year. Abbreviate all months except May, June, and July. End with a comma.

⑥ **Location (URL).** Give the URL without "http://." End with a period.

When citing an entire Web site, include the name of the editor or author (if available), followed by the title of the site, the publisher, the publication date, and the URL.

b. Web site without an author or an editor

Center for Financial Security. U of Wisconsin, 2016, cfs.wisc.edu/.

If a Web site lacks an author or an editor (as many do), begin with the title of the site.

36. Wiki

"Podcast." *Wikipedia.* Wikimedia Foundation, 6 Apr. 2016, en.wikipedia.org/
wiki/Podcast.

To cite an entry from a wiki, give the entry title, the site title, the publisher (if different from the title of the Web site), the publication date, and the URL.

37. Undated Web source

"Clean Cars 101." *Union of Concerned Scientists,* www.ucsusa.org/our-work/
clean-vehicles/clean-cars-101#.Vwa-KfkrKM8. Accessed 7 Apr. 2016.

MLA style no longer requires access dates for all online sources. However, if the work you cite is undated, or if your instructor requires an access date, give it at the end of the entry preceded by Accessed.

Social Media

38. Post on a blog

Minogue, Kristin. "Diverse Forests Are Stronger against Deer." *Smithsonian
Insider,* 8 Apr. 2014, insider.si.edu/2014/04/diverse-forests-resist-deer-
better/2014.

Cite a blog post like a work on a Web site, giving the author, the title of the post, and information about the container. The example gives the title of the blog, the publication date, and the URL. It does not give the name of the publisher because the name is clear from the title of the blog.

Cite an entire blog as you would cite an entire Web site (see model 35).

39. Post on a social-networking site

Literacy Network. Status update. *Facebook,* 5 Apr. 2016, www.facebook.com/
LiteracyNetwork/?fref=ts.

Give the name of the author (a person or an organization, as here), the type of post, the title of the site, the publisher (if different from the site title), the date of the post, and the URL.

40. Comment

Teka. Comment on "When a Feminist Pledges a Sorority." By Jessica Bennett,
     The New York Times, 9 Apr. 2016, www.nytimes.com/2016/04/10/
     fashion/sorority-ivy-league-feminists.

List the author's name or user name if the author uses a pseudonym
(as here). Then give Comment on followed by the title of the article or
post the comment responds to and the information for the container.
This example includes the author of the article the comment responds
to, the title of the site, the article's publication date, and the URL.

41. Tweet

Bittman, Mark. "Eating Less Meat Could Save up to $31 Trillion (and Many Lives)
     bit.ly/1UyYxyp." *Twitter*, 21 Mar. 2016, 2:21 p.m., twitter.com/bittman/
     status/712026468738404352?lang=en.

Give the author's name or user name if the author uses a pseudonym.
Give the entire tweet, using the author's capitalization, in quotation
marks. Then give the information for the container: the name of the
site (*Twitter*), the date and time of the tweet, and the URL.

42. Post to a discussion group

Williams, Frederick. "Circles as Primitive." *The Math Forum @ Drexel*, Drexel U,
     28 Feb. 2012, mathforum.org/kb/thread.jspa?threadID=2583537.

If a discussion-group post does not have a title, say Online posting instead. Then give the information for the container: the title of the discussion group, the publisher, the date, and the URL of the discussion
thread.

43. E-mail or text message

Green, Reginald. "Re: College Applications." Received by the author, 2 May 2016.

For an e-mail message, use the subject line as the title, in quotation
marks, with standard capitalization. Then name the recipient, whether
yourself (the author) or someone else. For a text message, give a descriptive label:

Soo, Makenna. Text message to the author. 16 Apr. 2016.

5 ▪ Visual, audio, and other media sources

44. Painting, photograph, or other work of visual art

a. Original artwork

Abbott, Berenice. *Soap Bubbles.* 1946, Museum of Modern Art, New York.

To cite a work of visual art that you see in person, such as in a museum, name the artist and give the title (in italics). Then give the

date of creation and the name and location of the place where you saw the work. You may omit the city if the name of the place includes the city.

b. Reproduction of an artwork in a print publication

Graham, David. *Bob's Java Jive, Tacoma, Washington, 1989. Only in America: Some Unexpected Scenery,* Alfred A. Knopf, 1991, p. 93.

To cite a reproduction of a work of visual art, give the artist and title of the work followed by information for the container in which you found it. In the example, the container is a print book with title, publisher, publication date, and location (a page number).

c. Work of art on the Web

O'Keefe, Georgia. *It Was Red and Pink.* 1959, *Milwaukee Art Museum,* collection.mam.org/details.php?id=6725.

To cite a work of art that you view on the Web, give the name of the artist or creator, the title of the work, and the date of the work (if any). Then give information for the container: the title of the Web site, the publisher of the Web site (if different from the title), and the location of the work (here, a URL).

d. Artwork in a digital file

Girls on the playground. Personal photograph by the author, 10 Aug. 2015.

To cite an unpublished artwork in a digital file that you are reproducing, such as personal photograph or work of art, give a description of it, the photographer, and the date.

45. Advertisement

a. Advertisement without a title

Apple iPhone SE. Advertisement. *Vogue,* May 2016, p. 3.

To cite an advertisement without a title, start with the name of the company and/or product followed by Advertisement. Then give information for the container of the source, in this case a print magazine: title, date, and location (page number).

b. Advertisement with a title

Honey Maid. "This Is Wholesome." *YouTube,* 10 Mar. 2016, youtu.be/2xeanX6xnRU.

Many companies post titled advertisements on their Web sites and on *YouTube.* To cite such an ad, give the company's name and/or product followed by the title of the ad in quotation marks. Then give information for the container: the site where you viewed the ad, the date, and the URL.

46. Comic strip or cartoon

a. Titled comic strip

Johnston, Lynn. "For Better or Worse." *San Francisco Chronicle*, 22 Aug. 2015,
   p. E6.

Cite a titled comic strip with the artist's name, the title of the strip (in quotation marks), and the information for the container—here, the title of the newspaper, the date, and the page number.

b. Individual cartoon

Sipress, David. Cartoon. *The New Yorker*, 7 Apr. 2016, www.newyorker.com/
   cartoons/daily-cartoon/daily-cartoon-thursday-april-7th/.

To cite a cartoon that is not part of a comic strip, start with the name of the artist. If the cartoon has a title, give it in quotation marks. If it does not have a title, provide the description Cartoon (as in the example), without quotation marks or italics. Then give information for the container of the work—here, the title of the Web site, the date, and the URL.

47. Map, chart, or diagram

List the illustration by its title (model a) unless the creator of the illustration is given on the source (model b). Put the title in italics if it is published independently or in quotation marks if it is contained in another source (model a). If the illustration does not have a title, provide a description in place of the title (model b). End with publication information for the source.

a. Titled map, chart, or diagram

Eastern United States Area Map. H. M. Gousha, 1992.

"Water Cycle Diagram." *Earthguide*, Scripps Institution of Oceanography, 2014,
   earthguide.ucsd.edu/earthguide/diagrams/watercyclel/index.html.

b. Untitled map, chart, or diagram

Tufte, Edward R. Diagram. *Envisioning Information*, Graphics Press, 1990, p. 63.

48. Television episode or series

To cite a television series or episode, start with the title (model a) unless you are citing the work of a person or persons (model b). Give the names of contributors if they are important to your project. To cite contributors to specific episodes, give the name(s) after the episode title (model b). To cite contributors to an entire series, give the names(s) after the series title (models c and d).

a. Broadcast TV episode

"Sink or Swim." *Nurse Jackie*, season 6, episode 1, Showtime, 2014.

This example gives the episode title and information for the container: the series title, the season and episode numbers, the name of the network, and the date.

b. Web TV episode

Peretz, Jesse, director. "Sink or Swim." By Clyde Phillips. *Nurse Jackie*, season 6,
   episode 1, Showtime, 2014. *Netflix*, www.netflix.com/watch/80065552.

This example gives the director and title of the episode. The writer is given next because he wrote this episode, not the entire series. Container 1 includes the name of the series, the season, and the episode number. Container 2 gives the streaming service, *Netflix*, and the URL.

c. TV episode on DVD, Blu-ray, or videocassette

"Sink or Swim." *Nurse Jackie Complete Collection*, created by Liz Brixius, Linda
   Wallem, and Evan Dunsky, performance by Edie Falco, season 6, episode 1,
   Lion's Gate, 2016, disc 7.

This example gives the episode title followed by the information for the container, a DVD set. The creators of the series and the actor who played the central character are named, followed by the season and episode numbers and publication information about the DVD.

d. TV series

Nurse Jackie. Created by Liz Brixius, Linda Wallem, and Evan Dunsky,
   Showtime, 2009-15.

This example gives information on the series as a whole: the title, the creators, the network, and the years during which the series aired.

49. Radio program

To cite a radio program, start with the title of the program (model a) unless you are citing the work of a person or persons (model b). Then give information about the container: the title of the radio show, any contributors you wish to include (model a), and broadcast or Web publication information. (To cite a podcast, see model 53.)

a. Broadcast radio program

On the Media. Hosted by Brooke Gladstone and Bob Garfield, WNYC, New York,
   5 Feb. 2016.

This example gives the name of the radio program, the main contributors, the station that produces the show, and the date.

b. Web radio program

McEvers, Kelly. "Opioid Epidemic Sparks HIV Outbreak in Tiny Indiana Town." *All
   Things Considered*, National Public Radio, 31 Mar. 2016, www.npr.org/2016/03/
   31/472577254/opioid-epidemic-sparks-hiv-outbreak-in-tiny-indiana-town.

MLA

56b

Radio content streamed from a Web site may give the names of reporters and titles of stories. This example gives the name of the reporter, the title of the story, and information about the container: the name of the program, the publisher (because it is different from the title of the site), the date, and the URL. If instead of listening to the story you consulted the written transcript, add Transcript at the end of the entry, followed by a period.

50. Interview

This section provides models for interview you heard or saw. For a published interview that you read, use a format for an article (models 7-12) or for a selection from an anthology (model 27). For an interview you conducted yourself, see model 57.

a. Broadcast interview

Morrison, Toni. Interview. By Terry Gross. *Fresh Air*, National Public Radio, WHYY, Philadelphia, 20 Apr. 2015.

Begin with the person interviewed. Follow the name with Interview (not italicized or in quotation marks) in place of a title unless the interview has one. Then give the interviewer's name and information for the container: the title of the program and broadcast information.

b. Web interview

Mosley, Walter. Interview. By Tavis Smiley. *Tavis Smiley*, Public Broadcasting Service, 29 June 2016, www.pbs.org/wnet/tavissmiley/interviews/author-walter-mosley/.

After the name of the person interviewed and Interview, give the interviewer's name and information for the container: the title of the Web site, the publisher (if different from the site title), and the URL.

51. Film or video

Start with the title (model a) unless you are citing the work of a person or a corporation (models b and c). Generally, list the director. You may also cite other contributors and their roles after the title (model b).

a. Film

Chi-Raq. Directed by Spike Lee, Amazon Studios, 2015.

For a film you see in a theater, end with the distributor and the date.

b. DVD, Blu-ray, or videocassette

Balanchine, George. *Serenade*. 1991. Directed by Hilary Bean, performance by the San Francisco Ballet, PBS Video, 1999.

For a DVD, Blu-ray disc, or videocassette, include the original release date after the title (as here) if it is relevant to your use of the source.

c. Video on the Web

CBS News. "1968 King Assassination Report." 4 Apr. 1968. *YouTube*, 3 Apr. 2008, youtube/cmOBbxgxKvo.

For a film or video you view on the Web, give a creator, if available, and atitle or a description. Then give information for the container: the title of the Web site, the date (if available), and the URL. If the video's original publication date is significant, give it after the title, as in the example.

52. Sound recording

Sound recordings include music on vinyl LPs, CDs, the Web, and other devices. They also include spoken-word recordings.

a. Song

Springsteen, Bruce. "This Life." *Working on a Dream*, Columbia, 2009.

Start with the name of the artist and the title of the song. Treat the album like a container, giving the title, publisher, and date.

For a song you stream on the Web, treat the service like a second container:

Jackson, Michael. "Billie Jean." *Thriller*, MJJ Productions, 1982. *Spotify*, play.spotify.com/track/5ORmAhIMRTcisVlB6jShJl.

b. Album

Shocked, Michelle. *Short, Sharp, Shocked.* PolyGram Records, 1988.

Give the name of the artist and the title of the album. Then give information about the container: other contributors if relevant, the recording company (as in the example), and the date of release. For an album on the Web, add the name of the streaming service and a URL, as in the Jackson example above.

If you are citing a musical work identified by form, number, and key, see model 54.

c. Spoken word

Dunbar, Paul Laurence. "We Wear the Mask." Narrated by Rita Dove. *Poetry Out Loud,* Poetry Foundation / National Endowment for the Arts, 2014, www.poetryoutloud.org/poems-and-performance/listen-to-poetry.

Spoken-word performances include readings, recitations, monologues, and the like. This example, of a poem read aloud, gives the author of the poem, the title, the narrator, and the container information: the Web site, the publishers (separated by a slash), the date, and the URL.

53. Podcast

Sedaris, David. "Now We Are Five." *This American Life*, Chicago Public Media, 31 Jan. 2014, www.thisamericanlife.org/podcast/episode/517/day-at-the-beach?act=4.

This podcast lists the author of a story on the program, the title of the story, and information about the container: the title of the program, the publisher, the date of the broadcast, and the URL.

54. Live performance

Beethoven, Ludwig van. Symphony no. 9 in D-minor. Performance by Ricardo Muti and the Chicago Symphony Orchestra, 8 May 2015, Symphony Center, Chicago.

The New Century. By Paul Rudnick, directed by Nicholas Martin, 6 May 2013, Mitzi E. Newhouse Theater, New York.

For a live performance, place the title first (second example) unless you are citing the work of an individual (first example). After the title, provide relevant information about contributors as well as the date of the performance, the performance venue, and the city (if it is not part of the venue's name).

If you are citing a work of classical music identified by form, number, and key (first example), do not use quotation marks or italics for the title.

55. Lecture, speech, address, or reading

Fontaine, Claire. "Economics and Education." 7 June 2015, Museum of Contemporary Art, North Miami. Address.

Give the speaker's name and the title of the talk (if any), the date of the presentation, the name of the venue, and the city (if it is not part of the venue's name). If the presentation occurred at a sponsored meeting, add the title of the meeting and the sponsor's name before the date. You can also give the type of presentation (Lecture, Speech, Address, Reading) if doing so will help readers understand what you are citing.

To cite a classroom lecture in a course you are taking, adapt the preceding format by giving a description in place of the title:

Cavanaugh, Carol. Class lecture on teaching mentors. Lesley U, 4 Apr. 2016. Lecture.

To cite a video of a lecture or other presentation that you view on the Web, see model 51b.

56. Video game, computer software, or app

Notch Development. *Minecraft: Pocket Edition.* Version 0.14.1, Mojang, 6 Apr. 2016, minecraft.net.

For a video game, computer program, or app, give the name of the developer or author, the title, the version, the publisher, the publication date, and the URL.

6 ▪ Other sources

57. Personal interview

Greene, Matthew. Personal interview. 7 May 2016.

Begin with the name of the person interviewed. For an interview you conducted, give a description of the interview—Personal interview, Telephone interview, or E-mail interview—and then give the date.

See also model 50 to cite a broadcast interview or a video of an interview on the Web.

58. Unpublished or personal letter

a. Unpublished letter

James, Jonathan E. Letter to his sister. 16 Apr. 1970. Jonathan E. James papers, South Dakota State Archive, Pierre.

For an unpublished letter in the collection of a library or archive, give the writer, a description in place of a title, and the date (if the letter is dated). Then give the information for the container: the title of the archive and the location.

See also model 32 to cite a published letter.

b. Personal letter

Murray, Elizabeth. Letter to the author. 6 Apr. 2016.

For a letter you received, give a description in place of the title and the date. To cite an e-mail message, see model 43.

59. Dissertation

McFaddin, Marie Oliver. *Adaptive Reuse: An Architectural Solution for Poverty and Homelessness*. Dissertation, U of Maryland, 2007. UMI, 2007.

Treat a published dissertation like a book, but after the title insert Dissertation, the name of the degree-granting institution, and the year.

60. Pamphlet or brochure

Understanding Childhood Obesity. Obesity Action Network, 2015.

Most pamphlets and brochures can be treated as books. In this example, the pamphlet has no listed author, so the title comes first. If your source has an author, give the name first, followed by the title and publication information.

Exercise 56.1   Writing works-cited entries

Prepare works-cited entries from the following information. Follow the MLA models given in this chapter unless your instructor specifies a different style. Arrange the finished entries in alphabetical order, not numbered.

1. An article titled "Who's Responsible for the Digital Divide?" in the March 2011 issue of the journal *Information Society*, volume 27, issue 2. The article appeared on pages 92–104. The authors are Dmitry Epstein, Erik C. Nisbet, and Tarleton Gillespie. You found the article in the online database *Academic Search Complete*. The DOI for the article is 10.1080/01972243.2011.548695.

2. A Web article titled "Who's Not Online and Why" on the Web site *PewResearch Internet Project*. The author of the article is Kathryn Zickuhr. The publisher of the site is the Pew Research Center. The article is dated September 25, 2013. The URL for the article is www.pewinternet.org/2013/09/25/whos-not-online-and-why/.

3. A Web article with no listed author on the Web site *Digital Divide Institute*. The publisher of the site is DigitalDivide.org. The title of the article is "Banking the Unbanked" and the date is January 24, 2014. The URL for the article is www.digitaldivide.org/#!dd-banking.

4. A print book titled *Technology and Social Inclusion: Rethinking the Digital Divide* by Mark Warschauer. The book was published in 2003 by MIT Press.

5. An article in the newspaper *The New York Times,* published on March 20, 2013, on page B1. The author is Jane L. Levere. The title is "Reaching Those on the Wrong Side of the Digital Divide." You found the source in the database *LexisNexis Academic*. The URL for the article is www.lexisnexis.com/lnacademic/HEADLINE(Reaching+those+wrong%2C+side+divide)%1B2013.

6. A government report you consulted online. The title of the report is "A Nation Online: Entering the Broadband Age." It was published in September 2004 on the Web site of the National Telecommunications and Information Administration, an agency of the US government that is also the author and publisher of the report. The URL for the report is www.ntia.doc.gov/report/2004/nation-online-entering-broadband-age.

7. An e-mail interview you conducted with Naomi Lee on April 23, 2014.

8. A blog post to the Web site *Code for America* by Jacob Solomon. The title is "People, Not Data." The post is dated January 6, 2014. The publisher of the site is Code for America Labs. The URL for the post is www.codeforamerica.org/blog/2014/01/06/people-not-data/.

56c   Format the paper in MLA style.

The MLA's Web site (*style.mla.org*) provides guidelines for the format of a paper, with just a few elements. For guidelines on type fonts, headings, lists, illustrations, and other features that MLA style does not specify, see pages 61–68.

The samples opposite show the formats for the first page and a later page of a paper. For the format of the list of works cited, see page 429.

First page of MLA paper

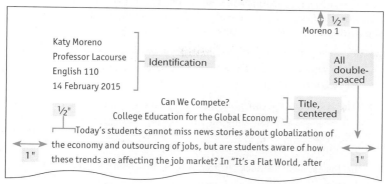

Katy Moreno
Professor Lacourse
English 110
14 February 2015

— Identification

Moreno 1   ½"

All double-spaced

½"

Can We Compete?
College Education for the Global Economy

Title, centered

Today's students cannot miss news stories about globalization of
the economy and outsourcing of jobs, but are students aware of how
these trends are affecting the job market? In "It's a Flat World, after

1"   1"

Later page of MLA paper

1"   Moreno 3   ½"

1"   time, they kept their jobs because they were experienced at figuring
out the company's IT needs, planning for changes, researching and

1"

1"   however, I have decided to take courses in English and history as well.
Classes in these subjects will require me to read broadly, think critically,

1"   1"

1"

Margins Use one-inch margins on all sides of every page.

Spacing and indentions Double-space throughout. Indent the first lines of paragraphs one-half inch. (See the next page for treatment of poetry and long prose quotations.)

Paging Begin numbering on the first page, and number consecutively through the end (including the list of works cited). Use Arabic numerals (1, 2, 3) positioned in the upper right, about one-half inch from the top. Place your last name before the page number in case the pages later become separated.

Identification and title A title page is not required. Follow the first sample above, providing your name, the date, and other information requested by your instructor. Place this identification an inch from the top of the page, aligned with the left margin and double-spaced.

Double-space again, and center the title. Do not highlight the title with italics, underlining, boldface, larger type, or quotation marks. Capitalize the words in the title according to the guidelines on page 338. Double-space the lines of the title and between the title and the text.

Poetry and long prose quotations Treat a single line of poetry like any other quotation, running it into your text and enclosing it in quotation marks. You may run in two or three lines of poetry as well, separating the lines with a slash surrounded by space.

> An example of Robert Frost's incisiveness is in two lines from "Death of the Hired Man": *"*Home is the place where, when you have to go there */* They have to take you in*"* (119-20).

Always set off from your text a poetry quotation of more than three lines. Use double spacing above and below the quotation and for the quotation itself. Indent the quotation one-half inch from the left margin. *Do not add quotation marks.*

> In "The Author to Her Book," written in 1678, Anne Bradstreet characterizes her book as a child. In these lines from the poem, she captures a parent's and a writer's frustration with the imperfections of her offspring:
>
> > I washed thy face, but more defects I saw,
> > and rubbing off a spot, still made a flaw.
> > I stretched thy joints to make thee even feet,
> > Yet still thou run'st more hobbling than is meet. (13-16)

Also set off a prose quotation of more than four typed lines. (See pp. 397–98 on when to use such long quotations.) Double-space and indent as with the preceding poetry example. *Do not add quotation marks.*

> In the influential *Talley's Corner* from 1967, Elliot Liebow observes that "unskilled" construction work requires more skill than is generally assumed:
>
> > A healthy, sturdy, active man of good intelligence requires from two to four weeks to break in on a construction job. . . . It frequently happens that his foreman or the craftsman he services is not willing to wait that long for him to get into condition or to learn at a glance the difference in size between a rough 2 × 8 and a finished 2 x 10. (62)

Do not use a paragraph indention for a quotation of a single complete paragraph or a part of a paragraph. If the quotation contains more than one paragraph, indent the first lines of the second and any subsequent paragraphs.

56d A sample paper in MLA style

The sample paper beginning on page 468 follows the eighth edition of the *MLA Handbook* for overall format, in-text citations, and the list of works cited. Annotations in the margins highlight features of the paper: those in blue boxes address format and documentation; the others address content.

Note Because the sample paper addresses a current topic, many of its sources come from the Internet and do not use page or other reference numbers. Thus the in-text citations of these sources do not give reference numbers. In a paper relying solely on printed sources, most if not all in-text citations would include page numbers.

A note on outlines

Some instructors ask students to submit an outline of the final paper. For advice on constructing a formal or topic outline, see pp. 23–24. Below is an outline of the sample paper following, written in complete sentences. Note that the thesis statement precedes a formal topic or sentence outline.

Thesis statement: Although green consumerism can help the environment, consumerism itself is the root of some of the most pressing ecological problems. To make a real difference, humans must consume less.

I. Green products claiming to help the environment both appeal to and confuse consumers.

   A. The market for ecologically sound products is enormous.

   B. Determining whether or not a product is as green as advertised can be a challenge.

II. Green products don't solve the high rate of consumption that truly threatens the environment.

   A. Overconsumption is a significant cause of three of the most serious environmental problems.

      1. It depletes natural resources.

      2. It contributes to pollution, particularly from the greenhouse gases responsible for global warming.

      3. It produces a huge amount of solid waste.

   B. The availability of greener products has not reduced the environmental effects of consumption.

III. Since buying green products does not reduce consumption, other solutions must be found for environmental problems.

   A. Experts have proposed many far-reaching solutions, but they require concerted government action and could take decades to implement.

   B. For shorter-term solutions, individuals can change their own behavior as consumers.

      1. Precycling may be the greenest behavior that individuals can adopt.

         A. Precycling means avoiding purchase of products that use raw materials and excessive packaging.

         B. More important, precycling means avoiding purchases of new products whenever possible.

      2. For unavoidable purchases, individuals can buy green products and influence businesses to embrace ecological goals.

Identification: writer's name, instructor's name, course title, date.	Justin Malik Ms. Rossi English 112-02 24 April 2015
Title centered. Double-space throughout.	The False Promise of Green Consumerism
Introduction: establishes the issue with examples (first paragraph) and background (second paragraph).	They line the aisles of just about any store. They seem to dominate television and print advertising. Chances are that at least a few of them belong to you. From organic jeans to household cleaners to hybrid cars, products advertised as environmentally friendly are readily available and are so popular they're trendy. It's easy to see why Americans are buying these things in record numbers. The new wave of "green" consumer goods makes an almost irresistible appeal: save the planet by shopping.
Citation form: no parenthetical citation because author is named in the text and DVD has no page or other reference numbers.	Saving the planet does seem to be urgent. Thanks partly to former vice president Al Gore, who sounded the alarm in 2006 with the documentary film *An Inconvenient Truth*, the threat of global warming has become a regular feature in the news media and a recurring theme in popular culture. Unfortunately, as Gore points out, climate change is just one of many environmental problems competing for attention: the rainforests are vanishing, the air and water are dangerously polluted, alarming numbers of species are facing extinction, and landfills are overflowing. The warnings from Gore and others can be overwhelming, and most people feel powerless to halt the damage. Thus it may be reassuring that people can make a difference with small changes in what they buy—but that is
Thesis statement.	not entirely true. Although green consumerism can help the environment, consumerism itself is the root of some of the most pressing ecological problems. To make a real difference, humans must consume less.
Background on green products (next two paragraphs).	The market for items perceived as ecologically sound is enormous. Experts estimate that spending on green products already approaches $500 billion a year in the United States
Citation form: author and page number; author not named in the text.	(Broder 4). Shoppers respond well to new options, whether the purchase is as minor as a bottle of chemical-free dish soap or as major as a front-loading washing machine. Not surprisingly, companies are responding by offering as many new eco-products

Malik 4

as they can. The journalist Rebecca Harris reports in *Marketing Magazine* that the recent "proliferation of green products" has been a revolution for business. She cites a market research report by TerraChoice: in the first decade of this century, the number of new packaged goods labeled as green increased by approximately 75% each year, and now nearly five thousand consumer items claim to be good for the environment. These products are offered for sale at supermarkets and at stores like Walmart, Target, Home Depot, Starbucks, and Pottery Barn. Clearly, green consumerism has grown into a mainstream interest.

Determining whether or not a product is as green as advertised can be a challenge. Claims vary: a product might be labeled as organic, biodegradable, energy efficient, recycled, carbon neutral, renewable, or just about anything that sounds environmentally positive. However, none of these terms carries a universally accepted meaning, and no enforceable labeling regulations exist (Atkinson and Rosenthal 34-35). Some of the new product options offer clear environmental benefits: for instance, LED lightbulbs last fifty times longer than regular bulbs and draw about 15% of the electricity ("LED Lightbulbs" 25), and paper made from recycled fibers saves many trees. But other "green" products just as clearly do little or nothing to help the environment: a disposable razor made with less plastic is still a disposable razor, destined for a landfill after only a few uses.

Distinguishing truly green products from those that are not so green merely scratches the surface of a much larger issue. The products aren't the problem; it's humans' high rate of consumption that poses the real threat to the environment. People seek what's newer and better—whether cars, clothes, phones, computers, televisions, shoes, or gadgets—and they all require resources to make, ship, and use them. Political scientists Thomas Princen, Michael Maniates, and Ken Conca maintain that overconsumption is a leading force behind several ecological crises, warning that

> ever-increasing pressures on ecosystems, life-supporting environmental services, and critical natural cycles are

---

Citation form: no parenthetical citation because author is named in the text and article (in HTML format) has no page numbers.

Common-knowledge examples of stores and products do not require source citations.

Citation form: source with two authors; authors not named in the text.

Citation form: shortened title for anonymous source.

Environmental effects of consumption (next four paragraphs). Writer synthesizes information from half a dozen sources to develop his own ideas.

Quotation over four lines set off without quotation marks. See page 466.

Ellipsis mark signals omission from quotation.

Citation form with displayed quotation: follows sentence period. Authors named in text, so not named in parenthetical citation.

Text refers to and discusses figure.

Figure presents numerical data visually.

Figure caption explains the chart and gives complete source information.

First effect of overconsumption

Brackets signal capitalization changed to integrate quotation with writer's sentence.

driven not only by the sheer number of resource

users . . . but also by the patterns of resource use

themselves. (4)

Those patterns of resource use are disturbing. In just the last century, gross world product (the global output of consumer goods) grew at five times the rate of population growth—a difference explained by a huge rise in consumption per person. (See fig. 1.) Such growth might be good for the economy, but it is bad for the environment. As fig. 1 shows, it is accompanied by the depletion of natural resources, increases in the carbon emissions that cause global warming, and increases in the amount of solid waste disposal.

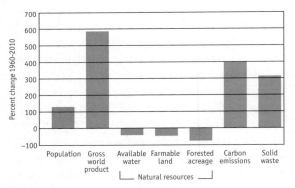

Fig. 1. Global population, consumption, and environmental impacts, 1960-2010. Data from United Nations Development Programme; *Human Development Report: Sustainability and Equity—A Better Future For All*, Palgrave, 2011, pp. 32, 37-38, 165; and from "Data Center," *Earth Policy Institute*, 16 Feb. 2014, www.earth-policy.org/?/data_center/C22/.

The first negative effect of overconsumption, the depletion of resources, occurs because the manufacture and distribution of any consumer product depends on the use of water, land, and raw materials such as wood, metal, and oil. Paul Hawken, a respected environmentalist, explains that just in the United States "[i]ndustry moves, mines, extracts, shovels, burns, wastes, pumps, and disposes of *4 million pounds of*

Malik 4

material in order to provide one average . . . family's needs for a year" (qtd. in DeGraaf et al. 78; emphasis added). The United Nations Development Programme's 2011 *Human Development Report* warns that many regions in the world don't have enough water, productive soil, or forests to meet the basic needs of their populations (4-5). Additional data from the Web site of the Earth Policy Institute confirm that as manufacturing and per-person consumption continue to rise, the supply of resources needed for survival continues to decline ("Data Center"). Thus heavy consumption poses a threat not only to the environment but also to the well-being of the human race.

> Citation form: source with three authors; "qtd. in" indicates indirect source (Hawken quoted by DeGraaf et al.); "emphasis added" indicates italics were not in original quotation.

> Citation form: article cited by title because names of corporate author and publisher are the same; no page numbers given because online source lacks page or other reference numbers.

In addition to using up scarce natural resources, manufacturing and distributing products harm the earth by spewing pollution into the water, soil, and air. The most worrisome aspect of that pollution may be its link to climate change. Al Gore explains the process as it is understood by most scientists: the energy needed to power manufacturing and distribution comes primarily from burning fossil fuels, which releases carbon dioxide and other greenhouse gases into the air; the gases build up and trap heat in the earth's atmosphere; and the rising average temperatures will raise sea levels, expand deserts, and cause more frequent floods and hurricanes around the world. This view is reflected in the bar chart of fig. 1, which shows that carbon emissions, like the production of consumer goods in general, are rising at rates out of proportion with population growth. The more humans consume, the more they contribute to global warming.

> Second effect of overconsumption

> Signal phrase introduces summary, which reduces a lengthy explanation to one sentence.

> Citation form: no parenthetical citation because Gore is named in the text and DVD has no page or other reference numbers.

> Writer's own conclusion from preceding data.

As harmful as they are, gradual global warming and the depletion of resources can be difficult to comprehend or appreciate. A more immediate environmental effect of buying habits can be seen in the volumes of trash those habits create. A US government study found that in a single year (2012), US residents and organizations produced 251 million tons of municipal solid waste, amounting to "4.38 pounds per person per day" ("Municipal Solid Waste Generation" 1). Nearly a third of that trash came just from the wrappers, cans, bottles, and boxes used for shipping consumer goods. Yet the mountains of trash left over from consumption are only a part of the

> Third effect of overconsumption.

problem. In industrial countries overall, 90% of waste comes not from what gets thrown out, but from the manufacturing processes of converting natural resources into consumer products (DeGraaf et al. 192). Nearly everything people buy creates waste in production, comes in packaging that gets discarded immediately, and ultimately ends up in landfills that are already overflowing.

Unfortunately, the growing popularity of green products has not reduced the environmental effects of consumption. The journalist David Owen notes that as eco-friendly and energy-efficient products have become more available, the "reduced costs stimulate increased consumption" (80). The author gives the example of home cooling: in the last fifty years, air conditioners have become much more affordable and energy efficient, but seven times more Americans now use them on a regular basis, for a net gain in energy use. At the same time, per-person waste production in the United States has risen by more than 20% ("Municipal Solid Waste Generation" 10). Greener products may reduce our cost of consumption and even reduce our guilt about consumption, but they do not reduce consumption and its effects.

If buying green won't solve the problems caused by overconsumption, what will? Politicians, environmentalists, and economists have proposed an array of far-reaching ideas, including creating a financial market for carbon credits and offsets, aggressively taxing consumption and pollution, offering financial incentives for environmentally positive behaviors, and even abandoning market capitalism altogether (de Blas). However, all of these are "top-down" solutions that require concerted government action. Gaining support for any one of them, putting it into practice, and getting results could take decades. In the meantime, the environment would continue to deteriorate. Clearly, short-term solutions are also essential.

The most promising short-term solution is for individuals to change their own behavior as consumers. The greenest behavior that individuals can adopt may be precycling, the term widely used for avoiding purchases of products that involve the

Annotations (left margin):

Citation form: source with three authors; authors not named in the text.

Environmental effects of green consumption.

Citation form: author is named in the text, so page number only.

Writer's own conclusion from preceding data.

Solutions to problem of consumption (next three paragraphs).

Long-term solutions.

Citation form: author's name only, because scholarly article on the Web has no page or other reference numbers.

Short-term solution.

use of raw materials. Precycling includes choosing eco-friendly products made of nontoxic or recycled materials (such as aluminum-free deodorants and fleece made from discarded soda bottles) and avoiding items wrapped in excessive packaging (such as kitchen tools strapped to cardboard and printer cartridges sealed in plastic clamshells). More important, though, precycling means not buying new things in the first place. Renting and borrowing, when possible, save money and resources; so do keeping possessions in good repair and not replacing them until absolutely necessary. Good-quality used items, from clothing to furniture to electronics, can be obtained for free, or very cheaply, through online communities like *Craigslist* and *Freecycle,* from thrift stores and yard sales, or by trading with friends and relatives. When consumers choose used goods over new, they can help to reduce the demand for manufactured products that waste energy and resources, and they can help to keep unwanted items out of the waste stream.

> Common-knowledge definition and writer's own examples do not require source citations.

Avoiding unnecessary purchases brings personal benefits as well. Brenda Lin, an environmental activist, explained in an e-mail interview that frugal living not only saves money but also provides pleasure:

> Primary source: personal interview by e-mail.

> You'd be amazed at what people throw out or give away: perfectly good computers, oriental rugs, barely used sports equipment, designer clothes, you name it. . . . It's a game for me to find what I need in other people's trash or at Goodwill. You should see the shock on people's faces when I tell them where I got my stuff. I get almost as much enjoyment from that as from saving money and helping the environment at the same time.

> Quotation of over four lines set off without quotation marks. See page 466.

> Ellipsis mark signals omission from quotation.

Lin's experience relates to research on the personal and social consequences of consumerism by the sociologist Juliet B. Schor. In one study, Schor found that the more people buy, the less happy they tend to feel because of the stress of working longer hours to afford their purchases (*Overspent* 11-12). Researching the opposite effect, Schor surveyed thousands of Americans who had drastically reduced their spending so that they would be less dependent on paid work. For these people, she discovered, a deliberately lower

> Citation form: no parenthetical citation because author is named in the text and interview has no page or other reference numbers.

> Citation form: shortened title for one of two works by the same author.

Malik 7

standard of living improved their quality of life by leaving them more time to socialize, get involved with their communities, and pursue personal interests (*True Wealth* 126-27, 139). Reducing consumption, it turns out, does not have to translate into sacrifice.

For unavoidable purchases like food and light bulbs, buying green can make a difference by influencing corporate decisions. Some ecologists and economists believe that as more shoppers choose earth-friendly products over their traditional counterparts—or boycott products that are clearly harmful to the environment—more manufacturers and retailers will look for ways to limit the environmental effects of their industrial practices and the goods they sell (de Blas; Gore). Indeed, as environmental business consultant Joel Makower and his coauthors point out, Coca-Cola, Walmart, Procter & Gamble, General Motors, and other major companies have already taken up sustainability initiatives in response to market pressure. In the process, the companies have discovered that environmentally minded practices tend to raise profits and strengthen customer loyalty (5-6). By giving industry solid, bottom-line reasons to embrace ecological goals, consumer demand for earth-friendly products can magnify the effects of individual action.

Careful shopping can help the environment, but green doesn't necessarily mean "Go." All consumption depletes resources, increases the likelihood of global warming, and creates waste, so even eco-friendly products must be used in moderation. Individuals can play small roles in helping the environment—and help themselves at the same time—by not buying anything they don't really need, even if it seems environmentally sound. The sacrifice by each person in reducing his or her personal impact on the earth is a small price for preserving a livable planet for future generations.

Citation form: page numbers indicate exact locations of information in source.

Writer's own conclusion from two sources.

Benefits of green consumerism.

Citation form: two works in the same citation.

Citation form: authors are named in the text, so page numbers only.

Conclusion: summary and a call for action.

Works Cited

Atkinson, Lucy, and Sonny Rosenthal. "Signaling the Green Sell: The Influence of Eco-Label Source, Argument for Specificity, and Product Involvement on Consumer Trust." *Journal of Advertising,* vol. 43, no. 1, 2014, pp. 33-45. *Business Source Premier,* doi:10.1080/00913367.2013.834803.

Broder, John M. "Complaints Abound in 'Green' Certification Industry." *The New York Times,* 1 June 2013, p. F4. *LexisNexis Academic,* www.lexisnexis.com/ lnacademic/ HEADLINE(Complaints+abound+green+certification+2C+ industry) %4F2013.

"Data Center." *Earth Policy Institute,* 16 Feb. 2014, www. earth-policy.org/?/data_center/C22/.

deBlas, Alexandra. "Making the Shift: From Consumerism to Sustainability." *Ecos,* no. 153, 2010. www.ecos. net/?paper=EC153p10.

DeGraaf, John, et al. *Affluenza: The All-Consuming Epidemic.* 3rd ed. Berrett-Koehler Publishers, 2014.

Gore, Al. *An Inconvenient Truth.* Paramount, 2006.

Harris, Rebecca. "Greenwashing: Cleaning Up by 'Saving the World.'" *Marketing Magazine,* 25 Apr. 2013, pp. 37-40. *MasterFILE Premier,* www.masterfile.com/marketingmag/ greenwashing-cleaning-up-by-saving-the-world-77259.

"LED Lightbulbs." *Consumer Reports,* Oct. 2010, pp. 26-28.

Lin, Brenda. "Re: Interview about Living Green." Received by the author, 21 Mar. 2014.

Makower, Joel, et al. "State of Green Business Report 2014." *Greenbiz,* Jan. 2014, www.greenbiz.com/research/ report/2014/01/19/state-green-business-report-2014.

"Municipal Solid Waste Generation, Recycling, and Disposal in the United States: Facts and Figures for 2012." *US Environmental Protection Agency,* Feb. 2014, www3.epa.gov/ wastes/nonhaz/municipal/pubs/2012_msw_dat_tbls. pdf.

Owen, David. "The Efficiency Dilemma." *The New Yorker,* 20 Dec. 2010, pp. 78-85. *Points of View Reference Center,* www.ebscohost.com/points-of-view/ article=AN159870231.

Introduction to a print anthology.	Princen, Thomas, et al. Introduction. *Confronting Consumption,* edited by Princen et al., MIT P, 2002, pp. 1-20.
Book with one author.	Schor, Juliet B. *The Overspent American: Upscaling, Downshifting, and the New Consumer.* Basic Books, 1998.
Second source by author of two cited works: three hyphens replace author's name.	---. *True Wealth: How and Why Millions of Americans Are Creating a Time-Rich, Ecologically Light, Small-Scale, High-Satisfaction Economy.* Penguin, 2011. *Ebrary,* site.ebrary.com/lib/reader.action?docID=10493613.
Book with a corporate author that is named because it's different from the publisher.	United Nations Development Programme. *Human Development Report: Sustainability and Equity—A Better Future for All.* Palgrave, 2011.

MLA
56d

57 APA Documentation and Format

In *Brief*

- In your text, document your sources with citations (below).
- Prepare an APA list of references (p. 481).
- Follow APA guidelines for paper format, including margins, spacing, headings, long quotations, illustrations, and other elements (p. 497).

Visit MyWritingLab™ for more resources on APA documentation and format.

The style guide for psychology and some other social sciences is the *Publication Manual of the American Psychological Association* (6th ed., 2010). The APA provides answers to frequently asked questions at *www.apastyle.org/learn/faqs*.

In APA documentation style, you acknowledge each of your sources twice:

- **In your text, a brief citation adjacent to the borrowed material directs readers to a complete list of all the works you refer to.**
- **At the end of your paper, the list of references includes complete bibliographical information for every source.**

Every entry in the list of references has at least one corresponding citation in the text, and every in-text citation has a corresponding entry in the list of references.

57a Use APA style for in-text citations.

In APA style, citations within the body of the text refer the reader to a list of sources at the end of the text. See the box on the next page for an index to the models for various kinds of sources.

Note When you cite the same source more than once in a paragraph, APA style does not require you to repeat the date beyond the first citation as long as it's clear what source you refer to. Do give the date in every citation if your source list includes more than one work by the same author(s).

1. Author not named in your text

One critic of Milgram's experiments questioned whether the researchers behaved morally toward their subjects (Baumrind, 1988).

When you do not name the author in your text, place in parentheses the author's last name, the date of the source, and sometimes the page number as explained on the next page. Separate the elements with commas. Position the reference so that it is clear what material is being documented *and* so that the reference fits as smoothly as possible into your sentence structure. (See pages 426–27 for guidelines.)

APA
57a

APA in-text citations

Unless none is available, the APA requires a page or other identifying number for a direct quotation and recommends an identifying number for a paraphrase:

In the view of one critic of Milgram's experiments (Baumrind, 1988), the subjects "should have been fully informed of the possible effects on them" (p. 34).

Use an appropriate abbreviation before the number—for instance, p. for *page* and para. for *paragraph*. The identifying number may fall by itself in parentheses, as in the preceding example, or it may fall with the author and date: (Baumrind, 1988, p. 34). See also model 11, page 480.

2. Author named in your text

Baumrind (1988) insisted that the subjects in Milgram's study "should have been fully informed of the possible effects on them" (p. 34).

When you use the author's name in the text, do not repeat it in parentheses. Place the source date in parentheses after the author's name. Place any page or paragraph reference either after the borrowed material (as in the example) or with the date: (1988, p. 34).

3. Work with two authors

Bunning and Ellis (2014) revealed significant communication differences between teachers and students.

One study (Bunning & Ellis, 2014) revealed significant communication differences between teachers and students.

When given in the text, two authors' names are connected by and. In a parenthetical citation, they are connected by an ampersand, &.

4. Work with three to five authors

Pepinsky, Dunn, Rentl, and Corson (2010) demonstrated the biases evident in gestures.

APA
57a

In the first citation of a work with three to five authors, name all the authors.

In the second and subsequent references to a work with three to five authors, generally give only the first author's name, followed by et al. (Latin abbreviation for "and others"):

> In the work of **Pepinsky et al.** (2010), the loaded gestures included head shakes and eye contact.

However, two or more sources published in the same year could shorten to the same form—for instance, two references shortening to Pepinsky et al., 2010. In that case, cite the last names of as many authors as you need to distinguish the sources, and then give et al.: for instance, (Pepinsky, Dunn, et al., 2010) and (Pepinsky, Bradley, et al., 2010).

5. Work with six or more authors

> One study **(McCormack et al.**, 2013) explored children's day-to-day experience of living with a speech impairment.

For six or more authors, even in the first citation of the work, give only the first author's name, followed by et al. If two or more sources published in the same year shorten to the same form, give additional names as explained with model 4.

6. Work with a group author

> The students' later work improved significantly **(Lenschow Research, 2014)**.

For a work that lists an institution, agency, corporation, or other group as author, treat the name of the group as if it were one person's name. If the name is long and has a familiar abbreviation, you may use the abbreviation in the second and subsequent citations. For example, you might abbreviate American Psychological Association as APA.

7. Work with no author or an anonymous work

> One article **("Leaping the Wall,"** 2014) examines Internet freedom and censorship in China.

For a work with no named author, use the first two or three words of the title in place of an author's name, excluding an initial *The*, *A*, or *An*. Italicize book and journal titles, place quotation marks around article titles, and capitalize the significant words in all titles cited in the text. (In the reference list, however, do not use quotation marks for article titles, and capitalize only the first word in all but periodical titles. See p. 482.)

For a work that lists "Anonymous" as the author, use that word in the citation: (Anonymous, 2015).

8. One of two or more works by the same author(s)

At about age seven, most children begin to use appropriate gestures to reinforce their stories (Gardner, 1973a).

When you cite one of two or more works by the same author(s), the date will tell readers which source you mean—as long as your reference list includes only one source published by the author(s) in that year. If your reference list includes two or more works published by the same author(s) *in the same year,* the works should be lettered in the reference list (see p. 485). Then your text citation should include the appropriate letter with the date: 1973a above.

9. Two or more works by different authors

Two studies (Marconi & Hamblen, 1999; Torrence, 2013) found that monthly safety meetings can dramatically reduce workplace injuries.

List the sources in alphabetical order by their authors' names. Insert a semicolon between sources.

10. Indirect source

Supporting data appeared in a study by Wong (as cited in Gallivan, 2014).

The phrase as cited in indicates that the reference to Wong's study was found in Gallivan. Only Gallivan then appears in the list of references.

11. Electronic or Web source

Ferguson and Hawkins (2015) did not anticipate the "evident hostility" of the participants (para. 6).

Many electronic and Web sources can be cited like printed sources, with the author's last name, the publication date, and page numbers. Others are missing one or more pieces of information:

- **No page numbers:** When quoting or paraphrasing a source that numbers paragraphs instead of pages, provide the paragraph number preceded by para., as in the preceding example. If the source does not number pages or paragraphs but does include headings, list the heading under which the quotation appears and then (counting paragraphs yourself) the number of the paragraph in which the quotation appears—for example, (Endter & Decker, 2014, Method section, para. 3). When the source does not number pages or paragraphs or provide frequent headings, omit any reference number.
- **No author:** For a source with no listed author, follow model 7.
- **No date:** For a source that is undated, use n.d. ("no date") in place of the date.

57b   Prepare an APA reference list.

In APA style, the in-text citations refer readers to the list of sources at the end of the text. Title this list References and include in it the full publication information for every source you cited in your paper. Place the list at the end of the paper, and number its page(s) in sequence with the preceding pages.

The following sample shows the format of the first page of the APA reference list:

APA reference list

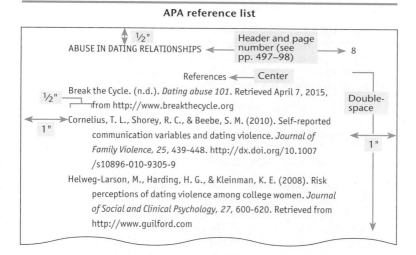

Arrangement Arrange sources alphabetically by the author's last name. If there is no author, alphabetize by the first main word of the title.

Spacing Double-space the title and all the references, as shown in the sample, unless your instructor requests single spacing. (If you do single-space the entries themselves, always double-space *between* them.)

Indention As illustrated in the sample, begin each entry at the left margin, and indent the second and subsequent lines one-half inch. Your word processor can create this so-called hanging indent automatically.

Punctuation Separate the parts of the reference (author, date, title, and publication information) with a period and one space. Do not use a final period in references that conclude with a DOI or URL (see the next page).

APA

57b

Authors For works with up to seven authors, list all authors with last name first, separating names and parts of names with commas. Use initials for first and middle names even when names are listed fully on the source itself. Use an ampersand (&) before the last author's name. See model 3 (opposite) for the treatment of eight or more authors.

Publication date Place the publication date in parentheses after the author's or authors' names, followed by a period. Generally, this date is the year only, though for some sources (such as magazine and newspaper articles) it includes the month and sometimes the day as well.

Titles In titles of books and articles, capitalize only the first word of the title, the first word of the subtitle, and proper nouns; all other words begin with small letters. In titles of periodicals, capitalize all significant words. Italicize the titles of books and periodicals. Do not italicize or use quotation marks around the titles of articles.

City and state of publication For sources that are not periodicals (such as books or government publications), give the city of publication, a comma, the two-letter postal abbreviation of the state, and a colon. Omit the state if the publisher is a university whose name includes the state name, such as University of Arizona.

Publisher's name Also for nonperiodical sources, give the publisher's name after the place of publication and a colon. Shorten names of many publishers (such as Morrow for William Morrow), and omit *Co., Inc.,* and *Publishers.* However, give full names for associations, corporations, and university presses (such as Harvard University Press), and do not omit *Books* or *Press* from a publisher's name.

Page numbers Use the abbreviation p. or pp. before page numbers in books and in newspapers. Do *not* use the abbreviation for journals and magazines. For inclusive page numbers, include all figures: 667-668.

Digital Object Identifier (DOI) or retrieval statement At the end of each entry in the reference list, APA style requires a DOI for print and electronic sources (if one is available) or a retrieval statement for electronic sources.

APA
57b

- **DOI:** Many publishers assign a DOI to journal articles, books, and other documents. A DOI is a permanent URL that links to the text and functions as a unique identifier. When a DOI is available, include it in your citation of any print or electronic source. DOIs appear in one of two formats, as shown in model 7a (p. 486) and model 10 (p. 490). Use the format given in the source.

▪ **Retrieval statement:** If a DOI is not available for a source you found in a database or on the Web, provide a statement beginning with Retrieved from and then giving the URL of the periodical's or Web site's home page (model 7c, p. 486). You need not include the date you retrieved the source unless it is undated (model 22b, p. 493) or is likely to change (model 29, p. 495). If the source is difficult to find from the home page, you may give the complete URL. If you have questions about whether to include a home-page URL or a complete URL, ask your instructor.

Do not add a period after a DOI or a URL. Break a DOI or URL from one line to the next only before punctuation, such as a period or a slash, and do not hyphenate.

An index to the following models appears on the next two pages. If you don't see a model for the kind of source you used, try to find one that comes close, and provide ample information so that readers can trace the source. Often you will have to combine models to cite a source accurately.

1 ▪ Authors

1. One author

Rodriguez, R. (1982). *A hunger of memory: The education of Richard Rodriguez.*
    Boston, MA: Godine.

The initial R. appears instead of the author's first name, even though the author's full first name appears on the source. In this book title, only the first words of the title and subtitle and the proper name are capitalized.

2. Two to seven authors

Nesselroade, J. R., & Baltes, P. B. (1999). *Longitudinal research in behavioral studies.* New York, NY: Academic Press.

With two to seven authors, separate authors' names with commas and use an ampersand (&) before the last author's name.

3. Eight or more authors

Wimple, P. B., Van Eijk, M., Potts, C. A., Hayes, J., Obergau, W. R., Smith, H., ... Zimmer, S. (2001). *Case studies in moral decision making among adolescents.* San Francisco, CA: Jossey-Bass.

For a work by eight or more authors, list the first six authors' names, insert an ellipsis mark (three spaced periods), and then give the last author's name.

APA references

4. A group author

Lenschow Research. (2014). *Trends in secondary curriculum.* Baltimore, MD: Arrow Books.

For a work with a group author—such as a research group, a committee, a government agency, an association, or a corporation—begin the entry with the group name. In the reference list, alphabetize the work as if the first main word (excluding any *The, A,* or *An*) were an author's last name.

5. Author not named (anonymous)

Merriam-Webster's collegiate dictionary (11th ed.). (2008). Springfield, MA: Merriam-Webster.

Resistance is not futile. (2014, April 5). *New Scientist, 221*(15), 5.

When no author is named, list the work under its title and alphabetize it by the first main word (excluding any *The, A, An*).

For a work whose author is actually given as "Anonymous," use that word in place of the author's name and alphabetize it as if it were a name:

Anonymous. (2015). *Teaching research, researching teaching.* New York, NY: Alpine Press.

6. Two or more works by the same author(s) published in the same year

Gardner, H. (1973a). *The arts and human development.* New York, NY: Wiley.

Gardner, H. (1973b). *The quest for mind: Piaget, Lévi-Strauss, and the structuralist movement.* New York, NY: Knopf.

When citing two or more works by exactly the same author(s), published in the same year, arrange them alphabetically by the first main word of the title and distinguish the sources by adding a letter to the date. Both the date and the letter are used in citing the source in your text (see p. 480).

When citing two or more works by exactly the same author(s) but *not* published in the same year, arrange the sources in order of their publication dates, earliest first.

2 ▪ Articles in journals, magazines, and newspapers

7. Article in a scholarly journal

Some journals number the pages of issues consecutively during a year, so that each issue after the first begins numbering where the previous issue left off—say, at page 132 or 416. For this kind of journal, give the volume number after the title (models a, b, c). Other journals as well as most magazines start each issue with page 1. For these journals and magazines, place the issue number in parentheses and not italicized immediately after the volume number (model 8).

a. Print, database, or Web journal article with a DOI

Hirsh, A. T., Gallegos, J. C., Gertz, K. J., Engel, J. M., & Jensen, M. P. (2010). Symptom burden in individuals with cerebral palsy. *Journal of Rehabilitation Research & Development, 47,* 860-876. doi:10.1682/JRRD.2010.03.0024

See pages 488–89 for an explanation of this format and the location of the required information on a source. The format is the same for any journal article that has a DOI—print, database, or Web.

Note DOIs appear in one of two formats, as shown above and in model 10 (p. 490). Use the format given in the source.

b. Print journal article without a DOI

Atkinson, N. S. (2011). Newsreels as domestic propaganda: Visual rhetoric at the dawn of the cold war. *Rhetoric and Public Affairs, 14,* 69-105.

If a print journal article does not have a DOI, simply end with the page numbers of the article.

c. Database or Web journal article without a DOI

Maness, D. L., & Khan, M. (2015). Disability evaluations: More than completing a form. *American Family Physician, 91,* 102-109. Retrieved from http://www.aafp.org/journals/afp.html

If a journal article you found in a database or on the Web does not have a DOI, use a search engine to find the home page of the journal and give the home-page URL, as in the preceding example. Generally, do not give the name of a database in which you found an article because readers may not be able to find the source the same way you did. However, do give the database name if you cannot find the home page of the journal on the Web, as in this example:

> Smith, E. M. (1926, March). Equal rights—internationally! *Life and Labor Bulletin, 4,* 1-2. Retrieved from Women and Social Movements in the United States, 1600-2000, database.

8. Article in a magazine

For magazine articles, give the month of publication as well as any day along with the year. If the magazine gives volume and issue numbers, list them after the title of the magazine. Italicize the volume number and place the issue number, not italicized, in parentheses.

a. Print magazine article

> Newton-Small, J. (2014, February 18). Blood for oil. *Time, 181*(6), 22.

b. Database or Web magazine article

> Weir, K. (2015, March 4). Our forgotten years. *New Scientist, 271*(11), 35-37. Retrieved from http://www.newscientist.com

If a magazine article includes a DOI, give it after the page numbers. Otherwise, give the URL of the magazine's home page in a retrieval statement. If you do not find the home page, give the name of the database in which you found the article (see the Smith example above).

9. Article in a newspaper

For newspaper articles, give the month and day of publication with the year. Use *The* in the newspaper name if the paper itself does.

a. Print newspaper article

> Zimmer, C. (2014, May 4). Young blood may hold key to reversing aging. *The New York Times,* p. C1.

Precede the page number(s) with p. or pp.

b. Database or Web newspaper article

> Angier, N. (2015, January 12). No time for bats to rest easy. *The New York Times.* Retrieved from http://www.nytimes.com

Give the URL of the newspaper's home page in the retrieval statement. If you do not find the home page, give the name of the database in which you found the article (see the Smith example above).

APA
57b

(continued on p. 490)

Citing journal articles: Print, database, or Web with DOI

Print journal article

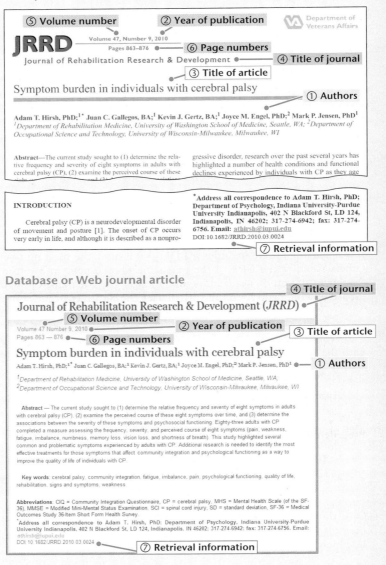

⑤ **Volume number** ② **Year of publication**

JRRD Volume 47, Number 9, 2010

Pages 863–876 — ⑥ **Page numbers**

Journal of Rehabilitation Research & Development — ④ **Title of journal**

③ **Title of article**

Symptom burden in individuals with cerebral palsy

① **Authors**

Adam T. Hirsh, PhD;[1*] Juan C. Gallegos, BA;[1] Kevin J. Gertz, BA;[1] Joyce M. Engel, PhD;[2] Mark P. Jensen, PhD[1]
[1]*Department of Rehabilitation Medicine, University of Washington School of Medicine, Seattle, WA;* [2]*Department of Occupational Science and Technology, University of Wisconsin-Milwaukee, Milwaukee, WI*

Abstract—The current study sought to (1) determine the relative frequency and severity of eight symptoms in adults with cerebral palsy (CP), (2) examine the perceived course of these ... gressive disorder, research over the past several years has highlighted a number of health conditions and functional declines experienced by individuals with CP as they age

INTRODUCTION

Cerebral palsy (CP) is a neurodevelopmental disorder of movement and posture [1]. The onset of CP occurs very early in life, and although it is described as a nonpro-

*Address all correspondence to Adam T. Hirsh, PhD; Department of Psychology, Indiana University-Purdue University Indianapolis, 402 N Blackford St, LD 124, Indianapolis, IN 46202; 317-274-6942; fax: 317-274-6756. Email: athirsh@iupui.edu
DOI:10.1682/JRRD.2010.03.0024

⑦ **Retrieval information**

Database or Web journal article

④ **Title of journal**

Journal of Rehabilitation Research & Development (*JRRD*)

⑤ **Volume number**

Volume 47 Number 9, 2010 — ② **Year of publication**

Pages 863 — 876 — ⑥ **Page numbers** ③ **Title of article**

Symptom burden in individuals with cerebral palsy

Adam T. Hirsh, PhD;[1*] Juan C. Gallegos, BA;[1] Kevin J. Gertz, BA;[1] Joyce M. Engel, PhD;[2] Mark P. Jensen, PhD[1] — ① **Authors**

[1]*Department of Rehabilitation Medicine, University of Washington School of Medicine, Seattle, WA;*
[2]*Department of Occupational Science and Technology, University of Wisconsin-Milwaukee, Milwaukee, WI*

Abstract — The current study sought to (1) determine the relative frequency and severity of eight symptoms in adults with cerebral palsy (CP). (2) examine the perceived course of these eight symptoms over time, and (3) determine the associations between the severity of these symptoms and psychosocial functioning. Eighty-three adults with CP completed a measure assessing the frequency, severity, and perceived course of eight symptoms (pain, weakness, fatigue, imbalance, numbness, memory loss, vision loss, and shortness of breath). This study highlighted several common and problematic symptoms experienced by adults with CP. Additional research is needed to identify the most effective treatments for those symptoms that affect community integration and psychological functioning as a way to improve the quality of life of individuals with CP.

Key words: cerebral palsy, community integration, fatigue, imbalance, pain, psychological functioning, quality of life, rehabilitation, signs and symptoms, weakness

Abbreviations CIQ = Community Integration Questionnaire, CP = cerebral palsy, MHS = Mental Health Scale (of the SF-36), MMSE = Modified Mini-Mental Status Examination, SCI = spinal cord injury, SD = standard deviation, SF-36 = Medical Outcomes Study 36-Item Short Form Health Survey.
*Address all correspondence to Adam T. Hirsh, PhD; Department of Psychology, Indiana University-Purdue University Indianapolis, 402 N Blackford St, LD 124, Indianapolis, IN 46202; 317-274-6942; fax: 317-274-6756. Email: athirsh@iupui.edu
DOI 10.1682/JRRD.2010.03.0024

⑦ **Retrieval information**

APA 57b

References entry: Print, database, or Web journal article
with DOI

Hirsh, A. T., Gallegos, J. C., Gertz, K. J., Engel, J. M., & Jensen,
①

M. P. (2010). Symptom burden in individuals with cerebral
②   ③

palsy. *Journal of Rehabilitation Research & Development, 47,*
④   ⑤

860-876. doi:10.1682/JRRD.2010.03.0024
⑥   ⑦

① **Authors.** Give each author's last name, first initial, and any middle
initial. Separate names from initials with commas, and use & before the last author's name. Omit *Dr., PhD,* or any other title. See
models 1–6 (pp. 483 and 485–86) for how to cite various numbers and kinds of authors.

② **Year of publication,** in parentheses and followed by a period.

③ **Title of article.** Give the full article title and any subtitle, separating them with a colon. Capitalize only the first words of the
title and subtitle, and do not place the title in quotation marks.

④ **Title of journal,** in italics. Capitalize all significant words and end
with a comma.

⑤ **Volume number,** italicized and followed by a comma. Include
just the volume number when all the issues in each annual volume are paginated in one sequence. Include the issue number
only when the issues are paginated separately (see model 7).

⑥ **Inclusive page numbers of article,** without "pp." Do not omit
any numerals.

⑦ **Retrieval information.** If the article has a DOI, give it using the
format here or as shown in model 10. Do not end with a period.
If the article does not have a DOI, see models 7b and 7c. (See pp.
482–83 for more on DOIs and retrieval statements.)

(continued from p. 487)

10. Review

Bond, M. (2008, December 18). Does genius breed success? [Review of the book *Outliers: The story of success,* by M. Gladwell]. *Nature, 456,* 785. http://dx.doi.org/10.1038/456874a

If a review has no title, use the bracketed information in its place, keeping the brackets.

11. Interview

Shaffir, S. (2013). It's our generation's responsibility to bring a genuine feeling of hope [Interview by H. Schenker]. *Palestine-Israeli Journal of Politics, Economics, and Culture, 18*(4). Retrieved from http://pij.org

List an interview under the interviewee's name and give the title, if any. If there is no title, or if the title does not indicate that the source is an interview, add a bracketed explanation, as above. End with publication information for the kind of source the interview appears in— here a journal on the Web, which requires retrieval information.

See model 32 (pp. 495–96) to cite a recorded interview. See model 30 (p. 495) to cite an interview you conduct, which should be treated like a personal communication and cited only in the text.

12. Supplemental periodical content that appears only online

Anderson, J. L. (2014, May 2). Revolutionary relics [Supplemental material]. *The New Yorker.* Retrieved from www.newyorker.com

If you cite material from a periodical's Web site that is not included in the print version of the publication, add [Supplemental material] after the title and give the URL of the publication's home page.

13. Abstract of a journal article

Thomas, N. L. (2014). Democracy by design. *Journal of Public Deliberation, 10*(1). Abstract retrieved from http://www.publicdeliberation.net/jpd

When you cite the abstract of an article, give the full publication information for the article, followed by Abstract and information about where you found the abstract.

3 ▪ **Books, government publications, and other independent works**

14. Basic format for a book

a. **Print book**

Ehrenreich, B. (2007). *Dancing in the streets: A history of collective joy.* New York, NY: Holt.

Give the author's or authors' names, following models 1–4. Then give the complete title, including any subtitle. Italicize the title, and capitalize only the first words of the title and subtitle. End the entry with the city and state of publication and the publisher's name. (See p. 482 for how to treat these elements.)

b. Web or database book

Reuter, P. (Ed.). (2014). *Understanding the demand for illegal drugs.* Retrieved
   from http://books.nap.edu

For a book available on the Web or in an online library or database, replace any print publication information with a DOI if one is available (see model 7a) or with a retrieval statement, as above.

c. E-book

Waltz, M. (2013). *Autism: A social and medical history* [Kindle version].
   Retrieved from http://www.amazon.com

For an e-book, give the format in brackets and a retrieval statement.

15. Book with an editor

Dohrenwend, B. S., & Dohrenwend, B. P. (Eds.). (1999). *Stressful life events:
   Their nature and effects.* New York, NY: Wiley.

List the names of the editors as if they were authors, but follow the last name with (Eds.).—or (Ed.). with only one editor. Note the periods inside and outside the final parenthesis.

16. Book with a translator

Trajan, P. D. (1927). *Psychology of animals* (H. Simone, Trans.). Washington, DC:
   Halperin.

17. Later edition

Bolinger, D. L. (1981). *Aspects of language* (3rd ed.). New York, NY: Harcourt
   Brace Jovanovich.

18. Work in more than one volume

Lincoln, A. (1953). *The collected works of Abraham Lincoln* (R. P. Basler, Ed.).
   (Vol. 5). New Brunswick, NJ: Rutgers University Press.
Lincoln, A. (1953). *The collected works of Abraham Lincoln* (R. P. Basler, Ed.).
   (Vols. 1–8). New Brunswick, NJ: Rutgers University Press.

The first entry cites a single volume (5) in the eight-volume set. The second entry cites all eight volumes. Use Vol. or Vols. in parentheses and follow the closing parenthesis with a period. In the absence of an editor's name, this description would follow the title directly: *The collected works of Abraham Lincoln* (Vol. 5).

APA
57b

19. Article or chapter in an edited book

Paykel, E. S. (1999). Life stress and psychiatric disorder: Applications of the
    clinical approach. In B. S. Dohrenwend & B. P. Dohrenwend (Eds.),
    Stressful life events: Their nature and effects (pp. 239-264). New York,
    NY: Wiley.

Give the publication date of the collection (1999 here) as the publication date of the article or chapter. After the article or chapter title and a period, say In and then provide the editors' names (in normal order), (Eds.) and a comma, the title of the collection, and the page numbers of the article in parentheses.

20. Article in a reference work

Wood, R. (1998). Community organization. In W. A. Swatos, Jr. (Ed.), *Encyclope-*
    dia of religion and society. Retrieved from http://hirr.hartsem.edu/ency
    /commorg.htm

If the entry you cite has no named author, begin with the title of the entry and then the date. Use a DOI instead of a URL if the source has one.

21. Government publication

a. Print publication

Hawaii. Department of Education. (2014). *Kauai district schools, profile 2013-14.*
    Honolulu, HI: Author.

Stiller, A. (2012). *Historic preservation and tax incentives.* Washington, DC: U.S.
    Department of the Interior.

If no person is named as the author, list the publication under the name of the sponsoring agency. When the agency is both the author and the publisher, use Author in place of the publisher's name, as in the first example.

For legal materials such as court decisions, laws, and testimony at hearings, the APA recommends formats that correspond to conventional legal citations. The following example of a congressional hearing includes the full title, the number of the Congress, the page number where the hearing transcript starts in the official publication, and the date of the hearing.

Medicare payment for outpatient physical and occupational therapy services:
    Hearing before the Committee on Ways and Means, House of Representatives,
    110th Cong. 3 (2007).

b. Web publication

National Institute on Alcohol Abuse and Alcoholism. (2015, July). *Underage*
    drinking [Fact sheet]. Retrieved from http://pubs.niaaa.nih.gov
    /publications/UnderageDrinking/Underage_Fact.pdf

For a government publication on the Web, add a retrieval statement.

22. Report

a. Print report

Gerald, K. (2003). *Medico-moral problems in obstetric care* (Report No. NP-71). St. Louis, MO: Catholic Hospital Association.

Treat a printed report like a book, but provide any report number in parentheses after the title, with no punctuation between them.

b. Web report

Anderson, J. A., & Rainie, L. (2014, March 11). *Digital life in 2025.* Retrieved from Pew Research Internet Project website: http://www.pewinternet.org

For a report on the Web, give the name of the publisher in the retrieval statement if the publisher is not the author of the report. Generally, provide the URL of the Web site's home page.

If the work you cite is undated, use the abbreviation n.d. in place of the publication date and give the date of your access in the retrieval statement:

U.S. Census Bureau. (n.d.). *Men's marital status: 1950-2013.* Retrieved April 23, 2015, from https://www.census.gov/hhes/families/files/graphics /MS-1a.pdf

23. Dissertation

a. Dissertation in a commercial database

McFaddin, M. O. (2007). *Adaptive reuse: An architectural solution for poverty and homelessness* (Doctoral dissertation). Available from ProQuest Dissertations and Theses database. (ATT 1378764)

If a dissertation is from a commercial database, give the name of the database in the retrieval statement, followed by the accession or order number in parentheses.

b. Dissertation in an institutional database

Chang, J. K. (2003). *Therapeutic intervention in treatment of injuries to the hand and wrist* (Doctoral dissertation). Retrieved from http://medsci .archive.liasu.edu/61724

If a dissertation is from an institution's database, give the URL in the retrieval statement.

4 ▪ Web sources and social media

Specific types of Web sources are covered under their respective categories, such as articles in periodicals (models 7a, 7c, 8b, 9b), books (model 14b), and reports (model 22b). When citing URLs, APA recommends giving the home-page URL unless the source is difficult to find from the home page. In such a case, provide the complete URL.

24. Part or all of a Web site

American Psychological Association. (2014). Information for students with disabilities [Web page]. Retrieved from http://www.apa.org

To cite a page or document on a Web site, give the author (if any), the date (or n.d. if the page or site is undated), the title of the page or document, a description in brackets, and a retrieval statement.

Cite an entire Web site just in the text of your paper, giving the name of the site in your text and the URL in parentheses:

The Web site of the Cyberbullying Research Center provides information on the causes and nature of cyberbullying among teenagers (http://cyberbullying.us).

Although APA does not require you to include entire Web sites in your list of references, some instructors ask for such references. Then you can use the format shown in the first example, substituting the title of the Web site for the title of the Web page or document.

25. Post to a blog or discussion group

Kristof, N. (2014, March 22). Confronting the netherworld of child pornography [Blog post]. Retrieved from http://kristof.blogs.nytimes.com

Include postings to blogs and discussion groups in your list of references only if they are retrievable by others. (The source above is retrievable by a search of the home-page URL.) Follow the message title with [Blog post], [Electronic mailing list message], or [Online forum comment]. Include the name of the blog or discussion group in the retrieval statement if it isn't part of the URL.

26. Blog comment

Peter. (2014, March 23). Re: Confronting the netherworld of child pornography [Blog comment]. Retrieved from http://kristof.blogs.nytimes.com

27. Post to a social-networking site

Environmental Defense Fund. (2014, May 1). Extreme weather = extreme consequences [Facebook status update]. Retrieved from https://www.facebook.com/EnvDefenseFund?fref=ts

28. Tweet

Bittman, M. [bittman]. (2015, February 24). Unraveling the #gluten-free trend: bit.ly/1BMYTJ8 [Tweet]. Retrieved from http://twitter.com/bittman

29. Wiki

Clinical neuropsychology. (2013, November 12). Retrieved April 15, 2015, from
    Wikipedia: http://en.wikipedia.org/wiki/Clinical_neuropsychology

Give your date of retrieval for sources that are likely to change, such as this wiki.

30. E-mail or other personal communication (text citation)

At least one member of the research team has expressed reservations about the design of the study (L. Kogod, personal communication, February 6, 2015).

Personal e-mail, personal letters, interviews that you conduct yourself, and other communication that is not retrievable by others should be cited only in the text, not in the list of references.

5 ▪ Video, audio, and other media sources

31. Film or video recording

If you cite a film or video as a whole, begin with the producer's name as in the first example below. Otherwise, cite the name or names of the creator, director, or other contributor, followed by the function in parentheses. Add the medium in brackets after the title: [Motion picture] for film, [DVD], [Videocasette], or [Video file].

a. Motion picture or DVD

American Psychological Association (Producer). (2001). *Ethnocultural psycho-therapy* [DVD]. Available from http://www.apa.org/videos
Tyrrell, C. (Director). (2010). *The Joneses* [Motion picture]. United States: Bjort Productions.

For a work in wide circulation (second example), give the country of origin and the studio that released the picture. For a work that is not widely circulated (first example), give the distributor's address or URL.

b. Video on the Web

CBS News (Producer). (1968, April 4). *1968 King assassination report* [Video file]. Retrieved from http://www.youtube.com/watch?v=cmOBbxgxKvo

In the retrieval statement, give the home-page URL unless the video you cite is difficult to locate from the home page. In that case, give the complete URL, as in the example.

32. Recorded interview

Ambar, S. (2015, April 1). Interview by T. Smiley [Video file]. Retrieved from http://www.pbs.org/wnet/tavissmiley

For an interview you view or listen to on the Web, give the name of the interviewee, the date, and the title of the interview, if any. Then give the interviewer's name if you wish, the type of file ([Video file] or [Audio file]), and a retrieval statement.

For an interview you see on television or hear in a podcast, adapt the preceding example using model 33b or 35.

33. Television series or episode

a. Television series

Rhimes, S. (Executive producer). (2015). *Grey's anatomy* [Television series]. New
  York, NY: ABC.

For a television series, begin with the producer's name and function. Add [Television series] after the title, and give either the city and name of the network or a Web retrieval statement.

b. Broadcast episode of television program

McKee, S. (Writer), & Wilson, C. (Director). (2014). Do you know? [Television
  series episode]. In S. Rhimes (Executive producer), *Grey's anatomy*. New
  York, NY: ABC.

For a TV episode, begin with the writer and then the director, identifying the function of each in parentheses, and add [Television series episode] after the episode title. Then provide the series information, beginning with In and the producer's name and function, giving the series title, and ending with the city, the state, and the name of the network.

c. Web episode of a television program

Randall, T. (Writer & Director). (2012). How smart can we get? [Television
  series episode]. In J. Cort (Executive producer), *Nova*. Retrieved from
  http://www.pbs.org/wgbh/nova

Cite a TV episode you view on the Web as you would a broadcast episode, giving a retrieval statement rather than the city, state, and network name.

34. Musical recording

Springsteen, B. (2002). Empty sky. On *The rising* [CD]. New York, NY: Columbia.

Begin with the name of the writer or composer. (If you cite another artist's recording of the work, provide this information after the title of the work—for example, [Recorded by E. Davila].) Give the medium in brackets ([CD], [LP], [mp3 file], and so on). Finish with the city, state, and name of the recording label or a retrieval statement.

35. Podcast

Glass, I. (Producer). (2014, April 11). The hounds of Blairsville [Audio podcast]. *This American life.* Retrieved from http://www.thisamericanlife.org

36. Visual

Southern Illinois University School of Medicine. (n.d.). Reporting child abuse and neglect [Diagram]. Retrieved from http://www.siumed.edu/oec/Year4/how_to_report_child_abuse.pdf

United Nations Population Fund (Cartographer). (2015). *Percent of population living on less than $1/day* [Demographic map]. Retrieved from http://www.unfpa.org

37. Video game, computer software, or app

Mojang. (2015). Minecraft: Pocket edition (Version 0.10.4) [Mobile application software]. Retrieved May 7, 2015, from https://minecraft.net

For a video game, computer program, or app, give the following: the name of the developer or author, the date, the title, the version, a bracketed description of the program (such as [Video game], [Computer software], or [Mobile application software], as here), and a retrieval statement.

57c Format the paper in APA style.

Use the following guidelines and samples to prepare papers in APA format. Check with your instructor for any modifications to this format.

Note See pages 481–83 for the APA format of a reference list. And see pages 61–68 for guidelines on type fonts, lists, tables and figures, and other elements of design.

Margins Use one-inch margins on the top, bottom, and both sides.

Spacing and indentions Double-space everywhere. The only exceptions are under headers (triple-spaced) and in tables and figures, where related data, labels, and other elements may be single-spaced. Indent paragraphs and displayed quotations one-half inch.

Paging Begin numbering on the title page, and number consecutively through the end (including the reference list). Provide a header about one-half inch from the top of every page, as shown in the samples on the following pages. The header consists of the page number on the far right and your full or shortened title on the far left. Type the title in all-capital letters, and triple-space below it. On the title page only, precede the title with the label Running head and a colon. Omit this label on all other pages.

Title page Include the full title, your name, the course title, the instructor's name, and the date. (See below.) Type the title on the top half of the page, followed by the identifying information, all centered horizontally and double-spaced.

APA title page

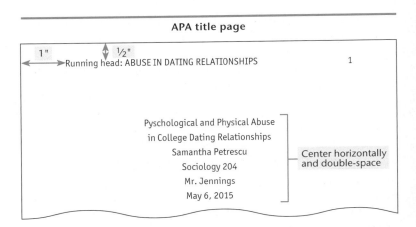

Abstract Summarize (in a maximum of 120 words) your subject, research method, findings, and conclusions. (See below.) Put the abstract on a page by itself.

APA abstract

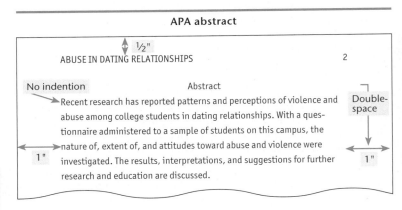

Body Begin with a restatement of the paper's title and then an introduction (not labeled). (See the next page.) The introduction presents the problem you researched, your method, the relevant background, and the purpose of your research.

First page of APA body

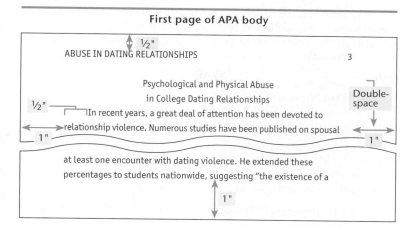

After the introduction, a section labeled **Method** provides a detailed discussion of how you conducted your research, including a description of the research subjects, any materials or tools you used (such as questionnaires), and the procedure you followed. In the illustration below, the label **Method** is a first-level heading and the label **Sample** is a second-level heading.

Later page of APA body

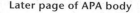

APA
57c

Format headings (including a third level, if needed) as follows:

First-Level Heading

Second-Level Heading

 Third-level heading. Run this heading into the text paragraph with a standard paragraph indention.

The **Results** section (labeled with a first-level heading) summarizes the data you collected, explains how you analyzed them, and presents them in detail, often in tables, graphs, or charts.

The **Discussion** section (labeled with a first-level heading) interprets the data and presents your conclusions. (When the discussion is brief, you may combine it with the previous section under the heading **Results and Discussion**.)

The References section, beginning a new page, includes all your sources. See pages 481–83 for an explanation and sample.

Long quotations   Run into your text all quotations of forty words or fewer, and enclose them in quotation marks. For quotations of more than forty words, set them off from your text by indenting all lines one-half inch, double-spacing throughout.

Echoing the opinions of other Europeans at the time, Freud (1961) had a poor view of Americans:

⟲The Americans are really too bad. . . . Competition is much more pungent with them, not succeeding means civil death to every one, and they have no private resources apart from their profession, no hobby, games, love or other interests of a cultured person. And success means money.⟳ (p. 86)

Do not use quotation marks around a quotation displayed in this way.

Illustrations   Present data in tables, graphs, or charts, as appropriate. (See the sample on p. 503 for a clear table format to follow.) Begin each illustration on a separate page. Number each kind of illustration consecutively and separately from the other (Table 1, Table 2, etc., and Figure 1, Figure 2, etc.). Refer to all illustrations in your text—for instance, (see Figure 3). Generally, place illustrations on pages by themselves immediately after the text references to them. (See pp. 63–68 for more on illustrations.)

57d   A sample research report in APA style

The paper on the following pages illustrates APA structure and documentation for a report of original research. See page 498 for the format of the title page and the abstract, which are required in APA papers, and for the margins and other elements of the text pages. See pages 481–83 for the format of the reference list.

ABUSE IN DATING RELATIONSHIPS   3

Psychological and Physical Abuse

in College Dating Relationships

In recent years, a great deal of attention has been devoted to relationship violence. Numerous studies have been published on spousal abuse and on violence among teenage couples. Violence among college-age dating couples has also been researched, as this study will discuss. Furthermore, published studies indicate that rates of relationship abuse have remained fairly consistent despite public attention to the problem. This study confirms that trend on one college campus.

Advocacy groups have defined dating violence as "a pattern of destructive behaviors used to exert power and control over a dating partner" (Break the Cycle, n.d.). These behaviors include both physical assault, from slapping to sexual coercion, and psychological abuse such as insults and threats. Recent studies have shown that such behavior is not uncommon in dating relationships. Kaura and Lohman (2007) found that 28.76% of respondents at Iowa State University had experienced premarital abuse. Similarly, a national poll revealed that 27% of college students have been subjected to possessive or controlling behaviors from a dating partner (Knowledge Networks, 2011). Another study (Helweg-Larsen, Harding, & Kleinman, 2008) found that so-called date rape, while more publicized, was reported by many fewer respondents (less than 2%) than was other physical violence during courtship (20%).

The purpose of the present study was to survey students on this campus to test whether the incidence of abuse was similar to the patterns reported in published studies.

Method

Sample

I conducted a survey of 200 students (109 females, 91 males) enrolled in an introductory sociology course at a large state university in the northeastern United States. Participants were primarily sophomores (67%) and juniors (18%), with an average age of 20. After I omitted from the analysis both incomplete questionnaires and responses from subjects who indicated they were married or not currently dating, the sample totaled 123 subjects.

The Questionnaire

A questionnaire exploring the personal dynamics of relationships was approved by the Institutional Review Board and distributed during class with informed consent forms. Questions were answered anonymously at home using a secure online survey system.

Margin notes:

Shortened title and page number.

Introduction: presentation of the problem researched by the writer.

Review of published research.

Citation form: undated source by group author, with no page numbers.

Citation form: source with two authors.

Citation forms: source with group author and source with three authors.

First- and second-level headings.

"Method" section: discussion of how research was conducted.

APA

57d

The questionnaire consisted of three sections. The first asked for basic demographic information such as gender, age, and relationship status. The second section required participants to assess aspects of their current dating relationships, such as levels of stress and frustration, communication between partners, and patterns of decision making. These variables were expected to influence the amount of violence in a relationship. The third section asked subjects to identify any psychologically or physically abusive behaviors they had experienced with their dating partner, from yelling to choking.

[The explanation of method continues.]

Results

The questionnaire revealed significant levels of psychological aggression among unmarried couples, consistent with the published studies. Of the respondents who indicated they were dating, just over half (62 of 123 subjects) reported that they had experienced verbal abuse at least once. Nearly 18% (22 of 123) had been shouted at by a romantic partner. In addition, almost 14% of respondents (17 of 123) had been threatened with some type of violence. (See Table 1.)

Rates of physical assault were also consistent with the published research. More than 16% of the study subjects reported being pushed or shoved by a partner, more than 12% had been slapped, and almost 6% had been kicked, bitten, or punched by a partner. Nine respondents (7.3%) indicated that an object had been thrown at them. One subject reported being attacked with a deadly weapon. (See Table 1.)

Discussion

Violence within premarital relationships has been widely acknowledged in the sociological research, and the present study confirms previous findings. On this campus, abuse and force occur among college couples. A high number of respondents indicated that they have been subjected to minor forms of abuse such as verbal aggression. Although the percentages of physical violence are relatively small, so was the sample. Extending the results to the entire campus population would mean significant numbers. For example, if the incidence of being kicked, bitten, or punched is typical at 6%, then 900 students of a 15,000-member student body might have experienced this type of violence.

As other studies have shown, participation in an abusive relationship can have lasting consequences. Miller (2011) found that those who don't

---

Margin notes:

"Results" section: summary and presentation of data.

Reference to table.

"Discussion" section: interpretation of data and presentation of conclusion

APA
57d

[New page.]

Table 1

Incidence of courtship violence

Type of violence	Number of students reporting	Percentage of sample
Psychological aggression		
Insulted or swore	62	50.4
Shouted	22	17.8
Threatened	17	13.8
Physical assault		
Pushed or shoved	20	16.3
Slapped	15	12.2
Kicked, bit, or punched	7	5.7
Threw something that could hurt	9	7.3
Used a knife or gun	1	0.8

Table on a page by itself.

Table presents data in a clear format.

[New page.]

label abusive behavior as such are more likely to perpetuate it and to accept it as victims, while Prather, Dahlen, Nicholson, and Bullock-Yowell (2012) discovered that violence tends to become more severe as relationships become more serious. Cornelius, Shorey, and Beebe (2010) concluded that for young men and women alike, premarital violence is a problem of "highly maladaptive interactional patterns" similar to those that surface in abusive marriages (p. 445).

These published studies suggest that a great deal is at stake for the participants in abusive relationships, not only in the present but for the future. This study extended research on this subject by contributing data on violence and abuse among college-age dating couples. The survey results provided an overview of the variables that may contribute to abusive relationships, the rates and types of dating abuse, and perceptions of abusive behaviors. The study found that rates of abuse are similar to those in published studies. If the courtship period sets the stage for later relationships, including marriage, then more attention should be given to educating young people to recognize and stop the behavior.

Citation forms: sources with four and three authors, named in the text.

Conclusion: summary and implications for further research.

New page for
reference list.

[New page.]

ABUSE IN DATING RELATIONSHIPS   7

References

Page on a Web
site with retrie-
val information.

Break the Cycle. (n.d.). Dating abuse 101 [Web page]. Retrieved April 7,
2015, from http://www.breakthecycle.org

Journal article
with a Digital
Object Identifier
(DOI).

Cornelius, T. L., Shorey, R. C., & Beebe, S. M. (2010). Self-reported communication variables and dating violence. *Journal of Family Violence, 25*,
439-448. http://dx.doi.org/10.1007/s10896-010-9305-9

Journal article
accessed
through a data-
base, with jour-
nal home-page
URL.

Helweg-Larsen, M., Harding, H. G., & Kleinman, K. E. (2008). Risk perceptions of dating violence among college women. *Journal of Social and
Clinical Psychology, 27*, 600-620. Retrieved from http://www.guilford
.com

Kaura, S. A., & Lohman, B. J. (2007). Dating violence victimization,
relationship satisfaction, mental health problems, and acceptability
of violence: A comparison of men and women. *Journal of Family Violence, 22*, 367-381. doi:10.1007/s10896-007-9092-0

Report from the
Web site of an
organization.

Knowledge Networks. (2011). *College dating violence and abuse poll.*
Retrieved from http://www.loveisrespect.org/pdf/College_Dating
_And_Abuse_Final_Study.pdf

Miller, L. M. (2011). Physical abuse in a college setting: Perceptions and
participation. *Journal of Family Violence, 26,* 71-80. doi:10.1007
/s10896-010-9344-2

Prather, E., Dahlen, E. R., Nicholson, B. C., & Bullock-Yowell, E. B. (2012).
Relational aggression in college students' relationships. *Journal of
Aggression, Maltreatment, and Trauma, 21.* doi:10.1080/10926771
.2012.693151

APA
37d

Commonly Misused Words

This glossary provides notes on words or phrases that often cause problems for writers. The recommendations for standard American English are based on current dictionaries and usage guides. Items labeled nonstandard should be avoided in speech and especially in writing. Those labeled colloquial and slang occur in speech and in some informal writing but are best avoided in the more formal writing usually expected in college and business. (Words and phrases labeled *colloquial* include those labeled by many dictionaries with the equivalent term *informal*.)

Note Two lists in the text supplement this glossary: idioms with prepositions, such as *part from* and *part with* (p. 171); and words that are pronounced the same or similarly but spelled differently, such as *heard* and *herd* (pp. 328–29).

a, an Use *a* before words beginning with consonant sounds, including those spelled with an initial pronounced *h* and those spelled with vowels that are sounded as consonants: *a historian, a one-o'clock class, a university.* Use *an* before words that begin with vowel sounds, including those spelled with an initial silent *h*: *an organism, an L, an honor.*

Using *a* or *an* before an abbreviation depends on how the abbreviation is to be read: *She was once an AEC undersecretary* (*AEC* is to be read as three separate letters). *Many Americans opposed a SALT treaty* (*SALT* is to be read as one word, *salt*).

See also pp. 261–62 on the uses of *a/an* versus *the.*

accept, except *Accept* is a verb meaning "receive." *Except* usually means "but for" or "other than"; when it is used as a verb, it means "leave out." *I can accept all your suggestions except the last one. I'm sorry you excepted my last suggestion from your list.*

advice, advise *Advice* is a noun, and *advise* is a verb: *Take my advice; do as I advise you.*

affect, effect Usually *affect* is a verb, meaning "to influence," and *effect* is a noun, meaning "result": *The drug did not affect his driving; in fact, it seemed to have no effect at all.* But *effect* occasionally is used as a verb meaning "to bring about": *Her efforts effected a change.* And *affect* is used in psychology as a noun meaning "feeling or emotion": *One can infer much about affect from behavior.*

aggravate *Aggravate* should not be used in its colloquial meaning of "irritate" or "exasperate" (for example, *We were aggravated by her constant arguing*). *Aggravate* means "make worse": *The President was irritated by the Senate's indecision because he feared any delay might aggravate the unrest in the Middle East.*

agree to, agree with *Agree to* means "consent to," and *agree with* means "be in accord with": *How can they agree to a treaty when they don't agree with each other about the terms?*

all ready, already *All ready* means "completely prepared," and *already* means "by now" or "before now": *We were all ready to go to the movie, but it had already started.*

all right   *All right* is always two words. *Alright* is a common error.

all together, altogether   *All together* means "in unison" or "gathered in one place." *"Altogether* means "entirely." *It's not altogether true that our family never spends vacations all together.*

allusion, illusion   An *allusion* is an indirect reference, and an *illusion* is a deceptive appearance: *Paul's constant allusions to Shakespeare created the illusion that he was an intellectual.*

almost, most   *Almost* means "nearly"; *most* means "the greater number (or part) of."* In formal writing, *most* should not be used as a substitute for *almost*: *We see each other almost* [not *most*] *every day.*

a lot   *A lot* is always two words, used informally to mean "many." *Alot* is a common misspelling.

among, between   In general, use *among* for relationships involving more than two people or for comparing one thing to a group to which it belongs. *The four of them agreed among themselves that the choice was between New York and Los Angeles.*

amount, number   Use *amount* with a singular noun that names something not countable (a noncount noun): *The amount of food varies.* Use *number* with a plural noun that names more than one of something countable (a plural count noun): *The number of calories must stay the same.*

and/or   *And/or* indicates three options: one or the other or both (*The decision is made by the mayor and/or the council*). If you mean all three options, *and/or* is appropriate. Otherwise, use *and* if you mean both, *or* if you mean either.

ante-, anti-   The prefix *ante-* means "before" (*antedate, antebellum*); *anti-* means "against" (*antiwar, antinuclear*). Before a capital letter or *i*, *anti-* takes a hyphen: *anti-Freudian, anti-isolationist.*

anxious, eager   *Anxious* means "nervous" or "worried" and is usually followed by *about*. *Eager* means "looking forward" and is usually followed by *to*. *I've been anxious about getting blisters. I'm eager* [not *anxious*] *to get new running shoes.*

anybody, any body; anyone, any one   *Anybody* and *anyone* are indefinite pronouns; *any body* is a noun modified by *any*; *any one* is a pronoun or adjective modified by *any*. *How can anybody communicate with any body of government? Can anyone help Amy? She has more work than any one person can handle.*

any more, anymore   *Any more* means "no more"; *anymore* means "now." Both are used in negative constructions. *He doesn't want any more. She doesn't live here anymore.*

are, is   Use *are* with a plural subject (*books are*), *is* with a singular subject (*book is*).

as   *As* may be unclear when it substitutes for *because*, *since*, or *while*: *As the researchers asked more questions, their money ran out.* (Does *as* mean "while" or "because"?) *As* should never be used as a substitute for *whether* or *who. I'm not sure whether* [not *as*] *we can make it. That's the man who* [not *as*] *gave me directions.*

as, like   In formal speech and writing, *like* should not introduce a main clause (with a subject and a verb) because it is a preposition. The preferred choice is *as* or *as if: The plan succeeded as* [not *like*] *we hoped. It seemed as if* [not *like*] *it might fail. Other plans like it have failed.*

assure, ensure, insure   *Assure* means "to promise": *He assured us that we would miss the traffic. Ensure* and *insure* are often used interchangeably to mean "make certain," but some reserve *insure* for matters of legal and financial protection and use *ensure* for more general meanings: *We left early to ensure that we would miss the traffic. It's expensive to insure yourself against floods.*

awful, awfully   Strictly speaking, *awful* means "awe-inspiring." As intensifiers meaning "very" or "extremely" (*He tried awfully hard*), *awful* and *awfully* should be avoided in formal speech or writing.

a while, awhile   *Awhile* is an adverb; *a while* is an article and a noun. *I will be gone awhile* [not *a while*]. *I will be gone for a while* [not *awhile*].

bad, badly   In formal speech and writing, *bad* should be used only as an adjective; the adverb is *badly. He felt bad because his tooth ached badly.* In *He felt bad*, the verb *felt* is a linking verb and the adjective *bad* describes the subject. See also pp. 255–56.

being as, being that   Colloquial for *because*, the preferable word in formal speech or writing: *Because* [not *Being as*] *the world is round, Columbus never did fall off the edge.*

beside, besides   *Beside* means "next to," while *besides* means "except," "in addition to," or "in addition": *Besides, several other people besides you want to sit beside Dr. Christensen.*

better, had better   In *had better* (meaning "ought to"), the verb *had* is necessary and should not be omitted: *You had better* [not just *better*] *go.*

between, among   See *among, between.*

bring, take   Use *bring* only for movement from a farther place to a nearer one and *take* for any other movement. *First take these books to the library for renewal; then take them to Mr. Daniels. Bring them back to me when he's finished.*

but, hardly, scarcely   These words are negative in their own right; using *not* with any of them produces a double negative (see p. 258). *We have but* [not *haven't got but*] *an hour before our plane leaves. I could hardly* [not *couldn't hardly*] *make out her face.*

but, however, yet   Each of these words is adequate to express contrast. Don't combine them. *He had finished, yet* [not *but yet*] *he continued.*

can, may   Strictly, *can* indicates capacity or ability, and *may* indicates permission or possibility: *If I may talk with you a moment, I believe I can solve your problem.*

censor, censure   To *censor* is to edit or remove from public view on moral or other grounds; to *censure* is to give a formal scolding. *The lieutenant was censured by Major Taylor for censoring the letters her soldiers wrote home from boot camp.*

cite, sight, site   *Cite* is a verb usually meaning "quote," "commend," or "acknowledge": *You must cite your sources.* *Sight* is both a noun meaning "the ability to see" or "a view" and a verb meaning "perceive" or "observe": *What a sight you see when you sight Venus through a strong telescope.* *Site* is a noun meaning "place" or "location" or a verb meaning "situate": *The builder sited the house on an unlikely site.*

climatic, climactic   *Climatic* comes from *climate* and refers to the weather: *Recent droughts may indicate a climatic change.* *Climactic* comes from *climax* and refers to a dramatic high point: *During the climactic duel between Hamlet and Laertes, Gertrude drinks poisoned wine.*

complement, compliment   To *complement* something is to add to, complete, or reinforce it: *Her yellow blouse complemented her black hair.* To *compliment* something is to make a flattering remark about it: *He complimented her on her hair.* *Complimentary* can also mean "free": *complimentary tickets.*

conscience, conscious   *Conscience* is a noun meaning "a sense of right and wrong"; *conscious* is an adjective meaning "aware" or "awake." *Though I was barely conscious, my conscience nagged me.*

contact   Avoid using *contact* imprecisely as a verb instead of a more exact word such as *consult, talk with, telephone,* or *write to.*

continual, continuous   *Continual* means "constantly recurring": *Most movies on television are continually interrupted by commercials.* *Continuous* means "unceasing": *Some cable channels present movies continuously without commercials.*

could of   See *have, of.*

credible, creditable, credulous   *Credible* means "believable": *It's a strange story, but it seems credible to me.* *Creditable* means "deserving of credit" or "worthy": *Steve gave a creditable performance.* *Credulous* means "gullible": *The credulous Claire believed Tim's lies.* See also *incredible, incredulous.*

criteria   The plural of *criterion* (meaning "standard for judgment"): *Our criteria are strict. The most important criterion is a sense of humor.*

data   The plural of *datum* (meaning "fact"). Though *data* is often used as a singular noun, many readers prefer the plural verb, and it is always correct: *The data fail* [not *fails*] *to support the hypothesis.*

device, devise   *Device* is the noun, and *devise* is the verb: *Can you devise some device for getting his attention?*

different from, different than   *Different from* is preferred: *His purpose is different from mine.* But *different than* is widely accepted when a construction using *from* would be wordy: *I'm a different person now than I used to be* is preferable to *I'm a different person now from the person I used to be.*

differ from, differ with   To *differ from* is to be unlike: *The twins differ from each other only in their hairstyles.* To *differ with* is to disagree with: *I have to differ with you on that point.*

discreet, discrete   *Discreet* (noun form *discretion*) means "tactful": *What's a discreet way of telling Maud to be quiet?* *Discrete* (noun form *discreteness*) means "separate and distinct": *Within a computer's memory are millions of discrete bits of information.*

disinterested, uninterested   *Disinterested* means "impartial": *We chose Pete, as a disinterested third party, to decide who was right.* *Uninterested* means "bored" or "lacking interest": *Unfortunately, Pete was completely uninterested in the question.*

don't   *Don't* is the contraction for *do not,* not for *does not*: *I don't care, you don't care,* and *he doesn't* [not *don't*] *care.*

due to the fact that   Wordy for *because.*

eager, anxious   See *anxious, eager.*

effect   See *affect, effect.*

elicit, illicit   *Elicit* means "bring out" or "call forth." *Illicit* means "unlawful." *The crime elicited an outcry against illicit drugs.*

emigrate, immigrate   *Emigrate* means "to leave one place and move to another": *The Chus emigrated from Korea.* *Immigrate* means "to move into a place where one was not born": *They immigrated to the United States.*

ensure   See *assure, ensure, insure.*

enthused   Avoid using colloquially to mean "showing enthusiasm." Prefer *enthusiastic*: *The coach was enthusiastic* [not *enthused*] *about the team's prospects.*

et al., etc.   Use *et al.,* the Latin abbreviation for "and other people," only in source citations: *Jones et al.* Avoid *etc.,* the Latin abbreviation for "and other things," in formal writing, and do not use it to refer to people or to substitute for precision, as in *The government provides health care, etc.*

everybody, every body; everyone, every one   *Everybody* and *everyone* are indefinite pronouns: *Everybody* [*Everyone*] *knows Tom steals. Every one* is a pronoun modified by *every,* and *every body* a noun modified by *every.* Both refer to each thing or person of a specific group and are typically followed by *of*: *The game commissioner has stocked every body of fresh water in the state with fish, and now every one of our rivers is a potential trout stream.*

everyday, every day   *Everyday* is an adjective meaning "used daily" or "common"; *every day* is a noun modified by *every*: *Everyday problems tend to arise every day.*

everywheres   Nonstandard for *everywhere.*

except   See *accept, except.*

except for the fact that   Wordy for *except that.*

explicit, implicit   *Explicit* means "stated outright": *I left explicit instructions. Implicit* means "implied, unstated": *We had an implicit understanding.*

farther, further   *Farther* refers to additional distance (*How much farther is it to the beach?*), and *further* refers to additional time, amount, or other abstract matters (*I don't want to discuss this any further*).

fewer, less   *Fewer* refers to individual countable items (a plural count noun), *less* to general amounts (a noncount noun, always singular). *Skim milk has fewer calories than whole milk. We have less milk left than I thought.*

flaunt, flout   *Flaunt* means "show off": *If you have style, flaunt it. Flout* means "scorn" or "defy": *Hester Prynne flouted convention and paid the price.*

flunk   A colloquial substitute for *fail*.

fun   As an adjective, *fun* is colloquial and should be avoided in most writing: *It was a pleasurable* [not *fun*] *evening.*

further   See *farther, further.*

get   This common verb is used in many slang and colloquial expressions: *get lost, that really gets me, getting on. Get* is easy to overuse: watch out for it in expressions such as *it's getting better* (substitute *improving*) and *we got done* (substitute *finished*).

good, well   *Good* is an adjective, and *well* is nearly always an adverb: *Larry's a good dancer. He and Linda dance well together. Well* is properly used as an adjective only to refer to health: *You look well.* (*You look good*, in contrast, means "Your appearance is pleasing.")

good and   Colloquial for "very": *I was very* [not *good and*] *tired.*

had better   See *better, had better.*

had ought   The *had* is unnecessary and should be omitted: *He ought* [not *had ought*] *to listen to his mother.*

hanged, hung   Though both are past-tense forms of *hang*, *hanged* is used to refer to executions and *hung* is used for all other meanings: *Tom Dooley was hanged* [not *hung*] *from a white oak tree. I hung* [not *hanged*] *the picture you gave me.*

hardly   See *but, hardly, scarcely.*

have, of   Use *have*, not *of*, after helping verbs such as *could, should, would, may, must,* and *might*: *You should have* [not *should of*] *told me.*

he, she; he/she   Convention has allowed the use of *he* to mean "he or she": *After the infant learns to creep, he progresses to crawling.* However, many writers today consider this usage inaccurate and unfair because it seems to exclude females. The construction *he/she*, one substitute for *he*, is awkward and objectionable to most readers. The better choice is to use *they*, to rephrase, or, sparingly, to use *he or she*. For instance: *After infants learn to creep, they progress to crawling. After learning to creep, the infant progresses to crawling. After the infant learns to creep, he or she progresses to crawling.* See also pp. 164 and 248–49.

herself, himself   See *myself, herself, himself, yourself.*

hisself   Nonstandard for *himself.*

hopefully   *Hopefully* means "with hope": *Freddy waited hopefully for a glimpse of Eliza.* The use of *hopefully* to mean "it is to be hoped," "I hope," or "let's hope" is now very common; but try to avoid it in writing because many readers continue to object strongly to the usage. *I hope* [not *Hopefully*] *the law will pass.*

idea, ideal   An *idea* is a thought or conception. An *ideal* (noun) is a model of perfection or a goal. *Ideal* should not be used in place of *idea*: *The idea* [not *ideal*] *of the play is that our ideals often sustain us.*

if, whether   Use *whether* rather than *if* when you are expressing an alternative: *If I laugh hard, people can't tell whether I'm crying or not.*

illicit   See *elicit, illicit.*

illusion   See *allusion, illusion.*

immigrate, emigrate   See *emigrate, immigrate.*

implicit   See *explicit, implicit.*

imply, infer   Writers or speakers *imply*, meaning "suggest": *Jim's letter implies he's having a good time.* Readers or listeners *infer*, meaning "conclude": *From Jim's letter I infer he's having a good time.*

incredible, incredulous   *Incredible* means "unbelievable," while *incredulous* means "unbelieving": *When Nancy heard Dennis's incredible story, she was frankly incredulous.* See also *credible, creditable, credulous.*

individual, person, party   *Individual* should refer to a single human being in contrast to a group or should stress uniqueness: *The US Constitution places strong emphasis on the rights of the individual.* For other meanings *person* is preferable: *What person* [not *individual*] *wouldn't want the security promised in that advertisement? Party* means "group" (*Can you seat a party of four for dinner?*) and should not be used to refer to an individual except in legal documents. See also *people, persons.*

infer   See *imply, infer.*

in regards to   Nonstandard for *in regard to, as regards,* or *regarding.*

insure   See *assure, ensure, insure.*

irregardless   Nonstandard for *regardless.*

is, are   See *are, is.*

is because   See *reason is because.*

is when, is where   These are faulty constructions in sentences that define: *Adolescence is a stage* [not *is when a person is*] *between childhood and adulthood. Socialism is a system in which* [not *is where*] *government owns the means of production.* See also p. 283.

its, it's   *Its* is the pronoun *it* in the possessive case: *That plant is losing its leaves. It's* is a contraction for *it is* or *it has*: *It's* [*It is*] *likely to die. It's* [*It has*] *got a fungus.* Many people confuse *it's* and *its* because possessives are most often formed with *-'s*; but the possessive *its*, like *his* and *hers*, never takes an apostrophe.

kind of, sort of, type of   In formal speech and writing, avoid using *kind of* or *sort of* to mean "somewhat": *He was rather* [not *kind of*] *tall. Kind, sort,* and *type* are singular and take singular adjectives and verbs: *This kind of dog is easily trained.* Agreement errors often occur when the singular *kind, sort,* or *type* is combined with the plural adjectives *these* and *those*: *These kinds* [not *kind*] *of dogs are easily trained. Kind, sort,* and *type* should be followed by *of* but not by *a*: *I don't know what type of* [not *type* or *type of a*] *dog that is.*

Use *kind of, sort of,* or *type of* only when the word *kind, sort,* or *type* is important: *That was a strange* [not *strange sort of*] *statement.*

lay, lie   *Lay* means "put" or "place" and takes a direct object: *We could lay the tablecloth in the sun.* Its main forms are *lay, laid, laid. Lie* means "recline" or "be situated" and does not take an object: *I lie awake at night. The town lies east of here.* Its main forms are *lie, lay, lain.* (See also p. 210.)

leave, let   *Leave* and *let* are interchangeable only when followed by *alone*: *leave me alone* is the same as *let me alone.* Otherwise, *leave* means "depart" and *let* means "allow": *Jill would not let Sue leave.*

less   See *fewer, less.*

lie, lay   See *lay, lie.*

like, as   See *as, like.*

like, such as   Strictly, *such as* precedes an example that represents a larger subject, whereas *like* indicates that two subjects are comparable. *Steve has recordings of many great saxophonists such as Ben Webster and Lee Konitz. Steve wants to be a great jazz saxophonist like Ben Webster and Lee Konitz.*

literally   This word means "actually" or "just as the words say," and it should not be used to qualify or intensify expressions whose words are not to be taken at face value. The sentence *He was literally climbing the walls* describes a person behaving like an insect, not a person who is restless or anxious. For the latter meaning, *literally* should be omitted.

lose, loose   *Lose* means "mislay": *Did you lose a brown glove? Loose* means "unrestrained" or "not tight": *Ann's canary got loose. Loose* also can function as a verb meaning "let loose": *They loose the dogs on intruders.*

lots, lots of   Avoid these colloquialisms in college or business writing. Use *very many, a great many,* or *much* instead.

may, can   See *can, may.*

may be, maybe   *May be* is a verb, and *maybe* is an adverb meaning "perhaps": *Tuesday may be a legal holiday. Maybe we won't have classes.*

may of   See *have, of.*

media   *Media* is the plural of *medium* and takes a plural verb: *All the news media are increasingly visual.* The singular verb is common, even in the media, but many readers prefer the plural verb, and it is always correct.

might of   See *have, of.*

moral, morale   As a noun, *moral* means "ethical conclusion" or "lesson": *The moral of the story escapes me. Morale* means "spirit" or "state of mind": *Victory improved the team's morale.*

most, almost   See *almost, most.*

must of   See *have, of.*

myself, herself, himself, yourself, ourselves, themselves, yourselves   Avoid using the *-self* pronoun in place of personal pronouns: *No one except me* [not *myself*] *saw the accident. Michiko and I* [not *myself*] *planned the ceremony.* The *-self* pronouns have two uses: they emphasize a noun or other pronoun

(*Paul did the work himself; he himself said so*), or they indicate that the sentence subject also receives the action of the verb: *I drove myself to the hospital.*

nowheres   Nonstandard for *nowhere.*

number   See *amount, number.*

of, have   See *have, of.*

off of   *Of* is unnecessary. Use *off* or *from* rather than *off of*: *He jumped off* [or *from*, not *off of*] *the roof.*

OK, O.K., okay   All three spellings are acceptable, but avoid this colloquial term in formal speech and writing.

on the other hand   This transitional expression of contrast should be preceded by its mate, *on the one hand*: *On the one hand, we hoped for snow. On the other hand, we worried that it would harm the animals.* However, the two combined can be unwieldy, and a simple *but, however, yet,* or *in contrast* often suffices: *We hoped for snow. However, we worried that it would harm the animals.*

owing to the fact that   Wordy for *because.*

party   See *individual, person, party.*

people, persons   In formal usage, *people* refers to a general group: *We the people of the United States. . . . Persons* refers to a collection of individuals: *Will the person or persons who saw the accident please notify. . . .* Except when emphasizing individuals, prefer *people* to *persons.* See also *individual, person, party.*

per   Except in technical writing, an English equivalent is usually preferable to the Latin *per*: *$10 an* [not *per*] *hour; sent by* [not *per*] *parcel post; requested in* [not *per* or *as per*] *your letter.*

percent (per cent), percentage   Both these terms refer to fractions of one hundred. *Percent* always follows a number (*40 percent of the voters*), and the word is often used instead of the symbol (%) in nontechnical writing. *Percentage* stands alone (*the percentage of voters*) or follows an adjective (*a high percentage*).

person   See *individual, person, party.*

persons   See *people, persons.*

phenomena   *Phenomena* is the plural of *phenomenon* (meaning "perceivable fact" or "unusual occurrence"): *Many phenomena are not recorded. One phenomenon is attracting attention.*

plenty   A colloquial substitute for *very*: *The reaction occurred very* [not *plenty*] *fast.*

plus   *Plus* is standard as a preposition meaning "in addition to": *His income plus mine is sufficient.* But *plus* is colloquial when it relates main clauses: *Our organization is larger than theirs; moreover* [not *plus*], *we have more money.*

precede, proceed   *Precede* means "come before": *My name precedes yours in the alphabet. Proceed* means "move on": *We were told to proceed to the waiting room.*

prejudice, prejudiced   *Prejudice* is a noun; *prejudiced* is an adjective. Do not drop the *-d* from *prejudiced*: *I knew that my parents were prejudiced* [not *prejudice*].

pretty   Overworked as an adverb meaning "rather" or "somewhat": *He was somewhat* [not *pretty*] *irked at the suggestion.*

principal, principle   *Principal* is an adjective meaning "foremost" or "major," a noun meaning "chief official," or, in finance, a noun meaning "capital sum." *Principle* is a noun only, meaning "rule" or "axiom." *Her principal reasons for confessing were her principles of right and wrong.*

proceed, precede   See *precede, proceed.*

question of whether, question as to whether   Both are wordy substitutes for *whether.*

raise, rise   *Raise* means "lift" or "bring up" and takes a direct object: *The Kirks raise cattle.* Its main forms are *raise, raised, raised. Rise* means "get up" and does not take an object: *They must rise at dawn.* Its main forms are *rise, rose, risen.* (See also p. 210.)

real, really   In formal speech and writing, *real* should not be used as an adverb; *really* is the adverb and *real* an adjective. *Popular reaction to the announcement was really* [not *real*] *enthusiastic.*

reason is because   This colloquial and redundant expression should be avoided in formal speech and writing. Use a *that* clause after *reason is: The reason he is absent is that* [not *is because*] *he is sick.* Or: *He is absent because he is sick.* (See also p. 283.)

respectful, respective   *Respectful* means "full of (or showing) respect": *Be respectful of other people. Respective* means "separate": *The French and the Germans occupied their respective trenches.*

rise, raise   See *raise, rise.*

scarcely   See *but, hardly, scarcely.*

sensual, sensuous   *Sensual* suggests sexuality; *sensuous* means "pleasing to the senses." *Stirred by the sensuous scent of meadow grass and flowers, Cheryl and Paul found their thoughts growing increasingly sensual.*

set, sit   *Set* means "put" or "place" and takes a direct object: *He sets the pitcher down.* Its main forms are *set, set, set. Sit* means "be seated" and does not take an object: *She sits on the sofa.* Its main forms are *sit, sat, sat.* (See also p. 210.)

shall, will   *Will* is a helping verb for all persons: *I will go, you will go, they will go.* The main use of *shall* is for first-person questions requesting an opinion or consent: *Shall I order a pizza? Shall we dance? Shall* can also be used for the first person when a formal effect is desired (*I shall expect you around three*), and it is occasionally used with the second or third person to express the speaker's determination (*You shall do as I say*).

should of   See *have, of.*

sight, site, cite   See *cite, sight, site.*

since *Since* mainly relates to time: *I've been waiting since noon.* But *since* is also often used to mean "because": *Since you ask, I'll tell you.* Revise sentences in which the word could have either meaning, such as *Since I studied physics, I have been planning to major in engineering.*

sit, set See *set, sit.*

site, cite, sight See *cite, sight, site.*

so Avoid using *so* alone or as a vague intensifier: *He was so late.* So needs to be followed by *that* and a statement of the result: *He was so late that I left without him.*

somebody, some body; someone, some one *Somebody* and *someone* are indefinite pronouns; *some body* is a noun modified by *some*; and *some one* is a pronoun or an adjective modified by *some*. *Somebody ought to invent a shampoo that will give hair some body. Someone told Janine she should choose some one plan and stick with it.*

sometime, sometimes, some time *Sometime* means "at an indefinite time in the future": *Why don't you come up and see me sometime? Sometimes* means "now and then": *I still see my old friend Joe sometimes. Some time* means "a span of time": *I need some time to make the payments.*

somewheres Nonstandard for *somewhere.*

sort of, sort of a See *kind of, sort of, type of.*

such Avoid using *such* as a vague intensifier: *It was such a cold winter. Such* should be followed by *that* and a clause that states a result: *It was such a cold winter that Napoleon's troops had to turn back.*

such as See *as, like.*

supposed to, used to In both these expressions, the *-d* is essential: *I used to* [not *use to*] *think so. He's supposed to* [not *suppose to*] *meet us.*

sure Colloquial when used as an adverb meaning *surely: James Madison sure was right about the need for the Bill of Rights.* If you merely want to be emphatic, use *certainly: Madison certainly was right.* If your goal is to convince a possibly reluctant reader, use *surely: Madison surely was right.*

sure and, sure to; try and, try to *Sure to* and *try to* are the correct forms: *Be sure to* [not *sure and*] *buy milk. Try to* [not *Try and*] *find some decent tomatoes.*

take, bring See *bring, take.*

than, then *Than* is used in comparisons, whereas *then* indicates time: *Holmes knew then that Moriarty was wilier than he had thought.*

that, which *That* introduces an essential element: *We should use the lettuce that Susan bought* (*that Susan bought* limits the lettuce to a particular lettuce). *Which* can introduce both essential elements and nonessential elements, but many writers reserve *which* only for nonessential elements: *The leftover lettuce, which is in the refrigerator, would make a good salad* (*which is in the refrigerator* simply provides more information about the lettuce we already know of). Essential elements (with *that* or *which*) are not set off by commas; nonessential elements (with *which*) are. See also p. 296.

that, which, who   Use *that* for animals, things, and sometimes collective or anonymous people: *The rocket that failed cost millions. Infants that walk need constant tending.* Use *which* only for animals and things: *The river, which flows south, divides two countries.* Use *who* only for people and for animals with names: *Dorothy is the girl who visits Oz. Her dog, Toto, who accompanies her, gives her courage.*

their, there, they're   *Their* is the possessive form of *they*: *Give them their money. There* indicates place (*I saw her standing there*) or functions as an expletive (*There is a hole behind you*). *They're* is a contraction for *they are*: *They're going fast.*

theirselves   Nonstandard for *themselves*.

them   In standard American English, *them* does not serve as an adjective: *Those* [not *Them*] *people want to know.*

then, than   See *than, then.*

these kind, these sort, these type, those kind   See *kind of, sort of, type of.*

this, these   *This* is singular: *this car* or *This is the reason I left. These* is plural: *these cars* or *These are not valid reasons.*

thru   A colloquial spelling of *through* that should be avoided in all academic and business writing.

to, too, two   *To* is a preposition; *too* is an adverb meaning "also" or "excessively"; and *two* is a number. *I too have been to Europe two times.*

too   Avoid using *too* as a vague intensifier: *Monkeys are too mean.* When you do use *too,* explain the consequences of the excessive quality: *Monkeys are too mean to make good pets.*

toward, towards   Both are acceptable, though *toward* is preferred. Use one or the other consistently.

try and, try to   See *sure and, sure to; try and, try to.*

type of   See *kind of, sort of, type of.* Don't use *type* without *of*: *It was a family type of* [not *type*] *restaurant.* Or better: *It was a family restaurant.*

uninterested   See *disinterested, uninterested.*

unique   *Unique* means "the only one of its kind" and so cannot sensibly be modified with words such as *very* or *most*: *That was a unique* [not *a very unique* or *the most unique*] *movie.*

usage, use   *Usage* refers to conventions, most often those of a language: *Is "hadn't ought" proper usage? Usage* is often misused in place of the noun *use*: *Wise use* [not *usage*] *of insulation can save fuel.*

use, utilize   *Utilize* can be used to mean "make good use of": *Many teachers utilize computers for instruction.* But for all other senses of "place in service" or "employ," prefer *use.*

used to   See *supposed to, used to.*

wait for, wait on   In formal speech and writing, *wait for* means "await" (*I'm waiting for Paul*) and *wait on* means "serve" (*The owner of the store herself waited on us*).

ways   Colloquial as a substitute for *way*: *We have only a little way* [not *ways*] *to go.*

well   See *good, well.*

whether, if   See *if, whether.*

which, that   See *that, which.*

which, who, that   See *that, which, who.*

who, whom   *Who* is the subject of a sentence or clause (*We don't know who will come*). *Whom* is the object of a verb or preposition (*We do not know whom we invited*). (See also pp. 242–43.)

who's, whose   *Who's* is the contraction of *who is* or *who has*: *Who's* [*Who is*] *at the door? Jim is the only one who's* [*who has*] *passed. Whose* is the possessive form of *who*: *Whose book is that?*

will, shall   See *shall, will.*

would be   *Would be* is often used instead of *is* or *are* to soften statements needlessly: *One example is* [not *would be*] *gun-control laws. Would* can combine with other verbs for the same unassertive effect: *would ask, would seem, would suggest,* and so on.

would have   Avoid this construction in place of *had* in clauses that begin with *if* and state a condition contrary to fact: *If the tree had* [not *would have*] *withstood the fire, it would have been the oldest in town.* See also p. 227.

would of   See *have, of.*

you   In all but very formal writing, *you* is generally appropriate as long as it means "you, the reader." In all writing, avoid indefinite uses of *you*, such as *In one ancient tribe your first loyalty was to your parents.* See also p. 253.

your, you're   *Your* is the possessive form of *you*: *Your dinner is ready. You're* is the contraction of *you are*: *You're bound to be late.*

yourself   See *myself, herself, himself, yourself.*

Credits

Text and Illustrations

Index

Page numbers in boldface refer to the primary definition of the term in the text.

Index

Index

Index

Inde*

Index

Index

Index

Index

Editing Symbols

Boldface numbers and letters refer to chapters and sections of the handbook.

ab	Faulty abbreviation, **49**	⌄	Comma, **39**
ad	Misused adjective or adverb, **33**	;	Semicolon, **40**
agr	Error in agreement, **29, 31**	:	Colon, **41**
ap	Apostrophe needed or misused, **42**	⌄̓	Apostrophe, **39**
appr	Inappropriate word, **18a**	" "	Quotation marks, **40**
arg	Faulty argument, **11b–d**	— ( ) . . . [ ] /	Dash, parentheses, ellipsis mark, brackets, slash, **44**
awk	Awkward construction	par, ¶	Start new paragraph, **7**
cap	Use capital letter, **47**	¶ coh	Paragraph not coherent, **7c**
case	Error in case form, **30**	¶ dev	Paragraph not developed, **7d**
cit	Missing source citation or error in form of citation, **54e**	¶ un	Paragraph not unified, **7b**
coh	Coherence lacking, **3b-3, 7c**	pass	Ineffective passive voice, **28a**
con	Be more concise, **20**	pn agr	Error in pronoun-antecedent agreement, **31**
coord	Coordination needed, **15c**	ref	Error in pronoun reference, **32**
crit	Think or read more critically, **10a–d**	rep	Unnecessary repetition, **20c**
cs	Comma splice, **36**	rev	Revise, **5**
d	Ineffective diction (word choice), **18**	run-on	Run-on (fused) sentence, **36**
		shift	Inconsistency, **26d, 27b, 28b, 32e**
des	Ineffective or incorrect document format, **8**	sp	Misspelled word, **45**
		spec	Be more specific, **7d, 18b-2**
det	Error in use of determiner, **33f**	sub	Subordination needed or faulty, **15d**
dm	Dangling modifier, **34b**	t	Error in verb tense, **26**
emph	Emphasis lacking or faulty, **15**	t seq	Error in tense sequence, **26e**
exact	Inexact word, **18b**	trans	Transition needed, **7c-6**
frag	Sentence fragment, **35**	und	Underline or italicize, **48**
fs	Fused sentence, **36**	usage	See "Commonly Misused Words," p. 505
gram	Error in grammar, **21–24**	var	Vary sentence structure, **17b**
hyph	Error in use of hyphen, **46**	vb	Error in verb form, **25**
inc	Incomplete construction, **19**	vb agr	Error in subject-verb agreement, **29**
ital	Italicize or underline, **48**	w	Wordy, **20**
k	Awkward construction	ww	Wrong word, **18b-1**
lc	Use lowercase (small) letter, **47**	//	Faulty parallelism, **16**
mixed	Mixed construction, **37**	#	Separate with a space
mm	Misplaced modifier, **34a**	⌣	Close up the space
mng	Meaning unclear	⸙	Delete
no cap	Unnecessary capital letter, **47**	the	Capitalize, **47**
no ⌄	Comma not needed, **39h**	The	Use a small letter, **47**
no ¶	No new paragraph needed, **7**	teh	Transpose letters or words
num	Error in use of numbers, **50**	x	Obvious error
p	Error in punctuation, **38–44**	^	Something missing, **19**
. ? !	Period, question mark, exclamation point, **38**	??	Document illegible or meaning unclear

Throughout this handbook, the symbol (CULTURE LANGUAGE) signals topics for students whose first language or dialect is not standard American English. These topics can be tricky because they arise from rules in standard English that are quite different in other languages and dialects. Many of the topics involve significant cultural assumptions as well.

No matter what your language background, as a college student you are learning the culture of US higher education and the language that is used and shaped by that culture. The process is challenging, even for native speakers of standard American English. It requires not just writing clearly and correctly but also mastering conventions of developing, presenting, and supporting ideas. The challenge is greater if, in addition, you are trying to learn standard American English and are accustomed to other conventions. Several habits can help you succeed:

- **Read.** Besides course assignments, read newspapers, magazines, and books in English. The more you read, the more fluently and accurately you'll write.
- **Write.** Keep a journal in which you practice writing in English every day.
- **Talk and listen.** Take advantage of opportunities to hear and use English.
- **Ask questions.** Your instructors, tutors in the writing center, and fellow students can clarify assignments and help you identify and solve writing problems.
- **Don't try for perfection.** No one writes perfectly, and the effort to do so can prevent you from expressing yourself fluently. View mistakes not as failures but as opportunities to learn.
- **Revise first; then edit.** Focus on each essay's ideas, support, and organization before attending to grammar and vocabulary. See the revision and editing checklists on pages 31 and 37.
- **Set editing priorities.** Concentrate first on any errors that interfere with clarity, such as problems with word order or subject-verb agreement. The following index can help you identify the topics you need to work on and can lead you to appropriate text discussions. The pages marked * provide exercises for self-testing.

Detailed Contents

← "Editing Symbols" and " CULTURE LANGUAGE Guide"